Library of
Davidson College

THE POETRY

OF THE

MINOR CONNECTICUT WITS

THE POETRY

OF THE

MINOR CONNECTICUT WITS

FACSIMILE REPRODUCTIONS

EDITED WITH AN INTRODUCTION

BY

BENJAMIN FRANKLIN V

GAINESVILLE, FLORIDA

SCHOLARS' FACSIMILES & REPRINTS

1970

SCHOLARS' FACSIMILES & REPRINTS
1605 N.W. 14TH AVENUE
GAINESVILLE, FLORIDA 32601, U.S.A.
HARRY R. WARFEL, GENERAL EDITOR

SBN 8201-1066-3

L. C. CATALOG CARD NUMBER: 68-17015

MANUFACTURED IN THE U.S.A.

CONTENTS

INTRODUCTION xi
NOTES xxiii
ACKNOWLEDGMENTS x

COLLABORATIONS

The Echo, with Other Poems (1807)
  Table of Contents ix
  The Democratiad (1795): Supplementary Notes to
    pages 127-140 333
  The Guillotina (1796): Supplementary Notes to
    pages to 219-232 349
  The Political Greenhouse (1799): Supplementary
    Notes to pages 234-259 352
  Index 361
  Supplementary Index 371
  The Echo, No. II 379
  The Echo, No. III 381

RICHARD ALSOP (1761-1815)

The Charms of Fancy (1856) 387
  Contents 389
  Biographical Sketch of the Author 391
*The Enchanted Lake of the Fairy
  Morgana* (1806) 603
*A Poem: Sacred to the Memory of George Washing-
  ton* (1800) 679
Aristocracy. An Epic Poem 701

An Elegy, Written in February, 1791   735
Versification of a Passage from the Fifth Book of Ossian's *Temora*   739
Habbakuk, Chapter III   747
Runic Poetry: Twilight of the Gods. From the *Edda*   749
Extract from *The Conquest of Scandinavia*   755
Ode to the Sheer Water   769
Verses to the Shearwater—On the Morning after a Storm at Sea   770
Hymn to Peace [I]   772
Hymn to Peace [II]   774
The Oath of Hannibal. From *Silius Italicus*, Book I   775
Description of Hannibal. From *Silius Italicus*, Book I   778
A Song. From the Italian   779
Description of an African Serpent. From *Silius Italicus*, Book VI   780
Addressed to an Infant Boy with a Small Toy-Watch   786
Inscription for a Family Tomb   788

ELIHU HUBBARD SMITH (1771-1798)

Edwin and Angelina; or The Banditti. An Opera, in Three Acts (1797)   791
Democracy; An Epic Poem (1794)   863
Epistle to the Author of *The Botanic Garden* [Erasmus Darwin]   883
ELLA-BIRTHA-HENRY POEMS

    1. Ella: The Volunteer Laureat. For the Birth-Day of the President of the United States: "Oft has the Poet's venal song"   889

CONTENTS

2. Ella: Sonnet I: "Fair shows the rose, but soon its beauty fades" 891
3. Ella: Sonnet II: "Blest is the Poet if his songs can raise" 891
4. Birtha: To Ella: "Strike, strike again thy silver-sounding lyre" 892
5. Ella: Sonnet III: "Now o'er the world hath sober Evening spread" 892
6. Birtha: Sonnet: "The incense-breathing lily rears her head" 893
7. Ella: Ode to Birtha: "Poor and unknown, a stranger to the great" 893
8. Ella: Sonnet IV: "Adown the melancholy stream of life" 894
9. Birtha: Sonnet: "Behold that woe-wild Maiden in yon Cell" 895
10. To Ella: "No skill I boast, no forceful art" 895
11. Ella: Sonnet V: "'Say, what is Life?' the sons of sorrow cry" 898
12. Ella: Sonnet VI: To Egwina: "Go verse, soft-whispering to Egwina say" 898
13. Ella: Ode to Birtha: "Soft o'er my soul the voice of music breathes" 899
14. Henry: Sonnet: "Hark! hear'st thou not the sweetly swelling strain" 900
15. Ella: Sonnet VII: "Hail Son of Morning! thou, whose orient Smile" 900
16. Ella: Ode to Henry: "What bliss the voice of music gives" 901
17. Ella: Sonnet VIII: To the Moon: "Bend from thy throne fair Empress of the Night" 902
18. Birtha: To Ella: "Ah! vainly, do I hear thy lute complain" 902

CONTENTS

19. Henry: To Ella: "Alighted from the azure sky a Seraph stood" — 904
20. Ella: Ode to Birtha: "And does disease thy bosom grieve?" — 904
21. Ella: Ode to Henry: "With what an anxious, trembling, joy" — 906
22. Birtha: Sonnet to Reflection: "*The Lord of Light* has journey'd down the sky" — 907
23. Ella: Laura and Mary: "Why drops the pearly tear from Laura's eye?" — 907
24. Ella: Ode, Written on Leaving the Place of My Nativity — 910
25. Birtha: To Ella: "Hark! while I sound my trembling shell" — 912
26. Birtha: Sonnet to Joy: "Hail! heaven-descended Queen!" — 914
27. Ella: Sonnet IX: To Mr. John Trumbull [the painter] — 914
28. Ella: Ode to Birtha: "With every changement of the varying mind" — 915
29. Ella: A Fragment [re Ralph Earl, a painter] — 917
30. Henry: Sonnet to Caroline: The Smile: "Hast thou not seen upon some night serene" — 918
31. Birtha: To Ella: "Again thy sweetly warbled strain" — 918
32. Birtha: Ode to Time: "Thou wast ere Worlds began to be" — 921
33. Ella: A Fragment in Imitation of Spenser: "Ah me! how black misfortune clouds the day!" — 923
34. Henry: Song: "Away each soft and tender bliss" — 926

CONTENTS ix

35. Ella: Ode, The Farewell: "Hope, holy sister of the cherub Peace!"	926
Occasional Address Spoken by Mr. Hodgkinson, on the Opening of the New Theatre, in New York, Monday, the 29th of January, 1798	928
New Year's Wish	932
From a Gentleman, to a Lady, who had presented him with a Cake Heart	934

LEMUEL HOPKINS (1750-1801)

Epitaph on a Patient Killed by a Cancer Quack	939
The Hypocrite's Hope	941
On General Ethan Allen	944
Psalm LXXXVIII	945
The Democratiad (see pages 127 and 333)	
The Guillotina (see pages 219 and 349)	

THEODORE DWIGHT (1764-1846)

Moll Carey	949
[African Distress]	958
Ode to Conscience	961
Lines on the Death of Washington	964
Lines Addressed to a Mother, Who Had Been Absent from Home Several Weeks, on Seeing Her Infant Child	966
Woman	968

ACKNOWLEDGMENTS

Grateful acknowledgment is made for permission of the following to permit the reproduction of materials in their possession.

THE AMERICAN ANTIQUARIAN SOCIETY: Richard Alsop, *Aristocracy*.

THE AMERICAN PHILOSOPHICAL ASSOCIATION: Ella, "Ode to Henry" and "Ode, Written on Leaving the Place of My Nativity"; Birtha, "To Ella" and "Sonnet to Reflection"; Henry, "To Ella" and "Song."

WILLIAM K. BOTTORFF: Poems from *American Poems*, ed. by E. H. Smith.

THE BROWN UNIVERSITY LIBRARY: E. H. Smith, "Epistle to the Author of *The Botanic Garden*" and Theodore Dwight, "Moll Carey."

THE HARVARD UNIVERSITY LIBRARY: Theodore Dwight, "Woman."

THE KENT STATE UNIVERSITY LIBRARY: Richard Alsop, "Verses to the Shearwater"; Thodore Dwight, "Lines on the Death of Washington" and "Lines Addressed to a Mother."

THE LIBRARY COMPANY OF PHILADELPHIA: E. H. Smith, *Democracy*.

THE OHIO STATE UNIVERSITY LIBRARY: Richard Alsop, *The Charms of Fancy* and *A Poem: Sacred to the Memory of George Washington*.

THE UNIVERSITY OF CHICAGO LIBRARY: Richard Alsop, "Ode to the Sheer Water" and "Addressed to an Infant Boy."

THE UNIVERSITY OF PENNSYLVANIA LIBRARY: The Ella-Birtha-Henry poems (with the exception of those from the American Philosophical Association).

THE YALE UNIVERSITY LIBRARY: *The Echo*, "The Echo, No. II," and "The Echo, No. III"; Richard Alsop, *The Enchanted Lake* and "A Song from the Italian"; E. H. Smith, *Edwin and Angelina*; Lemuel Hopkins, "Psalm LXXXVIII."

INTRODUCTION

John Trumbull, Timothy Dwight, David Humphreys, and Joel Barlow dominated the American literary scene in the last two decades of the eighteenth and the first decade of the nineteenth century. These poets, all born between 1750 and 1754 and all graduates of Yale College, wrote poetry that for the most part praised the history and the society of our new nation. All but Barlow were politically, socially, and religiously conservative and were the first Americans to speak out against the freethinking and, as they saw them, ignorant masses. Contemporary to and closely associated with these poets was another literary coterie that included Richard Alsop (1761-1815), Mason Fitch Cogswell (1761-1830), Theodore Dwight (1764-1846), Lemuel Hopkins (1750-1801), and Elihu Hubbard Smith (1771-1798). These nine men have been known collectively as the Connecticut, or Hartford, Wits, but in 1907 Annie Russell Marble correctly divided them into a "major" (the former) and a "minor" (the latter) group (*Heralds of American Literature* [Chicago, 1907], p. 150). With the exception of the Deist Smith, the Minor Wits held the same cultural beliefs as the major group, the average age of the Minors was ten years younger than the Majors, and Cogswell (in 1780) and Smith (in 1786) earned degrees at Yale while Alsop, Theodore Dwight (both in 1798), and Hopkins (in 1784) were awarded honorary degrees there. The most noticeable distinction between the two groups is the amount of poetry they produced. The Major Wits were prolific to the extent of tedium, while, the Minor Wits do not equal in quantity the collected poems of a Barlow or a Timothy Dwight.

At the time the English literati were aware of the newnesses of the *Lyrical Ballads*, the Minor Wits, as did all Federalist poets, emulated the poetics of the English neoclassicists in general and of Pope in particular. The logical patterns of parallel and contrast, the metaphoric meanings, puns, diction, and heroic couplets—all derived from Pope and the Augustans—may be seen in the poetry of the Minor Wits. Gordon E. Bigelow has noticed that the American poets writing around 1800, not unlike the Augustans, "looked upon these 'ornaments,' as the 'enamel,' 'painting,' or 'colors' which a poet could apply, as it were, from the outside, which could be manipulated or revised according to rules which had no reference to the inner intent of the particular poem" (*Rhetoric and American Poetry of the Early National Period* [Gainesville, 1960], p. 41). Although not every poem by the Minor Wits contains all of these devices, almost all of their poems include some of them.

The eighteen numbers of "The Echo" which were collected in *The Echo; With Other Poems* are the basis

INTRODUCTION   xiii

for whatever fame or notoriety the Minor Wits today possess. It is generally agreed that Alsop edited these parodies, burlesques, satires, and lampoons, but Cogswell, Dwight, Hopkins, and Smith either co-authored various numbers with Alsop or wrote some individually. The individual "Echoes" attack the elderly Samuel Adams, the philosophy of H. H. Brackenridge, speeches by John Hancock, the general behavior of the Jacobins or Democrats, the French Revolution, and the archenemy of the Federalists, Thomas Jefferson. The Federalist *Echo*, then, ridicules in heroic couplets the principles of the Democrats. Alsop and the other Minor Wits, "using every tactic of the smear and the big lie, . . . branded the republican Tammany sometimes as 'Jacobin,' a term equivalent to the modern 'Red' or 'Commie,' and hurled personal abuse at men of their own kind . . . whose espousal of republican principles made them traitors to their class. They stirred up class prejudice against 'high-flying mushrooms,'—against newly-made citizens of Irish birth in particular—and against native born 'people's friends' like John Hancock of Massachusetts, who not only fraternized with foreigners but treated 'Negroes to a royal dance' " (Mary Dexter Bates, "Columbia's Bards: a Study of American Verse from 1783 through 1799," Unpub. diss., [Brown Univ., 1954], p. 36).

The spirit of *The Echo* is accurately captured in the plates by the miniature painter Elkanah Tisdale (1771-   ). Tisdale, who allegedly wrote and illustrated the political satire entitled *The Gerry Mander*

INTRODUCTION

(Salem, 1812), was also responsible for the plates in Trumbull's *M'Fingal*. It appears that since Tisdale did the plates in both *The Echo* and *M'Fingal*, two of the most important volumes in our early National period, he possessed at least the spirit of the Wits. Scholarship into the *ethos* of Tisdale the man and the artist might well be a fruitful venture.

In another joint effort Alsop teamed with Dwight and Hopkins to write *The Political Green-House, for the year 1798*. This political satire was patterned after the new year's verses of the day; like *The Echo*, it denounces Jefferson, the Democrats, and the Jacobins. It vividly limns post-Revolutionary France as a wasteland, and it praises the state of Vermont for purging its government of Jacobins. This poem praises Benjamin Rush, but it lampoons the Major Wit Joel Barlow, the conservative turned Democrat.

The remainder of Alsop's poetry is non-political. His most ambitious effort was *The Charms of Fancy*, a work written in 1788 but not published until 1856. If this is Alsop's most ambitious poem, it is not his most successful. The notes are ponderous, the diction is stilted, and "in all its 2300 lines of heroic couplets [it] contains not a fresh image or an original idea" (William P. Trent, *et al.*, ed., *Cambridge History of American Literature* [New York, 1917], I, 165).

Alsop's two best poems are two of his shortest. In "Verses to the Shearwater—On the Morning After a Storm at Sea" (or "Ode to the Sheer Water"), the poet effectively captures the sailor's thoughts after an uneasy night, and he neatly juxtaposes the tumult of the waves and the civilization of the sailor with the simple existence of the bird. "Song from the Italian" may well not be a translation at all since there is nowhere a reference to a specific Italian verse. This *carpe diem* poem, while not possessing the urgency of Marvel's "To His Coy Mistress," is nonetheless a delightful attempt by the speaker to seduce, by means of logic, the "fair Iola." It may be true that "as a poet Alsop was often elegant, but his verse was generally without energy" (Rufus W. Griswold, *The Poets and Poetry of America* [Philadelphia, 1842], p. 59); still, these two short poems indicate that on occasion Alsop's "powers were certainly above the ordinary level of our native authors" (Samuel Kettell, *Specimens of American Poetry* [Boston, 1829], II, 55).

Alsop, proficient in several languages, translated a number of poems into English, especially from the Italian. His longest translation is *The Enchanted Lake of the Fairy Morgana*, a translation of the second book of the comic Italian poet Francisco Berni's *Orlando Inamorato*. Alsop is here "unhampered by that self-consciousness and stiffness of expression which are the most common faults of the inexperienced translator" (William B. Otis, *American Verse 1625-1807* [New York, 1909], p. 275), and the poem is enhanced by the poet's own corrections and notes.

Elihu Hubbard Smith, editor of *American Poems, Selected and Original*, the first anthology of American poetry, produced little poetry himself. Smith's version of Goldsmith's ballad "Edwin and Angelina," the opera *'Edwin and Angelina, or the Banditti, an Opera in Three Acts,* contains the abundance of romanticism that was characteristic of the late eighteenth century. It was performed only once on the New York stage. This first American drama of outlaws probably influenced Dunlap to write the second outlaw drama, *The Man of Fortitude* (Marcia E. Bailey, *A Lesser Hartford Wit, Dr. Elihu Hubbard Smith 1771-1798* [Orono, Maine, 1928], p. 107).

In "Occasional Address" Smith apotheosizes the theater. He traces the history of the theater from the mystery plays to the English actor Barton Booth (d. 1733), and he believes that a play should delight,

> But greater still, and far more nice the art,
> To fix the impressive moral in the heart.

Smith also begs his audience to be patient and not to chide actors or dramatists who do not compare favorably with Shakespeare, Dryden, or Colley Cibber. Although it contains an abundance of names and allusions and although it is at best a minor occasional piece, this poem appears to be ideally suited for the theater audience to which it was presented by the actor John Hodgkinson.

Smith also wrote twenty-one of the thirty-five poems in the Ella-Birtha-Henry correspondence. Smith, who signed his name "Ella" in a 1791 letter to Cogswell, was

"Ella," Joseph Bringhurst, Jr., was probably "Birtha," and Mason Fitch Cogswell was "Henry." These poems were published in the *Gazette of the United States* (Philadelphia) from February to August, 1791.

During the eighteenth century the sonnet became an ignored poetic form. Five of Smith's sonnets were written in 1788 and are characterized by the "overstrained sensibility of his period, by the usual colorless personifications, and by an amount of inversion and ineptness in adjusting his structure and rhymes to the Italian sonnet scheme which are in striking contrast to his later fluency, and are doubtless due to the immaturity of the writer" (Bailey, p. 33). Smith's mature poetry, while infested with unimaginative diction, possesses a sincerity, especially in "Ode Written on Leaving the Place of My Nativity," that makes his poetry more readable than that of many of his contemporaries.

There has been little written about the poet Theodore Dwight, the younger brother of Timothy. It is known that, next to Alsop, Dwight wrote most of *The Echo*, that his effort in *The Political Green-House* was equal to that of Alsop and Hopkins, and that he wrote the "Triumph of Democracy, A Poem" and "Sketches of the Times, For the Year 1807" which are included in *The Echo* volume. However, only a few other of his poems are extant. Jared P. Kirtland's notes to "Jefferson and Liberty" (not reprinted here) attribute "Moll Carey" to Dwight. Dwight wrote "Moll Carey" to satirize the Democrats' singing of "Jefferson and Liberty" in which they commemorated Jefferson's election to the Presidency. Dwight is biting, sarcastic, and unfair throughout the poem, and his are the most caustic comments made toward the Democrats by the Minor Wits.

In "Lines Addressed to a Mother" Dwight sensitively captures a mother's feelings for her child, and in "Lines on the Death of Washington" he skillfully avoids the temptation to which Alsop succumbed in his poem on the same subject. Alsop was unable to limit his poem; it is weakened by the long and superfluous summary of a life that was well known to all Americans. Dwight's eulogy is straightforward and concise, and it is only when he ranks the dead hero above all the ancient sages and refers to our "widow'd country" that his emotion becomes overly patronizing. (See William A. Bryan, *George Washington in American Literature 1775-1865* [New York, 1952], pp. 154, 156 for statements on these poems by Alsop and Dwight.)

Lemuel Hopkins composed "Echo XVIII"—which was published separately as *The Democratiad*,—and *The Guillotina*, both of which comment on repercussions from the Jay Treaty. He also was co-author of *The Political Green-House* and was, with Humphreys, Trumbull, and Barlow, one of the authors of *The Anarchiad*. (The reader is referred to *The Anarchiad*, ed. by William K. Bottorff, [Gainesville, Florida: Scholars' Facsimiles & Reprints, 1967], for a reprint and for a more detailed discussion of that poem).

INTRODUCTION   xix

Hopkins is perhaps best known for his three shortest poems. When he wrote "Epitaph on a Patient killed by a Cancer Quack" in 1785, the medical profession was in its infancy and was in danger of becoming overwhelmed by folk remedies and superstition. In medicine there were many able and outstanding doctors, but there was also an abundance of quacks (Richard H. Shryock, *Medicine and Society in America, 1600-1860* [Ithaca, 1962], pp. 5, 143). It was those quacks that the poet-physician Hopkins satirizes in his masterfully crafted poem. Leon Howard has noticed that in this poem Hopkins "announced in almost every line, the appearance of a new writer whose rough, nervous wit was as stimulating in its matter-of-fact purpose as it was unpretentious of the 'higher' literary aims of more ambitious men" (*The Connecticut Wits* [Chicago, 1943], p. 171). Both "The Hypocrite's Hope" and "On General Ethan Allen" are similar harsh attacks on hypocrisy and Deism, or, as Hopkins saw it, atheism. Hopkins aided Barlow in versifying Dr. Watts's Psalms in 1785. Despite a considerable controversy over who versified the individual Psalms, it is generally agreed that Hopkins did Psalm LXXXVIII.

Hopkins had no literary ambitions, but his caustic writing makes him the most easily identifiable of the Minor Wits. He possessed a good power of description, a keen sense of satire, and an original and pungent humor. Stanley T. Williams has observed that "Hopkins' verses indicate the inclination among the Wits, not merely toward the grandiose aims of Humphreys,

Barlow, and Dwight, but toward poetry as a kindly, witty instrument for daily incidents and human foibles" (*The Literature of Connecticut* [New Haven, 1936], pp. 13-14). Hopkins did indeed comment on "daily incidents and foibles" in poetry that was far from kindly. This poet's lampoons are among the most vicious poems written by the Minor Wits.

Mason Fitch Cogswell is the most perplexing of the Minor Wits. His name is continuously mentioned as a member of the coterie; yet with the exception of a few unenumerated lines in the "Henrico Echo" ("Echo X") and the "Henry" poems, we possess none of his poetry. Kettell records that Cogswell was present at William Brown's office in Hartford with Alsop, Theodore Dwight, and "a few others" when the idea for *The Echo* was conceived (*Specimens of American Poetry*, II, 55); Francis Parsons claims, without foundation, that Cogswell was "one of the chief contributors to 'The Echo' " (*The Friendly Club, And Other Portraits* [Hartford, 1922], p. 30); and Leon Howard, also without foundation, contends that Cogswell "was too modest about his literary ability to cooperate fully with the others, although he wrote copiously in secret" (*The Connecticut Wits*, p. 201). Aside from a 1793 letter from Alsop to Cogswell which proves that Cogswell helped compose *The Echo,* conclusive evidence that Cogswell wrote poetry is found in a letter from Smith to Cogswell in March, 1791: "I have written to Theodore [Dwight] on the subject of a poetical cor-

INTRODUCTION

respondence and I hope you will be persuaded to cast in your contributions, even if it be like the poor widow's mite. I have begun and done something in the business and am prepared to carry it on somewhat further. To receive assurance of support from you will encourage me to act with the more vigour and attention. You have already many small pieces in your hands and it requires neither much time or much severity of application to produce others" (Quoted from Bailey, p. 46). The "poetical correspondence" is the Ella-Birtha-Henry correspondence. This letter leaves no doubt that Cogswell was "Henry": he was aware of the correspondence, Smith asked him to enter into the correspondence which was already begun, and Henry did not contribute a poem until two months after the correspondence began in February, 1791.

Grace Cogswell Root, a descendent of Cogswell, grants that Trumbull, the two Dwights, Humphreys, Hopkins, Alsop, and Smith were "part of M.F.C.'s background, and occasionally of his foreground, in Hartford," but she doubts that the belief "that he was an official member of 'the Hartford Wits' has any corroborating testimony" (*Father and Daughter, A Collection of Cogswell Family Letters and Diaries, 1772-1830*, [West Hartford, Connecticut, 1924], p. 35). It must be recalled that membership in this coterie was not "official"; Cogswell's literary status, while still undefined, rests somewhere between the claims of Parsons and Root. Cogswell was probably not a major contributor to *The Echo*, and he was probably the least prolific of the Minor Wits. Nonetheless, there is no discussion of the Minor Wits that fails to include Cogswell as at least a confidant to the others of that group. Even if he was not an "official member" of the Minor Wits, Cogswell, like Tisdale, embodied the spirit of that group.

In this volume I have attempted to cull all of the poems of the Minor Wits that have previously been published. It is always impossible to locate every fugitive piece, but the republishing of the Ella-Birtha-Henry correspondence, Alsop's translations from Silius Italicus, and other lost poems are the fruits of such a search. The authorship of several of these poems is in doubt, but for the sake of completeness such works as *Aristocracy. An Epic Poem* and Psalm LXXXVIII, works often attributed to one of the Minor Wits, are included. It is with great satisfaction that these poems are for the first time collected and published for the scholar or dilettante who is interested in "the first significant group of American men of letters" (Williams, p. 1).

BENJAMIN FRANKLIN V

University of Michigan
January, 1967

NOTES

Following the page number of this edition is given the first printing of the item. An occasional explanatory statement is also included.

1: The twenty units in *The Echo* appeared (with the exceptions noted) in *The American Mercury,* Hartford, Connecticut. Numbers II and III, which were omitted from the book, are printed on pages 379 and 381. Other items in *The Echo* are listed under the appropriate page number. "Epistle to The Echo" on page xv is said to be by John Quincy Adams.

      I: August 8, 1791.
    IV: October 3, 1791.
     V: November 21, 1791.
    VI: January 23, 1792.
   VII: March 12, 1792.
  VIII: October 29, 1792.
    IX: January 14, 1793.
     X: January 21, 1793.
    XI: February 25, 1793.
   XII: May 6, 1793.
  XIII: Not previously printed.
  XIV: July 8, 1793.
   XV: September 2, 1793.
  XVI: November 11, 1793.
 XVII: August 25, 1794.
XVIII: September 8, 1794.
  XIX: *Connecticut Courant,* Hartford, August 20, 1798.
   XX: Not previously printed.

187: *Gazette of the United States,* Philadelphia, May 1, 1798.

xxiv NOTES

195: See page 863 where the original pamphlet containing Canto I is reprinted. The extracts in *The Echo* alone survive of Canto II. The poem has been ascribed without evidence to Henry Brockholst Livingston (1757-1823). M—k on page 197 is Timothy Matlack (1733-1829), an active member of the Democratic Society in New York City.
210: *Connecticut Courant,* January 1, 1795.
219: *Ibid.,* January 1, 1796. See also pages 349-351.
233: See pages 352-360.
267: Not previously printed.
283: *Connecticut Courant,* January 7, 1802.
295: *Ibid.,* January 4, 1804.
313: *American Mercury,* July 11, 1791.
379: *Ibid.,* August 22, 1791
381: *Ibid.,* August 29, 1791.
387: The editor is Theodore Dwight, Jr., the son of the poet.
679: Some copies of *A Poem* have the following after line 8:

> In swelling phrase and terms unmeaning veils
> Her hellish plots, her dark designs conceals,

735-768: *American Poems* (New York, 1793), ed. by Elihu Hubbard Smith, pp. 251-284.
769: *The Port Folio,* April, 1818, p. 227.
770: *Specimens of American Poetry* (Boston, 1829), 3 vols., ed. by Samuel Kettell, II, 60-61.
772: *The Port Folio,* Philadelphia, March 1818, p. 241.
774: *The Poets of Connecticut* (5th ed., Hartford, 1843), ed. by Charles W. Everest, pp. 103-104.
775: *The Monthly Magazine and American Review,* New York, July, 1799, pp. 319-320
778: *Ibid.,* July, 1799, p. 320.
780: *Ibid.,* December, 1800, pp. 477-480.
786: *The Port Folio,* October, 1817, pp. 349-350.
788: *The Poets of Connecticut,* p. 104.
889: The Ella-Birtha-Henry poems originally appeared in *The Gazette of the United States* in 1791.

    1. February 23, p. 759.
    2. March 9, p. 774.
    3. March 19, p. 787.

NOTES

4. March 23, p. 791.
5. March 26, p. 795.
6. March 30, p. 799.
7. April 2, p. 803.
8. April 9, p. 810.
9. April 13, p. 815.
10. April 16, p. 818.
11. April 20, p. 823.
12. April 23, p. 825.
13. April 27, p. 831.
14. April 27, p. 831.
15. April 30, p. 2.
16. May 7, p. 10.
17. May 11, p. 15.
18. May 14, p. 17.
19. May 14, p. 18.
20. May 21, p. 25.
21. May 25, p. 29.
22. May 25, p. 30.
23. May 28, p. 33.
24. June 1, p. 38.
25. June 4, p. 42.
26. June 8, p. 47.
27. June 11, p. 51.
28. June 18, p. 57.
29. June 22, p. 62.
30. June 25, p. 67.
31. July 2, p. 73.
32. July 6, p. 78.
33. July 16, p. 90.
34. July 20, p. 94.
35. August 3, p. 110.

928: *The Monthly Magazine*, June, 1799, pp. 239-240.
932: *American Poems*, pp. 219-221.
934: *The American Magazine*, April, 1788, pp. 345-346; reprinted from *American Poems*, pp. 221-222.
939: *Connecticut Courant*, November 7, 1785; reprinted from *American Poems*, pp. 137-139.
941: *The Columbian Magazine*, Philadelphia, May, 1787, p. 445; reprinted from *American Poems*, pp. 139-141.

NOTES

944: *The Columbian Magazine,* March, 1787, p. 344; reprinted from *American Poems,* p. 142.
945: *Dr. Watts's Imitation of the Psalms of David* (Hartford, 1785), ed. by Joel Barlow, pp. 164-165.
949: *Connecticut Courant,* March 3, 1803; reprinted from an untitled pamphlet, in the Brown University Library, containing "Song of Jefferson and Liberty" and "Moll Carey."
958: *American Magazine,* August, 1788, p. 675.
961: *American Poems,* pp. 284-287
964: *Monthly Magazine,* September-December, 1799, pp. 477-478.
967: *Specimens of American Poetry,* II, 73-74.
969: *The Euterpeiad: An Album of Music, Poetry, and Prose* (New York, June 1, 1830), p. 32.

THE POETRY

OF THE

MINOR CONNECTICUT WITS

THE ECHO

THE ECHO,

WITH OTHER POEMS.

1807.

District of New-York, ss. BE IT REMEMBERED, That on the 17th day of January, in the thirty-first year of the Independence of the United States of America, NOAH BAILEY, of the said district, hath deposited in this office, the Title of a Book, the right whereof he claims as proprietor, in the words and figures following, to wit:

" The Echo—with other Poems—1807."

In CONFORMITY to the Act of the Congress of the United States, entitled, " An Act for the encouragement of Learning, by securing the " Copies of Maps, Charts, and Books, to the Authors and Proprietors " of such Copies, during the times therein mentioned;" and also to an Act, entitled, " An Act supplementary to an Act, entitled, An Act for " the encouragement of Learning, by securing the copies of Maps, " Charts, and Books, to the Authors and Proprietors of such Copies, " during the times therein mentioned, and extending the benefits there-" of, to the Arts of Designing, Engraving, and Etching historical and " other prints."

EDWARD DUNSCOMB,
Clerk of the District of New-York.

The Echo.

Printed at the Porcupine Press
by Pasquin Petronius

Tisdale pinx.   *Leney sculp.*

Mercy's Angel
pouring down
Heaven's liquid blessing   *Echo 1. page 4.*

PREFACE.

THE principal poems in this volume, under the title of THE ECHO, owed their origin to the accidental suggestion of a moment of literary sportiveness, at a time when pedantry, affectation and bombast, pervaded most of the pieces published in the gazettes, which were then the principal vehicles of literary information. Willing to lend their aid to check the progress of false taste in American literature, the authors conceived that ridicule would prove a powerful corrective, and that the mode employed in THE ECHO, was the best suited to this purpose. A description of a thunder-storm, in one of the Eastern papers, furnished them not only with the hint, but with a suitable subject for the commencement of their plan. The favourable manner in which this first essay was received, determined them, occasionally, to continue the numbers.

But the ridicule of a vitiated mode of writing was not long the sole object of THE ECHO. The important political changes which soon after occurred, not only in Europe, but in America, produced a corresponding change in the republic of letters; and some of the principal gazettes of this country, exhibited a disgusting display, not only of a perversion of taste in composition, but a still greater perversion of principle, in that hideous morality of revolutionary madness, which, priding itself in an emancipation from moral obligation, levelled the boundaries of virtue and vice, while it contemptuously derided the most amiable and sacred feelings of our nature.

Disgusted with the cruelties exhibited by the French revolution, at a very early stage of its progress, and viewing it as a consuming fire, which, in the course of its conflagration, threatened to destroy whatever was most valuable in society, the authors wished to contribute their efforts in stemming the torrent of jacobinism in America, and resolved to render THE ECHO subservient to that purpose. They, therefore, proceeded to attack, as proper objects of satire, those tenets, as absurd in politics as pernicious in morals, the visionary scheme of equality, and the baleful doctrine that sanctions the pursuit of a good end by the most flagitious means.

Whatever may be the merit of this work, the plan is presumed to be novel. The *poetry of the Anti-Jacobin* forms a species of the burlesque which, perhaps, the most resembles THE ECHO; but that resemblance is remote, and to be found in its general scope and character alone, not in the management of the subjects, in its great outline, not in the minute discriminations of form and feature. In *those* brilliant effusions of wit and genius, the satire is exhibited in a happy burlesque imitation of the peculiar style and sentiments of the writers intended to be ridiculed: in

THE ECHO it consists in occasionally elevating the low style of the original to the solemn dignity of the mock-heroic, in introducing ludicrous images, or quaint and common sayings, and in exhibiting the folly, or pernicious tendency of the opinions advanced, by pursuing them in a train of burlesque reasoning, or by giving a turn to the sentiments and expressions, which may serve to hold them up to ridicule or detestation.

If, like the Epopea or the Drama, satire was restricted by arbitrary rules, sanctioned by long established authority, THE ECHO, as corresponding with no existing model of this species of writing, would, no doubt, be considered as an inexcusable innovation. But Satire, in its plan and conduct, appears to be unshackled by the forms of critical regulation; and is as various in its manner as the various objects which present themselves to the imagination, or the capricious and fanciful combinations suggested by its muse. In scourging the vices of the age or country, or the crimes of individuals, in ridiculing folly, or in delineating the odious or ludicrous traits of the villain or the coxcomb, satire is confined to no prescribed path or beaten road; but employs, at pleasure, the solemn severity of Juvenal, the sportive ease and sprightly wit of Horace, the mock gravity of Tassoni, or the sententious burlesque of Butler.

As a satirical poem, THE ECHO possessed some superior and appropriate advantages. From its free and unconfined nature, it readily admitted the introduction of any circumstance or character, however apparently remote or unconnected with its subject. It is distinguished also by its sudden transitions from the gay to the grave, from the burlesque to the serious; this, and the frequent use of proverbs and vulgar phrases, form its peculiar characteristics. Should it be objected, that many of the lines are flat and prosaic, and the style, sometimes, too low for poetry, the authors would observe, that these circumstances are not only in general conformity with their plan, but in many cases necessarily arise from the nature of the subject. Uniformly to have clothed the ridiculous effusions which formed the subject of their satire in pompous verse, would, in their opinion, not only have rendered the versification more dull and monotonous, but have prevented the ludicrous effect intended to be produced by the striking contrast which it occasionally exhibits.

Though many of the subjects may be considered as local and transitory, and some of them merely sportive, it has been thought proper to retain parts of the whole, excepting the second and third *Echoes;* from the others many passages have been expunged, but without essentially injuring the connection of their constituent parts. Whether the plan adopted by the authors was judicious, or otherwise, it is for the public to determine; they had reason to be pleased with the reception which these verses met with at their first appearance; and they cannot but feel some degree of self-complacency from having, thus early, evinced a decided disapprobation of those pernicious principles which have since produced so much distress and misery to mankind. However unavailing their efforts may have been to check the progress of this alarming evil, they have the satisfaction to reflect, that they have endeavoured to oppose the destructive torrent which threatened to overwhelm every thing good and estimable in private life, every thing venerable and excellent in political society.

Tindale pinx.   Infant Liberty nursed by Mother Mob.   Lowry sculp.

TABLE OF CONTENTS.

	PAGE.
Boston Thunder Storm,	1
Echo,	2
Truth, No. I. Or Birth of Liberty. By I. P. Marten,	5
Echo,	6
Tell it not in Gath. Or, an Eulogy on Samuel Adams. By I. P. Marten,	10
Echo,	12
Newtonian Philosophy controverted,	20
Echo,	22
Concluding Thoughts on the Indian War. By H. H. Brackenridge, of Pittsburgh,	29
Echo,	32
Monier's Advertisement for a School,	40
Echo,	42
Speeches of Governor Hancock to the Legislature of Massachusetts, Nov. 8, 1792,	48
Echo,	51
Impromptu, by Henrico, on the report that the Electors of Virginia, in consequence of their having voted for Governor Clinton as Vice-President, were contumeliously called Jacobins,	60
Echo,	63
Address to Mr. James Blanchard,	73
Echo,	75
G. Or, no Friend to Kings, from the Diary of April 13, 1793,	82
Echo,	84
Echo, No. 13. Extracts from,	93
Norwich Thunder Storm,	96
Echo,	97
A Son of Liberty, from the New-York Journal,	101
Echo,	103
A Frank, in answer to Americanus, from the Diary of October 28, 1793,	110
Echo,	112

	PAGE.
Cassius,	119
Echo,	121
Letter of S. T. Mason to B. F. Bache, inclosing an abstract of the British Treaty, June 29, 1795,	127
Echo,	128
Proceedings of the Town-meeting in Boston, relative to the Treaty,	141
Reply of President Washington to the Address of the Selectmen of Boston,	145
H. H. Brackenridge's Address to the Electors of the Western Counties of Pennsylvania, 1798,	147
Echo,	150
Echo, No. 20, March 4, 1803,	162
Versification of a Letter from a political character in Philadelphia, to his friend in Connecticut, March, 1798,	188
Extracts from Democracy, an Epic Poem—Canto First,	196
from the same—Canto Second,	200
New-Year's Verses for the Connecticut Courant, January 1, 1795,	210
Guillotina, or the Annual Song of the Tenth Muse—January 1, 1796,	220
The Political Green-House for the year 1798—January 1, 1799,	234
Extract of a letter from a gentleman in Philadelphia, to his friend in Hartford, on occasion of Mr. Nicholas's having read in Congress, a passage from the Green-House, January, 1799,	259
Complimentary Address to the Hon. John Nicholas,	260
Triumph of Democracy, for the Connecticut Courant, January 1, 1801,	268
Symptoms of Millennium for 1801—January 1, 1802,	284
Sketches of the Times for 1803—January 1, 1804,	296
Prospect of Happiness for the Jews,	313
Supplementary Notes to the Echo,	319
Supplementary Notes to pages 127-143, Echo, No. XVIII	333
Supplementary Notes to pages 219-232, Guillotina	349
Supplementary Notes to pages 234-259, The Political Green-House,	352
Index,	361
Supplementary Index,	371

CORRECTIONS.

Page	Line	Correction
3	12	for " those" read *the*.
14	25	" bellowing" *bellowings*,
15	5	" boobies" read *loobies*.
15	21	" When" read *While*.
23	13	" For" read *That*.
—	16	after " light." dele period.
—	18	after " so" insert period.
24	1	for " waistcoat's" read *waistcoats*.
27	3	" bid" read *bade*.
—	26	" system" read *system's*.
—	6	" Beholds" read *Behold*.
—		Note, line 3 for " a" read *the*.
—		Note, line 4 dele " home-made."
34		Note, line 20 for " refus'd to" read *would not*.
37	17	" Cyclops" read *Cyclop*.
38	14	" turn'd" read *turn*.
44	18	after " bick'rings" read *e'er*.
48	6	" her" read *his*.
55	6	for " hoops" read *whoops*.
66		Note, line 14 for " and" read *in*.
69		Note, line 3 for " it was said" read *it was stated*.
93	11	of introductory observations, for " councils read *council*.
117	7	" more with" read *with more*.
158	25	In consequence of expunging some lines from this passage a grammatical inaccuracy has been introduced, which, was not discovered in time for correction ; the readers therefore, is desired to substitute the following variation

That man avoid, his vile communion shun,

In black corruption all his counsels run ;

He is a Jacobin of spirit fell,

His breath is poison, and his haunt is hell.

117	1	" for it constitutes" read *'twould constitute*.
180		Note, line 4, for " light" read *slight*.
181	23,	for " pass" read *hap*.
201		Note, line 9, for " any" read *that*.
246		25 & 26 corrected as follows.

To all the ills of war combin'd

Want, sickness, and despair consign'd.

331		dele the first four lines.

Kidale pinx. *Tracy sculp*.

in crowds the Ladies ram,
All wish'd to see and touch the tawny man!. Echo 7 page 37.

LIST OF PLATES.

	PAGE.
1. Engraved Title Page and Vignette,	
2. Mercy's Angel, to front the Title Page.	
3. Infant Liberty, nursed by Mother Mob—Echo 4,	7
4. Blind Sam. the Royal Indian—Echo 7,	37
5. There was a Piper had a Cow—Echo 10,	67
6. Negro Ball—Echo 13,	94
7. Terror excited by a Crow's Nest—Echo 19,	154
8. Ludicrous scene in a Barber's Shop—Democracy,	205

The Plates, in the order given above, are placed in this edition on the Frontispiece and in the facsimile of *The Echo* on pages viii, xii, xiv, xvi, 66, and 67.

☞ THE EDITORS, while they return their grateful acknowledgments to those Gentlemen who have subscribed to this work, regret that, owing to the small number of subscription papers which were returned in season, they have been under the necessity of omitting a list of the subscribers' names.

Terror excited by a Crow's nest.

Echo 19 page 153.

XV

The following elegant Address to THE ECHO, *was received by the Mail from Boston, and printed in the American Mercury of Feb.* 4, 1793 : *It is stated to have been from the pen of a gentleman, who ranks high in the scale of literary and political eminence.*

EPISTLE TO THE ECHO.

Enchanting nymph, whose imitative tongue,
Returns so sweet whate'er is said or sung ;
Accept the tribute of my plausive lays,
For even Echo loves deserved praise.
With thee, sweet maid, the Muses all rejoice,
To hear the vast improvements of thy voice ;
Oft have I woo'd thee, at the midnight hour,
When my fond bosom own'd Miranda's power ;
Oft call'd on thee to fan my tender flame,
And thou, indulgent, didst repeat her name.
But, lovely maid, thy powers were then confin'd
To speak the language of thy prompter's mind ;
Thy voice as each successive speaker taught,
With wit and dullness was alternate fraught :
But now no more thy mimic arts are found
Contracted to the shadow of a sound.—
To nobler faculties thy voice aspires,
And lends to dullness all the Muse's fires.
Where, beauteous nymph, didst thou the talent get,
To hear rank nonsense, and return it wit ?
Where learn the art, like Phrygia's king of old,
To turn the vilest substances to Gold ?
From Folly's brow to tear the mask away ;
Make Vice himself his dirty face display.—
The petty monarch's strutting state deride,
And laugh to scorn the pedant's paltry pride.
Yet, peerless nymph, thy new acquired art
Gives not the same delight to every heart ;
The knave and fool, by thee to shame consign'd,
Nor wit, nor music, in thy voice can find ;
And made the theme of laughter and disdain,
Feel not the charms of thy responsive strain.

* * * * * *

Still gentle nymph, the tuneful verse prolong,
Still taste and virtue shall approve thy song.

"Damn, damn the Author, Publisher I say!" p. 205.

THE ECHO.

NUMBER I.

Boston, July 14th, 1791.

"ON Tuesday last, about 4 o'clock, P. M. came on a smart shower of rain attended with lightning and thunder, no ways remarkable. The clouds soon dissipated, and the appearance of the azure vault, left trivial hopes of further needful supplies from the *uncorked bottles of heaven.* In a few moments the horizon was again overshadowed, and an almost impenetrable gloom mantled the face of the skies. The wind frequently shifting from one point to another, wafted the clouds in various directions, until at last they united in one common centre and shrouded the visible globe in thick darkness. The attendant lightning, with the accompanying thunder, brought forth from the treasures that embattled elements to awful conflict, were extremely vivid, and amazing loud. Those buildings that were defended by electric rods, appeared to be wrapped in sheets of livid flame, and a flood of the pure fire rolled its burning torrents down them with alarming violence. The majestic roar of disploding thunders, now bursting with a sudden crash, and now wasting the rumbling Echo of their sounds in other lands, added indescribable grandeur to the sublime scene. The windows of the upper regions appeared as thrown wide open, and the trembling cataract poured impetuous down. More salutary showers, and more needed, have not been experienced this summer. Several previous weeks had exhibited a melancholy sight : the verdure of fields was nearly destroyed ; and the patient husbandman almost experienced despair. Two beautiful rainbows, the one existing in its native glories, and the other a splendid reflection of primitive colours, closed the magnificent picture, and presented to the contemplative mind, the angel of mercy, cloathed with the brilliance of this irradiated arch, and dispensing felicity to assembled worlds.

" It is not unnatural to expect that the thunder storm would be attended with some damage. We hear a barn belonging to Mr. Wythe of Cambridge caught fire from the lightning, which entirely consumed the same, together with several tons of hay, &c."

HARTFORD, AUGUST 8, 1791.

" *Those mighty tales which great events rehearse,*
" *To fame we consecrate in deathless verse.*"

ON Tuesday last great Sol, with piercing eye,
Pursued his journey thro' the vaulted sky,
And in his car effulgent roll'd his way
Four hours beyond the burning zone of day;
When lo! a cloud, o'ershadowing all the plain,
From countless pores perspir'd a *liquid* rain,
While from its cracks the lightnings made a peep,
And chit-chat thunders rock'd our fears asleep.
But soon the vapoury fog dispers'd in air,
And left the azure blue-eyed concave bare:
Even the last drop of hope, which dripping skies
Gave for a moment to our straining eyes,
Like *Boston Rum*, from heaven's *junk bottles* broke,
Lost all the corks, and vanish'd into smoke.
But swift from worlds unknown, a fresh supply
Of vapour dimm'd the great horizon's eye;

The crazy clouds, by shifting zephyrs driven,
Wafted their courses through the high-arch'd heaven,
Till pil'd aloft in one stupendous heap,
The seen and unseen worlds grew dark, and nature
      'gan to weep.
Attendant lightnings stream'd their tails afar,
And social thunders wak'd ethereal war,
From dark deep pockets brought their treasur'd store,
Embattled elements increas'd the roar—
Red crinkling fires expended all their force,
And tumbling rumblings steer'd their headlong course.
Those guarded frames by thunder poles* secur'd,
Tho' wrapp'd in sheets of flame, those sheets endur'd,
O'er their broad roofs the fiery torrents roll'd,
And every shingle seem'd of burning gold.
Majestic thunders, with disploding roar,
And sudden crashing, bounc'd along the shore,
Till, lost in other lands, the whispering sound
Fled from our ears and fainted on the ground.
Rain's house† on high its window sashes op'd,
And out the cataract impetuous hopp'd,
While the grand scene by far more grand appear'd
With lightnings never seen and thunders never heard.
  More salutary showers have not been known,
To wash dame Nature's dirty homespun gown—
For several weeks the good old Joan's been seen,
With filth bespatter'd like a lazy quean.
The husbandman fast travelling to despair,
Laid down his hoe and took his rocking chair,

  * Vulgarly lightning rods.
  † The old gentleman from whose cellar the junk bottles and demi-johns were taken.

While his fat wife the well and cistern dried,
Her mop grown useless hung it up and cry'd.

   Two rain-bows fair that Iris brought along,
Pick'd from the choicest of her colour'd throng;
The first-born deck'd in pristine hues of light,
In all its native glories glowing bright,
The next adorn'd with less refulgent rays,
But borrowing lustre from its brother's blaze;
Shone a bright reflex of those colours gay
That deck'd with light creation's primal day,
When infant Nature lisp'd her earliest notes,
And *younker Adam* crept in petticoats:
And to the people to reflection given,
" The sons of Boston, the elect of heaven."
Presented Mercy's Angel smiling fair,
Irradiate splendors frizzled in his hair,
Uncorking demi-johns * and pouring down
Heaven's liquid blessings on the gaping town.

   N. B. At Cambridge town, the self-same day,
A barn was burnt well-fill'd with hay.
Some say the light'ning turn'd it red,
Some say the thunder struck it dead,
Some say it made the cattle stare,
And some it kill'd an aged mare;
But we expect the truth to learn,
From Mr. Wythe, who own'd the barn.

   N. B. The design of these verses is to respond to the public ear, from time to time, as they occur, those news-paper performances which may justly claim superior merit, that the fugitive efforts of American genius may be preserved, " Till moons shall wax, and wane no more."

   * Otherwise called demi-jars; but the above is preferred as the most elegant, being a species of the prosopopeia.

ECHO.....NO. IV.*

From the Boston Argus of August 5th, 1791.

TRUTH, No. I.

"LIBERTY, that goddess, which is destined to render happy our world, was born yesterday; she now lies smiling in her cradle. The angels of benignity attend her infancy, and the face of nature is changed into joy and festivity. The people of the ancient world expected her; they worshipped her in many forms, but all were deceptive, and led them astray.

"She dwells on the principle of NATURAL EQUALITY—The voice of NATURE, which is the voice of GOD, says, that "He made of our blood all the nations who dwell on the face of the earth." They were all spoke into being by divine omnipotence; they are all instamped with his image, and all bear the distinguishing mark of reflection, and rationality. To them he gave, without right of exclusion, the surface of the ponderous globe, and the riches of the mighty deep. As he gave them being, so, at his sovereign pleasure, they are recalled to their primeval dust, and laid equally among the forgotten dead. But LIBERTY cheers the vale of life; creates in the rational mind the temper of angels; and attunes the soul for the joys of heaven!

* * * * * * * * * * * * * *

"The people of ATHENS long since worshipped a deity, which they believed to be LIBERTY. Each one when he approached the shrine, advanced with four thousand of his fellow men in

---

* The subject of the second and third Numbers of the Echo being of a local kind, or allusive to circumstances not generally known, the authors have thought it expedient to omit them altogether in the present collection.

chains; with the toils of these wretched beings, he purchased the incense he burned at her altar; with their labours he was enabled to present her with the richest gifts! but she was not there, the demon of vassalage had assumed her divine form, and under the guise of freedom had enslaved the world.

" The world has been for ever in the expectation of the day which we enjoy: and that divine system of revelation, which was intended to give, " peace on earth, and good will to men," would have long ago made the human race happy; but, the tyrant ATHANASIUS, wedded; *unnaturally* wedded, the *church* to the *state*. He believed, and what he believed, he decreed—that all men should believe with him.

* * * * * * * * * * * * * *

" The moment the arm of civil authority is extended between the man and his god, that moment he loses the light of the divinity, within him, and in that moment he becomes a slave. How dare the worms of the dust thus trample upon the sacred rights of each other?"

HARTFORD, OCTOBER 3, 1791.

" *With strange astonishment our eyes behold,*
" *Those wond'rous scenes which wond'rous men unfold;*
" *And still to merit and to genius true,*
" *In broken echoes we the theme pursue.*"

THE other day there chanc'd a dreadful rout,
For lo! old mother SPUNKY had " sent out."
The gossips and the granny had a frolic,
And eat and drank themselves into the cholic;
When, to our joy supreme, on yester morn,
A full twelve-pounder—LIBERTY was born.

In swaddling clothes they pinn'd the baby up,
And laid her smiling in a chicken-coop;
While mother MOB, that steady wet-nurse, press'd
The sturdy infant to her milky breast.
Around benignant angels joyous flock'd,
Some air'd her clouts and some her cradle rock'd,
While grandame Nature shook her grisly chin,
And ey'd the urchin with transporting grin.
In ancient days before the deluge-rain,
Mankind expected she would come in vain;
Before her shrine, in many a changing form,
Of shark, of wild-cat, porcupine and worm,
They used to worship, squabble, sing and pray,
But jack-a-lantern-like she always ran away.
The EQUAL RIGHTS of man her mansion form,
She soars superior to Oppression's storm.
Great NATURE's voice, which now is understood,
To mean the same thing as the voice of GOD,
(That is to us, who all the *twenty* own,
GOD NATURE ranks at least at number one,)
Says of *our* blood all things at first were made,
All wear one image, all pursue one trade,
Claim to this pond'rous globe an equal right,
At times to trade on, and at times to fight,
Sometimes to speculate with mighty sweep,
Sometimes to plunge head foremost in the deep,
Sometimes an outcast on a foreign shore,
Begging with *clouted shoes* from door to door.*
And as he gave us life and being, first
Formed us of clay and particles of dust.

* See Supplementary Notes.

So at his sov'reign will we backward tread,
Hang down our heads, and live among the dead.
But LIBERTY cheers up this vale of woe,
With fallen angels fills the world below,
Makes us feel tuneful as the toad* of even,
And bears us *poose-back* to the joys of Heav'n.

* * * * * * * * * * *

Long since thy Gentile sons, O Athens! paid
Their pure devotions to the sainted Maid,
Her fane adorn'd with richest spoils of war,
And heap'd their offerings round her splendid car,
And, what must yield her goddess-ship delight,
Four thousand men in chains, (a pretty sight,)
Around her shrine, with steps sedate and even,
Solemn as saints who've miss'd the road to heav'n,
In pairs advanc'd, as Noah's cattle mov'd
From the green pastures and the meads they lov'd;
While the good sire, conspicuous at their head
In Sunday wig, the strange procession led,
And Shem and Ham and Japhet in a row,
With goads and cudgels clos'd the goodly show,
Sore vex'd at CAPTAIN NOAH's plan to roam
And leave their sweethearts and their wives at home,
Not relishing a pleasure voyage with hogs,
Skunks, toads and rattle snakes, and *prairie dogs*,†
Their lives at stake, their property afloat,
Raw hands on board, no compass and no boat.

* Commonly called the tree-toad.
† An animal known to the Ante-Diluvians by the name of Woodchuck. For a further account of this wonderful quadruped see Supplementary Notes.

Yet notwithstanding all the vows they paid,
Their grand processions and their proud parade,
When they the Goddess found it was not she,*
But Vassalage to whom they bow'd the knee;
For as, one night with Lemnian wine o'ercome,
The goddess slumber'd in an outer room,
That thievish crony the occasion took,
And stole her clothes, her attributes and look.
* * * * * * * * * * * * * * * *
The world has been for ever and for aye
In expectation of this jovial day.
And that Religion which, from realms above,
Brought peace to earth, and rules the world by love,
Would long ago have made the human race
Blest in th' enjoyment of supernal grace,
Had not the tyrant ATHANASIUS wed
The Church to State, and forc'd the bride to bed:
The unnatural union op'd a devious way,
And, like coquettes, led foolish man astray.
And yet he thought 'twas right—he did indeed—
That all mankind should swallow down his creed.
* * * * * * * * * * * * * * * *
When Civil Power, whose life is but a span,
Extends his arm betwixt the God and man,
That moment stripp'd of all his inward light
He sinks a recreant slave in tenfold night—
How dare these worms, ordain'd the ground to crawl,
And on their bellies in the dust to sprawl,
Mount up, like man, erect on hinder feet,
And kick the shins of every worm they meet.

* For this elegant specimen of hibernianism see the text.

c

ECHO.....NO. V.

From the Argus of November 1, 1791.

" TELL IT NOT IN GATH."

" ON the morning after your last town-meeting, I was on Beacon-Hill, and casting my eyes on the Eastern side of the Monument, read these words——" AMERICANS, WHILE FROM THIS EMINENCE, SCENES OF LUXURIANT FERTILITY, OF FLOURISHING COMMERCE, AND THE ABODES OF SOCIAL HAPPINESS, MEET YOUR VIEW, FORGET NOT THOSE, WHO, BY THEIR EXERTIONS, HAVE SECURED TO YOU THESE BLESSINGS."

You need not wonder that the singular occurrence of the preceding evening, at Faneuil-hall, rushed into my mind. Shall Europe hear, shall our Southern brethren be told, that *Samuel Adams rose to speak in the midst of his fellow citizens, and was silenced!*

That, while others, who were born but in season to enjoy the blessings, which he earned, were applauded, SAMUEL ADAMS *could not be heard!*

Long may we remember that he rose to speak against the THEATRE in Boston, *and could not be heard!* Was he in fault that he wished to speak the sentiments of his heart, and to deliver the language of enlightened religion and truth? Do you blame him, that he wished at death, to leave his country *virtuous* as well as free?

RICHLY HAS HE EARNT THE RIGHT TO SPEAK, AND TO BE HEARD!

Is his voice weak?—That voice once made the proudest kingdom in Europe tremble to its centre. Does his hand shake?— That hand was once firm, strong were its sinews, and ably did it enforce the feelings of a firm heart.—*In whose service has he grown grey? Was it difficult to hear him?* We would have listened with double attention.—*Did we doubt whether he would speak with wisdom?* Then we had lost our memories.

Did we doubt whether he would speak the truth?—Then we must have lost our senses. Had such a thing happened in the days of enlightened Greece, we should never have read it, without being told of the marked disapprobation, with which the good, the virtuous, and the free regarded it. Such, I am happy to say, did on this occasion, discover (some by looks, and some in words) this generous spirit. Our measures are not to be carried by noise and cabal; not by silencing and drowning the voices of those who oppose us. The well-informed advocates of a Theatre did not wish nor attempt it. Judicious arguments and eloquence were used on both sides; but several men as well as boys, did unite to silence an eminent patriot.

It remains that I make a proposal, which will terminate this affair to the honour of the town.

Let the inscription which I have quoted, be copied into the vacant niche, left in the hall door, and under it these words,

" Translated from the monument, to this place,
" In honour of Samuel Adams. The name needs
" No title, nor testimony of applause."

Long may Americans revere the Saviours of their country, and on the records let the occasion be noted with the marked disapprobation of the town. Thus shall future generations of Americans, taught by our example the virtues of 1791, be ashamed to move their tongues, or their feet, when future ADAMS's shall rise to speak.

J. P. M.

HARTFORD, NOV. 21, 1791.

"*Echo unnotic'd lets no rumblings pass,*
"*From mighty Thunder to the Bull-frog's bass.*"

WHERE Gath's proud Beacon lifts its awful form,
Climbs o'er the clouds, and smiles above the storm;
Where Mercy's Angel mounts her lovely bow,
Rides o'er the town, and wets the world below;
Where genius grows to great Goliah's frame,
And leans majestic on a weaver's beam;
Where simple style its classic light displays,
Undeck'd with bombast's meretricious blaze;
Where wax-work Belles assail the wond'ring heart,
And Bowen's Indians make the Ladies start——
And mighty Achish, leader of the state,
By gouts untroubled, rules the still debate,
And Bel and Dragon lend their useful aid,
And John the Baptist shakes his bloody head,
While the Old Hermit* from the realms of light,
Spurs gaping boobies to behold the sight;
Where Nature's Gossips† their strange orgies hold,
This story never, never must be told.

---

* The Old Hermit. A gentleman fortunately rescued from oblivion by Mr. B——, who published a faithful narrative of his life and extraordinary adventures, and has since consigned him to immortality, in ever-during wax. The Echo with pleasure mentions this publication, as it serves to establish this fact, incontrovertibly—that a simple story, unaccompanied with any thing marvellous, is the proper subject of history.—this having been the first successful attempt of American genius in Biography.

† Mother Mob, and the other assistants at the birth of Liberty. See the preceeding Number.

On that sad morn, when Sol's astonish'd ray,
Rose pale and languid from town-meeting day,
On Beacon-Hill my footsteps chanc'd to go,
And my thoughts wander'd o'er a world of woe.
At length I sigh'd so loud it was a groan,
While my eyes read the monumental stone—
" Columbia's sons ! while from this lofty height
" Luxuriant objects crowd the raptur'd sight,
" While blooming small-craft rises up to view,
" And three-mast vessels lie in goodly shew,
" Where social joy spreads out her gay abode,
" And carts and coaches roll along the road;
" Forget not those whose arm of mighty power
" Scar'd British Regulars from this happy shore,
" Who tarr'd and feather'd every Tory's frock,
" And made a tea-pot of your spacious dock."
  Say can you wonder that, in colours bright,
Rush'd on my mind the doings of that night
When Faneuil-Hall with wild amazement shook,
And fain like Balaam's ass had silence broke
To manifest its wrath—but ah ! 'twas plain
No tongue had Faneuil-Hall to vent its pain.
Shall Europe hear, shall Gallia's king be told,
That Prince so spirited, so wise and bold,
Whose duteous subjects, anxious to improve
On common forms of loyalty and love,
Took from their sovereign's hands the reigns of state,
For fear his royal nerves could not support the weight;
And shall our worthy brethren of the South
Be told Sam. Adams could not ope his mouth ?
That mouth whence streams of elocution flow'd,
Like tail of saw-mill, rapid, rough, and loud—

Sweet as the honey-dews that Maia pours
O'er her green forests and her tufts of flowers—
That potent mouth, whence issued words of force
To stun an ox, or terrify a horse.
Be told, that while those brats whose feeble sight
But just had op'd on Freedom's dawning light,
Born in the nick of time that bliss to know
Which to his great and mighty toils we owe,
Receiv'd applause from Sages, Fools, and Boys,
The mighty Samuel could not make a noise—
Be told, that silenc'd by their clam'rous din,
He vainly tried one word to dove-tail in ;
That though he strove to speak with might and main,
His voice and strivings equally were vain.
Thus when on bleak Norwegia's iron shore,
Mid rocky straits, where Ocean's billows roar,
If chance the unwieldy Kraken heedless stray
To make discoveries in the wat'ry way,
Though there the Nations of the deep resort,
And Whales at leisure play, and Grampi sport,
Yet wedg'd in rocks, or grounded on the sands,
For many a league his island bulk expands,
And while the Maelstrom wildly raves around,
And heaven re-echoes to the dreadful sound,
In vain with bellowing loud and fearful cries,
He lifts his voice in thunder to the skies,
Lost and confounded in the mightier roar ;
But silent lies at length, and gives his efforts o'er.

   Long may our souls the fond remembrance prove,
How, with a bosom crowded full of love,
To blast a wicked stage his voice he rear'd
And yet that thundering voice could not be heard.

With equal toil, half-burn'd with Etna's heat,
Thus strives Enceladus to find his feet,
While o'er his back, convuls'd with dreadful pain,
A fiery deluge floats along the plain;
Around th' affrighted boobies stand and stare,
And ask what dreadful creature tumbles there.
Was he in fault that he should wish t' impart
The smoaking feelings of his red-hot heart?
Perhaps Religion would have cloth'd the song,
And truth and bombast roll'd the strains along.
Thus when th' Old Dragon op'd his mighty mouth
Out burst a flood of overwhelming froth,
Down the soft tide three unclean spirits float,
Like frogs in semblance and like frogs in note.
Was he to blame when, struck by mighty death,
He wish'd, by puffing his expiring breath,
To raze the pillars of a vicious stage,
And scatter virtue in his holy rage?
Thus Samson, when Dalilah cut his hair,
Mutter'd and clank'd his fetters in despair,
When Gaza's nobles fill'd the spacious court,
And laugh'd to see the blinded monster's sport,
When lo! the two-legg'd Mammoth rais'd his back,
And down they tumbled with prodigious crack.

Hard has he toil'd and richly earn'd his gains,
Ruin'd his fingers and spun out his brains,
To acquire the right to ope his ponderous jaws,
As the great champion of Sedition's cause.
Once his soft words, like streams of melted tar,
Stuck in our ears and led us on to war;

But now we hear the self-same accents flow,
Unmov'd as quails when buried up in snow.
  Is his voice weak? that dreadful voice we're told,
Once made King George the Third thro' fear turn
    cold.
Europa's kingdoms to their centre shake,
When mighty Samuel bawl'd at freedom's stake,‡
Thus when provok'd at hell's eternal gate,
Grim Cerberus opes his jaws and shakes his pate,
O'er the black regions swells the horrid roar,
Dark Styx affrighted quits his wonted shore,
The sound rolls dreadful through the dire domains,
And coward devils scud across the plains.——
Does his hand shake?—When Sam cried out for war,
His potent hand spread many a coat of tar,
That sinewy hand the feathers scatter'd o'er,
Till Tories' jackets made their bellies sore.
Say for whose sake has Time, that Barber gruff,
O'er his wise noddle shook his powder puff?
Was the task hard to hear the sage's noise?
Perhaps the aweful sound had frighten'd boys;
But we, the sons of wisdom, fond to hear,
With joy had held the breath and op'd the ear.
Did we e'en doubt that Solomon had spoke?
If so, has memory vanished into smoke.
  Could we who oft have known the hoary sage,
With godlike zeal, in party feuds engage—
Those disquisitions calm in which the mind
To candour's season'd, and to truth inclin'd—

‡ Otherwise called a liberty pole.

Say, could we doubt his Jack-a-lantern light
Would guide at length our wandering steps aright
To where Dame Truth, afraid of being found,
In her dark hole lies skulking under ground;
Still as all Nature ere the earthquake stirs,
Hush as a mouse when near Grimalkin purrs;
If so, I think our brains have taken flight,
And bade for aye our foolish heads good night.
Had this event in those bright days been known,
When Greece with glory's blaze illumin'd shone,
Then had we read, and wonder'd as we read
Where sense had gone, and where discretion fled.
What crime so base can with this crime compare?
What deed so dark but match'd with this is fair?
If ancient realms had witness'd this sad tale,
The sun had darken'd, and the skies grown pale;
For sun and sky, more modest in those places,
Were wont full oft in shame to veil their faces.
Some, with much happiness, I'm proud to say,
Did their great spirit wond'rously display;—
While part, by swaggering looks, with force express'd,
The full grown feelings of the swelling breast:
Thus, first of birds, the Turkey-Cock so bold
Around the dunghill ranging uncontroll'd,
With all the pride of self-importance big,
Struts, and looks stately at each passing pig,
While geese and hens around at distance stare,
And wonder who the devil marches there.
Others in words " *sung out*" their discontent,
Like new-made cider struggling for a vent;

Or as when Sirius sheds his sultry ray,
And pours oppressive languor o'er the day,
While the shrunk stream scarce laves its pebbly bed,
And one brown hue is o'er the landscape spread,
In thund'ring prayers the bull-frogs call for rain,
And pond to pond repeats the solemn strain.
Not by such windy sounds, all noise and fume,
Can we our points to carry e'er presume;
Vain, vain the hope by empty blasts t'o'erwhelm
The firm, the mob-lov'd leader of this realm;
This many knew who oft had tried before
With words of sense to still his clam'rous roar.
Sound arguments, like hail-stones, thick were show-
    er'd,
And streams of eloquence on all sides pour'd;
But boys and men, with clamours vile and rude,
Shut up the mouth of that old man so good.
As when, high-soaring in the fields of air,
The guardian hen-hawk fill'd with tender care,
Eyes, with solicitude and keen regard,
The chickens feeding in the poultry yard—
Physician kind, with fondest love preparing
To give the little souls a pretty airing!
The congregation, filled with wild affright,
Hens, geese, and ducks in one shrill scream unite,
And loud to heaven with cries discordant pray
To keep the too-kind gentleman away.

  My text thus prov'd—all that remains behind,
Is to apply the subject to the mind—
By inference clear I'll make the truth go down,
And thus relume the honour of the town.

To ease the torments of the great man's ghost,
Transplant th' inscription here from yonder post,
And in the vacant niche, on glory's boards,
In golden letters write the following words.—
" To honour Sam this bright inscription's made ;—
" 'Twas hither brought with wonderful parade—
" Astonish'd meteors throng'd the realms of day
" While Sam's pure honours streak'd along the way."
 Thus when sublime, by rapid whirlwinds driven,
A kite majestic scales the vault of heaven,
Bright through the air its tail in splendour flies.
And paper glory blazes round the skies.
 Long, O Philistia! shall thy sons revere
Their country's saviours and its Sampsons fear,
While thy fair records this occasion note,
That Wisdom disapprov'd the last town-meeting vote.
Thus shall our sons, and eke our daughters rise,
Stare at our length and wonder at our size:
Whilst we their sires, as time's long race we run,
Boast of the deeds of A. D. Ninety-One.
And should misrule in future times return,
And unborn Demaguoges with faction burn,
Should tar and feathers come again in vogue
And Patriot stand synonimous with rogue—
Perchance some second Sam may rise to day,
And o'er mob-meetings hold an equal sway.

ECHO.....NO. VI.

From the Connecticut Gazette, of October 20, 1791.

[Some time since a writer in the Connecticut Gazette attacked the Newtonian Philosophy with such astonishing force of argument, that many of its friends trembled for its fate. However, as he rested a considerable period, they fondly hoped it would survive the shock. A week or two since, he poured forth another volley, which has induced the Echo to speak in an audible voice, what he had before uttered in a whisper.]

" *Messrs. Green,*
" *Your inserting the following in your useful paper will oblige one of your readers and perhaps make others reflect.*

" THE Newtonian philosophy accounts for all the phenomena of nature by one principle, which it supposes to pervade all material nature: and the principle is this, viz.—that matter attracts matter. But, that this principle never did, nor does now, nor never will exist, I thus prove.

" If matter attracts matter, either there must be an universal plenum, or matter must act where it is not. But, that there is not an universal plenum in material nature has been mathematically demonstrated by all Newtonians of any note: and that matter can act where it is not, is an impossibility, for it is an impossibility that matter should be where it is not—therefore a much greater impossibility that it should act where it is not, and therefore matter, never did—does not now—nor ever will attract matter.

" Nay, farther, even upon the hypothesis of an universal plenum, in material nature, matter's attracting matter would be physically inconsistent with the essence of matter. For, though in a plenum all the particles would be perfectly coherent or contiguous to each other, yet their coherency or contiguity would not be the effect of the attraction of the particles, but of something else, namely, immaterial impulse *ab extra*. The principal essential property of matter, which is to resist all change of its present state of rest or motion, is absolutely inconsistent with the idea of matter's attracting matter: for, since a particle of matter, from its *vis inertiæ*, cannot possibly change its own state of rest or motion, it must be absolutely impossible, that it should change the state of rest or motion of an extraneous particle.

"To go still farther, if matter should be supposed unresisting, that is, deprived of its *vis inertiæ*, that it would be still more unfavourable to the Newtonian principle, that matter attracts matter, may be easily demonstrated. Hence, let the Newtonians no more pretend to account for the various phenomena of nature by their favourite principle, till they refute these arguments and many more ready to be adduced. ANONYMOUS."

HARTFORD, JANUARY 23, 1792.

" *Lo* ECHO *from her solemn sounding shell,*
" *Again strikes up the philosophic knell !*
" *While borne along the whispering tide of air,*
" *The ghost of Genius seems to stop, and stare.*"

DEAR Messrs. Green, with diffidence extreme,
I ask a corner for my humble theme,
In your most useful paper, which appears
To grow in wonder, as it grows in years,
(How much more pleasing than that hackney'd road
By other papers, and by Nature, trod ;
For Wonderment, like Love, delights to spread
Her airy phantoms round the youthful head,
But soon retires, when Age's wint'ry snow,
Sheds its white honours o'er the wrinkled brow.)
'Twill, kind as dews on Hermon that distil,
One reader's breast with sweet sensations thrill,
In rich manure the seeds of knowledge sow,
And, like a hot-bed, make reflection grow.

THAT *Matter's* chain'd to *Matter*—seems to be
The underpinning of philosophy
By Newton taught—the wonder-working sage,
With this idea blotted many a page ;
This favourite truth the wizard thought he found
On sea, and land, above and under ground—
A kind of cord of love, more strong than leather,
Which ties bears, snakes, and owls, and men toge-
    ther—

A sort of yoke, how strange so'er it seem,
That makes creation one stupendous team.
But to those souls who'll condescend to list,
I'll prove this principle did ne'er exist,
And never will—Nay more—with all their clatter,
I'll prove that *Matter* never heard of *Matter*.
  If *Matter* is by *Matter* still attracted,
This only proves that *Matter* is distracted,
Or else this self-same *Matter* must act most
Where *Matter*, motion, time, and space are lost.
But that dame Nature ne'er a plenum makes,
We know by this, dame Nature ne'er mistakes;
For she abhors this monster more than space,
More than a Quaker hates a golden lace,
More than the tuneful choir the bird of night,
Or more than Atheists hate Religion's light.
Newtonians fain would prove—but well we know
'Tis not—nay more—if 'tis, it shan't be so,
For if this magic Plenum fills all nature,
And holds in durance every struggling creature,
Even Nature's self must be content at home,
Nor even a "*groaning*," force her steps to roam—
Besides, that *Matter* should find cords to pull
Beyond where space with *something* is fill'd full,
Is just as likely as that sense should be
Found in those skulls were dwells *Inanity*:
And hence this *ergo*—Matter does not now,
Nor ever did, nor ever will, find how
By word, or deed, or any juggling tricks,
To make discordant atoms friendly mix.
  If plenum fills up all, both far and wide,
Why then 'tis plain we're full on every side,

Our waistcoat's stuff'd and plenteously lin'd,
With flesh, and fish, and fowl of every kind;
And much I fear dame Nature will complain,
And wring, and twist her sides, in cholic pain;
Unless good Dr. B——e† will assist her,
And make a vacuum with his sovereign clyster.
For tho' a goose, or turkey, may delight
In being stopp'd and cramm'd so very tight;
Yet we, a fowl of somewhat different palate,
Had rather have the meat without that sallad.
But if amidst this vast terrestrial ball,
One universal Plenum fills up all,
And *Matter's* parts are wedg'd as close together,
As three in bed, or pigs in stormy weather,
Yet, not conjoin'd by Love's attractive power,
No smiling Hymen waits the nuptial hour;
But by external impulse made to wed,
Are forc'd reluctant to the marriage bed.
In all things, great or small, this fact we see,
That ne'er with motion *Matter* can agree:
For can a log of wood, or stack of hay,
Take leg, or wing, and bear itself away?
No—when we wish such things to move, of course
We take a team of cattle, or a horse.
This fully proves that *Matter* has no motion
And Newton's system all an idle notion.
'Tis true, in times of old, when Orpheus sung,
When stones were tender soul'd, and Nature young,

---

† The learned gentleman, who has lately so ably defended the Newtonian system; and proved incontrovertibly, that Matter may exist with Motion,

When brick-kilns went to school,† & quarries spoke,
And music trembled from the lofty oak,
To sound of human voice the rocks would prance,
And elms and maples join in country dance.
Now less polite, their feelings callous grown,
No voice of music stirs a stick, or stone,
And we in vain our sweetest notes might raise,
In these barbarian and degenerate days,
And fairly fret away both lungs, and liver,
Before a stump, or stone, would condescend to quiver.
 This inference then is fair, and plain to see,
If join'd with *Motion*, *Matter* ne'er can be,
Where ever *Motion* comes, when e'er 'tis known
To act on timber, metal, clay, or stone,
Whate'er the agent that directs its force,
Air, water, fire, man, cattle, mule, or horse,
Matter, like Rat, when Guinea-pig too night‡
Offends his savoury nose, and shocks his eye,
Vex'd at the intrusion, in a mighty huff,
Packs up her duds, and surlily goes off,
And as she takes her leave (so sweet and civil)
Wishes the clownish fellow to the devil.
Thus in a torrent swell'd with wintry rains,
That rends the hills, and deluges the plains,
Bears wild destruction on its foaming wave,
And sweeps the pumpkins to a watery grave;
Or in a kettle, where some house-wife good,
Prepares the Mush, § her children's homely food,

† Supposed to mean singing schools.   ‡ A curious fact in natural history.   § Otherwise called hasty pudding.

While urg'd by fires beneath, the mingled mass,
High o'er the brim, hoarse muttering strives to pass;
No *Matter* can reside, for Motion's power
Impels the pudding's rise, and torrent's roar;
But when the torrent in a pond subsides,
By storms unruffled, and unmov'd by tides,
When freed from fire, the pudding swells no more,
And e'en its last faint, dying, sputtering's o'er,
Quick to her wonted home, the foe now gone,
Matter returns, and occupies her throne.

Yet should we farther go, and e'en suppose
That *Matter* no resistance will oppose,
But fir'd with saintly, Methodistic pride,
Bear like an ox the basting of his hide,
Patient as Fakir,‡ who from high rais'd chair,
Exhorts the crowd with sanctimonious air,
And fill'd with somewhat singular a notion,
Makes of his rump a pin-ball of devotion—
That is, her *vis inertiæ* wholly gone,
And left poor *Matter* empty, and alone,
Still no assistance to their systems vain,
These idle sons of Newton will obtain,
For ne'er by strong attraction's impulse led,
Will brother *Matter* sister *Matter* wed,
As we can prove by father Nile's† assistance,
When FURTUM keeps the Moon at proper distance.

† A peculiar kind of devotees in India, who prove the fervency of their piety, by sitting upon cushions made of ten-penny nails.

† A wicked wizard, who by the assistance of a magical type, in which the Planet Furtum and the Moon, occupy the principal places, pretends to surprising discoveries, and has been sentenced by a court of justice to pay an exemplary fine, as the righteous retribution of practising the black art.

Long has the world been lur'd by Newton's schemes
His systems strange, and philosophic dreams,
And long has fashion bid all ranks proclaim,
In terms of loud applause his hallow'd name,
From the Astronomer whose piercing eyes,
Beholds events dark-pictur'd in the skies,
Young bratling planets in their cradles sleeping,
And stars as yet unhatch'd in egg-shells peeping,
To Show-man wondrous, who, by feats so rare,
With magic lantern makes the children stare,
Thus when Redress from Stamp-act's dreary night,
O'er fair Columbia shed its morning light,
The cheering ray thro' all her regions ran,
And grateful incense warm'd the heart of man,
While each bright city from Bostonia's shore,
To southern Charlestown join'd in glad uproar,
Gilt with their streaming fires the shades of even,
And bade the cannon tell the news to heaven;
Fair Hebron felt inspir'd, and from a stump
Her sons, for lack of cannon, fir'd a pump.†
But hence Newtonians vain no longer dare
With heaven-taught truths your sophistry compare,
Nor with your brittle arguments essay
To prove that Matter's legs, and runs away;
Why *Moodus*‡ groans in such convulsive frolics,
And why Hull's physic cures all sorts of cholics,

† Vide Peters' history of Connecticut—a performance so celebrated for a close adherence to Truth, that many people have conjectured the holy divine pumped the old lady out of her well by the assistance of a Hebron Cannon.

‡ A place celebrated for a kind of home-made earthquakes, which will probably at some future day make a conspicuous figure in the natural history of this country.

Relinquish then the unvailing strife,
For while I've matter left, or breath, or life,
I'll prove, should logic fail, by force of fist,
That Plenum *Vacuums* every where exist ;
Then will you gladly own yourselves mistaken,
And give your tenets up to save your bacon.
So when proud Pharaoh, loth with Jews to part,
Froze his dark soul, and steel'd his harden'd heart,
Though frogs, and lice around the monster pour'd,
Fleas bit his back, and thunder o'er him roar'd,
Though murrain, boils, and blains attack'd his hide,
Yet nought could start him 'till his children died.

ECHO.....NO. VII.

From the National Gazette.

" FARTHER AND CONCLUDING THOUGHTS ON THE INDIAN WAR, BY H. H. BRACKENRIDGE, OF PITTSBURG.

" I CAN easily excuse those, who, from motives of humanity, call in question the justness of our cause in the war against the Indians. But could I make my observations theirs with respect to the ruthful disposition of a savage, that is not soothed continually by good offices, or kept down by fear; could I give my knowledge, recollection, and impression of the accumulated instances of homicide committed by the tribes with whom we are at war, the humane would be more humane, for their feelings would be more awake, not in favour of these people, but of the persons butchered by them in cold blood, or dragged to that pole seen by the soldiers under General HARMAR, by the Miami village, where the ground was beat like a pavement by the miserable victims moving round the stake to avoid the still pursuing tortures, which the circle of black coals, at a distance from the piles burned, shewed whence they brought their brands and heated gun-barrels to afflict the object. All this, though there have been but three instances since the conclusion of the war with Britain, where an Indian has been hurt on our part; one on the Susquehanna, and two on the Ohio: with respect to one of which instances, that of M'Guire and Brady, it is a doubt whether they were hostile or peaceable.

" I consider men who are unacquainted with the savages, like young women who have read romances, and have as improper an idea of the Indian character in the one case, as the female mind has of real life in the other. The philosopher, weary of the vices of refined life, thinks to find perfect virtue in the simplicity of the unimproved state. He sees green fields and meadows in the customs and virtues of the savages. It is experience only can relieve from this calenture of the intellect. All that is good and great in man results from education ; and an uncivilized Indian is but a little way removed from a beast, who, when incensed, can only tear and devour, but the savage applies the ingenuity of man to torture and inflict anguish.

" A great dependance seems to be placed on Cornplanter and his party. I know Cornplanter, and Big-Tree, and Half-Town ; they are good, as Indians, and are well disposed to us, because they can be of little or no account on the other side. Brandt treats them with contempt, and adheres to the British. Instead of bringing them down at a great expense, and presenting them in Philadelphia, and appropriating 800 dollars for their maintenance and vestment, were things put upon a right footing, and Presqu'isle garrisoned, we should have no more occasion for Cornplanter, or Big-Tree, or Half-Town, than they would have for us ; and if we gave them goods, they would give us furs.

" I have seen a certain blind Sam, so called, because blind of an eye, taken down to this city, passed for a warrior, dining at clubs, and have heard of him presented at a ball, on his way down : the favoured ladies looking upon themselves as beatified in receiving the salute of a king. When he returned, with a laced waistcoat, the vulgar Indians that before thought him one of them, laughed immoderately at the farce.

" As these are desultory observations, I remark and conclude that some think me rather rash in presuming that the king of Britain has given any countenance, directly or indirectly to the Indian depredations or armaments. I should be sorry to do injustice to any power, and it was with great difficulty that I admitted the idea, but I have been convinced of it, and can have no doubt, because that government could not but have heard of the hostilities, and by one simple word of the commandant of Detroit to M'Kee and Brandt, we should have had a perfect peace. But M'Kee and Brandt, when messengers were sent to call the Indians to the treaties at Muskingum and at Miami, advised them not to go: witness——I shall suppress my authorities. It may perhaps injure these men in their future trade with the Indians or connections at Detroit. Good God! that an island where I drew my first breath, where a Milton and a Hume have lived, where a Howard has sacrificed to humanity—there can be those who can aid, at least not disarm, what may be in their power, the savage of his axe, battered on the skulls of their species, in the cottage or the fields of the settlements adjoining their province—they could do this by the surrender of the posts, for at that moment I proclaim peace to to the westward, and ensure safety.

"It may be thought that I am inhumane in my sentiments towards the savages; It is a mistake; I am inhumane to no man or men; but in order to be humane, let me have it in my power. Let myself first be safe, and then I can shew what humanity dictates. The question is, Whether we shall submit ourselves to the savages or they to us? I say, let us conquer because we cannot depend upon them, for the weaker ever distrusts the mightier, and the unenlightened man, the sensible; but when we shall have it in our power, let us dispense treaties on principles of reciprocity (to use the term of the diplomatists) and let them know that we are not about to purchase a treaty, but to make one and preserve it. These principles, founded in nature and truth, will strike the mind of the savage, that we ask no more than he ought to give, or that we give more than he has a right to ask. By the immortal gods! (a Roman oath, but sworn with christian devotion,) if this principle could be made the basis of our negotiations, we should govern not only these people, but all the world with whom we have to do. When I say *govern*, I mean *command* of them all, that is our right on principles of the laws of nations or of nature. But in our affairs with the western Indians, we have for a series of years pursued a sickly tampering system of half peace, half war, from which nothing could result but half success. A bold and decisive act of effective hostility at the conclusion of the war with Britain would have composed these Indians, and preserved in existence the countless numbers that have fallen victims to torture or death on the bourne of the wilderness. It was therefore inhumane not to have adopted this system, which would have been effectual. But I saw, and lamented the circumstance of the Congress beseiged with candidates for agencies and commissionships, and messengers, and runners, to negotiate with these tribes.

"There was not a thing that had ever seen a squaw or a half king, or a chief, or had heard the guttural sound of a Kickapoo, or a Delaware, but would have it that he understood fifty Indian languages, and could interpret, and could draw all the tribes after him just as a boy would whistle pigeons. Hence, treaty, and not war."

HARTFORD, MARCH, 1792.

" And every time they fir'd it off,
" It took a horn of powder,
" It made a noise like Father's gun,
" Only a nation louder."

[The foregoing sounds made by H. H. BRACKENRIDGE, have reached the ECHO, which in faithfulness she is obliged to respond. It is presumed there were others equally important, but, being indistinct, they are lost to immortality.

I GRANT my pardon to that dreaming clan,
Who think that Indians have the rights of man;
Who deem the dark skinn'd chiefs, those miscreants base,
Have souls like ours, and are of human race;
And say the scheme† so wise, so nobly plann'd.
For rooting out these serpents from the land,

† The talents of the Secretary at war, however generally esteem'd, have been too long concealed under the shade of a peaceful administration. We

To kill their squaws, their children yet unborn,
To burn their wigwams, and pull up their corn;
By sword and fire to purge the unhallow'd train,
And kindly send them to a world of pain,
Is vile, unjust, absurd :—as if *our* God
One single thought on Indians e'er bestow'd,
To them his care extends, or even knew,
Before Columbus told him where they grew.

O could I, pois'd on Observation's wings,
Point whence the Indian's ruthless temper springs,
That ruthless temper which, like bear unchain'd,
Is proof to kindness, nor by fear restrain'd,
Could that vast knowledge which my skull contains,
Once find its passage from my wilder'd brains,
And spring to view with recollection fraught,
Of all I've ever dreamt, or ever thought;
Then would I tell of homicides so dire,
Of tom'hawk, scalping-knife, and torturing fire,
Of wicked pole at the Miami town,
Which Harmar went on purpose to pull down,
While roused to pity by the potent strain,
Humanity herself would grow humane;
The soul would shudder, and the cheek turn pale,
And uncork'd feelings foam like bottled ale;

sincerely congratulate the public on *their* late glorious emersion from that obscurity. The well concerted plan, and skilful arrangements, of the two late expeditions, have discovered a genius for war, and a foresight scarce to be paralleled in the annals of time. The sacrifice of two armies, in order to lull the savages into such perfect security as to render them an easy conquest to General Scott, and the brave Kentucky Militia, is a stroke of masterly and unprecedented policy; and more especially when we consider the armies thus wisely sacrificed, as consisting mostly of men whose services were worth but two dollars a month—a cheap purchase of the lives and properties of the noble sons of Kentucky.

Not for those soulless heathen of the wood,
But christian folks of kindred flesh and blood,
Pity, meek habitant of yonder sky,
Wipes the full tear-drop from her dewy eye,
As, from her throne of never fading light,
O'er western worlds she bends her anxious sight,
Thy LAMBS,† Kentucky! claim her darling care,
Expos'd to all the miseries of war;

† In order fully to shew the singularly peaceable, and gentle disposition of these good people (not to mention the massacre of the Moravian Indians, when, under pretence of celebrating divine worship, their white brethren convened them in the church and piously dashed their infants against the wall) I shall select two instances out of the many which are related of their extraordinary humanity. Not many years since the legislature of Kentucky, from the purest motives, no doubt, proclaimed a bounty of a hundred dollars for any Indian scalp. A gentleman in that country, who, in his intercourse with the natives, had married one of their women, by whom he had several children, inspired with true patriotic zeal, and parental affection, made a visit to the unsuspecting family, and, while they were asleep, kindly dismissed them to the Indian paradise, took off their scalps as a memorial of love, received the premium of his noble services, and was advanced to a post of honour and profit under that government.

The other is as follows.——In the summer of 1788, Col. Logan, with a party of Militia from Kentucky, sat out on an expedition against the Pickewa town. They were discovered by some young warriors, out on a hunting party, who immediately returned, and gave information to their old Chief Melaanthee. But relying on the faith of a Treaty, executed but the preceding spring, he refused to believe that any injury was intended by the Whites to him, or his people; and in full assurance of a friendly reception, advanced to meet them, displaying in one hand the treaty signed by the American commissioners, and in the other the flag of the United States, which he had received at the same time. Being informed of their intention to put him to death, he told them—" That he and his people were the friends of the thirteen fires, and had faithfully observed the Treaty made with their Chiefs."—and holding up the flag—" this," said he, " I have received from your Chiefs, as the mark of friendship, and on this I place mine and my people's protection."—Yet all these marks of unsuspecting confidence, attended with the most artless protestations of friendship, could not impose upon these ex-

Unkindly left, without defence or stay,
To savage Wolves a weak unshielded prey;
Those savage Wolves, in cruelty grown old,
Who torture prisoners when their blood is cold.

   All this;—while on our part, so mild and **good**,
No one e'er thought of spilling Indian blood,
Save once, when Susquehannah's trout-fill'd† **wave**,
And twice Ohio form'd their watery grave:
Though those whom valiant Brady sent to **pot**,
Perhaps were friendly, and perhaps were **not.**
But best it is, as ancient proverbs say,
Never to let occasion run away:
And pat another proverb meets my eye,
While the sun shines, spread out your **hay to dry**;
As haply that good Man would ne'er again
Have caught a chance to tap an Indian's **brain**;
Yet mild humanity inspir'd the deed,
And gave those wandering savages to bleed,
For as, with toil severe, fatigu'd, they plied
Their bark, fur-laden, down the rapid tide,
Kind Brady took compassion on their woes,
And bade in endless sleep their weary labours close.
But circumstances strong arise to shew
That these were foes, of foes the vilest too;
For tis a fact well known our parts throughout,
A friendly Indian can't be worth a groat.

perienced men, who thought it much less safe to trust an Indian in this world than the other, and, in conformity to this humane sentiment, put a speedy period to his existence with the tomahawk, and the standard thus gloriously obtained, was for several weeks triumphantly displayed on the Court-House at Lexington, as a trophy sacred to humanity.

  † For the aptitude and beauty of this epithet, see the speech of the Hon John Vining, on the question for altering the Seat of Government.

Therefore, where'er we can a savage find
Who has a skin or blanket to our mind,
Presuming they were stole, since well we know
Nor furs, nor blankets, can on Indians grow,
We ought forthwith to kill the hostile brute,
And strip him of his goods, and scalp to boot;
While this reflection gives no small relief,
That after all 'tis nought but stealing from a thief.

  I view the men, who ne'er a savage saw,
Like those young girls whose minds begin to thaw,
In Fancy's spring, when wild romances start
The mind to mischief, and to love the heart.
The one is solely bent on plotting evil;
The other thinks an Indian is the devil;
The first employs her industry and art
To raise a bobbery in the human heart;
The last with pure devotion worships God
By offering incense sweet of scalps and blood.
The sage Philosopher, by ign'rance fir'd,
Of genteel vice, and common follies tir'd,
Thinks Virtue's hallowed form alone is found
Where squaws cut capers o'er the desart ground.
He sees green spring in their rude minds appear,
And their brown skins disclose the falling year.
Experience only can the pill dispense,
Which purges off this calenture of sense.
All that is great in man, I do suppose,
From education, and from College flows,
And those brown tribes, who snuff the desart air,
Are aunts and cousins to the skunk and bear.
  I know Cornplanter, and I know Big-Tree,
I know Half-Town, and I know all the three:

They're very clever; but do what you will,
Indians and rum, are rum and Indians still.

From desart wastes a mighty Indian came,
Robb'd of an eye, blind Sam his royal name;
Brought to this Town,* in wampum richly gay,
At balls he pass'd the night, at clubs the day;
In crowds the ladies to his Levee† ran,
All wish'd to see, and touch, the tawny man.
Happy were those who saw his stately stride,
Thrice happy those who felt his naked hide.
As school-boys, when a monkey comes in sight,
Forsake their games, and chase him with delight;
View with astonishment the stalking creature,
So sleek and pretty in a state of nature;
Thus sparkling belles the Indian flock'd around,
Charm'd with his melting eye, his voice's silver sound,
And as the Cyclops graciously held up
His copper lips to give them all a sup,
Some thought for very joy they should have died,
Some thought they were bewitch'd, and some beati-
    fied.

All gracious heaven! can that high favour'd isle
Where at my birth Creation tried to smile,
When pigs and ram-cats trill'd their tuneful strains,
And geese quack'd grateful anthems o'er the plains;
Where, on a car of fire sublimely borne,
Great Milton soar'd beyond the blaze of morn;
Where bonnie Hume on raven pinions flew,
And croak'd more truths than science ever knew,

  * Philadelphia.
  † It is presumed that Royal Sam had his Levees as well as other distin-
guished personages.

Where, from the shrines of slavery and despair,
Howard's rich incense floats along the air.—
Bear up a wretch whose bloody arm can aid
An Indian's knife to scalp a White-man's head,
Or from his vengeful hand forbear to pull
The axe all batter'd on the soldier's skull,
That skull by nature harden'd for the toil
Of butting Indians on Kentucky's soil?
This might be done if, bursting through the charm,
Britain would stretch her old, big, pestling arm,
From that blest hour war's crimson ensign furl'd,
Her throne a wigwam in the western world,
Peace at my word, shall walk the carnag'd field,
And turn'd to pot-lid every savage shield.
Let me be safe, and then I'll plainly shew
The de--l may take the Squaws and Indians too.
The question is which of us shall obey?
Shall we make brooms and baskets—or shall they?
I say let's fight, regardless of their groans,
And bring the wretches on their marrow bones;
For every man who lies beneath his foe,
Dreads the deep bruising of the fateful blow.
When I say *govern* I'd be understood
To mean the simple right to shed their blood,
That right which Nature, ever good and kind,
Wrote with her finger on the White-man's mind.

Was there a single *thing* that ever saw
A chief or half a king, or all a squaw;
Or heard of Kickapoos the guttural sound
Rumble like earthquakes stifled under ground,
But thought he understood th' incongruous strain,
Of those erst scatter'd over Shinar's plain

And had no doubt without or force or law
His whistle-pipe these pigeons wild would draw
Tame to his coop, where he them safe might pen,
Pluck off their plumes and make them look like
       men,§
No more with these dark devils let us chase
A mongrel system of half war, half peace;
'Tis nonsense all—the word is—fight, or yield—
An Indian master, or a bloody field.

§ Mr. B*********** in contra-distinction to Lord Monboddo's theory, seems to have been of the opinion of that Naturalist who considers man as belonging to the class of birds; that is, a two-legged animal without feathers.

ECHO.....NO. VIII.

From the Diary, &c. of October 10, 1792.

TO THE PRINCIPAL GENTLEMEN AND LADIES OF THE CITY AND COUNTRY.

" HAVING, before the late Revolution, had the honour when every body and every thing in America and Old England understood one another; and in 1763, that period also being calm and serene; I had likewise the honour to hold or sustain two important offices in this state, viz. the Post Office and the Commissariat; and during that period, I had also the honour to correspond with the first gentlemen at that time in the country; I will mention the first gentlemen at that time in the country. The Honourable Sir William Johnson, Baronet; the Honourable Hugh Finlay, at Quebec; Sir John Johnson, Baronet; Hugh and Alexander Wallace, Esquires; and all the gentlemen printers on this vast continent.

" From my correspondence with men and a good library of books, I think I have sufficient knowledge to take upon me the education of a few country gentlemen's children; say six boys, from twelve to fifteen years of age, my situation will be near the city, in a very *healthy desirable stand*, near perhaps to the Israelitish Burying Ground; I will study or teach none but English Syntax and refined sentiment. I know nothing of the business of a country schoolmaster, who would positively take one whole sheet of paper to communicate his ideas, when any of my scholars possessed with the least share of sense, shall do it with propriety and elegance in six lines. My plan therefore will be to take only six gentlemen's children for six months, when they shall be fitted for business. The elegance of double entry, or the Italian method of Book-keeping, shall be taught (if they please) with propriety. The young gentlemen may then, if they please, leave the Academy for six months, to re-enter, and so on a regular and uniform succession of them.

Mr. Monier's plan will be to board them, wash them, and lodge them. Mrs. Monier is of a respectable Dutch family, and will not suffer one dirty matter about the house, nor about the gentlemen's children—this by way of further introduction to his plan.

Mr. Monier further acquaints his friends and the public, that five whole days in the week he means to devote his time to the children; but Saturdays a total relaxation from business, when his pupils may then visit their friends in comfort. Terms of entrance and schooling to be made known, and made easy to the public.

JOHN MONIER,
Late Deputy Post-master, and Agent at Albany.

N. B. The subscriber will begin to take in subscribers' names the 8th instant, and open the Academy the 22d.

New-York, Oct. 16, 1792.

HARTFORD, OCTOBER 29th, 1792.

" *Once more shall drowsy* ECHO *rise,*
" *Lift up her head and rub her eyes,*
" *Quit* BRACKENRIDGE *for* JOHN MONIER,
" *And give the pedagogue a cheer.*"

Ye city dames who roll the streets around,
Ye country Joans who till the furrow'd ground,
Around whose board a tribe of noisy brats,
Throng thick as mice in absence of the cats,
If to my school for six short months you'll send 'em,
I'll teach them all I know, and scour and mend 'em,
I neither ask nor wish a moment more,
For all I know, I learn'd in less than four.

BEFORE the Briton left his distant shore,
To drench Columbia's peaceful plains in gore,
When men and things each other understood,
And Bute and North turn'd pale to think of blood,
I had the honour——and in sixty-three,
(A cloudless period, from commotion free)
I also had the honour to sustain
A post of honour, and a post of gain—
Post-Office first——then Commissariate,
As good a chance as any in the state—
For in the first, I frank'd my numerous letters,
And in the last I learn'd to cheat my betters.
Alas! how swiftly flew this age of gold!
Surpassing that by fabling poets told;

To me more dear the storms of Kingly sway,
Than the clear sun-beams of fair Freedom's day.
But thirdly—during this same happy time,
When writing letters was not deem'd a crime,
When no committees prowl'd the streets around,
And whigs and tories no existence found,
It also was my honour'd lot to spend
A leisure hour in writing to a friend.
To every gentleman of any note,
By every opportunity I wrote—
I'll tell you every gentleman of note,
To whom each opportunity I wrote.
Sir William Johnson, Baronet, was one,
A jovial prig, who liv'd on Indian fun;
Hugh Finlay, of Quebec, Esquire, another;
And next Sir John, Sir William's son, or brother;
'Squire Alexander Wallace, and 'squire Hugh,
Both as fine blades as ever wore a shoe;
And then with all those typographic fellows—
With Mills and Hicks, with Goddard, Hall and Sel-
    lers,
With Jemmy Rivington, and Robert Bell,
Old Holt, Hugh Gaine, Tim Green, and Edes and
    Gill,
Good deacon L——, that puritanic fidge,
And "Ebenezer Watson, near the bridge."
  From men like these and books almost as good,
The turtle-fat of intellectual food,
I think my knowledge is so sturdy grown,
That I at length may dare to make it known,

And now declare it to be my intent,
To teach the children of the country *gent*—
Those little shabby lads, who ne'er before
Stray'd half a mile beyond their father's door;
Give them to know the world as well as me,
And doff their hats to every man they see;
Thus by good fortune they may hope in time,
Up to the top of my renown to climb—
Say half a dozen awkward boys, between
The sprightly years of twelve, and wild fifteen
That blooming season when they first begin
To shew the fruits of father Adam's sin:
That sin, bequeath'd in true paternal grace,
A loving legacy to all his race,
And though we still the inheritance divide,
Yet every one is fully satisfied;
And what is seldom seen in such affairs,
Nor suits nor bickerings disturb the heirs.
For though 'tis said Cain broke poor Abel's pate,
To rob his children of their just estate;
Yet since that day we find no eldest son,
Who claims a double portion for his own.—
Near this great city will my school be plac'd,
A monument of judgment, and of taste;
For health selected—long I search'd around,
At length a spot to suit my mind I found.
Near that white wall which rears its form on high,
Where cold in death the sons of Israel lie,
Forgot each wonted care, the thirst of gain,
The wish of pleasure, and the dread of pain;

O'er whose green graves unthinking mortals **tread,**
Nor heed the loud monitions of the dead.
Nor can this city boast so sweet an air,
A spot so charming or a view so fair;
What air more fragrant to a christian nose,
Than from the mouldering Hebrew daily flows;
What scene more pleasing to a christian eye
Than where the sons of circumcision lie.
Mere vulgar business does not suit my mind,
Be that to country pedagogues confin'd,
Who to my knowledge take a world of pains,
To beat ideas into children's brains,
Though afterwards I make no kind of doubt,
The boys would give the world to get them out.
And oft I've witness'd with extreme dismay,
A whole clean sheet of paper thrown away
By these vile fellows, who ne'er seem to think,
What vast expense they make of pen and ink.
Far different is my mode; for well I ween,
That all my pupils, those of sense I mean,
Shall in six lines, without incumbrance, put
All their ideas, and my own to boot.
Six children in six months alone I'll bring
To know so much their empty skulls shall ring,
While common schools will take a year or two
To run this wond'rous stock of knowledge **through.**
In the vast sphere of sentiment refin'd,
Now ranges free as air my active mind,
By English Syntax borne sublime along,
Beyond the boundaries of my mother tongue,

Which I in former correspondence learn'd,
Now cheaply sold, though then so dearly earn'd.
I'll teach the lads, without much toil or trouble,
To make their entries elegantly double;
And if they please, and can so foolish be,
It shall be taught them with propriety;
For 'tis a fact, propriety's a clog
To every man who means to be a rogue.
But when the tedious period has expir'd,
The learned lads will probably be tir'd;
Then to their homes and friends they may repair,
To spend their mighty acquisitions there,
And should they prove industrious six months more,
They'll be as knowing as they were before,
And, if they please, they may retrace the road
Back to my school, and take another load.

 Mr. Monier is such a clever man,
He means to state at length his useful plan—
He'll keep a table, bed, and soap and tub,
Wherein the little nasty dogs he'll scrub.
Thus the kind guardian of the pen, who sees
His bristly charge oppress'd with scurf and fleas,
Amid the squeeling gentry takes his stand,
The cob scrubbific waving in his hand,
To each in turn the grateful rub applies,
While grunts of pleasure echo through the sties.

 Mrs. Monier is of the Holland breed,
Rather more famous for the dray, than speed;
She ev'ry now and then, from room to room,
Will waddle round, well arm'd with brush and broom,

Breed in the house a most tremendous rout,
And all the dirty matters kick about,
And then, her plans more fully to disclose,
She'll seize the little blockheads by the nose,
Comb out their snarly bristles in a trice,
And clear their numbsculls both from nits and lice.
   For five whole days his time he will devote,
But Saturdays he'll let his pupils out,
When where they please the learned lads may go,
And John will never say " Why do ye so?"

ECHO.....NO. IX.

[The Echo, unwilling that the sublime and cautionary speeches of the Governor of the State of Massachusetts, should be lost to posterity, has thought proper, as they possess such uncommon excellencies, to introduce them together, to the notice of the public; and has only omitted such passages as did not seem so immediately to concern the two grand objects of her laudable apprehensions.]

From the Columbian Centinel, of Nov. 10, 1792.

CONCORD, NOVEMBER 8.

" *Gentlemen of the Senate, and*
" *Gentlemen of the House of Representatives,*

"I SHOULD for my own, as well as for your convenience, have been glad to have met you at the ancient seat of our Government; but as it has pleased the Most High, to visit that, as well as many other of our towns, with a troublesome and contagious disease, I have, with the advice of the Council thought it most for your safety and comfort to convene you at this place.

" Gentlemen,

" I am urged, by sense of duty, to communicate to you my mind upon a transaction, which I cannot but consider as an open insult upon the Laws and Government of the commonwealth.

" In the year one thousand seven hundred and fifty, the legislature of this then province of Massachusetts-Bay, passed an act, entitled, " An Act to prevent Stage Plays, and other Theatrical Entertainments."

" The preamble of the Act is in these words, " For preventing and avoiding many great mischiefs, which arise from public Stage-Plays, Interludes, and other Theatrical Entertainments; which not only occasion great and unnecessary expenses, and discourage industry aud frugality; but likewise tend generally to increase immorality, impiety, and a contempt of religion."

" The act is now a law of the commonwealth; the principles upon which it is predicated, have been recognized by, and derive support from the consideration of several legislatures; and surely it ought to claim the respect and obedience of all persons who live or happen to be within the Commonwealth. Yet a number of aliens and foreigners, have lately entered the State, and in the metropolis of the Government, under advertisements insulting to the habits and education of the citizens, have been pleased to invite them to, and to exhibit before such as attended, *Stage-Plays, Interludes, and Theatrical Entertainments*, under the stile and appellation of " Moral Lectures." This fact is so notorious, that it is in vain to attempt a concealment of its coming to our knowledge.

" Whether the Judicial Departments, whose business it is, have attended to this subject or not, I am unable to determine; but this I am convinced of, that no measures have been taken to punish a most open breach of the Laws, and a most contemptuous insult upon the powers of the Government.

" You, Gentlemen, are the guardians of the Commonwealth's dignity and honour; and our fellow-citizens rely upon your vigilance and wisdom, for the support of the sovereignty and importance of the Government. I therefore refer this matter to your determinations; and cannot but hope that your resolutions and measures will give efficacy to the laws, and be the means of bringing to condign punishment those who dare to treat them with contempt or open opposition.

" *Gentlemen of the Senate, and of the*
" *House of Representatives*,

" BY the Constitution of the United States of America, each State is to appoint, in such manner as the legislature shall direct,

Electors of President and Vice-President. By a late act of Congress, it is enacted, " That the Supreme Executive of each State SHALL cause three lists of the names of the Electors of such State to be made and certified, and to be delivered to the Electors on or before the first Wednesday in December."

" I feel the importance of giving every constitutional support to the General Government: and I also am convinced that the existence and well-being of that Government depends upon preventing a confusion of the authority of it with that of the States separately. But that Government applies itself to the People of the United States in their natural, individual capacity, and cannot exert any force upon, or by any means controul the officers of the State Governments as such: Therefore, when an act of Congress uses compulsory words with regard to any Act to be done by the Supreme Executive of this Commonwealth, I shall not feel myself obliged to obey them, because I am not, in my official capacity, amenable to that Government.

" My duty as Governor, will most certainly oblige me to see that proper and efficient Certificates are made of the appointment of Electors of President and Vice-President; and perhaps the mode suggested in the Act above-mentioned, may be found to be the most proper. If you, Gentlemen, have any mode to propose with respect to the conduct of this business, I shall pay every attention to it.

" *Gentlemen,*

" I do not address you at this time from a disposition to regard the proceedings of the General Government with a jealous eye, nor do I suppose that Congress could intend that clause in their Act as a compulsory provision: but I wish to prevent any measure to proceed through inattention, which may be drawn into precedents hereafter, to the injury of the people, or to give a constructive power where the Federal Constitution has not expressly given it."

HARTFORD, JANUARY 14th, 1793.

> " *Again shall* ECHO *strike the lyre,*
> " *While deeds sublime the song inspire:*
> " *To* HANCOCK *pass from* JOHN MONIER,
> " *And give the* ROYAL JOHN *a cheer.*"
>
> Western Star.]

GENTLES, of either kind, both small and great,
Props of *our* laws, and pillars of *our* state;
Tho' words would fail, and language' self prove weak,
My joy, in seeing you once more, to speak;
While in this fleshly bottle closely pent,
Strong expression struggles for a vent,
Ere I can draw the cork, I fear, alas!
'Twill burst the frail contexture of my glass.
Yet, had this joy been even *more* complete
Could I have met you at our ancient Seat,
Near Faneuil Hall, to me forever dear,
Where first I enter'd on *my* great career;
Whose walls, so oft, *my* presence bade rejoice,
Which oft in transport echoed to *my* voice,
When rose, 'gainst Britain, its tremendous roar,
And shook her distant isle, from shore to shore;
So when stern JOVE, to vengeful anger driven,
Rolls the black tempest o'er the expanse of heaven,
Loud peals of thunder on the storm arise,
And the red lightning quivers o'er the skies;

From central depths disturb'd the Ocean raves,
And high to heaven upheaves his briny waves;
From its deep base the cloud-veil'd mountain shakes;
The firm rock trembles, and the valley quakes;
All nature, shuddering, owns the dreadful nod,
And shrinks before the terrors of the God.
There FREEDOM, then a chick, unfledg'd and bare,
I kindly brooded with a mother's care;
Taught her to creep, to hop, to run, to fly,
And gave her wings to lift herself on high,
'Till perfect grown, she came, at length, to soar
To heights unthought of, but by *me*, before.
In that loved spot, O could you but have met!
" But fate denies, and man must yield to fate;"
Since the SMALL-POX, *Death's* Vicar here on earth,
Who, stern, respects nor dignities, nor worth,
O'er that sad place, now sunk in dire dismay,
Waves his pale banners, and extends his sway,
Wide pours contagious poison from his breath,
Deforms the face, and shuts the eyes in death,
And still uncheck'd, his grisly triumph leads,
Nor votes regards, nor resolutions heeds;
Those *votes*, by which, that man of patriot soul
Who o'er Town-Meetings held unmatch'd controul,
Far-fam'd SAM ADAMS thought to fright away
This curst disease, for ever, and for aye:
Therefore it is, by heaven's peculiar grace,
That I've thought fit to call you to this place.
  But Gentlemen! a thing unmention'd yet,
Enough to throw you in a dog-day sweat;

A thing, perchance, which you, as well as *I*,
Have seen, some time, with many an aching eye;
Since, above measure bold, it scorns disguise;
And proudly stares us in the face and eyes;
A thing, most vile, most dreadful in its kind,
Hangs, like a mill-stone, heavy on my mind:
By conscience urged, in duty's cause made bold,
To you this wicked thing I shall unfold,
Since plain enough to *me* is its intent,
An open insult on *my* government.

Long since, while Britain, with maternal hand,
Cheer'd the lov'd offspring of Columbia's land;
Ere proud oppression bade that offspring brave
Assert their rights, and scorn the name of slave;
Ere o'er the world had flown my mob-rais'd fame,
And George and Britain trembled at *my* name;
This State, then Province, pass'd, with wise intent,
An ACT, *Stage-Plays*, and such things to prevent:
You'll find it Sirs, among the Laws sky blue,
Made near that time on brooms when Witches flew,
That blessed *time* when Law kept wide awake,
Proscribed the *faithless*, and made Quakers *quake;*
And thus, in terms sublime *I* state the fact,
Runs the *Preamble* of this precious *Act.*

Both for preventing, and avoiding, all
Those various evils which would sure befall
Our sober people, and their sober ways,
From *Interludes*, and vile *Theatric Plays;*
To wit, all fiddling, fighting, gaming, raking,
Swearing profane, high broils, and sabbath breaking;

This Act, so full of wisdom and so good,
Has now become a Law well understood;
Since it has often been confirm'd, you see,
By many a Legislature great as we.
Yet, notwithstanding this, some chaps uncivil,
Grand Emissaries of our foe the Devil,
Aliens, and *Foreigners*, and *Actors* funny,
Who less esteem our morals than our money;
Even in *our* holy Capital, of late,
Have dared insult the majesty of state,
And to exhibit publicly, propose,
Stage-Plays, and *Interludes*, and *Heathen Shows;*
Which, in the garb of *Moral Lectures* drest,
Of our good, sober manners make a jest.
Yet so obnoxious to the people's notions,
So strange, so foreign to their constitutions,
That well *I* am convinced they never go,
From motives of amusement, to the Show;
But, like good, honest folks, with mere intent,
To keep these Actors under some restraint.
Judge, Gentlemen! *my* feelings, when at first,
This information, on my ear-drum burst:
Not more was Israel's hapless King appall'd,
When Endor's Witch the Ghost of Samuel call'd,
And, slowly rising from the shades of night,
The frowning spectre met his startled sight.
Not more *bold* ELDERKIN* with terror shook,
Not more dismay was pictured in his look,

* For a particular account of this remarkable occurrence, extracted from Peters' History of Connecticut, see Supplementary Notes.

When Windham's Sons, at midnight's awful hour,
Heard, from afar, the hoarse discordant roar
Of Bull-Frog sorrow groaning on the wind,
Denouncing death and ruin to mankind;
While one supposed the *tawny Myriads* near,
And heard their War-hoops thunder in his ear;
Another thought *Old Nick* was sure a coming,
Since none but Belial's bands could make such drumming;
Yet each, prepar'd, his proper weapon took,
While one his bible hugg'd, and one his musket shook.
Wild consternation on my visage hung,
Congeal'd my blood, and every nerve unstrung;
O'er my whole frame a palsying horror flew,
And *sense*, retiring, bade a long adieu.
So Cain, the fratricide, when deep disgrace
Fix'd its black brand upon his guilty face,
Fled from the crime of brother Abel's blood,
And took lone lodgings in the *Land of Nod*.
  Whether the Magistrates all this have known
I do not know; but this I know, that none
Have taken care, whatever their intent,
These Fellows' *pranks*, and *postures*, to prevent;
  Ne'er have laid hold of them with Law's strong hand,
And fairly brought the scoundrels to a stand,
Nor to the whipping-post the rogues have tied,
Where oft cash-pay is chang'd to pay in hide.
With joy extreme, O Gentlemen! in you
The firm upholders of the Laws I view,

On you devolves the *task* (I grant it great,)
To keep unstain'd the chasteness of our *State*:
Since that *good Lady* is beset so sore
By rakes and libertines full many a score,
That much I fear me, do whate'er you can,
She'll be debauch'd by that unrighteous clan.
But this at least I hope, that, if unable
To keep with all your might, her virtue stable,
You will not fail to shew this wicked sect,
You know to punish, though you can't protect;
And whate'er punishment you shall devise,
As to your noble judgments seemeth wise;
Whether you burn, drown, knock them on the head,
Or hang them by the neck, 'till dead, dead, dead—
Or with a neighbour State, so very tender,
Loth to extend the neck of an offender,
Prefer the hanging business to commute
For *private prayers* and some *small goods*† to boot—
I hope a great example it will stand,
And *in terrorem* guard *our* pious land.

 Once more, ye Gentles! to my voice give heed,
While things unthought of from my lips proceed,
Things of high import and of utmost weight,
Which much concern *our* Sovereignty of State.
The Constitution most expressly says:
" Each several *State* shall, in such modes and ways,

 † For an explanation of the above, vide the Archives of Connecticut, wherein it may be found that on a certain occasion of commutative justice, the sheriff was directed to furnish the criminal with the consolation of his prayers.

" As to adopt *its* Rulers are content,
" Appoint Electors for the President."
Yet in an act has Congress said of late,
That the Supreme Executive of State
Shall—what a word to *Governors to use*,
By men unworthy to unloose their shoes!
Shall—I repeat the *abusive term* once more,
That dreadful offspring of usurping pow'r—
Cause with th' Electors names to be supply'd
Three proper lists all duly certified;
These to be given them *on or ere* that day
The Wednesday first that owns December's sway.
Though not unconscious of what mighty weight
Would prove my count'nance, and my aid how great,
Should I stretch forth my hand, with kind intent,
To prop the frame of General Government—
And eke am conscious that the public good
Would better be consulted if *I* should;
Yet when the Congress in compulsive phrase,
Pretend to teach *me* how to guide *my* ways,
Shall I, who not from them my power have got,
Shall I obey them?—sooner will I rot—
For from my head to foot I feel all o'er
The vast importance of *Official power*.
Shall I obey them, tremble at their nod,
And, school-boy like, most humbly kiss the rod?
I who first led the way to wond'rous things,
To humbling nobles and unkinging kings?
I who have done what man ne'er did before,
Quell'd the old British Lion's frightful roar?

I who first taught the Pole* t' ascend on high,
While flaming Tar-tubs kindled up the sky;
When, thick as feathery snows fast-flitting fall,
Or quails and manna at the Prophet's call,
The *Tar* and *Feathers* at my voice appear'd,
And every Tory thought himself a bird?
I who most nobly burst the *chests* of *tea*,
And with those wicked cargoes strew'd the sea,
Till Boston's dock might rival in its store
Kiangsi's plains, or Canton's busy shore—
That drink Circean, whose bewitching charm,
Had tied our tongue, unnerv'd our sinewy arm,
Chill'd the warm breast, transform'd the man to ape,
And given to Freedom Slavery's brutish shape?
No—I ne'er will—for *Governors* I'm sure
If any thing are from their power secure.

 As Presidents it seems must be elected,
Perhaps the mode which Congress has directed
Is full as good as any we can find:—
Yet Gentlemen! if any strikes your mind
Of different feature, mien, shape, air, or stature,
By which you would conduct this weighty matter,
Congress shall know it—and from *me* shall hear
That once they've caught the wrong pig by the ear.

 Pray, Gentlemen! do not suppose that *I*
Regard the Government with jealous eye;
Or have the smallest hope, or wish, that you
Should with a jealous eye regard it too.

   * Liberty Pole.

I do not think that Congress ever meant
That *Clause* to construe to such base intent;
It must be a mistake, the careless work
Of careless Printers, or more careless Clerk.
I only meant a gentle hint, or so;
For, to the wise, a hint's enough you know;
I only wish'd such measures to prevent,
As might, in time, grow up to precedent,
To raise *constructive power*, as high as steeple,
On the tir'd shoulders of the grumbling people.

ECHO.....NO. X.

From the Virginia Gazette.

RICHMOND, DECEMBER 6, 1792.

" Mr. Carey,

" The following impromptu was written on the report that the Electors of this State in consequence of their having unanimously voted for Governor Clinton as Vice-President, were contumeliously called Jacobins.

" Having remarked and admired the freedom of your press, I have submitted it through your medium to the public.

" If any one shall suppose it personal as to himself, with him you are at liberty to effect an interview with the author.

" Rejoice! Republicans rejoice! your inestimable privileges are secure. The genius of America is awake. The tutelary saint of Virginia is roused. The electors of this state have unanimously given their suffrages to Governor Clinton, as Vice-President. Governor Clinton is a republican both in principle and practice. The principles of Mr. Adams, the late Vice-President, are reprobated—his book—his writings—his sentiments—his late conduct—his love of, and his having recommended hereditary monarchy, and hereditary aristocracy, are all, all, reprobated. The monocrats, aristocrats, highflyers, mushrooms, all hang their heads; and while the friends of men sing psalms, hallelujahs, and anthems, to the tune of regenerating freedom, they who were conspiring to dethrone the sacred majesty of the people may perform the last funeral obsequy and sing the last melancholy dirge to Adamitical principles.

"Yes! ye men of Belial, regeneration is at your heels, and ere long she will hold you up hated and avoided, as you are now suspected and despised. Your chariots, your pomp, your gala-days, your court etiquette, your cries of sedition, and your reproaches against tried republican characters, will not avail. All eyes will be opened; the fatal issue of your abominable schemes will be developed; then you will hate and execrate each other, yourselves, as you now deserve it, from all the race of man.

"You call the electors Jacobins, as a mark of contumely; in that view they despise you and ask, that a man shall avow himself. But why say, Jacobins? Are they not the authors of the greatest and most glorious revolution of which the annals of history can boast? Have they not loosed the shackles of slavery from thirty millions of people? Have they not fanned the sacred blaze of liberty, in every region of the earth? Have they not dethroned tyranny, monarchy, aristocracy, priestcraft, and all their satellites? Have they not set up and crowned the mighty majesty of human kind over the punyism of individuals? Yes! the Jacobins of France have done all this. The French have no longer a king; they are no longer slaves; they are free; and therefore you despise them.

"But future ages, when they trace the history of man, when they contemplate the catalogue of woes, which blacken the pages of antiquity, will at this eventful epoch make a complacent pause, and drop the tear of gratitude to the memory of those who so much contributed to emancipate the human race.

"The revolution has blasted your hopes; the kings or tyrants of Europe have leagued against them; and why do you not go? The duke of Brunswick will receive you; he will embrace you, and you will shew the ne plus ultra of human depravity; Americans aiding and abetting kings and tyrants to reduce to bondage thirty millions of people, whose blood and treasure were exhausted to purchase your country's freedom. Go hence and take with you the last seed, the last shoot, the last scion of your stock ; and let that bold essayist, as your crusading champion, whose head, heart, and hand have been employed to sap the imprescriptible and defined rights of his countrymen be announced to kings and their cut-throats, by his herald as a voluntary fugitive from a country where men will cease to be, or live free.

"Thanks to you, electors; all the friends of human liberty will thank you; future ages will revere and venerate your names: Heaven and your own consciences will reward you.

"HENRICO."

HARTFORD, JANUARY 21st, 1793.

" Echo with transport turns her eyes
" Where Old Virginia's realms arise;
" Bright POKAHONTAS'* *noble name*
" Shall consecrate the lay to fame.

With love of freedom, Mr. Carey! smitten,
In ancient realm was this Impromptu written,
Where POKAHONTAS left a noble breed
All other men in science to exceed;
On the report as Jacobins denoted,
Were our Electors who for Clinton voted.

Having oft seen the offspring of the brain
Drop from your press, with small parturient pain,
Through your pure medium I have thought it right
To let my strange ideas see the light.
If any one a personal meaning smell,
I'll pack him off, or he shall me, to hell.

REJOICE, ye Democrats! I say rejoice!
See fix'd secure your privileges choice!
Columbia's Genius has our cause espous'd,
Virginia's tutelary Saint† is rous'd,

---

* POKAHONTAS, a celebrated Squaw, who married one of the first settlers of Virginia; and from whom the Virginians are proud to derive some of their most considerable families. It has not a little puzzled many American Politicians, in considering the political situation of Virginia, where the manners of the Planters are *naturally* and *habitually* Aristocratic, to ac-

† Saint Tammany.

That Saint so mighty whose extended sway
Ancient Dominion's wide domains obey,
Who while War hover'd o'er our fertile coast,
Sent forth her reg'ments, an *unnumber'd* host,
Where *fifty* officers, in martial pride,
Strutted with five poor soldiers at their side.
That saint who marks, with clear sagacious ken,
Low in the scale the gen'ral race of men,
While high his vot'ries stand—by him decreed
The guides of worlds—to follow where they lead.
Lo! fill'd with joy, he staggers o'er the land,
His *whisky bottle* shaking in his hand:
To us he cries—" Behold this bottle big!
" Come on my boys, and take another swig!
" This magic juice will second-sight restore,
" And make you see things never seen before."
Waked by his speech Virginia's sons arise,
His grateful liquor sparkling in their eyes;
And her Electors, with consenting voice,
Have made George Clinton their united choice.

count for the greatest number of our high-spirited Democrats having originated from that state. A very ingenious Civilian, of our times, has thrown much light on this subject, by deducing the origin of the Democratic part of the Ancient Dominion, from the famous Pokahontas; and he gives two very satisfactory reasons why her descendants should rather partake of the Levelling, than of the Aristocratic principle, although the offspring of royal ancestors. For, *first*, he remarks, that the Whites were inclined to treat the *Natives* as an inferior order of beings; which naturally created in *them*, and *their descendants*, a disposition to reduce all to one standard: and, *secondly*, which is a still more convincing argument, as being founded in the constitution of nature, he remarks, that the sovereignty among the Indians, was merely nominal; and that they, universally, preserved the most perfect Democracy in their Governments.

Him for our head we mount o'er every bar,
His voice our compass, nod our polar star.
For, with severe and unremitted hate,
We urge illustrious Adams on to fate;
Condemn his principles, his book detest,
Misquote his sentiments, his conduct wrest,
Charge him with loving what ourselves we love,
Charge him with hate of what we disapprove,
And load with vilest terms of reprobation
The very phantom of our own creation.
The monocrats, aristocrats lie low,
High-flying mushrooms sink in deadliest woe,
The toad-stool too, with sympathy opprest,
Feels his soft heart lie heavy in his breast,
And, as he hangs his head, he oft applies
The handkerchief to dry his moisten'd eyes.
While joyous sing the people's friends and prance,
And treat the Negroes to a royal dance,*

* The following description of the celebrated Equality Ball given to the Negroes of Boston by Governor Hancock is extracted from the New-Year's Verses for the American Mercury, for 1793:—

"And lo! where o'er the Eastern shores,
Bostonia lifts her haughty towers,
What motley scenes salute our eyes!
What wonders upon wonders rise!
There each succeeding day still brings
A mixture strange of various things.

* * * * * *

There plays their *heathen names* forsake,
And those of Moral Lectures take,

And loud to Anarchy their voices raise
In hallelujahs and in hymns of praise,
To the sweet Tune of *Freedom born anew ;*
That Tune so charming, and so novel too,

While, thus baptis'd, they hope to win
Indulgence for all future sin.
Now, Hancock, fir'd with patriot rage,
Proscribes these morals of the stage,
Claps Harper under civil durance,
For having dared, with vile assurance,
By *Interludes* and *Plays profane*
Pollute the glories of his reign.
Now, prompt to assert the *rights of man*,
On Nature's most extensive plan,
Behold him to his splendid hall
The noble sons of Afric call :
While as the sable bands advance,
With frolic mien, and sportive dance,
Refreshing clouds of rich perfume
Are wafted o'er the spacious room.
With keen delight the Sage surveys
Their graceful tricks, and winning ways ;
Their tones enchanting raptur'd hears,
More sweet than music of the spheres ;
And as he breathes the fragrant air,
He deems that Freedom's self dwells there.
While CUFFEY near him takes his stand,
Hale-fellow met, and grasps his hand—
With pleasure glistening in his eyes,
" Ah! Massa Gubbernur !" he cries,
" Me grad to see you, for de peeple say
" You lub de Neegur better dan de play."

"Cuffey near him .... grasps his hand". Page 165. Knnow m.

Tisdale pinx.t   Leney sculp.t

"A piper had a Cow"

page 67.

That Tune by tinkers sung, by coblers lov'd,
Which to the Cow* of old so fatal prov'd,
That from this world with joy she took her flight.
And bade her ancient friends a long Good Night;
Those who his *Majesty of Mobs* disown,
And seek that *Holy Sovereign* to dethrone,
When Grandsire ADAM's *principles* shall fail,
And flesh and blood, from keeping long, grow stale,
May sing the funeral dirge in mournful stave.
And get old Burkitt† too to dig the grave.
  Rejoice! ye Pokahontian Tribes rejoice!
In loud *Te Deums* raise your clam'rous voice!
Proclaim from Anarchy what blessings spring!
" Shall CLINTON reign and HENRICO not sing?"
  Yes, men of Belial! had ye sense to feel,
You'd find Regeneration at your heel,
And not far distant is the awful day
When your base clan a reckoning dire shall pay,
When old Virginia shall resume the reins,
And yield a rich reward for all your mighty pains.
Then shall your dress, your mimickry of state,
Your chariots, servants, equipage and plate,
Your brilliant levees, and your gala-days,
Your court-parade, your frankincense of praise,

    * There was a piper had a Cow—
    He had no hay to give her—
    He took his pipe and began to play—
    " Consider, Cow, consider."

     † A well known Sexton.

Your cries seditious 'gainst Virginia's sway,
Which all the other states were made to obey;
Against her Statesmen too, who're born to show
A truth which first or last the world must know,
That the best way a Government to raise
Is to destroy its pillars and its base,
All these to aid your sinking cause shall fail,
ADAMS *must* fall, and CLINTON *shall* prevail.
Soon, very soon, will every open'd eye
The fatal issue of *your* schemes espy;
While in equality *our* days shall flow,
And licence unrestrain'd its choicest gifts bestow.
    Rejoice! ye Anti-fed'ral Clan rejoice!
'Gainst *Bank* and Funding-system raise your voice!
Declare from *Ruin'd Faith* what honours spring!
" Shall CLINTON reign, and HENRICO not sing?"
    You call th' Electors Jacobins—what then?
Are not the Jacobins the first of men?
Most certainly they are, I do protest,
Of men the very first and very best;
With fist and stick this truth will I maintain;
For arguments I never rack my brain;
No—to poor drivelling souls I leave such things,
Whom right and reason hold in leading-strings.
The Jacobins, once more I say, are good,
Staunch, noble fellows, fond of letting blood—
The Jacobins— I dwell upon the name,
My admiration and my homage claim—
To wond'ring nations do they not display
A noble generous spirit every day?

With much politeness and with equal skill,
Do they not torture whom they mean to kill?
And fir'd with zeal to render man humane,
Bear high on pikes the heads of children slain?
Do they not curse that chosen man of God
Old David call'd, who shed Uriah's blood,
And swear, indignant, that they'll never sing*
The psalms compos'd by that adult'rous king?
And shall not we, inspir'd with equal hate,
Reject the Psalms of Brady, Watts and Tate?
Have they not heav'd Oppression's iron yoke
From off the necks of thirty million folk?
With strength Sampsonian broke the chains of power,
And freed their legs, from long confinement sore?
Have they not fill'd Old Freedom so with fire
That the good Dame is ready to expire?
And e'en at length have worn her bellows out
In blowing Faction's flame the world about?
Have they not tumbled from his splendid throne
Our Ally, once so good, great Louis down,

---

* This curious fact, among the multifarious events of the French Revolution, may still exist in the recollection of some of our readers. A member of one of the French legislative bodies, it was said, about this time seriously proposed the rejection of the psalms of David from the service of their churches for the reason above assigned. This reminds us of the story of the Cape Cod man who had removed to a town in Connecticut; and on the introduction of the psalms of Dr. Watts in place of the former New-England Version into the Churches of that State, declared with much indignation to his clergyman, that he was determined never to attend Divine Service in his Church while he persisted in singing the psalms of that Isaac Watts, whom he had very well known at Cape Cod, and who was the greatest drunkard in the place.

And keep him closely in the *Temple* pent,
Like some fine stall-fed ox for slaughter meant?
Have they not plunder'd of their goods and cash
All those Aristocrats who *cut a dash?*
Have they not made the Priests renounce their vows,
And pluck'd the mitre from their hallow'd brows,
While their Satellites, the Monks and Friars,
Have furnish'd glorious fuel for their fires?
Have they not, fraught with sentiments refin'd,
Crown'd the big *Majesty of Human Kind?*
Set up, on high, that many-headed God,
And bade the world bow down before his nod?
So, wrought in gold, with dazzling jewels spread,
On Dura's plain the Image rear'd its head,
While awe-struck thousands at the King's decree,
Bow'd the proud head, and bent the stubborn knee.
All this the Jacobins have done and more,
And France no longer owns monarchic power;
Set loose from law, from moral shackles freed,
Her sons have gain'd fair freedom's fullest meed.

 Rejoice! ye pious Jacobins, rejoice!
Ye graceful Fishwomen strain high your voice!
Proclaim from bloody heads what transports spring!
" Shall CLINTON reign and HENRICO not sing?"
 But future ages when they come to trace
The varied history of the human race;
When they regard the list of woes so black,
That left such bloody weals on Time's old back;
Will at this epoch complaisantly pause,
And wet with tears their cheeks and drop their grate-
  ful jaws.

To those good souls, by charity inspir'd,
And meek-ey'd pity's soft enthusiasm fir'd,
Who kindly clubb'd their wits and eke their power,
To speed poor Frenchmen on their saintly tour,
And, with a world of pains, so hard have striven
To boost their brethren o'er the walls of heaven.
Sons of benevolence! my heart o'erflows,
When I but think from what a weight of woes,
From what dread injuries, what pain, what grief,
Your neighbours, through your cares, have gain'd
    relief;
In Mr. Giles's classic phrase, though they
Had rather* manag'd matters their own way;
Had rather taken their own time to go;
Had rather staid a longer while below;
Had rather jogg'd more softly on their course;
And rather not have mounted Death's white horse.
  Cold are those hopes which once your bosoms
    warm'd,
Those sanguine hopes that Order's sons had from'd,
O'er those bright scenes, which erst your fancies fed,
The Revolution's mildewing blast has spread.
Then why don't you to Europe's monarchs go,
And join those tyrants 'gainst your common foe?
The Duke of Brunswick will be glad, no doubt,
Of such strong aid the Jacobins to scout,
With tender Indian hugs he'll squeeze you to him,
For you can fully *ne plus ultra* show him.

  † For examples of this elegant phraseology, see the Debates in Congress—Article, Mr. Giles.

Americans, abetting tyrants base
To bring in bonds the *virtuous* Gallic race,
Once more to make them wear their rusty chains,
And go to fiddling for their master's gains,
Those thirty million folk, whose sweat and blood
Stream'd in such torrents for your country's good;
I—by my power almighty—bid you hence !
Go—and take that with which we can dispense !
Take the last seed, shoot, scion of your stock,
Nor leave the poor old stump our nerves to shock !
Take every virtue with you as you go,
Leave us our Clinton, Jefferson and Co ;
These shall amuse us in the daily papers,
And Johnny Hancock give us Negro capers.

   Thanks be to you most wise and great Electors !
Freedom's old Cronies hail you her protectors !
Bald Father time, with mouldy tooth and nail,
In vain your fame, so bulky, shall assail !
Gabriel shall crack his trumpet with hard blowing,
To tell the names of folks so mighty knowing ;
While your own consciences shall need new cases,
Grown thin and thread-bare in so many places.

   Rejoice ! ye noble Levellers rejoice !
Ye democratic Tribes exalt your voice !
Declare what joys from prostrate morals spring !
" Shall CLINTON reign, and HENRICO not sing ?"

ECHO.....NO. XI.

From the National Gazette, of January 9, 1793.

"TO MR. JAMES BLANCHARD.

"Sir,

"After having served your country with distinguished honour and integrity, during the late arduous contest for freedom and independence, you have now nobly and intrepidly stepped forth, to vindicate your own rights and those of your fellow soldiers, by calling on your country for that justice to which you have so righteous a claim and which has so long been denied—you have attacked speculation in its strong hold. No doubt the nest you have disturbed will send forth a howling tribe about your ears, but persevere in the good cause—be not deterred by the open threats or secret frowns of men in office—we have long been amused with hints and insinuations respecting the dark intrigues of Congress-men—It was reserved for you Sir, to point out the culprits. Neither names nor stations should screen public blunderers from public execrations; go on, Sir, in the noble work you have begun—state facts, produce your vouchers, name your men, lay open the whole scene of iniquity, and let vengeance fall on the guilty—strip off the mask that conceals the speculator under the guise of the patriot—drag forth to daylight the men let them be who they will; whether they be Presidents, Vice-Presidents, Judges, Senators, Representatives, Secretaries, Comptrollers, Auditors, Commissioners, Registers, Clerks, Collectors, Supervisors, Inspectors, Agents, Contractors, Quartermasters, Generals, Colonels, Governors, State Comptrollors, Treasurers, Accountants, or whatever else may be named. Let the Augean stable be cleansed, though the world be turned inside out or topsy-turvy—order will spring out of confusion, light will flash out of chaos, rogues will be exposed, justice shall appear, and the war-worn soldier, the pennyless officer, and the long cheated real public creditor shall bless the name of Blanchard. Having entered on the arduous undertaking, having collected materials in your late southern tour, having an able friend, adviser and counsellor in that independent and truly disinterested friend of the *poor soldier*, the author of " the poor soldiers' plea"—you must be armed at all points, your enemies cannot assail you with advantage ; they shall retire from your attack, and the whole herd of speculators, from the first man in the government, to the despicable wretch who prowling through the country for prey, has bought the soldier's or widow's mite, for a song, shall crouch and refund their ill-gotten gains.—Cloth'd with the impenetrable armour of honour, faith, a good conscience and an unspotted character, you will effect your object, though Appollyon and all his host of treasury blood-suckers should stand in your way.

A FELLOW LABOURER."

HARTFORD, FEBRUARY 25th, 1796.

> "*Alas!* '*tis strange, that* not a sigh
> "Can *pass this babbling creature by;*
> "*To give true answers she'll pretend,*
> "Yet almost *lie to gain her end.*"

HAVING, with courage fill'd, with honour stor'd,
Drawn in your country's cause your trusty sword,
While yet the scales of conquest doubtful swung,
And Freedom trembling on the balance hung,
Once more most nobly have you strutted forth,
In conscious pride of dignity and worth,
And us'd conveniently the soldier's name,
To make for further pay a *modest* claim—
A claim so righteous, rational and strong,
'Tis strange how Congress could reject so long:
For 'tis in politics a maxim known,
That those who've had the meat should pick the bone.
So round the skeleton of some old horse,
Far fam'd for beauty, matchless in the course,
Strut the voracious crows in sable pride,
And pick the ribs, and glean the shrivell'd hide;
While the insatiate band, who long before
Had shar'd a double portion, call for more,
And bitterly complain how poor the pay,
For having snatch'd the carcass from decay.
  Move on brave sir, in Quixote state advance,
Rear your strong shield, and shake your magic lance,

At your approach alarm'd, that Giant old,
Proud Speculation, trembles in his hold;
Dreads lest your potent arm should lay him low,
His treasures plunder, and his pomp o'erthrow.
No doubt the nest you've stirr'd inflam'd will rise
And jump in angry swarms before your eyes;
Their sting-fraught tails those waspish dogs will rear,
And buzz most dreadful howlings in your ear.
Be persevering in the cause, be bold,
And to the point in view your progress hold;
Keep a taught rein, coax, whip, and spur your horse,
Nor stop him short, nor deviate from the course;
Nor let the open frown, or secret threat
Of Men in office make you quit your seat:
For should you, be assur'd, some means they'll find
To crupper-gall your steed, & make him kick behind.
   Long we've been pleas'd with stories, not a few,
Of Congress-men, and *Congress-Women* too,
Their private bargains, and their party leagues,
Their public brothels, and their sly intrigues,
Their assignations, and their tricks at play,
Their debts of honour, paid in *honour's way*.
For neither station, title, rank, nor place,
Should screen a public robber from disgrace;
But round his steps let injur'd Justice bawl,
And on his head a nation's curses fall.
Pray sir go on—complete the work begun,
State facts, produce your vouchers one by one;
On whom soe'er your wise suspicions light,
Call forth the villains, be they wrong or right—

Yoke up your "*minute men*," hitch fast a chain,
Grease Faction's wheels, and drag them o'er the plain;
Load the old Cart with every crippled dog,
Each speculating, money-asking rogue;
No matter who, nor what—if once they're taken
We'll smoke the rascals into human bacon.
Where'er a villain's form to lurk is seen
Beneath a jacket, strip him to the skin,
Make him sans culottes, tear away his shirt,
And lay the scoundrel sprawling in the dirt.
Perhaps some future time when worth is fled,
When truth is exil'd, and when Virtue dead,
When FREEDOM'S SAVIOUR meets the fatal doom,
And sinks his country's glory in the tomb—
While o'er her Washington's illustrious urn,
The Genius pale of Liberty shall mourn—
Some future President, with impious feet,
Shall dare ascend the exalted patriot's seat,
And o'er Columbia's wretched land display
The mournful blightings of a tyrant's sway.
And then look sharp to find some smaller rogue
Crept somewhere in this lengthy catalogue—
Vice-Presidents, and Registers, Inspectors,
Old Gifford Dallies,† Senators, Collectors,
Comptrollers, State-Comptrollers, Office-writers,
Drummers and Fifers, Minters and Auditors
Accountants, Representatives, and Runners,
Clerks, Colonels, Treasurers, Quarter-masters, Gunners,

† Gifford Dally, the name of the Door-keeper of Congress.

Post-masters, Supervisors, Secretaries,
Chaplains, Philosophers, and Antiquaries,
Whate'er their shape, importance, state or name,
How great so e'er their wealth, or small their fame,
Pluck off the mask, the face infernal shew,
And hold the monster up to public view.
    Thou modern Hercules! whose deeds sublime,
Shroud in eclipse each deed of former time,
Urge thy great work by labours undismay'd,
And cleanse the Augean stable with thy spade,
Pitch pile on pile, on ordure ordure spread,
And give the heap to lift on high its head :
While all mankind shall view with wondering eyes,
The fragrant pillar of thy fame arise.
Though dire misrule should riot o'er the world,
And Nature's systems be in ruin hurl'd,
All things chang'd inside out, from man to mouse,
Like corn when parch'd, or tripe prepar'd for souse,
The laws of sober Decency be spurn'd,
And men and women wrong-end upwards turn'd,
From black Confusion's womb shall order rise,
And blinking chaos ope in light his eyes;
Rogues shall be naked stripp'd, of all bereft,
Nor e'en a pair of fig-leaf breeches left.
Justice so long asleep shall leave her bed,
Pull off her night-cap, wash, and comb her head;
And the poor soldier worn in fields of strife,
Whose scanty pittance scarce suffices life;
The hapless officer whose pockets low,
Nor bills of credit, gold, or silver know ;
The real creditor by power oppress'd,
So long defrauded, and so long distress'd;

Shall bid on high their acclamations rise,
And hoist thy glory, Blanchard, to the skies,
Sing to the wondering stars thy wondrous name,
And make them scowl with envy at thy fame.
As late thy Namesake in his airy car,
Hail'd by their christain-names each well known star,
Told them the glorious* news, that France was treat-
    ing
The wicked Austrians to a woful beating;
And since such bright examples France had given,
'Twas time to talk Equality in heaven—
Nor did he fear the important point to gain,
If means could be contriv'd to bring up PAINE.
And having thus the arduous task begun,
Your warp well twisted, and your filling spun,
Bring forth your loom, your ardent shuttle seize,
And weave the web of Faction as you please—
You've had full time this useful trade to learn,
And in your southern tour have purchas'd *yarn*—
Then, when your cloth is wove, and bleach'd, and
    dress'd,
The nap well *teazled*, and the folds well press'd,
To every state present a yard or two—
(Perhaps for some a smaller piece will do)
A precious scrap to feed Rebellion's fire,
'Till Peace and Freedom in the flame expire.
The Levite thus to every Hebrew tribe,
Sent a small *boiling* from his wanton *Rib*,
That while his brethren ey'd the novel food,
War, rage, and murder might inflame their blood;

* See a southern Advertisement, enjoining this important task on Mr. Blanchard, when making his late *cheap*, and useful aerial voyage.

Astonish'd Jebus saw her race expire,
Her town in ruins, and her fields on fire,
Merely because inspir'd by love and wine,
The sons of Belial kiss'd a concubine.
What strange ideas govern'd in those days,
When things so slight so fierce a strife could raise,
How much improv'd the morals of our time
When kissing concubines is held no crime.
 An able friend to counsel and advise,
To hatch new schemes and manufacture lies,
You must have found in him, whoe'er he be,
Who wrote that wondrous thing " The soldiers' plea."
Arm'd at all points, no foe will dare assail
Your barricadoed head, and guarded tail;
While your attack shall make the dastards run,
And death, or something worse, catch every mother's son.
When lazy Sol at both ends clips the day,
And chill November calls out beasts of prey,
Like you great Sir, well charg'd with awful spunk,
From his deep burrow struts the stately skunk;
While men and beasts with upturn'd noses fly,
As the pied Warrior rears his tail on high,
Nor look behind, nor breathe, 'till far without
The direful scatterings of his watry shot—
From the best man that ever shod his feet,
To the poor soul that barefoot treads the street,
From him who stole the war-worn soldiers' right,
And gave but nothing for the widow's mite,
To that extorting sneaking under-bidder,
Who gave but half of that and took the widow,

We'll force the dogs by dint of whips and chains,
To yield again their store of ill-got gains.
In honour's garb impenetrable clad,
Faith's old fusil, and Conscience' shining blade,
A spotless character, a pious shield,
Like Bunyan's saint thou now may'st take the field.
And if again,† as in Death's shadowy vale,
Apollyon's arm should try the strength of Hell,
Thyself, with " Mr. Great heart"§ at thy side,
Shalt bruise the devil's pate, and scotch his hide,
Knock the old scoundrel's horns off at a blow,
And send him howling to the world below.
And tho' blood-suckers to thy legs should stick,
And while thou fightest make thee swear and kick;
Yet thou at last a victory shalt obtain,
And on thy shins shall Honour's scars remain.

† See Pilgrim's Progress.
§ Author of " The poor soldier's plea."

ECHO.....NO. XII.

From the Diary, &c. of April 13, 1793.

Messrs. Printers,

"It is grating to the feelings of the friends of *Liberty*, to hear dastardly base men, protected by the mild laws of a plentiful Republican Country, come forward in public company, among a free, enlightened, and generous people, whose country heretofore flowed with the blood of *Warren, Montgomery,* and the rest of Heroes and American Worthies, who gloriously fell, in opposing the unlawful rights of a King; I say shall the refuse of the human species, the enemies of man (I mean the friends and advocates of kings and despots) dare stigmatize the French nation in the hearing of American patriots, with the cruel epithets of murderers, assassins, madmen, regicides, and the like, for decapitating Louis XVI. Do those ignorant prejudiced wretches not remember that the French nation's moderation and partiality to Louis, exceeded every thing that in reason could be expected from a people emerging from the vilest state of slavery, (in which they had been kept for ages past by king-craft and priest-craft united) to the pinnacle of importance and power; have they not sufficiently proved their attachment to him, by erasing from their memories the remembrance of their late bondage and past grievances under a brood of kings, and confirming him in the regal power? In forming their constitution, have they not given him sufficient authority and support? Have they not made the Crown hereditary in his family, if they would prove themselves worthy? Was there any thing necessary for the honour and dignity of the king of a free people, (if such can exist under a king) but was granted him? How has he requited them for their predilection in his favour? Did he not break the solemn oaths he had taken, and sacred vows he had made, to be faithful to the nation, and govern it agreeable to the constitution he had accepted? Did he not openly despise the love of the nation for him, in attempting repeatedly to fly to the enemy? Did he not support the emigrant princes (rather devils) and their army, composed of a species of beings not far distant from the brute creation, raised in the principalities of despots, with an intent to enter France with fire and sword? Patience would fail me, indignant horror would overwhelm me, and the callous heart of a Hessian, or an uncouth S———n, would shudder to enumerate all the arts, plots, hypocrisies, perjuries, murders, conspiracies, &c. &c. that Louis and his base adherents have been guilty of, to effect a counter revolution in favour of despotism, which he well knew could not be done but by the effusion of blood.

O! cursed thirst for absolute power, thou offspring of hell, and companion of kings, how deceitful are thy false charms to swerve men from their duty to God and man: but nothing is pleasing to God, which is not useful among men, consequently in Louis, (for the first) was verified an old Proverb, " Evil to him that evil thinks," or in other words, he that deviseth the blood of the innocent in his heart, (as Louis did) shall fall by the sword of the just.

It is said by some, that Louis is the best King the French had since the reign of Henry IV.—Granted; but that does not prove him a good one, for out of 100 arrant villains, one no doubt is more humane than the rest, though all very bad. Did he not know there was a bastile, an engine of terror to awe his subjects? Why did he not demolish that fabric of cruelty, the grave and receptacle of innocent men doomed to destruction, perhaps men torn from the arms of a beloved wife and the offsprings of affection? In a word, I think Louis has proved himself unworthy of the honour the French intended him, that is, of being their king. And let some of their base calumniators remember, that it is more honourable to put a King to death for good and sufficient reasons, than to sell him for 4d. a man. And let some more of them think that but a few years ago, during the American war, if they had Louis in Old England that they would serve him as they did M. de Lamot, for sending fome trifling information into Ostend, a neutral country.

G,
Or no Friend to Kings.

HARTFORD, MAY 6th, 1793.

" *Still daring* Echo *wakes the tuneful strain,*
" *And —— pun, and C——r prints in vain.*"

Vide Echo, no. xiii.

How dire, how grating to that lawless clan,
Who build up freedom on a novel plan,
To hear each day a pack of dastards base—
Mere water-gruel of the human race—
In this our land, where freedom sprung to birth,
The fairest portion of the spacious earth;
Where in strange union, Law and Peace we meet,
And full-fed Plenty waddling thro' the street;
I say—how dire to see this rascal throng,
With all the pride of self-importance strong,
Come into company among such free,
Such bold, enlighten'd, generous folks as we,
Whose bleeding country pour'd a purple flood,
And blush'd with Warren's and Montgomery's blood;

With other chiefs whom I've forgot by name,
Tho' doubtless number'd on the rolls of fame.
Shall this vile refuse, this ungodly clan,
The foes of every *native right of man*—
The right of doing whatsoe'er he list,
By secret stratagem or force of fist—
I say, shall these thus impudently dare,
Pour their vile scandals in a patriot ear,
And call the French a pack of cruel dogs,
Murderers, assassins, regicides, and rogues;
Merely, because by soft compassion led,
They've taken off their hapless monarch's head;
From all his woes a kind release have given,
And sent him up an extra post to heaven—
To tell their Maker *they* intend to go
Where all are *equal* in the world below.
Do not these wretches know that generous nation
The French exceed all men in moderation,
And that they lately have become, 'tis plain,
E'en to a proverb, gentle and humane?
'Tis true such instances we seldom find,
In this degeneracy of human kind,
Such virtue as transcends whate'er I thought,
That pious people ever could have wrought.
What generous feelings in their bosoms glow!
How prompt to soothe the pangs of royal woe!
Have they not proved mid every trying scene,
Their love most strong for Louis and his Queen?
First, in forgetting what a brood of kings,
Old Despotism had fledg'd beneath her wings;

Then in depriving him of legal sway,
Lest he should take *French leave* and scud away;
Next in confining him with so much care,
From the rude peltings of external air;
And lastly, what I deem by far the best,
Of love and loyalty the happy test,
In cutting off his head, to save his life
From scenes of woe, of horror, and of strife;
And thus, by *certain means*, to keep away
Old age, that mournful period of decay.
Then why this bluster, why this causeless blame?
'Tis crime enough to wear a pompous name.
I hate all titles of what kind soe'er,
King, Duke, Stadtholder, President or Mayor;
And had I but my will each dog should swing
That e'er has had the power or stile of King:
If good or bad, I'd no distinction make—
The good should perish for the wicked's sake.
And since *our* government's so prosperous grown,
I think it best to try to pull *that* down:
For much I dread, lest made by errors wise,
Columbia's sons refuse to blind their eyes,
And, tired of anarchy, should grow content
With the mild blessings of good government.
   Yet cannot these absurd defamers feel
What glorious views inspire a Frenchman's zeal?
Lie, rob and murder, drench the earth with blood,
Break faith with man and spurn the laws of God,
Each kindred tie, each charity deride,
If good the end the means are sanctified:

Indeed such means more efficacious prove,
As more deserving of Almighty love.
Then since base acts a saving grace confer,
Those who adopt such means can never err—
Such means, O France ! thy great redeemers use,
Such good Egalite with zeal pursues.
Hail chief! renown'd for deeds of blackest shame,
D'Orleans, Egalite whate'er thy name,
Whose head and heart with equal lustre shine,
And in thyself both fool and villain join !
With admiration and surprize we see
One vast monopoly of vice in thee,
In thee, whose changeful life alone has stood
Unchanged, in constant enmity to good,
While ne'er one solitary virtue shined,
To light the Memphian darkness of thy mind.
See young Lambelle, in closest ties allied,
By thee corrupted, ruin'd and destroy'd,
By darkest plots his lovely wife pursued,
And stripp'd of wealth to pay thy ruffian brood,
The vile De Genlis and his athiest clan,
Sworn foes to God and direst pests of man.
Yet still the glorious work imperfect lay,
Nor less than blood thy pious zeal could stay ;
By thee accused the hapless Princess dies,
To human fiends a wretched sacrifice—
While that loved form and that enchanting face,
Where peerless beauty shone with every grace,
The brutal throng in savage fury tear,
And shouts of horror fill the the tortured air.

Proceed great man! on murder murder pour,
Till satiate cruelty is gorg'd with gore,
And the poor remnant of what worth remains,
Is exiled far from Gallia's hapless plains.
But joy ye race oppress'd! ere long the day
Shall come when guilt a reck'ning dire shall pay;
When the full measure of his crimes complete,
Abhorr'd Egalite his doom shall meet,
And that deluded throng by him misled,
Shall wreak their vengeance on his guilty head.

   Have not the French declar'd, in terms most strong,
That royal Louis could commit no wrong,
Inviolability's stiff buckler spread,
To guard from each mischance his sacred head,
Given to his heirs, in fee, the domination,
But taken care they ne'er should get possession?
Yet for these wondrous proofs of loyal zeal
What gratitude did Louis ever feel?
Did he not break the solemn oath he took,
Though held in durance when he kiss'd the book?
Did not this Louis, with his child and wife,
Flee from their hands to 'scape the assassin's knife,
And thus in open terms most plainly prove,
His fear and trembling at the nation's love?
And when amidst his native land arose
A band more hostile than external foes,
When fell Revenge unsheath'd his bloody knife,
And hell-born Murder urged the fatal strife,
When from the ax, suspended o'er their head,
His dearest friends and royal brothers fled,

Scarce 'scaped with life, proscribed, deserted, poor,
Unfriended exiles on a foreign shore,
Did he not basely from his purse supply
Those dogs, nor leave them in the streets to die?
Patience would fail, a Hessian's heart would swell,
Ere half the devilish tricks my pen could tell,
The arts, the cheats, the perjuries and plots,
Conspiracies, and murders, and what nots,
Accomplish'd by that powerful band of strife—
By prisoner Louis and his prisoner wife:
For since the tribe of murderers first began,
To make their inroads on the life of man,
Full well they knew no artifice or flood,
Can hide the guilt, or wash the stain of blood.

  O cursed thirst of absolute controul,
The youngest offspring of Hell's fiery hole!
Sworn friend to tyrants, emperors and kings,
Thy smiles coquettish are most dangerous things.
By thee betray'd we lose the narrow way,
From virtue swerve, and far from duty stray,
And like Dupont, the pious, brave, and good,
Hurl bold defiance to the arm of God,
His altars raze, his holy temples burn,
And hold Religion up to public scorn.
For nought the sacred Majesty can please,
But what conduces to his creatures' ease;
And France has proved, that what mankind abhor,
Fire, murder, rapine, Jacobins and war,
Are far more useful, than that truth and peace,
Should bid the jarring world from slaughter cease,

By laws promulged upon this novel plan,
These heroes fought t' assert the rights of man—
By laws like these the royal Louis tried,
And villains batten'd while their sovereign died.
  'Tis said by some that since the great Navarre,
That pride of peace, that soul and strength of war,
France has not seen a king so mild and good
As the last Louis—yet they've shed his blood—
Granted—but then pray what does all this prove?
Are they at all events obliged a king to love?
Must they who've nobly burst through every tie,
And bravely dared each sacred law defy,
Drench'd Paris' streets with waves of human blood,
Spurn'd at religion and blasphem'd their God—
Shall souls like these at length be forced t' obey,
And basely crouch beneath a mortal's sway?
No—France, like Titan's sons, shall boldly rise,
And claim *equality* in yonder skies.
Suppose a hundred rogues grown old in evil,
And all, but one poor scoundrel, beat the devil—
Must we that sneaking fellow love?—no, no,
Send him to hell and let him better grow.
Besides beyond a doubt this Louis knew
Where the Bastile, that human stable, grew;
Why did he not that dreadful place destroy,
Where chains and famine murdered human joy,
Where many an honest man has wasted life,
Torn from his bed, his children and his wife,
While power's stern voice has bade him rise, be gone,
With scarcely time to pull his breeches on?

In short I think 'tis proved, as clear as lead,
That Louis Capet ought to lose his head.
And that upon his neck, for ours unfit,
The crown of martyrdom will nicely sit.
And let calumniators recollect,
That 'tis a greater mark of true respect,
That a mild king, for reasons wise and good,
Should *thus be tapp'd* and lose a little blood,
Than vile Egalite, that monster fell,
That scourge of man, that inmate fit of hell,
That prince of robbers and his *equal* clan
Should bid him off at four pence to a man.*

* The Echo acknowledges that there is a sublime obscurity in this part of the text, which it is difficult to comprehend, but in responding it literally its beauties will at least be faithfully transmitted to the public ear.

Portrait of Philip Egalite, ci-devant Duke of Orleans, taken from a London paper "The life of this man has been the scandal of his age. A swindler and debauchee, in early youth he corrupted and destroyed his brother-in-law the Prince de Lambelle, and afterwards accused and caused to be assassinated the Princess his wife, whom he had before contrived to plunder of the greatest part of her fortune. He carries in his bosom the pestilential germ of corruption, and after dishonouring his own bed he dishonours that of another, and blasts what little remains of the family of the celebrated Buffon, whose daughter he made the instrument of his debauchery. In his attempt to build the Palais Royal he plunged thousands of families into ruin, who had entrusted him with their property, by a fraudulent bankruptcy, which he committed with the most cynical impudence. His treasures and his fortune have been employed to pay the crimes of the tenth of August, second of September, the fifth of October and the twenty-first of January. Thus has heaven been lavish of its favours only to render vice more conspicuous. He was educated in dignity, that his villainy might be more prominent; he was rich and powerful only that his vices might be more numerous and despised; he was stationed near the throne only to overturn it with more public disgrace. and thus offer a terrible lesson to nations and to kings.—His friends and his agents were homogeneal with himself. La Clos, the author of Les Liaisons Dangereuses, Sillery de Genlis, a man the most

And let each heir of this auspicious land,
Where infant FREEDOM led her daring band,
With grateful bosoms call to mind the hour,
When generous Louis raised an arm of power,
Stretch'd forth his hand a sinking world to save,
And snatch'd its honours from an early grave.

deeply depraved of any of the present age, figured in his councils in conjunction with that execrable and atheistical priest, who at the end of the eighteenth century disgraces the name of Perigord. To these we may add that villain La Touche, and Biron, enlarged from an English prison, to appear at the head of the armies of the revolution. Such were the colleagues of Philip Egalite: such were his coadjutors in that series of guilt which wanted nothing to its completion but calling in to his assistance the butcher Le Gendre, Robespierre, the nephew of Damiens, and the malefactors of every country. Such were his secretaries, his directors, his chancellors, his familiars and his bosom friends."

By thee accused, &c. The following beautiful and pathetic lines upon the unfortunate Princess de Lambelle, who was barbarously murdered by a ferocious populace on the memorable second of September, 1792, are extracted from the New-Years' Verses for the American Mercury for 1793, and are the production of a much regretted friend, as estimable for the virtues of his heart, as distinguished for his literary talents, who in the fatal fever of 1798 in New-York, fell a victim to his active benevolence in the exercise of his professional duties, and his humane attention to an unfortunate foreigner of distinguished literary acquirements. Some passages in a few of the earlier Echoes were likewise furnished by the same hand.

" Rage, Rapine, Horror stalk around;
The palace thunders to the ground;
Babes, parents, patriots glut the grave;
Nor could imperial beauty save
Thy form where long she joy'd to dwell,
Loved, lost, unfortunate Lambelle!"

ECHO.....NO. XIII.

The text of this Echo was a publication under the signature of "Mirabeau," which appeared in one of the Philadelphia papers in the spring of 1793. This was a virulent attack on the Federal Printers in the Eastern States, particularly those of Hartford, and contained many illiberal general reflections. The Echo itself was nearly completed when some circumstances induced the authors to lay it aside, and it was never after resumed. As specimens of the manner in which it was written the following passages are given; the first being an Echo of the writer's attack on New-England, and the second the portrait of a conspicuous public character in our national councils.

Well may the name of sycophant agree
With all opposed in sentiment to me;
And chief New-England's sons deserve that name,
Those foes of primal right and native claim,
Who think that sober government should bind
In vile restraint the passions of mankind,
And that e'en legal justice has a claim
On those inspired with Freedom's holy flame.

But ne'er in Pennsylvania's unkind soil
Will those rank weeds reward the planter's toil,
But fix'd in Hartford, with attentive care
Rear'd in her *hot-bed*, nurtured by her air,
With rapid growth their towering heads shall rise,
Above the dwarfish plants of southern skies,
And in wide-spreading majesty expand
A grateful shade o'er each congenial land:
While HARTFORD COURANT, like a pedlar's cart,
Shall *lug* their goodly fruits to every part.
Hartford! curst corner of the spacious earth!
Where each dire mischief ripens into birth,
Whence dark cabals against our statesmen rise
And spread a black'ning cloud o'er eastern skies:
Whose impious sons, by decency unsway'd,
Nor check'd by prudence, nor by fear dismay'd,
Each solemn thing have turn'd to constant jest,
From John Monier to Boston's civic feast,
From Pokahontas' breed, prime lords of all,
To Hancock glorious at his Negro ball:
For still proud Echo wakes the tuneful strain,
And ****** pun and C****** prints in vain.
Hartford detested more by faction's race
Than harden'd sinner hates the call of grace,
Not more the owl abhors meridian light,
Not more the generous steed the camel's sight,
Not more the skulking thief the fatal tree,
Than Faction's brood abhor thy sons and thee!

See where in black yon champion takes his stand,
The firm file-leader of the daring band!
His early youth with fairest prospect shone,
Exulting Genius claim'd him as her own,
With rapid step through learning's realms he ran,
And Science gazed delighted at the man:
Awhile with seeming zeal inspired he stood,
And preach'd the Gospels of the Son of God;
Bade round his native land the trumpet blow,
Swell'd with the clangor of eternal woe;
'Till sacred peace her olive wand display'd,
Removed Columbia's foes and spoil'd his trade:
Then dropp'd the veil, the pious mask he drew,
His real character shone forth to view,
Self stood confess'd, through every varying plan,
The sole unchanging object of the man.

ECHO.....NO. XIV.

From the Norwich Packet, of June 20, 1793.

MONDAY the 27th inst. being very warm, there appeared in the N. W. several small clouds, which indicated what the earth greatly stood in need of, viz. showers of rain, which afterwards collected and directed their course to the northward of this place, till about three o'clock when a cloud clothed in sable black gathered in the west, arose and passed in a direct line over this city; wafted with uncommon violence by the wind fluctuating in various directions, presented to the human mind a spectacle alarming to behold ; it was highly charged with the electric fluid, and almost incessantly burst in streams of crimson fire, which streaked the heavens with astonishing lustre ; several of which, from the near connection between the blaze and report must have reached the earth not far distant, though we do not learn of any consequential damages sustained. It continued to disburden itself of its contents with unremitted ardour and violence until the shades of evening had spread around us the curtains of the night, when it gradually disappeared; and the horizon shone again clear and bright. Gay *Luna* who in majestic sway was now travelling the downward skies shone with unusual splendor, and the star bespangled canopy of Heaven furnished a scene at once beautiful to the eye of the beholder. The feathered tribe who during the storm were hushed in silence now erected their plumy wings, asone, attuned to the God of nature their feeble songs of praise, and the neighboring groves amidst creation's smiles harmonized music echoed through the skies ! the earth has received a goodly supply of rain, and the works of nature, undisturbed, laugh and rejoice; let audible gratitude awake the voice of man on this occasion for one of the choisest of heaven's blessings.

We hear that three cows were killed at Bolton last Monday evening, by the lightning.

HARTFORD, JULY 8th, 1793.

"*Our song resounds a thunder storm once more—*
"*But Norwich' far transcends Bostonia's roar.*"

ON Monday last, the sun with scorching ray,
Pour'd down on Norwich rocks a red-hot day,
Along the streets no verdant weeds appear'd,
No blades of grass the geese and goslings cheer'd,
No brook, nor pond, mud-puddle, slough, nor pool,
Where ducks might paddle, and where pigs might cool,
But all was so completely burnt and bare,
That had old Babel's king been pastured there,
On such *short feed* (I do not mean to joke)
He never would have staid without a poke.
At length, slow rising up north-western skies,
Some little clouds about Elijah's size,*
Told us in hints and indications plain,
That they were sensible we wanted rain.
At first the teazing showers our patience tried,
By sailing northerly at distance wide,

* I. Kings, Chap. 18th.

'Till three o'clock—when lo! a wondrous cloud,
Full dress'd in *sable black* like funeral shroud,
Rose in the west, and climb'd its awful way,
In proud defiance of the god of day,
Who soon perceived his rays were vainly shed,
And therefore rashly stripp'd, and went to bed.
But not much used to blankets in the heat
Of June, his godship soon began to sweat,
And snore, and puff, and piteously complain,
Which we mistook for thunder, wind and rain.
This reverend cloud came on with dreadful rumpus,
Wafted by winds which blew all round the compass,
And to the mind (the medium of sight)
A scene presented pregnant with affright.
For overcharg'd with true electric shot,
(Which all who've felt well know are rather hot)
As musket loaded deep on training day,
When Captain Flip commands to " *bouze away,*"
From breech to muzzle splits in splinters dire—
The cloud incessant burst in streams of fire;
While o'er the inky vault the lustre spread,
And streak'd the concave with surprising red.
Some of these streaks were follow'd by a roar,
Which came so near the streak that went before,
That if the first the earth did ever find,
The latter surely was not far behind.
And though we have not heard which way they went,
What place they stopp'd at, where their fury spent,
When e'er they're found, like birds of equal feather,
I'll lay my ears you'll find them both together.

The ardent cloud continued to unlade,
Like sea-sick man in violent cascade,
'Till Evening's shades afraid to see the light,
Took care to spread the curtains of the night,
But all in vain—old Sol his sweating o'er,
Kick'd off the clothes, and still'd his tuneful snore,
Just raised his head and oped his drowsy eyes,
And gave one flash of lightning through the skies,
When lo! the stars who thought the night begun,
In wild amazement started back and run;
While nodding Phœbus, trimm'd in slumbering cap,
Yawn'd out a smile and took his evening nap.
But Luna somewhat wiser than the rest,
Stepp'd softly out, in pink and silver dress'd,
And trode with cautious step the western way,
To see if all were safe where Phœbus lay:
For well she knew if Sol again should rise,
And catch her idly flaunting round the skies,
He'd make her strip to gratify his ire,
And dress herself in every day's attire.
But when she found he certainly reposed,
His lamp in truth burnt out, his eye-lids closed,
Round heaven's high arch her car celestial roll'd,
O'er starry pavements gem'd with living gold,
From orb to orb her fiery coursers flew,
And new-born splendours cloth'd th' etherial blue.
The feather'd tribe o'erjoy'd to lose the storm,
Now ventured forth in many a cackling swarm.
Aud fill'd with noise upraised the plumy wing,
And stretch'd on tiptoe oped their throats to sing,

And all around, from every stump and tree,
Proceeded songs of praise, and songs of glee;
While men and beasts stood staring all the while,
To see creation ope her mouth and smile.
The earth has got of rain a good supply,
And every thing is wet that late was dry—
Now Nature's self with mighty legs and voice,
May skip in earthquakes and in songs rejoice,
While man the master of the tuneful throng,
Shall sound the pitch, and lead the choral song.

   P. S. As such a storm does rarely fly
For nought across the azure sky,
'Tis said, that on the self-same night
Three cows were kill'd at Bolton by't!
Poor Mr. Wythe two years ago,
Had his barn burnt exactly so.

ECHO.....NO. XV.

From the New-York Journal, &c.

CITIZEN GREENLEAF,
By inserting the following in your useful paper, you will much oblige a CONSTANT READER.
Fellow sons of Liberty!

WHEN I reflect on our present political situation, my heart is too big for its little cabin: On the one hand, I observe a host of hellish despots conspiring against the liberties of mankind; on the other, a magnanimous people staking their all, and bravely resisting the torrent of universal misery.——But what are my feelings, when I consider, that this very people, proud of our example, and stimulated by our virtuous career, have pledged every thing dear for us as well as themselves. Is it possible, can America coldly see her early, her only prop, her bosom friend, her sister republic, weighed with unrelenting fury to the ground?—— And do we expect to purchase peace and liberty by a degrading pusillanimity? No—The dæmons of despotic sway, if they succeed against our only hope, will soon send their engines of destruction among us—This devoted country they consider as the primary cause of the enlightened state of Europe. Methinks I see the Genius of Liberty, on the plains of France, veiling her eyes, and while with one hand she is wiping away the falling tear, the other is stretched towards America, in awful suspence—Behold her ye sons of Freedom—Ye, who revere the Cap of Liberty —This divine form, this celestial maid, groans over you—press her, press her to your bosoms! Could we see him, who for us had, and would again, risk every thing, lift up his hand, while sinking in the storm, without a generous effort to rescue him?— And can we be tame spectators to the struggles which the brave people of France are now making, to obtain that blessed state of political happiness which, through the exertions of the allied arms, we now enjoy? If we do, the indignation of Heaven will rest on our heads. Let us tell the diseased courts of Europe, we wish well to all mankind: but that we dearly love our brethren, the citizens of France—Let us entreat them to desist from their abominable cruelties to our friends—Let us use every peaceable, every laudable method, to intercede for them—Let us particularly, urge the Spaniards to assist their old friends and neighbours; and if they will not hear, let the Eagle of America spread her covering wings, and strike home among their southern settlements, and open a free trade for our citizens to those rich provinces, which heaven and nature intended to be free. If Frenchmen cannot stay at home, let the generous souls come here, and we will soon help them to the countries of their enemies.——If America proves unjust, I will take my children, and flee to the woods, where the hell-hounds of human misery cannot sail with their ships: From the cliffs of the Allegany hills, I will show them the ungrateful country which once was free: I will early open their young minds to the light of knowledge and the detestation of tyranny; I will teach them all the arts of war, and sing the praises of liberty; and while we plough the ground, I will inspire their minds with grateful sensations towards their beneficent Creator; and, if my country should rise, and look for aid, I will seize my rifle, and with my boys, descend into the plains, and hurl destruction on the enemies of freedom, or fall in the attempt.

A SON OF LIBERTY.

HARTFORD, SEPTEMBER 2d, 1793.

" *Ye lineal heirs of Doctor Faust,**
" *By watchful freedom hourly crost,*
" *Who like your Sire*† *yourselves have sold,*
" *And leagu'd with hell for G————'s gold,*
" *Look up, and see with guilty dread,*
" *The vengeance bursting o'er your head.*"

Good Master GREENLEAF,§ thou, whose press still teems
With riot's visions, and with faction's schemes,
Whose owlish eyes the dark recess explore,
Where hid in ambush lie the slaves of power,
And, strange to tell, have grown so very keen,
As to see things that never yet were seen—
Such things as other eyes will ne'er behold,
'Till Time's last era into birth is roll'd—
Have found the secret spot—that spot unblest,
Where regal Tyranny had built her nest,
Where once each year she hatch'd her cursed brood,
And let them loose to prey on human blood,

---

* The inventor of printing, commonly called Dr. Faustus.
† The story of the Devil and Dr. Faustus, is well known.
§ Of this worthy promoter of anarchy honourable mention is made in the following lines taken from a poem lately written, descriptive of Citizen G————t's intended journey through the eastern states:

    ' TOM GREENLEAF, with a mighty horn,
      Before him proudly rode
    And stoutly ever and anon
      With all his might he blow'd.'

For a further account of this poem see Supplementary Notes.

Thence slily stole the addled eggs away,
To throw at Hamilton, at King and Jay—
Thou patriot cit, to whom all gracious Heaven,
A kind supply of impudence has given,
And privileg'd most other men beyond,
To rail at merit wheresoe'er tis found.
While brother Freneau groans in deep dismay,
Lest you at length should steal his trade away,
While Franklin's grandson, thunder-gotten Bache,‡
Declares thy tones are far beyond his reach,
(Though from his venal press big sounds arise,
And Pascal's bleatings fill th' astonish'd skies),
And Cockey Adams from Bostonia's shore,
Responds to every bray and every roar—
To thee this offspring of my brain I send,
That your kind hand its fostering aid may lend,
And through the medium of your paper give
The little brat at least nine days to live.

M<small>Y</small> heart with politics so big is grown
Its little cabin scarce can hold its own;
As where luxuriant waves the corn on high,
In verdant rows alluring to the eye,
If chance some ox by strong temptation woo'd
Crams his keen stomach with the luscious food,
Too late he finds, too proud to be controul'd
His granary bigger than his skin can hold.
On the one hand, we see with weeping eyes,
A host of despots against Freedom rise;
And on the second, a tremendous people,
Hanging their friends on lantern-post and steeple;

‡ In Greek Boanerges.

And on the third, a minister sent o'er
To raise the devil on this peaceful shore.
But what strange feelings blow me up with **wonder,**
And burst my breeches and my brain asunder,
When I reflect that this religious race,
These pious heirs of heaven's peculiar grace,
These bosom friends of every mother's son,
Who wears a star, a diadem or crown,
For us, themselves, and all creation's sake,
Have martyr'd Liberty at Faction's stake;
And having much seditious truck to spare,
Determine all mankind shall have a share,
And bent on holy crusade, lend a hand
To spread confusion over every land;
And though to some, *French freedom* is a pill,
They'll force it down their throats against **their will!**
And Doctor Genet for Columbian phthisic,
Has brought a store of this new kind of physic,
And says 'twill be agreeable to France,
To change our Asthma to St. Vitus' dance,
And " *si vous plait* permettez moi one trial,
" Vill donnez vous le contents of mon phial."

And can it be? Can this ungrateful soil,
Look careless on and see her neighbour toil,
Her bosom friend, her old substantial prop,
At war with reason, scarce in sight of hope,
By hellish despots, tumbled to the ground,
Her ancles fetter'd and her elbows bound?
And how can we in such a case succeed?
The brave escape where paltry cowards bleed;

And these curst demons of despotic sway
Will prick our backsides if we run away.
Against our only hope if they prevail,
They'll hither come as fast as they can sail;
Old England hates us, and she'll scull them over,
And try once more her foothold to recover,
That she may have a place some future day,
Whene'er she breaks to stow herself away.
   Methinks I see, convuls'd with dreadful pains,
Fair Freedom's Genius stretch'd on Gallia's plains;
Around her butcher'd sons in millions lie,
Beneath the ax the heirs of virtue die,
While Law and Peace are into exile fled
Her temples prostrate, and her Louis dead;
With stern disdain her kindling looks inflame,
To view the murders sanction'd by her name;
Around her head a bandage tight she binds,
Her deep-drawn sighs increase the passing winds;
While with one hand she wipes her dewy eyes,
The other stretches towards Columbia's skies
In awful silence—Freedom's sons draw near!
Ye who the Cap of Liberty revere!
That sacred Cap, which fools in order sped,
In grand rotation, round from head to head—
That Cap, by Liberty and Lice inspired,
Which every wearer's head with courage fired—
E'en aged Sam. of Freedom always full,
Bar'd to this wond'rous Cap his doating skull,

And Captain S——s proclaim'd that one and all,
Should bend the knee before this modern Baal.*
This form divine, this bright celestial maid,
With heart-distressing groans implores your aid;
For lo! assail'd by cholic pangs severe.
No pill of Hull† to take, no H——d near,
Soon will the lovely maid resign her breath,
And kick life's bucket to the shades of death.
Then press her, press her, with a strict embrace,
Nor spare an Indian hug in such a case;
Perhaps a proper squeeze may do her good,
Rouse up her faculties, and stir her blood.
Can we stand tamely by and see the French
In such a sea of Despots take a drench,
And yet refuse a helping hand, to save
The half drown'd wretches from a watery grave?
If we do this, by all indignant Heaven,
Doubtless our heads will in two parts be riven.
To Europe's courts, now faint and sick at heart,
Of each disease that braves the healing art,
The story tell, that we to party blind,
In our own way, wish well to all mankind.
Let us entreat, eat humble-pye, and beg
With abject crouching, and with bended leg,
That they no more will draw the murderous dirk,
But leave the French to do that kind of work.

* See the accounts published of the celebration of a civic feast on board of the Ambuscade Frigate in Boston, when Governor Adams decorated himself with this glorious insignia of Jacobinic freedom; and of the grand proccssion in New-York, in honour of the French victories.

† A celebrated medicine for the cholic.

But more especially, we'll try again,
To tie them fast to their old cousin Spain.
But if the stubborn Dons refuse to hear,
And nought can make the rascals ope the ear,
Then let Columbia's Eagle spread her tail,
And on her hovering wings adventurous sail.
Then, then, no doubt, the German troops will fly,
Like chickens frighted when the hawk is nigh—
Then shall this Eagle ope an easy trade,
Where Spanish silver—Spanish gold is made,
Their southern settlements to us will fall,
For heaven intends that we shall have them all.
For since the Frenchmen cannot live at home,
Where villains govern, and where murderers roam,
Let them but cross th' Atlantic's spacious flood,
To teach our citizens the use of blood.
Oh glorious time! when this too peaceful realm,
Shall find some Robespierre to take the helm,
Some pious Danton, or some mild Marat,
To mend our morals and to save the state,
Some good Dupont,* to whom alone 'tis given,
To show mankind the *modest* road to heaven.
Some beauteous females of the Poissard race,
Their country's glory and their sex's grace,
For soul-attracting charms not more renown'd
Than sweet-toned voices of enchanting sound;

---

* This virtuous member of the French Convention, in the course of a debate, took an opportunity publicly to avow himself an atheist, and this candid declaration was received with great applause by the majority of that enlightened body.

Those tones which Pity's self might joy to hear,
Which smote so sweetly on the dying ear,
When Paris waked her festivals of death,
And mangled thousands yielded up their breath.
  But should America prove so unjust,
So much opposed to kicking up a dust,
As thief or murderer, fearful of the law,
Flies for his life to 'scape the bailiff's paw,
So with my boys I'll fly to yonder wood,
Where human hell-hounds cannot smell my blood.
There safely lodg'd in wood-chuck burrow deep,
Secure from ships, we'll suck our paws and sleep;
Save now and then, upon a rainy day,
When all is still along the desart way,
From Allegany's cliffs I'll let them see
The land, the ungrateful land *that will be free.*
Teach them to praise the works of Anarch's hand,
And always ready for a bobbery stand.

ECHO.....NO. XVI.

From the Diary, &c. of October 29, 1793.

Answer of a Frank *to the author of a printed writing, under the name of* Americanus *in the Daily Advertiser of the 25th of October.*

LEARN you who are unworthy of the glorious name with which you cover your baseness;—that all the reproaches which you make to an honest man whom his love for the cause of liberty, and his hatred to tyrants, together with his attachment to the real interests of his country, induced to give a kind reception at Charleston to the Minister of the French Republic, are as destitute of foundation as of reason.

I will not follow you in the fastidious verbosity with which you speak of the motives which may have induced one free man to ask another free man whom he esteems, if it be true that he used certain discourses which his enemies seem to propagate with intention to injure him in a country which has not yet recovered from paying idolatrous worship to men. I will not give myself the trouble to refute the machiavelian maxims which you would wish to introduce into the free government of the United States, the Venetian silence to which you, and all who resemble you, would subject the members; I will only inform the public, whom you endeavour to deceive, that the brave MOULTRIE, in paying to the envoy of a great people the honours due to his character, when constrained by the winds, the ship of war which carried him landed him at Charleston, did no more than follow the general custom observed in all countries towards foreign ministers provided with passports from their sovereigns; that the vessels which were fitted out at Charleston, were fitted out by virtue of treaties, at a time when they had not yet been interpreted by the author of Pacificus and his followers: that the orders for hindering the Custom-house officers to oppose the going out of those vessels, were given only at the request of the consul of the Republic acknowledged by the government of Carolina; that the commissions of the Executive Council, delivered to the above-mentioned vessels, were delivered by the same consul, who had received direct instructions for that purpose, only by virtue of a resolution taken in the Committee of general safety of the National Convention; in a word, that Gov. Moultrie, in permitting those acts of the French agents, did only his duty, because they were authorised by treaties; because no law of the United States forbade a nation, in alliance and friendship with them, to arm in their ports when in danger; that the *generous* and *grateful* proclamation of the President had not then arrived at Charleston: that the federal judges had not yet been convened at Philadelphia, to know if the executive power could take upon itself to make laws under the form of decisions; that those zealous defenders of the sovereignty of the people, had not yet given their *patriotic* consent to this *constitutional* innovation, and that in supposing even that those historical monuments had been published—the governor of South Carolina who is also a depository and executor of the acts of the United States, having it at his option to follow laws sanctioned by the people, or arbitrary decisions which destroy the sense of those laws, would probably have determined to give preference to the latter.

As for your astonishment at Mr. Moultrie's conceiving a friendship for Citizen Genet in the course of a fortnight, know that this phœnomenon is not new. There exists among men of sensibility and virtue, a certain sympathy and similitude of affections, which quickly forms intimacies between them; as on the other hand their exists between virtuous men and scoundrels—such an aversion that from the first moment they never can agree.— Wherefore, *Mr. pretended American*, I here end my correspondence with you, not having any desire to continue it longer.

A FRANK.

HARTFORD, NOVEMBER 11th, 1793.

" *Ah! much I ween mistaken is that man,*
" *The fated tool of vile Sedition's clan,*
" *Who quits his father's ways and house of prayer,*
" *In their dark orgies and their plots to share !*
" *Ah better far ! had he, with pious grace,*
" *Roll up his eyes and lengthen down his face,*
" *(So haply he, in time with honour meet,*
" *May fill his father's place in Deacon's seat)*
" *Than from his press continue to defame*
" *The first of patriots' and of heroes' name.*"

Young Mr. Loudon, *si vous plait* I'll try
To give Americanus a reply;
Though in your language I am still but young,
And write but badly in the English tongue,
Yet with the highest pleasure I perceive
Your Diary in works of darkness thrive,
Therefore you'll please to print, *of my inditing*,
This civil answer to his printed writing.

LEARN you, who're worthless of that glorious name,
With which (sans culottes) you conceal your shame,
That all the vile reproaches which you throw
On that *great statesman*, our mild Plenipo,
Who burns with love of Faction's sacred cause,
Hatred to peace, to government and laws,
Whose soul corrupt disgusted turns from good,
But glows with transport at the thoughts of blood,
Who feels no tie sufficient to restrain
His heart from mischief, and his hands from gain;
Are void of truth, bereft of all support,
And weak as *Envoys out of grace at court.**

  But, sir, I shall not enter on the task
Of answering all the questions you may ask,
In this blest land what motives may induce
A saucy Frank his betters to abuse?
T' asperse with daring tongue that spotless name,
Which shines unsullied on the roll of Fame—
A Frank whose matchless impudence would dare,
To plunge Columbia in a deadly war,
O'er her blest soil the seeds of Discord sow,
And whelm the nation in the gulph of woe?
Why he should 'scape, when Law and Justice urge
To mark the culprit with their blackest scourge?
Nor will I here attempt a refutation,
Of all the maxims which this infant nation,
Has brought from every kingdom, state, and clan,
To fix the rights, and guard the peace of man—

* Mr. G——t is of the Brissotine party, which has lately been overpowered by its more daring opponents; and Mr. Brissot, with several of his adherents, thrown into prison.

That peace, which philanthropic Frenchmen find
A dangerous jewel for the human kind,
And worn too long, will grow so bright and fair
That Heaven will watch it with peculiar care:
For here we find the bliss of Eden grows,
And here will flourish 'till Time's last repose,
Unless some envious blight from Gallia's shore,
Shall blast its blossom and its stem devour.
But here I'll whisper to the public ear,
A fact which doubtless they'll be glad to hear –
On that blest day when first we came to land,
Great Mr. Moultrie took us by the hand,
Survey'd the ships, admired the motley crew,
And o'er the Envoy friendship's mantle threw,
Received the sans-culotte with soft embrace,
And bade him welcome with the kindliest grace;
While Genet thus was lovingly carest,
The tender passion touch'd his gentle breast,
With fond fraternal love he oped his arms
And ardent clasp'd his Excellency's charms.
And can we be astonished when we find
A Frenchman lost to sense, to reason blind,
O'erpower'd with soft affection, weak, and wild,
And from an Envoy wasted to a child?
This is the natural course of Love—at once
The heir of Wisdom changes to a dunce,
Peasants grow great and scorn their humble breed,
And kings, Love-smitten, bow the haughty head.
Howe'er employ'd among the wise and great
In schemes of empires and in plots of state

Howe'er design'd by Nature's high command,
To mow down nations with destructive hand,
Yet man must yield to Love—his mighty sway
Envoys and Generals, knaves and fools obey.
  By treaties too which never did exist,
Save where they treat by musquet and by fist,
From Charleston Monsieur *Genet* fitted out
A ship or two, which made a cursed rout.
For being then by pomp, and Love betray'd
Moultrie's attention turn'd the Frenchman's head,
Until Pacificus by reasoning strong,
Convinced the hair-brain'd Envoy he was wrong.
When pale Columbia plunged in deepening woe,
Saw Anarch's arm her purchas'd bliss o'erthrow,
When Public Faith lay prostrate on the ground,
And Freedom's bosom felt the deadly wound,
At Wisdom's voice the States new sprung to birth,
And songs of triumph fill'd th' astonish'd earth:
Forth stepp'd the SAGE, in war and peace rever'd,
By Freedom reverenc'd, and by tyrants fear'd,
The voice of millions lured his feet to stray,
From bliss domestic to the toils of sway.
Blest by that POWER whose all-pervading ken,
Descries the thoughts, and sees th' affairs of men,
The state supplied with life and health anew,
Advanced in size, in daily vigour grew,
Forth from the dust reviving CREDIT sprung,
Her air attractive, and her aspect young,
Bade round the realm her morning-sun display
The certain promise of a perfect day:

Close at her side Pacificus appear'd,
Her steps directed, and her spirits cheer'd;
With voice persuasive charm'd her cautious feet,
Up the bright pathway to her lasting seat;
While near the throne the anxious Guardian stands,
Secures her peace and issues her commands;
Regardless of each dark insidious wile,
The noise of Demagogues, the scribbler's toil,
Of Giles's brayings, ******** artful leer,
Old Findley's stubbornness, and Mercer's sneer,
The schemes of M******* whose solemn face
Clokes dark designs beneath the masque of grace,
And all that tribe of venal apes which tries
Through Freneau's press to drown the world with lies.
  'Tis true that when those ships were fitted out
The Proclamation had not got about,
Therefore we thought, besure, we might go on,
And largely taste of privateering fun;
But this vile law, which keeps us all so trim,
Knocks on the head full many an honest scheme.
E'en now methinks I see her anger rise,
And flash like lightning from her flaming eyes,
While o'er my head her stern terrific form
Frowns a black onset to the threat'ning storm.
Nor had the judges, at that lucky hour.
Arm'd with the awful rod of legal power,
Bade traitors tremble, pirates flee the light,
And all our party skulk away from sight.
  What wond'rous sympathy of soul we find
Among the various race of human kind!

Though born in distant lands, of different breed,
Of varying language and opposing creed,
Still with fond love the kindred spirit glows,
Though foreign climes and hostile faiths oppose,
Not all these obstacles its force controul,
It clings attracted to its kindred soul.
Not more with certainty the vulture brood,
Allured by carnage, seek the field of blood;
Not with more joy the crow voracious hies
Where some fresh carrion greets his greedy eyes,
Or more attracted by congenial smell
The skunk explores his cousin pole-cat's cell;
" Than by the impulse of attraction led"
Congenial souls to souls congenial speed.
Thus all who Freedom's *genuine* ardour feel,
Whose souls are warm'd with Jacobinic zeal,
Felt at first sight love's keen electric flame,
And thrill'd with transport at *Sieur Genet's* name;
With raptured eye in him they saw disclos'd
The man on whom their fondest hopes repos'd,
Whose factious breath the flames of war might light,
And 'gainst our PATRIOT CHIEF their force unite.
So mid old Ocean's caves and deep retreats,
If chance the Sword-fish with the Thresher meets,
'Till then though neither met each other's eyes,
Unlike in figure and unlike in size,
Yet tastes congenial knit in strict embrace,
And join in friendship's bond the cruel race;
While the same impulse moves them to assail
With various force combined the lordly Whale.

But yet, however it may seem to you,
This strange phenomenon is not so new,
That man in man should sudden love inspire,
And sympathetic feelings wake desire.
For ever since that day renown'd of yore,
When pale Gomorrah felt the fiery shower,
When Lot in terror from the city fled,
O'er Asian climes this *manly* passion spread.
From thence to Europe's shores imported came,
And brighter splendours mark'd its growing flame:
But chief in Paris glows this *love divine*,
By Sodom's sons entail'd on Gallia's line.

Nor is this sympathy *to love* confin'd—
A *sympathy of hate* we frequent find.
The subtil knave beneath his dark disguise,
The virtuous man with scowl malignant eyes;
And as his virtues shine to view confest,
Still deadlier hate corrodes his hostile breast.
Wherefore Americanus you may see,
That you and I ne'er will nor can agree;
On my own plan I cannot be your friend,
So here at once our intercourse must end—
My signature's A FRANK—my name is P--s--l—
As you are honest—I must be a r———l.

ECHO.....NO. XVII.

[*When a man has ventured into the regions of prophecy, it is highly gratifying to his pride, to have his predictions fulfilled. In the following passage, Cassius appears in the character of a prophet. It did not require any supernatural aid, to foresee the effect his writings would produce; but as the prophecy is made, a fulfilment is as necessary, to save Cassius's reputation and pride, as ever it was for Simon Magus, Jemima, or Christopher Love. For this important purpose* ECHO, *ever intent on doing good, and preventing mortifications, has awakened from a long sleep, just caught his last words as they passed along, and thus sent the* SEER *on a voyage to immortality.*]

But my countrymen, this is plain dealing. Alas! it is too plain to sit easy on men long accustomed to office. It is lifting *up* the curtain and looking *in* upon their conduct. They will therefore exert themselves to cast a mist before the eyes of the people. For this purpose they have numerous expedients. They have dependants tools and sycophants, men of wit, of satire and invective, at their service; and they well know, that ridicule and drollery are able to turn the most serious and important subjects into laughter, and often into ridicule itself. They will therefore exert their utmost to throw every man who dares advance in defence of the people, into a ridiculous point of view; they will strain every nerve to twist all relations of facts and principles into distortions, and having fashioned the real interests of the people into a deformed picture, they will laugh at it themselves, and strive to get the people to join with them in the shout. But the Freemen of Connecticut will neither *laugh at*, nor be *laughed out* of their liberties. They will be upon their guard, and will be guided by facts and solid arguments, not by fiction, sophistry, disguise and witty conceits. But if any inquirer should think it his duty to face the facts and principles, which have been, or may be advanced, let him come forward into the field of free and fair discussion, and men of candour will affix upon him no imputation. They will meet him as a brother and a philosopher, not to wrangle and dispute, but to investigate and aid the cause of truth. In the mean while the real friends of the people in every part of the State, will feel it their duty, as free and independent Citizens, to contribute their assistance in establishing the facts and principles advanced on the people's behalf. For himself, regardless of ridicule, aspersions and invective, Cassius is resolved to steer on and lay before the public a further relation of instances, in which he conceives the Upper House have opposed the interests of the people; and this he will do with the most perfect freedom, because he sincerely believes himself in the discharge of his duty, and because he also believes, that he shall be supported by the great body of his Fellow-Citizens.

CASSIUS.

HARTFORD, AUGUST 25th, 1794.

> "*Seldom he smiles and smiles in such a sort,*
> "*As if he mock'd himself and scorn'd his spirit*
> "*That could be moved to smile at any thing.*
> "*Such men as he are never at heart's ease,*
> "*While* they behold a greater than themselves."
> SHAKESPEARE.

PERCHANCE my countrymen, my windy strain
To some nice ears will seem a little plain;
They'll think, perhaps, I mean to give offence,
Or (which is false) have very little sense;
That none but fools would lay out such a plan;
And that, instead of *nine*, I sha'n't turn out a man.
I fear my food your stomachs will not fit,
You're used to eating much more wholesome meat;
While I, alas! no better dare to boast,
Than *water-gruel*, or a *stew* at most.
But 'tis no wonder—all my thoughts of late
Have been employ'd to benefit the State.
Call'd by my *town* to act a public part,
Their interest lies *the second* from my heart;
(My own, be sure, employs the nighest room,
For *Christian* charity begins at home.)
Indeed, so much I've ponder'd on these things,
So much with politics my skull-bell rings,
So much I wish the Council should retreat,
And leave for me in Upper House a seat;

So much I've watch'd, and toil'd, and wrote in vain,
That I begin to think't has turn'd my brain.
How much I've strove the *candid air* to keep,
That air which lays Suspicion fast asleep:
How oft has Cassius shifted in his gait,
To suit the ruling party in the State,
Argued with blockheads to preserve their right,
Prov'd white is black, and then prov'd black is white.
How oft, when call'd t' uphold the moral cause,
By feeble aid of temporary laws,
My heart, attracted by its genial guide,
O Vice! has always labour'd on thy side!
My *real feelings* scarce I dare disclose,
My friends may sneer—ah what will say my foes!
To tell the honest truth in simple speech,
I'm sadly troubled with politic itch;
So much it spreads, and makes me so uneasy
That I must either scratch, or run quite crazy;
So great its power, not Mercury's self can quell,
Nor all the fire and brimstone this side hell.
Once my bold wishes vainly dar'd to aspire,
" Above the vulgar flight of low desire;"
I fondly hoped the Federal-Hall to reach,
And there, 'mongst other great men, make my speech.
Alas, in air that cheating vision floats!
The stubborn freemen will not give their votes:
In vain I flatter, fawn, shake hands and write,
The *Nomination's* doom'd to be my height.

   Robb'd of this hope, I turn my anxious eyes
To where the Council into honour rise.

In firm belief, what proverbs old have said,
That "*half a loaf* is better than *no bread*,"
I'm now resolv'd, urg'd on by keen despair,
To gain, if possible, a station there,
That there are thorns and hedges in the way,
Which check my progress and enforce delay,
Alas! is true;—no vacancy remains,
To soothe my spirits and reward my pains.
What can be done to ease this heart of mine?
To stand some kind of chance, I'll turn out *nine:*
I'll pray the freemen to adopt my plan,
And sweep the board, and scarcely leave a man;
Three, three alone of all that haughty band,
Shall 'scape to scourge, betray and spoil the land.
As when pale Sodom saw with dire dismay,
Heaven's fiery tempest shroud the face of day,
While tenfold thunder roll'd the concave round,
And hurrying torrents whelm'd the guilty ground,
Lot, with *two* daughters, shunn'd *alone* the shower,
By fleeing early to the town of Zoar.
Or as, when Noah, taught from yonder sky,
Read Fate's dark volume with prophetic eye,
Prepar'd his spacious Ark of Gopher-wood
To sail triumphant o'er the mighty flood,
While all his neighbours met an awful doom,
Swept by the deluge to an early tomb,
With *snakes* and *toads* the patriarch lay secure,
Rode out the storm, and reach'd his promis'd shore.
 If any fear the State will be bereft,
When *nine* are taken, and but *three* are left,

There's nought to fear depend upon't—I know
Of eight, beside myself, who're all prepar'd to go.
  Doubtless the Council will together rise,
And cast a mist before the people's eyes,
They'll say, perhaps, *we* wish to get their seat—
This I've confess'd and need not now repeat—
They'll say (alas! 'tis true) they've acted well,
Used all their powers injustice to repel,
As reason taught, or conscience led the way
Pleased they pursued, nor wish'd to disobey,
Nor though ten thousand knaves and blockheads prate,
Will they turn rogues and sacrifice the State.
But what assails me with superior dread,
And makes me shudder from the heel to head,
Is Satire's gang; that devilish hornet crew,
Who always sting intriguers through and through.
I know they'll ridicule, and laugh, and jeer,
Expose our plans, and raise the public sneer;
Perhaps some nick-name to our club they'll stick,
A stale, old-fashion'd, Stelligeri* trick,
From which a man no more can wash him clean,
Than Adam's sons can wash out Adam's sin.
But O my friends, I beg, beseech, and pray,
You will not laugh my *only hope* away;
As said the frog, this useless waste of breath
May be your pleasure, but to me 'tis death.
I hope no honest man will deign t' appear,
My writings read, and all my troubles hear;

---

* Stelligeri, a band of *patriots* so called from their meeting by star-light, for the *praise-worthy* object of effecting a *reform* in the government of the State of Connecticut.

For when he sees how poor and wan I grow,
Borne down with fear, and all ambition's woe,
If e'er one passion touch'd his generous heart,
To see a beggar stripp'd of every art,
Whose tricks have fail'd, whose schemes have been
　　betray'd,
While Ruin hovers o'er his guilty head,
He'll feel his honest indignation rise,
And drive me trembling from his flashing eyes.
　Sometimes, indeed, I feel my strength so great,
I dare to face the force of all the State;
But these bold fits are short—cold fear returns,
And dim the lamp of expectation burns;
I recollect when Satire's potent spell,
Show'd these my comrades in their darksome cell,
Expos'd their plots, their wond'rous schemes o'er-
　　threw,
And routed all the Stelligeri crew.
Grown wise by suffering, lo! the Club no more,
Moves to the field courageous as before,
Trembling they skulk along the path of life,
Praying to rocks to shield them from the strife.
Thus Succoth's sons, when Midian's tribes were fled,
Before great Gideon bent the haughty head;
But the brave warrior, with terrific face,
By thorns and brambles taught the cringing race.
　If, if indeed, mine were an honest cause,
If Cassius loved his country, and her laws,
If he could overcome his love of pelf,
And once forget that ugly thing—HIMSELF,

Then, then he'd dare to brave the witty throng,
With all the force of satire and of song.
But oh! alas! mine's not an honest cause!
I do not love my country, and her laws!
I cannot overcome my love of pelf!
Nor once forget that ugly thing---MYSELF!
Therefore I fear the truth will flash around,
For *Truth* is *Satire* to a *heart unsound*.

ECHO.....NO. XVIII.

From the Aurora.

[AUTHENTIC.]

"Philadelphia, June 29th, 1795.

"Sir,

"I HAVE seen in your paper of this date an abstract from the Treaty between the United States and Great Britain, which, though not perfectly correct, is nearly so.

"As the publication will probably excite newspaper discussion, it is of importance that the people should possess a full and accurate knowledge of the subject to which their attention may be drawn, and which I think has already been improperly withheld from them. Lest therefore the Treaty should be presumed more favourable, or be represented to be less so than it really is, I send you herewith a genuine copy, which you may correct your statement by, or make such other use of as you please, for the purpose of giving to the citizens of America full information respecting this momentous business.

"I am, sir, your obedient servant,
"STEB. THOM. MASON."
[One of the Senators from Virginia.]

To B. F. BACHE, *Editor of the Aurora.*

HARTFORD, AUGUST, 1795.

"*Lo the dire Hedge-Hog, from another sty,**
"*At titled Folly lets his arrows fly.*"

THOU great descendant of that wond'rous man,
Whose genius wild through all creation ran—
That man who walk'd the world of science o'er,
From ink and types to where the thunders roar—
To thee, friend Bache, these lines I now address,
Prepar'd on purpose for thy hallow'd press.
  In thy blest paper, which, like clouds of night,
Lets in the darkness and shuts out the light,
I've seen an abstract of the Treaty dire,
Design'd to light the democratic fire.
As that has had full time to work its way,
And call the public spirit into play,
Before their passions have a chance to flag,
I'll let the cat out of the senate bag.
For ten long days my soul has been confin'd,
My thoughts all shackled, chain'd my free-born mind;
For though in secret whilst the Senate sat,
I did not figure greatly in debate,

---

* In reference to the circumstance of the Echo having been, at this time, transferred to a different newspaper. The Hedge-Hog, or Porcupine, was its constant device.

Indeed I did not much *incline* to speak,
Yet my heart's sound although my head be weak.
And yet, in this respect, I'm not alone,
Eight other tongues were silent as my own;
Save once, when Johnny Langdon silence broke,
And for the space of half a minute spoke;
But finding out that he had started wrong,
He seal'd thenceforward his uneasy tongue.
On Burr alone our hopes and wishes lay,
Burr was our spokesman, counsellor, and stay,
In him we trusted for the last relief,
In times of trouble, and in hours of grief.
But though we could not reason quite so strong,
Discuss so ably, nor declaim so long,
Yet we'll convince them on the other side,
That our free tongues no longer shall be tied:
No haughty Senate, by its tyrant laws,
Shall longer lock our democratic jaws;
Perish their secrets—laws were made for fools,
We laugh to scorn the Senate and its rules.
In pure Republics secrets ne'er exist,
Knowledge like wind should blow where'er it list,
No man can claim a right exempt to *know;*
Science and Truth in common streams should flow.
Where each at will his parched bill may dip,
And, as occasion calls, enjoy a sip;
Thus borne away, a drop by every hand,
Knowledge will bless each corner of the land.

s

Hard, very hard would be the poor man's lot,
If every one might hoard up all he'd got,
From whence no common man supplies may draw,
Without transgressing some despotic law,
And thus establish, spite of all our pains,
A dreadful *aristocracy of brains*.

 We're all determin'd (*we* the virtuous *ten*,
The major part of thirty common men;
For by the rules of democratic lore,
Twenty is less than ten by three or four,)
I say that we're determin'd, one and all,
That Jay's vile treaty to the ground shall fall.
Doubtless the subject will much heat excite,
Blockheads will prate, and demagogues will write,
From Club to Club the uproar will expand,
Fill all our towns and spread throughout the land.
But chief in towns, as long experience shows,
Each factious plant in rank luxuriance grows;
For there collects the scum of human race,
The dark-soul'd plotter, and the villain base.

 O thou, my native land, by Heaven design'd
As the last refuge of the human kind,
The land where Freedom built her blest abode,
Where lavish Nature all her blessings strew'd,
Where Health and Plenty hand in hand appear,
And pleasure wantons through the varied year,
Oft thy horizon blackening storms o'ercast,
And bend thine honours to the sweeping blast,

To civic feasts, dark clubs, and riots fell,
The plots of traitors and the lies of hell.
But let us overhaul this mighty *ten*,
(This major part of thirty common men)
On whom their country's glory seems to rest,
Safe as a secret in a gossip's breast.
First Irish James, a red-hot blust'ring blade,
By nature honest, but so so by trade.
His eye-sight reaching only to his nose,
He thinks the world beyond is fill'd with woes,
And thus beclouded mid a flood of light,
Each object startles, empty sounds affright;
While one short maxim rules his heart and tongue—
" *What I can't see through certainly is wrong.*"
Pierce Butler next, a man of *sterling worth*,
Because he justly claims a *noble birth*;
Doubtless great Ormond's Duke foresaw in thee,
The heir of freedom and *equality*.
North Carolina boasts her number *twain*,
Men form'd *to vote*, but never *to explain*.
Obedient still, they do as they are bid,
And follow where their wiser masters lead.
Ah Thomson Mason! long thy fame shall rise
With democratic incense to the skies!
Long shall the world admire thy manly soul,
Which scorn'd the haughty Senate's base controul,
Came boldly forward with thy weighty name,
And gave the treaty up for public game,

Expecting, doubtless, that thy praise would sound,
When the full glass, and *patriot* toast went round.
But be assur'd, that though the sons of rout,
When drunk, may push thy name with glee about,
Though Faction's slave, Ben Austin, lifts the hand,
And hails thee saviour of the sinking land—
Yet honest men with indignation fraught,
Will search thy bosom to the inmost thought,
And on thy brow will fix a deeper stain,
Than ting'd the murderous front of guilty Cain.
Decent thy Colleague is, a man of merit,
Though tinctur'd strong with Jacobinic spirit.
Kentucky from her mountain heights afar,
Sends forth John Brown t' engage in *treaty war*.
Next in the train the courtly Burr is seen,
With winning aspect, and with varying mien;
Though small his stature, yet his well-known name,
Shines with full splendour on the roll of fame.
Go search the records of intrigue, and find
To what debasement sinks the human mind,
How far 'tis possible for man to go,
Where interest sways and passions urge the blow;
While pride and pleasure, haughtiness and scorn,
And mad ambition in his bosom burn.
Next from New-Hampshire, fill'd with feverish fire,
To climb ambition's steep a little higher,

See Johnny Langdon, searching every side,
To find where patriots safest can abide :
But when at length our Southern brethren saw,
His ballast was not proof against a flaw,
They told the foolish fellow how to steer,
Which point his course to lay, and when to veer,
And as a rich reward, with kindly grace,
They'd try to hoist him into Adams' place.
Poor doting Moses! wherefore dost thou stray?
Is the good rougher than the evil way?
Or can thy stupid undiscerning head,
Alone by Faction and her sons be led?
Thou weak old man! 'tis little short of crime,
On thee to waste the smallest space of time.

  Believe me, Sir, I've not the smallest doubt,
That when this publication shall come out,
Our countrymen will in a ferment glow,
And wage dire war where e'er news papers go.
Long has the Treaty lurk'd beneath the shade,
And long the work of mischief been delay'd,
But game like this don't offer every day,
I'll throw it out and let the bull-dogs play.
Full well I see how Democrats will meet,
And drink seditious toasts at every treat,
Roar out to Liberty to save the land,
And damn a treaty they don't understand.
Full well I see how every mother's son,
In wild disorder through New-York will run,

While hosts of cartmen, tinkers, sweepers bawl,
" *Damnation seize the Treaty, Jay and all!*"
To these succeed a patriotic train,
Of whigs scarce rescu'd from *their brethren slain ;*
Old whigs of seventy-six—whom fate decreed,
Not for the cause of liberty to bleed;
But Irish whigs, accomplish'd in the art,
To take of others' property a part,
Who nightly risqued the stretching of the neck,
To rob a hen-roost, or a pocket pick.
Perchance three quarters of this patriot band,
Within three months first saw this suffering land;
Sold for their passage, from the gallows sav'd
That this vile country need not be enslav'd.
   Far to the south, where on her oozy bed,
Like some sick sea-nymph, Charleston bows her head
Her languid sons collect in solemn state,
To join their sages in the grand debate.
But chief on Boston's* sons our hopes rely,
There Expectation turns her anxious eye ;
There Faction hatches first her glorious brood,
There Riot finds perpetual stores of food,
There wild Disorder all her poison sheds,
There Insurrection lifts her hundred heads.

  * It may be proper here to mention, that by this general expression, it is not intended to include the great body of the inhabitants of the town of Boston. The ECHO is no stranger to their character, and respects them for their zeal and firmness in support of the government of the country, and for their exertions in quelling the spirit of Jacobinism.

Do thou, friend Bache, the Treaty bear along,
Post haste to shew it to the Boston throng;
Drive through Connecticut with swiftest speed;
Stop not to sleep, nor scarcely stop to feed;
For Democrats find sure destruction there,
As quick as toads and snakes in Irish air,
And bid (of late though rather under par)
Great Jarvis wage again the wordy war,
Again attempt with Federal strength to cope,
And not forget that while there's life, there's hope,
Bid him pursue Sedition's beaten way,
Town-meetings lead both knaves and fools astray.

  Now see the Demagogue in haste advance,
Seize his broad shield, and shake his trusty lance,
In Faction's cause for furious fight prepare,
Unfurl her flag, her bloody standard rear.
See at his nod his spaniel, Adams, run—
" Fire! fire!" he cries, " the world is all undone!
" The awful day of Judgment's near at hand!
" Hell's flames already kindle in the land!
" Help! help! O Faction! stretch thy arm to save,
" Thy sons, thy cause, sink downward to the grave."
Thus wretched Type runs raving round the streets,
Accosting every democrat he meets——
" Call a town meeting, call, for God's sake call,
 ' Or soon our Club, and eke our Cause will fall!
" Soon will disgrace our every step attend,
" And all our prospects in confusion end."

The day arrives, a day o'ercast with gloom,
" Big with the fate of Cato and of Rome."
From every hole, behold the shabby throng,
To Fanueil-Hall creep anxiously along——
A Club which treaties never knew nor saw,
A Club much better known to civil law;
Too poor to profit should the Treaty stand,
Too poor to lose if ruin whelms the land;
But proper tools for Jarvis to employ,
Prepar'd to riot, pillage, and destroy.

Now loud and clam'rous the debate begins...
Jarvis his thread of tropes and figures spins;
And often pauses, often calls aloud,
On every member of the gaping crowd,
To shew him, if the Treaty should go down,
Why Faction's hopes were not forever flown---
" And here, my friends, I solemnly declare,
(And by your looks I shall not make you stare)
'Tis not John Jay that calls your speaker here,
'Tis not against the Treaty I appear—
To read it through I ne'er have taken pains,
And scarcely know a sentence it contains—
But government, 'tis government I dread,
Which hangs like Sinai o'er the pilgrim's head.
The time is come when Jacobins must make
Their last exertions for Sedition's sake,
When Federal measures, Federal men must fall,
Or ruin seize ourselves, our plans, and all.

This Treaty cuts us off from every chance,
Of fighting Britain, and of helping France;
Of course, no hope of war will then remain,
And we must settle down in peace again.
Now who would wish to live in endless peace,
To see his wealth and happiness increase?
And yet so long as government shall stand,
'Twill spread its terrors o'er this dastard land,
And what its wisdom e'er shall choose to say,
We Democrats must tremble and obey,
A dismal proof of this we lately saw,
When Faction yielded, and when triumph'd law;
When, boldly rang'd along rebellion's field,
Our Whiskey brethren rais'd the daring shield;
When all our Clubs with expectation view'd,
The hopeful prospect of a time of blood;
When low in dust our government should lie,
And peace and safety from our country fly;
When true French Freedom from th' abyss of hell,
On misery bent, and ravening fierce to kill,
Arm'd with her bloody knife and flaming brand,
Should roll her car tremendous o'er the land.
But soon appear'd great Freedom's awful form,
Still grew the thunder, disappear'd the storm,
Back shrunk Rebellion from her flashing sight,
And all our prospects vanish'd into night.
Now I'm for living free, entirely free,
God never made a man to govern me;

And hence this inference I most clearly draw—
That we may prostrate government and law.
And let us now the glorious work begin,
To flinch is cowardice, to doubt is sin.
All who attempt the treaty to uphold,
W'ell swear are traitors, bought by British gold:
One of that sort has impudently said,
He should be glad to hear the Treaty read:
He wish'd delays—delays must not be had,
I've never read it, but I swear 'tis bad;
If it goes down, I'll bet my ears and eyes,
It will the people all *unpop'larize*,*
Blockheads may hear it read ere they decide,
I move it quickly be *unratified.*"

So said—so done—with Democratic view,
They saw the direful Treaty through and through;
And standing thus unread, and unexplain'd,
They found much in it that it ne'er contain'd:

* The Doctor said this in a manner that would have done honour to Cicero—says his printer, Mr. Adams. Pray Mr. Adams, who ever told you any thing about Cicero? Why did not you say, which would have done honour to a *Joseph Blake, jun.* the classical young orator, who seconded the Doctor in putting down Mr. Hall? You might then have appealed for proof to an Oration he spoke a few years ago on the 4th of July, in which, among other things, he says——that this *Continent* is very happily situated, being "*barricaded on one side by vast regions of soil.*" Be so good, Mr. Blake, before you decide on the merits of the British Treaty, as to tell us, which side of this Continent it is, that is *barricaded by vast regions of soil.*

The vote was pass'd, each booby rais'd his hand,
And thought himself, no doubt, the saviour of the
    land.
  Now great Honestus from his seat arose,
Thrice strok'd his chops, and thrice survey'd his toes,
Thrice strove his mighty project to declare,
Thrice paus'd to see if G******r was there;
For well he knew the satirizing priest,
Would hang him up a scare-crow and a jest,
If once he saw his wayward footsteps stray,
But a small distance in the factious way.
Ah cautious man! thou nothing hadst to dread,
Among thy Club appear'd no honest head,
No satirist was there thy steps to trace,
Or paint the guilty terrors of thy face.
At length the struggling patriot silence broke,
And every traitor chuckled as he spoke—
" Had it not been for Thomson Mason's care,
We had been tangled in a mighty snare,
This treaty vile would in the dark have lain,
And we to damn it wish'd, but wish'd in vain.
Thus should this mob, whites, negroes, boys and all,
Presumptive tenants of this mighty Hall,
We should, my friends, we *fifteen hundred men*,
Been forc'd to yield to twice the number ten.
But we have acted well in Faction's cause,
We've shown ourselves superior to the laws,

And if the President could only see,
How well agreed and resolute we be,
Though he already may have set his name,
To Jay's eternal monument of shame,
He'd think it best, to stop the growing rout,
To dash his name across, and dash it out.
To Thomson Mason then, a vote of thanks I move,
A genuine proof of democratic love."
   O WASHINGTON! How stands thy dauntless breast?
Do scenes like these disturb thy nightly rest?
Though mobs assemble, and town-meetings swarm,
And the sky darkens with a gath'ring storm;
Yet shall thy heart so often us'd to share,
Dangers and toils too great for man to bear,
Shrink back appall'd, its fortitude resign,
When pigmies bluster and when knaves combine?
ILLUSTRIOUS MAN! thy indignation show,
And frown in terror on thy country's foe!
Then turn thine eye, this mighty realm survey,
See Federal virtue bless thy glorious sway,
See infant states beneath thy plastic hand,
Stretch in vast numbers o'er the boundless land,
The desert blossom, towns and cities rise,
And Peace and Freedom hail their kindred skies;
While all earth's empires, states, and kings behold,
Millennial scenes of happiness unfold.

The following account of the town meeting in Boston on the subject of the Treaty, will serve as an explanation to some parts of the preceding Echo.

BOSTON, JULY 13, 1795.

TOWN-MEETING—ON THE TREATY.

THE commercial Treaty between the United States and the British nation, as agreed to by Mr. Jay, having been made public by Mr. Mason, one of the Senators from Virginia—the citizens of this town, after having perused the same, and finding that the commerce of this country and almost every privilege as a free, sovereign and independent nation had been surrendered to the British, could not refrain from expressing their disapprobation of the instrument. A petition was handed to the Selectmen, signed by a number of respectable and independent citizens, requesting them to call a meeting to know the sentiments of the inhabitants on this important question.

On Friday last the citizens accordingly assembled—consisting of about 1500 persons. The merchants, tradesmen, and other citizens formed the assembly, and after choosing the Hon. Thomas Dawes, for Moderator, they proceeded to consider the subject on which they were called together.

After reading the petition, Dr. Jarvis opened the meeting, by observing that the crisis was important—that the happiness and future tranquillity of this country were in a great measure hazarded on the principles involved in the Treaty—If it was ratified, the commerce of the United States must eventually fall a sacrifice to the embarrassments of the British—That no reciprocity was contemplated in any article, and that it was an insidious plan on the part of the British to injure our allies the French, and might involve this country in a war with that powerful Republic. The Doctor repeatedly paused and called on the citizens to show in what instance the United States could be benefited by the adoption?

At length he was answered by Mr. J. Hall, who did not pretend to vindicate any part of the Treaty, but only observed as to the propriety and constitutionality of the town acting on the subject. That we had constituted the respective departments of the government, and that it was our duty to suppose that they had acted from the best evidence before them, for the interest of the United States.

Doctor Jarvis and Mr. J. Blake, jun. replied to his objections, by advocating the right of the people, more especially of a town in its corporate capacity, to assemble to express their sentiments on all matters in which their interest was concerned—that by the Constitution this privilege was allowed them and that it was an inherent principle in a free government for the people to exercise this right. He adverted to the calling the people together to approbate the President's proclamation for impartial neutrality, and retorted that those persons who were secretly and openly opposed to this meeting, were some of the very persons who called the town together on that occassion. That if the people then had a right to *approbate*, they now had an equal right to *disapprobate*;—more especially as a Treaty was an instrument of that nature, that when it was ratified, it could not be set aside by the Legislature, which was the only security the people had in case of legislative acts being disapproved of by them—That there was no doubt but that the opinion of the people on this subject would be agreeable to the President; for as he acted for the general interest, he could not be displeased at their expressing their sentiments on so interesting a question.

Mr. Hall again observed that if that meeting was not altogether *unconstitutional*, it would at least look like an attempt to *controul* the doings of the Executive—it would (if he might be allowed the expression) be " *unsenatorizing the Senate.*"

Dr. Jarvis in reply, said that the observation of the gentleman was not strictly true—How could the proceedings of this town " *unsenatorize the Senate?*"—Will not the Senators at the next Congress assemble as usual, notwithstanding the meeting of this town? They were elected by the people, but they could not be broken by them—But, says the Doctor, (with an expression that would have done honour to a Cicero) I fear that if the opinion of that gentleman prevails, it will " *unpopularize the people!*"

A motion was made to read the Treaty, but it was observed that as it had been so universally read by the citizens, it would be a needless delay of the business. The subject was accordingly considered at large, and most of the articles observed on, and proved to the satisfaction of the audience, that it was ruinous and destructive to the commerce, rights, and interest of this country.

The question was then called for, and put by the Moderator, whether the citizens of the town approved of the Treaty? Not a single hand appeared in favour of it? But when the negative was called for, a cloud of near fifteen hundred hands were displayed in the Hall.

The spirit and order of the meeting was as great as ever appeared on any former interesting subject.

The Hon. Judge Dawes, Judge Tudor, Wm. Cooper, and Dr. Eustis, spoke in terms most unequivocal and decidedly against the Treaty and of the propriety of the meeting. In fact there seemed but one mind on the subject—unanimity prevailed in condemning the Treaty in all its parts. The only question was the right of acting, and this was the objection of but one man. But the people felt themselves degraded in the suggestion, and spurned with a manly indignity, at the revival of a sentiment agitated during our struggles against the arbitrary measures of George the Third.

A committee of fifteen gentlemen were appointed to report the reasons *in writing*, which led to the disapprobation of the Treaty, viz.——

Charles Jarvis, Thomas Dawes, William Tudor, Benjamin Austin, jun. William Little, Thomas Walley, William Cooper, Nathaniel Fellows, Samuel Brown, Stephen Gorham, John Sweetser, Perez Morton, William Eustis, George Blake, and Joseph Blake, jun.

The town meeting was accordingly adjourned to Monday (this day) at ten o'clock.

It is requested a general attendance will be given this day, to hear the report of the committee.

MONDAY.

At ten o'clock, agreeably to adjournment, the inhabitants again met at Faneuil Hall, in numbers equal to the meeting of Friday.

Dr. Jarvis observed, the committee thought it improper to proceed upon the Treaty before it was publicly read. He moved the reading of it, which accordingly took place.

After the perusal of the Treaty was over, Dr. Jarvis, in the name of the committee, made a report of the resolutions they had drafted, for the consideration of the town. On motion of Judge Tudor, these resolutions were taken up by paragraphs, in which manner they were severally unanimously adopted.

[*The Selectmen conceiving it would be indecorous to suffer a copy to be published before they were laid before the President, we are deprived of the opportunity of laying these important Resolutions before our readers; and a deference to the Selectmen, prevents our giving that partial sketch which memory might enable us to do.*]

On motion, it was ordered, that an express be immediately dispatched to the President, by the Selectmen, with the Resolutions which have been passed.

After passing the resolutions, on motion of Mr. Austin, a vote of thanks was passed to Stephens Thomson Mason, one of the Senators from Virginia, for his patriotism in publishing the copy of the TREATY, which has enabled us to prevent the impending danger of its ratification.

A vote of thanks passed to the Moderator, and the meeting was dissolved.

The following is the answer of President Washington to the address of the Selectmen of Boston, in pursuance of the directions of the before mentioned Town Meeting.

GENTLEMEN,

IN every act of my administration, I have sought the happiness of my fellow-citizens. My system for the attainment of this object has universally been, to overlook all personal, local and partial considerations; to contemplate the United States as one great whole; to consider that sudden impressions, when erroneous, would yield to candid reflection; and to consult only the substantial and permanent interests of our country.

Nor have I departed from this line of conduct on the occasion which has produced the resolutions contained in your letter of the 13th instant.

Without a predilection for my own judgment, I have weighed with attention every argument which has any time been brought into view. But the Constitution is the guide which I never can abandon. It has assigned to the President the power of making treaties, with the advice and consent of the Senate. It was doubtless supposed that these two branches of government would combine without passion, and with the best means of information, those facts and principles upon which the success of our foreign relations will always depend; that they ought not to substitute for their own conviction the opinions of others; or to seek truth through any channel but that of temperate and well-informed investigation.

Under this persuasion, I have resolved on the manner of executing the duty now before me. To the high responsibility attached to it I freely submit; and you, gentlemen, are at liberty to make these sentiments known, as the grounds of my procedure. While I feel the most lively gratitude for the many instances of approbation from my country I can no otherwise deserve it than by obeying the dictates of my conscience.

With due respect,
I am—gentlemen,
Your obedient
GEO. WASHINGTON.

United States,
28th July, 1795.

ECHO.....NO. XIX.

From the Aurora, of July 28, 1798.

THE Electioneering campaign has already opened in the Western counties of this State. John Woods, the present State Senator from Alleghany, is held up by the Federalists as their candidate for a seat in the Federal House of Representatives from the district composed of Alleghany, Washington, and Green.— H. H. Brackenridge has come forward, and in an address to those counties, replete with the sense and wit which generally mark his writings, opposes Mr. Woods' pretensions.

His address concludes as follows:

" But John Woods, as he never reads, has no occasion for acquired knowledge. His academic education was extremely limited, and his literary application since none; but it is his genius —his native power that made amends for all.

I give it up then. I admit then he has no occasion for improvement. But, as to occupying place, there might be a propriety in letting older though weaker lights be carried to the upper chamber, and go out first: or at least in letting some other lights exist at the same time. When I left Philadelphia, almost twenty years ago, I saw no chance of being any thing in that city, there was such great men before me, Chew, Dickinson, Wilson, &c. I pushed my way to these woods whence I thought

I might emerge one day, and get forward myself in a congress or some other public body. But what has been my surprise to find a youth of Bedford county in my way; whereas, when I passed the hills, I would just as soon believe that a crow's nest could come to a perriwig. But I see my fate and am resigned to it.

"To avoid offence, I do not deny, as I have already said, that he is a prodigy. What is more, I admit he is far from being ignorant of this himself. It might be a quere whether the lion knows whether he is the king of beasts, or the jack-daw that it has variegated feathers; out there can be no question but that John Woods knows all his pre-eminencies, and perhaps adds to them in his own imagination. He is none of your people that is not acquainted with himself. The *Gnothi seauton* of the Greeks is his motto; not just in the sense the philosophers intended, but in the meaning, that he thinks more of himself than any thing else. Some are troubled with what is called absence of mind; this is not his defect. He has continual presence of mind, a rare qualification for a general. His thoughts are never abroad; no more than if there was not an animal in the creation but himself. His ideas centre where they first arise. He feels no blush at the precedence of others, because they are never the subject of his thoughts.

He must be a candidate for Congress, must he? At the academies, we used to play at what they call leap the Bullock; that is, some leaned their heads, until others leaped upon their shoulders, or leaped over. But it was the rule for those who leaped last to lean their heads next. I suffered John Woods to leap over last year; and I think it hard that I, or somebody else, should not leap now. The truth is I have no thoughts of leaping; but I do not like to see one overgrown youth leaping always. The play, man and boy is the same; we cannot easily endure what is assuming and arrogant; I never suffered it at school, nor will

I suffer it in life without protesting against it. For though I might allow this in John Woods, himself merely considered, yet the principles are dangerous and of bad example; it is this same fire of ambition, and disregard to age, experience, moderation and self-denial, in the elections of the Primary Assemblies of France, that has carried forward such unwrought materials and produced such unfledged politicians as have disgraced the noble cause in which she was engaged, and enslaved the people. When you see any man domineering and taking place of his seniors at home without a blush, can you expect a regard to equal liberty and right abroad?

No; let John Woods reduce his mind within a reasonable compass; let him wait till he is called upon for his services, and then they may be valued. Dropping irony, let him occupy the present interval to improve himself in books; for most assuredly he is not without the need of this. I am now in the fiftieth year of my age, and have been forty-five a severe student; and yet *because I know something* I should tremble were I to think of a seat in the legislature of the Union, at not knowing more. Perhaps from what we have heard of that house last year, John Woods may think it is but a game of cudgeling to act a part there. Indeed, from the half of their speeches, it is pretty evident, that a bear garden would suit some better, than a hall of Philosophers; but ought we not to labor a reform? If there are a number of harsh, haughty, intolerant, and at the same time ignorant young men in that assembly, why carry coals to New-Castle and increase the store from our stock? Suggesting these things to your consideration, citizens, I close the discourse.

H. H. BRACKENRIDGE.

HARTFORD, AUGUST 20th, 1793.

Hark ! From fair Ohio's wave,
What sounds familiar borne along,
Waken Echo in her cave,
And again inspire her song.

JOHN WOODS ne'er reads, nor need he read, I trow,
As he who nothing knows, ne'er wants to know,
No way to knowledge is this reading sure,
I am for Nature, unadulterate, pure—
Nature, who surely never meant that man
Should be restrain'd by such a narrow plan.
Nor spelling-book, nor primmer, well I wot,
Had mother Eve, or Father Adam got,
When shame first introduc'd the taylor's trade,
And taught how fig-leaf Overalls were made,
While all so blithely, mid the sun and rain,
They strutted sans-culotte around the plain.

But, to return to Woods,—to speak my mind,
His education was of narrow kind ;
Nor has he since to learning much applied,
But smil'd with calm contempt on pedant pride.
His mental powers, howe'er, superior shine,
His genius glows with energy divine.

But when with mine in competition plac'd,
How low his powers, his genius sink debas'd.
Has not my genius shone with peerless ray,
And o'er Ohio pour'd the blaze of day?
Have not my writings spread abroad my name,
And bards* consign'd me to immortal fame?
Then shall John Woods with me presume to vie,
The brightest star that decks the western sky?
But though John Woods may no improvement want,
Though lack his wit, his knowledge though but scant,
Yet why should he, to upper rooms be sent,
Ere older lamps their feeble rays have spent?—
For 'tis, I deem, but fair that each awhile
However dry his wick, or poor his oil,
Should have his turn to light his torch-wood fire,
To smoak his time out, and in funk expire.
This maxim oft revolving in my mind,
" Ne'er where they're known, do prophets honor
    find,"
Full twenty years ago, to try my luck,
I Philadelphia's beauteous walks forsook,
Convinc'd that there I never could obtain,
" A post of honor, or a post of gain"—
Resolv'd to quit the social haunts of men,
And seek the bear's retreat, the satyr's den,

*See Echo No. VII. Concluding thoughts on the Indian War, by H. H.
Brackenridge.

Left each attachment Penn's fair city shews,
Its yellow fever, and its crowded stews,
Left its fair dames, with all their *winning* charms,
And clasp'd an ocher'd beauty in my arms;
For tho' with Wilson, Dickinson, and Chew,
Great as I was, the contest vain I knew,
Yet in my breast I felt a lively hope,
That with a simple Indian I could cope,
And in some future day by them be sent
To Congress, Powaw, or to Parliament.
But what astonishment, what deep surprise,
Possess'd my soul, to see John Woods arise,
This Bedford county youth, whom t'other day
No mortal knew, now strut across my way!
O shame, disgrace, to be thus strangely foil'd,
When I for days, for months, for years have toil'd,
Spent all my vigour, all my prowess flown,
My wit exhausted, and my wisdom gone!
And this by one, who ne'er reclin'd his head,
Midst piles of learning upon learning spread; †
Where Philadelphia's dome attracts the eyes,
And *Bingham's Franklin* seems to threat the skies.

When o'er these western hills my footsteps ran,
Driven by stern Justice from the haunts of man,
Close at my heels, the fatal bailiff trode,
And far before me stretch'd the land of Nod.*

† Mr. B——e is stated to have been in the habit of frequently indulging himself in a nap, with a folio or quarto for his pillow, in the City Library of Philadelphia.
* Kentucky.

Dark o'er me wav'd the hemlock's frightful shade,
And at my elbow gleam'd the savage blade;
While the gaunt wolf amid the shades of night,
Prowl'd by the pallid moon's uncertain light;
In quest of carnage roam'd the rugged bear,
The panther's hideous yell assail'd my ear;
And the brown bittern's dismal clang was heard,
Join'd with the shriekings of the funeral bird;
And every leaf that rustled on the heath,
Seem'd the dread harbinger of instant death—
When lo! an object of terrific size,
By the faint glimmering caught my wondering eyes;
Exalted high in air, amid the wood,
This strange phenomenon suspended stood,
Fix'd on a lofty tree's far spreading bough,
And gloom'd with deeper dye the shades below.
Chill horror nail'd me to the shuddering ground,
Froze my heart's blood, my jaws distended bound,
Cold sweat my limbs bedew'd, my nerveless tongue,
Stretch'd at its length, adown my bosom hung.
Swift through my mind each fearful image pac'd,
Hell seem'd to hover o'er the howling waste;
Some shaggy beast of awful size was there,
Some mighty scalp was floating in the air,
Some Indian Giant, as Goliah big,
Had hung on high his mighty perriwig;
Great Mammoth here, perchance his levee keeps,
And not remote, amid his courtiers sleeps;

What being else so large a wig could wear,
Who else could carry such a load of hair?
And who but him, his burthen'd skull to ease,
For barber's block could use the tallest trees?
All petrified with fear, aghast, amaz'd,
On this dread object rivetted I gaz'd—
I saw, methought, the dreaded monster nigh,
Wild fury sparkling in his brutal eye,
Already felt myself within his paws,
And saw the inside of his hideous jaws:
When lo! that moment, to relieve my pain,
And save from dread insanity my brain,
A Crow, like that to old Elijah sent,
When to his boarding-house (the woods) he went,
With cawing hoarse, from off the branches flew,
And straight discover'd to my raptur'd view,
So clear my stupid eyes the truth could see,
A Crow's nest built upon a hemlock-tree.

 To avoid offence, how'er, I'll not deny
Where e'er you find him, John's a prodigy,
A *rara avis* running on so fast,
No one imagines where he'll stop at last.
To me 'tis clear, without some good advice,
He'll outgrow Pittsburgh steeple in a trice.
And what is strange methinks, and also wrong,
John knows, as well as I, his legs are long,
And if he does not shortly catch a fall,
Colossus like, he'll straddle o'er us all.

I hardly think the Lion knows the length
To which he's able to extend his strength;
More modest than John Woods, he growls around,
But leaves to other beasts their own peculiar ground.
Not so with John—he's every rival's foe,
And on to Congress seems resolved to go.
And go he will, unless I make a rout,
And by my wisdom try to cut him out.
    John Woods is truly a surprising elf,
He's perfectly acquainted with himself;
" *Gnothi Seauton,*" thus the oaf translates,
" I've beat old Brackenridge as sure as rates."
Some men are troubled with an absent mind,
To all that's passing either deaf or blind;
And though we *sages* loud their ears assail,
And still rehearse the oft repeated tale,
Alas! we're treated with extreme neglect,
Our hoary hairs gain not the least respect.
Some people's thoughts are ever wont to roam;
But John's reflections never stir from home;
His mind is but a dunghill fowl at most,
Before the door all day, at night at roost.
Nought can disturb his muscles, raise a blush,
For me or mine he does not care a rush.
    To Congress now it seems John Woods must go,
To try his skill in saying " *aye*" and " *no;*"
But if permitted, I will let him see
I can say aye and no as well as he.

At school, I recollect, full many a day
A game call'd Bullock's-leap we us'd to play;
I for this game by nature was prepar'd,
My skull was thick and tough, my horns were hard,
Full half a bullock from my birth was I,
No calf in school with Brackenridge could vie.
It was the fashion then *by turns* to jump,
And now exalt the head, and now the rump—
John leap'd last year, I let him leap you know,
But John declines to let me leap him now,
Though stiff my joints, my former vigour gone,
Since John leaps me, why should not I leap John?
Tis true that now my jumping days are o'er,
Nor do I wish to play the bullock more,
But if too old to leap, too weak to stand,
At least *at falling* I can try my hand.
But my soul sickens and my cheeks grow pale,
Whene'er of Woods I hear the wond'rous tale;
Ah why should this young calf of Bedford breed,
Be ever leaping o'er some messmate's head?
E'en when a boy at school, at this lov'd play
I ne'er could bear a rival in my way,
But chose to have my ample share of fun
And do myself what leaping there was done.

   All things consider'd, since I can't prevent
John Woods' election, I would e'en consent,
Did not the principle so dangerous seem,
Were not the example fatal in the extreme.

For if young men such confidence obtain,
No chance for older ones will long remain.
What, but a want of deference to age,
To tried experience, and to counsel sage,
What, but ambition's all-devouring fire,
The pride of youth, of power the wild desire,
By want of proper self-denial nurs'd—
With such deep woes " regenerate France" has curs'd.
Where politicians not yet fledg'd are seen,
With scarce a bit of down to shade their chin;
And like young quails with egg-shell on their back,
Run wildly round, and sense and knowledge lack.
As the red meteor, mid the shades of night,
O'er the wide cope of heaven emits its light,
Shines with portentous beams, while youthful eyes,
With pleasure view its progress thro' the skies,
But cautious Age beholds with deep regret,
This sign of woe and messenger of fate;
So these, amid its wild politic gloom,
Appear'd the Gallic hemisphere t' illume,
And hoary Statesmen with experienc'd view,
From thence presages dire of horror drew.
Nor long the period, ere by Faction nurs'd,
Involv'd in flame the dread tornado burst,
O'er Gallia's realm impell'd its dreadful force,
And mark'd with ruin its destructive course.

While swept in blended heaps together lay,
To Anarchy and wild Misrule a prey,
Law, order, government, the ties that bind
In civil harmony the human kind,
Each sweet relation of domestic life,
The friend, the parent, offspring, husband, wife;
The fanes of God by impious rage o'erturn'd,
Each moral bond, each social duty spurn'd,
Fair Liberty, by ruffians' hands profan'd,
Fled in wild horror from the fated land;
While in her stolen robes, exulting stood,
Fell Faction howling o'er the scenes of blood.

 When e'er a man, elate with conscious pride,
Marches about with meanness at his side,
Among his seniors fawning, cringing, base,
Among his equals fill'd with *equal* grace,
Yearning for power, yet worshipping the crowd,
In morals mild, in praise of freedom loud,
Of law the foe, the " sovereign people's" friend,
Of means regardless, anxious for the end,
Of tyrants fearful, *candid*, *meek*, and *just*,
The rights of man his sole, and sacred trust,
Bankrupt in purse, the foe of all that's good,
Hostile to peace, and fierce for shedding blood—
Such men avoid, their vile communion shun,
In black corruption all their counsels run;
They're Jacobins—French tools, of spirit fell,
Their breath is poison, and their haunts are hell.

No; let John Woods, instead of all this rumpus,
Reduce his mind, within some sort of compass,
Let him take physic, feed awhile on air,
Or bring himself to water-gruel fare;
Let him wait patiently until his time—
In me he has an instance most sublime.
Have I not linger'd on from day to day,
Have I not loiter'd years and years away,
In hopes some opportune, some lucky chance,
To fair promotion might my steps advance?
Vain hope! for lo! the rays of favour shine,
On other heads, while shadows rest on mine.
Ah how unlike this Woods, by most belov'd,
By all with fond partiality approv'd;
In love with peace, yet freedom *he'll defend*,
Fell faction's foe, of government the friend,
From school-boy age to manhood's sober hour,
Has fortune joy'd on him her choicest gifts to shower
Tis hard that Brackenridge, grown old in toil,
Should always stumble on some barren soil,
That he, within whose skull such wisdom floats,
Can't go to Congress *for the want of votes*.
But irony apart—let John Woods read,
Of this, most sure, the fellow stands in need.
Let him begin where others have begun,
That is, buy books, and read them one by one.

If to improve's his aim, why let him o'er
Both Young Squire Webster, and Tom Dilworth pore;
And he, like me, in time perchance may learn,
That Noah's Ark had neither stem nor stern.
Tis almost fifty years since I could tell,
The fatal cause why Eve and Adam fell.
How Lot from Sodom ran with visage pale,
And how great Jonah swallow'd up a whale,
How Daniel kept the lions still as mice,
Nor could they Shadrach better burn than ice;
All this I know, and, knowing, can repeat;—
And yet, perchance should I obtain a seat,
By hook or crook, sublime in Congress Hall,
Fear, shivering fear, my senses would appal;
For there, no doubt, some men would meet my eye,
Possess'd of knowledge full as much as I.
And yet, perhaps, from news arrived of late,
Of Griswold's breaking Lyon's leaden pate,
John Woods may think, for empty is his head,
The cudgel's force of sense will stand in stead.
This would be true, if in Creation's round,
Another Matthew Lyon could be found,
Blows in that case would take the place of words,
And reason yield the palm to " Wooden Swords."
If to Newcastle we should carry coals,
The world would call us all a pack of fools,

'Twere nonsense all—we might expect as well
To retail brimstone from a store in hell.
These things just mentioned, let them have their force
And here I end my notable discourse;
If John this time should cross the Congress bridge,
'Twould do the job for
>> H. H. Brackenridge.

ECHO.....NO. XX.

March 4, 1805.

" On taking this station on a former occasion, I declared the principles on which I believed it my duty to administer the affairs of our commonwealth. My conscience tells me that I have, on every occasion, acted up to that declaration, according to its obvious import, and to the understanding of every candid mind."

* * * * * * * * * * *

" I have said, fellow-citizens, that the income reserved had enabled us to extend our limits; but that extension may possibly pay for itself before we are called on, and in the mean time may keep down the accruing interest; in all events it will replace the advances we have made; I know the acquisition of Louisiana has been disapproved by some, from a candid apprehension that the enlargement of our territory may endanger its union.

" But who can limit the extent to which the federative principle may operate effectively? The larger our association the less will it be shaken by local passions; and in any view is it not better that the opposite bank of the Mississippi should be settled by our brethren and children, than by strangers of another family? With which shall we be most likely to live in harmony and friendly intercourse?

" The Aboriginal inhabitants of these countries, I have regarded with the commiseration their history inspired : endowed with the faculties and the rights of men, breathing an ardent love of liberty and independence, and occupying a country which left them no desire but to be undisturbed, the stream of overflowing population from other regions directed itself on these shores : without power to divert, or habits to contend against it, they have been overwhelmed by the current or driven before it : now reduced within limits too narrow for the hunter state, humanity enjoins us to teach them agriculture and the domestic arts ; to encourage them to that industry which alone can enable them to maintain their place in existence, and to prepare them in time for that state of society, which to bodily comforts adds the improvement of the mind and morals. We have therefore liberally furnished them with the implements of husbandry and household use : we have placed among them instructors in the arts of first necessity ; and they are covered with the Ægis of the law against aggressors from amongst ourselves.

" But the endeavours to enlighten them on the fate, which awaits their present course of life, to induce them to exercise their reason, follow its dictates, and change their pursuits with the change of circumstances, have powerful obstacles to encounter, they are combated by the habits of their bodies, prejudice of their minds, ignorance, pride, and the influence of interested and crafty individuals amongst them, who feel themselves something in the present order of things, and fear to become nothing in any other. Those persons inculcate a sanctimonious reverence for the customs of their ancestors ; that whatsoever they did must be done through all time ; that reason is a false guide, and to advance under its counsel in their physical, moral, or political condition, is perilous innovation ; that their duty is to remain as their creator made them, ignorance being safety, and knowledge full of danger ; in short among them also is seen the action and counteraction of good sense and of bigotry : they too have their anti-philosophers, who find an interest in keeping things in their present state, who dread reformation, and exert all their faculties to maintain the ascendency of habit over the duty of improving our reason and obeying its mandates."

* * * * * * * * * * *

"During this course of administration, and in order to disturb it, the artillery of the press has been levelled against us, charged with whatever its licentiousness could devise or dare. These abuses of an institution so important to freedom and science, are deeply to be regretted, inasmuch as they tend to lessen its usefulness, and to sap its safety : they might indeed have been corrected by the wholesome punishments reserved to and provided by the several states against falsehood and defamation ; but public duties more urgent press on the time of public servants, and the offenders have therefore been left to find their punishment in the public indignation. Nor was it uninteresting to the world that an experiment should be fairly and fully made, whether freedom of discussion, unaided by power, is not sufficient for the propagation and protection of truth.—Whether a government, conducting itself in the true spirit of its constitution, with zeal and purity, and doing no act which it would be unwilling the whole world should witness, can be written down by falsehood and defamation. The experiment has been tried, you have witnessed the scene; our fellow citizens have looked on cool and collected ; they saw the latent source from which these outrages proceeded ; they gathered around their public functionaries, and when the constitution called them to the decision by suffrage, they pronounced their verdict, honourable to those who had served them, and consolatory to the friend of man, who believes he may be intrusted with his own affairs.

" No inference is here intended, that the laws provided by the state against false and defamatory publications should not be enforced: he who has time renders a service to public morals and public tranquillity, in reforming these abuses by the salutary coercions of the law. But the experiment is noted to prove that, since truth and reason have maintained their ground against false opinion in league with false facts, the press, confined to truth, needs no other legal restraint.

* * * * * * * * * * *

" Contemplating the union of sentiment now manifested so generally, as auguring harmony and happiness to our future course, I offer to our country sincere congratulations.—With those too, not yet rallied to the same point, the disposition to do so is gaining strength; facts are piercing through the veil drawn over them, and our doubting brethren will at length see that the mass of their fellow-citizens, with whom they cannot yet resolve to act, as to principles and measures, think as they think, and desire what they desire; that our wish, as well as theirs, is that the public efforts may be directed honestly to the public good; that peace be cultivated, civil and religious liberty unassailed, law and order preserved, equality of rights maintained, and that state of property, equal or unequal, which results to every man from his own industry, or that of his fathers. When satisfied of these views, it is not in human nature that they should not approve and support them; in the mean time let us do them justice, and more than justice, in all competitions of interest: and we need not doubt that truth, reason, and their own interests will at length prevail, will gather them into the fold of their country; and will complete that entire union of opinion, which gives to a nation the blessing of harmony and the benefit of all its strength."

" Wak'd from long sleep her tuneful shell,
" Shall sportive Echo strike again,
" While loud its tones melodious swell,
" As nobler themes inspire the strain."

" 'T IS just four years, this all-eventful day,
Since on my head devolv'd our country's sway,
When at the undertaking's magnitude
With lowly rev'rence I most humbly bow'd.
You well remember with what modest air
I first approach'd the Presidential Chair,
How blush'd my cheek, what faultering in my gait,
When first I squatted on the throne of state!
But as, protected by supernal power,
We all surviv'd that most tremendous hour,
Let us rejoice, and trust that not in vain
Four years have brought us to this place again.
A foolish custom forc'd me to declare
Off-hand what point of compass I should steer;
But knowing well that every Fed'ral eye
On me was fix'd some mischief to descry,
I tun'd my fiddle for the vulgar throng,
And lull'd suspicion by a soothing song.

An old companion in my bosom keeps
A constant watch, save when perchance he sleeps,
From early youth in friendship sweet we've play'd,
And hand in hand through life's vast circuit stray'd.
Last night I ask'd him freely to declare,
(And he was here before, and heard me swear)
How far I'd kept my first inaug'ral speech,
And whether Candour could allege a breach.
He boldly answer'd—' Sir, on each occasion,
You've acted e'en beyond your declaration :
Thus, when you promis'd to be just and true
To *all*, and give to every man his due,
Could *Candour* possibly have understood
That the term *all men* could your foes include ?
No, Sir, on me let all the mischief fall,
If aught except *your friends* was meant by *all*.
Nor shall the Fed'ralists, perverse and base,
On grounds like these lay claim to hold their place.
Again, when toleration was your theme,
What stupid mortal could a moment dream
You meant to drop at once your choicest grace,
The right to turn the Fed'ralists from place :
What though you said, with soft persuasive tone,
That Fed'ralists and Democrats were *one ;*
Yet you, and I, and Candour fully knew
By *one* you meant nor more nor less than *two*.
And shall a man of broad capacious mind
Be to one meaning rigidly confin'd ?

The ancient proverb's wiser far, I trow,
" *'Tis best to keep two strings to every bow.*"
This maxim oft, amid this world of strife,
Has prov'd the solace of your varied life,
Charm'd the rapt ear with soft and double tongue,
And gain'd applause by sweet ambiguous song.
Now, Sir, since I have set all matters right,
Conscience will bid the President good night.

* * * * * * * * * *

" Among the deeds economy has wrought,
High rank the num'rous tracts of land we've bought;
Our country's limits constantly extend
O'er boundless wilds and rivers without end,
Nations are bargain'd for by sleight of hand,
We soon shall purchase old Van Diemen's land,
Beyond Cape Horn our speculations roll,
" And all be our's around the Southern pole,"
What though no boundary to our views are set,
And every bargain swells the public debt,
Unlike all other modes of gaining pelf,
Before we're sued this debt *will pay itself.*
And though our title deeds, by strange mischance,
Instead of Spain are sign'd and seal'd by France,
The limits too, not definitely fix'd,
Lie somewhere *this* and *t'other world* betwixt,
For fear some quarrel should hereafter rise
We've given our obligations for the price.
I grant some minds, of weak and fearful mould,
Instead of buying think we'd better sold,

Lest first or last, by some unseen mishap,
So greatly stretch'd, our union cord should snap—
'Tis true, indeed, a leather string will break
If stretch'd too far; but much do I mistake
If ever mortal broke a string of leather
By tying first a dozen strings together.
And can it be that as we larger grow
At the same moment we grow smaller too?
This does not quadrate with dame nature's course;
She gives to pigmies weakness, giants force;
The mighty Mammoth stronger is by half
Than the slim stag, the bullock than the calf.
Thus should this great Republic once expand
From shore to shore and cover every land,
In like proportion would our strength abide,
And we could manage all the world beside.

And when our children leave our fost'ring arms
And roam the western wilderness for farms,
On banks remote to see them peaceful toil,
Lords of the stream, and masters of the soil,
Is better far than on the self same place
To meet with squatters* of a different race,
With whom, perhaps, possess'd of better right,
We cannot get along unless we fight.

* * * * * * * *

Oft have the dark-skinn'd natives of the wild
Our tenderest thoughts engag'd, Our love beguil'd;

* Persons who settle on vacant lands in the wilderness, without title, and who are with much difficulty removed.

At their sad story oft We've felt Our breast
With soft compassion's throbbing pangs opprest,
That story sad, by Fiction's hand adorn'd,
Where hapless Logan for his offspring mourn'd,†
What time, by cruel Cresap's murd'rous knife,
Poor Squaw and Poppoose both were reft of life.
Long since We've prov'd from Philosophic ken,
That Squaws are women and their Sanaps men;
Though, far unlike our European race,
No bristly beards their polish'd chins disgrace.
O'er their smooth frames no hairs unseemly spread,
Nor aught displays that covering but the head,
Yet nature prompts them with the same desires,
And with like feelings and like passions fires.
 When, fresh from Sov'reign Nature's plastic hand,
Shone in the bloom of youth this blissful land,
Good, simple, harmless, nor with blood defil'd,
Liv'd the poor Indian mid the desart wild.
Close by some crystal stream his wigwam stood,
The skins of deer his dress, their flesh his food;
Few were his wants, and his desires but few,
No bliss beyond his pipe and Squaw he knew,
Small as his wants his homely household gear
Inspir'd, from nightly theft, no cause of fear,
With various hues his deer-skin mantle dyed,
By night his covering, and by day his pride,

† For this story, see Notes on Virginia, and for its authenticity the letters of Luther Martin Esquire.

A pot of stone, his succotash§ to boil,
And huge samp-mortar, wrought with patient toil,
These were his riches, these his simple store,
And having these he sought for nothing more :—
Thus liv'd he blest, what time from Cambria's strand,
Advent'rous Madoc sought this unknown land.
With swords and bibles arm'd the Welch appear,†
Their faith to 'stablish and their empire rear ;
Struck with surprize the simple savage sees
The pictur'd dragon waving in the breeze,
Hears with delight the harp's wild music play,
As sweet the strings respond to Gryffidd's lay ;
But when th' advancing squadrons forward move,
Their arms bright gleaming mid the dusky grove,
Joy yields to fear, as now, approaching nigh,
Their ress and uncouth features meet his eye ;—
And when their barb'rous Celtic sounds he hears,
That grate discordant on his *tender* ears,
Fill'd with wild terror from the scene he scuds,
And seeks retreat amidst impervious woods,
While, in pursuit, behind th' affrighted man
' *The o'erflowing stream of population ran,*'

§ The Indian name for the mixture of Indian corn, or maize, with beans.

† One of these very bibles is said to have been discovered, not many years since, in the possession of the Welch Indians, who have excited so much curiosity, and who preserved with *a sanctimonious reverence* this relic of their ancestors, although they were unable to read it and ignorant of its use. It is to be hoped that the gentleman appointed by the President to explore the western part of this Continent may, in his researches, be so fortunate as to fall in with this tribe and obtain from them this curious and invaluable deposit.

His wigwam swept away, his patch of corn,
Before the fury of the torrent borne;
Drove him from wood to wood, from place to place,
And now for hunting leaves him little space.
　　Then since, beneath this widely-spreading tide,
Sunk are the grounds that Indian wants supplied,
Few are their deer, their buffaloes are dead,
Or o'er the lakes with mighty Mammoth fled;
Humanity has whisper'd in Our ear,
Whose dictates ever have We held most dear,
To teach them how to spin, to sew, to knit,
And for their stockings manufacture feet,
Since by their ' energies' exertions' sole
Can they e'er figure on *Existence*' roll.
We therefore liberally to them have sent
Such household matters as for use are meant,
Pots, kettles, trenchers, dripping-pans, whate'er
Their kitchens lack, their victuals to prepare,
And with them skilful men to teach them how
To still their whisky their tobacco *grow*;—
While, to secure them from domestic harm,
We've lifted o'er them, with Our thundering arm,
The *Law's* broad *Egis*, under which as still
And safe they lie " as thieves within a mill."
　　But vain th' attempt to this IMPERIAL DAY
To light their dusky souls with reason's ray,
To make them quit their guns and scalping knives,
And stay at home contented with their wives;

Most powerful obstacles this scheme prevent,
Thwart my fine plans, and frustrate my intent :—
Firstly their bodies' habits different are,
And different med'cine claim, and different care,
No neutral mixture will for them suffice
Of gentle acids and mild alkalies;
But powerful *Blood-root*, *Oil of Rattle-snake*
Jerusalem Oak, and *Gum of Hacmetac*.
Nor simple blood lettings their pains assuage,
Warm their cold chills, and quell their fever's rage,
Means far more potent their tough frames require,
And the free use of lancets and of fire.
Besides as ne'er the Indian's chin appears
Mark'd with a beard, howe'er mature his years,
Of course no *Barber's* hand, with razor keen,
No *Barber's pole* amidst the tribes is seen.—
Great marts of knowledge, form'd the world to bless,
The seats of scandal, politics and dress!
From *Barber's shops* what benefits we trace?
How great their 'vantage to the human race?
That source of civil culture unpossess'd,
What wonder reason slowly fills the breast?
Thou knight renown'd! possess'd of equal skill
The comb to flourish, or to ply the quill,
Whose bright effusions, wond'ring, oft I see,
And own myself in message beat by thee,

O would'st thou, HUGGINS, to the Indians go,†
And on their chins give mighty beards to grow,
Soon should thy shop o'er all their wigwams rise,
And painted pole attract their *curious* eyes,
While the glad tribes would thither thick repair,
And claim in turn the honours of thy chair.
Methinks amid the newly-bearded band,
With brush and lather arm'd, I see thee stand,
And as each visage gleams with foamy white,
And wields thy dexter hand the razor bright,
Thy eloquence pervades, refines the whole ;
And pours the beams of reason o'er their soul,
While white-wigg'd savages, with loud acclaim,
Thee as the *People's Friend*, and *President* shall name.

   Thrice happy time ; when, freed from Error's night,
Reason's broad beam shall shed her mid-day light,
O'er realms regenerate ope unbounded day,
And bless the Indians with its brightest ray.
Drive the thick mist from their bewildered eyes
Give them their former habits to despise,
While they partakers of our equal right,
In civic feasts and whiskey shall delight.

   † Though the Echo is disposed to allow to a certain great philosopher every credit for his zeal for political and moral reform, she has doubted whether the solicitude expressed for the illumination of the savages by this novel, though doubtless efficacious method, may not, in part, have had its origin in a jealousy of the rival talents of the celebrated character, so strongly urged to this philosophic mission, and a disposition to remove him to a greater distance, by this species of honourable exile, as even the greatest men are not always entirely devoid of that passion, and " like the Turk, can bear no rival near the throne."

But much We doubt that ne'er within Our reign,
Will Indian manners such refinement gain;
For ah! among them live some crafty dogs,
Change-haters, anti-philosophic rogues,
Chaps who, though something, are of nothing **made,**
Mere forms of air and phantoms of the shade:
Who say 'tis better in the ancient way
Safe to go on, than in new paths to stray,
Where bogs and precipices lurk beneath,
And ignes fatui point the way to death,
That civic feasts with Indians suit but ill,
And Rum and Whiskey are contriv'd to kill,
That what the whites the light of reason call
Is but another name for cheating all,
And that by *equal right* is meant, 'tis plain,
The right by force or fraud whate'er they list **to gain.**
Thus like the Feds to reason they pretend
Suspect Our motives, and decry Our end.
  Where *Action* too with counteraction jars,
And wild Misrule 'gainst Order fiercely wars,
Anti-Philosophers with scorn reject
Th' enlightning doctrines of Our favour'd sect;
Bigot's of mouldy creeds, that long ago
The Goddess Reason taught were idle show,
Their superstitious whims and habits hold,
Reject the new and cleave unto the old:
In vain Reform in Gallic mantle drest,
Unbinds her zone, and wooes them to her breast,

And Innovation's meretricious smile
Attempts their rigid firmness to beguile.
Strange that such Prejudice in chains should bind
In our enlighten'd days the human kind!
Fools must they be, by dullness sure possess'd,
In their old way contented to be blest,
When Novelty, with all-alluring charms
Of untried systems, lures them to her arms.

* * * * * * * * * * *

  E'er since the day when first we took Our seat,
As Lord High Admiral of our nation's fleet,
The busy goose-quill has pursued its trade,
And the Press kept a constant cannonade,
Charg'd with the dreadful cartridges of wit;
Our head is batter'd, and Our heart is hit.
That scoundrel Scotchman, from his awful chest,
For weeks and months disturb'd Our nightly rest,
'Till freed from fear we heard the joyful sound
That Callender at last was safely drown'd,
Old Gabriel Jones the next in row appears,
And rings his story in Our tortured ears;
The old curmudgeon rummag'd up a feat
Of Ours, when fav'ring law allow'd to cheat,
Merely because We wish'd to pay, in trash,
A trifling quantity of borrow'd cash,
And makes as much disturbance at it *now*
As if it happen'd but a week ago.
Besides, the chance is even in Our mind
That Jones was anti-whiggishly inclin'd,

If so, it constitutes Our brightest glory
To've done Our very best to trick a Tory.
Such tales with other things of trifling charge,
(For Us too tedious to detail at large,)
Mere peccadilloes, fir'd with deadly hate,
The paltry printers sound from State to State.

   Nor even here has ceas'd the thundering press,
But still invades Our quiet, " more or less:"
If from Our lips some contradictions fall,
These Fed'ral Warriors from their ambush crawl,
With direful War-whoop break upon Our ear,
And rend Our bosom with distracting fear.
Sometimes We're timid, other times too rash,
Penurious now, now prodigal of cash,
Sometimes We talk in hypocritic strain,
Sometimes We're hand and glove with atheist **Paine**,
Sometimes Our style is mere bombastic sound,
Sometimes 'tis mean and grovelling on the ground,
Sometimes We're sulky, insolent and proud,
And sometimes drinking cyder with the croud,
Now in imperial state beheld with dread
Now seen with jack-knife slicing beef and bread.
So the Old Man, to please the *many*, tried
His Ass to lead, to carry, and to ride,
While the base herd, from charity exempt,
Call'd *him* a Jack-ass for each vain attempt.
Nor stop We here—Our nerves receive a shock
Whene'er is nam'd that terrible "*dry dock;*"

A a

That mount of salt, so monstrous high and long,
Is made the theme of many a '*caustic*' song,
Lead mines are laugh'd at, jeer'd are *horned frogs*,
And every booby sneers at *prairie dogs*.
These ills, too great for mortals to sustain,
Make Us at times most bitterly complain,
But then so far We've bolster'd up our cause
By loudly railing at Sedition Laws,
We've thought it prudent to entrust Our fates,
For kind protection to the sev'ral States.
Besides 'twas well to feel the public mind,
And know tow'rds Us how far it stood inclin'd,
To try if free discussion could remove,
Or aught impair the " sovereign people's love."
This has been done—and you have witness'd all
How vain th' attempt has proved to work Our fall;
How round Us throng'd the *worthies* of the land,
" Ready, aye ready" at Our high command—
" True whigs of seventy-six," a goodly store,
Imported fresh from Erin's peaceful shore,
Time-serving changelings, faction's desperate band,
And all the *virtuous* refuse of our land,—
Thick as the flies that round some carcase pour.
Or lice that punish'd Pharaoh's sins of yore;
And kindly gave Us through their *patriot* cares,
In our own way to *gest*§ our own affairs.

§ No apology, it is presumed, will be thought necessary by the literary reader for the introduction of this very expressive word into our language, as the use of it substantively, is sanctioned by such high authority, in that elegant phrase, " the gestion of our public affairs."

No inference still must old offenders draw
That We dislike the vengeance of the law;
But being press'd with more important cares,
And loaded deep with national affairs,
We have not leisure now to throw away,
Nor wish for lawyer's fees our cash to pay;
Yet he who loves in court his time to spend
Perchance the public morals may amend,
The slanderous Press of all its rage disarm,
And shield Our public character from harm,
To Fed'ralists a useful lesson teach
To drop their pens, and curb the use of speech,
And though, in Washington's and Adams' reign,
It was *Our* right 'gainst rulers to complain,
Though Freneau's labours faithfully were tried,
And year by year Duane and Cheetham lied,
Yet now the table's turn'd, we hold the sway,
Our lying Dogs at length have got their day,
'Tis therefore clear we cannot get along
Unless We shackle every Federal tongue,
Our fame in garb inviolable dress,
And bind in chains the Freedom of the Press.
And tho' with them 'twere base, with us 'tis fit
" Since one man's poison is another's meat,"
Nor does the adage in this case hold true,
" That sauce for goose is sauce for gander too."
But our success we merely note t' unfold
That since in reason's spite Our ground we hold,

All that the Feds can do We deem full light,
Though with opinions false,* *false facts* unite,
In league against Us harmless are they found,
These truths untrue a jingle mere of sound;
Nor need the Press, to Us devoted, e'er
Of harpy law the griping talons fear.

● ● ● ● ● ● ● ● ● ● ●

Joy to Our friends, to all sincerest joy
Who share Our favours, or Our care employ,
Scarce can Our breast its load of joy contain
As ope to view the glories of Our reign!
Lo! all conjoin'd in one great bond of peace,
Contention dies, and oppositions cease!
Ourselves in social intercourse combin'd,
One spirit actuates, and one gen'ral mind,

* Next to invention, that first qualification of a writer, and the prime characteristic of genius, may be rank'd the happy talent of accommodating the *felicitous* thoughts or expressions of others to his own purposes; particularly when he possesses the art of giving them, by a light variation, the appearance and effect of originality. A rare specimen of this talent seems to occur in the above beautiful antithesis, for which, it is presumed the writer must have been indebted to the celebrated Ben Towne, a royalist printer in Pennsylvania, during our revolutionary war with Great Britain.— This noted character, in a confession of his politico-typographical sins, which he addressed to the good people of that state, acknowledged himself guilty of having, in imitation of his friend and model Jemmy Rivington, often stated in his paper, "*facts that never happened.*"

Nor e'er shall varying systems rudely jar,
And 'midst Our bands excite intestine war,
Or furious Discord with unlovely mien,
Among *Fraternal Union's* sons be seen.
Hereafter free from care, Our skiff shall glide,
Its compass folly, theory its guide,
Adown the stream of state, no rocks t' impede
No federal shoals to intercept its speed;
And should, perchance, from Eastern climes arise
The howling storm and darken o'er our skies,
Though the rent sails be driv'n before the blast,
The cordage snap and spring the groaning mast,
Yet on *one* anchor firm can We confide,
And all the perils of the storm deride;
The People's favour is that anchor sure,
With which through every gale We ride secure,
And though, from want of skill, 'midst breakers cast,
That ever safely brings Us up at last.
As trout, by tickling, so the Mob are ta'en,
This long we've known, and practis'd not in vain,
And now do what We may We need not fear,
Applause is sure to greet Our raptur'd ear,
For, should aught luckless pass, the stupid elves
Would shut both eyes and ears to cheat themselves.
O thou, to whom my present state I owe,
To whom whate'er of future hope I know,
Flatt'ry, great master, who, with magic art,
Mov'st at thy will the springs of every heart!

O still propitious prove, still give my tongue
With honied sounds to lure the blinded throng!
Give them to trust, implicit, in my word,
Howe'er fallacious, and howe'er absurd!
Make them believe whatever I propose
From purest zeal for public welfare flows!
That those my fav'rite projects who decry
Are urg'd by malice, or mean jealousy!
That I alone the proper course can see,
And all of wisdom emanates from me!
Then shall our *doubting brethren*, who, as yet,
To *rally* round Us have delay'd " a bit,"
When they so pleas'd and wonderstruck shall hear
That *all republican, all fed'ral* are;
That in all questions that betwixt us rise,
Where party passions clash, and interest vies,
Justice her scale holds so much more than even†
The balance ever to our side is given;
When they shall see this blissful state, tis plain
'Tis not in human nature to refrain,

† The Echo acknowledges herself to have been at first not a little puzzled to discover the meaning of the expression *more than justice*; the explanation however fortunately presents itself in the first dramatic production of this country, the celebrated Mercenary Match of the Honorable Barna Bidwell; who puts into the mouth of his heroine, in addressing herself to her confidante, these striking and highly poetical words " My *more than Maid*, my ever constant Betty." As more than maid must necessarily be there intended to mean something very different from that pure and icicle state of virginity, so finely described by Shakespeare, so it may fairly be presumed,

Within Our fold in droves those sheep will run,
And joyful take Our ear-crop, every one,
And as a proof of love when safely penn'd,
Their silly fleece We'll shear, their mutton vend.
So when in quest of game the Indian roves
Amid his native wilds and piny groves,
If chance, amidst the branches perch'd on high,
The yellow Wappernocker meets his eye,‡
Instant, as if transform'd to powder'd beau,
He bows and cringes with politest show,
While, pleas'd, the simple beast wide opes his eyes,
And views the tawny juggler with surprize;
But, grown familiar with his antic feats,
He grin for grin and bow for bow repeats,
Drawing still near and nearer by degrees,
'Till in his reach his prize the savage sees,

in the present instance, that *more than justice* signifies something widely different from that stern unrelaxing principle, which, without regard to friends or foes, perseveres inflexibly in the course of impartial rectitude ; of this construction, the numerous removals from office, and other official acts of the present administration, will furnish a happy exemplification. At the same time the Echo is highly gratified in finding such respectable authority for the use of this expression, the ambiguity of which is so little in unison with the usual *plain* and *lucid* style of our Executive communications.

‡ Wappernocker, the Indian name for the Marten. For this remarkable mode of taking that animal, see Peters's history of Connecticut, or some other work of equal veracity.—A similar device is said to be practised in the Bahamas for taking the Iguana.

When o'er his neck the treacherous cord he throws,
And closely draws the suffocating noose;
Then cease the bows, and drops the courtly air,
As the poor victim gasps within the snare;
While with stern joy he eyes th' expiring prey,
And bears elate his furry spoil away.

A
Poetico-Political Olio,

CONSISTING OF EXTRACTS FROM DEMOCRACY, AN EPIC
POEM; GREEN-HOUSE, AND OTHER
NEW-YEARS' VERSES,
&c. &c.

VERSIFICATION

Of a Letter from a Political Character in Philadelphia to his Friend in Connecticut.

To the Printer of the Middlesex Gazette,
March, 1798.

" SIR,

YOUR paper of the 9th instant, contains an extract of a letter, said to be written by a gentleman in Philadelphia, to a friend of his in this state. It was no doubt written there, and unquestionably with the *purest* intention. The author, it is understood, has long been in the habit of labouring in this manner for the public good; and it is to be hoped that his virtuous efforts may meet with their due reward. In order to give all possible currency to this excellent production, and promote its circulation, (as such truly patriotic sentiments should never be forgotten, but inculcated strongly on the mind of every one,) it has been thought proper to render some of the most striking passages into verse, which has long been considered as the surest vehicle to fame; and has this advantage over plain prose, that it is much more easily retained in memory.

There exists in this country a party or two,
And each has its object, and each has its view.
To the Jacobin party you know I belong,
For, by nature, I take to the side that is wrong.
Against us are pitted the good, and the great,
The lovers of order, the props of the state :
These fellows intend to leave *us* in the lurch,
As sneaking as girls, when confessing at church.
But we will convince them we'll hold up our noses,
Tho' the Devil himself all our plotting discloses.

Our government's deem'd an OLD CART, by these clubs,
They grease up the axle—*we* split off the hubs,
They whip up the cattle to drag it up-hill,
We throw down obstructions chock under the wheel.
This cart, we contend, was most wretchedly made,
That its *timbers* already are sadly decay'd,
That its *spokes* are all loose, broken down are the *raives*,
And nothing is sound but the *tongue* and the *naves*.
And since it has shewn such a proneness for wearing,
Our Club has resolv'd it is not worth repairing,
We have therefore determin'd by one mighty lift,
To tumble it over, or set it adrift.
These Fed'ralists have a strange plan of their own,
For when we so crabbed, and factious are grown,
That neither their threats, nor there coaxings can move,
The scoundrels will *hire us* their measures to love,
And no Jacobin ever a *bribe* could resist,
No, not if 'twere offered by Beelzebub's fist.
Thus Mr. Fauchet, in his flour-merchant trade,
Found Randolph hung back, when he wanted his aid;
But yet, when the patriot told him *his price*,
From the bargain the Frenchman flew off in a trice,
Resolv'd a while longer his dollars to keep,
Tho' Edmund was willing to sell him dog-cheap.

The House, too, they view on the same scurvy plan,
A kind of excrescence, like a *wart* on a man,
Like a *wen* on an ox, or a *corn* on the toes,
Or a *carbuncle* hung to a dram-drinker's nose.

They have been in the habit of borrowing as much
Ready cash as they could by the way of the Dutch,
But since poor Mynheer has become sans culotte,
He has lost with his breeches both guilder and groat;
While Grandmamma Europe. stripp'd down to the bone,
Much fonder of borrowing than lending is grown;
And still scarcer with us is that "Root of all evil,"
That widow of Mammon and child of the Devil:
So that now it is obvious to every eye,
That the stream has dry'd up and the grist has gone by.
Besides, it won't answer to strain over hard,
Lest they carry away all their sails by the yard,
And give smugglers a chance, now and then, to pop in
An anchor of brandy or stone-jug of gin;
Hence it is that these fellows are ever contriving
Some plan for preventing *our* calling from thriving,
Since this creed we all hold, both black, red and white,
"To steal from the Public's a Jacobin's right."
Thus they tax our molasses to keep us from cheating,
So you see they're resolv'd we shall pay for good eating,

Our sugar, our salt, as if like Lot's wife,
They thought us well pickled for the rest of our life.
And in getting their cash they've a damnable way
That is—the most easy for people to pay.
Now a tax that's direct I advocate laying,
That each may enjoy the full pleasure of paying,
And give occupation to sheriffs a score,
And country collectors a thousand or more,
Thus to grind down the poor to their own native dirt,
And strip a poor fellow that has not a shirt.
At the opposite party, I'll just take a glance,
They were hatch'd by Genet, when he first came from France.
One never need look at a prettier set,
The sire, and the brats, are "hale fellows, well met,"
Thieves, bankrupts, and drunkards, pickpockets, and all,
Well branded with brimstone, and cropp'd at the fall.
We do all in our power to persuade the blind people,
That Adams's legs are as long as a steeple,
That he straddles about at a terrible rate,
Now over a puddle, now over a gate;
While "THE MAN OF THE PEOPLE," great Thomas, so pale,
Works along like a tad-pole, by wriggling his tail.
These Fed'ralists, too, are an insolent race,
They won't e'en permit us to spit in their face.
In Congress behold a great LYON appears,
From Ireland imported, and *purchased with steers;*

He just took the license on Griswold to squirt
A stream of mundungus, not thinking of hurt;
When lo! the fierce Yankee flew into a passion,
And gave the bog-trotter a notable threshing.
The KING of the BEASTS most lustily roar'd,
At his army acquaintance, the old WOODEN-SWORD.
No Christian, I'm sure's this Connecticut shaver,
He ought not to've grumbled, but swallow'd the sla-
 ver,
The Testament says, you should turn t'other cheek,
And not go to using the hickory stick.

   But in order to carry our schemes to effect,
We're oblig'd to conduct with peculiar respect.
One weapon, all-potent, as wielded by us,
Is constantly preaching on guarding the purse.
And so far our plan of economy reaches,
We intend to abolish the *wearing* of *breeches*.
Another contrivance we mean to pursue,
Which has hitherto serv'd us, we hope 'twill still do.
Our dead-and-alive country has sunk in a trance,
And has lost all affection for fighting and France.
Our farmers too seem to have outgrown their merit,
And given themselves up to a peaceable spirit.
But some-how or other, we'll break down the charm,
Make them handle the musquet, and give up the
 farm.
'Tis the duty of all, if the Frenchmen should need
 'em
To offer their lives on the altar of Freedom;

'Tis to France you're indebted for all you have got,
Your freedom, religion, your farms, and what not,
And as they once bought you, in *our* firm opinion,
You're their slaves, first by purchase, and then by dominion.
These being the facts, you perceive my intent—
If once you affront them, they'll make you repent;
These sans-culotte butchers are terrible heroes,
More valiant than Cæsars, more bloody than Neroes,
They'll come over on *rafts*, or perhaps on the *ice*,
As thick as musquitoes, or Pharoah's lice.
In time then be wise—mind the words of my text—
Go to France in the first place—to *hell* in the next.

EXTRACTS
FROM DEMOCRACY,
AN EPIC POEM,
BY AQUILINE NIMBLECHOPS.

The following extracts are from a poem entitled Democracy, the first Canto of which was printed in New-York, in March, 1794, and at the time excited no inconsiderable share of the public attention. This poem was written in consequence of a tumultuous meeting of the citizens of that place, instigated by a few popular demagogues, for the purpose of prescribing to Congress the adoption of hostile measures against Great Britain. The second Canto, which was of much greater length, was prepared for the press immediately after the appearance of the first, but the timidity of the booksellers, and the peculiar circumstances of the times prevented its publication.

EXTRACTS FROM CANTO FIRST.

HERE clos'd the wond'rous speech—hoarse-braying, loud,
In tones of thunder echoing from the crowd,
The murmurs of applause, resounding far,
In one deep column rush'd upon the ear;
While separate sounds their light detachments spread,
Lurk'd in the rear, or skirmish'd at the head.
Thus, when the vernal sun's prolific ray
Paints with rich flowers the verdant robe of May,
When the green citizens of ponds prepare
To hold their first town-meeting of the year,
Some leading frog, with croaking talents blest,
For strength of lungs distinguish'd o'er the rest,
Perch'd on his chair of log in solemn state,
With notes sententious opes the grave debate:

'Tis silence round—at length begins the strain,
The notes applausive echo o'er the plain,
Deep, deeper swells the undulating sound,
And one vast croaking vibrates o'er the pond.

* * * * * * * * * * *

Now mighty M*****k, by success inspir'd
With bold resistless elocution, fir'd
(Perch'd as he was on balcony so high)
The crowd who watch'd his most expressive eye:
" With joy, O friends! with rapture vast I view
What union'd hearts this day's proceedings shew—
Sure from this day democracy shall rise,
Spread through the earth and triumph o'er the skies;
Before its power all government shall fly,
And at its presence each republic die,
An age of gold once more delight the earth,
With years not number'd from a saviour's birth,
Decades, not weeks, our days shall hence divide,
And o'er the globe democracy preside.
Such, such effects from your *Resolves* shall flow,
Which best, I think, some future day will show.
Not at this time can your committee frame
Such *Resolutions* as your zeal would claim;
Some day next week we better can proceed."
" Thursday!" the crowd exclaim'd—and Thursday
    was decreed.

Again he speaks—" By that time we shall have
The prudent doings of *Bostonians* brave ;
Those men so fam'd for true, consistent merit,
And not behind us much in proper spirit ;
Them will we join, with them go hand in hand,
Fall if they fall, and if they stand we'll stand.
No ' *act of milk and water*' shall be ours—
Fragrant and strong as urinary showers,
To our foes' sores no comfort shall *it* give
But make them smart while yet *it* lets them live."
As when vast billows break upon the shore,
Applause now burst in one tremendous roar ;
Hats, caps and wigs, and leathern aprons flew,
And puffs of wond'rous size, and jerkins blue.
Not less the noise when, 'mid the watery way,
The wounded whales in anger lash the sea ;
Not less the noise when, 'neath beleagur'd walls,
The deep mine bursts, the whelmed city falls ;
Nor less the rout when, out of *Meeting* read,
The mighty M*****k bent his sable head.

  Soon was the tumult hush'd, and soon was heard
A voice, but neither face or form appear'd.
At length, beneath the chairman's arm, was seen,
Of wond'rous aspect, and of fearful mien,
A human head, if head it might be nam'd,
Which scarce to man the least resemblance claim'd.
Like the full moon, but of a darker dye,
The visage was—disastrous beam'd an eye

On either side of what was meant for nose,
Which from each cheek quadrangularly rose ;
Below a chasm tremendous op'd to view,
Whence, with hoarse groans, these words the spectre
    drew.
" As yet of ships delay'd, and men misus'd,
Of vessels captur'd, and of wealth abus'd,
Whether by Algerines the mischief came,
Or yet by Britons of notorious shame—
No proper list—no facts by them believ'd,
From any place has CONGRESS yet receiv'd."
" You lie !" the crowd exclam—" I have not lied !"
Sternly the hideous mouth, direct, replied.
Tumult and rout now drown'd the speaker's voice,
His own all vanquish'd by the people's noise.
" Order !" sage GRIPUS screams—and P**** R.
Begs that the throng the speaking CRANE would hear.
" He ! he a CRANE !" cried one, with horrid howl—
" I swear he's cousin german to an OWL."
" Hear him !" again the Chairman bellows loud ;
And hush'd in peace attentive stood the crowd.
" I hope that our Committee will take care
A long account for CONGRESS to prepare
Of all the mischiefs by the British done,
And brand the devils every mother's son."
" Huzza ! huzza !" through all the streets resounds;
" Huzza ! huzza !" from every wall rebounds ;
The distant lanes reverberate the roar,
And echoes break on either river's shore.

EXTRACTS FROM CANTO SECOND.

It may be proper to observe, that the ludicrous scene delineated in the following extract, is not the mere creation of poetic fancy; an incident very similar to the one described having actually taken place in New-York, when the publication of the first Canto was announced in the newspapers, accompanied with a comprehensive account of its subject. The following extract from the argument to the first Canto, is the particular passage in the advertisement which is supposed to have excited the irascible feelings of the character intended: 'Strange spectre appeareth—speaketh—interrupted—how a CRANE may be mistaken for an OWL—spectre proceeds,' &c. &c.

" HE said—nor long they hesitate—the voice
Of *Esculapius' Son* resolv'd their choice;
His *Resolutions* they adopt with speed,
And pleas'd he saw his every wish succeed.
Far different thoughts his rival's bosom fill'd,
His brightest hopes by keen frustration chill'd.
With less surprise amid the fields of air
Pale superstition views the comet's glare;
With less the bumpkin, petrified with fear,
Thinks he beholds a ghost approaching near;
With less dismay VERMONT's religious son,
That *granny statesman*, far for wisdom known,
Who shines, array'd in *senatorial* pride,
The guard of congress and his country's guide,

Heard I———n* declare that not within
A meeting-house for twenty years he'd been,
And though in singing great *their* skill might be,
No proper judge of psalmody was he;
Than felt that rival when at length he found
His labours fall unfruitful to the ground,
Spite of his speech his propositions lost,
His hopes all blasted, and his wishes crost.
Home as he went, the MEETING now dissolv'd,
Sad thoughts within his troubled breast revolv'd:
At length, distracted with tormenting pain,
Forth from his bosom burst this mournful strain:
" And have I liv'd this awful hour to see!
This hour to faction fatal as to me—
To me—who, during a long course of years,
Through floods of sorrow, and through hosts of tears,
From fame's eternal shipwreck oft have fled,
To be thus forced to bow my haughty head.

* A certain *great man*, a few years since, in a tour through Vermont, passed the Sunday in Bennington, at the house of a person of some consequence in that state. Agreeable to the custom of the place, he was kindly treated with New-England rum, and taken to the Meeting-House, to attend the celebration of divine service. On returning, his host, inquired of him, how he liked their singing, and whether he did not think it fine. He replied, much, as it may be presumed, to the surprise of the inquirer, that not having, for many years, attended any kind of public worship, he was a very incompetent judge of psalm singing; that for aught he knew, they might sing very well or they might not.

Disgrace on me her heaviest weight has hung,
O'erpower'd my faculties, and stopp'd my tongue.
No more in mobs its oily sounds shall flow ;
No more the bar its strong persuasions know ;
Poor thing ! in painful silence must thou lie ;
Dumb are thy fountains and thy channels dry :
No more among committees shall thy strains
Melodious burst through reason's iron chains:
That cursed Doctor, with his milk-sop schemes,
Has brought to dust my high-built airy dreams.
Ah painful sight to see our fame decay !
Our name grows dark as moments flit away—
Our name, which once with awful splendour shone,
The haughty rival of the noon-day sun,
Now turns to night—while spread from pole to pole,
Clouds of contempt and storms of ruin roll.

* * * * * * * * * * *

Thus oft some youth, by fond, paternal care,
Fill'd with the folly of a wealthy heir,
Sees round his board, while plenty holds her reign,
The pimp, the gamester, parasite and vain :
But when bleak penury chills his drear abode,
And gain no longer tempts the faithless brood,

Far from his house the ravening vultures fly,
And leave the wretch to weep, despair and die.
   The hostage sure of lov'd though short repose,
Meekly the venerable Sabbath rose;
Nor noise disturb'd the Town, nor rout was heard,
'Till the next day-star in the heavens appear'd.
Clear rose the Morn in robes of rosy hue,
Before her car the lingering shades withdrew;
The *Printer's Boy*, now risen from his bed,
From door to door the daily news had spread;
When C—— whose mighty soul disdain'd to feel
Aught of less import than the public weal,
Who still on that great object kept his eye—
Keen as the greyhound when the fox is nigh,
Keen as the fish-hawk watching for her prey—
As if he fear'd 'twould from him run away;
And still intent a careful watch to keep,
Had scorn'd that night the privilege of sleep;
Now sallied forth in hopes, by Barber's aid,
To deck at least the *outside* of his head:
For shrewdly thus he thought "t'improve that part
" Perchance is not beyond the reach of art,
" For well I know that proverbs old have said—
" Half of a loaf is better than no bread;"
" And though the Scriptures recommend, as meet,
" To keep the inside of our vessels neat,
" Yet, when that's past all hope, we sure are right,
" To make the outside of the platter bright."—

In pride important seated in the chair,
While Puff his visage soap'd, and sleek'd his hair,
The tedious moments anxious to amuse
He seiz'd the herald of the daily news,
With eager gaze from page to page he flew,
At length an *Advertisement* met his view—
" What's this? what's this? DEMOCRACY! he cries,
While joy transcendant sparkled in his eyes;
" Can it be true, does AQUILINE the great
" Our deeds in strains immortal celebrate?
" Such, such applause will nobler acts inspire,
" And heat our bosoms with a hotter fire."
Thus he, exulting in the fame bestow'd,
While marks of transport on each feature glow'd.
 Alas! how fleeting are our schemes of bliss!
How frail the tenure of our happiness!
Mid mists of error still involv'd we stray,
And blindly grope along a slipp'ry way:
Too oft from specious good our sorrows flow;
And joy mistaken leads to certain woe.
Bright smiles the sun, the vernal breezes move,
And waft a fragrance from the blossom'd grove
Fair glows each scene arround—with pride elate,
Man spreads the sail and tempts the depths of fate,
O'er halcyon seas his careless course pursues,
While hope allures him and while pleasure wooes;
Nor sees that, veil'd beneath the fair disguise,
On death's dark pinions soon the storm shall rise.

Again he reads, but ah! how chang'd the scene!
What sudden clouds, O C―――! obscure thy mien?
What frowns terrific o'er thy brow are hung!
And what has chain'd the music of that tongue.
　Say hast thou been at turtle party e'er,
At City Feast of Alderman and Mayor?
If so—perchance some wight thou may'st have
　　view'd,
Who too intent on cramming down his food,
Had let the unchew'd morsel go astray,
And choke the passage of the narrow way:
Witness'd the open'd mouth, the starting eye,
The cheek deep-ting'd with crimson's darkest dye,
The rigid limbs in strong convulsions thrown,
The hideous quackle and the rattling groan.
So C――― appear'd—his eye-balls glow'd with ire,
Red grew his face like shins expos'd to fire,
He tries to speak but rage his voice confounds,
And words are lost in undistinguish'd sounds:
He stamp'd, he foam'd, at length his speech found
　　way,
Damn, damn the author, publisher I say!
On the whole tribe may stores of curses fall,
And hell's hot flames consume them one and all."
Thus speaking, from the chair, half-shav'd, he flew,
And seiz'd his hat, and from the shop withdrew;
Along the street invoking curses loud,
He stalk'd, the wonder of the gazing crowd,

Who stood amaz'd to hear from mouth of C——e,
Such hideous crunkings* and such notes profane;
While, bawling loud, the suds-drench'd barber stood,
" Bring back my towel, Mister —— d—n your blood!
" If e'er again"—exclaims he in surprise—
" I shave a crazy *Shitepoke*,† blast my eyes."
   Nor did less noise the Coffee-room pervade,
Nor less disturbance there the *Papers* made.
The Chiefs seem'd glad; their followers, weak of mind,
Nothing but satire in the song could find:
Where most the Poet prais'd, there most they swore,
The more of truth they saw they raged the more.
And O what oaths terrific, threatnings dread,
What direful curses on the Poet's head,
What ills denounc'd 'gainst those who dar'd to vend,
Resounded through the room, from end to end!
They swore and rag'd, and rav'd, and fum'd, and vapour'd,
Shook fists, and sung and danc'd, and kick'd, and caper'd:
But 'gainst the Press their fiercest rage was bent,
And on its freedom *all* their curses vent.

  * The peculiar noise made by a certain bird.

  † The vulgar name for the lesser bittern, frequently applied as a general appellation to birds of that genus.

" Let the Press perish" loud the *patriots* cry—
" Let the Press perish" echoing walls reply—
" Flourish Democracy" the shout goes round—
" Flourish Democracy" the walls resound—
" Damn all the Friends of Order" next they bawl—
And echo dies along the wearied wall.

NEW-YEARS' VERSES.

For the Connecticut Courant, January 1, 1795.

THE events of all-evolving time,
In this, and many a distant clime,
The tuneful new-year's Muse rehearses,
In *novel strain* of new-year's verses ;
Which, by degrees, with proper pains,
We hope will rise to epic strains.
   Nor shall we court the *nine old maids*,
By former poets us'd for *aids*,
Since MUSE *the tenth* has slop'd her way,
To these Hesperian walks of day.
O ! late arriv'd from *Georgium Sidus*,
Vouchsafe t' inspire the song, and guide us !—
While men of *law* and *rule* grow weary,
O ! deign to celebrate the *æra !*—
Hark ! how the music of her tongue,
Makes thread bare subjects fresh and young !
   See, dim beneath the arctic pole,
Rude Russian hosts of ruffians roll
A sea-like wave—in barb'rous pride
The Poles to conquer, and divide !
See Frederick aid the base design,
And march his legions from the Rhine !
And see KOSCIUSKO rouse the Poles,
While indignation fires their souls,

That tyrants leagu'd should still essay
To bend their necks to foreign sway!
O *Son* of our great Son of Fame,
May deeds like his, exalt thy name.
May fated Poland yet be free,
And find a Washington in thee.

   The French still fight like veriest witches,
Both those who have, and *have not breeches;*
And scarce a decade passes o'er,
But sees them wade knee deep in gore;
Sees hosts of foes, though men of might,
Put all their trust in speedy flight;—
And oh! how quick their news is hurl'd,
From realm to realm—from world to world;
For has not *Telegraphe* the merit,
To make French feats out race a spirit?
Cannot *Balloons* as high arise,
To tell them through th' astonish'd skies?
While *Guillotine* quick lets them know,
By headless ghosts, in realms below.

   Nor can the Muse forget the year,
That seal'd the fate of Robespierre;
But 'mid th' aristocratic laugh,
Will here inscribe his epitaph;
Which, in some proper time to come,
We hope will grace his mournful tomb.

   "Long, luckless chief! thy guileful form
Astride the whirlwind, rein'd the storm;

That storm, where streams of human blood,
Drench'd towns and realms like Noah's flood;
Till hurl'd beneath the *Guillotine*,
Where gasp'd thy nobles, king, and queen,
Where daily swell'd thy bounteous store,
Of headless trunks and spouting gore;
Where Science' sons and daughters bled,
And priests by hecatombs fell dead—
Its rushing blade thy members freed,
From sins their tyrant head decreed;
And sent thy ghost to shades of night,
To prove, with Danton, which *of right*,
Should have in hell the highest seat,
An *atheist* or a *hypocrite*."

 May heaven our favourite planet bear
Far, far from Gallia's blazing star;
Ye lights of Europe shun its course,
Or order yields to lawless force,
As though a random-comet hurl'd,
Should dash at once and melt the world.

 But though the French are giant sinners,
Yet have we not *Tom Thumb* beginners?
Which though a molish sort of mice,
May grow to rats like nits to lice,
Gnaw thro' our vessel's lower quarter,
And fill, and sink her in deep water.
See fraught with democratic lore,
Genet arriv'd on Charleston shore,

But, as was meet, first broach'd his mission,
To men of sans-culotte condition;
Who throng'd around with open throats,
As round old *Crusoe* flock'd the *goats,*
And learn'd his sermon, to his wishes,
As *Austin* taught huge shoals of *fishes;*
Made all the antifederal presses,
Screech shrill hosannas, styl'd addresses;
And while to Court he took his way,
Sung hallelujahs to *Genet;*
But still our Palinurus saw,
With cool contempt this stormy flaw,
And, spite of all the Belial band,
Steer'd safe our leaky bark to land.
Like Hessian flies, imported o'er,
Clubs self create infest our shore.
And see yon western rebel band,
A medly mix'd from ev'ry land;
Scotch, Irish, renegadoes rude,
From Faction's dregs fermenting brew'd;
Misguided tools of antifeds,
With clubs anarchial for your heads,
Why would ye make with cost and trouble
Yourselves of warlike flames the stubble?
Tire down the arm out-stretch'd to save,
And freedom's cradle make her grave?
  See next the veteran troops of Wayne,
March o'er the savage bands of slain,

And scatter far, like noxious air,
Those victors of the fam'd St. Clair;
While blust'ring Simcoe, as requir'd,
To bleak Canadian climes retir'd,
And let his tawny friends remain,
To sue for proffer'd peace again.

   Here Fame reports, in vast expanse,
A clime extends that baulks romance,
Where sea-like rivers wind their way,
Through vast savannas to the sea;
Clear lakes extend, huge mountains rise,
And spicy vales perfume the skies;
Whatever earth maternal yields
To deck the groves, or cloathe the fields,
All fruits and flow'rets flourish here,
And bloom like Eden's gorgeous year:
Birds bask in air, the game in woods,
And finny nations crowd the floods.
Here then Columbians seek your farms,
When warlike Wayne shall quell alarms;
But let not speculations vain,
Exhaust the purse and turn the brain,
Nor grudge the roaming Indian rude
To hunt his native wilds for food.

   Though tir'd I might pass on to mention
Our second Middletown convention;*

---

* In consequence of the prevalence of the yellow fever in New-Haven, in the autumn of 1794, the Legislature of Connecticut held its session at Middletown.

How all the Stelligeri brood,
Their subterranean plots renew'd;
Made speeches with long periods rounded,
Like Babel's masons when confounded;
Strove hard and harder still to hit it,
But got most wofully outwitted;
For lo! on Court-House wall appear'd,
That hand which old Belshazzar fear'd,
And wrote in characters full plain,
HIS MENE TEKEL o'er again.
All gaz'd aghast at one another,
And smote each *jaded* knee its brother.

   Yet where BOSTONIA lifts her spires,
Like Phenix from devouring fires,
See federal Virtue take her stand,
And ward Destruction from the land.
Hail Nurse of Heroes! Statesmen sage!
The guard and glory of the age!
Above the mists of mouldering time,
Thy Fame, O ADAMS! soars sublime,
Who first the British lion spurn'd,
And gave the terms when peace return'd;
Cull'd from the lapse of ages past,
And fram'd a Work with time to last;
Display'd in truth's celestial light,
How *Freedom*, *Law*, and *Power* unite.
May choicest flowers with tears bedew'd,
O'er thy brave WARREN's grave be strew'd;

And long heroic LINCOLN stand,
The laurel'd bulwark of the land.
 But still no flowers of greatness grow,
Where thorny plagues lurk not below:
There swarms *Honestus' rabble throng*,
And *Lawyer Incest* joins the song;
While *Jarvis* with his *bob-tail* crew,
Retreats before great AMES's view.
 And now, O Muse! throw Candour's veil,
O'er aged SAM. in dotage frail;
And let past services atone,
For recent deeds of folly done;
When late aboard the Gallic ship,
Well fraught with democratic flip,
He praying fell on servile knees,
That France alone might rule the seas;
While Sense and Reason took a nap,
And snor'd in *Jacobinic cap*.
 Now north the Muse revolves her eyes,
Where domes Albanian *fright* the skies;
And sees the wisdom of the State
Collected, both to legislate,
And to obtain, by slight of hand,
A further tract of Indian land.
At length they send an envoy, greeting,
To bid the natives to a meeting—
And lo! the Indian deputation,
Approach'd the Council of the nation,

Who found too late, by *Benson* told,
Their *deep-laid* scheme would never hold;
Since Congress, in all Indian treating,
Had stopp'd the separate States from **cheating.**
Not more amaz'd Philistia's race,
Beheld old Dagon's sore disgrace,
When by the Ark, in ruin spread,
He lay depriv'd of stumps and head—
Than each pale legislator star'd,
When this unwelcome news he heard.
  Arriv'd, the speculating band
Shake Squaws and Indians by the hand,
And on each cheek of paint and grease,
Imprint the true fraternal kiss.
Huge mugs of cyder and of flip,
With gin and rum, salute the lip.
Four weeks they liv'd like pigs in clover,
At length the feasting moon was over;
Their friends who found they'd nought **to gain,**
Would fain dismiss the greedy train;
Yet still to keep them somewhat *quiet,*
Resolv'd to have one general *riot,*
Where all should join, with frisky heads,
The grand *Pawaw* of *whites* and *reds.*
Now opes the dance, a pleasing sight
Of brothers red and brothers white;
A royal Squaw with brooches grac'd,
Superbly clad in Indian taste,

With due regard for rank and place,
Is given great Clinton's hand to grace.
They stamp, they reel, loud whoops resound,
As high in savage haze they bound,
'Till frolic fires in Clinton burn,
And bid his second youth return;
He seiz'd the Squaw, and warmly prest
The ocher'd beauty to his breast;
When lo! the Sachem's jealous ire
Flash'd from his eyes vindictive fire.
" Heeiyuh, Big Chief! 'tis Indian's law,
" All Sanup stick um fast his Squaw."
He said, and dealt a furious blow,
Which laid the sportful hero low.
But here the time would fail to tell,
How high each Indian rais'd his yell;
How each pale legislator glar'd,
As round in wild dismay they star'd;
And how, afraid of scalping knives,
They broke their shins to save their lives;
All which, Fate willing, shall appear
In Epic Song another year.

Hartford, January 1, 1795.

GUILLOTINA;

OR

THE ANNUAL SONG OF THE TENTH MUSE.

For the Connecticut Courant, January 1, 1796.

COME Guillotina, Muse divine!
Whose voice o'erawes the tuneful nine,
Come sing again! since Ninety-Five,
Has left some *Antis* still alive;
Some Jacobins as pert as ever,
Tho' much was hop'd from Yellow-fever;
One TRAITOR, fond to enrol his name,
With Judas on the list of fame;
A host of unhang'd *Democrats*,
And Speculators thick as rats;
Some lurking hoards, by patriots hated,
Stil'd very aptly " self-created,"
Since neither heathen God, nor Devil,
Would own engendering such an evil—
'Tis these, in contrast with the GREAT
Whose virtue saves the unhinging State,
That makes the music of thy rhyme,
Flow annual down the stream of time.

 Last winter prov'd a *trying season*,
The State resum'd its wonted reason,
The Council kept a steady pace,
And STELLIGERI dropp'd the chase;
Peace shed her poppies o'er the State,
And all cry'd out *appropriate;*

For well they knew a dire distemper,
That makes the brains and purses scamper,
Had seiz'd on every kind of creature,
And turn'd him to a speculator;
And though our title none could tell,
Yet all agreed 't would do to sell.

   Soon FAME's shrill trumpet told the tale,*
That *We* had western lands for sale.
Forth from the East and West, alack,
Nor did the North or South keep back.
Much people—both the high and low,
The squire, the deacon and the beau,

---

* This passage was intended to ridicule the *mania* for lands peculation, which at that time pervaded the United States in general, but raged with increased violence in the Eastern States. The year 1795, was particularly remarkable for this species of adventure, in which nearly every class and description of people engaged with an almost inconceivable degree of ardour. In addition to the immense quantities of land thrown into the market by the sale of the Georgia Territory, the Legislature of Connecticut had authorised the sale of an extensive country belonging to this state, situated on lake Erie, and known by the name of the Western Reserve. It had likewise ceded to a company of its own citizens, the claim of the state to a tract called the Gore, situated within the jurisdiction of New-York, but supposed to be included in the charter of Connecticut, on condition of the purchasers completing the State house in Hartford. To these may be added speculations in Virginia mountains; in Susquehannah title deeds that never existed; in the pine barrens of the south, and the frozen desarts of the north; in fine, in every thing that bore the name of land.

With judges, generals, legislators,
(All melted down to Speculators)
Flow'd in amain, from every quarter,
Like Windham frogs from dry'd-up water.
A host like this the northern hoard,
O'er pale Ausonia never poured,
Nor did a more inflated band,
Avenge, long since, the holy-land,
Nor, in our days, seek money hid,
From shore to shore by Captain Kid.—
Thus when old Noah op'd his gate,
And advertis'd to take in freight,
Swift at the all inviting sound,
All kinds of cattle throng'd around,
From which the patriarch cull'd the best,
And let the Deluge take the rest.—
Conven'd they sever'd into *squads*,
And talk'd of townships, miles, and rods,
With night-hawk wildness in their faces,
Like *scrip-men* bent on swiftest chases;
While each at other cast an eye,
At once determin'd, cross and sly,
And deem'd by dint of purse or brain,
The largest *wastes* of woods to gain;
But when they came to prove their skill,
And purse met purse, and will met will,
Till what they brought for stock in trade
Was spent and tavern-bills unpaid,

They all agreed to coalesce,
And in the immense of profits mess.
This done, at eve the bargain clos'd,
And all in south-sea dreams repos'd;
Yet waking found their *bonds* and toil,
But won the right to buy the soil;
Which though they think to get with ease,
The terms must be as *Indians please.*

And had the anarchial powers that dwell,
In unform'd wilds, 'twixt earth and hell,
Come forward, or sent on a letter,
To sell their realm for worse or better,
In breadth from where *Arcturus* glows,
To where the *Bull* turns up his nose,
In length from hence to where in terror,
The wicked find out Chauncey's* error,
They'd bought it off like Georgia land,
And paid for't *down* in *notes of hand*,
Then *quarrell'd* which should have the most,
Where matter, time and space are lost.
Nay, had there been a narrow *Gore*,
Close in upon the Stygian shore,
Claim'd neither by the abodes of pain,
Nor forms that roam the vast *Inane*,
We should no doubt, from thence be able,
To rear a second modern Babel.‡

* The celebrated Advocate of Universal Salvation.

‡ Alluding to the State-House in Hartford, the building of which was completed by certain persons on condition of receiving

How stormy is thy sea of troubles,
How hoar with *froth*, how full of *bubbles*,
Oh SPECULATION! how thy waves,
Toss up and down thy greedy slaves:
For one that makes thy *golden coast*,
What myriads of thy *Tars* are lost;
This hour beholds them proudly float,
The next sees each a sans-culotte;
And though the boldest borrow breeches,
And tempt again thy main for riches,
Some whirlpool vast or billowy swell,
May land them and their schemes in —*

Ere Jay had reach'd that pigmy coast,
Where Pitt and Grenville rule the roast,
Where once the Lion us'd to roar,
But late has chang'd it to a snore,—
The *Anti-Treaty* noise began,
Club answer'd Club—man echo'd man;
From town to town the cue was caught
By Faction's Telegraphe of thought.

At length on rapid wings of fate,
Ardent to save the sinking State,
The Envoy came—his steady eye,
Was fix'd upon the distant sky,

from the Legislature of Connecticut a grant or quit claim of the right of that State to the tract of land called the Gore.

* "A reverend Dean, preaching at the" British "Court, threatened the sinner with punishment in a place he thought not decent to name in so polite an Assembly."—Pope.

Regardless of the boisterous scene,
Which seem'd prepar'd to intervene.
No party rage disturb'd his rest,
No vile detraction shook his breast,
But rooted deep in Virtue's soil,
And cultur'd long by patriot toil,
His honours a bright harvest yield,
And wave around his country's field.
Firm in his hand the statesman shows
A *solace*† for his country's woes,
Peace on his path her sun-beams spread,
And glory arch'd around his head.

  Swift starting from their darksome den,
The nightly haunt of thieves and *men*,
Our democrats, broke forth in fury,
And sentenc'd Jay *sans* judge or jury.
Great Mason saw a precious hour,
Which chance had thrown within his power,
And join'd with Benny Bache to seize
A little cash their wants to ease.
Forth from the Anti-federal mint,
A half-false‡ Treaty came inprint;
For telling truth so long had stray'd
From Bache, he had forgot the trade.
Soon, crowded forward into birth,
The full grown Child was usher'd forth.

  † The Treaty.
  ‡ The abstract of the Treaty " published from recollection."

His face so like his Sire's appear'd,
Such innate worth his visage cheer'd,
That Bache and Mason fled amain,
And swore old Jay was born again.
While thus the slumbering Infant lay,
With eyes just open'd to the day,
A dark revengeful coward brood,
Laid a deep scheme to spill his blood.
Soon far and near the tidings ran,
All swore he ne'er should grow to man.
Among the rest, though scarce alive,
Old Sam crawl'd out and swarm'd his Hive,
(Consisting of the stingless Hone§
That Humble-Bee, that shrivel'd Drone,
With all old Falstaff's‖ trainband, come
Inspir'd by patriotic Rum)
While Jarvis rung the pan with greeting,
To make them settle in Town-meeting.
At York stout Nicholson, whose zeal,
Burns greatly for the public weal,
Collects the vagabond and traitor,
With many a " dare Hibernian cratur."
At Philadelphia Blair the great,
That Irish guardian of the State,
Rais'd his hard foot to give the blow,
And cry'd " to hell the child must go."

§ A creature of the doubtful gender, called Honee, Honestus, or Ben Austin, Jun.
‖ See Shakspeare's Henry IV.

Still further south the mongrel throng,
Responsive bray'd the factious song.
At Portsmouth too, poor Johnny's seed,
Produc'd a short-liv'd blust'ring breed,
Whose courage soon began to fail,
When Gilman pointed to the jail.
In Vermont, where the Reverend Niles,
To his own state confines his wiles,
And where the saintly Robinson
Prays that the Will of Burr be done—
The Green-woods politicians met,
To hew the timber of the State;
There printer Haswell, Col. Fay,
The Treaty damn'd—and Mr. Jay;
'Till PRINCE,¶ Equality's dark son,
Grew weary of their wit and fun,
And, seizing Haswell by the cheek,
He cried out " Brurrur let me peak.
" You tear my libber from my maw,
" Gor dam a man all ober jaw."
 Alas! how vain are mortal dreams,
How flit away the wisest schemes!
Who would have thought this infant JAY,
Could have found means to get away?

¶ This incident, as related, is stated to have occurred at Bennington at the time of discussing the merits of the Treaty. The conduct of Prince, upon this occasion, is a striking proof of that happy consciousness of the dignity of his nature, which ever distinguishes man, when emancipated from the shackles of restraint.

Yet, strange and wond'rous to relate,
By some surprising spell of Fate,
A Giant from the cradle rose,
And frown'd indignant on his foes,
With step tremendous stalk'd along,
And trampled on the dastard throng.

As now in song the muse proceeds,
Let tears bedew her sable weeds.—
Here lies an Officer of State,
Who met alas! a *timely* Fate:
A Fate which Jacobins regard,
As their full measure of reward;
For here the deadly secret's told,
Who 'tis that fingers foreign gold;
That " patriots" stripp'd to state of nature,
Bear strong resemblance to the traitor;
That each disorganizing scoffer,
Will take a bribe if any offer.
Come then ye democratic band,
Who yearn t' enthral this favour'd land,
To Edmund's dismal tomb draw near,
And vent your lamentations here,
In groans, as Rachel groan'd at Rama,
Hic cinis—sed—*ubique fama.*¶

¶ His ashes here—but—every where his Fame. This is the Epitaph of the late celebrated King of Prussia; but we hope his *manes* will not be offended that we apply it to a character equally GREAT *in a different way*.

Yes there are men who fiercely burn
Your Constitution to o'erturn;
To blast the Sages of your choice,
They wield the pen and ply the voice;
Nor long will Talents tempt th' affray,
Where Virtue gains Contempt for pay;
But men of fell and factious prate
Shall mount the faithless Car of State.
　　Where Ignorance sheds his sooty beam,
And rays of Science rarely gleam,
There, fed with lies from day to day,
From venal presses in French pay,
Fell Faction broods—and scents afar,
Predestin'd fields of civil war.
And will the men who till their farms,
Who Freedom love—whom Freedom warms,
Who live in plenty, peace and ease,
Be vex'd by *living plagues* like these?
They will—have been—and still must be;
For Faction thrives where States are free,
As plants of baleful form and nature,
Thrive in fat soils, by plenteous water;
And thrive it must while there are fools,
And knaves to shape them into tools.—
Spread Knowledge then; *this only Hope*,
Can make each eye a *telescope*,
Frame it by *microscopic* art,
To scan the hypocritic heart;

And can, at least, keep Faction under,
As butting rams are aw'd by thunder.
 The French have beat all other elves,
And now are beating fast themselves;
In which we wish them to succeed,
Just as the Fates, long since, decreed;
But how that is no mortal ken
Can spy, no more than how and when
New suns shall wake the blaze of day,
Where Chaos holds Eternal sway.
 From themes like these th' indignant Muse
Turns, and th' applausive strain pursues.
 Prompt at thy Country's call to work,
Thy pathless way where *vipers lurk*,
Where darksome wastes before thee lay,
Unbless'd but by thy mental ray,
O HAMILTON!—that ray how clear,
How like the Sun's resplendent sphere,
When too intense for *clouds of flies*,
He makes his zenith in the skies.
 Let " CALM OBSERVER" hear the Song,
Shrink from the day and bite his tongue;
Far, far above his base controul,
Self-balanc'd stands sage WOLCOTT's soul,
A Patriot firm—to toils inur'd,
Long for the public weal endur'd,

Who, when the pestilential burst,
Laid Philadelphia's Pride in dust,
Mov'd unassuming and sedate,
The various tardy wheels of State.
  Now Muse survey this land of peace,
Of Virtue, Law, and Happiness.
The Clime how blest! how rich a soil
Repays the labourer's cheerful toil,
How safe *we* till the field for food,
While EUROPE tills the field of blood;
Our sons how tranquil o'er the main,
But their's in hostile navies slain;
Their Anarchists still prowl for prey,
But ours are held, like wolves, at bay;
Their towns, while Emigrations drain,
Rise in our wilds and bloom again;
The Isles rejoice to heap their stores,
In plenty on our smiling shores;
Proud Albion, mistress of the waves,
With France and Spain, our Commerce craves;
Wayne barricades the west frontiers,
And peace is made with grim Algiers.—
Here while the North deep snows infold
The Georgian orange beams in gold;
And here the various climates rear,
Unblasted harvests through the year.

Bold FREEDOM feeds her Vestal Fires,
And every heart and tongue inspires;
While, still in Courts, as once in Fields,
Great WASHINGTON her Glory shields;
Long may his Sun unclouded shine,
And set " full orb'd."

Hartford, January 1, 1796.

[This and the preceding New Year's Verses were principally written by a late eminent physician in Connecticut, distinguished both for his literary talents and professional skill; several of the passages in the Green-House were likewise furnished by him.]

THE
POLITICAL GREEN-HOUSE,
FOR THE YEAR 1798.

The Political Green-House, for the year 1798.
Hartford, January 1, 1799.

OFT has the NEW-YEAR'S Muse essay'd,
To quit the annual rhyming trade,
Oft has she hop'd the period nigh,
When fools would cease, and knaves would die;
But each succeeding year has tax'd her
With " more last words of Mr. Baxter;"
And most of all, has Ninety-Eight,
Outstripp'd the years of former date.
And while a Jacobin remains,
While Frenchmen live and Faction reigns,
Her voice, array'd in awful rhyme,
Shall thunder down the steep of Time.
 Scarce had the New-Year's wintry sun,
His short-liv'd daily course begun,
When lo! a strange offensive brute,
Too wild to tame, too base to shoot,
A Lyon of Hibernian breed,
In Congress rear'd his shaggy head.
What speculations might be made,
Were men acquainted with the trade?
In countries new, the market price
Will often take a wondrous rise,
And things to day are held for nought,
Which scarce to-morrow can be bought.

This beast, within a few short years,
Was purchas'd with a yoke of steers;
But now, the wise Vermonters say,
He's worth six hundred cents per day.
When erst Britannia's hostile hosts,
Ravag'd our long extended coasts,
This Lyon, Falstaff-like, impell'd
By " *instinct*," shunn'd the dangerous field.
And yet, in him, our patriot props,
Had center'd all their darling hopes,
That he, by spirit, would obtain,
What they had talk'd for long in vain.
It chanc'd one memorable day,
'Mongst gentlemen he happ'd to stray,
Where, ignorant what to say, or do,
His monkey tricks he 'gan to shew,
When Griswold's stick of vigour full,
Knock'd *gently* on his solid skull;
By courage, strength, and sleight forsaken,
Not " *instinct*" now could save his bacon,
But as he drew his " WOODEN-SWORD,"
He roar'd and kick'd, and kick'd and roar'd.
With less of Lyon, than of sheep,
The beast retires to wash, and weep;
While Elmendorf and Havens join,
To bathe his wounds with oil and wine.

   Long had the Jeffersonian band,
Determin'd here to take their stand,

To *us*, their vile intrigues impart,
And old Connecticut subvert.
Firm on her rock, sublime she stood,
And all their arts indignant view'd;
With smiles beheld them, fill'd with plot,
Come sneaking round that precious spot,
Where erst the Stelligeri Club,
Held converse sweet with Peter Grubb,*
And where, though lost their quondam Clerk,
They still keep Records in the dark.
Here then our Jacobins resort,
For *business* some, and some for *Court*,
Each *unsuspicious* of the rest,
(No *mischief rankling in his breast*)
But each, as order'd, took his station,
And rattled up a Nomination.
Mix'd up of various sorts, and kinds,
Themselves ahead, a few for blinds,
The rest, a coarse, outlandish Crew,
Which scarce a single creature knew.
As harbinger of sure success,
'Twas next agreed to fill the press,
And through the weekly prints, enlighten
The people's stupid skulls by writing.
Soon our " impartial paper" teems†
With deep laid plots, and cunning schemes:

* Peter Grubb. The supposed secretary of the Stelligeri, at their midnight caucuses.

† The American Mercury.

Don Quixotte,† knight of woeful face,
Led on the Revolution race;
Then follow'd on a nameless tribe,
Too poor to mention or describe,
While Granger fill'd with weightier matters,
Employ'd his time in gutting letters.
This precious story soon took wind,
Out turn'd the aged, deaf, and blind,
All honest men from small to great,
Combin'd their force to save the state,
Tumbled each caitiff from his station,
And purg'd the chequer'd Nomination.
Poor Gideon, with astonish'd eye,
Beheld the stroke of Fate draw nigh,
And like Ahithophel the Sage,
In deep despair, commix'd with rage,
Saddled his ass, took leave of pelf,
Wrote No. 4, and hang'd himself.

Long had our Ministers of Peace,
The insults borne of Gallia's race.
At length the envoys deign'd to tell us,
They had to deal with scurvy fellows,
With Autun, and the five-head Beast,
And half the Alphabet at least.
The budget, op'd in Congress, show'd
The whole contrivance of the brood,
And that their heads were bent on brewing
Subjection, infamy, and ruin.

† The signature of a writer in the American Mercury.

While joy each Federal feature crown'd,
And triumph glow'd the Hall around;
Each Jacobin began to stir,
And sate, as though on chesnut burr.
Up the long space from chin, to forehead,
Sate every feature of the horrid;
Their moon-ey'd leaders stood like beacons,
Or as a drove of Satan's Deacons,
When from the burning lake, in ire,
They sat their feet on solid fire,
To find if war, or sly pollution,
Could raise in Heaven a revolution.
Pale melancholy mark'd their features,
The most forlorn of human creatures;
While shame, deep-stamp'd as though with thunder,
Reliev'd th' unmeaning stare of wonder.
At length, from lethargy profound,
Congress awoke, and star'd around:
The major part, with heart and hand,
Extend protection to the land,
Dissolve our treaties, arm our hosts,
And drive the robbers from our coasts.
Next from the press the tidings ran,
From state to state, from man to man,
In Freedom's cause they all combine,
And Georgia, and New-Hampshire join.
The warlike spirit fills the presses,
And teems the nation with addresses,

Answers, Resolves, and Toasts in throngs,
Orations, Sermons, Prayers, and Songs.
The spirit freed of righteous hate,
Like wild-fire spreads from state to state,
And made thy sons, Columbia, see
The extreme of insult heap'd on thee—
Made thee behold the just renown
Of HIM, who wears thy laurell'd crown,
And gave his heaven-directed pen,
New themes in civic walks of men,
Which, through the world shall waft thy fame,
Beneath the banners of his name.

 Eas'd now of much incumbent weight,
Proceeds the business of the State.
Rais'd by the sound of war's alarms,
Our ardent youth all fly to arms,
And from the work-shop, and the field,
The active labourers seize the shield;
While on the silver'd brow of age,
Relumes the fire of martial rage.
Our veteran Chiefs, whose honour'd scars,
Are trophies still of former wars,
Appointed move beneath their SHIELD,
To reap the ripen'd martial field.
And lo! From Vernon's sacred hill,
Where peaceful spirits love to dwell—
Where twice retir'd from war's alarms,
Slept, and awoke, his conquering arms,

The HERO comes!—whose Laurels green,
In bloom eternal shall be seen;
While Gallic Ivy fades away,
Before the scorching eye of Day.
He comes!—he comes! to re-array
Your hosts, ye heroes, for th' affray!
Him for your head—collect from far
The shield, the sword and plume of war;
Indignant earth rejoicing hears,
Fell insult bristling up your spears,
And joins her hosts to crush the foes
Of virtue and her own repose.

   Now see each jacobinic face,
Redden'd with guilt, with fear, disgrace,
While through the land, with keenest ire,
Kindles the patriotic fire!
See J******** with deep dismay,
Shrink from the piercing eye of day,
Lest from the tottering chair of state,
The storm should hurl him to his fate!
Great Sire of stories past belief!
Historian of the Mingo Chief!
Philosopher of Indian's hair!
Inventor of a rocking chair!
The Correspondent of Mazze'!
And Banneker less black than he!
With joy we find you rise from *coguing*
With judge M'Kean, and "*foolish Logan,*"

And reeling down the factious dance,
Dispatch the Doctor off to France,
To tell the Frenchmen, to their cost,
They reckon'd here without their host.
  See next, brave Massachusetts' Sires,
Whose breasts still burn with Freedom's fires,
Whose dauntless bosoms never yield,
Nor shun the foe, nor quit the field;
Where Independence took her stand,
And shot her light'ning through the land,
Again their true-born zeal display,
Again to Freedom lead the way.
To save our Country from disgrace,
Her Councils shut from Aliens base,
Bostonia's valiant sons combine,
And call their sister states to join.
The fire has caught, the flames arise,
And spread throughout the northern skies.
And shall our southern friends forbear
In Freedom's glorious cause to share?
When blest with sons of brightest name,
Alive to all its growing fame,
Shall they stoop downward to disgrace,
And crouch beneath a foreign race?
Forbid it pride—Each manly soul,
Disdains the renegade's controul,
Columbia's sons shall bear the sway,
In southern, as in northern day.

Behold! along yon western plains,
Where wild Misrule with Mischief reigns,
Behold that dark Intriguer steer
A devious course, through Faction's sphere!
Not yet matur'd to Freedom's sun,
His seven short seasons† scarcely run,
The brogue still hobbling on his tongue,
His brows with rank rebellion hung,
See him with brazen forehead stand,
Among the fathers of the land,
With daring voice her glory mar,
And gash her face with many a scar.
Ye heirs of Penn's undying name,
Where is your spirit, where your shame!
Rouse from your base degenerate state,
And chace this hireling from his seat.

 Once more, far-stretch'd from South to North,
The Pestilence stalks dreadful forth,
And arm'd with subtler venom frowns,
To thin our marts and crowded towns;
He walks unseen the midnight way,
And wasteth at the noon of day.
In vain to check his fell career,
Apollo‡ waves his shield and spear;

---

† By the Constitution of the United States, no foreigner can be elected a Representative in Congress, until he has been seven years a citizen of the United States.

‡ Apollo the God of Physic.

Where'er the *yellow* Fiend draws nigh,
He fills with death the tainted sky,
The city wraps in midnight gloom,
And marks whole myriads for the tomb.
In vain from crowded towns they haste,
His shafts unseen their flight arrest;
Man flies from man, as though pursued
In vengeance of a brother's blood,
But finds no refuge from the grave,
Alas! no altar blest to save.
When erst th' Almighty's vengeful ire
Wrapp'd Sodom's guilty domes in fire,
Lot from the scene of horror flew,
And safe to friendly Zoar withdrew;
But here no place a shelter yields,
No Zoar the friendless exile shields.
No rules by which the wisest live,
No aid that Med'cine knows to give,
When Pestilence bursts dreadful forth,
Can save the fated sons of Earth.
Nor bright endowments of the mind,
With learning fraught and taste refin'd,
Nor pitying heart for others woe,
Can turn aside the fatal blow;
Else had his shafts that wing'd the sky,
Pass'd thee, O SMITH§ uninjured by—
Thy friends' delight, thy parents' stay,
Fond hope of their declining day;—

§ Doctor Elihu H. Smith of New-York.

Nor had those floods of sorrow, burst,
Lamented COOPER,‖ o'er thy dust;
Nor mourning Science wept forlorn,
O'er learn'd SCANDELLA'S¶ timeless urn.

‖ Doctor —— Cooper of Philadelphia.

¶ Doctor I. B. Scandella of Venice, who died in New-York during the prevalence of the Yellow-fever in the Autumn of 1798. The fate of these gentlemen, all of whom possessed distinguished talents, and bade fair to become ornaments to their profession, was attended with some peculiarly interesting circumstances.— During the Yellow-fever in Philadelphia, Doctor Cooper was seized with that malady; a friend of his kindly attended him during his illness. Unfortunately, before he had recovered, that friend was taken sick; strongly impressed with a sense of the obligations he was under, he could not be dissuaded from attending him. A relapse was the consequence, and his life became the sacrifice of the high sense of gratitude which he entertained.

From a congeniality of taste and a similarity in their literary pursuits, Doctor Smith had recently formed an intimacy with Doctor Scandella, who had been but a short time in this country. The latter while at New-York waiting for the sailing of the packet in which he had taken his passage for Europe, learned that a lady in Philadelphia, a foreigner, to whose daughter he was tenderly attached, was sick with the fever. He instantly hastened thither to aid and alleviate the distress of the family; but his exertions were in vain, both the mother and the daughter died. Scandella, in a state of mind much easier to be conceived than described, returned to New-York. There, a stranger, coming from a place highly infectious, and apparently indisposed himself, he found no one who would consent to receive him. In this situation he wrote, stating his embarrassment, to Doctor Smith, who, with a

Learn then COLUMBIANS, ere too late,
If not to cure, to ward the fate;
For when swart skies find filth beneath,
They breed swift messengers of death.
Let BELGIAN neatness mantle o'er
The marts and towns around your shore;
And ere the Dog Star's sultry rays
Dawn and decline with solar blaze,
Stretch daily in warm baths your limbs,
Or lave you o'er in tepid streams.
Let no late revels break your rest,
Nor passion rankle in the breast;
The strictest temperance of the board,
And glass, can potent aid afford.

warmth of feeling which did honour to his heart, immediately invited him to his house. Scarcely was he established there, when he was taken with the fever. Doctor Smith was indefatigable in his attention to aid and solace his unfortunate friend, but his anxiety for his fate, and fatigue in attending to the duties of his profession, at a time when most of the physicians had quitted the city, combining with a pestilential atmosphere, soon rendered the attention he had paid to his friend, necessary to himself; he was taken sick, and his disorder from its commencement exhibited the most malignant symptoms. A friend with whom he lived, and on whom, after his sickness, the care of Doctor Scandella devolved, did every thing that friendship and active benevolence could suggest for their relief, but to no effect. Scandella died, and Smith soon after followed him to the grave.—*See Supplementary Notes.*

From ardent spirits most refrain,
Dire sources of disease and pain.
Ye heirs of wealth! to rural seats
Retire from summer's scorching heats,
And let the virtuous sons of want,
Throng gladd'ning round the sylvan haunt,
On tented plains; and often taste
With you the simple plain repast.
  Strange as it seems, this happy land,
Nurses a Jacobinic band,
Who, their united force employ,
Its richest blessings to destroy,
And, in the place of all that's good,
To mark our fate with guilt and blood.
But ere that mighty change is wrought,
Pause for a moment from the thought;
Across the Atlantic wing your way,
And Gallia's wretched land survey.
There the foul breath of every crime,
Contaminates th' extended clime.
There crush'd, and trodden to the ground,
In ten-fold chains the poor are bound,
Their pittance stripp'd by ruffian hands,
Their offspring forc'd to distant lands,
To sickness, and to want a prey,
And wars more fatal far than they.
There the rich soil neglected lies,
No harvest meets the wandering eyes,

Commerce reclines her drooping head,
And Industry the land has fled.
Where Justice rears her awful seat,
The blockhead, and the villain meet,
While Law astonish'd quits the place,
And blushing Virtue hides her face.
There a whole Nation sinks deprav'd,
Corrupted, plunder'd, and enslav'd,
Its dignity forever flown,
Its manners lost, its honour gone;
High on the ruins of a throne,
Behold the base-born tyrants frown,
Rapacious, cruel, proud, and vain,
Far spreads the mischief of their reign.
Of each inherent right bereft,
Not Freedom's name, nor semblance left,
The dastard people kiss the rod,
And bow beneath the tyrant's nod.

 Hence, let the searching vision bend,
And o'er the moral scene extend.
There Vice unshackled holds her reign,
And binds the nation in her chain.
At WEISHAUPT's midnight orgies nurs'd,
Th' *Illuminated* band accurs'd,
Spread mischief with destructive hand,
Through every corner of the land.
There Discord sows the seeds of strife,
There Murder whets the bloody knife,

Foul Incest seeks the eye of day,
And Theft, and Robbery mark their prey.
Forth from her sacred Temples thrust,
Her honours prostrate in the dust,
Religion from the Nation flies,
And wings her passage to the skies;
While Blasphemy usurps her seat,
And Atheists triumph in her fate,
Behold! this dark mysterious band,
In myriads spreads through every land,
Steal slily to the posts of state,
And wield unseen the Nation's fate!
Where Virtue builds her still retreats,
Where learning holds her sacred seats,
Behold! array'd in semblance fair,
The fell Illuminatus there!

In scenes like these, let those who dare
E'en wish this peaceful land to share,
Change their dark purpose ere too late,
Or else prepare to meet their fate.

Behold! array'd on Gallia's coast,
A ragged, death-devoted host,*
Resolv'd at all events, to land
On Albion's sea-surrounded strand.
Already yields her naval force,
And nought obstructs their daring course.
While London's tempting plunder lies
Unfolded to their greedy eyes.

* The swaggering " Army of England."

What though no ships their harbours grace,
Great rafts will well supply their place,
They'll " *condescend* to cross the sea,
And *set the slaves of England free.*"
" Men," says the ancient proverb sound,
" Born to be hang'd will ne'er be drown'd"—
This is the source from whence must flow,
The strong inducement Frenchmen show
To quit their home, all dangers share,
And tempt their fate no matter where.
Oft has this silly scheme been laid,
And oft the mighty effort made,
And just as oft, the boasting race
Have met disaster and disgrace.
  As every victim of despair
Has all to hope and nought to fear,
With Napper Tandy for their guide,
Again they tempt the dangerous tide,
Among the Irish Bulls, to teach
" The rights of man," and pow'rs of speech.
Her standard swift Rebellion rais'd,
And o'er the bogs her fury blaz'd;
Teague his potatoe-field forsook,
His harp and mattock Paddy took,
The White-boy, deep in den conceal'd,
Rush'd fearless to the bloody field,
Determin'd, one and all, to dare
In Faction's cause the storm of war.

Brave Albion frowns—their courage fails,
In crowds they flock from camps to jails;
Law's awful mandates intervene,
And hemp, as usual, ends the scene.
  Intent to sow the seeds of strife,
To mar each bliss of human life,
Spread wide Corruption's putrid flood,
And bathe the nations round in blood,
Extinguish Freedom's last remains,
And rivet Slavery's galling chains;
From *France*, behold! a savage band
Invade Helvetia's free-born land;
Where factions, jealousies, and hate,
Those fell destroyers of a state,
To French intrigues had op'd the way,
Their force to weaken and betray.
In vain her virtuous sons contend
Their rights to save, their soil defend,
Fell Faction's schemes their views oppose,
And timid Caution aids the foes.
Through threats, and artifices vile,
Corruption base, or secret wile,
Th' Helvetic troops, compell'd, remain
Inactive on the marshall'd plain.
Meanwhile, approach the hostile force,
No arms oppos'd to check their course,
Nor longer deign, with friendly show,
To mask the treach'ry of the foe.

Impell'd by courage and despair,
Berne's gallant youth rush forth to war;
But vain their courage, to oppose
Th' o'erwhelming myriads of their foes,
Yet nobly brave they scorn to yield,
And but with death resign the field.
Illustrious STEIGNER!* o'er thy grave
Shall Virtue's freshest laurels wave,
And Freedom long lament thy fate,
With many a tear of deep regret!
Thou gallant SWISS! the praise was thine,
In council as in arms to shine;
Though Faction base, and wav'ring Fear,
Thy just monitions scorn'd to hear,
Though vain thy efforts, to inspire
The sordid soul with patriot fire;
Yet o'er thy country's closing day,
When Freedom shed its parting ray,
With soul sublime, thou scorn'dst to wait
A witness of her mournful fate,

* At the time when these lines were written, it was the generally received opinion that this venerable patriot had fallen in an engagement between the Bernese and the French. The account of his death was afterwards contradicted, and it appeared that though badly wounded in the battle, he had escaped with life.— This respectable magistrate died in 1799, during the period that Zurich was occupied by the Austrian and Russian troops, and his remains were accompanied to the grave by the principal officers of the army, and interred with military honours.

With desp'rate courage sought the war,
And bar'd thy bosom to the spear.
O! had thy counsels firm and good,
Thy vet'ran counsels been pursu'd,
Helvetia still had freedom known,
Nor bent beneath the despot's frown;
Nor seen her fertile fields laid waste,
Her hamlets burn'd, her temples raz'd,
Her cities levell'd in the dust,
Her fair a prey to fiend-like lust,
In heaps, the dying and the dead,
Hoar Age and feeble Childhood spread,
By tempests smote, whose pale remains
Lie whitening o'er their native plains!

  O then, COLUMBIA! from her fate
A warning draw ere yet too late;
For, from Destruction's lurid sky,
The *Fiend* has mark'd thee with his eye,
In hope, already shakes thy chains,
And revels o'er thy wasted plains.
Howe'er his varying features show,
If smiles or frowns impress his brow,
Still fix'd, his views remain the same,
Nor once he deviates from his aim.
Then, from his smiles indignant turn,
His proffer'd love with horror spurn,
Beneath those smiles lurks deadly hate,
That friendship but conducts to fate.

So, cloth'd in fair and treach'rous guise,
Morocco's image* meets the eyes—
Her face in soft allurements drest,
She hides the dagger in her breast,
And, while her arms the wretch surround,
Her poniard gives the deadly wound.
  Behold the Chief, whose mighty name
With glory fills the trump of fame !
Before whose genius, smote with dread,
The veteran hosts of Austria fled,
Th' imperial Eagle droop'd forlorn,
His plumage soil'd, his pinions torn,
And Conquest's self, 'mid fields of blood,
Attendant on his footsteps trode ;
To gain new palms on Afric's coast,
Lead o'er the deep a chosen host.
And lo ! at first, with fav'ring ray,
Kind fortune lights him on his way ;
Those ramparts, Europe's ancient pride,
Which erst the Turkish power defy'd,
By stratagem and force compell'd,
To him the towers of Malta yield.
Victorious, thence to Egypt's coast
He leads his fell marauding host ;
In vain the Turks oppose their force,
To stop the fierce invader's course,

  * An image of a beautiful woman, said to be kept by the Emperor of Morocco, for the purpose of punishing his refractory subjects. Such persons are ordered to embrace the image, at which moment, a dagger concealed in it, pierces them to the

Nor Alexandria's time-worn tow'rs,
Nor Cairo long resist his pow'rs;
By desp'rate courage fierce impell'd
The Mam'luke squadrons tempt the field;
But vain the bold, undaunted band
In close and furious contest stand;
Against the column's solid force,
In vain impel their scatter'd horse,
And wake anew, by deeds of fame,
The ancient glories of their name—
Foil'd, slain, dispers'd, the routed train
In wild confusion quit the plain.

 But lo! the ever-varying queen,
Delusive Fortune, shifts the scene:
To crush the towering pride of France,
Behold brave NELSON firm advance!
Beneath his rule, in close array,
The Britons plough the wat'ry way;
To fam'd Rosetta bends his course,
Where deem'd secure from hostile force,
The fleet superior of the foe
A lengthen'd line of battle show.
Lo! from the west, the setting ray
Slopes the long shades of parting day!
The fight begins;—the cannon's roar
In doubling echoes rends the shore;
Wide o'er the scene blue clouds arise,
And curl in volumes to the skies,

heart. History informs us, that one of a similar construction, was applied by the tyrant Nabis to the same purpose.

While momentary flashes spread
Their fleecy folds with fiery red.
More desp'rate still the battle glows
As night around its horrors throws.
Long lines of fire enkindling sweep
A blueish splendour o'er the deep,
Then swells the dread displosive sound,
While deeper darkness closes round.
Yon sable volume, roll'd on high,
With thicker gloom obscures the sky;
And lo! emerging from its womb,
What sudden flames the shade illume!
Evolving slow the clouds retire,
Red glows the wide-extended fire,
And rears sublime a column white,
High as the eagle wings his flight,
'Till veil'd 'mid clouds of pitchy hue,
It shrinks diminish'd from the view;
Wide o'er the seas the splendours play,
In radiance like the blaze of day;
With reflex beams the waves are bright,
Bichierrian heights emerge in light,
While o'er the distant hills and dales,
Night's deepest gloom the landscape veils.
At length, disparting, from the waves
The giant ship concussive heaves;
Still wider spreads the glare of light,
With momentary splendour bright,

Far heard, the wild, tremendous sound
In dire explosion roars around—
The lifted surges wide expand,
And dash with refluent waves the strand;
The Nile receding seeks its head,
And pale Rosetta shakes with dread—
Huge burning beams are hurl'd on high,
And masts and yards obscure the sky—
Burnt, mangled, torn, and dy'd in blood,
The Gallic sailors strew the flood,
While the rent hulk, with groaning sound,
Sinks plunging, whirl'd in eddies round.
'Tis silence all:—the cannon's roar
In deaf'ning thunder rings no more;
No light is seen to mark the gloom,
Still as the stillness of the tomb.
Such the dire gloom, in days of yore,
That darken'd Egypt's fated shore,
When Plagues pursued the Prophet's word,
And terror pal'd her haughty lord.
Not long the pause; for lo! once more
Resounds the loud terrific roar,
Flash answering flash, alternate plays,
And lightens ocean with its rays.
But when the Morning's golden eye
Beheld the dusky shadows fly,
Wild Havoc frowning o'er the flood,
His giant form exulting show'd;

The Gallic navy foil'd and torn,
With pale discomfiture forlorn,
Wide scatter'd o'er Rosetta's bay,
In prostrate ruin helpless lay;
Two shatter'd fly; the rest remain
To wear the valiant victor's chain;
While o'er the wreck-obstructed tide
The British ships in triumph ride.
All-anxious, from Abucar's height,
The Gallic leaders view the fight,
And desp'rate see their fleet compell'd
To force inferior far to yield.
So when, by night, o'er Memphis trod
Th' avenging minister of God,
At morn pale Egypt view'd with dread,
Her first-born number'd with the dead.

Ambitious Chief! in dust laid low,
Behold the honours of thy brow,
The laurels cull'd on Egypt's shore
Shall wither ere the day be o'er;
Thy armies thinn'd, reduc'd thy force,
Fell Ruin waits thy onward course,
While of thy country's aid bereft,
No safety but in flight is left,
And victory's self but seals thy doom,*
And brings thee nearer to the tomb.

* It will not, we imagine, be deemed requisite to apologize for the retention of the above lines; since the events of the French

I see destruction wing her way,
I see the eagles mark their prey,
Where pent in Cairo's putrid wall,
In heaps thy dying soldiers fall;
Or, mid the desart's burning waste,
Smote by the Samiel's fiery blast;
Or press'd by fierce Arabian bands,
With thirst they perish on the sands.
While Bonaparte's dreaded name
Shall shine a beacon's warning flame,
To point to times of future date
Unprincipled ambition's fate.

Revolution, and particularly the fortunes of this most extraordinary man, have been such as to set conjecture at defiance, and baffle all human foresight. That the prediction has in part been fulfilled cannot, however, be denied; witness the repulse and slaughter at Acre, the toilsome and distressful march across the desart, which proved fatal to such numbers of the army, and lastly, the abandonment of that army by the flight of their commander, who, by this means alone, most probably, escaped death or capture. At any rate, if our prediction has not held true in its fullest sense, we have at least the satisfaction of having failed in respectable company. The author of the Pursuits of Literature has fallen into a similar mistake in the following line:

" And Pompey points to Buonaparte's tomb."

These instances among many others, may be adduced to prove, that like their predecessors of ancient days, the bards of modern time possess the spirit of vaticination, with only this slight difference, that, whereas, the former foretold what was to happen, the prophecies of the latter are seldom or never accomplished.

What fruits shall on this victory grow,
All climes shall see, all ages know;
Earth's eastern realms that long have view'd
Descending suns go down in blood,
Now with the western world shall frame
Loud Pæans, Nelson, to thy name.

Shield, still Britannia, shield from harm
The Nations with thy naval arm;
And blighted Europe soon shall see
Her freedom guaranteed by thee.

HARTFORD, JANUARY 28.

Extract of a letter from a gentleman in Philadelphia, to his friend in this City.

" On Thursday when Mr. Griswold's bill was the subject of debate, the evil genius of Mr. Nicholas prompted him to quote " THE POLITICAL GREEN-HOUSE." He read part of it as an authority to prove, that Connecticut wished to produce a war, and not a peace, with France. Is it uncharitable to suppose, that he thought it a favourable opportunity for aiming a *severe* stroke at Connecticut? Unfortunately, however, for the Virginian wight, he mistook the sense of the poet, and stumbled on a mischievous place. He cited, as descriptive of the disposition of Connecticut, part of the passage which depicts the scene in Congress, on reading the " Dispatches," commencing with

" Long had our Ministers of peace,
" The insults borne of Gallia's race."—

and read with much solemnity, until he had brought the Jacobins to *set on chesnut burrs*. The house and galleries tittered while he was reading, and at last broke out into pretty loud laughter, which continued until the Speaker had called *to order* several times.

Dana at length rose, and after speaking generally on the bill, closed his speech with a vindication of the members of Congress, and the people of Connecticut, and read again the passage which had been read by Nicholas, and the lines following, ending with

"Could raise in heaven a revolution"—

and appealed to the house for the accuracy of the description.— As most of the members were present, when the dispatches were first read in the hall, there appeared a very general suffrage in favour of the Poet, and to the great confusion of the *good citizen*, a general laugh at his expense. Here follows the passage, which was so *aptly* quoted by citizen Nicholas:

" Long had our Ministers of peace,
The insults borne of Gallia's race;
At length the Envoys deign to tell us,
They had to deal with scurvy fellows—
With Autun, and the Five-head Beast,
And half the Alphabet at least.
The budget op'd in Congress, shew'd
The whole contrivance of the brood,
And that their heads were bent on brewing,
Subjection, infamy, and ruin.
While joy each Fed'ral feature crown'd,
And triumph glow'd the Hall around,
Each Jacobin began to stir,
And sate, as though on chesnut burr."

The remainder was added by Mr. Dana.

" Up the long space from chin to forehead,
Sate every feature of the horrid;
Their moon-ey'd leaders stood like beacons,
Or as a drove of Satan's Deacons,
When from the burning lake in ire,
They sate their feet on solid fire,
To find if war, or sly pollution,
Could raise in heaven a revolution."

Complimentary Address to the Hon. John Nicholas.

The following verses were written in consequence of Mr. Nicholas's having read a passage from the Green-House in proof of his assertions, that the state of Connecticut were desirous of a war with France.

HAIL worthy wight, Virginia's wond'rous son!
For *candour* fam'd, for *calm* discussion known—
Fain would the muse thy worth to sing essay,
Fain in thy praise would tune the various lay;
Would tell to distant lands thy deeds sublime,
And register thy name to latest time:
But, as the copious subject meets her eyes,
She sees new Andes upon Andes rise—
Yet, though despairing in her humble lays
To reach the towering summit of thy praise,
Still, by the call of gratitude impell'd,
She tempts with timid step the dangerous field.
  Hard is the task thy virtues to rehearse,
And harder still to crowd them into verse;
But, lest confounded by the numerous throng,
Let white rob'd Candour lead th' approving song—
In candour's paths thy feet by instinct run,
Alas! for candour, who can equal John?

Not Randolph when the "*thousand dollars*" shone;
Not Johnny Langdon when his speech was done;*
Not Thompson Mason, when, with visage pale,
He rescu'd Callender from Leesburg jail;
Not *** the spouter as, with graceful grin,
He rais'd his hand extatic to his chin,
To tell his transports, when, through *second sight*,
His father burnt his barn for candle light
To read the treaty, which by Franklin's aid,
A *twelvemonth after*,† with the French was made;
Not Gallatin, when march'd the patriot band,
And crush'd Rebellion's host in whiskey land;
In Freedom's toils, from party spirit free,
E'er dealt in candour, citizen, like thee.

 But chief thy modesty demands our lays—
Thy modesty, beyond compeer, or praise—

* This able statesman is said to have spoken once in the Senate for *five minutes*.

† A year or two since this patriotic Orator broke out into a violent rhapsody upon the pleasure which glistened in all eyes, on the reading of the Treaty made between the United States and France, in the late war; which Treaty, he observed, was read by the light of the flames which consumed his father's dwelling. It is, no doubt, true that the old gentleman's house was burned; but unless we are misinformed, it was a year or eighteen months previously to the signing of the Treaty. It is probable that Mr. L—— had adopted the sentiments of his friend Swanwick, in the famous debate upon wigs, that, *an Orator ought not to be confined too closely to truth.*

Which spreads its maiden blushes o'er thy face,
And decks each gesture with a nameless grace,
As, with a downcast eye and reddening cheek,
We see thee rise, with diffidence, to speak.
Oft, when the interests of our wavering state
Have swell'd tumultuous into warm debate;
When every forward youth has rais'd his voice,
And fill'd our Congress Hall with senseless noise;
When doubtless one sweet-ton'd persuasive speech
Had put the question out of danger's reach,
Our anxious eyes have seen, with wondering stare,
The shame-fac'd spirit nail thee to thy chair.
Yet, true it is, too oft this lamb-like guest,
This charming inmate of the feeling breast,
Impels the brave, the noble, and the wise,
To shun the eager glance of wondering eyes.
Too oft, by her induc'd, is genius led
Midst solitude's deep shades to hide his head:
And this, with real pain, great John! we see
Unfortunately verified in thee:
For 'tis with deep regret, with grief we find
That thou a re-election hast declin'd.
In this, how much alike thy colleague, Giles,
The late companion of thy patriot toils,
In whom sweet Diffidence beheld, with pride,
Herself in human form personified—
He too, so bashful, like thyself, withdrew
(In this most modest) from the public view.

Ah! why does blushing Modesty desire
From scenes of public notice to retire?
Why will she e'er compel the good and great
Thus to relinquish privilege and state?
Ah! yet, if not too late, thy plan forego;
Ah! do not leave thy friends to bitterest woe—
Think, too, what evils must the step pursue,
O! what will E............e without thee do!
How will that tender plant, 'mid tempests stand
All unsupported by thy fostering hand!—
Ah! quit him not on danger's giddy brink,
Oppress'd with diffidence he sure must sink;
No Giles, alas! his untaught steps to stay,
No Nicholas to guide him on his way—
That hopeful plant, beneath too hot a sun,
Will hang its head and wither e'er 'tis noon.
 Oh! if thy skill in reading can compare
With that enlightened taste, that judgment rare,
Which taught thy fine discriminative eye
To choose so well, so happily apply,
When strange astonishment each face o'erspread,
As with selection nice the verse you read—
What joy, what transport must have glow'd around
In all who heard the soul-attractive sound!
Methinks midst Congress-Hall I see thee stand,
The Green-House blooming in thy genial hand,
Thy form displaying dignity and grace,
The smile of pleasure lighting up thy face,

Round whose red sides no waving tresses flow,
Since Time, with razor keen, has shorn thy brow—
Propitious Time! resolv'd a face like thine,
Without obstruction in full glow should shine,
Nor have by locks obscur'd, or ringlets crost,
The sweet expression of one feature lost:
While thy Stentorian voice, with silver sound,
In tuneful echoes makes the Hall rebound;
With pleas'd surprise, to hear such accents sweet,
The Muses listen from their sacred seat,
Pan drops his lute, Apollo quits his lyre,
All stop to hear, to wonder, and admire;
While she, whose voice of music thrills the soul,
As still at morn she cries the smoking roll,
In vain to reach thy tones mellifluous tries,
And o'er her basket droops with downcast eyes;
And e'en the *Sweep*, of far superior skill,
Feels jealousy his sable bosom thrill,
Sick of his trade, he quits the sooty throng,
Resigns his blanket, and gives up his song.
Thou patron kind, through whose auspicious care,
The GREEN-HOUSE shines renew'd, in charms more
    fair—
O! still extend thy kind protecting hand,
Still let its blooms beneath thy smile expand,
Again in *Congress* read it, read once more,
And only quote as aptly as before.

So shall th' admiring Muse consign thy name
As first of *Quoters* to eternal fame.
Vain, vain would be th' attempt, in prose or verse,
At large thy various merits to rehearse;
How strong thy patriot feelings and how great
Of Gallic principles thy virtuous hate,
Of French exactions how thou loath'st to hear,
And scarce to TRIBUTE lend'st a patient ear.—
All these, and more, perchance, some future time,
The Muse shall consecrate in deathless rhyme;
'Till then accept this humble mite of praise,
Which grateful feeling to thy merit pays.

NEW-YEARS' VERSES,

FOR THE PRESENT CENTURY.

THE TRIUMPH OF DEMOCRACY,

A POEM.

TRIUMPH OF DEMOCRACY.

PRECISELY twelve o'clock, last night,
The Eighteenth Century took its flight.
Full many a calculating head,
Has rack'd its brains, its ink has shed,
To prove by metaphysics fine,
A *hundred* means but *ninety-nine;*
While at their wisdom others wonder'd,
But took *one more* to make a hundred.
Thus, by an unexampled riddle,
The world's divided in the middle—
The Century, waking from its bed,
Finds half mankind a year a-head,
Whilst t'other half, with lingering pace,
Have scarcely started in the race.
Strange! at " *the Eighteenth Century's close,*
When light in beams effulgent glows,"
When bright " *Illumination's*" ray,
Has chac'd the Darkness far away,
Heads fill'd with mathematic lore,
Dispute if *two and two make four.*
Go on, ye scientific sages,
Collect your light a few more ages,
Perhaps as swells the vast amount,
A century hence you'll *learn to count ;*

Whilst we, more usefully employ'd,
Will traverse back the mighty void,
With keen researching eye, discern
Some lessons for the world to learn.
Nor will we venture far to stray,
Lest *in the dark* we lose our way;
A single year, perchance, or so,
Is all the length we mean to go—
A *bastard year*, which none will own,
A pauper thrown upon the town,
A year, that no where does belong,
Shall be the subject of our song.
 Last New-Year found our land in tears
Absorb'd in grief, and fill'd with fears;
Our nation's strength, and pride, and stay,
Her hope, her day-star fled away.
Faction, with raptur'd eye, beheld
Her foe forever quit the field;
And doom'd no more in dens to lurk,
Began afresh her deadly work—
And lo! her angry meteor shines,
The billows roll, the storm begins;
From state to state the Demon strides,
And howling on the whirlwind rides.
Each Democrat, with hand and heart,
Equips himself to play his part;
Resolv'd, JOHN ADAMS should go home,
When e'er " *the Ides of March*" should come;

That humble, in his native state, he
Might *otium* mix with *dignitate;*
Whilst, all our losses to repair,
Mazzei's " SAMPSON "* takes his chair,
Whose mighty Ass's jaw shall slay,
Each Philistine that clogs his way,
'Till at the last, as fortune veers,
He pulls an *old house* round his ears.
The Democrats *all* means prepare,
From telling lies, to aping prayer;
(For Democrats can pray for evil,
Their gods are Frenchmen and the Devil)
While to the Union's utmost bounds
The Jacobinic Tocsin sounds.
Thieves, traitors, Irish renegadoes,
Scape-gallowses, and desperadoes,
All sorts of rogues stripp'd off the mask,
And enter'd on the glorious task,
Prepar'd to flounce with highest glee,
In JEFFERSON'S " *tempestuous sea.*"
Each in prophetic view beheld
The *Washingtonian* charm dispell'd;
No longer by enchantment bound,
No longer sunk in awe profound,
The horde from deepest silence broke,
And thus in wildest transports spoke—

* See Jefferson's letter to Mazzei.

—" The *Fed'ralists* are down at last,
The *Monarchists* completely cast,
The *Aristocrats* are stripp'd of pow'r,
Storms o'er the *British faction* low'r.
Soon *we Republicans* shall see,
Columbia's slaves from bondage free.
Lord! how the Fed'ralists will stare
At JEFFERSON in ADAMS' chair!
What glorious times! when great men wait,
And *little ones* direct the state;
When *Tom*, and *Dick*, and *Harry*, rise
Two feet above their common size;
When Reason quits the reins to Passion,
And Revolutions are the fashion;
When Rulers must in turn obey,
That ' *Every Dog may have his day;*'
And we, whom now the laws expose
To pillories, or the halter's noose,
May then the seats of honour grace,
And hang our Rulers in our place!"

   The LEADERS soon complete their plan;
His task's assign'd to every man—
The orders given—Lo, far and wide,
The Democratic couriers ride!
In every state the mischief works,
In every town some villain lurks;
And if too weak to guide the trade,
His lies are furnish'd ready made.

'Twould stretch the limits of our song
To notice all the virtuous throng,
Thousands must pass—the noblest game
The honours of our annals claim.

Resolv'd her sister states to lead,
And, first or last, to be their head,
" The ANCIENT STATE" begins—and lo!
Plac'd at her helm one *J. Monroe !*—
Alas! the powers of language fail,
For such a head to name the tail!
Behold! in Tom's " tempestuous ocean,"
" The old dominion's" wayward motion!
Things follow there " the Rights of Man,"
(That is the topsy-turvy plan)
The people hold the sovereign sway,
Rulers are chosen to obey;
Their President and Congress folks,
Are only *Tom,* and *John-a-nokes,*
Their servants, by themselves appointed,
To shew *they're not the Lord's Anointed.*
Doctrines profound—display'd much better
In Randolph's " *Raggamuffin*" letter.†

---

† That Rulers are " *servants* of the people," is one of the favourite doctrines of modern times. That many rulers are fitter for *servants,* than they are for masters, in every thing unless it may be *honesty,* will be granted. And hence we may learn the true source of much mischief in the world—It is putting those into power, who ought to be in *servitude.* " Set a beggar on horseback, and he will ride to the devil," *says the proverb.*

Charm'd with a democratic sway,
Knaves flock amain the southern way,
United Irishmen, and thieves,
Virginia's open arms receives.
In such a virtuous congregation,
Some fruits must ripen for the nation—
And lo! in meretricious dress,
Forth comes a strumpet call'd "THE PRESS"*—
Whose haggard, unrequested charms,
Rush into every blackguard's arms.
Ye weak, deluded minds, beware!
Nought but the outside here is fair!
Then spurn the offers of her sway,
And kick the loathsome hag away,
 Let Callender in jail remain,
Ripe for the halter, and the chain;
His horizon contracts apace;
His "PROSPECT'S"† circumscrib'd by CHASE—

* "THE PRESS."—A newspaper established the last year in VIRGINIA, for the avowed purpose of forwarding Mr. *Jefferson's* election. The *paper* was to be disposed of *dog-cheap;* and to those who would not buy it, and would read it, it was to be sent gratis. In many instances, it was sent to the wrong people. Whether it be yet alive, we do not know.

† "THE PROSPECT BEFORE US."—A book published by this vile Scotchman, who, let it be remembered, was convicted by a Virginia jury! It is said that the Insurrection planned by the negroes at Richmond this fall, was occasioned by the hand-bills

Ne'er may it lengthen to his sight,
'Till perch'd upon the ladder's height,
While round, as far as eye can reach,
The crowd admire his *dying speech*.

 Proceed great state—thy arts renew,
With double zeal thy course pursue,
Call on thy sister states t' obey,
And boldly grasp at sovereign sway—
Then pause—remember ere too late,
The tale of St. Domingo's fate,
Though *Gabriel* dies, a host remain
Oppress'd with slavery's galling chain,
And soon or late the hour will come,
Mark'd with Virginia's dreadful doom.

 In Pennsylvania where M'KEAN
Extends his mild and gentle reign,
Where birds, of every name and feather,
Flock, and at times *get drunk* together,
TENCH COXE, from his interior draws
His weekly *Tape-worm* in the cause—*

which this culprit uttered from his prison. His apology in the newspapers, was, that he published his hand-bills to forward Mr. Jefferson's election. This may be called launching on *the Black Sea of Liberty*.

 * A dull long-winded series of political publications written by this turn-coat.

Just finishing the factious round,
TENCH finds his vessel fast aground,
A parted cable, shiver'd mast,
Foul bottom, and a squally blast.
Despair not TENCH—thy brother FRIES,
Beneath the gallows heav'd his sighs,
Jack-Ketch stood ready with his cord,
And only waited for the word,
When lo! by force of magic spell,
Tattoos succeed the funeral knell;
In place of robes of sable hue,
Gay regimentals rise to view,
Instead of hangman's knot, appear
Bright Epaulettes beneath each ear,
And fairly slipping from the noose,
A *Colonel* from *the halter* goes.
Thou too, O *Tench!* as times come round,
Beneath the gallows *may'st* be found;
And should *M'Kean* then hold his place,
Wilt doubtless meet with equal grace,
And rise from Fate's successive knocks,
The famous, half-hang'd Colonel COXE.
   Nor *Coxe* alone this state can boast—
DALLAS commands a numerous host.
As things their various courses push,
Slight help is gain'd from Doctor Rush:

PRIESTLEY† with pious fervour labours,
Among his *dear Northumbrian neighbours;*
JUDGE BRACKENRIDGE,‡ great sire of laws!
Turns *Jew* to aid the Christian cause.
But chief DUANE amid the throng,
Demands the notice of our song.
When ROBIN-HOOD's illustrious name,
When LITTLE-JOHN of equal fame,
GEORGE BARRINGTON, and CAPT. KYD,
In black oblivion's shade are hid,
DUANE, more fam'd than all the gang,
Like tavern-sign on high shall hang.

Now further eastward let us run,
(Coiling our rope *against the sun*)
To where New-York, with pride, displays
Her turrets to the noon-tide blaze—
Here, when all other measures fail,
To turn the newly balanc'd scale,

---

† See *Priestley's* factious letters to the people of Northumberland County, (Penn.) in which he takes special care to address his readers by the endearing title of " My friends and neighbours."

‡ *Brackenridge* is one of McKean's Judges. He has lately set up a printing press at Pittsburgh, for the purpose of moulding the people of that state to the manners and morals of their Governor. Brackenridge's partner in the printing office, is one Israel, a Jew, to whose religion the Judge is said to be strongly disposed to become a proselyte, in hopes to have a double chance for safety, viz. both as Jew, and Gentile.

Manhattan's Bank* pours in its stream,
The Fed'ral party kick the beam—
A Bank contriv'd on system new,
A various purpose to pursue—
A Bank, upon occasion's spur,
To *discount notes* for *Colonel Burr*—
A *Bank of Water*, to supply
The citizens when running dry—
Pipes *under ground* the streams convey,
Supplies are copious, *conduits* play,
" Line upon line" the people share,
" A little here, a little there."
New-York, well water'd, brings forth fruit,
Decay'd *old Trees* revive and shoot,
Dire *Storms* ensue, so fame relates,
Old *Broomes* sweep clean, and creak old *Gates*†
What marvel, if with helps like these,
The Livingstons should raise a breeze,
If Burr should multiply his tools,
Aided by dotards, knaves and fools,
Or, if there now and then appears
A poor Elector stripp'd of ears.‡

* The change in the politics of the state of New-York, is universally ascribed to the skilful operation and effect of the " *surplus capital*" of the Manhattan Bank.

† See the names of the members of the House of Representatives, in the Legislature of New-York, chosen by the city, last spring.

‡ One of the Electors for the state of New-York was some years ago convicted of forgery in Rhode-Island.

But let our wandering eye-sight roam,
O'er scenes a little nearer home;
For though we claim a right to stray,
Where'er the spirit points our way,
Yet, surely, 'tis no more than fair,
Our charity should finish there.
But, who is able to relate
The storms that shook this *stubborn state*,
The projects vast, the deep intrigues,
The printed hand-bills, solemn leagues;
KIRPLUCK and *Squab* worn out *with trying*,
OLD LARRABE laid up *a drying*,
"POTBELLY" too, so pure and mild,
And eke "DELUSION's spurious child,
Sedition's last and feeblest hope,
All over mark'd—"*Keep this side up.*"*
Though all the list cannot be brought in,
Yet Sandy† must not be forgotten—
Sandy, the delicate and chaste,
With modesty so amply grac'd—
No wonder that Sedition draws
Such creatures to support her cause;
Nor need we be surpris'd to find
"The DISHITE"‡ to her side inclin'd—

* See a celebrated oration on Political Delusion, by ABRAHAM BISHOP, and "THREE LETTERS addressed to him."

† A river in Virginia.

‡ Dishite—a word evidently of oriental origin, signifying, from, or belonging to the land of Dishes; in like manner as the in-

A forward, vain, and frothy youth,
Too fond *of talk* to stick to truth—
The cause his powers exactly suits,
A second ANACHARSIS CLOOTZ,*

    These *patriots* had their nightly meetings,
Chose sub-committees, " held their sittings,"
Rang'd round the state, " *attended courts*,"
Gave orders, and " receiv'd reports ;"†
All on one generous purpose bent,
All fill'd with patriot intent—

habitants of that portion of Canaan, a country emphatically called the " Land flowing with milk and honey," which was most abundant in the latter article, were very appropriately designated by the appellation of *Hiveites*. The present term furnishes an instance of no less felicity, as Suffield, the birth-place of this distinguished character, has ever been celebrated for its great traffic in wooden dishes ; respecting which, many humourous stories are related, strongly evincive of the genius and adroitness of its inhabitants in this species of traffic.

    * *Anarcharsis Clootz* was a Prussian, who, upon the breaking out of the Revolution, went into France, and became a member of the National Convention. He used to call himself—" *The Orator of the Human race.*"

    † See an anonymous letter printed in one of the New-London papers, last September. Mr. Clootz assumed the letter to himself, declared it a forgery, promised to search out its origin, and engaged that the public should *know the result*. As the public has heard no more about it, probably he dropped his plan, or else found it to be genuine.

This peaceful state with storms to shake,
Our strength to wither, union break,
" *The strait-hair'd folks* from office hurl,
Destruction's purple flag unfurl,
Raise knaves and blockheads into place,
And brand our name with foul disgrace.
    CONNECTICUT!—thou wond'rous STATE!
Forever firm, forever GREAT!
Oft faction here her tools employs,
And oft we hear a mighty noise,
That government is full of evil,
The nation running to the devil—
The blindest eyes begin to wink,
The thickest skulls begin to think.
The *little ones* are growing big,
" The tail has got on t'other pig"—
But when the hour of trial's o'er,
These short liv'd tempests cease to roar,
Sedition's vermin sneak from day,
And all goes on *the good old way*—
Still the *old Council* keep their seats,
Still wisdom there with honour meets,
Still *Granger* keeps his humble station,
Just at the tail of nomination,
Prepar'd as seasons come about,
Once more to slip and tumble out.
    Here, mid the vast, and wild uproar,
Which rends the earth's remotest shore,

This small, this blest, secluded STATE,
Still meets unmov'd the blasts of fate—
Here Justice still extends her sway,
Here Virtue sheds her blissful ray,
Churches our villages adorn,
And Infidels are laugh'd to scorn.
ALMIGHTY GOD, still let us lie,
Safe as the apple of thine EYE,
Still, still protect our happy land,
Within the hollow of thine HAND!

But hark! what noises rend the air!
What acclamations make us stare!
News from the regions of the south,
Wide opes each democratic mouth;
For Faction's reign prepare the way,
The democrats have gain'd the day!
South-Carolina's votes are come!
" Sound the trumpet, beat the drum!
Let every voice with triumph sing—
JEFFERSON is chosen king!
Ring every bell in every steeple,
T' announce the " Monarch of the People!"
Stop—ere your civic feasts begin,
Wait 'till the votes are all come in;
Perchance, amid this mighty stir,
Your Monarch may be— Col. BURR!
Who, if he mounts the sovereign seat,
Like BONAPARTE will *make you sweat.*

Your Idol then must quaking dwell,
'Mid *Mammoth's* bones at *Monticelle*,
His country's barque from anchors free,
On " *Liberty's tempestuous sea ;*"
While all the Democrats will sing—
THE DEVIL TAKE THE PEOPLE'S KING."

SYMPTOMS OF THE MILLENNIUM,
IN THE YEAR 1801.

Symptoms of the Millennium, in 1801.

HARTFORD, JANUARY 7, 1802.

OFT has the period been foretold,
By Prophets, and by Seers of old,
When men, and beasts should all be blest
With long, and universal rest—
When fists no more 'gainst fists should rise,
No bloody nose, nor blacken'd eyes,
When gaols should into taverns turn,
The gallows be cut up to burn,
" *Oppress'd humanity*" no more,
Should wander to *Botania's** shore—
But birds of every note, and feather,
And snakes, and toads should flock together,
And bears, and wolves should learn to browse,
And go to pasture with our cows—
Then every child well brac'd with health,
Well fed, well cloth'd, and fill'd with wealth,
No sorrows in his bosom rankling,
Shall die *as old as Doctor Franklin ;*†

* Vulgarly called Botany-Bay. Probably President Jefferson forgot this asylum for " *oppressed humanity*," when he so pathetically sung (by proxy) his requiem over our Naturalization Law.

† " The ornament of human nature," three or four years older than DEACON BISHOP. See Mr. J—n's reply to the remonstrance of the Merchants of New-Haven, on the appointment of DEACON BISHOP as collector.

And Satan, source of all our evils,
" CHIEF CONSUL" of the other Devils,
Shall, for his sins, and tricks, and strife,
To the State Prison be sent for life.
 That this blest morn approacheth nigh,
Behold the beams in yonder sky!
The cock has crow'd; from spray to spray,
The songsters greet the God of Day;
The day-spring fires the east with red,
And smiles on every mountain's head.
But who the symptoms can relate,
Which verify *the book of fate?*
Whose eagle-eye 'mid guilt, and crimes,
Can mark the *Signs of coming Times?*
Not heedless all—through toil and pains,
A little remnant yet remains—
A DAVID AUSTIN still is found,
Shouting with wild, ecstatic sound,
That *Babel's haggard, painted Whore,*
Shall dance " *the Dragon's-Tail*" no more;
That " *True and Faithful*" from the Cross,
Rides *General Washington's old horse;*
That soon, *the Gentiles,* and *the Jews,*
In his new Church will purchase pews,
The *Four-and-twenty Elders* come,
Bright from their everlasting home,

Adorn'd with pearls, and golden crowns,
To dress themselves in *Hum-hum* gowns,*
A Parson Leland,† too, at ease,
High mounted on a " *Mammoth-Cheese*,"
From curds, and skippers lifts his sight,
Like Moses on mount Pisgah's height,
Through whey and rennet darts his eye,
And sees new-milk beyond the sky,
With exultation swings his hat,
As flows the nectar to his vat,
And while the mighty mass is pressing,
Drops on his knee, and asks a blessing.

* See some of the works of this rational Divine, in which he proves, *clearly*, that the white horse which General Washington used to ride, the white horse which the Marquis La Fayette rode, and the white horse which Bonaparte rides, are the horses which were prefigured by that in the Apocalypse, on which was seated him whose name was Faithful and True. In the same book is particularly described the dance of the Whore of Babylon. It is storied of this extraordinary man, that having discovered that the Millennium would begin at New-Haven, and knowing that the Jews were fond of trading, he built a long row of stores for them and the Gentiles; and that he procured four-and-twenty long white hum-hum garments to be made for the four-and-twenty Elders.

† The elegant author of a " *Blow at the Root*," and a " *Stroke at the Branch*," of all order and government; and also the Guardian Genius of Curds and Whey, at Cheshire, Massachusetts.

I too, perchance, before we part,
May act with skill the prophet's art,
Point out events which clearly show,
The world is getting rid of woe,
And when a few more years have run,
Mankind will tread knee-deep in fun.
Nor shall our proofs be drawn from far,
From former years, " *before the war,*"
Lest Infidels, from mere vexation,
Should plead the act of limitation.

Scarce had the world with tearful eye,
Bade the OLD CENTURY " good bye,"
When lo! there rose a mighty stir,
'Twixt JEFFERSON and COL. BURR.
A direful contest then ensued,
Which *some* suppos'd would end in blood.
At length a *Lyon** grim and bold
For desperate warfare fam'd of old,
Declar'd himself Behemoth's friend,
And brought the combat to an end,
Bade dire hostility to cease,
And hush'd " *Republicans*" to peace—
Then join'd the Presidential flocks,
And ate the herbage like an ox;

---

* It must be a very gratifying reflection to the native inhabitants of the United States, that the important point—*who should be their President*—was settled by the power of *Matthew Lyon.*

And still around the pasture strays,
Among his master's beasts to graze.
  Quick from the midst of strife and storm,
Starts up the Presidential form,
Like Daniel from the Lion's Den,
Unhurt stalks forth " *the first of Men,*"
With cautious step, and measur'd stride,
(Perambulator* at his side)
Unblush'd his cheek, no fear nor quaking,
Though *humbled at the undertaking*,
And climbs with bold unhallow'd feet,
GREAT WASHINGTON's exalted seat—

* * * * * * * *

But stop this course, this strain forbear,
There's no Millennial symptom here—

* * * * * * * * *

But hark! what soft and dulcet note,
Pours from his philanthropic throat?
" Behold I come, prepar'd to heal
All bruises in the Commonweal,

---

* It is said that a certain great man has invented a piece of machinery called a *Perambulator*, which, when hung to his thigh, will tell him—*how many steps he has taken* in any of his perambulations.—What a useful thing this must be. Certainly such a genius must make a good President. This discovery, at least as far as appearances go, is equivalent to contriving for mankind *a third leg*; which is equal to *a fifth wheel to a coach*.

Sweet Harmony again restore,
Blest Intercourse shall bleed no more.
We're brothers of the self-same breed,
A Demo-*Janglo*-Federal seed.
Soon shall this land from sorrow rest,
" And all the sons of want be blest."
Vox populi through ether rings
And brings to pass surprising things;
An *Irish-howl* our land pervades,
And overpow'rs our statesmen's heads,
Bursts through the doors of Honour's shop,
Steals all her cash, and locks it up.
Soon " *Labour's mouth*" its jaws shall ope,
And feed on Metaphor and Trope,
Soon a *cheap government* shall see
An end, to our felicity."

 Scarce do the honied accents cease,
Ere the whole land is drown'd in peace,
Conciliation fiercely burns,
And Harmony in droves returns,
Concord like yellow-fever rages,
And sweeps all sizes, ranks and ages.
Goodrich and Chester lead the bands,
And at their heels go Fish, and Sands.
While to do honour to the nation,
Gelston and Osgood take their station;
To pay for Abra'm Bishop's speaking,
An office lights upon the *Deacon*,

Though plough'd with wrinkles, stamp'd with age,
And tott'ring off life's rugged stage,
Like fabled fool he bends his back,
And takes a Jack-Ass for his pack.
  Now reigns the philanthropic spirit,
And men are guag'd alone by merit;
Regardless where they found their birth,
Here, or some foreign spot of earth.
For what are kingdoms, states, or nations?
Does Geography confine our stations?
And are not men, where'er they're found,
The tenants of great Nature's ground,
All brothers of the human race,
Uninfluenc'd by time, or space?
These arguments resistless prove,
That no man should his country love
Exclusively—the world is common,
The property of *Man* and *Woman*.
And hence we find that our affairs,
Our laws, our interests, and our cares,
Our Constitution—all, are whole
Beneath a foreigner's controul—
That renegades a numerous bevy,
From England, Ireland, and Geneva,
A pure disinterested race,
From motives kind of love, and grace,
To govern us will condescend,
And lead us to a prosperous end.

If the MILLENNIUM were not near,
Would *Duane** bask and batten here?
Would *Dallas*, insect of an hour,
Roll round in splendour, wealth and power?
Would Jackson's† " *seeds*" so early sown,
Have to *such pods* of " *greatness*" grown?
Or *Gallatin* have found a seat,
Just *where our cash, and credit meet* ?

Lo! now an era new begins,
Each star with new-born lustre shines—
Old *Clinton* from his dotard den,
Once more crawls out to govern men.

Rhode-Island too, with virtuous zeal,
Has puk'd and purg'd the Commonweal,
White-wash'd old *Fenner's* smoky coat,
Prov'd him " *Not Guilty*" *by a vote*,
By numbers borne Judge Dorrance down,
And *warn'd thanksgiving out of town.*

* Duane, an Irish " fugitive and vagabond," holds a birth under the present administration, which is computed to be worth TEN THOUSAND DOLLARS A YEAR. Could not some native citizen, some officer of our Revolutionary War, have been found, oppressed by poverty, to whom such a chance to reap a little of that harvest which he helped to sow, would have been received with thankfulness?

† General Jackson, an Irishman, has lately been Governor of Georgia; and is now a Senator in Congress. His speeches *after mid-day*, are said to be fairly represented by that which he lately made in Savannah.

And see the "Worcester Farmer"* draws
His goose-quill in his master's cause!
Deals out his literary bastings,
To turn the vote 'gainst Mr. Hastings,
Sets up a wind-mill of his own,
And grinds out nonsense for the town,
Becomes Attorney for all classes,
Like Balaam talks with men and asses,
Holds dialogues with trees and sheep,
And wades with stone-walls to the deep.

The spirit too has wander'd here,
Connecticut has had her share.
At Wallingford it first broke out,
And show'd itself in noise and rout;
Men grew voracious, ate like swine,
Drank freely *different sorts* of *wine*,
O'ercharg'd, and snor'd till break of day,
Then quitted, *but forgot to pay*,
Following the Prophet's sage advice,
To buy their milk without a price.
Yet here "*the People's friends*" exist,
See *Hyde* and *Wilcox's* Protest!
Wolcott and *Potter* coalesce,
The moral field *to dung and dress;*

* Called in the *National Ægis*, a *Junius*. This reminds us of the Dutchman's picture, which no one could tell the design of, until he wrote at the bottom—" This is a Bear."

Though *Gid.* no more in taverns teaches,
Yet *Gemmill* prays, and *Griswold* preaches,
And *Babcock* promises *this year*,
Truth in the Mercury shall appear.
  And lo! what accents rend the air,
And make the wondering thousands stare!
Each post, and packet, mail, express,
Bears home a copy of th' *Address.*
Soft to our ears its warblings reach,
A new " *inauguration speech.*"
" See through the earth war's tumults cease!
Blest be the power that gives us peace!
To him let gratitude be show'd,
Be he or *Bonaparte* or *God!*
But, while you feel the general joy,
Let other themes your minds employ."
" The Enterprize" in combat fair,
Has beat a Tripoline Corsair,
Kill'd half his men, his vessel taken,
Plunder'd his guns—but *sav'd his bacon.*"
" The Indians too, so fame relates,
Begin to throng around these states,
Their numbers rapidly increase,
An earnest strong of future peace;
Therefore with joy we ought to yearn,
O'er every popoose that is born.
And here a stimulus we find,
To propagate the human kind;

Then let us all with heart and hand,
Fulfil, at least, this one command ;
And let " *our energies*" obey,
What Indians and the bible say."

  O happy people ! happy land !
What can thy bright career withstand ;
When " *Labour's mouth*" is cramm'd with bread,
When nought is *tail,* and all is *head,*
When taxes all are swept away,
And " LIVING CHEAP" 's the only play—
What stupid mortal's head can doubt,
The Devil's time is almost out,
That Gog, and Magog must retreat,
And own their troops are fairly beat,
And that our country soon will find,
A FRENCH MILLENNIUM TO HER MIND.

SKETCHES OF THE TIMES,
FOR THE YEAR 1803.

Sketches of the Times.

HARTFORD, JANUARY, 1804.

WHAT vast advantages we find
Result from Poets to mankind?
Borne on their sure recording page,
Fame sounds her trump from age to age;
And though Destruction's besoms sweep
Whole nations to Oblivion's deep—
Though heroes, patriots, sages die,
And in the grave unnotic'd lie—
Yet Poesy, with magic pen,
Relumes the fading fame of men,
In deathless numbers sings their story,
And rears their pyramid of glory.
Without the aid of Homer's song,
Where would have been the Grecian throng;
Who would Achilles' name have known,
Or who old Priam's god-like son?
Who bore his venerable Sire,
Safe through the midst of Ilium's fire,
On Latium's shores that flag unfurl'd,
Which wav'd in triumph o'er the world,
Ask Mantua's Bard——

And shall the great of modern days,
Fail of the meed of future praise?

Shall not remotest ages see
The lights of EIGHTEEN HUNDRED THREE?
Shall Jefferson, grown old and spleeny,
In dudgeon quit his "*red Arena,*"
From fame "*occluded,*" dark and dreary,
Plunge headlong into death's "*vast prairie*"?
Shall Johnny Randolph cease to bloom?
Shall Paine *reel* silent to the tomb?
Shall Gallatin unheeded stray
Adown Time's dark and cheerless way,
Without one friendly tongue to tell,
Who "*stopp'd of government de veel*"?
Or Farmer Lincoln drag his name,
Through "*oppugnation*" up to fame?
Shall nought of Granger be rehears'd,
But, that the *bag of wind* is burst?
Shall Fate's "*Recorder*" only say—
"*Cheetham and Dun were hang'd to day*"?—
Justice forbid—Their names shall ring,
Till the last Poets cease to sing;
And though old Homer's spirit's fled,
Though Virgil's number'd with the dead;
Some genius, fir'd for humbler lays,
Shall register their claim to praise,
To unborn Homers transmit down,
Their *memoranda* of renown.

But, as the weather grows severe,
We'll just survey the country here,

Pick up the patriots few that stray,
And drag their merits into day,
Mark how the *Rights of Man* are further'd,
Then spend the winter at the Southward.

And here, in erring reason's spite,
'Mid storms of truth, and floods of light,
Unmov'd by threats, unaw'd by fears,
CONNECTICUT her front uprears.
On Democratic frontiers plac'd,
By spirits base and foul disgrac'd,
Annoy'd with Jacobinic engines,
And doom'd to Governmental vengeance,
Strait on her course she firmly steers,
Nor gibes, nor tacks, nor scuds, nor veers,
Not the whole force they all can yield,
Can drive her vet'rans from the field.
The same pure, patriotic fires,
Which warm'd the bosoms of their Sires,
That generous, that effulgent flame,
Which glow'd in Winthrop's deathless name,
Unsullied through their bosoms runs,
Inspires and animates their sons.

Last spring, the atmosphere was hazy,
The tempest lower'd, the path was mazy;
All hearts prognosticated evil,
And all seem'd running to the devil.
But luckily, the means were taken,
And just in time to save our bacon,

The Democrats for conquest striving,
The trumpet sounded for Thanksgiving.
By Libertines and Deacons sign'd,
The summons call'd on deaf and blind,
On knaves and blockheads, old and young,
Of every colour, craft, and tongue,
Through mud and mire, *in March* to meet,
And draggle round New-Haven street,
Recount each Democratic duty,
Show General Hart in all his beauty,
" *Lead up*" their sweethearts and their spouses,
To dalliance sweet in " *private houses,*"
Get drunk by day—and snug by night,
Chaunt forth " Moll Carey"*—" *Tune Delight,*
When lo!—to circumvent the matter,
Poor Abra'm dropp'd his circ'lar letter!!!
Like wildfire round the story flew,
And the whole plot disclos'd to view.
And though Tim Dexter's hopeful son,
Kept sentry o'er the morning gun,
And as the " ragged throng" pass'd by,
Shot " *Memorandums*" through the sky;
Though Judd and Kirby came prepar'd,
To reap *the Democrat's reward,*
Though General Hart, when all was still,
Bravely retir'd to make his will,

* A song written for the occasion of the Democratic Thanksgiving at New-Haven.

Though Paine got drunk, and was not there,
And David Austin made a pray'r,
And rang'd by Powell, grave and sage,
Twelve of the sleekest grac'd a stage—
Yet all in vain——The farce was o'er,
And Democrats give thanks no more;
Resolv'd henceforward to grow wise,
And trust their cause to fraud and lies,
Abandon every childish caper,
And rest their hopes on Babcock's paper.

   Poor souls—before this stubborn State,
To Democrats resigns its fate,
Your growth of timber must be shifted,
Your character from filth be lifted.
Will Freemen virtuous, just, and brave,
Of tempers firm, and manners grave,
To Freedom born, by Plenty fed,
By TRUMBULL and by ELLSWORTH led,
Bow down their necks to Slavery's bands,
And trust themselves in Kirby's hands?
Shall Abraham Bishop guard their morals?
And Wolcott settle all their quarrels?
But let us leave New-Haven racket,
And go to New-York in the packet;
Where we shall find the Clinton band,
Of morals pure, of manners bland,
With swords, and staves, and whip and spur,
Rush forth to war with *Col. Burr.*

So have I seen, with fiery rage,
A Hawk and Snake, in fight engage,
For such a combat nothing loth,
Nor'd care if Satan had them both.

  Poor Pennsylvania sweats amain,
Beneath the rod of Tom M'Kean.
This rich, this proud, degraded state,
Is hastening onward to its fate.
Here foreign rogues of every tongue,
Like Pharaoh's frogs by thousands throng;
On posts of honour fix their eyes,
O'erpower the good by fraud and lies,
Drive Justice from her sacred seat,
Tread Law and Order under feet;
By falsehood fire the rabble rude,
And loose the dogs of war and blood.
No kingdom underneath the sun,
No state, nor nation but our own,
E'er spread such tempting lures, or gave
Such rich rewards to every knave.

  And yet, each grumbling tory dares
Arraign the "*gestion of affairs*"—
When were they manag'd half so well,
In point of prudence, or of skill?
Our President, as each one knows, is
As strong as Sampson, meek as Moses,
As Solon good, as chaste as ice,
(Black Sal is all a heap of lies)

Not quite so brave as old Suwarrow,
But loaded with the people's sorrow;
And spite of all old Jones can say,
Knows how to borrow, *and to pay.*
Beneath his kind and fostering hand,
What blessings overwhelm the land.
Our debt is paid with so much vigour,
'Tis grown about a quarter bigger;
Sal'ries which were so high before,
Have hoisted up a quarter more;
The taxes too are done away,
And Labour's mouth has nought to pay;
Loaf sugar free from duty passes,
And Jersey people drink molasses.
What stupid Fed'ralist shall dare,
Wolcott with Gallatin compare?
Roll'd on his tongue, our language mends,
He holds finance at finger's ends;
And while his former Whiskey neighbours,
Reap the rich harvest of his labours,
Pour down dog-cheap th' enlivening rill,
All hot, and luscious from the still;
Yet still our patriot merchants pay,
And save our Treasury from decay.
This is the true Virginia plan,
Built on *the equal rights of man*—
" *That Commerce should the burthens bear,*
" *And Labour's mouth be free as air*"—

For where does Commerce spread her sails,
Where brave the storms, or court the gales?
Along Virginia's sullen shore,
Scarce floats a barque, or strikes an oar,
No hardy seaman mounts the mast,
Nor whistles at th' approaching blast.
But Eastward turn the searching eye—
What fairy scenes before us lie?—
There Commerce spreads unnumber'd sails,
There braves the storms, and courts the gales,
Vast fleets old Ocean's bosom ride,
And wealth flows in with every tide.
Hence springs that firm resistless pow'r,
Which meets unmov'd the threat'ning hour,
That spirit which no fears controul,
That fire which warms the freeborn soul.
 Nor stands the Genevese alone—
A chosen club surround the throne.
The Farmer can his goose-quill draw,
On politics as well as law;
Dearborne performs his duty well,
Except when call'd upon to spell;
And when depriv'd of every shift
Paine takes a sling, and gives a lift.
For though, when sober, Tom is dull,
Stupid, and filthy as a gull,
Yet give him brandy, and the elf,
Will talk all night *about himself;*

And whilst his patron stands amaz'd,
Waiting to hear himself be-prais'd,
The drunken sot does nought but cry,
And sing, and write, of Mr. I.
Such skill have Granger's projects shew'd,
O'er those which Habersham pursued,
So nicely does his compass traverse,
In shifting men for "*faithful service*,"
That ere two years have run their race,
By travelling *nights* as well as days,
The Income's risen through *Hobbles* dirty,
From *Eighty Thousand, down to Thirty*.
Our councils too are well conducted,
Resolves well drawn, laws well constructed;
Claibornes and Cloptons take the lead,
And Triggs, and Nincompoops succeed,
Dawson presides in high debate,
And Randolph's Minister of State.
What though sometimes the club gets puzzled,
By Griswold's Fed'ral cunning muzzled,
And the affrighted, speechless throng,
Close first the doors, and then the tongue,
Though Nancy Dawson lisps surmises,
And little David's choler rises,
And CENTUM VIR* on knees devout,
Begs Septon's aid to bear them out,

* Centum Vir.—Sometime since, that prodigy of learning, Dr. Mitchill, wrote a letter, in Latin, to the king of Naples, beg-

Yet Dana brings them to a stand,
And bids their silent jaws expand,
The doors unclose, their hinges creak,
And the dumb Legislature speak.
Our philosophic Chief prepares
" Essays tow'rds statements of affairs ;"
Wakes once a year from fancy's dreams,
And hatches a whole brood of schemes—
Behold ! secure from leaks, and worms,
From tides, from shipwreck, and from storms,
From privateers, and dashing waves,
Rocks, whirlpools, and old Ocean's caves,
Safe in a hovel, high and dry,
Flat on their sides our ships shall lie.
No corsair there shall dare intrude,
No pirate show his visage rude,
Not e'en Goose-creek† shall dare to lave,
Their Lordly timbers with its wave.

ging his Majesty to make him a present of a book. This letter the Doctor subscribed with his name, and added the words, ' CENTUM VIR." One of his friends asked him the meaning of the title; the Doctor said it meant, that he was a member of Congress. This was before the late census, when the House of Representatives consisted of 105 members. How the Doctor should sign himself now there are more than 130, must be settled by himself.

† Goose-creek was the vulgar name of the stream, which in the scheme for a Dry-Dock, was exalted by the President into the TIBER.

Thus arm'd, what pow'r shall dare invade
Our harbours, or annoy our trade?
While proud Potowmac rolls her flood
Unruffled o'er her native mud,
The Dry-Dock cannon's awful roar,
Shall guard Penobscot's distant shore.
Nay, ships henceforth, shall plough the strand,
And ride secure from land to land;
While arm'd *en flute*, shall Granger's mail,
On turnpike roads hoist every sail,
Through wilds unknown, undaunted steer,
Give every Indian tribe a cheer,
Pass Mississippi's new toll-bridge,
And anchor on the Salt mount's ridge.
How slow the human mind proceeds
In that bright path, where Science leads!
How sluggishly up Reason's steeps,
Dull Common Sense phlegmatic creeps!
Eustis this useful plan derided,
(Great men will sometimes be divided)
E'en that great reasoner, Friar Bacon,
Said—" No Sir,"—when the vote was taken.
Thus was this brilliant theory lost,
And thus philosophy was crost—
Dry-Docks are jeer'd at as a whim,
And vessels now must sink or swim,
Men risk their necks 'mongst rocks and caves,
And now and then find wat'ry graves.

But let us trace this mighty mind,
Form'd to amaze, and bless mankind—
See him commence Land-Speculator,
And buy up half the realm of nature,
Towns, cities, Indians, Spaniards, '*prairies*,'
Salt-petre vats, and buff'loe dairies,
Harvests all ripen'd for the sickle,
And salt enough the world to pickle—
Salt, which in rain and shine has stood,
From Adam's fall through Noah's flood,
And yet enough remains behind,
To cure the pork of all mankind.
Here too we find a soil so deep,
Wool grows on stumps as well as sheep;
And shrubs and trees, if e'er they grew,
Have lost their foothold, and slump'd through;
And men dare not, so soft's the road,
Without their snow-shoes walk abroad.
At random here the Mammoth browses,
As large as common meeting-houses;
Snakes reach the size of saw-mill logs,
And rats and mice as large as dogs;
Musquetoes weigh as much as crows
And man to such a giant grows,
So long, so wide, that at a meal,
He'll eat a loin of Mammoth veal.
 O'er this Canaan blest presides
The man, who all our interests guides—

Judge, Sheriff, President, and King,
Lawyer, Bum-Bailiff, every thing.
Beneath his philosophic sway,
A pure republic springs to day,
Free from Aristocratic pests,—
Soldiers, and Citizens, and Priests—
Here all pursue their strong desires,
Sires know no sons, and sons no sires,
Wives follow nature's high behest,
Try half a dozen, and choose the best,
And boys and girls, in wanton droves,
Indulge in unforbidden loves.

Nor only in this distant sky,
Does light break in upon the eye;
The SPIRIT dire of *Reformation*,
Has rear'd her standard in the Nation—
What, though "*the Lilliputian ties,*"
Snap one by one before their eyes,
What, though the public wealth is squander'd,
The great and good by villains slander'd,
The hoary patriot robb'd of bread,
Pale Justice from the nation fled,
Though foreign outlaws blast our name,
Though vengance hunts our native fame,
Base falsehoods sneak, and slanders crawl,
And shakes the Union to its fall—
Still, still unmov'd the people stand,
And see fell Ruin mark the land—

See Freedom's Edifice decay,
Its lofty pillars torn away,
By Gothic hands its splendours soil'd,
Its dome defac'd, its turrets spoil'd.
 The " *Sovereign People*" who compose?
The friends of freedom, or its foes?
Those are they who in dread array,
Dauntless met Britain in the affray—
Who (when War's ensigns, wide unfurl'd,
Spread tumult through the western world)
Seiz'd the rude musket, sword, and shield,
And throng'd by thousands to the field;
That little remnant which remains
From Bunker's heights, and York-**Town's plains**—
A glorious few, whose forms still bear,
The fearless front, the victor's scar—
Bright trophies in hard conflict won,
When led by Fame's IMMORTAL SON?
Or are the owners of the soil,
Proud of the spot on which they toil,
Attach'd by habit, and by birth,
To freedom, government, and worth—
Are these the men whose voice is heard,
Whose wishes, or whose will rever'd?
Far other powers these States obey,
A different sovereign holds the sway—
A foreign, outcast, needy brood,
Blighted with crimes, and ripe for blood—

Those renegado gallows trains,
Which Ireland from her dungeons drains,
And pours, with an unceasing hand,
Like Egypt's plagues upon our land.
Who steal our letters, rob our stores,
Who lurk with firebrands round our doors,
Who plunder records of the State,
The virtuous blast, belie the great?
A foreign, outcast, needy brood,
Blighted with crimes, and ripe for blood.
These are the miserable tools,
By which the proud Virginia rules.
In myriads, lo! the miscreants come,
In search of freedom, and of rum,
Scarce do their footsteps reach the strand,
Scarce do they press the fated land,
Ere their whole souls with freedom burn,
And convicts into patriots turn:
On posts their greedy optics fix,
Fir'd with the spark of *Seventy-six*,
Call Adams, Jay, and Ellsworth tories,
Rob Washington of all his glories,
Claim for their own our Revolution,
And fondly brood the Constitution.

 Where are New-England's hardy sons?
How slow their ancient spirit runs?
Can they stand cold and tamely by,
And see in dust their country lie?

To Independence they were bred,
For Freedom oft they fought, and bled.
And shall the prize be basely lost,
Which so much blood, and treasure cost?
Forbid it shame—Then ere too late,
Ward off the dark impending fate.
That Party which now holds the helm,
Will ruin, or will rule the realm.
Go backward, all their footsteps trace,
Mark every winding of their race,
Their measures to one purpose tend,
All to one favourite object bend.
Arm'd at all points, they scour the field—
Our Union ties already yield,
Our Constitution's strength is gone,
Its pride, its Justice overthrown.
Lo! now the servile Band engage,
With party fire, and madd'ning rage,
To force our freeborn souls t' obey,
And bow beneath a despot's sway,
To fix their Man, through noise and strife,
Our KING or PRESIDENT FOR LIFE!
In one vast vortex sink the fates
And freedom of the Northern States,
Place in Virginia's hands the reins,
And bind our Sovereignty in chains.
What palsy numbs the Public hand!
What madness overspreads the land!

To Gallia turn the searching eye,
See millions there in bondage lie,
In adamantine fetters bound,
Oppress'd, and trodden to the ground.
See Switzerland in ruin spread,
See Holland number'd with the dead,
Half Europe kiss the iron rod,
And tremble at a Ruffian's nod.
Here let us pore on Freedom's tomb,
Here read our own approaching doom—
That doom from Anarchy which springs,
More dreadful than the worst of kings—
And from example, learn to save
The birthright which our FATHERS gave—
LAWS equal, mild, and just, and pure,
FREEDOM from anarchy secure,
FIRESIDES where heavenly bliss has flow'd,
And ALTARS consecrate to GOD.

PROSPECT OF HAPPINESS
FOR THE JEWS.

PROSPECT OF HAPPINESS FOR THE JEWS.

THE following extracts are from a Poem entitled The Prospect of Happiness for the Jews, which was written in the summer of 1791 by the authors of the Echo and printed in the American Mercury. It was a mere *Jeu d'Esprit*, suggested by an event which at that time excited some attention, and would probably never have been rescued from the dust of a newspaper file, had not the late imperial decree of Napoleon for convoking a delegation of that dispersed people, with the professed intention of re-establishing them in their ancient country, have recalled it to mind and convinced the authors that their effusions, like the leaves of the sybil were pregnant with fate, and may equal in inspiration the prophecies of those celebrated characters, Christopher Love, Richard Brothers, or David Austin.

REJOICE! ye wanderers of the earth, rejoice!
Ye Hebrew tribes exalt your grateful voice!
Where'er dispers'd o'er earth's wide realms ye stray!
From Lapland's frozen night, to Congo's torrid day!
Whatever shape by fortune doom'd to wear,
The humble pedlar, or rich usurer,
Attend the call, the joyous summons wait,
And hail the omen of your bright'ning fate!
Lo! the glad day by sacred promise given
Glows from afar, and lights the western heav'n,
The glorious day, to Amos' raptur'd son
By heav'n's own hand in clearest vision shown;

When by his native streams the Seer survey'd
Fate's mystic volume to his view display'd,
And thus o'er wond'ring Judah pour'd along
His strains prophetic in sublimest song.
  Ye chosen few of Jacob's favour'd race,
Bright heirs of fame, and heav'n's peculiar grace!
For you the fates superior bliss design,
And beams of glory shed o'er David's line.
I see pourtray'd 'mid shades of mystic night
Your future fame in characters of light.
Though, for long years, the earth condemn'd to roam,
Your name reproachful to the world become,
A hissing vile, a bye-word of disgrace,
Fair nature's blot, and stain of human race;
Yet when revolving time shall wake to birth
New scenes and empires o'er the spacious earth,
Your lot shall change, the world your sway confess,
And gladd'ning nations hail the reign of peace.
Then shall the lion leave the gloomy wood,
His rage forgot, and quell'd his thirst of blood,
O'er flowery meads with sportive heifers stray,
And join the lambkin in his wanton play;
Beneath one shade the wolf and kid shall rest,
One tree contain the dove's and falcon's nest;
The doe in friendship with the leopard graze,
And on on his spotted beauties fearless gaze;
To marriage bed the cat and dog shall move,
And former hatred lose in joys of love.

The little child with fearless hand shall grasp
The fire-ey'd cockatrice and frigid asp;
The mink and musquash social compacts make,
And one firm tie unite the frog and snake,*
The fox and goose hymeneal transports share,
And fraud and folly mark the future heir;
The painted tribes in fields of horror bred,
By vengeance prompted and by murder led,

* It is pleasing, as it affords a striking proof of the near advent of the Millennium, to remark the completion of this part of the prediction, in the late important discovery of the wonderful friendship subsisting between the snake and horned frog, who with the celebrated Prairie Dog are joint tenants of the same habitation; and there is little cause to doubt that all the other animals mentioned are in a state of rapid social progression. With respect to the savages, we are enabled to affirm from high authority that the prophecy respecting them is accomplished in spirit, if not in " very deed." That most *enlightened* statesman, Governor Wright, of Maryland in his late letter to the Legislature of that State, notifying his acceptance of that office, observes, that he has most cordially cooperated with the present virtuous administration in the measures which it has pursued; and among other things recapitulated, in the attention that has been paid to our native brethren the savage tribes, in instructing them in agriculture, and manufactures, and in inducing them "to convert their scalping knives into pruning hooks, and their tomahawks into implements of husbandry, and both by precept and example teaching them to prefer the pacific olive to the bloody laurel." He who cannot perceive in all these concurring circumstances the arrival of the long expected age of gold, must surely have his intellectual vision obscured with an impenetrable film.

Grown mild, shall own the gentle arts of peace,
Bid slaughter stay its hand and discord cease,
And, long disus'd, their rusty tomahawks
Shall beat and polish into knives and forks,
Whilst erst that steel with brains of chieftains gor'd
Shall carve the sirloin at the festal board.
———————————Lo! from revolving years
The first glad day-spring of that morn appears,
The clouds disperse so long o'er Israel spread,
And bright Success uplifts her radiant head:
Led by the hand of *Gain* the Goddess comes,
Sublime she moves, and waves her golden plumes,
With potent voice, in words transporting cries,
From your low state ye heirs of promise rise;
No longer doom'd o'er various realms to roam,
No clime your country and no soil your home,
No longer doom'd the general hate to meet,
Be scorn'd by Gentiles, and compell'd to cheat:
Be deem'd the refuse of the world no more,
By laws unguarded and oppress'd by power,
Outcasts from man, of every virtue foes,
By heav'n in mercy, not from merit chose.—
Far diff'rent scenes ensuing days unfold,
A life of rapture and an age of gold:
No more contemn'd your wealthy sons shall rise
The first of men, the favour'd of the skies.

* * * * * * * * * *

All hail! illum'd with glory's splendid ray,
Ye harbingers of joy's approaching day!
In you the bliss, by ancient Seers foretold,
Those various scenes of promis'd good unfold;
In you th' extremes of warring nature join'd
Form a sweet solace for the social mind.

* * * * * * * * * *

* * * * * * * * * *

And lo! from op'ning skies, with look serene,
Mild Peace descends, and glads the bright'ning scene,
Bliss smiles on all, the Hours in transport move,
And ev'ry Hebrew heart is tun'd to joy and love.
   Rejoice! ye wand'rers of the earth, rejoice!
Ye tribes of Israel raise your grateful voice!
Where'er dispers'd o'er earth's wide realms ye stray,
From Lapland's frozen night, to Congo's torrid day.

SUPPLEMENTARY NOTES.

Begging with clouted shoes from door to door.—Page 7.

THE reputed author of the text to this Echo, as well as the following, both under the signature of S. P. Marten, is no less a personage than the son-in-law of the late Tim. Dexter of Newburyport, of speculating memory, the author of Political Delusion, alias the present Collector for the District of New-Haven. The above lines allude to a singular circumstance in the life of this celebrated character. Not long after the re-establishment of peace between Great-Britain and America Mr. B——p, as is stated, smitten with a strong desire to see foreign lands and foreign fashions secretly quitted his paternal roof with a small sum of money, and took passage on board of a ship bound to a port in Europe, with a view to visit the principal places in that part of the world. On his arrival he resolved to make the grand tour on foot, which he accordingly performed, having traversed great part of France and Italy in that manner, subsisting principally on the charitable donations of the hospitable. On his return to his native place, he presented the shoes in which he had performed this wonderful journey, as having had the honour of pressing classic ground, to the late President of Yale College, Dr. Stiles, a gentleman noted for his curiosity and love of antiquity; they were received and deposited with care in the College Museum. But alas! such was the want of taste, such the barbarism of one of the Tutors of that seminary, that after having occupied for some time this post of honour, to the no small admiration of the curious, they were by him rudely and without any regard to their classic dignity tossed out of the window, to " rot unheeded mid vulgar dust."

Skunks, toads, and rattle snakes and " Prairie Dogs."—Page 8.

THIS wonderful quadruped, a non-descript, as it would seem, is supposed by certain unbelievers to be nothing more than a ground hog, or woodchuck; indeed some who pretend to have seen it affirm that it is the same, with merely a variation in size, being somewhat smaller, and that it perfectly resembles that animal both in form and colour, in its food and habits. But without attempting to decide this question, it may be proper to notice one very singular trait of character which it is said to possess and which has nothing in common with the woodchuck, or any other animal that we are acquainted with, which is, that instead of consorting with one or more of its own species, it has a strange predilection for the society of a certain snake and frog, which, by the way, is an instance of a still more singular association. These three co-partners inhabit the same burrow, they give each other warning on the approach of danger, and appear to be inseparable friends. As for some years it has been our opinion that the Millennium had actually commenced, we entertain not the smallest doubt of the authenticity of this account; and although the learned Mr. Dobbs, in his Letters on the Prophecies, seems to be fully persuaded that the Millennium is to commence in Ireland, we think that he is evidently mistaken, and that instead of the shores of the Shannon or the Liffy, those of the Missouri are destined to witness the commencement of this blissful era. Many very learned and weighty reasons might be adduced in support of this theory; but this single fact of the snake and the frog living in such harmony together, is amply sufficient, and worth more than volumes of the most ingenious reasonings. Impressed with this conviction, we cannot therefore sufficiently applaud the prescience of our wise administration in obtaining possession, at any price, of a country marked with so auspicious a destiny.

You'll find it, Sirs, among the laws sky blue.—Page 53.

BLUE-LAWS, an appellation given to the Statutes of the Colony of New-Haven, prior to its union with that of Connecticut; a code of absurd and rigourous laws framed in the true spirit of puritanic fanaticism. Were we disposed to swell this volume with notes, we could select a number of these singular ordinances, and instances of severe and oppressive penalties having been incurred on the slightest and most whimsical occasions. The process against the witches at Salem, and the persecution of the quakers, would likewise furnish an ample store of materials; but for this we shall refer the reader to the History of Connecticut, Mather's Magnalia, and other records of those times.

Note to Page 54.

The following is extracted from Peters's History of Connecticut.

" THE town of Windham is situated on Willimantic river. Strangers are very much terrified at the hideous noise made on summer evenings by the number of frogs, in the brooks and ponds. There are about thirty different voices among them, some of which resemble the bellowing of a bull. Persons accustomed to such serenades are not disturbed by them; but one night in July 1758, the frogs of an artificial pond, three miles square, and about five from Windham, finding the water dried up, left the place in a body, and marched, or rather hopped, towards Willimantic river. They were under the necessity of taking the road, and going through the town, which they entered about midnight. The bull-frogs were the leaders, and the pipers followed without number. They filled a road forty yards wide for four miles in length, and were for several hours passing through the town unusually clamourous. The inhabitants were equally perplexed and frightened: some expected to find an army of French and Indians; others feared an earthquake and dissolution of nature. The consternation was universal. Old and young, male and female, fled naked from their beds, with worse shriekings than those of the frogs. The event was fatal to several women. The men, after a flight of half a mile, in which they met with many broken shins, finding no enemies in pursuit of them, made a halt, and summoned resolution enough to venture back to their wives and children: when they distinctly heard from the enemy's camp these words, *Wight, Elderkin, Dyer, Tete.* This last they thought meant treaty; and plucking up courage, they sent a triumvirate to capitulate with the supposed French and Indians. These three men approached in their shirts, and begged to speak with the general; but it being dark, and no answer given, they were sorely agitated for some time betwixt hope and fear; at length, however, they discovered that the dreaded inimical army, was an army of thirsty frogs going to the river for a little water."

With all due respect for the talents of the reverend author, we cannot but think that his account of this incident displays much less felicity of description than usually marks his writings.—Perhaps the affinity of the story to truth, by restraining the flights of his fancy, may have rendered his description in this part less vivid, than while his inventive genius, unshackled by restraint, was free to expatiate in the flowery regions of fiction. We must however except from this remark the passage relative to the numbers of the croaking army, and the space of ground occupied by them as being in the author's best manner. But he has strangely omitted a ludicrous circumstance, perfectly familiar to the inhabitants of Connecticut. As these formidable enemies approached, one division of them repeatedly and vociferously demanded " Col. Dyer," while another as loudly and imperiously required " Elderkin too ;" of course, as may well be imagined, these gentlemen, two distinguished law characters, were particularly alarmed and thrown into the greatest consternation.

Good Master Greenleaf thou whose press still teems.—Page 103

AS a specimen of the poem written on occasion of citizen Genet's projected journey through the Eastern States, the following descriptive lines are taken, which are from the pen of a gentleman of refined literary taste, who, had he cultivated his talents for poetry, would have held a distinguished rank among the favourites of the Muse.

" These heroes when the Plenipo
  Advanc'd with all his train ;
Went quickly forth their zeal to show,
  And his applause obtain:

Approaching first, with cap in hand,
  In courtly guise so clever,
Blithe Toby, as before he'd plann'd,
  Cried, " Genet live forever !"

But while Genet with pleasure heard
  Bold Toby's salutation,
A spectre strange to him appear'd,
  Which caus'd much speculation.

Straight from his steed he seem'd to rise
  So stiff, so tall and slim,
A wig's snug border touch'd his eyes,
  And stretch'd was ev'ry limb.

His right hand, with majestic grace,
  A cane enormous grasp'd,
With stiff-topp'd glove, in strict embrace,
  His left the bridle clasp'd.

Beneath the shadow of his hat
A visage pale and thin,
Which long had bade adieu to fat,
Appear'd with horrid grin.

" *what time from Cambria's strand
Adventurous Madoc sought this unknown land.*"—Page 171.

SINCE printing the above, we have fortunately met with a publication relative to the Welch Indians, which we esteem of the greatest importance to elucidate the subject. We shall make no apology for inserting it at length, convinced that the public will feel equally interested with ourselves in this very important question.

To the Editor of the Kentucky Palladium.

Frankfort, 12th December, 1804.

Sir,

No circumstance relating to the history of the western country, probably, has excited, at different times, more general attention and anxious curiosity, than the opinion that a nation of white men, speaking the Welch language, reside high up the Missouri. By some the idea is treated as nothing but the suggestion of bold imposture and easy credulity :—whilst others regard it as a fact fully authenticated by Indian testimony and the report of various travellers worthy of credit. The fact is accounted for, they say, by recurring to a passage in the history of Great-Britain, which relates that several years before the discovery of America by Christopher Columbus, a certain Welch prince embarked with a large party of emigrants—that after some time a vessel or two came back with the account that they had discovered a country far to the westward, and that they set sail again with a fresh reinforcement and never returned any more. The country which these adventurers discovered, it has been supposed, was the continent of North-America, and it has been conjectured, that they landed on this continent some where in the gulph of Mexico, and from thence proceeded northwards till they got out of the reach of the hostile natives, and seated themselves in the upper country of Missouri. Many accounts accordingly have been published within the last thirty years of persons who in consequence either of accident or the ardour of curiosity have made themselves acquainted with a nation of men on the Missouri, possessing the complexion of Europeans, and the language of Welchmen. Could the fact be well established, it would afford, perhaps, the most satisfactory solution of the difficulty occasioned by a view of the various ancient fortifications with which the Ohio country abounds, of any that has ever been offered. Those fortifications were never made by the Indians. The Indian art of war presents nothing of the kind. The probability too is that the persons who constructed them were *at that time* acquainted with the use of iron; the situation of those fortifications, which are uniformly in the most fertile land of the country, indicates that those who made them, were an agricultural people, and the remarkable care and skill with which they were executed, afford traits of the genius of a people, who relied more on their military skill than on their numbers. The growth of the trees upon them, is very compatible with the idea that it is not more than 300 years ago that they were abandoned.

These hints, however, are thrown out rather to excite inquiry, than by way of advancing any decided opinion on the subject. Having never met with any of the persons who had seen these white Americans, nor even received their testimony near the source, I have always entertained considerable doubts about the fact. Last evening however, Mr. John Childs, of Jessamine county, a gentleman with whom I have been long acquainted, and who is well known to be a man of veracity, communicated a relation to me, which at all events, appears to merit serious attention. After he had related it in conversation, I requested him to repeat it, and committed it to writing. It has certainly some internal marks of authenticity. The country which is described was altogether unknown in Virginia, when the relation was given, and was probably very little known to the Shawanese Indians; yet the account of it agrees very remarkably with later discoveries. On the other hand, the story of the large animal, though by no means incredible, has something of the air of fable; and it does not satisfactorily appear how the long period which the party were absent was spent—though Indians are however, so much accustomed to loiter away their time, that many weeks and even months, may probably have been spent in indolent repose.

Without detaining you any more with preliminary remarks, I will proceed to the narration, as I received it from Mr. Childs.

Maurice Griffith, a native of Wales, which country he left when he was about 16 years of age, was taken prisoner by a party of Shawanese Indians, about 40 years ago, near Vosse's fort, on the head of Roanoke river, in Virginia, and carried to the Shawanese nation. Having staid there about two years and a half, he found that five young men of the tribe, had a desire of attempting to explore the sources of the Missouri. He prevailed upon them to admit him as one of the party. They set out with six good rifles, and with six pounds of powder a piece, of which they were of course very careful. On reaching the mouth of the Missouri they were struck with the extraordinary appearance occasioned by the intermixture of the Missouri, and the clear, transparent stream of the Mississippi. They staid two or three days amusing themselves with the view of this novel sight: they then determined on the course which they should pursue, which happened to be so nearly in the course of the river, that they frequently came within sight of it as they proceeded on their journey. After travelling about thirty days through pretty farming wood land, they came into fine open *prairies*, on which nothing grew but long, luxuriant grass. There was a succession of these, varying in size, some being eight or ten miles across, but one of them so long, that it occupied three days to travel through it. In passing through this large *prairie* they were much distressed for water and provisions, for they seldom saw either beast or bird, and though there was an abundance of salt springs, fresh water was very scarce. In one of these *prairies*, the salt springs ran into small ponds, in which, as the weather was hot, the water had sunk and left the edges of the ponds so covered with salt, that they fully supplied themselves with that article, and might easily have collected bushels of it. As they were travelling through the *prairies*, they had likewise the good fortune to kill an animal which was nine or ten feet high, and of a bulk proportioned to its height. They had seen two of the same species before, and they saw four of them afterwards. They were swift footed, and they had neither tusks nor horns. After having passed through the long *prairie*, they made it a rule never to enter on one which they could not see across, till they had supplied themselves with a sufficiency of jerked venison, to last several days. After having travelled a considerable time through the *prairies*, they came to very extensive lead mines, where they smelted the ore and furnished themselves with what lead they wanted. They afterwards came to two copper mines, one of which was three miles through, and in several places they met with rocks of copper ore as large as houses.

When about fifteen days journey from the second copper mine, they came in sight of white mountains, which though it was in the heat of summer, appeared to them to be covered with snow. The sight naturally excited considerable astonishment, but on their approaching the mountains, they discovered, that instead of snow, they were covered with immense bodies of white sand. They had, in the mean time, passed through about ten nations of Indians, from whom they received very friendly treatment. It was the practice of the party to exercise the office of spokesman in rotation; and when the language of any nation through which they passed was unknown to them, it was the duty of the spokesman, a duty in which the others never interfered, to convey their meaning by appropriate signs.

The labour of travelling through the deep sands of the mountains, was excessive, but at length they relieved themselves of this difficulty by following the course of a shallow river, the bottom of which being level, they made their way to the top of the mountains, with tolerable convenience.

After passing the mountains they entered a fine fertile tract of land, which having travelled through for several days, they accidently met with three white men in the Indian dress. Griffith immediately understood their language, as it was pure Welsh, though they occasionally made use of a few words with which he was not acquainted. However, as it happened to be the turn of one of his Shawanese companions to act as spokesman, or interpreter. he preserved a profound silence, and never gave them any intimation that he understood the language of their new companions.

After proceeding with them four or five days journey, they came to the village of these white men, where they found that the whole nation were of the same colour, having all the European complexion. The three men took them through their village for about the space of fifteen miles, when they came to the council house, at which an assembly of the king and chief men of the nation was immediately held. The council lasted three days, and as the strangers were not supposed to be acquainted with their language, they were suffered to be present at their deliberations. The great question before the council was what conduct should be observed towards the strangers.—From their fire-arms, their knives and their tomahawks, it was concluded they were a warlike people—it was conceived that they were sent to look out for a country for their nation, that if they were suffered to return, they might expect a body of powerful invaders, but that if these six men were put to death, nothing would be known of their country, and they would still enjoy their possessions in security. It was finally determined that they should be put to death. Griffith then thought it was time for him to speak. He addressed the council in the Welsh language. He informed them that they had not been sent by any nation: that as they were actuated merely by private curiosity, they had no hostile intentions: that it was their wish to trace the Missouri to its source, and that they should return to their country satisfied with the discoveries they had made, without any wish to disturb the repose of their new acquaintances. An instant astonishment glowed in the countenances not only of the council but of his Shawanese companions, who clearly saw that he was understood by the people of the country. Full confidence was at once given to his declarations: the king advanced, and gave him his hand. They abandoned the design of putting him and his companions to death, and from that moment treated them with the utmost friendship. Griffith and the Shawanese continued eight months in the nation: but were deterred from prosecuting their researches up the Missouri, by the advice of the people of the country, who informed him that they had gone a twelve months journey up the river but found it as large there as in their own country. As to the history of this people, he could learn nothing satisfactory. The only account they could give was that their forefathers had come up the river from a very distant country. They had no books, no records, no writings. They intermixed with no other people by marriage; there was not a dark skinned man in the nation. Their numbers were very considerable. There

u u

was a continued range of settlements on the river for fifty miles, and there were, within this space, three large water courses which fell into the Missouri, on the banks of each of which, likewise, they were settled. He supposed that there must be 50,000 men in the nation, capable of bearing arms. Their cloathing was skins well dressed. Their houses were made of upright posts and the bark of trees. The only implements they had to cut them with were stone tomahawks. They had no iron, their arms were bows and arrows. They had some silver, which had been hammered with stones into coarse ornaments, but it did not appear to be pure. They had neither horses, cattle, sheep, hogs, nor any domestic or tame animals. They lived by hunting. He said nothing about their religion.

Griffith and his companions had some large iron tomahawks with them. With these they cut down a tree and prepared a canoe to return home in :—but their tomahawks were so great a curiosity, and the people of the country were so eager to handle them, that their canoe was completed with very little labour. When this work was accomplished, they proposed to leave their new friends, Griffith, however, having promised to visit them again. They descended the river with considerable speed, but amidst frequent dangers from the rapidity of the current, particularly when passing through the white mountains. When they reached the Shawanese nation, they had been absent about two years and a half. Griffith supposed that when they travelled, they went at the rate of about fifteen miles a day.—He staid but a few months with the Indians after their return, as a favourable opportunity offered itself to reach his friends in Virginia. He came with a hunting party of Indians to the head waters of Coal river, which runs into New river not far above the falls.—There he left the Shawanese, and easily reached the settlements on Roanoke.—Mr. Childs knew him before he was taken prisoner, and saw him a few days after his return, when he narrated to him the preceding circumstances. Griffith was universally regarded as a steady, honest man, and a man of strict veracity. Mr. Childs has always placed the utmost confidence in his accounts of himself and his travels, and has no more doubt of the truth of his relation, than if he had seen the whole himself. Whether Griffith be still alive or not he does not know.

Whether his idea be correct or not, we shall probably have a better opportunity of judging on the return of captains Lewis and Clark—who, though they may not penetrate as far as Griffith alleged that he had done, will probably learn enough of the country to enable us to determine whether the account given by Griffith be fiction or truth.

I am, Sir, your humble servant,
HARRY TOULMIN.

Though those whom valiant Brady sent to pot.—Page 35.

SINCE the preceding notes were printed, accidentally recurring to Hole's remarks on the Arabian Nights' Entertainments, a work containing much curious research and information, we have met with a singular account of the derivation of the vulgar saying " gone to pot," which, as it may serve to amuse our readers, we have thought proper to throw into the form of a note to the above line. Mr. Hole observes that, notwithstanding its being apparently indigenous, it was imported to England from the extremity of the globe, the metropolis of Tartary : " We are told that a tailor of Samarcand, who lived near the gate which led to the burial ground, whenever a corpse was carried by, threw a little stone into an earthern pot fixed to his cupboard, to calculate the number of deaths in a certain space of time. At length the tailor himself died ; and a passenger, observing his shop to be shut up, inquired of a neighbour after him and was answered: " The tailor is *gone to pot* as well as the rest."

333

SUPPLEMENTARY

NOTES TO PAGES 127-140,

ECHO, No. XVIII

The poem, together with a Preface and the "authentic" letter by Thomson Mason, appeared in a twenty-two page pamphlet entitled *The Democratiad, A Poem in Retaliation* for the "Philadelphia Jockey Club" (Philadelphia: Thomas Bradford, 1795). The title page and Preface are given below, together with variant readings. The first number gives the page in *The Echo, with Other Poems;* the number after the colon identifies the line.

128:6   Ten lines follow. In line 8 of the following passage the word *"accidental"* carries a footnote: "Otherwise called *come-by-chances*."

I've pick'd thee out becaufe I highly prize,
Thy grandfire's memory, and thy knack at lies.
That good old man behind him left a name,
Unmatch'd in *luftre* on the rolls of fame—
A love of fcience—and a love of fun—
Witnefs our lightning-rods and many a hopeful fon,
Among thofe fons, perhaps not one remains
More worthy Franklin's *accidental* * pains,
Than thee, Ben Franklin Bache—to Faction's foul
Dear as the ftreams which thro' life's channels roll.

128:8   Read "shuts" for "lets."
128:16   Three lines follow:

No damn'd black negro e'er was clofer pent,
Nor ftrain'd new cyder harder for a vent.
'Tis true, that all the time the Senate fate,

128:18   "Indeed, I did not *once* attempt to speak."
128:19   Read "But" for "Yet."
129:12   Eight lines follow:

In short, you'll be astonish'd when you know,
How far our party first and last would go—
Old Robinson, borne down with factious care,
As *usual* † tried to help himself by prayer ;
But finding heaven had turn'd a deafen'd ear,
Nor deign'd to answer, nor appear'd to hear,
As *ne plus ultra* turn'd to Burr his course,
And gain'd relief from that more handy source,

† As a proof that this senator relies *generally* upon divine assistance, the following story is related of him. One of his brother Senators, whose political tenets differed widely from Mr. Robinson's, taxed him with having propagated a story about him which injured his character. The old man found himself in difficulty ; and knew no better way to get out than to evade the conversation. Accordingly, he told the gentleman that it had given him great pain that they should differ in sentiment——that in consequence of that pain he had often prayed to heaven, that if he was wrong, he might be led to think like the gentleman—or if the gentleman was wrong, that he might be led to think like Mr. Robinson—for he could not bear to think differently from such a sensible man, even if that man was wrong in his opinions.—

129:20   "True Democrats despite the Senate and their rules."
130:3   "From which no *common man* his 'rights' may draw."
130:5   Read "o'er these happy plains" for "spite of all our pains." Lines 5-6 precede line 3.
130:10   A note reads:

THE
DEMOCRATIAD,

A

POEM,

IN

RETALIATION,

FOR THE

"*PHILADELPHIA JOCKEY CLUB.*"

Lo ! the dire Hedge-Hog from *another* ity,
At titled Folly lets his arrows fly.

By a Gentleman of Connecticut.

PHILADELPHIA.

PUBLISHED BY THOMAS BRADFORD, PRINTER,
BOOK-SELLER & STATIONER,
No 8, SOUTH FRONT STREET.
1795.

PREFACE.

IT is clear that the title of the pamphlet called the "Philadelphia Jockey Club", is an imitation of that of an English pamphlet; but, in what respect it is applicable to the American performance must be left to the ingenious Imitator to explain. Certainly no mortal, besides himself, would ever have discovered a resemblance between the Gentlemen, Merchants and Traders of Philadelphia, and the Sportsmen at New Market. It is not a little wonderful, that this author should express such an aversion to the funding system, when, at the same time, he makes no bones of borrowing, without leave or licence, from every unhappy author that falls under his fingers. His last loan, besides its being a forced one, is of a nature diametrically opposite to those made by other poor brainless authors, who, though they, like him, make very free with the insides of books, always take special care to have an original Title; but our Jockey-Clubman has refined upon borrowing to a degree that would justify the use of a paradox in describing him; with truth may it be said, that he is an Original Imitator; the hard-hearted wretch spares nothing; he seizes on inside and outside, guts and giblets, all, from Title Page to FINIS.

PREFACE.

But, be the *Jockey-Club* an imitation of an original or an original imitation, the poem here presented to the public appeared to the editor to be an excellent counter-part to it; the *Jockey-Club* is certainly imperfect without the Democratiad.

This poem has, as *Wilkes* expressed it with respect to one of *Churchill's* Satires, the three Ps; it is Personal, Poetical, and Political. Its merits alone would, therefore, have rendered it an object of the Editor's attention; but, as one of the Jockeys, he has an additional motive in the publication of it. The very learned and candid author of the *Jockey-Club* could not, it seems, find any thing worse against him than his having published the works of *Mr. Porcupine,* while he refused to publish those of a certain literary out-law; but, if he reccollects that the Editor prints books to sell, he will at once see the reason of his refusal, and will conclude that the Editor would refuse *(even to* a second time *)* the performances of the Author of the Jockey-Club.

‡ The common principle in Reprefentative governments, *" that the majority fhall decide,"* feems to have a fingular conftruction among our democrats. In common cafes one more than half is a majority. In the cafe of eftablifhing Treaties, the Conftitution requires *two thirds*. Still thefe *patriotic* Democrats would perfuade us that we ought to obey *one third*, let *two thirds* fay what they may. It is this kind of majority that the Democrats in the United States compofe. However what they want in numbers *they fay* they have in *merit*.

130:13   Lines 13-20 replace the following:

The fubject we expect will raife a heat.
In every town were Clubs and Traitors meet.
From thence extend itfelf from fhore to fhore,
'Till Peace and Government exift no more.
For well the truths of fage Experience fhow,
That Faction's plants in towns and cities grow;
For there collect the refufe of mankind,
Prepared for treafons, and for plots defign'd,
There every traitor hides his forfeit head,
There finds protectors, and there looks for aid,
There noify demagogues their ftandards raife,
Sedition's fparks there kindle to a blaze.

131:3   Lines 3-8 replace the following:

To Bradford, Jarvis, Madifon and Giles,
Old Adams' weaknefs, and old Clinton's wiles.
But, to return, examine all this TEN,
And fee if they don't form a fet of men,
On whom their country's happinefs may reft,
Safe as a fecret in a goffip's breaft.
Firft, General Jackfon—he's a fiery blade,
Ay *nature* honeft—but *fo fo* by trade.

131:13 "While by this maxim he has acted long."
131:17 A footnote states:

* It is faid to be a fact that this doughty Republican, is defcended from the family of the Duke of Ormond.

131:19 Lines 19-22 rewrite the following:

North-Carolina counts her number, TWO,
Who each can lift the hand, and make a fhew,
Further than this, they do as they are bid,

132:2 "Patriot toast" carries this note:

‖ This was a very natural calculation. A man who had not decency fufficient to comply with an injunction of fuch a refpectable body of men as the Senate of the United States, ought to expect to be toafted by drunken Democrats.

132:3 "But, Sir, remember, tho' the sons of Rout."
132:11 Lines 11-14 replace the following:

Thy colleague is a decent fort of man,
But tinctured with the Jacobinic plan;
And thinks that every thing the Frenchmen do,
No matter what—we ought to do fo too.
Kentucky fends John Brown, a peaceful man,
A likely Chieftan of a mountain Clan.
More fit by far, with fierce maurauding force,
To fcour the Miffifippi's lengthen'd courfe,
To drive the Spaniards from their native foil *

* My readers will doubtlefs recollect that a few years ago a certain gentleman was planning an expedition down the Miffifippi, for the virtuous purpofe of driving off the Spaniards, and taking poffeffion of their country.

Feaſt on their tears and fatten on their ſpoil.
Cut Indians' throats, their huts and fields deſtroy,
And riot in the waſte of human joy;
Than to ſit down and form a fooliſh plan,
To guard the peace and happineſs of man.

132:16   Read "piercing look" for "winning aspect."
132:24   A footnote states:

> † For the remainder of this character ſee *Ariſtocracy* an epic poem, lately publiſhed.

133:3   "At length our southern brethren clearly saw."
133:5   "Accordingly they told him how to steer."
133:7   Lines 7-9 replace the following:

Told him the ſtory of the *French receit*, ‡
(A kind of Couſin to a common cheat,)
But yet, if he poſſeſs'd ſufficient ſkill,
To ſhift and tack to ſuit their various *will*,
They to reward him for his glorious race,
Would *try* to vote him in to fill John Adam's place.

> ‡ A certain great man boaſts much of the ſacrifices he made during the war. This probably alludes to one of them. It may have been the caſe that he made many more ſuch, as he proved a very wealthy man at the cloſe of the war.

133:10   Read *"harder"* for "rougher."
133:12   A footnote states:

> * It is a common fact, that perſons naturally poſſeſſed of great mental weakneſs, and yet not abſolute idiots, are exceedingly prone to miſchief.

133:14 Two lines follow:

Thefe are the virtuous, patriotic TEN,
The major part of *thirty common* men.

133:21 "But as such game don't offer every day."
133:22 Read "see" for "let."
134:1 Read "carmen" for "cartmen."
134:2 Thirty lines follow:

With joy I fee great Brokholft lead the van,
That honeft, peaceful, modeft, humble man—
A man whom every democrat adores,
Becaufe he feeds them from his fcanty ftores,
Stores never fwell'd by fpeculations vile,
But gather'd *flowly* by the hand of Toil.
O Brockholft Livingfton, thou wondrous man!
Sure Nature form'd thee on her wifeft plan!
When opportunity prefents, thy mind
Ne'er lingers Opportunity behind.
Thou'ft learn'd the art to make all objects bend,
To help thee forward to thy favourite end;
And when that end is good---for inftance, GAIN---
All means are juft which may that end attain---
I mean to cheat, or break, to encreafe thy pelf,
And now and then perchance *to ftab thyfelf*; *

* If this allufion fhall perplex any perfon, for an explanation, let him trace out a quarrel which happened fome years ago in New-York, between a certain Lawyer (now a great Democrat) and a Mr. Smith, during which the former tho't proper to fall down in the ftreet one night, and fay he was affaffinated, but in the end it was ftrongly fufpected he had wounded himfelf, in order to fave a caning, and injure the character of his antagonift.

I'd rather take the *day-light* * from his face.
Than that his potent, all-commanding hand,
Should feal deftruction to Sedition's band."

* This undoubtedly means *Gouging according to law*, or in a *Judge-like manner.*

134:19 The footnote reads:

¶ It may be neceffary for the Author to mention, that this general expreffion does not mean to include the great body of the wealthy, refpectable, and orderly inhabitants of the town of Bofton. He is no ftranger to their character, and reveres them for their firmnefs in fupport of the government of their country and their unparallelled exertions to difcomfit thofe fons of fedition and anarchy—the Jacobins, or Democrats.

135:1 Read "Ben" for "friend."
135:3 A footnote states:

* It is faid, that this great Printer, hired a conveyance to carry him thro' a part of Connecticut on *Sunday*, in order that he might outftrip the ftage, and have a chance to fell his treaties; or elfe for fear of catching Ariftocracy.

135:7 Read "tho' late he's" for "of late though."
135:10 A footnote states:

† Surely this maxim muft have often occured to the political Doctor in the courfe of his extenfive practice; at leaft one would think fo from his holding out in fome political cafes to prefcribe, even when the coffin of his patient was making.

135:17 A footnote states:

In short to run the Livingstonian round,
Where every trick of knavery is found.
Close at his heels trots cousin Peter R.!
And Maturine, a younger feebler star!
Two hopeful brothers of a hopeful breed,
Two thrifty plants of well approved seed,
Who long have tried by arts and measures base,
To lift from filth the remnant of their race----
A race so sunk, by habit so deprav'd,
So long by vice and infamy enslav'd,
So weak, so haughty, pompous, proud and mean,
Indeed so black, so shameful and obscene, †
That nought but strength omnipotent can save
Their name deep sinking in Oblivion's wave.

† As one might reasonably expect from this character, these people are *true* Democrats.

134:6 Two lines follow:

Whigs not employ'd by freedom, to withstand
The force of Britain in this desperate land---

134:12 Read "suffering" for "sinking."
134:14 Two lines follow:

But still a club to Livingstons allied ‡
By every string that ever nature tied.

‡ As a proof of the facts stated in this passage, the following story is related. A party of *these Whigs of* 1776 (which had just arrived from Ireland, assisted Mr. Peter R. Livingston at the late *town-meeting* in New-York, in burning the Treaty. Within a few days after this *patriotic* transaction, fourteen of

them were taken up, and confined in New York goal for theft and burglary. How could master Peter find out these sons of Liberty and Equality so soon, unless by the force of *Sympathy* ?

134:18 Sixty-two lines follow:

There like the vision in the sacred book,
Old Gadsden's dry bones in a whirlwind shook,
But o'er the rest chief justice Rutledge stands,
Stamps with his feet, and boxes with his hands,
And 'mid the applauses of the gather'd crowd,
Shews what a judge can do by bawling loud,
That zeal intemperate helps a desperate cause,
And Passion much adorns a *Minister of laws*.
Thou learned Judge, whose eloquence can move
Tag, Rag, and Bobtail loudly to approve,
What pirate, that may hear thee talk of war,
Would fear to stand a prisoner at *thy bar*,
Assur'd that Sympathy so strong as thine,
Would save him harmless from the hempen line ?
But let us hear, sir, what you have to say
Against the Treaty—alias, Mr. Jay.
" I tho't when Mr. Jay was sent to treat,
That Britain was *to lose* and we *to get* ;
Instead of which, it seems that Mr. Jay
Basely agrees to meet them half the way.
How foolish ! how ridiculous a plan,
To take an inch when he might had a span !
He ought at least to have made them promise well,
Even if he knew they never would fulfil,
This is the rule I practice every day,
I *often promise, but I seldom pay* ;
A truth my friends will all believe, who know
How *cheap* my bonds in daily market go. *

* What, judge, have they got below the old price of ten shillings in the pound ?

† It is ſaid, that this patriotic printer opens his mouth for Doctor Jarvis to ſpit in. That he had a principal hand in collecting the Boſton town-meeting is an undoubted fact; and might eaſily have been gueſſed, by their mode of proceeding.

135:21	Read "great goddess" for "O Faction."
135:23	Read "Now" for "Thus."
135:26	"Or soon our 'self-created club' shall fall."
135:27	Read "shall" for "will."
136:24	A footnote states: *"See Bunyan."*
137:9	"And when in wisdom IT shall choose *to say.*"
137:15	Read "While" for "When."
138:7	*"One of that sort* just now got up and said."
138:13	Read "Boobies" for "Blockheads."
138:21	"And tho' it stood unread, and unexplain'd."
139:1	Read "blockhead" for booby."
139:3	Read "sage" for "great."
139:6	Read "G******r" for "G."
139:11	Read "timid" for "cautious."
139:13	Read "No satirist" for "No parson G."
139:14	Read "And" for "Or."
139:22	Read "Prescriptive" for "Presumptive."
140:6	Read "pen" for "name," and "blot" for "dash."
140:7	"To Thomson Mason . . ."
140:8	Two lines follow:

**And then to Mr. Bache, his worthy poſt,
A ſingle dollar for his ſweat and coſt."**

140:9	The caption "SUMMING UP" precedes this line.
140:11	Lines 11-12 replace:

If Mr. Jay had bluster'd round a while,
And swore he'd have at least the British isle,
His Majesty, no doubt, with cap in hand,
To appease our wrath would give us up the land.
For now Great Britain has so aged grown,
That she has hardly strength to stand alone,
And had we only seized her by the throat,
She would have snuffled like a strangled shoat.
I'm satisfied our Envoy did not know,
What he was sent for, what he had to do;
He has not shewn a common school-boy's skill,
Or else he'd had it SHALL instead of "WILL."
How scandalous a cession! how absurd!
I'd sooner lost the Treaty, than the *Word*.
We'd better much have fought a year or two,
Than yielded up a word that was not due.
I never lik'd a Treaty, nor its end—
These " Laws Supreme" our stubborn necks may [bend;
I see no reason why they should exist,
Let laws be settled by the force of fist ;
Then unrestrain'd, our Pirates may at ease,
In countless swarms securely scour the seas,
On plunder bent, with force resistless go,
And hurl destruction upon friend and foe.
But if this Treaty should be ratified,
Snug in our ports our privateers must ride.
And spite of all Democracy can say,
Instead of *plundering*, we shall have *to pay*,
By Heaven! I'd sooner draw my trusty knife,
And take from Washington his useless life,
(Altho' I love him so, I make no doubt,
That I should cry my eye-sight almost out)
Or, in the common Carolina phrase,

Tho' Charleston mob, like lice in Egypt, swarms,
Tho' Rutledge rages, and tho' Pinkney * storms,
Tho' Bache and Mason join † to print, *and sell,*
Tho' Hydrop Blair ‡ " the treaty kick to hell,"
Tho' Thieves and Livingstons with patriot ire,
Commit the accursed paper to the fire.
Tho' Jarvis ‖ thundering from the murkey cloud,
Sheds night and terror o'er the astonish'd crowd,

* This used to be a very *virtuous* man when he was in the old Congress ; I do not know how it is with him now. " Two whores already in my chariot ride. *Biograph. Amer. Art. Pinck.*
† It is not uncommon for members of Congress from the southward to be out of cash at the end of a session ; and this was a good plan to supply the revenue.
‡ The rest of this man's name is *M'Clenachan.*
‖ " The names and character of the New-York Chamber of
" Commerce, is given to the public in this days Chronicle—
" The public will judge between them, and a Rutledge, a *Pink-*
" *ney,* a Muhlenburg, a *Livingston,* a Cooper, a Dawes, a
" *Jarvis,* a Ramsey, a Cadsden, and a host of *other* uniform pa-
" triots who were opposed to the Treaty." Boston Chronicle, Aug. 13. 1795. Yes, Mr. Adams, by the aid of *the Democratiad*, the public will be able to do it very fairly. And what do you think will be that judgment. I can tell you. That it is very fortunate that you have got one or two Lots, which may possibly save your Sodom. But, *as they are,* I very much doubt whether even Belzebub would take them, without you put them down 13 to the dozen, as Bakers do biscuit.

140:18   "And plunge them headlong where they ought to go."
140:26   A footnote states:

* Since the author finished his Response, he has seen the President's answer to the Selectmen of Boston, and he felicitates them on their marvellous *success*. For tho' the Hawk-eyed Mr. Adams has found out by reading this answer, that at the date of it, the Treaty *was not signed*, yet is to be hoped there is discernment enough among so many Selectmen, to see, that instead of the information which Mr. Adams has found, it contains a firm dignified disdain of the clamour of a rabble, even if it be composed of 1500 men, with Doctor Jarvis at their head; and that the author understands the character of GEORGE WASHINGTON; at least as well as a Boston Town-Meeting. There is now nothing left for you gentlemen, Jacobins, to do, but to attack the President, swear that he is bought by British Gold, and that you will all be damned if he is ever elected President again.

As for the Livingstons, and their Irishmen, they will have some reason to believe, that what Mr. S. Smith has stated to them as the President's answer to the New-Yorkers, *is true*, when they see the letter to the Bostonians. Otherwise they might certainly *doubt*, for the *signature* does not afford "the "best evidence the nature of the case will admit of."

349

SUPPLEMENTARY NOTES TO PAGES 219-232,

GUILLOTINA

This poem was published in a sixteen-page pamphlet as *The Guillotina, or a Democratic Dirge, A Poem* "By the Author of 'Democratiad'" (Philadelphia, 1796). Variant readings refer to that publication.

221:7   The footnote is not in the pamphlet.
222:5   "A host like this the northern dome,"
222:6   "Pour'd never o'er affrighted Rome."
222:7   Read "less" for "more."
225:16   The footnote is not in the pamphlet.
225:26   The footnote is not in the pamphlet.
226:19   Read "fat" for "stout."
226:22   Two lines follow:

Large hofts of theives, the fons of foot,
And all the Livingftons to boot.

227:2   A comma closes the line. Four lines follow:

Led on by Rutledge, fkill'd to fhun
The Bailiff and the daily dun,
But unexpert to hold the Seat,
Where HONOUR, WORTH, and JUSTICE meet.

227:3   Read "Johnny's" for "Johnny."
227:15   The footnote is not in the pamphlet.
227:18   Lines 18-20 are reproduced to show the dialect variants. Eight lines follow in the pamphlet.

THE
GUILLOTINA,
OR A
DEMOCRATIC DIRGE,
A
POEM.

By the AUTHOR of the "DEMOCRATIAD."

"For here the deadly secret's told,
"Who 'tis that fingers foreign gold;
"That " patriots" stripp'd to state of nature,
"Bear strong resemblance to the traitor;
"That each disorganizing scoffer,
"Will take a bribe if any offer.
"Come then ye democratic band,
"Who yearn to enthrall this favor'd land,
"To Edmund's dismal tomb draw near,
"And vent your lamentations here,
"In groans, as Rachel groan'd at Rama,
"*Hic simis--but--ubique fama.*"

PHILADELPHIA:
SOLD AT
THE POLITICAL BOOK-STORE,
South Front-Street,
No. 8.

He cry'd out " Brurrur lem me peak,
" You tear my body from my maw,
"Gorra dam a man all ober jaw."
In several other trifling places,
The factious dar'd to shew their faces;
Charlestown and Dracut tho't no doubt,
That they were big enough to vote
At Plymouth too, a string of boys,
About the treaty made a noise,
Headed by *master* Henry Warren,
Like crows around some new-found carrion.

228:24   Read "but" for "sed."
231:9   Read "tend" for "till."

352

SUPPLEMENTARY NOTES TO PAGES 234-259,
"THE POLITICAL GREEN-HOUSE"

"The Political Green-House, for the Year 1798," was first printed in *The Connecticut Courant*, Hartford, February 11, 1799. It was issued as a pamphlet of twenty-four pages under date of January 1st, 1799, in Hartford, printed by Hudson & Goodwin.

The following notes give the variant readings found in the pamphlet. The first number gives the page in *The Echo, with Other Poems;* the number after the colon identifies the line.

234:20   The line ends with a period.
236:8   There is no note on Peter Grubb.
236:25   The "impartial paper" is not identified.
237:1   "Don Quixotte" is not identified.
237:3   A note reads: "See the vile, seditious publications in the Middlesex Gazette, &c. last spring."
238:16   A semicolon closes the line, and these two lines follow:

Yet blended with fell caſt of guilt,
Like Cain's when Abel's blood was ſpilt.

239:26   Two lines follow:

Yet, where ſome warrior-angel ſhews,
How Heaven was purg'd of helliſh foes,

239:27   Read "thrice" for "twice."
239:28   Read "thy" for "his." Two lines follow:

Where late, and laſt from more renown,
Than glitters o'er an eaſtern crown,——

THE

Political Green-House,

FOR THE YEAR 1798.

ADDRESSED TO THE READERS OF
THE CONNECTICUT COURANT,

JANUARY 1ſt, 1799.

PUBLISHED ACCORDING TO ACT OF CONGRESS.

HARTFORD:
PRINTED BY
HUDSON & GOODWIN.

240:17 "Jefferson."
241:2 "Send Deborah's husband off to France."
241:4 A semicolon closes the line; thirty-six lines follow:

Whilſt thou, to ſmooth the ills of life,
Held ſweet communion with the wife.
  Lo ! now too diſmal forms† draw nigh,
And cloud the Jacobinic ſky,
While awful Juſtice lours around,
And Law's loud thunders rock the ground.
Each factious alien ſhrinks with dread,
And hides his hemp-devoted head ;
While Slander's foul ſeditious crew,
With gnaſhing teeth retire from view.
See yon vile Beaſt, while Freedom ſmiles,
Led by ſtern Juſtice in her toils,
Undaunted to the Judgment Seat,
Where upright freemen ſeal his fate ;
When, lo ! dejected, and forlorn,
The Lyon from his viſage torn,
He ſhews a Calf from head to tail,
And barters Congreſs for a jail.
In Boſton too, whoſe garden bears
Some plants as vile as Nature rears,
Uplifts the hideous form of Law,
And on Tom Adams lays his paw.
" Deſerted at his utmoſt need,"
By thoſe whoſe lies he long has ſpread,
Before the bar the culprit ſtands,
With not a wretch to eaſe his bands.
Poor guilty daſtard ! ſtand aſide !
Already gapes the priſon wide !
Nat Fellows, and old Thompſon,* eke,

---

† The Alien, and Sedition Law.

* The *worthy* gentlemen who finally gave bail for this contemptible tool of Faction.

Cannot redeem thy forfeit neck ;
The dungeon walls shall teach thee reason,
At least shall make thee sick of Treason.
From these dread scenes of wild affright,
Bache and Tom Greenleaf took their flight,
The Yellow Fever clos'd their date,
And sav'd two halters to the State.

244:4   The footnote is as follows:

* Doctor I. B. Scandella of Venice, who died in New-York during the prevalence of the Yellow fever this fall.

The fate of these three gentlemen, was attended with some interesting circumstances. During the Yellow Fever in Philadelphia, Doctor Cooper was seized with the distemper. He was kindly attended by a friend; who before the Doctor's recovery was taken ill. Doctor Cooper, considering himself indebted to his friend, insisted on taking care of him—a relapse was the consequence—and he fell a victim to his high sense of gratitude.

Doctor Smith had contracted an intimacy with Doctor Scandella. The latter was at New-York, waiting for the English Packet, to take passage for Europe. He there heard that a foreign lady in Philadelphia, to whose daughter he was attached, was sick of the Yellow Fever. He returned there to alleviate the distress of the family. The mother and the daughter both died. Doctor Scandella returned to New-York disconsolate; but could find no person who dared to take him as a lodger. He wrote the fact to Doctor Smith, who cheerfully invited him home; where he was immediately attacked with the distemper. Doctor Smith attended him, until he was also seized, and obliged to be removed. A friend of his, who lived with him, took care of Doctor Scandella until he expired—and then had the same melancholy task to perform for Doctor Smith. The gentlemen were all distinguished for their genius, and erudition, and had fair prospects of being extensively useful in their profession.

246:3   Lines 3-8 precede lines 1-2.
246:8   Sixty-two lines follow:

Time fails, to tell you how the Peft,
When firft he thrills may be repreft;
This then, and whence the Hydra fprings,
What aids, or blunts, his venom'd ftings,
And how from earth to make him flee,
Is left, O learned RUSH! with thee.
 Train'd in Illumination's fchool,
And hir'd by rogues to play the fool,—
His mafter Barras to reward,—
Lo now the " Hafty-pudding" Bard,
His wandering wits, and cunning call'd in,
Writes o'er " *his book*" to Parfon Baldwin.
This book, by regular gradation,
From Baldwin mounts to Thomfon Mafon;
From Mafon naturally progreffes,
And comes to light in Lyon's preffes.
What eye can trace this Wifdom's fon,—
This " Jack-at-all trades, good *at one*,"
This ever-changing, Proteus mind,—
In all his turns, thro' every wind;
From telling finners where they go to,
To fpeculations in Scioto,
From pleading law, and taxing crimes,
To ftealing Colonel Humphrey's rhymes,[*]

---

[*] In the Confpiracy of Kings, publifhed by Mr. Barlow, fince his refidence in Europe, are feveral paffages taken literally from No. 10 of American Antiquities, which were written by Col. Humphreys. As Mr. Barlow wrote a part of the fame No. it is probable he knew the fact abovementioned and therefore did not infert them *without marks of quotation, by miftake*. It is, however, a prominent trait in the Jacobinical character, to *take* what belongs to others, without leave, and without paying for it.

From morals pure, and manners plain,
To herding with Munroe and Paine,
From feeding on his country's bread,
To aping X, and Y, and Z,
From preaching Christ, to Age of Reason,
From writing psalms,† to writing treason.
  Beyond the Apalachian height,
Let poor Kentucky shew her spite,
Pass many a factious Resolution,
To *guard* the Federal Constitution,
And calculate, that foreign knaves,
Will save her sons from turning slaves.
And, 'tis at least worth Garrard's while,
When labouring thus to raise a broil,
To recollect one proposition—
A Governor can preach Sedition.
Some entertain the wise opinion,
That faction lurks in Old Dominion,
And, that the *fistula*‡ of Giles,
Is only one, of many wiles,
Which modern politicians play,
To shield their projects from the day ;

† When Mr. Barlow was about the business of correcting Watts's psalms, for the use of the churches in Connecticut, (a work executed much to the disadvantage of Watts's version) the celebrated Arnold, who has so often amused his acquaintance by his singular talent at rhyming, met Mr. Barlow, and addressed him in the following just, and prophetic lines—
  " Tis God's blest praise you've sought to alter,
  " And for your pains deserve a halter ;
  " You 've prov'd yourself a simple creature,
  " Murder'd great Watts, and ruin'd metre."
‡ A distemper among horses, called the POLL-EVIL, or as it is sometimes spelt POLE-EVIL. This disease attacks the head ; and when spelt in the former manner, means (among men) a strong propensity to obtain votes, *no matter how* ; in the latter, as strong a disposition to erect Liberty Poles.

And that mankind will quick difcern,
The Farmer, found from ftem to ftern,
Among his kindred fpirits ftand,
Hurling Rebellion o'er the land.
But let the Farmer, ere too late,
Remember Swanwick's* dreadful fate.
   Vermont a bright example fets,
To all her elder fifter States.
Her Councils fill'd with ftatefmen able,
Refolve to cleanfe the Augæan ftable,
To feize each Jacobinic Lout,
Strip off his mafque, and turn him out.
Not one of all old Mofes'† race,
Is fuffer'd to fuftain a place,
And the whole Lyon party find,
That Federal Juftice is not blind.

   * It is faid this Gentleman died of the diftemper which affects Mr. Giles.
   † Old father Robinfon's children fuffered much in the late purgation of ftate officers in Vermont.

   249:4   Ten lines follow:

'Tis but a ftep, the fhore's in view,
A half-way houfe at St. Marcou.
At St. Marcou the Frenchmen call'd,
And for admiffion loudly bawl'd,—
The tavern-keeper fhut his inn,
And begg'd *his friends* to call again;
He'd cuftomers enough that day,
Who, when they'd ate, would alfo pay.
Back fled the raggamuffin crew,
Curfing their luck at St. Marcou.

250:27 Lines 27 and 28 replace the following:

Nor longer deign with semblance fair,
Pretended friendship's mask to wear.
Too late convinc'd, in dread surprize,
Irresolution opes his eyes;

251:7 The footnote on Steigner is not in the pamphlet.

252:2 Two lines follow:

Nor life, of freedom reft, would have,
But rush'd indignant to the grave.

253:2 The final sentence in the footnote is not in the pamphlet.
253:14 Four lines follow:

While his dark enterprize unknown
Each nation dreads it for its own,
And pale suspended on its fate,
The anxious eyes of Europe wait;

254:5 Lines 5-12 replace the following:

But Mam'luke courage glows in vain,—
By Gallic swords they all were slain,
The rest were drown'd as Frenchmen say,
Besides some few that ran away.
All soil'd with ooze, with dripping beard,
His head Old Nile affrighted rear'd,
And gaz'd with anger and surprize,
On these new scenes that met his eyes,
As near his shores, defil'd with blood,
In human form these demons stood;
While Crocodiles in horror fled
Monsters more cruel and more dread.

" What!" faid he, kindling with difdain,
" Have the vile Jews come back again?
" For fure fuch fiends, fince Pharaoh's time,
" Ne'er curs'd Egyptia's fertile clime,
" When Jacob's offspring, all forlorn,
" Came down to buy a bag of corn,
" Tho' Pharaoh tho't they meant to fteal
" Inftead of buying Indian meal."

257:24 Two lines follow:

And e'en that laft refource deny'd,
Since Britain's navy rules the tide ;

257:25 Read "While" for "And."
259:10 Twelve lines follow:

  See far beneath the polar fkies,
The Ruffian warlike ftandards rife,
While o'er the feas her fleets advance,
To brave the Buccaniers of France.
And lo ! Germania's numerous ftates,
Pour countlefs thro' her hundred gates,
And ere Helvetia's final knell,
Shall rife up many a William Tell.
Him too, whofe faith the Koran fways,
And whofe ftern nod rules Egypt's Beys,
Sends forth his martial proclamation,
Againft " THE TERRIBLE GREAT NATION."

INDEX.

A

	PAGE.
Adam in petticoats	4
Adam and Eve become tailors	150
Adams Samuel, his eloquence compared to a saw-mill tail	13
puts on the Bonnet Rouge	106
prays for the success of the French	216
inscription in honor of	19
Adams John, vice-president	65
Austin David, a celebrated prophet and ranting divine	285
Albert Gallatin	297
A. Bishop and his father the deacon	297
drops his circular letter warning a democratic meeting	299
presents his shoes to Yale College	319
Athanasius's compulsive marriage of the church to the state	9

B

Beacon hill view from	13
Balaam's ass and Fanueil Hall	13
Bowen's wax-work	12
Blind Sam, the royal Indian's visit and reception at Philadelphia	37
Babel dispersion at	38
Blue laws, witches, &c.	53
Blanchard the æronaut, charged with a singular commission	79
Bastile description of	90
Burning of Gomorrah	118

INDEX.

	PAGE.
Burr Col.	132
Barber's shop, ludicrous scene in one	204
Boston town-meeting votes of, respecting the small-pox	52
Builders of Babel	215
British treaty	224
abstract of forwarded by S. S. Mason to B. F. Bache	225
Barber's shops advantages of, considered as schools of civilization	173
Ben Towne, a noted printer, and Jemmy Rivington	180
Bernese youth, gallant defence made by them	251
Bonaparte's invasion of Egypt	253-4
capture of Alexandria and Cairo	254
Battle of Aboukir	254-5
Brackenridge Judge, his conversion	276

C

Cerberus affrights the ghosts	16
Cornplanter, Big-tree, and Half-town, Indian chiefs	36
Cain murders Abel	44
flees to the land of Nod	55
Commutation of a capital punishment to the loss of member	56
Congress, allusions to secret history of	76
Christian's battle with Apollyon	81
Clinton Governor and the Oneidas	218
Connecticut Western Reserve lands, sale of	221
Legislature's session at Middletown	215
political situation of in 1800	280
in 1801	292
in 1803	298
Congress scene in, on reading the dispatches from the commissioners	238
Conscience, conversation with	167

INDEX.

	PAGE.
Cart government, compared to an old one	189
Crane mistaken for an owl	199
Callender liberated from jail by S. S. Mason	262
Clintonians and Burrites, contest between	300
illustrated by a battle between a hawk and snake	301
Centum vir, explanation of	304-5

D

Dragon of Revelation	15
Death of General Washington and change in the administration anticipated	77
Dupont, a member of the French National Convention	89
makes a public declaration of atheism	108
Dagon Image of, mutilated by the ark	217
Dutchmen stripped of their breeches	190
Dishite, a word derived from the Hebrew	278
Daniel in the Lion's den	288
Democratic thanksgiving at New-Haven	299
Dry Dock,	306
David and Uriah,	69
his psalms denounced in the French National Convention	69
Doctors Smith, Cooper and Scandella	243-4

E

Enceladus in Etna	15
Egalite Philip Duke of Orleans	87
his fate and that of his adherents predicted	88
Elijah the prophet's little cloud	97
in the wilderness	154
England, invasion of	248-9

INDEX.

	PAGE.
Egypt, darkness in	259
Election of Mr. Jefferson	281
contested by the adherents of col. Burr and finally settled by Matthew Lyon	287
Enterprize schooner takes a Tripolitan vessel	293

F

First born destroyed	257
Fakir seated in his chair of nails	26
Furtum, the planet Mercury so denominated	26
Funding system	68 115
Fishwomen of Paris	70 108
Freedom attacked with the cholic	107
French privateers fitted out of Charleston	115
Dr. Franklin	128
France, political and moral situation of, in 1798	246
Fatal consequences of the French Revolution	157-58
Fable of the old Man and his Ass	177
Fauchet and Randolph's flour contract alluded to	189-262
Frogs, Town meeting of	196
Freedom of the Press execrated by the Democrats	206
Fries pardoned and rewarded with a military commission	275

G

Ghost of Samuel	54
Mr. Giles, Classic phrase of	71
his modesty applauded	263
Gabriel's trumpet broken	72
Gabriel chief of the Southern revolted slaves	274
Genet's Citizen reception by Gov. Moultrie on his arrival	114
his journey	323
Gideon and the men of Succoth	125
Gnothi Seauton, singular translation of	155
Granger	297

INDEX.

	PAGE.
Granger compared to Ahitophel	231
Gog and Magog	294
Gone to pot, derivation of	329

H

Honey Dews	14
Hen-hawk and Chickens	18
Hebron firing of the Pump at	27
Hull's physic, a celebrated remedy for the cholic	27-107
Harmar Gen. and the Miami Town	33
Howard the Philanthropist	38
Hancock Governor, compared to Jove	51
quells the British Lion's roar	57
his Negro Ball	65
Hercules and the Stable of Augeas	78
Honestus, alias B. Austin, junior	139
Hand-writing on the wall	215
Haswell, the Bennington printer and Prince the Negro	227
Hamilton Gen.	230
Hints for the prevention of Pestilence	245
Hair-dresser, a celebrated	174

I

Indians killed on the Susquehannah	35
reasons in favour of plundering	36
Indians, primitive manners of	170
ægis of the law extended over them	172
new plan for civilizing	174
Indian medicines	173
Indian dance with the members of the New-York Legislature	217
Invasion of Italy by the Barbarians	222
Inscription for the tomb of a celebrated patriot	328

INDEX.

PAGE.

J.

Johnson, Sir William and John, Hugh Findley, Esq. &c.	43
Jewish Burying Ground, a favourable situation for a Christian school	45
Jacobins	68
Jacobin, a picture of	158
Jacobin creed	190
Jackson Gen. of Georgia	131
Image of a beautiful woman, an instrument of punishment	253

K

Kraken entangled among the Rocks of Norway	14
Kickapoos	38
Kosciusko and the Poles	210
Kid, Capt. the Pirate, and money diggers	222
Kirby, the Connecticut Democratic Candidate for Governor	299

L

Liberty, birth of	6
Liberty clothes stolen by Vassalage	7
Law of the Province of Massachusetts to prevent Plays	53
Louis the Sixteenth confined in the Temple	69-70
tenderness of the French towards him and his Queen how displayed,	85
Decapitation of	ib.
Levite and his Concubine	79
Lot flees from Sodom	123
Langdon, John	133
Lyon Matthew and the Wooden Sword	160—191
Leap Frog	156
Logan, the Mingo chief, and col. Cresap	170
Lincoln, General	16
Levi	297
Logan Doctor goes to France on a political mission	241

INDEX.

	PAGE.
Leland and the Mammoth Cheese	286

M

Matter attractive of Matter	22
incompatible with motion	24
illustrated by the boiling of Hasty Pudding	26
Magical effects of Tea	58
Music fatal to a Cow	67
Mason, Stevens T.	131
Mount Sinai and the Pilgrim	136
Madoc landing of in America	171
Mercenary Match	182
Mat—k W—e speech of	197
Moral Reflection	204
Mamelukes defeat and slaughter of	252
Manhattan Bank, its many properties	277
Moses on Mount Pisgah	286

N

Noah's Ark, embarkation on board	8
Nebuchadnezzar's golden image	70
Commodore Nicholson and Blair M'Clannachan	227
Napper Tandy and the insurrection in Ireland	249
Nelson tribute of praise to	259

O

Orpheus, wonderful effects of his music	25
Obstructions that oppose the civilization of the Indians	175
Oneida Chiefs arrive at Albany	217

P

Princess de Lamballe murder of	87-92
Prairie Dog	8
more particularly described	320
Pharaoh and his Plagues	28

INDEX.

	PAGE
Pokahontas	63
Plunder of the French Nobles, and Murder of the Priests	70
Public Officers list of	77
Paine, Tom	79
his egotism	304
Procession in New-York, in honour of the French Victories	107
Pacificus, writings of	115
Philadelphia Library and Statue of Dr. Franklin	152
Psalmody, a singular appeal with respect to its merits	201
Pestilence, description of	242
Pennsylvania and Governor M'Kean	300
Post-master General	304
Political State of France, Holland and Switzerland in 1803	312
Proofs of the Millennium	316-320

Q

Quails and Manna	58

R

Rat, its Antipathy to the Guinea Pig	25
Robespierre, Danton and Marat	108
Robespierre, Epitaph on	211
Robinson, Moses	133
Robinson Crusoe and his Goats	213
Rams terrified by thunder	230

S

Samson in the Temple of Gaza	15
Stamp Act Repeal of	27
Swineherd and his hogs	46
St. Tammany Tutelary Saint of Virginia	63
Skunk in a hostile attitude	80

INDEX.

	PAGE.
Sympathetic attraction instances of in the Crow, Skunk and Pole Cat	117
Socratic Love	118
Stelligeri, a club so called	124
Speculation, mad schemes of	215-223
Strange appearance exhibited to a Western Judge	153
Session of the Legislature of New-York at Albany in 1794	216
Switzerland Invasion of, by the French	250
Salt Mountain, horned Frog and Prairie Dog	178
Steigner, the Advoyer, a tribute of respect to his memory	251
Switzerland Desolation of	252
Second Sight, a remarkable instance of, relative to the American Treaty with France	262
Salt Mountain and Louisiana purchase	307

T

Tarring and Feathering	13-16-58
Truth in her Well	17
Turkey Cock and Pigs	ib.
Tea destroyed at Boston	58
Tories changed into Birds	ib.
Tench Coxe, and his Tape Worm	274

V

Virginia Regiments well supplied with Officers	64

W

Wythe's Mr. Barn Burnt	5
Washington's General proclamation of Neutrality	116
Washington and Hamilton	141
Whale attacked by the Sword Fish and Thresher	117
Warren, General	215
Western Insurrection	242-262
Wieshaupt and the Illuminati	247

INDEX.

	PAGE
Weppernocher, or Martin, how taken	183
Wayne General defeats the Indians	214
Warning to America	252
Wright, Governor of Maryland	316
Windham Invasion of by Frogs	55
Frogs	222
Welch Indians, letter relative to	324

SUPPLEMENTARY INDEX TO
THE ECHO, WITH OTHER POEMS

Abel, 44, 55
Abucar, 257
Achilles, 296
Achish, 12
Adam, 4, 44, 67, 124, 150, 160, 307
Adams, John, 60, 65, 68, 179, 215, 269, 271
Adams, Samuel, 10-11, 13-19, 52, 54, 104, 106, 107, 133, 135, 138, 191, 215, 216, 226, 310
Africa, 66, 253
Ahithophel, 237
Albanian domes, 216
Albion, 231, 248, 250
Alexandria, Egypt, 254
Algeria, 199, 231
Allegany Hills, 102, 109
Alleghany, Pa., 147
Ambuscade, 107
America, 4, 11, 34, 40, 60, 63, 101, 102, 109, 127, 319, 324
American Mercury, The (Hartford), xv, 65, 92, 236, 293, 314
American Revolution, 40
Ames, 216
Amos' son, 314
Andes River, 261
Apollo, 242, 265
Apollyon, 81
Arabia, 258
Arabian Night's Entertainment, 331
Army of England, 248
Asia, 118
Athanasius, 6, 9

Athens, Greece, 5, 8
Atlantic Ocean, 108, 246
Aurora (Philadelphia), 127, 147
Austin, Ben, Jr., 132, 144, 213, 226
Austin, David, 285, 300, 314
Austria, 79, 251, 253
Autun, 260

Baal, 107
Babcock, Elisha, 293, 300
Babel, 97, 215, 223, 285
Babylon, 286
Bache, B. F., 104, 127, 128, 135, 225-26
Bacon, 306
Bahama Islands, 183
Balaam, 13, 292
Banneker, 240
Barrington, George, 278
Bastile, 90
Baxter, 234
Beacon Hill, 10, 13
Bedford County, Pa., 148, 152, 156
Beezlebub, 189
Behemoth, 287
Belial, 55, 61, 67, 80, 213
Bell, Robert, 43
Belshazzar, 215
Bennington, Vt., 201, 227
Benson, 217
Berne, 251
Bidwell, Barna, 182
Big Tree, 30, 36
Biron, 92
Bishop, Abraham, 278, 284, 289, 299, 300, 319

SUPPLEMENTARY INDEX

Black Sal, 301
Blair, 226
Blake, George, 144
Blake, Joseph, Jr., 138, 142, 144
Blanchard, James, 73, 79
"Blind Sam," 30, 37
Bolton, Conn., 97, 100
Bonaparte, Napoleon, 258, 281, 286, 293, 314
Boston, 4, 10, 27, 58, 65, 94, 97, 104, 107, 134, 135, 141, 145, 198, 215
Boston Argus, 5, 10
Botany-Bay, 284
Bowen, 12
Brackenridge, H. H., 29, 32, 42, 147, 149, 151, 155, 156, 159, 161, 276
Brady, 35, 331
Brady, 69
Brandt, 30
Brissot, 113
Britain, 29, 30, 31, 42, 51, 53, 127, 137, 138, 141, 180, 196, 199, 215, 254, 257, 271, 309, 319, 324
British Lion, 57, 215, 224
Brothers, Richard, 314
Brown, John, 132
Brown, Samuel, 144
Brunswick, Duke of, 61, 71
Buffon, 91
Bunker Hill, 309
Bunyan, John, 81
Burkitt, 67
Burr, Aaron, 129, 132, 227, 277, 281, 287, 300
Bute, 42
Butler, 131
Butler, [Samuel], v

Caesar, 193
Cain, 44, 55, 132
Cairo, 254, 258
Callender, 176, 262, 273
Cambria, 171, 324
Cambridge, Mass., 2, 4
Canaan, 279, 307
Canada, 214

Canton, China, 58
Cape Cod, 69
Cape Horn, 168
Captain Flip, 98
Captain Kid, 222, 276
Carey, 60, 63
Cassius, 119-20, 122, 125
Cato, 136
Cerberus, 16
Charleston, S. C., 110-11, 115, 134, 212
Charlestown, 27
Chase, 273
Chauncey, 223
Cheetham, 179, 297
Cheshire, Mass., 286
Chester, 289
Chew, 147, 152
Childs, John, 325-26, 330-31
Cicero, 138, 143
Clairbornes, 304
Clark, William, 331
Clinton, George, 60, 63, 64, 67, 68, 70, 72, 218, 291, 300
Clootz, Anacharsis, 279
Cloptons, 304
Clos, Choderlos de la, 91
Coal River, 330
Columbia, 13, 27, 42, 53, 63, 77, 86, 95, 105, 106, 108, 113, 115, 214, 239, 241, 245, 252, 271
Columbian Centinel (Boston), 48
Columbus, Christopher, 33, 324
Congo, 314, 318
Connecticut, 69, 124, 135, 187, 192, 221, 236, 259-60, 261, 280, 292, 298, 321-22; Archives of, 56; Freemen of, 120; Legislature of, 214, 221, 224
Connecticut Courant (Hartford), 210, 220
Connecticut Gazette (New London), 20
Cooper, Dr., 244
Cooper, William, 143-44

SUPPLEMENTARY INDEX 373

Cornplanter, 30, 36
Coxe, Tench, 274-75
Crane, 199, 200, 206
Cresap, 170
Crusoe, 213
Cuffey, 66
Cyclops, 37

Dagon, 217
Daily Advertiser (Boston), 110
Dalilah, 15
Dallas, 275, 291
Dally, Gifford, 77
Damiens, 92
Dana, S., 260, 305
Daniel, 160, 288
Danton, 108, 212
David, 69
Dawes, Thomas, 141, 143, 144
Dawson, Nancy, 304
Democrats, 63, 64, 133, 135, 137, 138, 167, 220, 269-71, 282, 298, 299, 300
Detroit, 30, 31
Dexter, Timothy, 299, 319
Dickinson, 147, 152
Diemen, Anthony Van, 168
Dilworth, Tom, 160
Dobbs, 320
Don Quixote, 237
Dorrance, Judge, 291
Duane, 179, 276, 291
Dun, 297
Dupont, 89, 108
Dura's Plain, 70
Dutch, 190
Dyer, Colonel, 322

Eden, 114, 214
Edes, 43
Egalite, Philip, 87, 88, 91, 92
Egypt, 253, 256-57, 310
Elderkin, 54, 322
Elijah, 97, 154
Ellsworth, 300, 310
Elmendorf, 235
Enceladus, 15

Endor's witch, 54
England, 40, 84, 92, 106, 249, 290, 331
Esculapius' son, 200
Etna, 15
Europe, 10, 13, 16, 61, 71, 101, 107, 118, 190, 212, 231, 253, 259, 312, 325
Eustis, Dr. William, 143, 144
Eve, 150, 160

Falstaff, 226, 235
Faneuil Hall, 10, 13, 51, 136-44
Fauchet, 189
Faust, Dr., 103
Fay, Colonel, 227
Federalists, 147, 167, 179, 189, 191, 271, 302
Fellows, Nathaniel, 144
Fenner, 291
Findley, 116
Finlay, Sir Hugh, 40, 43
France, 61, 69, 70, 71, 79, 82, 83, 84, 85-92, 101, 102, 105, 107, 108, 110, 111, 114-18, 137, 141, 149, 157, 158, 168, 189, 191-93, 211, 212, 216, 229-31, 234, 241, 249, 250, 251, 254, 256-57, 259-60, 261, 262, 270, 279, 319, 321-22
Frank, A., 112, 113, 118
Frankfort, Ky., 324
Franklin, Benjamin, 104, 262, 284
Frederick, 210
Freedom, 14, 43, 52, 58, 66, 69, 72, 75, 79, 92, 93, 101, 104, 106, 115, 117, 130, 137, 192, 229, 232, 238, 241-42, 247, 250-51, 262, 300, 309, 311, 312
French Convention, 108
French Revolution, iv, 69, 71, 257-58
Freneau, Philip, 104, 116, 179

Gabriel, 72, 274

Gaine, Hugh, 43
Gallatin, Albert, 262, 291, 297, 302
Gallia, 13, 72, 88, 106, 114, 118, 157, 175, 212, 237, 246, 248, 256, 257, 259, 260, 312
Gath, 12
Gaza, 15
Gelston, 289
Gemmill, 293
Genet, 103, 105, 111, 113-17, 191, 212, 213, 323
Geneva, Switzerland, 290
Genevese, 303
Genlis, 87, 91
George III, 16, 53, 143
Georgia, 221, 223, 238, 291
German troops, 108
Gideon, 125, 237
Giles, 71, 116, 263-64
Gill, 43
Gilman, 227
Goddard, 43
Goliath, 12, 153
Gomorrah, 118
Goodrich, 289
Goose-Creek, 305
Gore, 221, 223, 224
Gorham, Stephen, 144
Granger, Gideon, 237, 280, 297, 304, 306
Greece, 11, 17, 148, 296
Green, 20, 22
Green, Pa., 147
Green, Tim, 43
Greenleaf, Thomas, 101, 103, 323
Grenville, 224
Griffith, Maurice, 326-31
Gripus, 199
Griswold, Roger, 160, 192, 235, 259, 293, 304
Grubb, Peter, 236
Gryffidd, 171
Gulf of Mexico, 325

Habersham, 304
Half-Town, 30, 36
Hall, 43, 138, 139, 142, 143
Ham, 8
Hamilton, Alexander, 104, 230
Hancock, John, 48-50, 51, 65-66, 72, 94, 227
Harmar, General, 29, 33
Harper, 66
Hart, General, 299
Hartford, Conn., 93, 94, 218, 221, 223
Hartford Courant, 94
Hastings, 292
Haswel, 227
Havens, 235
Hebrew, 45, 79, 314, 318
Hebron, 27
Helvetia, 250, 252
Henrico, 62, 67, 68, 70, 72
Henry IV, 83
Hercules, 78
Hessians, 89, 213
Hicks, 43
Hole, 331
Holland, 312
Holt, 43
Homer, 296, 297
Horace, v
Howard, 31, 38
Huggins, 174
Hull, 27, 107
Hume, 31, 37
Hyde, 292
Hymen, 24

Ilium, 296
India, 26
Indians, 29-39, 43, 152, 153, 170-76, 183, 216-18, 223, 240, 293, 306, 307, 321-22, 324-30; Delaware, 32; Kickapoo, 32, 38; Miami, 29, 33; Shawanee, 328-29; Welsh, 171, 324-25, 328
Indian War, 29
Ireland (Erin), 178, 191, 213, 226, 249, 270, 273, 289, 290, 291, 310, 320
Iris, 4
Irish Whigs, 134
Israel, 54, 276, 318

SUPPLEMENTARY INDEX

Paine, Thomas, 79, 177, 272, 297, 300; *Rights of Man*, 272, 298
Palais Royal, 91
Palinurus, 213
Pan, 265
Paris, France, 90, 109, 118
Pascal, 104
Penn, William, 152, 242
Pennsylvania, 94, 180, 301
Penobscot, 306
Perigord, 92
Peters, Samuel, 27, 54, 183, 321; *History of Connecticut*, 27, 54, 183, 321
Pharaoh, 28, 178, 193, 301
Philadelphia, 30, 37, 93, 111, 147, 151, 152, 187, 188, 226, 231, 259
Philistia, 19, 217
Phoebus, 99
Phrygia, xv
Pisgah, 286
Pitt, William, 224
Pittsburgh, 29, 154, 276
Plenipo, 110, 323
Poissard, 108
Pokahontas, 63-64, 94
Poland, 210, 211
Pompey, 258
Pope, Alexander, 224
Portsmouth, Conn., 227
Potowmac River, 306
Potter, 292
Powell, 300
Presqu'isle, 30
The Press (Richmond) 273
Priam's son, 296
Priestley, Dr. Joseph, 276
Prussia, 228, 279

Quakers, 23, 53
Quebec, 40, 43

Rachel, 228
Rama, 228
Randolph, Edmund, 189, 228, 262, 304
Randolph, John, 297
Republicans, 60, 271, 287

Rhine River, 210
Rhode Island, 277, 291
Richmond, Va., 273
Rivington, Jemmy, 43, 180
Roanoke River, Va., 326, 330
Robespierre, 92, 108, 211
Robin Hood, 276
Robinson, 227
Rome, 136
Rosetta River, 254, 256-57
Rush, Dr. Benjamin, 275
Russia, 210, 251

St. Clair, General, 214
St. Domingo, 274
Saint Tammany, 63-64
Salem, Conn., 321
Salt, 306
Samarcand, 331
Samiel, 258
Samson, 15, 19, 301
Sandy River, Va., 278
Savannah, Ga., 291
Scandella, Dr. I. B., 244-45
Scotch (Scotland), 213
Scott, General Winfield, 33
Sellers, 43
Septon, 304
Shadrach, 160
Shakespeare, 121, 182, 226
Shannon River, 320
Shem, 8
Shinar's Plain, 38
Simcoe, 214
Sinai, 136
Sirius, 18
Smith, Dr. Elihu H., 92, 243-45
Sodom, 118, 123, 160, 243
Sol, 2, 13, 80, 99
Solomon, 16
Solon, 301
South Carolina, 111, 281
Spain (Spaniards), 102, 108, 168, 231, 307
Spunky, 6
Stamp Act, 27
Steigner, 251
Stelligeri, 124, 125, 215, 220, 236

139, 140, 141, 144, 225-26, 262
Massachusetts, 241
Massachusetts Bay, 48
Mather, Cotton, 321
Mazzei, 240, 270
McKean, Thomas, 240, 274-75, 276, 301
McKee and Brandt, 30
Melaanthee, 34
Memphis, 257
Mercenary Match, 182
Mercer, 116
Mercury, 122
Mercy, 4, 12
M'Guire and Brady, 29
Middlesex Gazette, 188
Middletown, Conn., 214
Midian, 125
Mills, 43
Milton, 31, 37
Mirabeau, 93
Miranda, xv
Mississippi River, 162, 306, 326
Missouri River, 320, 324-26, 329-30
Mitchell, Dr., 304
Mob, 7, 12, 67, 181
Moll Carey, 299
Monboddo, Lord, 39
Monier, John, 41, 42, 46, 47, 51, 94
Monier, Mrs. John, 41, 46-47
Monroe, James, 272
Montgomery, 82, 84
Modus, 27
Monticelle, 282
Moon, 26
Morocco, 253
Morton, Perez, 144
Moses, 133, 286, 301
Moultrie, Governor, 110-11, 114, 115
Mynheer, 190

Nabis, 254
Naples, 304
National Gazette (Philadelphia), 29, 73

Nature, 3-4, 5, 7, 12, 17, 22, 23, 24, 38, 66, 78, 100, 115, 130, 150, 170, 290
Navarre, 90
Negroes, 65, 72, 94
Nelson, Horatio, 254, 259
Nero, 193
Newburyport, Conn., 319
New Castle, 149, 160
New Hampshire, 132, 238
New Haven, 214, 284, 286, 299, 300, 319, 321
New Jersey, 302
New London, 279
New River, 330
Newton, 22, 24, 26, 27
Newtonian Philosophy, 20-21, 22-28
New Year's Verses, 65, 92
New York, 107, 133, 196, 200, 221, 243, 244, 276-77, 300
New York Journal, 101
Nicholas, John, 259-60, 261, 263-64
Nicholson, 226
Nile (a wizard), 26
Nile River, 256
Niles, Nathaniel, 227
Nimblechops, Aquiline, 195, 204
Noah, 8, 123, 160, 212, 222, 307
Nod, Land of, 55, 152
North, 42
North Carolina, 131
Northumberland County, Pa., 276
Norwegia, 14
Norwich, Conn., 97
Norwich Packet, 96

Ohio country, 325
Ohio River, 29, 35, 150, 151
Old Nick, 55
Ormandy, Duke of, 131
Orpheus, 24
Osgood, 289
Ostend, 84

SUPPLEMENTARY INDEX 377

Israelitish Burying Ground, 40
Italy, 319

J. P. M., 11
Jackson, Andrew, 291
Jacob, 314
Jacobins, 60, 61, 63, 68, 70, 71, 89, 107, 117, 132, 134, 136, 158, 188, 189, 190, 216, 220, 228, 234, 236, 238, 246, 260, 270, 298
James, Irish, 131
Japhet, 8
Jarvis, Dr. Charles, 135, 136, 141-44, 216, 226
Jay, John, 104, 130, 134, 136, 140, 141, 224, 225-26, 227, 310
Jay's Treaty, 127-46, 224-28
Jebus, 80
Jefferson, Thomas, 72, 162-84, 191, 235, 240, 270-74, 281, 284, 287, 297, 303; *Notes on Virginia*, 170
Jemima, 119
Jessamine County, Ky., 325
Jews, 28, 276, 285-86, 314-18
John, the Baptist, 12
Johnson, Sir John, 40, 43
Johnson, Sir William, 40, 43
Jonah, 160
Jones, 302
Jones, Gabriel, 176
Jove, 51
Judah, 315
Judas, 220
Judd, 299
Juvenal, v

Kentucky, 33, 34, 38, 152
Kentucky militia, 33, 34
Kentucky Palladium (Frankfort), 324
Kiangsi, 58
King, 104
Kirby, 299, 300
Kosciusko, 210
Kraken, 14

La Fayette, 286
Lake Erie, 221
Lambelle, Prince de, 87, 91
Lambelle, Princess de, 91, 92
Lamot, M. de, 84
L[ang], 43
Langdon, John, 129, 133, 227, 262
Lapland, 314, 318
Larrabe, 278
Latium, 296
La Touche, 92
Leesburg, 262
Le Gendre, 92
Leland, John, 286
Lewis, Meriwether, 331
Lexington, Ky., 35
Liberty, 5-9, 12, 82, 101, 105, 133, 158
Liffy River, Ireland, 320
Lincoln, 216, 297
Little, William, 144
Little John, 276
Livingston, 277
Logan, Colonel, 34
Logan, Chief John, 170, 240
London, 91, 248
Lot, 118, 160, 191
Loudon, 112
Louis XVI, 69, 82-84, 85-92, 106
Louisiana, 162
Love, Christopher, 119, 314
Luna, 96, 99
Lyon, Matthew, 160, 191, 234-35, 287

Madoc, 171
Magus, Simon, 119
Maia, 14
Malta, 253
Mammon, 190
Manhattan Bank, 277
Mantua's Bard, 296
Marat, 108
Marten, S. P., 319
Martin, Luther, 170
Maryland, 316
Mason, Thomson, 127, 131,

SUPPLEMENTARY INDEX

Stiles, Dr. Ezra, 319
Stygian Snore, 223
Styx, 16
Succoth, 125
Suffield, 279
Susquehanna River, 29, 35, 221
Suwarrow, 302
Swanwick, 262
Sweetser, John, 144
Switzerland (Swiss), 251, 312

Tandy, Napper, 249
Tartary, 331
Tassoni, v
Tate, 69
Tete, 322
Theater, 10-11, 48-50, 53-56
Tiber River, 305
Titan's sons, 90
Toby, 323
Tory, 13, 16, 58, 177
Toulmin, Harry, 331
Towne, Ben, 180
Triggs, 304
Trumbull, Jonathan, 300
Tudor, William 143, 144
Turkey, 253

United States, 34, 110-11, 127, 141-42, 145, 221, 262, 287
Uriah, 69

Venice, 244
Vermont, 200, 201, 227, 235
Vining, John, 35
Virgil, 297
Virginia, 60, 63, 64, 67, 68, 127, 141, 144, 221, 259, 261, 273-74, 302, 303, 310, 311, 326

Virginia Gazette (Richmond), 60
Vosse's Fort, Va., 326

Wales, 326, 328-29
Wallace, Alexander, 40, 43
Wallace, Hugh, 40, 43
Walley, Thomas, 144
Wallingford, Conn., 292
Warren, Joseph, 82, 84, 215
Washington, George, 77, 140, 145-46, 179, 211, 232, 270, 285-86, 288, 310
Washington, Pa., 147
Watson, Ebenezer, 43
Watts, Isaac, 69
Wayne, General Anthony, 213, 214
Webster, 160
Weishaup, 247
Western Reserve, The, 221
Whiskey Rebellion, 137
Wight, 322
Wilcox, 292
Willimantic River, 321
Wilson, 147, 152
Windham, 321
Windham's Sons, 55
Winthrop, 298
Wolcott, Oliver, 230, 292, 300, 302
Woods, John, 147-49, 150-51, 152, 154-61
Worcester, Mass., 292
Wright, 316
Wythe, 2, 4, 100

Yale College, 319
York, 226
Yorktown, 309

Zoar, 123, 243
Zurich, 251

The ECHO. No. II.

From the Massachusetts Magazine for July 1791.
"Philadelphia. June 24, 1790.

"ONCE more, my dear Maria, I hold the pen of sweetly familiar scribble, sitting down, quite at my ease, to chat with a friend, who I am assured by the charming consciousness which plays about my heart, is prepared with indulgent candour to listen. I stand indebted upon the page of friendship for two letters, and to discharge the arrears with superior pleasure, I proceed. Charming was the tho't, which, on the wings of excursive fancy, bore you along, the companion of a journey, the pleasure of which you have thereby contributed largely to augment. Not a green bank, not a shady grove, not a glassy rill, can now present, but immediately, like one of the daughters of Paradise, arrayed in spotless white, I place thereby the beauteous image of my Maria.—In the arms of my imagination, I clasp the lovely form, and it animates, cheers, and adds a richer colouring to all the glowing scene.

* * * * * *

The departure of my cousin T—must have opened a new wound, in the gentle bosom of my ever lovely friend.

* * * * * *

It is strange indeed what could originate the story of T—'s matrimonial connection.—Doubtless it was forged in the wilds of conjecture, and the idea taking air, was soon in the prolific imagination of the notable Dowager, blown up to an authenticated certainty."

"Constant I am wherever found is heard—
"And only by the fool, and villain, fear'd."

ONCE more Maria, dearest, prizeless maid—
Dearer than daisy on the grassy glade—
My thumb and finger hold, with sweetest clasp,
The scribbling pen——love kindles at the grasp.

Quite at my ease, on stuff-chair sitting squat,
With you my pigeon dear I itch to chat ;
Assur'd by Love that plays about my heart,
And charming consciousness, devoid of art,
That you will deign to lend a listening ear,
And with indulgent candour stoop to hear.
On friendship's Ledger, in Truth's fair round-hand,
For two Epistles, I your debtor stand ;
To save myself from dunning, suit, or fine,
I tender your demand in paper coin.
    Charming the tho't (O how it frisks to sing ;)
Which, borne along on Fancy's wandering wing,
Shew'd you the sweet companion of the way,
When JOURNEY travelling all the live-long day,
Mail'd you behind, portmanteau like, to ease
The toils of trotting, and his back to please.
Not a green bank, and not a shady grove,
No glassy rill, where bull-frogs joy to rove,
Can rise to view, but I, by Fancy driven,
Strip you like girls in great Mohammed's heaven,
And, beaming forth each pure, celestial grace,
Seat you the beauteous *Houry* of the place.
With raptur'd arms I clasp the lovely form,
Imagination feels the image warm,
Red on each cheek the kindling blushes rise,
And love, and transport sparkle in her eyes ;
The cheering rays adorn the glowing scene,
And richer colouring tints the verdant green.

   *   *   *   *   *   *   *

    How I regret the loss of cousin T—'.
And do I not espy a wound in thee,
Thro' which the streams of soft affection roll,
Nor love can cure, nor patience plug the hole ?

   *   *   *   *   *   *   *

    Whence could the strange, & senseless story spring,
That cousin T— has tried the marriage ring ?
Doubtless 'twas forg'd where wild conjecture reigns,
In some vast garret destitute of brains ;
From thence, half-starv'd, the creature crept to air,
An embryo *Notion*, scarce enough to stare:
Then urg'd its flight like lightning, or the wind,
To the great Dowager's prolific mind—
There by her bellows blown to mighty size,
Abroad for Truth the windy monster flies.

The ECHO. No. III

From the MIDDLESEX GAZETTE.

"On the celerity of SCANDAL, No. III.

"Mr. Woodward,

"Whilst men are prolific with a fruitious brain to calumniate their neighbours, it's not (however irksome to the feelings of a gentleman) to touch a little upon where scandal hath its force more poignant than from a source where it never should be found. The Female sex, with whom prudence should be found without the general observation perpetually revolving in the mind, "That women govern the world." How many and innumerable are the women addicted to scandal, living a life of celibacy, groaning in their beds for the want of a protector, so easily remedied as a *silent tongue and unerring reflections?* Peace to your *exits, wisdom* to your *closing hours!* Numerous have been the instances thro' the course of my life, that I have witnessed compunction for scandalizing a friend, and blood shed through the medium of a liquid tongue, whispering at table some kind of vilifying jeers unworthy the dignity of a woman. It may be thought, that I bear too hardly upon the female sex—No one is a greater or better friend to them; but as I observed before, their influence is great with men; so that influence will effectuate, proportionably to the object aimed at: and the more exalted the station in life, the greater the weight falls on the person to whom such shafts of malignity are levied. It would be well for the Satirist to consider.

382

> "*Women are lovely dangerous things,*
> "*Have sweets like the bees, mingled with stings.*"

I have sat at the table of many a friend where numerous characters, under the veil of modesty, have whispered words of vital death against the innocent—Surmise is a pretty savory to interlard contuming a character.

It is too frequent in companies to observe whispering going on with an adder's tongue; when some character that is *virtuous* and *meritorious*, is lost thro' imaginary supposition. The dress of a person, or manner of expressing certain words give high exhilaration to the satirist, altho the sentiment or story is perfectly understood, and leads to knowledge."

> "Hark! hark to the sound! do but hear the words splutter,
> "And ECHO—poor ECHO! must stammer and stutter."

> *"To the tune of the Old Cow died of."*

Whilst men are prolific with fruitious brains,
And daub o'er their neighbours with calumny's stains,
(How irksome soever to feelings genteel)
It is not to touch it, and make scandal feel
In that delicate spot, where its feelings are found,
Than to find out a source that can never be found,
With the creature call'd female as you are alive,
Cold Prudence in clover should fatten and thrive,
Nor suffer the proverb to whirl in the mind—
"That women are witches, & men are stone blind"—
How many, and big are the women now blown,
To scandal addicted—Old maids—forc'd to groan
For the want of a jockey to sleep by their side,
Their silence to spur, their reflections to guide.

383

CHORUS I.

    Peace to your exits—
    Look out for next hits.

A great many times in the course of my days,
I've seen deep Compunction as red as a blaze;
And blood I've seen shed, like the stream of my song,
For belying a friend, thro' a long liquid tongue—
And whispering at table, and jeering—(a true man)
Unworthy the vengeance of what we call woman.
Perhaps some may think that in playing my card,
On the poor female women I bear rather hard—
But no one's more friendly to woman than me,
I love them all dearly, and so do they me.
But as I once said, so say I again,
They can do as they please with all us great men,
They can make us look silly, and make us look wise,
They can shoot thro' our livers, and wink out our eyes—
All this they can do, be the man great or small—
But let him look out, or he'll catch a sad fall;
For the higher he's been, when once on the ground,
The weight will fall on him like five hundred pound.

CHORUS II.

    Women are things
    As queer as you please—
    They carry honey like bees,
    And they prick with their stings.

I've sate at the table of many a friend,
Where they'd eaten so much they scarcely could stand;
Yet under the veil of their Modesty's guise,
They have whispered round stories we know to be lies;
And still we believe the pestilent breath,
Altho' the poor innocents died vital death.

CHORUS III.

Guessing is a savoury chink,
To mix with scandal, and with drink.

It is often the case where companies throng,
That whispering goes 'round with a dumb adder's tongue;
When alas! some poor creature of sweet disposition,
Is sent to de'el by supposed supposition.
A coat or a wig, the jacket or breeches,
Will kiddle up satire as keen as milk porridge,
And drive on the hero as fierce as dutch courage,
Tho' the story is told by a scholar from college,
Understood by the hearers, and leads on to knowledge.

CHORUS IV.

"There was a piper had a Cow,
"He had no hay to give her—
"He took his pipe and began to play,
"Consider Cow—consider."

THE POETRY

OF THE

MINOR CONNECTICUT WITS

RICHARD ALSOP

THE

CHARMS OF FANCY:

A Poem,

IN FOUR CANTOS,

WITH NOTES.

BY RICHARD ALSOP.

EDITED FROM THE ORIGINAL MANUSCRIPTS, WITH A BIOGRAPHICAL
SKETCH OF THE AUTHOR,

BY THEODORE DWIGHT.

NEW YORK:
D. APPLETON AND COMPANY,
346 & 348 BROADWAY.
M.DCCC.LVI.

ENTERED, according to act of Congress, in the year 1855,
BY JOSEPH W. ALSOP,
In the Clerk's Office of the District Court of the United States, for the Southern District of New York.

Contents.

	Page
Biographical Sketch of the Author, . . .	7
Argument to Book First, ...	12
Book First, ...	13
Notes to Book First, ...	37
Argument to Book Second, ...	44
Book Second, ...	45
Notes to Book Second, ...	75
Argument to Book Third, ...	110
Book Third, ...	111
Notes to Book Third, ...	151
Argument to Book Fourth, ...	182
Book Fourth, ...	183
Notes to Book Fourth, ...	211

Biographical Sketch of the Author.

RICHARD ALSOP was born at Middletown, Connecticut, on the 23d of January, 1761, and was the son of the principal merchant of that village, who bore the same name, and was distinguished for enterprize, system and probity in his business, and by honor and liberality in his intercourse with others, as well as by gentleness and affection in the midst of his family. To his love of reading and good taste his son owed much, as he found a library, large for the times, and well selected, at much pains and expense, ready provided for him in his earliest years.

The first American ancestor of the family came from England, and settled at Newtown, Long Island; and of him and his descendants some particulars may be found in Thompson's History of Long Island.

The father of the poet died in the year 1776, leaving a widow and seven children, three of whom were sons, and all of them young: Richard, the eldest child, being only fifteen years of age. Mrs. Alsop was a lady of uncommon energy of character, as was fully proved by her managing with success the complex affairs of her husband's business and estate, left as they were by his unexpected decease, and exposed to a thousand difficulties during the whole period of the Revolution, which had just commenced. Many of the debts she was obliged to cancel, after receiving little more than a nominal payment in Continental money, at its lowest grade of depreciation.

The following incidents have been furnished by one of the surviving sisters of the poet, who was most intimate with him from childhood, and a participator in his literary enjoyments. In her ninetieth year she wrote the following paragraphs, with her own hand, at the solicitation of the editor.

"It is my wish to comply with your request, for some of the little incidents which occurred in the life of my dear brother Richard, and were indicative of his character, his taste, and his pursuits.

"After the death of our father, in 1776, he studied mathematics, I believe at Branford, with a tutor of Yale College, by the name, I think, of Strong. My brother never entered college, though he had passed a good examination, his father intending him for a merchant. During the exciting times of the Revolution he was at home, with the exception of one voyage to Cape Français, in St. Domingo, his mother having hired a man in his stead, to serve during the war. He was ardent in his temper, and fearless of danger; and many were the risks he ran. One in particular I remember, when not more than twelve years of age. The flood was very high, and a great quantity of drift-wood was brought by it down Connecticut River. He was in a boat with some boys, engaged in catching it. In attempting to reach a log, he fell over and went down. On coming up by the side of the log, he flung his arm over it, and called out, ' Here, boys, here is the log !'

"He was much attached to books, eager for information, and particularly fond of poetry, and used to act the heroes of the Iliad. He was sociable, winning in conversation and fond of humor, and a general favorite with those of his own age in early life, and afterwards with those of the age of his children.

"You request me to inform you respecting his translation of Molina. He had two copies of Molina to translate, one of which was in Italian, the other in Spanish. While my brother was engaged in this work, Mr. William Shaler, who had been consul in Cuba, brought him a translation he had in part made, thinking it would be of service to him. But whoever is acquainted with a foreign language finds it easier to translate it into his own, than to compare another's translation with the original and correct it, and at the same time to secure a uniform style. This my brother told me was the case with the translation of Molina, by Mr. Shaler, and that he did not make any use of it.

"He was deeply interested in natural history; and all our walks and rides were rendered highly pleasing and instructive, by his remarks on the habits of animals in the woods, fields and waters, especially of the birds, of which he seemed to know every variety, and I might almost say every feather."

To this it may be added, that through life his intimacy with natural science, together with his admiration of fine scenery, his literary acquirements, and the warmth of his friendship, made him ever agreeable and instructive to persons of different classes and ages. He made small collections in natural history, and prepared several boxes of rare birds, stuffed with his own hands; some of which were particularly admired by Wilson, on his tour through the country, and one of which (the crimson-breasted Grosbeak) has a place in his "American Ornithology," drawn in the posture in which he found Mr. Alsop's rare specimen.

In the year 1786 Mr. Alsop accompanied two of his sisters and several young friends on a visit to the Springs of New Lebanon, Ballston and Saratoga. The journey was performed on horseback, and abounded in incidents, whose interest was much increased by the presence of the young poet. At that time there were only two houses at Ballston Spring, and three at Saratoga—all of them mere log-huts.

Mr. Alsop had a strong taste for the acquisition of foreign languages; and, notwithstanding the difficulty of procuring teachers and books at that time, and especially in his neighborhood, he early became a proficient in reading French, Spanish and Italian, perused various standard authors with a high relish in the originals, and made translations, both in poetry and in prose. Molina's History of Chile he published in two volumes, with extracts from the Araucana of Ercilla, in English verse.

Partly owing to his literary taste and habits, and partly to the fact that a large share of the property of his family had been left to him by his father, he never devoted himself to commercial business, but was one of the few men then in the country, chiefly devoted to a literary life, amidst all its discouragements.

It was his love of interesting novelties, combined with his philanthropy, which induced him to write the adventures of John R. Jewitt, an English sailor wrecked on the north-west coast of America, a work in which he imitated with some success the style of Robinson Crusoe, and of which he procured the publication for the benefit of that poor and friendless man, without giving his own name.

The composition of some of his works, and the publication of others, may be attributed in part to the coöperation of his brother-in-law, Isaac Riley, Esq., of New York, an enterprizing bookseller, who afforded him facilities which he could not have found elsewhere, in the existing state of the country. Mr. Riley laid the foundation of the auction system, which now controls the book-trade of the United States, and with his characteristic liberality and energy, encouraged and assisted the author in a career which the public were then ill prepared to sustain.

It seemed proper, in publishing a work of this kind, so many years after its composition, to retain some of the marks which it bore of the period of its production; and not only has the old authography in some places been retained, but other things still more strongly bears the stamp of the day. It will be instructive as well as interesting to the reader, to meet with some of the peculiarities of style and verse since superseded, and with views and opinions since corrected by the extension of inquiry, the investigations of science on the researches of travelers. And of these there are many examples to be noticed in the course of this poem: as both the text and the notes have been printed with scarcely a single alteration from the strict letter of the original, though considerable omissions have in some parts been made in the latter.

The reader will bear in mind the time and circumstances in which this work was written: most of it having been completed before the year 1788, so that it was the product of the very first years of our National Independence. The author was but a youth, a resident in a small interior village, and had shared in the anxieties attendant on the war, from the peculiar situation in which he had been placed by the death of his father. To a heart and mind like his, the position he occupied, as the oldest son of a fatherless family, had many and engrossing trials. His widowed mother, with all her energy of character, naturally leaned upon him: while the warm mutual affection that prevailed among her children, must have been intermingled with many exercises of feelings to the eldest son. When all these things are taken into view, it cannot but excite surprise to see, in the productions of his pen, evidence of so extensive knowledge, sound thought and laborious effort in the production of such a poem, with the record of so many of the materials of which it was framed.

But much else is indicated, which is not so formally displayed, particularly the amount of reading which he must have given to English poets, whose style he had insensibly adopted, often with a fluency, beauty and vigor, that would have done no discredit to some of the best of them. It is striking to reflect, that, many years before foreigners renounced the idea that America was unfavorable to the growth of taste, the "Charms of Fancy" should not only have been conceived, but completed: a poem in which many of the materials were drawn from English writers, and selected, compounded and used, with a degree of ingenuity, taste and poetical ability perhaps superior to any of their own poets of a similar class. Without any wish to overrate the merits of this work, we may ask our fellow-admirers of genuine English poetry to name a production of a similar kind and of superior merit.

THE

Charms of Fancy.

BOOK THE FIRST.

ARGUMENT OF THE FIRST BOOK.

INVOCATION to Fancy—Her powers over the Poet, Spenser; and the gifts she brings to Man. Fancy's Influence upon the Arts; inspires Painters; and wings aloft the Genius of the Muse. The soothing Charms of Music, and her power of subduing the Spirit of Affliction, Penury, or Dependence. The sway of Fancy over the Empire of Mind, in ruling alike the martial Youth and avaricious Miser; the poetic fire of Genius, and the restless ambition of the Daring. Then soaring grandly upon the wings of discovery, tempering the rule of Kings, or gently descending to domestic happiness, her powers are supreme. The varied charms of Fancy. Her Influence upon the Author; opens New Worlds of bliss to him—beautiful Landscapes; romantic Adventure; wild and fantastic Dreams; Elysian Scenes, with beauteous Groves, the frolics of lovely Maidens, and tuneful warbling of forest Songsters. A Churchyard Scene. The Bird of Sorrow. Phantoms, Spectres, Haggard Forms, and Monsters created by Fancy. Nature portrayed; her Vastness, Variety, and Beauty. Retrospective and prospective View of the Globe and its Inhabitants.

THE
CHARMS OF FANCY.

Book the First.

Thou visionary Pow'r, whose magic art
With boundless influence rules the feeling heart,
Whose potent charms can ev'ry sense control,
Acknowledg'd Empress of the Poet's soul:
To thee, thou source of animating song,
Fancy! To thee my earliest lays belong.
My artless verse, my first attempts inspire,
And give my Muse to glow with all thy fire;
Who dares, though conscious of the dangerous way,
O'er thy wide realm on vent'rous pinion stray.
    Indulgent Pow'r, O, lend thy timely aid:
Come to my view in all thy charms array'd,

CHARMS OF FANCY.

As erst o'er Spencer's infant form you hung,
His mind enraptur'd, and attun'd his tongue,
When Fairy-land, with all its magic throng,
First wak'd the visions of his future song.
Come with the raptur'd look, the heaven-turn'd eye,
In robes, loose-floating, of the rainbow's dye,
Thy auburn locks in careless beauty spread,
Thy crown of sun-beams glittering on thy head,
Thy golden wand, whose magic pow'r can raise
Th' events of past, and deeds of future days,
The gaudy dreams illusive Hope bestows,
The sable scenes Despair's dark mirror shows,
The Seraph forms that grace the seats of bliss,
Or hideous Fiends that darken hell's abyss.
Be present all thy visionary train,
That fire with life the Poet's glowing strain:
Soft sensibility in sorrow pale,
Hope sweetly smiling from her rosy veil,
Bright Mirth with laughing eye and careless heart,
Enchanting Pleasure and creative Art,
Young frolic Love in vest of vernal green,
And elder Friendship of sedater mien.

CHARMS OF FANCY.

Prone to indulge in thy creations gay,
Long has my soul confest thy sovereign sway
E'en from that age, when blithe Contentment's power,
With April sunshine, deck'd youth's fleeting hour,
And, bright in Expectation's flattering ray,
The alluring future shone, one cloudless day;
And still to thee thy humble votary pays,
In artless strains, his tributary praise;
Reckless though sordid minds the task condemn,
The heavy sons of dulness and of phlegm,
Whose half-formed, lifeless souls, with stupid **pride,**
Mock Fancy's powers and Genius' toils deride;
And, in the garb of Prudence masked, with zeal,
Decry those pleasures they can never feel.
From thee each nobler impulse springs to birth,
Each social virtue blooms with fairer worth,
Each sympathy attests thy high control,
Each keen sensation of the impassion'd soul;
Love's ardent hopes, and tenderest ties are thine
And Friendship hails thee as its source divine.

Enchanting Parent of each liberal art,
The mind that graces and improves the heart,

Alone to thee their magic powers thy owe,
To thee alone the pleasures they bestow.

  High in the foremost rank see Painting stand:
What bright creations rise at her command!
Nature's great rival in mimetic strife,
She bids the canvass glow with passion'd life.
Chain'd to yon' rock,[1] whose rude o'erhanging steep
Throws a dark horror o'er the storm-tost deep,
Behold a female form, divinely fair!
Wild glare her eyes with phrenzy's fearful stare;
The hurried glance, and eyeball's frantic roll,
Proclaim thy triumph, Madness! o'er the soul:
Yet heavenly beauty 'midst distraction glows,
And a sad lustre e'en o'er horror throws.

  Here Belisarius, o'er whose hoary age
The storms of Fortune shed their bitterest rage,
While lesson'd Grandeur hangs the pensive head,
Wretched and eyeless, asks a little bread;
Yet looks the Hero 'mid his abject state,
Sublime in misery and in ruin great.

  There opes in smiling skies a cheerful scene:
The peasants sporting on the village green,

Where, to the broken fiddle's well-known sound,
The rustic throng in awkward measures bound;
Mix'd with discordant notes we seem to hear
The hoarse laugh breaking on the tortur'd ear.

 Thou giv'st the Muse each passion to control,
With terror thrill, with glory fire the soul;
To flush the cheek with indignation's glow,
And Pity's eye to melt in kindly woe:
In vain the Critic with phlegmatic rules,
Those servile fetters of fastidious schools,
Fashion'd by Prejudice, by Meanness wrought,
Would chain the ardor of her freeborn thought;
On eagle-wings she tries the untempted height,
While Dulness' heavy eye in vain pursues her flight.

 Thine Music's melting tones, her airs divine,
And her full soul of harmony are thine.
Wak'd by thy touch she bids the passions start,
Or calms the tempests of the woe-torn heart,
In mute suspension locks the mental powers,
And wafts the rapt soul to celestial bowers.

 Tho' culture's force, or habit's varied sway,
May check thy ardor, or thy power display:

Thy birth deriv'd from no factitious source,
Alone from nature springs thy active force,
Connects with Genius, in the feeling breast,
In rapt'rous hour by fav'ring heaven imprest.
Not all the ills [2] that humble life await,
Penury's chill gloom, Dependance' abject state,
Improvement's want, Affliction's darkest hour,
Subdue thy spirit, or destroy thy power:
Nor in the groveling mind can toil bestow
Or favoring station wake thy genuine glow.

 With various sway thou rul'st the various mind,
By temper modified, by art inclined;
Thy magic mirror gives, in richest dye,
Its fav'rite wish to each illuded eye.
The dauntless youth, whom martial ardor warms,
Whom thirst of fame and proud distinction charms,
There views reflected, in the future bright,
The high rewards that valor's toils incite;
Sees conquest follow where he leads the way,
And Glory round him bear her solar ray,
While chiefs renown'd, the darling sons of fame,
Yield to the brighter splendors of his name.

Ambition there beholds, in rich array,   [sway;
Grandeur's meridian height, and Power's unbounded
Sees regal wreaths adorn his haughty brow,
Submissive realms in fearful homage bow,
O'er foreign climes his vast domain extend,
And crowns and sceptres on his nod depend.
And, tho' in Avarice' more than Arctic night,
Thy smother'd flame scarce gleams a feeble light;
Yet e'en the miser, 'midst his heaps of ore,
Owns the strong magic of thy boundless power,
When, with anticipation's airy hold,
He grasps in vision countless sums of gold.

But in full force, with influence unconfin'd,
Thou hold'st dominion o'er the Poet's mind,
Fir'd by thy touch divine, in brightest hue,
Each varied object meets his raptur'd view:
A lovelier dress the face of Nature shows,
Inspir'd with warmer life creation glows,
Far richer tints the robes of May adorn,
More splendent glories paint the blush of morn,
Sublimity a grander mein assumes,
And loveliness in fairer beauty blooms;

While scenes of wonder to his view arise
And all Elysium opens on his eyes.

 The hope-flush'd youth, whom views sublime inspire,
Whose glowing bosom boasts thy genuine fire,
Oft while unheeded pass the scenes of life,
Pleasure's mad chase or Gain's o'ertoiling strife,
Careless alike if Spring, with blossoms crown'd,
Beams her gay smile, if Summer laughs around,
If russet Autumn bends the blushing bough,
Or howling Winter whirls the drifty snow,
In thy strong spell confin'd, as, rapture-fraught,
Peculiar feelings sway the tide of thought,
Now shines in arms terrific o'er the plains
Where Horror frowns, and Death in triumph reigns,
Points the grim battle's rage, and joys to dare
The fiercest furies of unspairing war.
His matchless prowess turns the scale of fight,
And valor trembling shrinks before his might;
Where'er he moves whole ranks with slaughter gor'd,
Roll in wild heaps before his matchless sword,
While mad Revenge pursues the haggard train,
Gores their pale flight, and crimsons o'er the plain.

Now proudly rais'd on Grandeur's loftiest **height**
In all the blaze of sovereign splendor bright,
Like that glad Orb, whose life-inspiring beam
Through vast Creation wakes the genial flame,
With godlike pleasure from his bounteous **hand**
Dispensing blessings on a smiling land,
Shines the lov'd author of each useful plan,
Of arts the patron and the friend of man;
Opes the rich stores of learning's copious **spring,**
And bids Discovery lift a bolder wing;
His cheering rays illume the wintry shade,
In cold neglect where modest worth is laid,
With fostering warmth give genius' buds **to rise**
And spread their blossoms to indulgent **skies,**
While greatful hearts a glad obeisance **own,**
His people's love the basis of his throne.
Where late fell Tyranny with gore defil'd,
In fiend-like pleasure o'er his murders smil'd,
And ruffian Licence with unbridled might,
Boldly profan'd the sacred name of right,
His equal laws extend their blissful **power,**
Life to protect and property secure.

No more in nuptial loves the blooming bride,
Torn from her fond distracted lover's side
By Lust's stern force with unavailing cries,
Invokes the slumbering vengeance of the skies;
No more the native at the midnight hour,
Fears the dark ruffians arm'd with regal power,
Or views, aghast with horror and dismay,
His all to harpy violence a prey,
And while mad Riot revels o'er the prize,
Hangs o'er his famish'd babes, despairs and dies.
Where late wild Havoc with his ruthless train,
Mark'd with sterility the cultur'd plain,
Lo! wide-spread fields in ripening pomp unfold,
And to the breezes wave their seas of gold;
The spireless heath in sun-scorch'd brownness drear,
Smiles a green mead, and hails the auspicious year;
In fragrant pride, fruit, bending groves expand,
And a new Eden blossoms o'er the land.
 Or now, as schemes of less ambition fire,
Wrapt with the music of the Poet's lyre,
High in the list of song he stand's enroll'd,
Amid the sires of verse, the bards sublime of old;

While every muse auspicious, o'er his lays
Pours the full splendor of poetic praise,
And Wit and Genius, round his brows divine,
In union bright, their blooming laurels twine.
 Or, charm'd with private life's domestic scene,
Its social circle and its joys serene,
Happy in love-form'd union with the fair,
The beauteous object of his tenderest care,
With affluence crown'd, with mild contentment blest,
Of heaven's best gift, a feeling heart, possest,
His kind compassion yields the poor relief,
And wipes the tear-drop from the cheek of Grief;
Bids pale Dejection raise the languid eye,
And dumb Despair repress the anguish'd sigh.
A few lov'd friends, with genius, learning grac'd,
Of kindred manners and congenial taste,
His frequent hours with sprightly converse crown,
And make each social bliss peculiarly his own.
His are the joys that nature's scenery yields,
His are the health-fraught pleasures of the fields;
When the shrill cock awakes his matin cries,
And light's first dawnings break o'er eastern skies,

Oft with his dog and gun he joys to stray,
'Mid the pale twilight of uncertain day,
O'er the thin furze-clad heath, the hillock brown,
Near the brush-hedge, with frequent briars o'ergrown,
Through the rough thicket, pearl'd with trembling dew,
While with light steps he darts a heedful view,
Where, cowering close beneath the friendly wood,
The Quail or Partridge hides her timorous brood;
Or where the mist, in snowy volumes, spreads
Its shrouding mantle o'er the lilied meads;
Each reedy cove, each wonted haunt explores,
Along the windings of the fenny shores,
Where 'mid the bending rush, and colts-foot broad,
The Teal and Mallard wanton o'er the flood;
Or crested Wood-duck, [3] rich in all the dies
That tinge the fleecy robes of venal skies.

Thus in thy musings wild, the raptur'd breast
Partakes each varied bliss by man possest;
Shines in each different walk of changeful life,
In cool retirement's vale, in active strife;

Each glory shares that splendid station knows,
Each placid joy that private life bestows,
While glows the visionary prospect fair,
Nor gloom'd with sorrow, nor o'ercast with care;
For thy bright scenes no gathering clouds deform,
That o'er the real hang the frequent storm.

Oft has my bosom, in the gloomy hour,
Own'd the strong influence of thy soothing power;
Oft have thy warm creations, rising bright,
With noon-day radiance deck'd the shades of night;
In thy wild visions lost, with reckless toil,
Oft have I wander'd many a wildering mile,
O'er flowery meadows, o'er the sunburnt hill,
Through waving woods, or darkly winding dell,
When blaz'd the mid-day from his fervent throne,
When eastern hills with moon's pale glim'rings shone,
And o'er extended meads, in wreathings white,
The cold-breath'd mist, slow-spreading on the sight,
Look'd a vast lake, where groups of poplars show'd,
Like isles dim-gleaming through a watery cloud;
Hung o'er the cliff, from whose dark, beetling brow
Regardless Danger eyes the storm below;

Along the river's pebbly shore have stray'd,
When eve approach'd, in threat'ning glooms array'd,
While flocks of swallows o'er the surface throng,
Just dip the wing, and twittering, skim along;
And, heav'd without a breeze, the conscious wave,
In sounds low-murmuring, signs of tempest gave;
Scarce heeding aught, the landscapes varied scene,
Morn's grey-veil'd brow, or evening's cloudy mien,
As rose thy fairy scenes by rapture drest,
And every glowing nerve thy power confest.
  [4] Now, fir'd by tale of Knight or Hero old,
In wild romance or fabling legend told;
When wak'd to life, with brightest hues portray'd,
In tears all-winning, rose some hapless maid
To the dire gloom of Terror's lonely tower,
Confined by magic art, and giant power,
O'er dreary wastes, the regions of dismay,
O'er ghost-frequented fens have held my fancied sway.
Struggling through broken clouds, the lamp of night,
Reluctant sheds a melancholy light:
Now in full splendors from the glooms releas'd,
Gilds the wild horrors of the dismal waste,

Now swift retiring, hid in doubling clouds,
In ten-fold darkness every object shrouds.
Far seen, wild frowning o'er the sullen moor,
The Giant's castle lifts its ramparts hoar.
The time-struck towers seem tottering to their fall,
In frequent breaches yawns the rifted wall;
Slow opes, reluctant yielding to my power,
The massy gate, grating with hideous roar;
O'er the still dome the startling echoes roll,
Loud as when thunder rends the reddening pole:
Resolv'd I enter,—a blue magic flame,
Slow gliding onward, casts a dismal gleam.
By the faint livid light what scenes unfold!
Scenes at which Fancy's curdling blood runs cold:
The crimson-dropping walls, the treacherous floor,
With corses lin'd, and wet with human gore;
Around the bloody hall with ghastly stare,
Thin shadowy forms in pale succession glare;
With mournful looks the deathly train draws near,
And shriek their warnings in my tortur'd ear;
Amid the rest a wither'd form appears,
His grief-plough'd visage stain'd with wasting tears,

Waving his hand:—"O fly!" The phantom cries,
" Who e'er approaches to these walls, he dies!
" Say, wretched mortal! Art thou hither come,
" To share our fate, and find a certain tomb?
" Or can thy pride indulge this senseless hope,
" With magic powers and giant strength to cope?
" These ghastly forms that crowd this haunted room,
" Whose knelling shrieks prelude thy horrid doom,
" Like thee, advent'rous, dar'd these perils brave,
" And here their rashness found untimely grave;
" Doom'd to the same sad fate, thou too must fall,
" Thy mangled corse pollute the trophied wall!"
Vanish the flames,—now, all is night profound;
Deep tolls the turret bell a sullen sound,
Thrilling upon the heart. In chill dismay
O'er mangled limbs I grope my dreary way,
While each dire echo, murmuring thro' the gloom,
Sounds like the ghostly warnings of the tomb.
Rous'd at the unusual noise and hollow tread,
Starts the huge Giant from his iron bed;
Clad in bright arms he rears his monstrous size,
Revenge indignant flashing from his eyes:—

But vain his ponderous mace, his steely arms,
His size immense, his necromantic charms,
And more than human strength,—in bloody strife,
The caitiff falls, and yields his forfeit life.
The spells dissolve,—wide fly the iron doors,
Through the dark dungeon light unusual pours;
From its deep cells, the walks of pale despair,
Beyond all hope retrieved, I lead the Fair,
And to her long-lost lover's raptur'd arms,
Conduct her blushing in the pride of charms.

Now o'er Elysian scenes have held my way,
Such as the wizard's potent spell obey;
Whose charms to sing, whose various beauties paint,
Weak were the Poet's lays, the Painter's colors faint.
Fretted with gold, here gem-bright domes expand
Their beauteous wonders o'er enchanted land;
Here gardens bloom, in spring's luxuriance warm,
By liberal Nature deck'd in every charm,
Whose lucid streams, in tuneful mazes roll'd,
"O'er rocks of chrystal and o'er sands of gold,"
Here in smooth lakes, blue skies reflecting sleep,
There in cascades white hurry o'er the steep,

Or in jets d'eau their waves high-streaming throw,
And mock the beauties of the painted bow.
Here spar-roof'd grottos beam a placid light;
Here, wreath'd with woodbine, myrtle bowers invite;
The orange walk here spreads its grateful glooms,
The fragrant clove unfolds its crimson blooms,
The cinnamon, with spicy sweetness crown'd,
Wav'd by the Zephyr, breathes her odours round;
(5) And groves, with gold and silver foliage gay,
Bend their bright boughs, and sparkle to the day.
Beneath, each flower that scents the vernal skies,
Crowns the rich verdure with innumerous dyes;
In playful droves, the kid and tender fawn
Sport, lightly-bounding o'er the spangled lawn;
Or, wanton peering in the streamlet clear,
Start to behold a kindred face appear.
Here lovely maids, in snow-white silk array'd,
Range o'er the mead, recline beneath the shade;
Or, lur'd by sport, by frolic wildness fir'd,
Apart from ken of prying eye retir'd,
Beneath the chrystal wave their beauties hide,
And now emerging gambol o'er the tide,

Or laughing dart to shore, in cheerful play,
And near the banks in bright procession stray.
In rounds of pleasure, free from grief's alloy,
Flit their gay moments on the wings of joy;
While every songster wakes his tuneful notes,
And wide around the soul of music floats,
Ring the wild warblings o'er the echoing grove,
And all is beauty, melody and love.

 Thus, frequent rapt from morn to eve, **I 've strayed,
Regardless whither, through the woodland shade;**
And reckless view'd the sun's departing ray,
" Gilding the purple edge of closing day,"
Stretch the tall shadow of the trees afar;
Nor yet retir'd when beam'd the evening star;
Or, thron'd in full-orb'd majesty serene,
The pale moon, pensive, smiling o'er the scene,
Through op'ning boughs a trembling lustre play'd,
And softest silver chequer'd o'er the shade;
Till, from the dodder'd stump, or moss-clad **stone,
Whence through the night she pours her dismal moan,
While glimmer near the half-seen Church-yard throng,
The** [6] **Bird of sorrow wak'd her funeral song.**

Swift at the boding sound, the deathful cry,
The charms all vanish, and the beauties fly;
In quick succession hideous shapes arise,
And half-formed phantoms flit before my eyes;
While hollow groans my startled ear assail,
And shriek the spectres on the passing gale.
Now frowns, in terror's eye, a scene of fear,
A ruin'd pile, lone, desolate and drear;
Where, veil'd in midnight glooms, the sisters old
Unhallow'd rites and nameless orgies hold.
Around yon lamp, whose solitary light
Casts a dire paleness o'er surrounding night,
Lo! Where the haggard forms, with gore defil'd,
Writhe their blue lips, and roll their red eyes wild,
Low muttering o'er the sounds, whose potent spell
Calls up the dead, and bursts the gates of hell,
While, to their charms submissive, hover near
Monsters that want a name, the hideous brood of Fear.
 Oft have I rang'd o'er nature's wide domain,
And viewed the secrets of her ancient reign;
Where the dread Power, retir'd in central earth,
Moves Life's first springs and calls her atoms forth;

Explor'd the caverns of the rocky mine,
Where ripening gems in infant lustre shine,
Where glows the Gold in majesty of day,
And milder Silver beams the evening ray;
Have view'd, deep-sunk beneath old Ocean's waves,
The pearly treasures of her coral caves,
Where wealth immense, wide-spread in slighted heaps,
The spoil of nations and of ages, sleeps;
O'er realms of snow, on daring pinions whirl'd,
Survey'd the cheerless limits of the world;
The northern Pole, the ice-surrounded coast,
Lock'd in the rigors of eternal frost;
The straits impassable, where winter's hand
In thankless fetters chains the neighboring land;
Where rocks of ice on rocks of ice sublime,
The growth of ages since primeval time,
O'er the white-sailing clouds high-raised in air,
[7] Gleam bright in lucid green, and cast a chilling glare.
When, from the bosom cold of half-year night,
The Sun returning brings enlivening light,
And, slowly circling round the polar sky,
O'er the white verge just lifts his sparkling eye,

The emerald cliffs like fires wide-spreading glow,
And shine far-glittering o'er th' eternal snow;
Beamed from their sides the sunny splendors play,
And give new brightness to the Artic day.
Close screen'd in caves beneath their wintry sky,
Where chill Kamschatka's torpid natives lie;
Where the fierce Tartar leads his roving bands,
O'er Amor's banks, or Karakathai's sands;
Or where the Baikal [8] spreads, in grandeur lone,
His *sacred* waters o'er a world unknown,
Have held my way; and now excursive soar
O'er Nootka's floods, and bleak Anadir's shore;
O'er the vast Western world where nature reigns
Sublimely awful 'mid uncultur'd plains,
And grim in painted tribes, the tawny throng
Pour the dire shriek and raise the deathful song.
Where storm-tost Erie and Ontario rave,
Where the wild [9] Huron rolls its freezeless wave;
From its dark mountain cliffs sublimely rude,
Where Niagara heaves the raging flood
In one broad sheet of foam, while far around,
Woods, hills and vales repeat the thund'ring sound;

420

Where great Superior, mid surrounding wilds,
Boasts the rich scenery of his thousand isles,
And bids his ocean waves from eye impure
The Mighty [10] Spirit's lov'd recess secure;
Or where Missouri, through sequester'd woods,
And trackless deserts, leads his swelling flood;
Or Mississippi rolls his sovereign tide,
Or fair Ohio's mazy waters glide.
Hail lovely River! "Pride of future song!"
Bright as thou roll'st thy wildering waves along,
With what luxuriance vast thy banks are crown'd,
In nature's charms what beauty smiles around,
In savage grandeur frown what scenes sublime,
And what enchantments mark thy magic clime.
Here time-worn forests lift an awful shade,
O'er ancient [11] forts in lonely ruin laid,
Whose finish'd form and regular design,
Where geometric art and skill combine,
Proclaim that erst, in war's proud science skill'd,
This desert tract a powerful people fill'd,
Of e'en whose name no record now appears,
Lost in the ocean of revolving years;

Far different race from those barbarians rude,
By arts ne'er polish'd, nor by laws subdued,
Whose unsubmitting souls, with sternest pride,
Exult in death and torture's pangs deride,
In countless tribes far-spreading to the shores,
Where his broad wave the vast Pacific pours.
Here, midst savannah's vast of waving green,
Where not a tree diversifies the scene,
Mansoleums [12] rude the tombs of nations swell,
In frequent hillocks o'er the grass-grown dell.
Lo! op'd to view, the bursting heaps display
Their dark recesses to the eye of day:
The deep concealments of the unknown dead,
Where bones [13] of giant size on bones are spread;
While o'er them bending, with enraptur'd eyes,
Stands Admiration, fix'd in deep surprise.
Hence dark conjecture weaves her dubious veil,
And wild Invention forms her fairy tale
Of Cambrian hosts by princely Madoc led,
Of Jewish tribes from stern oppression fled,
When proud Assyria stretch'd her iron sway,
And saw the trembling East her nod obey.

NOTES TO THE FIRST BOOK.

[1] " Chained to yon rock." These lines allude to a painting by an American artist which possesses an uncommon degree of merit.

[2] " Not all the ills that humble life await, &c." These reflections were principally suggested from having read in the European Magazine for the year 1786 or 1787—an extract from the first poems of that inimitable minstrel of nature, Burns, accompanied with a short and interesting account of the author.

[3] " Or crested Wood-duck." This highly beautiful and graceful bird, is strikingly distinguished from others of its genus, by the richness and elegant distribution of its colors, by its long waving crest of green and purple intermixed with white, beautifully contrasted with its bright yellow and scarlet bill, and eyes that have the appearance of a coal of fire.

[4] " Now fir'd by tale of Knight, &c." The writer, in this place, readily acknowledges his obligation to the Fragment of Sir Bertrand: but to the Library of the ingenious author of the Village is he principally indebted, who, after a long silence and apparent consignment to oblivion, has recently received that reward of public applause which his distinguished talents so richly merit. The countenance of such respectable authority has determined me on the retention of this passage, which my matured judgment might otherwise have induced me to reject.

[5] " And groves with gold and silver foliage gay." At the Cape of Good-Hope are forests of a peculiar kind of tree, called the Gold and

NOTES TO THE FIRST BOOK.

Silver trees, the leaves of which resemble those metals in color and splendor.—Voyage to Mauritius.

⁶ "Bird of sorrow." By this appellation I have thought proper to designate the Whipperwill, a species of the Goatsucker, whose mournfully monotonous and funeral note appear to me to justify the term.

⁷ "Gleam bright in lucid green." The glacieres or cliffs of ice in the frozen ocean exhibit a splendid appearance, being of a vivid green, and rivalling the emerald in color and lustre.

The following Picturesque Description of the Icebergs in the Frozen Ocean is extracted from the Universal Magazine for 1785:—

The forms assumed by the ice in this chilling climate are extremely pleasing to even the most incurious eye. The surface of that which is congealed from the sea-water, for I must allow it two origins, is flat and even, hard, opake, resembling white sugar, and incapable of being slid on like common ice. The greater pieces, or fields, are many leagues in length; the lesser are the meadows of the seals, on which they sport by hundreds at a time. The motion of the lesser pieces is as rapid as the currents. The greater, which are sometimes two hundred leagues long, and sixty or eighty broad, move slow and majestically; often fix themselves for a time immoveable by the force of the ocean, and then produce near the horizon that bright white appearance, called by mariners the blink of the ice. The approximation of two great fields produces a most singular phenomenon; it forces the lesser out of the water and adds it to its surface; a second and often a third succeeds, the whole forming an aggregate of a tremendous height. These float in the sea like so many rugged mountains, and are sometimes five or six hundred yards thick, the far greater part of which is concealed beneath the water. These are continually encreased in height by the freezing of the spray of the sea, or the melting of the snow which falls upon them. Those which remain in this climate receive continual growth, others are gradually wafted by the northern winds into southern latitudes. The collision of the great fields of ice,

NOTES TO THE FIRST BOOK. 39

in high latitudes, is often attended with a noise, that for a time takes away the sense of hearing anything else, and the lesser with a grinding of unspeakable horror. The water, which dashes against the mountainous ice, freezes into an infinite variety of forms, and gives the voyager ideal towns, streets, churches, steeples, and every shape that imagination can frame. The Icebergs of Spitzbergen are among the principal wonders of the country; they are seven in number, but at considerable distances from one another; each fills the vallies for tracts unknown in a region totally inaccessible in the internal parts. One of them exhibits over the sea a front three hundred feet high, emulating the emerald in color; cataracts of melted snow precipitate themselves down various parts, and black spiring mountains, streaked with white, bound the sides, and rise, crag above crag, as far as the eye can reach in the back ground. At times immense fragments break off and tumble into the water, with an alarming noise. A piece of this vivid green substance has fallen, and grounded in twenty-four fathoms of water, and spired above the surface fifty feet. Frost sports also with these Icebergs, and gives them majestic as well as the most singular forms. Masses have been seen which assumed the shape of a Gothic church, with arched windows and doors, and all the rich tracery of that style, composed of what an Arabian tale would scarcely dare to relate, of crystal of the richest sapphirine blue; tables with one or more feet; and often immense flat-roofed temples, like those of Luxor, supported by round transparent columns of cœrulean hue, float by the astonished spectator.

* "Lake Baikal." The country, says M. Pullas, a little beyond the Lake Baical, produces the wild horse, called in the Mongul Dhiggetei. They were formerly seen in herds of from ten to thirty or upwards, but they are now rarely to be found except singly. The Dhiggetei is neither a horse nor an ass, but an intermediate species. Its form is handsomer than that of the mule; he is very slender and light, has fine limbs, a wild and sprightly air, and his skin is furnished with a good coat of hair. His ears (though long,) are better proportioned, shorter and straighter than those of the mule. The head is somewhat heavy, and the hoofs resemble those of the ass. He has also two other imperfections which injure his appearance, a long and square back, and a tail like that of a cow; his head is large, his breast broad and square below, and his chest somewhat contracted; his short and frizzled mane is like that of the ass; his shoulders are narrow, and as well as the breast less fleshy than those of the horse; his rump is more slender; all his limbs are thin but pretty high; his hair is a pretty bright brownish yellow, and the mane and tail are blackish; the whole spine of the back is marked with a handsome stripe of dark brown, a little broader at the small of the back, and considerably narrower near the tail. He carries his head very straight, and when he runs, his nose is in the air. It is asserted that the Dhiggetei surpasses all other animals in swiftness, and that the best horse is no match for him; he is extremely shy and can be taken or shot only by stratagem. All attempts that have been hitherto made to tame and domesticate this animal have proved unsuccessful.

The Lake Baical in Tartary is between four and five hundred miles in extent, but of very unequal breadth, not generally exceeding one hundred miles. The waters of this large lake are fresh; it is deep throughout, and abounds with excellent fish. The natives entertain a superstitious veneration for it, and have denominated it the Sacred Sea.

9 " Where the wild Huron rolls its freezeless wave." This is not peculiar to the Huron, but may be considered as equally applicable to all the larger lakes, which are never frozen, except around the shores and in the bays.

10 " The Mighty Spirit's lov'd recess." The principal island in Lake Superior is supposed by the Indians to be the favorite residence of the Great Spirit.

11 " O'er ancient forts." Remains of ancient fortifications, constructed agreeably to the modern principles of the art, have been

NOTES TO THE FIRST BOOK. 41

within a few years past discovered in the country, bordering on the
Ohio, on whose parapets were trees, some of which measured four feet
in diameter.

¹² " Mausoleums rude, &c." These tumuli are not unfrequently
met with on the vast plains of the Ohio ; they are filled with human
bones, some of which are said to be of an extraordinary size. On
opening some of them, bracelets of copper and other ornaments have
been found.

¹³ " Where bones of giant size." The bones found in these tumuli,
some of which are said to be of extraordinary size, must not, however,
be confounded with those occasionally found dispersed in various parts
of this country, but more particularly in a small salt pond, commonly
called the Big-Bone Lick, and which are supposed to have belonged to
an animal now extinct, known from the traditionary accounts of the
natives by the name of the Mammoth. This account has been detailed
at length by a celebrated philosophical writer of our own country ; but
without enquiring what degree of dependence, if any, is to be placed
on an Indian tradition, not improbably of recent fabrication, when we
take into consideration the inclination of those people to mislead and
deceive the whites respecting their country, the bones and the teeth in
themselves afford the most incontestible evidence of the existence, at
some remote period, of a race of animals in this country, surpassing the
elephant in size. A friend of the author, who had resided a long time
in the country on the banks of the Ohio, and who had examined with
care its most remarkable productions, informed him on a visit a few
years since to this part of the country, that he had in his possession a
tooth of this animal which weighed between eleven and twelve pounds,
and which he supposed to have been an incisor, as it was long and of a
different form from any other that he had met with. In relating the
manner in which the bones were found in the Lick above mentioned,
where he had employed some soldiers who were with him in collecting
some, he observed that there happened to be with him at the time—an

Indian belonging to the Seneca tribe or one of the Six Nations, and that when one of the soldiers first brought to him one of the teeth from the pond in which he had been groping, he showed it to the Indian, at the same time making him comprehend what it was, and enquiring if he knew how it came there. The man was at first so wholly incredulous on the subject that he would not be satisfied that it was not a trick to impose upon him, until he had procured one of the same kind himself by actual search, which, though of considerable weight, he carefully deposited in his frock in order to carry it home and exhibit it to his countrymen, declaring at the same time most solemnly, that he had never till then heard of such an animal, and that there was no account or tradition of anything like it among the Six Nations. "From this circumstance," said the officer, "together with what an old Shawanese chief had previously told me, I was led fully to conclude that not only such an animal was unknown by tradition to the Six Nations, but that it was equally so to the Shawanese, Delawares, Miamis and other tribes, at present occupying that part of the country, in or near which these remains are found. 'Indeed,' continued he, 'it is not to these who are but in a manner the people of yesterday that we must look for any real tradition on this subject; it is to the descendants of those nations who, previous to the first European Settlements on our Coast, inhabited these regions, and who, if they exist, will be found in the remotest western wilds, having been forced off by the other nations, as they have been successively driven westward by the Whites. He promised on his next visit, which he did not intend to have delayed long, to bring the remarkable tooth which was in his possession with him. Alas! he was destined never to return to his friends. Shortly after, rejoining the army, he was appointed second-in-command on the unfortunate expedition under General Harmer. He fell bravely at the head of his troops on the plains of the Miami in attacking the savages. In him fell the kind and generous friend, the brave soldier, the accomplished scholar, and the man of scientific research and investigation.'"

428

THE

Charms of Fancy.

BOOK THE SECOND.

ARGUMENT OF THE SECOND BOOK.

REFLECTIONS on the Power of Change.—Present rudeness and refinement of several countries, compared with their former state. Refinement of Manners, and Progress of Literature in America. Trumbull, Dwight, and Barlow. The country upon the Ohio. The scene of the misfortunes of the American Armies, and the first exploits of General Washington. Western shores of America. Pacific Ocean. Otaheitee. New Holland. Reflections on Man. New Zealand. Death of Captain Marion. Battle between the New Zealanders and the Crew of a French Ship. Voyages of Captain Cook. Apostrophe to Captain Cook. South America. Mexico and Peru; The Andes; The Condor; The rivers Oronoque and Amazon. Interior of Africa. Personification of Death and his attendants. The Lion, the Anaconda, &c. Barbarous nations inhabiting the interior. The Gallas, Jaggas, &c. Countries on the Coast. Whidda; Congo; River Senegal; Gambia; Boabab Tree. Slight mention of Europe; whence the author passes to Asia. Japan. General sketch of the manners of the inhabitants. China. City of Nankin; Porcelain Tower. Confucius, the Chinese Philosopher. Perfection of the Arts in China. Reverence entertained for the Laws by the Chinese. Their strict observance of Filial Duties. Reflections suggested by their national character. Great Wall of China. Tartarian Eruption and Conquest.

THE
CHARMS OF FANCY.

Book the Second.

How vast the power of Change! each passing day
Confirms her empire and extends her sway.
Wide o'er the earth she spreads despotic powers,
Now lifts with hope, or with dejection lowers,
Now bids the vernal beams of pleasure play,
With sorrow's wintry cloud now veils the glittering ray.
Here mighty realms, with wealth, with grandeur crown'd,
Whose sovereign sway far-distant nations own'd,
At her stern mandate, fled each former boast,
Sink, in the whelming waves of Ruin lost:
While petty states, of low, ignoble name,
She lifts to empire and adorns with fame.

O'er lands where polish'd Culture beam'd her rays,
And spreading Science pour'd her brightest blaze,
In barbarous pride now Ignorance profound
Throws the dark shades of native night around;
While climes, late plung'd in rudeness' deepest glooms,
Refinement's sun with cheering ray illumes.

 Lo Egypt's realms! where first the dawning light
Of new-born science burst the veil of night,
Beneath the yoke of vilest Ignorance groan,
Unknown to social love, to laws unknown;
Savage her sons, whose base, perfidious minds
No science softens, and no honor binds;
While Russian wilds, in former days alone
For manners rude and brutal fierceness known,
Whence o'er fair Italy the barbarous throng
In floods of ruin roll'd their course along,
Now in Refinement's brightening splendors glow,
And fair with Art's unfolding roses blow.

 E'en here, where late unknown to Culture's hand,
Thy glooms, Columbia! spread the savage land,
O'er whose wild walks, whose unfrequented shade,
The Indian sole, rude son of Nature, stray'd;

Now cultur'd plains extend, and cities smile,
And polish'd manners grace the favor'd soil:
Begrim'd with blood where erst the savage fell
Shriek'd the wild war-whoop with infernal yell,
The Muses sing; lo! Trumbull wakes the lyre,
With all the fervor of poetic fire.
Superior Poet! in whose classic strain
In bright accordance wit and fancy reign;
Whose powers of genius, in their ample range,
Comprise each subject and each tuneful change,
Each charm of melody to Phœbus dear,
The grave, the gay, the tender and severe.
Majestic Dwight, sublime in epic strain,
Paints the fierce horrors of the crimson'd plain;
And, in Virgilian Barlow's tuneful lines
With added splendor, great Columbus shines.

Nor less o'er Nature spreads her high control:
New lands she bids extend, new oceans roll;
Here plains to mountains swell'd aspiring rise,
And lift their snow-crown'd summits to the skies;
While here, as o'er them wasting time prevails,
The humbled mountains sink to lowly vales.

Where once proud cities rose in spiry pride,
Now rolls the surgy deep its billows wide,
And midst their palaces and gorgeous domes
Sea-monsters revel, and the Mermaid [1] roams;
Insidious foe of all, in ambush dark,
On death intent, there lurks th' unpitying Shark,
There poisonous Rays and chill Torpedoes swarm,
And the dread Sepia [2] spreads his hideous form.
The [3] Sea-snake there his proud dominion holds,
Waves his white mane, and coils his monstrous folds.
While erst, where Ocean [4] spread his dark-blue waves,
And branching coral redden'd o'er the caves,
Now in green pride tall forests rear the head,
And yellow harvests gild the waving mead.
O'er those once sea-wash'd vales, those shelly rocks,
The simple shepherd drives his bleating flocks,
And far from shrinking ocean's storm-beat shore,
Ne'er view'd the sea, " or heard the billows roar."
    And now, so long divergent from her way,
Mid fairy realms and primal worlds to stray,
Allur'd, the Muse resumes her pristine theme,
And hangs delighted o'er Ohio's stream.

CHARMS OF FANCY.

Mid these fair scenes, array'd in summer's bloom,
Where wilds of fragrance breathe a glad perfume,
And bright with every flower of richest hues,
One vast parterre, ⁽⁵⁾ each beauteous prairie shews;
Too oft in fatal strife the bloody plain
Has blush'd, Columbia! with thy heroes slain,
While o'er their mangled forms the savage smil'd,
And songs of triumph shook the echoing wild.
Here, patriot Chief! commenc'd thy first essay,
The morning promise of thy glorious day!
What time the foe their fatal ambush spread,
And Britain yielded, while her general bled :
Here first that martial genius shone display'd,
Destin'd in future time thy country's aid,
When stern injustice bade her gloomy band
In blood and ruin whelm the hapless land,
Oppression in his car exulting sate,
And Freedom trembled for Columbia's fate.
In thee thy country owns, with grateful pride,
Her shield in war, in peace her surest guide.
Long, generous Patriot! may that country share
Thy prudent councils, and thy guardian care;

Long happy in thy rule, in peace maintain
Those various blessings which she bled to gain;
While, borne to distant lands, thy deeds sublime
Shall brighten as they mark the page of time,
And ages yet unborn, with glad acclaim,
Pronounce a Washington's illustrious name.

 These scenes luxuriant left, mine eyes survey
The shores far-distant of descending day,
Where setting Phœbus, bright in parting smiles,
Beams his last splendors o'er the western isles.

 Lo! where a golden plain in sun-bright pride,
The vast Pacific spreads her slumbering tide;
O'er her smooth breast what numerous islands rise,
And gladdening smile beneath their blissful skies!

 Here Otaheitee, [6] beauty's favorite soil,
Sees Love in triumph revel o'er her isle:
Hail, happy climate! o'er whose joyous plains,
In genial pomp, exulting Nature reigns;
Hail, happy people! to whose lot are given
The brightest favors of indulgent heaven.
Here, no cold blasts of calumny annoy,
No clouds of coyness chill the buds of joy,

But the warm wish disdains concealment's art,
And love is nature springing from the heart.

 Wide o'er the immense of seas, in southern skies,
Within itself a world, ⁽⁷⁾ New Holland lies;
Shrouded in woods, in all the pomp sublime
Of nature's wildness, frowns the gloomy clime;
Where pensive Solitude, romantic maid,
Sits undisturb'd in robes of grey array'd,
And views, mild pleasure trembling in her eye,
Her favorite Kangaroo ⁽⁸⁾ light-bounding nigh.
Here, no gay bands in mirth their hours employ,
No vales resound the notes of festive joy,
No cheerful pipe, or soft-alluring song,
Wakes the brisk dance, or charms the sprightly throng,
No hamlets smile, no fields in culture gay
The first faint steps of social life display;
Scarce trod by man, it frowns, a dreary scene,
Where wears humanity its rudest mien,
And where, to nature's simplest wants confin'd,
No thirst of knowledge ⁽⁹⁾ marks the improving mind.
A few vile huts, in straggling loneness strewed,
Scarce made for shelter, hide the wretched brood.

Here see, oh Man! how low thy vaunted pride;
Thee from the brute what narrow bounds divide.
Thy vast pre-eminence o'er all, how vain :
The empty vision of an idle brain!
What regal marks, by forming power imprest,
Designate thee the Sovereign of the rest?
Rude in their origin, how near, we find,
Approach the human to the bestial kind.
The same wild appetites in either sway,
Each follows blind, as instinct points the way,
Impell'd by lust, or hunger's ruthless power,
Now propagate their kind, and now devour.
Is this the period—theme of lavish praise—
The age of innocence, the golden days?
The often-envied time by poets sung,
" When nature triumph'd, and the world was young;"
All arts alike unknown, while brutal man
Wild with his fellows of the forest ran,
Stranger to thought, with reason scarce endued,
And glean'd from woods and streams his scanty food?
Yes! these the scenes that oft have fir'd the Muse,
Scenes deck'd by Fancy in her brightest hues.

Here Terror, listening to the billowy roar,
Spreads her black pinions o'er New Zealand's shore,
And views with grim delight her dark-eyed band,
Thick-seam'd with gashes, prowl around the strand;
In all the fierceness of rude nature drest,
Nor rul'd by reason, nor by laws represt,
Unknown the tender, sympathetic glow,
Unknown the tear that melts at human wo,
Unknown philanthropy's exalted zeal,
Alone thy gloomy joys, Revenge, they feel.
By seeming friendship's treacherous lure trepann'd,
Thy blood, O Marion! [10] stain'd the barbarous land,
Thick o'er the beach the wondering natives pour,
With eager eye the stranger band explore,
In savage kindness with each other vie,
Proffer their aid, and all their wants supply;
While every face, in smiles of welcome drest,
Conceals the hatred rankling in the breast.
Lull'd by false calms, from dread of danger free,
Caution oft sleeps on Ruin's flattering sea;
O'er the wild plain, or through the frowning grove,
In straggling bands the careless strangers rove,

Boldly secure, unjealous of their wiles,
Nor deem that murder lurks beneath their smiles.
Meanwhile the tribes, with bloody hopes elate,
Silent conven'd, in secret ambush wait.
Sudden the dismal yell resounds afar,
And the hoarse clamors speak the savage war;
Furious as tigers, fir'd by thirst of gore,
Dark from their shades the frowning warriors pour,
Whelm the weak train, opprest with wild dismay,
And grin exulting o'er their mangled prey.
Now wide around triumphal flames aspire,
Red glows through night the melancholy fire;
In circling throngs their brutal feast they share,
Rend the warm limbs, the flesh yet panting tear,
With joy malignant gorge their horrid flood,
And dye their jaws with streams of human blood;
While swells the hideous roar of triumph round,
And hill and vale repeat the infernal sound.

 From the far ship the crew, with wild surprise,
Behold the fires red-kindling o'er the skies;
Their absent comrades wake the anxious thought,
And dark suspense, with all its terrors fraught,

Grows on each hour; at length, confirm'd their fears,
The dreaded truth in every horror glares;
Bursts the full drop from friendship's anguish'd eye,
And Detestation breathes the impassion'd sigh.
Crozet to vengeance moves; an ardent band
Pours from the ship and hastens to the strand;
Each sparkling eye indignant fury speaks,
Impatience reddening on their burning cheeks;
O'er the blue wave their snow-white standards stream,
Their arms bright glitt'ring to the morning beam,
The watchful chiefs behold the impending war,
Yells the dire summons through the woods afar;
Like blackening clouds that roll the gathering storm,
To the high Hippah [11] rush the savage swarm,
With threatening gestures dare the hostile train,
Brandish their arms, and taunt in fierce disdain.
Now first the cliffs repeat the cannon's roar,
And unknown thunders shake the affrighted shore:
But, firm as rocks, when howling tempests rave,
Dash their strong sides, and heave the angry wave,
The mat-clad [12] warriors stand; nor aught dismays,
The thundering sound, or lightning's mimic blaze.

Pierc'd by strange deaths, astonish'd they behold
Their friends around, in floods of crimson roll'd,
Yet unextinguish'd burns the rage of fight,
Nor knows one breast a distant thought of flight:
But valor vain, in martial arts unskill'd,
With arms inferior tempts the desperate field.
Loud bursts the war, thick clouds involve the morn,
Crash the strong pales, in shivering fragments torn;
Yawns a vast breach: within the opening wide
A frowning chieftain towers in dauntless pride.
Pierc'd in the breast, the gallant savage lies,
Roll'd in the pass, and glare in death his eyes;
On his yet breathing corse a second stands,
And fires the ardor of his native bands.
Stretch'd on his friend's pale form the warrior bleeds;
Instant another to the charge succeeds,
With emulation's generous glow elate:
Thus eight successive mount to certain fate,
At length their courage sinks, their leaders slain,
And pale dismay impels the remnant train;
Wide o'er the plains, in flight dispers'd, they pour,
And copious vengeance dyes the sword in gore.

Round these wild shores, by thirst of knowledge
    led,
Adventurous Cook his daring pinions spread.
Lo! seas unsail'd before, his streamers hail,
And willing breezes lift the spreading sail;
Where e'er he roves, see gladdening islands heave,
And worlds unknown their shrouds of darkness
    leave,
With smiles of welcome opes each joyous strand,
Wave the tall trees, and beckon him to land.
Round wild Kamschatka's winter-loaded coast,
Where Arctic regions pine in endless frost;
Or where, far south, Antartic billows roar,
Heave the white isles, and lash the freezing shore;
'Mid fields of ice in boundless horror spread,
'Mid floating rocks that cast a chilling shade,
The intrepid chief pursues his arduous way,
No perils daunt him, no fatigues dismay.
Ting'd by the low-hung sun's faint-beaming smiles,
In beauty dreadful glare the [13] purple piles,
In wintry pride, like towers, they rise on high,
Pierce the blue clouds and brighten in the sky;

Beneath the mass, hoarse groan the encumber'd tides,
High swell the waves, white-foaming o'er their sides,
Loud crash the dashing rocks, together driven,
Like shooting stars, their sparkles gleam to heaven,
O'er the drear waste concussive echoes pour,
And ocean trembles at the deafening roar.

Regretted chief! whom savage fury gave,
In bloom of honor, an untimely grave;
With generous thirst of enterprize inspir'd,
By foes respected and by friends admir'd,
A heart humane and dauntless spirit join'd,
With worth superior, grac'd thy active mind;
In cold neglect Discovery weeps thy doom,
And pensive droops, pale sickening o'er thy tomb.

Now Southern climes, in wealthiest pomp, unfold
Their silvery rocks and regions rich with gold:
Where Mexico, illum'd with grandeur's ray,
Saw Montezuma spread an envied sway;
But now, beneath the oppressive yoke of Spain,
Bends with the weight of slavery's galling chain:
Where high Peruvia breathes salubrious gales,
And nature revels o'er Chilesian vales.

CHARMS OF FANCY.

Enthron'd in star-crown'd majesty sublime,
Frown the vast Andes o'er the extended clime:
Cliff piled on cliff, high mounting to the skies,
Where e'en the soaring eagle fears to rise;
Vast rocks unverdur'd, here, in steep ascent,
Lift their grey sides, in yawning fissures rent; [brow,
Here, shagg'd with woods, project the threatening
And nod their horrors o'er the vale below.
Its topmost cliff, which yon tall granite shrouds
In blackening tempests and involving clouds,
With snows perpetual spread, with larch o'erhung,
'Mid storms enthron'd, the Condor [11] rears her young;
No ravenous bird, on airy pinions light,
Hither presumes to point his venturous flight,
No hungry serpent dares, in quest of prey,
To these dark eyries wind his dangerous way,
But, fill'd with terror, shuns the place where reigns
The dreaded tyrant of the ethereal plains.
Lost in the gloom, or brightening in the day,
Here numerous torrents roll their foamy way,
Through the rough clefts in whitening fury sweep,
Hoarse roaring, deafening, down from steep to steep,

445

And, hurrying o'er the heights with mingled swell,
In maddening tumult seek the distant dell;
Now, in wild eddies whirl'd, with dashing force,
'Twixt rifted rocks impel their furious course;
Now, far-releas'd, in placid beauty spread,
And gently-dimpling silver o'er the mead,
'Till mingling, streams of sovereign name they glide:
Hence Oronok rolls wild his rapid tide;
Hence Amazonia winds her lengthening train,
In weary progress to the Atlantic main.

 Excursive, hence o'er Africa's wilds I stray,
Scorch'd with the fiercest fires of vertic day.
Dire nurse of monsters! Whose envenom'd earth
Wakes every plague, and gives each poison birth;
Here, fierce exulting o'er the desert plains,
In all his horrors Death triumphant reigns;
And views, with baleful joy, around him wait
Submiss his deadliest messengers of fate:
The fiery [13] Dipsas and the Aspic cold,
And fell Cerastes, twin'd in horrent fold.

 Prompt to perform his will, with pois'nous breath,
Sweeps the blue Simoom o'er the blasted heath—

Mid fenny vapors and mephitic clouds
The purple Plague his form disgustful shrouds;
While Cruelty, with stern obdurate brow,
O'er the pale features of his dying foe,
Relentless cannibal, exulting lours,
Quaffs the warm blood, the quiv'ring flesh devours.
　Here, by the sun's hot ray sublim'd to blood,
Of size supreme, with greater strength endued,
To man more terrible, the savage beast,
With wilder fury, prowls the desert waste.
From the dark lair, his unknown, dire abode,
E'en by the native's fearless feet untrod,
By hunger's call impell'd, when silence reigns,
And midnight horrors gloom the lonely plains,
Stalks the fierce Lion: hark! his hideous roar,
In echoing thunder, rings the forest o'er,
Borne on the winds, wild terror pants around,
And firmness, self e'en trembles at the sound.
Terrific, glowing in his scaly arms,
Whose painted beauties lend to horror charms,
Like some tall cedar, length'ning o'er the plain,
The fell (16) Constrictor spreads his hideous train.

447

Where'er the dreaded monster sweeps along,
Before him trembling fly the savage throng;
In one promiscuous rout together roll'd,
The weak, the strong, the tim'rous and the bold.
To him oppos'd the Tiger's vigor fails,
Nor e'en the Lion's mightier force avails;
Proud in resistless strength he tow'ring moves,
And reigns the tyrant of the midland groves.
Of size minute, here nature's deadliest pest,
The [17] Seps, envenom'd, rears his vengeful crest.
Fraught with sure fate, his baleful poisons glide
Through the scorch'd channels of the vital tide;
With instant death defy the powers of art,
Dissolve the frame and burst the blood-swoln heart.

 Unknown to gentle pity's soft control,
Unknown to arts that harmonize the soul,
Strangers to peace, in wild ferocious bands,
Here sable nations blacken o'er the sands;
Compar'd with whom that fury of the wild,
Pity's stern foe, the fell Hyena's mild.
Here, scarce superior to his fellow beast,
The brutal Caffre spreads his filthy feast;

448

Mid time-coeval woods, unknown to day,
Here Goran's [18] sons in lonely wildness stray;
Here roams the Galla, [19] stain'd with streaming gore;
Here Anzikains [20] their mangled foes devour;
And here the Jagga, [21] nature's foe accurst,
In every crime and deed of horror nurst,
By hands maternal bids the infant die,
And kindred flesh his dire repast supply.

From these dread realms, in every terror drest,
Where savage tribes a savage clime infest,
And uncontrol'd, each social tie defied,
Relentless murder prowls in licensed pride,
I turn where nature cheers the favor'd shores,
Where royal Congo boasts her golden stores;
Where bright beneath her Paradisean skies,
Thy Eden, Afric, [22] Whidda's landscapes rise!
Where Senegal devolves his length'ning floods,
Through rice-clad fields and aromatic woods,
And views the jetty tribes his banks along,
With uncouth gestures raise their evening song;
Where, round the central tree, in circling rows,
The reed-built [23] hamlet's hive-form'd structures close;

As to the Banjo's hoarse, discordant sound,
The sprightly dancers trip in antic round,
While circling gourds, with luscious nectar fraught,
Fresh from the palm, supply their festive draught;
Where Gambia's wide-extended waves are roll'd
O'er regions rich in iv'ry and in gold,
Mid whose luxuriant scenes and fertile meads
Its forest shade the vast Boabab [24] spreads;
Or where, mid tracts unknown, in regal pride,
Mysterious Niger pours his mighty tide,
O'er citied plains, that mark inquiry's eye,
Where proud [25] Tombuctoo lifts her towers on high,
Where Houssa's domes and fair Ghanara gleam,
In bright reflection, from his parent stream.

    O'er Europe, now, enraptured hold my way;
Europe by arts refined, with social manners gay;
Where fav'ring freedom crowns the happy soil,
And peopled plains with beauteous cities smile:
Her forms of rule, her various laws survey,
The different customs different realms display,
The rich productions of each fertile coast,
Her splendid piles, of modern art the boast,

And hoar, superb remains of ancient days,
That still a solemn awe and mournful pleasure raise.
 O'er Asian climes—O come, thou source of song,
To whom description's brightest hues belong!
Propitious smile, thy fav'ring aid bestow,
With richest colors give the pen to glow,
That diffident attempts, in humble rhyme,
To trace the beauties of the Eastern clime.
Shall Greece and Rome, those thread-bare themes of praise,
Alone deserving claim the poet's lays?
Though ancient Greece, for arms, for science known,
In sages, heroes, bards superior shone,—
Though Rome, proud empress of the world, could boast
Her power unrivall'd and her patriot host,—
His martial lyre though there a Virgil strung,
And love's soft pangs enamor'd Ovid sung,—
Sublime in age, though yet her ruins roll
The tides of wonder o'er th' impassion'd soul,—
Still must the Bard for them employ the verse,
To sing their beauties and their fame rehearse;

With servile step pursue the common road,
The way-worn paths so oft by poets trod;
While yet unsung Palmyra's charms remain,
Unsung the wonders of Egyptia's plain?

Come, let me then those fav'rite scenes explore,
Where, borne by Fancy, oft I've ranged before.
And first Japon's extensive isle survey,
The distant region of the new-born day,
Where dark Suspicion bids her keen-eyed band
Guard from access the interdicted land.
No foreign eye its wonders e'er explores,
No foreign foot e'er treads the jealous shores;
From all divided and to all unknown,
In proud seclusion live her sons alone.
Ingenious skill th' industrious native warms,
Whence art mechanic wears her fairest forms:
But pagan faith, in dark'ning current, rolls
The waves of error o'er their blinded souls;
To imaged monsters rites divine they frame,
[26] And bow to Xaca and Amida's name.
Far as the utmost bounds of sight extend,
Imperial [27] Jeddo's glitt'ring piles ascend.

O'er all, sublime, her golden palace burns,
Another sun, and blaze for blaze returns.
Here wealth unequall'd beams its brightest smile,
And pours its envied bounties o'er the isle. [towers,
But, from these climes where ignorance proudly
In vain pre-eminence of fancied powers,
Whose haughty natives, to their shores confined,
Disdain all commerce with the human kind,
I haste where neighb'ring lands their charms display,
Where China boasts her wide-extended sway,
And, vain of antique fame, [28] infabling clouds
Of primal ages her high annals shrouds.

Here warm fertility her seat maintains,
In richest state; here [28] cultivation reigns,
With vivid hues impaints the various scene,
With gold the harvest and the mead with green;
The desert waste with ripening stores supplies;
Here spreads the herb, there gives the tree to rise;
Where black'ning forests pour'd an awful gloom,
She bids the Jaka [29] and the Lichi bloom;
Rears the rich Tea, [30] unfolds her snowy flowers,
And o'er her leaf-refreshing fragrance pours.

453

O'er the vast region, from Corea's lands,
Where distant Thibet on the west expands,
Whose sons, by servile superstition aw'd,
Pay adoration to a human [31] God,
From royal Pekin to the southern shores,
Its peopled wave where shining [32] Canton pours,
What figured arches bend, what pompous fanes,
What swarming [33] cities crowd th' extended plains!
But far o'er all ascend, in gorgeous view,
Where the deep Kiang [34] rolls his waters blue,
Nankin, thy piles, whose vast extent defy
The utmost vision of the aching eye,
Pouring in dazzling stream one boundless blaze,
An ocean beaming with meridian rays.
Amongst the rest, with golden figures gay,
Far seen, bright glowing in the noon of day,
Thy Porcelain Tower, [35] enrich'd with every dye,
Spires like a fir, in flames amid the sky.
As ants, when early autumn's nitrous breath
Reddens the leaf and dews the filmy heath,
Taught by wise instinct, with prudential care,
To brave the rigors of the wintry year,

Spread o'er their heapy town in toiling strife,   [life.
And the whole moving mole-hill seems inspired with
Thus o'er thy streets thick throng the busy train,
Lured by the all-enticing voice of gain.

Thee, happy China, great Confucius blest,
The first of sages as of men the best,
Whose institutions and whose laws divine
With social love and moral wisdom shine.
With wide benevolence his bosom glow'd,
Where every virtue fix'd its loved abode;
With judgment cool, discernment keen combined,
Superior genius mark'd his lofty mind.
Midst the bright beams that gild the vernal days,
When smooth prosperity's gay smile betrays,
Midst the dark clouds with wintry storms that lour,
When dire misfortune pours her baleful shower,
His soul, exalted in one calm serene,
Still shone the same mid every changing scene.
Above the lures that bribe the vainly great,
Wealth's dazzling glare, and grandeur's empty state,
The Patriot Sage, by no mean cares subdued,
Comprised all blessings in his country's good—

That end alone with zeal unwearied sought,
" And shone a mirror of the truths he taught."
Bright star of reason! thy diffusive light
Pierced the dark shades of superstition's night;
From fair religion threw the veil aside,
That craft had wove and ign'rance sanctified;
Show'd her true form to man's illumined mind,
In fair perfection's heavenly beams enshrined;
And taught that ne'er from reason's path she strays
Lured by bewild'ring creeds, or system's meteor blaze.

Blest realm, where nature gives each plant to rise,
That glows in torrid, smiles in temp'rate skies;
With richest sweets each nectar'd fruit endues,
And paints each fragrant flower with brightest hues.
Adorn'd with glossy gold and shining red,
The purple Mutang [37] rears its regal head;
By art's nice hand arranged in chequer'd rows,
The [38] Tallow grove with scarlet beauty glows;
Sprinkling its foilage red with snowy hue,
The fruit fair-opening forms a pleasing view:
Thus shows in sinking autumn's early morn
The hoar-frost whit'ning on the berried thorn.

There [39] art with life her gay creation warms,
And decks with richest dies their mimic forms;
In every vale of peace the lily blows,
And mild contentment opes her blushing rose.
Thy people blest, with arts industrious graced,
Whom cool-eyed prudence guards from thriftless waste,
Taught from their youth to hold, in rev'rent awe,
Their rulers' mandates as a sacred law,
And with obedience unreserved fulfil
The harshest dictates of a parent's will;
Submission hence and filial duty shine,
On every breast, in characters divine.
For them no charms has slaughter's crimson-field—
To them no pleasure martial honors yield;
Alone the gentle joys of peace they prize,
And war detest, though veil'd in glory's guise.

But, through life's varied paths, by heaven assign'd,
On good attendant, evil still we find;
Still near the virtues hundred vices lurk,
And blast perfection through all nature's work.
Though here, with bright invention's garland crown'd,
Ingenious art her roses strews around—

Yet far from nature's simple rules she strays,
To follow fancy through her wildest maze.
Though ne'er thy sons, by thriftless waste betray'd,
Quit the cool walks of prudence' guardian shade—
Yet wincing av'rice oft infects the root,
And blights the promised virtues ere they shoot.
Hence meanest [40] arts disgrace thy filial train,
Base fraud's low cunning and each trick of gain.
Though lust of war may dye the earth with blood,
And whelm the nations in misfortune's flood,
Yet love of peace her ills peculiar brings,
Which cherish'd thrive beneath her shelt'ring wings.
To glory lost alone her votaries please
The low delights of mean, disgraceful ease,
Whose baneful opiates, with lethargic art,
Deaden the noblest passions of the heart;
Hence trembling cowardice, the dastard's shame,
With base opprobrium brands thy recreant name.

 Urged by this spirit base in days of yore,
The sceptred rule when great Chi Ho Ham bore,
Thy timid race, with persevering toil,
Rear'd the vast bulwark of yon massy [41] pile—

O'er the wide realm unbroken holds its way,
From Tanguth's mountains to Leaotung's bay;
O'er far-stretch'd plains in length'ning line extends,
Through winding dells in course meand'ring bends,
Tow'ring ascends the craggy mountain's brow,
And sinks far less'ning in the vale below.
Enormous Work! alone with thee might vie
The tower that raised its sky-veil'd head on high,
When earth's proud sons, by mad presumption fired,
With mortal works to rival heaven aspired,
Till midst the builders fierce dissensions sprung,
And harsh confusion jarr'd on every tongue.

But walls in vain their rampired strength extend,
The languid sons of affluence to defend
From savage foes: the battle's dauntless brood,
By plunder fired and train'd to scenes of blood,
If lost to honor's voice, to glory's charms,
No martial virtues rouse the soul to arms.
This Rome experienced, when, in luxury lost,
Wide o'er her regions spread the Gothic host;
This China proved, when, prompt at rapine's call,
Rush'd the grim Tartars o'er the slighted wall.

As when a storm, in wild destructive flight,
Invades the golden grain with chilling blight,
Strews wide the orchard's shatter'd limbs around,
And with unripen'd fruitage loads the ground,
The hapless peasant, in despair aghast,
Surveys the ruins of the furious blast:
Thus, o'er thy realm, in careless ease betray'd,
The ruthless foe one scene of havoc spread;
Thus view'd thy sons their fertile fields laid waste,
Their treasures plunder'd and their cities razed,
Their kindred slain, with sacred blood distain'd,
The holy temples of their gods profaned—
Th' imperial throne to barb'rous foes a prey;
Their empire groans beneath a Tartar's sway.

NOTES TO THE SECOND BOOK.

[1] "Sea-monsters revel, and the Mermaid roams." Many doubts have been entertained of the existence of this animal; and it has generally been considered as nothing more than the fictitious offspring of the imagination. Many concurrent testimonies, however, appear to establish the fact, that a creature, in some degree resembling man, is an inhabitant of the ocean. The Tritons and Nereids of Pagan mythology have, no doubt, their origin from this source.

[2] "The hideous Sepia." The eight-armed Cuttle-fish, a species of the Polype, is said sometimes to grow to a monstrous size, and frequently to attack men or other animals that come within the reach of its monstrous arms and devour them. Pliny relates, that a fish-pond, belonging to one of the Roman Emperors, having been robbed of its fish in the night, a guard was placed, in order to watch and intercept the thief; but that, to their astonishment, the soldiers discovered the robber to be a Cuttle-fish, or Polype, of an enormous size, which came from the sea. This monster, after breaking down part of the bank of the pond, devoured the fish and returned to the sea, without the guard daring to molest it. It is likewise related of the celebrated Sicilian diver, Nicolo, that, on his return from Charybdis, into which he had been induced to dive by the persuasion and offers of Frederick, King of Naples, he mentioned, as one of the greatest dangers he had to encounter, the monstrous Polypi that adhered to the sides of the rocks, many of which were of the size of a man's body, and entangled with their long arms whatever living object came within their reach. An

ingenious writer has observed, that the fable of Scylla's destroying men, probably owes its origin to the number of these large Polypi, which in ancient times surrounded that rock.

³ "The Sea-Snake there his proud dominion holds." According to the account given by Pontopidan, Bishop of Norway, this serpent is frequently discovered by the fishermen in the Norwegian seas. It is described as having a head like a horse, with a long mane, and large eyes which shine like plates of silver; and it is added, that his immense folds, as he lies upon the surface of the waves, have the appearance of a great number of hogsheads, separated by small intervals from each other.

"Sea Serpent." The following extract from an account of Norway, by a learned and ingenious writer, will show the belief entertained by the Norwegians, relative to the existence of such a monster as the Serpent of the Sea: "In the year 1746, says the author, Captain Laurence de Torcy, of Bergen, shot a Sea-snake, which instantly disappeared, and when the boat was rowed near the place, the water appeared tinged with blood. The head of this animal, which it held at least two feet above the surface of the water, was of a greenish color, and resembled that of a horse; the mouth was very large and black; the eyes were of the same color, and a long white mane hung down from its neck and floated on the sea. Besides the head, they saw seven or eight coils of this snake about the distance of a fathom from each other. It is stated in Egede's Journal of the Greenland Missionaries, that, on the 6th of July, 1734, a large and frightful sea-monster raised itself so high out of the water, that its head reached above the main-topmast of the ship; that it had a long sharp snout, broad paws, and spouted water like a whale. The body seemed to be covered with scales; the skin uneven and wrinkled, and the lower part was formed like a snake. It plunged itself back in the water, and then raised its tail above the surface, a whole ship's length from the head. Though the dimensions of the Sea-snake cannot be accurately ascertained, it would appear, from the concurrent accounts of those who have seen it, that it is nearly an hundred fathoms in length, and of the size of a hogshead."

Since the above was written, several accounts of the Sea-snake have appeared, from which I have selected the two following, which serve to place its existence beyond a doubt. In, or about the year 1795 or '96, an account was published in one of the Boston newspapers, of the appearance of a monster of this description, in the Bay of Penobscot. It was contained in a letter from a clergyman, of the name of Maclean, residing on the Penobscot. The account stated, that certain persons, whose names are mentioned, being out in the bay fishing, saw at a distance, the weather being clear, what they thought to be a number of floating barrels, drifting at small intervals, which they supposed to have come from the wreck of some vessel. They immediately rowed thither, but, on approaching near, to their surprise and terror, perceived that the supposed casks were nothing more than the folds of an immense serpent, which lay floating on the surface of the waves. At their approach, the animal raised its head some feet above the water, but soon after dove and disappeared. The head was very large and had the form of that of a horse; the neck was furnished with a mane, and the eyes resembled two large shining pewter plates. It appeared to them to be of very great length; but, as only part of the body was visible, they could only form a conjectural calculation, from what they saw, that it was upwards of one hundred feet long. This account was accompanied with a certificate, signed by several very respectable gentlemen of that part of the country, in favor of the veracity of the relators.

The same, or a similar serpent, was seen some time during the American war, in the same bay, at, or about the time of the Penobscot expedition. It was discovered by a naval officer belonging to the State of Massachusetts, who gave a description of it, nearly similar to the preceding, to a gentleman of the author's acquaintance. But one circumstance which he mentioned, and which seems either not to have been known, or to have escaped the notice of those who have written of this snake, was, that its motion was very different from that of land serpents, being vertical, instead of horizontal ; for, though he was at first astonished, and not a little alarmed, at the appearance of a monster, of whose existence it would seem he had never heard, he resolved at all events to examine it as accurately as he could, and was particularly struck with the singularity of its movement over the waves.

At a meeting of the Wernerian Society of Natural History, at Edinburgh, on the 19th of November, 1808, Mr. P. Neill read an account of a great Sea-Snake, which was cast ashore in October, in Orkney. This curious animal, it appears, was stranded in Nothesholmer Bay, in the island of Stronsa. Malcolm Laing, Esq., being at Orkney at the time, communicated the circumstance to his brother at Edinburgh, upon whose estate the animal had been cast. Through this authentic channel, Mr. Neill received his information. The body measured fifty-five feet in length, and the circumference of the thickest part of it was about equal to the girths of an Orkney pony. The head was not larger than that of a seal, and was furnished with two blow-holes. From the back, a number of filaments, resembling in texture the fishing-tackle, known by the name of silk-worm-gut, hung down like a mane. On each side of the body were three large fins, shaped like paws and jointed. Mr. Neill concluded with remarking, that no doubt could be entertained that this was the kind of animal described by Ramusius, Egede, and Pontoppidan, (and called by the latter, the Soe-Ormen,) but which had hitherto been rejected by scientific Naturalists as ideal.

⁴ " While erst where ocean spread his dark-blue waves." On the mountain of Stella, in Portugal, there is a lake, in which wrecks of shipping have been found, though this mountain is more than twelve leagues distant from the sea. Sabinios, in his commentaries on the Metamorphoses of Ovid, observes, that, from historical records it appears, that, in the year 1460, an entire ship, with its anchors, was found in a mine on the Alps.

N. B. The latter may be adduced as a farther proof of the General Deluge.

NOTES TO THE SECOND BOOK.

⁵ "One vast parterre." The country on the banks of the Ohio, Miami, and other western rivers, is in the highest degree fertile and luxuriant; the prairies are productive of innumerable species of the most beautiful plants and flowers, and in the spring have the appearance of a vast garden, presenting to the view an enchanting variety of the rarest colors.

⁶ "Here Otaheitee, &c." This flattering description of the happiness of the Otaheitans, though, by no means conformable to the accounts of more recent navigators, cannot be considered as a mere picture of the poet's imagination. From the animated and glowing description given of that island by Sir Joseph Banks, it may fairly be considered as possessing at least a claim to a sufficient degree of poetical truth. The society of the Areoshoi, to which has been attributed the great decrease of population in Otaheitee, was, most probably, at the period of its being first visited by Captain Cook, confined to a few, and of recent origin, or much less profligate in its principle, than it has since been represented.

⁷ "Within itself a world, New Holland lies." The island of New Holland, by far the largest hitherto discovered, is two thousand miles in length, and surpasses Europe in the number of its square miles.

⁸ "Her fav'rite Kangaroo." An animal of New Holland, first described by Captain Cook. The head and ears resemble those of a hare, but it is of a much superior size, sometimes weighing nearly one hundred pounds. The hind legs are nearly three times as long as the fore. It is extremely difficult to be taken or shot, as it is very shy, and leaps forward upon its hind feet, by the assistance of its tail, with inconceivable swiftness.

⁹ "No thirst of knowledge, &c." The natives of New Holland have not only been remarked by navigators for their wretched appearance and mode of living, and utter ignorance of every art, even the most

simple and necessary, but also for their entire want of curiosity, a circumstance distinguishing them from most savages, more particularly from the islanders of the South Sea.

[10] " Thy blood, O Marion." Captain Marion, the commander of two French ships, on a voyage of discovery in the year 1772, was treacherously slain, with twenty-eight of his men, by the natives of New Zealand. The second in command, M. Crozet, with a small party of marines and the carpenters belonging to the ships, was at work in the woods, when he received information of the captain's death. He instantly set out to return to the ships; but, before he had gone far, he was surrounded by a great number of armed natives. He, however, with surprising intrepidity and presence of mind, effected a safe retreat with his men. Finding it necessary to procure new spars, he landed a few days after, attacked one of their fortifications with his cannon, and made a breach in it. An armed chief instantly stepped forward to occupy the pass. He was shot dead. Another took his place and shared his fate. In this manner fell in succession eight chiefs, attempting to defend this dangerous post. The remainder, after the loss of their chiefs, abandoned their fort, and fled precipitately to the woods.

[11] " To the high Hippah, &c." A fortified place in New Zealand, situated on a rock or eminence, and surrounded with palisades. A representation of a very curious fortification of this kind is to be seen among the prints to Cook's first Voyage.

[12] " The mat-clad warriors." The dress of the New Zealand warriors is a sort of cloak, resembling a mat, made of flags and the leaves of rushes.

[13] " In beauty dreadful glare, the purple piles." These floating rocks of ice are of a beautiful purple, frequently interspersed with a bright sapphire color.—Foster's Voyage of Captain Cook.

NOTES TO THE SECOND BOOK.   81

¹⁴ "The Condor rears her young." A monstrous bird, a native of Chili, whose wings, when extended, are said sometimes to measure eighteen feet. They are greatly dreaded by the inhabitants, whose sheep and calves they frequently carry off, and, in some instances, their children. Two of them, it is asserted, will attack and destroy an ox or bull. The following account is given by Brookes, in his Natural History: "The master of a ship, of the name of Strong, saw on the coast of Chili, a large bird, sitting upon a high cliff near the shore, which one of the crew shot with a bullet and killed. They were greatly surprised when they beheld its size; for the wings, when extended, measured thirteen feet. He asked the Spaniards the name of it. They told him it was called a Contus. They likewise informed him that it was a very rapacious bird, and they were continually in fear lest it should carry away their children. One of the quills was two feet, four inches long, and the barrel six inches and three quarters in length and an inch and a half in circumference; the color, a dark brown." The color of this bird is an intermixture of black and white; the head and neck are bare of feathers, and on the top of the head is a dark colored, fleshy excrescence, somewhat in the shape of the cone of a helmet. The noise of its wings, when it descends, is like the roar of a whirlwind. It builds its nest on the most inaccessible cliffs of the Andes. The Indians say, that it will carry off with ease a deer or calf in its talons; that its sight is piercing, and its appearance terrible. In the deserts of Pachomal, where it is chiefly found, men seldom venture to travel. Those wild regions are, of themselves, sufficient to inspire horror. Broken precipices, prowling panthers, forests vocal only with the hissing of serpents, and gloomy mountains, rendered still more terrible by the Condor, the only bird that ventures to make its residence in those deserted situations.

¹⁵ "The fiery Dipsas." The Dipsas, or Burning Serpent, derives its name from the effects of its bite, which immediately produces a glowing heat over the whole body, attended with an insatiable thirst, which soon ends in delirium and death. A more particular account

of this serpent will be found in Mr. D. Obsonville's Description of
the Poison and the Burning Serpent.

[16] "The fell Constrictor." The Boa Constrictor, Anaconda, or
Giant Serpent, a monstrous snake, inhabiting the deserts of Africa.
The strongest and most ferocious beasts are said to be frequently de-
voured by this monster, who conceals himself in the top of a large
tree, and waits the approach of his unsuspecting prey; when suffi-
ciently near, he throws himself upon it, and, inclosing it in his mon-
strous folds, soon puts an end to its existence. A species of this ser-
pent is found in Guiana, which sometimes exceed forty feet in length;
but the most formidable and destructive kind infest the wilds of
Africa, and some of the islands in the Indian sea. An account of one
of the latter, which was killed in the island of Ceylon, was many years
since published in one of the English Magazines, and afterwards re-
published in this country. It is contained in a letter from a gentle-
man who was an eye-witness, and who, after relating the circumstance
of the animal's first appearance, the alarm caused by it, and the pre-
cautions taken by himself and his companions for concealing them-
selves from the sight of the monster, on their approaching the tree on
which he had established himself, in order to obtain a nearer view of
him, thus proceeds with his narrative : " The next morning, having
assembled to the number of more than a hundred, we had the pleasure,
(if I dare call it so,) of finding our enemy still at his old post. He
seemed very fierce and hungry, and we soon had an opportunity of
witnessing the amazing effects. There is in this country a great plenty
of tigers, and one of a prodigious size, being not much less than a
common heifer, came under the serpent's tree. Instantly we heard a
dreadful rustling, and as swift as thought the serpent dropped upon it,
and seizing it across the back, a little below the shoulders with its hor-
rible mouth, took in a piece of the back bigger than a man's head.
The creature roared with agony, and, to our unspeakable terror, was
running with its enemy towards us. Its course was, however, soon
stopped, for its nimble adversary, winding its body three or four times

around the tiger, girt it so violently that it fell down in an agony. The moment the serpent had fixed its folds, it let go the back of its prey, and raising itself and twining round the head of the tiger, opened its mouth to its full extent, and seized the whole face of the animal, biting and grinding it in a most horrid manner, at once choking and tearing the creature to pieces. The tiger, on this, reared itself up again; but words are too poor to paint its agony: It writhed and tossed about, but all in vain; the enemy, wherever it was, was still with it, and its hollow roarings within the destroyer's mouth, were dreadful, beyond expression.

The tiger was a very strong and fierce creature; and though unable to free itself of its cruel enemy, gave it prodigious trouble. A hundred times would it rear up, and run a little way, but would soon fall down again, partly oppressed by the weight, and partly by the folds, and wreathed twists of the serpent around its body. But though the tiger fell, it was far from being entirely conquered, or at all manageable. After some hours it appeared to be much spent, and lay as if dead, when the serpent, which had many times violently girded itself around the tiger, vainly attempting to break its bones, now quitted its hold, twisting its tail only around the neck of its prey, which was in no condition either to resist or escape. It then made towards the tree, dragging its victim with some difficulty after it.

Having by degrees dragged the tiger to the tree, and the animal being unable to stand, the serpent seized it lightly a second time by the back, and set it on its legs against the trunk of the tree; then winding itself around the tiger and the tree together several times, it girded both with such violence, that the ribs and other bones began to give way, and by repeated efforts of this kind, it broke all the ribs, one by one, each of which gave a loud crack in breaking. It next attempted the legs, and broke them severally in the same manner, each in four or five different places; this employed several hours; during all which time the poor tiger remained alive, and at every crack of the bones gave a howl, not very loud, but piteous enough to pierce the most obdurate heart, and make even man forget his natural antipathy to the tiger and pity its misery. After the legs, the serpent attacked the skull in the same manner; but this proved so difficult a task, that the monster, overcome with fatigue, and seeing its prey in no condition to escape, left it for the night, at the foot of the tree, into which it retired to rest.

In the morning, on returning to the thicket, we beheld a most surprising change. The body of the tiger, which now seemed one red lump of shapeless matter, was dragged to some distance from the tree, and shone all over as if covered with glue or jelly. We soon discovered the cause of this—the serpent being still employed in producing that appearance. It had laid the legs, one by one, close to the body, and was now placing the head strait before, licking the body, and covering it with its saliva, which coated it over like a jelly, and rendered it fit for swallowing. Much time was employed in the business. At length, the serpent, having prepared the whole to its mind, drew up before its prey, and seizing the head, began to suck that, and afterwards the body down into its throat. This was the work of so much time, that I left the monster struggling at the shoulders, when I went home to dinner, and from the account of those who staid to watch, it was night before the whole was fairly swallowed.

The following day we assembled for the last time, when the very women and children followed, convinced that as it had gorged its prey, there was no danger to be apprehended. I was myself by no means satisfied of this, till I reached the place, when I found it true, as the serpent had so loaded its belly it could neither fight nor retreat. It attempted on our approach to re-climb the tree, but being unable, was soon dispatched, by striking it on the head with large clubs. We then measured it, and its length was thirty-three feet four inches, and it was as thick as a slender man's waist.

" Anaconda, or Boa Constrictor." By those who are unacquainted with the wonders of nature, (says the learned Dr. Shaw, in the Naturalist's Miscellany,) the descriptions given by Naturalists of some of the more striking and singular animals, are received with a degree of cautious scepticism, or even rejected as exceeding the bounds of credibility. Amongst these animals may well be numbered the prodigious serpents that are sometimes found in India, Africa, and America—serpents of so great a size, as to be able to ingorge even some of the larger quadrupeds, and of so enormous a length, as to measure twenty, twenty-five, and thirty feet. There is reason to believe that these immense serpents are become less common now than some centuries back; and that, in proportion as cultivation and population have increased, the larger species of noxious animals have been expelled from the haunts of mankind, and driven into the more distant and uncultivated tracts. They are still, however, occasionally seen, and sometimes approach the plantations and gardens of the districts nearest to their residence.

It is happy for mankind, that these gigantic serpents are not poisonous; they are, therefore, to be dreaded only on account of their vast size and strength, which latter is so great as to enable them to kill deer, cattle, and other animals, by writhing themselves around them, so as to crush them to death by mere pressure; after which they swallow them in a very gradual manner; and when thus gorged with their prey, grow almost torpid with repletion, and, if discovered in this state, may without much difficulty be dispatched.

Considered as one of the great destroyers of the animal world, this serpent must be viewed with horror; but if we take into consideration only its form and colors, we cannot deny it a very great share of external beauty; yet, like many of its tribe, it is apt to vary in color, and appears in a more or less vivid state, according to the period of life in which it happens to be found; but it is generally of a grayish color, variegated on the back and sides in the most curious manner, with large oblong patches and spots of bright reddish brown, which are still farther decorated by having black margins, surrounded both internally and externally with streaks of white and yellow; the belly is commonly of a yellowish white.

It was, in all probability, an enormous specimen of this very serpent, that once diffused so violent a terror amongst the most valiant of mankind, and threw a whole Roman army into dismay. Historians relate this surprising event in terms of considerable luxuriance. Valerius

Maximus thus mentions it from Livy, in one of the lost books, of whose history it was related more at large:—

"And, since we are on the subject of uncommon phenomena, we may here mention the serpent, so eloquently and accurately recorded by Livy, who says, that near the river Bagrada, in Africa, a snake was seen, of so enormous a magnitude as to prevent the army of Attilius Regulus from the use of the river; which, after snatching up several soldiers with its enormous mouth, and devouring them, and killing several others by striking and squeezing them with the spires of its tail, was at length destroyed, by assailing it with all the force of military engines and showers of stones, after it had withstood the attack of their spears and darts, so that it was regarded by the whole army, as a more formidable enemy than even Carthage itself; and, that the whole adjacent country being tainted with the pestilential effluvia proceeding from its remains, and the waters with its blood, the Roman army was obliged to remove its station. He also adds, that the skin of the monster, measuring one hundred and twenty feet in length, was sent to Rome as a trophy. This is said, by the learned Freinshemius, in his Supplement to Livy, to have been suspended in one of the temples at Rome, and to have continued there till the Numantine war."

The relation of this singular conflict, forms quite an episode in the 6th Book of Silius Italicus, from a poetical version of which, attempted by the author when a youth, the following lines, descriptive of its appearance, are taken:—

> Roused at the tumult, forth the serpent came,
> Emitting from his jaws sulphureous flame;
> From his broad front terrific lightnings fly,
> And rage vindictive sparkles in his eye;
> High-raised in air he lifts his head above
> The topmost branches of the towering grove.
> * * * * * * * * * * * * * *
> But when the trumpet's martial notes he heard,
> In threat'ning guise his form immense he rear'd,

And with his back reclined, his length comprest
In sinuous folds beneath his scaly breast,
Then swift unloosing his contorted train,
His glitt'ring bulk extended o'er the plain,
And on the shore advanced the fight to try,
While dread amazement glared in every eye.

The following account of one of these singular serpents, is from Booth's translation of Diodorus Siculus, Book 3, Chapter 3:—

"The inhabitants (of Ethiopia,) bordering upon the deserts, say, that there are in those parts divers sorts of serpents of an incredible bigness; for, as to those that say they have seen them a hundred cubits long, they are looked upon to be liars, not only by me, but by every one else.

"But we shall say something of the greatest serpents, (that ever were seen,) which were brought to Alexandria, in nets. For, Ptolemy the Second, (Philadelphus,) being very much given to the hunting of elephants, for that purpose encouraged with great rewards many that were skillful hunters of the strongest, wildest beasts, by which means many strange beasts that were never before seen, became known to the Grecians. Upon these considerations, some of the huntsmen, knowing the generosity of the king in his rewards for things of this nature, agreed together, with the hazard of their lives, to bring if it were but one of these monstrous serpents alive to the king, to Alexandria. It was a bold and difficult undertaking; but fortune crowned the enterprise, and prosperity effected the attempt. They spied a serpent lying in the standing pools, thirty cubits long, still and quiet, as it used to be at all other times, save when it spied any beast come to the water to drink, and then it suddenly leaped out, and with its wide jaws and the winding itself around about their bodies, held them so fast as that they could never escape.

"Hereupon, these persons, considering he was so very long, and naturally dull and slow, conceived some hopes of catching him in gins and chains—having all things ready prepared for the purpose; but the

473

nearer they came to him, the more they were terrified; and when they saw his eyes kindle like sparks of fire, his tongue slapping about his jaws, his terrible hissing, the sharpness of his scales, his rustling among the reeds and bushes when he began to stir himself, the greatness of his terrible teeth, his horrible aspect and high round, whereunto he had wound himself, they grew wan and pale with excessive fear, and with trembling hands they cast the gin upon his tail. As soon as it touched him, the monster rolled about with a terrible hiss, and lifting himself up above the head of the first that approached him, he snapped him up and tore him in pieces. The second he catched by the winding of his tail, at a great distance, when he was making off, and, (twisting himself around him,) held him fast by the middle. Thereupon, the rest were so affrighted that away they fled—however, what they could not do by force, they endeavored to effect by art, making use of the following contrivance: They made a toil of bulrushes, in shape like to a bosom-net, large enough to receive and hold the beast; and, observing his hole, and the time when he went out to feed and when he returned; and as soon as he was gone forth, they stopped up the mouth of his den with great stones and earth, and near to it dug another hole, and there placed the toil made of bulrushes, just over the mouth of the hole, so that the entrance might be plain and open. Then, as he returned from feeding, the darters, slingers, and a great number of horsemen, with trumpets, and other assailants, set upon him. The monster, (as he came nearer to them,) pricked up his head far above the heads of the horsemen, but none of the whole durst come near him, being made cautious by the former misfortune; but many cast darts at him all at once, at a great distance, so that by the sight of the horses, multitude of dogs, and the noise of trumpets, they terrified the beast, and pursued him cautiously by degrees, till he came to his hole, lest, by pressing too hard and close upon him, he should be too much provoked and enraged. Now, near approaching to the mouth of the den, before prepared for him, they all at once set up such a noise with beating upon their arms, and with such a multitude of men, and the noise and sound of trumpets, they exceedingly terrified the monster, who, not finding his former hole, and fearing the hunters, flies into the mouth of that which was open and near at hand. While he was filling the net, by rolling of himself round in it, some forthwith rode up with full speed to the place, who, (before the beast could wind up himself,) tied up the mouth of the net, which was made very long to the top, on purpose for quickness of dispatch in this business. Then, with all speed, they put rollers under the massy weight of the net, to lift it up, and so drew it forth. The serpent, being thus shut up, hissed most dreadfully, gnawing the bulrushes with his teeth, and tossing himself to and fro, as if he were just leaping out of the net; which the hunters exceedingly fearing what he would do, drew him upon the ground, and others, pricking him in the tail, caused him to snap and to bite there, where he was most sensible of pain. At length, they brought him to Alexandria, and presented him to the king—a most strange monster, and almost incredible; and to admiration, this creature was afterwards made tame. For, keeping him low in want of food, he abated in his fierceness, so as, by degrees, to be very gentle. Ptolemy liberally rewarded the hunters, and kept and fed the serpent thus tamed. A most wonderful sight to all strangers that traveled into his kingdom."

Jackson, in his account of Morocco, says, that the Boah, or Desert Snake, is from twenty to eighty feet long, as large as a man's body, and of a dingy color. The Arabs, in their figurative mode of expression, say, that, as it passes along the desert, it fires the ground with the velocity of its motion. It is impossible to escape it. It will twist itself around an ox, and after crushing its bones, swallow it gradually, and remain for several days motionless, until the process of digestion is performed.

The author was informed by a friend of his, in the year 1782, who had just returned from a privateering cruise in the West Indies, that the ship on board of which he was, having gone into Surinam, whilst lying at anchor in the river, they were, one morning about day-break, awakened by a singular noise, and running on deck, found, to their astonishment, a monstrous snake, just entering the ship by means of the cable; that Captain Chew, their commander, seizing an axe, had the good fortune to discover the creature's head, as it was extended over the gun-wale, so that it merely hung by the skin. Its size was about that of the thigh of a middle-sized man; the length, (as well as memory at this distant period can serve,) from thirty to thirty-six feet. He farther said, that the color of the whole body was black, a little paler on the belly, and the head of a beautiful yellow. It was begged of the captain by the negroes, for the purpose of eating it; and was supposed to have been attracted on board the ship by the hogs and poultry, which they had provided for stores.

[17] "The Seps envenom'd." The Seps of Lucan, otherwise called, from the peculiar activity and deadliness of its venom, the Poison Serpent. It is found in some parts of Africa and the East Indies. This serpent is about two feet in length; its bite causes immediate death, and, in a short time, an entire dissolution of the whole corporeal mass takes place. The following account of this serpent, and of the Burning Serpent, is taken from D'Obsonville's Philosophical Essays:—

"Among the serpents of India, that which I believe to be the most formidable, is but about two feet long, and very small. Its skin is freckled, with little traits of brown, or a pale red, contrasted with a ground of dirty yellow. It is chiefly found in dry and rocky places, and its bite is mortal in less than one or two minutes. In the year 1759, in the province of Cadapet, I saw several instances of it; among others, one very singular, in the midst of a corps of troops commanded by M. de Bussy. An Indian Gentoo merchant perceived a Mahometan soldier of his acquaintance going to kill one of these reptiles, which he had found asleep under his pack. The Gentoo flew to beg its life, protesting that it would do no hurt if it was not first provoked; at the same time, passing his hand under its belly to carry it out of the camp, when suddenly it turned round and bit his little finger. The unfortunate martyr of a fanatic charity gave a shriek, took a few steps, and fell down senseless. They flew to his assistance, applied the serpent-stone, fire, and scarifications, but they were all ineffectual—his blood was already coagulated. About an hour after, I saw the body, as they

476

were going to burn it, and I thought I perceived some indications of a complete dissolution of the blood."

The Burning Serpent is nearly of the same form with the preceding. Its skin is not quite so deep a brown, and is speckled with dark green spots; its poison is almost as dangerous, but it is less active, and its effects are very different. In some persons, it is a devouring fire, which, as it circulates through the veins, soon occasions death; the blood dissolves into a lymphatic liquor, resembling thin broth, pparently without having passed through the intermediate state of coagulation, and runs from the eyes, nose, and ears, and even through the pores. In other subjects, the poison seems to have chapped the very nature of the humors in dissolving them; the skin is changed and becomes scaly, the hair falls off, the limbs are tumified, and the patient feels all over his body the most excruciating pains, followed by numbness, and is not long in perishing. It is, however, said, that some have been cured by remedies well and soon applied. The poison of these reptiles appears to me, to be in general more powerful, according as they live in hot and dry places, where they feed upon insects that abound with saline, volatile, and acrimonious particles.

[18] " Here Goran's sons." Goran, or Goram, a nation of negroes who live wholly in the deserts, have no intercourse with any other, and have a language altogether peculiar to themselves. Leo Africanus says, that they are descended from the Zingani.

[19] " Here roams the Galla." Gallas, a cruel and ferocious nation, in the interior of Africa, of whom the Jaggas are supposed to be a colony.

[20] " Here Anzikains." A nation of cannibals, adjoining the Jaggas.

[21] " And here the Jagga." A warlike and powerful nation of Africa, the most cruel and blood-thirsty of all that are known.

The country in possession of this people, extends along Matambu and

Benguela, from north-east to south-west, about nine hundred miles in length, but is narrow in proportion, being no more than from one hundred to one hundred and fifty miles broad. This nation pays no attention to cultivation of any kind, but subsists wholly on plunder. The men are tall, stout, and strong, but very nimble and swift of foot, climbing up the steepest mountains and most craggy rocks with surprising agility. The women are large, well-formed, warlike, and active, and both sexes possess such a degree of intrepidity, that no enterprise is thought too hazardous for them, more especially when incited with the prospect of plunder, at which times they rush on their adversaries with a perfect unconcern for their lives. They esteem it a proof of bravery to attack the strongest and most ferocious animals, and as a still greater one, to be even more cruel and ferocious. This savage disposition is not confined to the nations they invade, but is extended to their own people, and even their kindred and children, whom, when they are in want of other food, they make no scruple to kill and eat. Their soldiers are neither well disciplined, armed, or clothed. Their offensive weapons are bows and arrows, spears, daggers, darts, and clubs; but, they are instructed to make more use of their defensive arms than their missive, being particularly directed to cover their bodies, which are almost naked, with their large oval shields, made of thick hides. This mode of combat proves of singular service in a retreat, as it secures them from the arrows and lances of their pursuers. After their enemies have expended their shafts upon their shields, they generally resume the attack with such vigor, as seldom fails of putting them to flight, which is always followed by a general slaughter, as they pay no respect to sex or condition, whenever victory declares itself in their favor. Battel, who resided amongst them several years, in describing the manner of educating their soldiers, observes, " These are not their own offspring, but the children of captives made by them in their excursions."

The following extract from Brunet's " Parallel of Religions," published at Paris in 1792, relative to the institutions of the Jaggas, will conclude this note :—

NOTES TO THE SECOND BOOK.

"It is not certainly known whether the horrible institutions of the Jaggas still remain in force. It is, however, certain, that they have been governed by thirty princes, since the time when Caluximbo, their sovereign, perished by the hands of his infamous subjects, for persisting in his refusal to drink the blood and eat the flesh of his fellow men. Caluximbo succeeded Chinguri, who was killed in battle, and who was himself the successor of Culemba, who, from a common soldier, became the husband of Tem-ban-Dumba, and poisoned her, to avoid the fatal consequences of the change which he perceived had taken place in the inclinations of that diabolical woman, who is said to have induced the Jaggas to adopt their barbarous laws, called Quixillas."

22 "Thy Eden, Afric, Whidda's landscapes rise." The kingdom of Whidda, is said to possess the finest soil, and one of the happiest climates in the world; the whole country has the appearance of a highly cultivated garden, and is adorned with the richest and most beautiful landscapes.

23 "The reed-built hamlets, &c." The Negro villages on the banks of the Senegal and the Gambia, are composed of huts built in a conical form, from reeds woven or twisted together, which make a very compact covering. The houses form a number of circles, one within the other, surrounded by palisades, or a quick fence of lime-trees, &c. There is usually a large tree in the centre of each village, under the shade of which the inhabitants are accustomed to assemble, for the purposes of council or festivity.

24 "The vast Boabab spreads." This tree, the largest production of the vegetable kingdom, though never exceeding seventy feet in height, is of an almost incredible size, the trunk frequently measuring upwards of twenty-five feet in diameter, and the branches, which extend themselves horizontally, are from forty-five to fifty feet long, and of such size that each branch is equal to the largest trees in Europe.

[25] "Where proud Tombuctoo, &c." The city of Tombuctu, from late accounts, is said to be very wealthy, and almost as large as London, and to carry on a very extensive commerce, principally in slaves, with all parts of Africa. The cities of Houssa and Ghanara are also represented as very rich and populous.

"Where Houssa's domes," &c. Since the original note to this passage was written, our knowledge of the interior of Africa has been greatly increased by the industrious researches of a Brown, a Park, and a Hernemann; the two last of whom have, unfortunately, fallen victims to their laudable thirst of inquiry, and their zeal for the promotion of science, in the exploration of this almost unknown country. Indeed, the discovery of the true course of the Niger, has rendered it necessary for the author to make some material alterations in the lines themselves, as, when they were written, in conformity to a very commonly received opinion, he had supposed the Niger to be the same river with the Senegal.

(Addition to the information obtained by Mr. Park.)

Jackson, in his account of Morocco, describes Tombucto, from the information of merchants, who had gone thither in the caravans, as not only very large and populous, and containing many handsome edifices, but adds, that the inhabitants are much more courteous and civilized, and much less bigoted to their religion, and inveterate against the Christians, than M. Park was led to believe, from the accounts he had received; that the king, who is very powerful and immensely rich, has one of the largest libraries in the world, consisting of many thousands of volumes, principally in the Arabic language, on various subjects; among which are numerous translations from the ancients. To the accounts of later travelers, I am induced to add some notices of Tombuctu, and the cities of the Niger, by the Nubian Geographer, and Leo Africanus, taken from a translation of some passages from them, contained in an old book, entitled, "Travels into the inland parts of Africa, by Francis Moore." The Nubian, who has divided his work into Climates, gives the following account of several cities on the Niger, in Part 2, of Climate 1:—

"In Ghana, are two cities,"—(it appears, that the author's meaning, is, that the great city of Ghana, as he denominates it elsewhere, was divided by the river or lake, into two parts,)—" situated on the two opposite shores of what they call a fresh-water sea, and is the largest, most populous, and wealthiest, in all the Negro countries ; and thither the rich merchants resort, not only from all the neighboring places, but also from the remotest parts of the West. Its inhabitants are Musselmen ; and the king, who derives his pedigree from Abi Taleb, is absolute, although he pays obedience to Abbasaeus, Emperor of the Musselmen," (one of the Caliphs of the Abbassides.) " He hath a palace, which is a strong and well-fortified structure, on the bank of the Nile," (thus he denominates the Niger,) " with apartments adorned with various engravings, paintings, and glass windows. The aforesaid palace was built in the five hundred and tenth year of the Hegira." " And, from the confirmed reports of the people who come from (that country) the West, there is in the palace of the king, an entire lump of gold, not cast, nor wrought by any instrument, but perfectly formed by the Divine Providence only, of thirty pounds weight, which has been bored through, and fitted for a seat to the royal throne : And truly, it is a most extraordinary thing, granted to no other but to him, by which he procures to himself a peculiar glory, in comparison of all the Negro kings. And that king, as is reported, is the most just of all men." (The Geographer then proceeds to detail his mode of administering justice, which was daily done by him, in going through the city on horseback, accompanied by his guards ; when he listened to the petitions of all who had been aggrieved.) " He generally wears a habit of sattin, or a black mantle, after the Arabian manner, with drawers, and leathern sandals on his feet. He always goes on horseback. He has abundance of rich ornaments ; and horses, with most sumptuous trappings, on solemn days, led before him. He has many troops, who march, each with their colors under his royal banner ; elephants, camels, and various kinds of animals, which are found in the Negro countries, precede him." "From the city of Ghana, to the confines of the country of Vancara," (Wangora, as called by some authors,) " is a journey of eight days ;

and this" [country] ." of Vancara, is most famous for the excellency and plenty of its gold. It is an island of three hundred miles in length and one hundred and fifty in breadth, which the Nile surrounds all the year. But, the month of August approaching, and the scorching heat increasing, and the Nile overflowing, that island, or at least the greater part of it, is covered with water, and remains so, as long as the Nile is wont to overflow. But, when the waters decrease, and the Nile begins to gather itself in its proper channel, all who are in the kingdom of the Blacks, living in those islands, return to their habitations; and every day in which the Nile decreases, they slightly dig the earth, and not one of them is disappointed in his labor; but, whosoever he be, by digging, finds more or less of gold, according to the gift of God."

"Next to the cities of the country of Vancara, lies the great and populous city Tirca, distant from Ghana six days journey; the road lies along the banks of the Nile. From Tirca to the city Marasa, is reckoned six days; and from this to the country of Seemara, is also six days journey. From that to the city Semagda, is eight days. The last is a beautiful and neat city, situated on the shore of a fresh-water sea, and distant from the city Reghebil nine days. Also from the city Seemara to the city of Reghebil, towards the South, is a journey of six days. The city Reghebil lies also on the shore of a fresh-water sea, and is of a beautiful form and bigness, situated under a mountain, which hangs over it, on the South side. Between the city Reghebil, towards the West and Ghanara, there is a distance of eleven days. The city Ghanara is on a bank of the Nile, inclosed with a strong wall, and inhabited by a numerous and robust people. Also, from this city to that of Ghana, is a journey of eleven days, where water is very scarce. All these countries are under the dominion of the king of Ghana."

Leo Africanus, as he relates, in his youth, accompanied his uncle to Tombuctoo, who was sent thither as an ambassador from the king of Fez, and, as it appears, was there a second time. Such is his description of the kingdom of Tombuctoo, called by him Tombuto. "The name of this kingdom is modern. It was so called," (as some think,) "from the name of a certain town, which, they say, was built by king Mense

NOTES TO THE SECOND BOOK.

Suliman, in the year of the Hegira 610, situate within twelve miles of a branch of the Niger. The houses here are built in the shape of bells; the walls are stakes or hurdles, plastered over with clay, and the houses covered with reeds; yet, there is one stately mosque, the walls of which are made of stone and lime. The royal palace is also built of stone, by an excellent artist from Grenada, as also many of the shops of the artificers and merchants. Here are great numbers of weavers of cotton cloth; and hither the cloth of Europe is brought by the Barbary merchants. It is customary here for all the women to go with their faces covered, except the maid-servants, who sell food. The inhabitants, especially the strangers that reside there, are very rich, insomuch that the present king gave both his daughters in marriage to two rich merchants. Here are many wells, the water of which is excellent; and, as often as the Niger overfloweth, its water is conveyed into the town by certain sluices. There is great plenty of corn, cattle, milk, and butter in this region, but a scarcity of salt, which is brought hither by land from Tegaza, five hundred miles distant. When I, myself, was here, I saw one camel's load of salt, sold for eighty ducats. The rich king of Tombuto, hath in his possession many golden plates and sceptres, some whereof are thirteen hundred ounces in weight, and he keeps a splendid and well furnished court. In traveling, he rideth himself upon a camel, and one of his greatest officers leads his horse after him. He also in war rideth a camel, but all his soldiers ride on horses. Whosoever will speak to the king, must prostrate himself at his feet, and then taking up dust, must sprinkle it on his own head and shoulders, which custom is observed by them that never saluted the king before, or who come as ambassadors from other princes. His attendants consist of three thousand horsemen, and a great number of footmen, who use poisoned arrows. They have frequent skirmishes with those that refuse to pay tribute; and their captives they sell to the merchants of Tombuto. There are not many horses bred here, and the merchants and courtiers have certain little nags to ride upon; but their best horses come from Barbary. When the king is informed of a merchant coming to town with horses, he orders a certain number to be brought to him, and, chosing the best, he payeth a great price for him. He hath such an inveterate hatred against the Jews, that they are not allowed admittance into his city; and whatsoever Barbary merchants he finds to traffic with them, he immediately commandeth their goods to be confiscated. The king, at his own expense, liberally maintaineth here great numbers of doctors, priests, judges, and other learned men. There are manuscripts brought hither out of Barbary, which are sold for more money than any other merchandise. Instead of money, they use bars of gold; and in matters of small value, certain shells, which are brought hither from the kingdom of Persia, four hundred of which are worth a ducat. The inhabitants are of a mild and gentle disposition, and are wont to spend great part of the night in singing and dancing. They have many men and women slaves, and their town is very apt to be set on fire; when I was there the second time, almost half the town was burnt down in the space of five hours. Without the suburbs are neither gardens nor orchards."

The same author says of the kingdom of Ghinea, called by the natives, Genna, that it is nearly five hundred miles in length, extending two hundred and fifty miles along the river Niger; that there is neither town or castle throughout this region, but one great village, which is inhabited by the prince, together with his priests, doctors, merchants, and all the principal men. The houses are of the shape of a bell, with clay walls, and roofs covered with reeds. The dress of the inhabitants is black or blue cotton, except the priests and doctors of the law, who wear white. The overflowings of the Niger, annually, surround this country in manner of an island, during the three months of July, August, and September, during which time the merchants of Tombutu bring their wares hither in canoes.

He also mentions among other kingdoms situated on or near the Niger, that of Melli, (which extends almost three hundred miles along the bank of a river that runs into the Niger,) and is bordered on the north on Ghinea. This kingdom contains a town of six thousand families, called Melli, from whence the kingdom has received its name. In this town resides the king. The country abounds with corn, flesh,

NOTES TO THE SECOND BOOK.

and cotton. Strangers are honorably received and entertained by the king. The inhabitants are rich, and have among them a great number of artificers and merchants. There are likewise many mosques, priests, and professors. The people are, in wit, civility, and industry, superior to all the other Negroes, and were the first who embraced Mahometanism."

[26] "And bow to Xaca and Amida's name." Xaca, a god of the Japanese, the supposed founder of idolatry among them. His mother dreamed of a white elephant, whence the predilection is supposed to have arisen, which the kings of Japan, Siam, and some of the other Eastern princes, have for elephants of that color. Xaca withdrew into a desert, where he invented his system of worship; and, on his re-appearance in the world, soon obtained proselytes to the number of eighty thousand, from whom he selected one thousand to preach and disseminate his doctrines. His disciples pretend that he passed through eighty thousand transmigrations, his soul having inhabited the bodies of so many different animals before his reception among the gods. He is sometimes represented with three heads; at others with but one, in the figure of a man, sitting in the Japanese manner, and extending his hands like a devotee. Around his neck he has a chain of gold shells, set with precious stones; his arms are adorned with ribbons, with ornaments at the ends like tassels, and he has a silken sash about his waist. On either side of him are golden scales suspended, and the table on which he sits is decorated with censers, hung by golden chains, in which incense is continually burnt. His followers practise the greatest austerities, and even starve themselves, in order to obtain the prize of martyrdom. (See Bell's Pantheon.)

Amida, another god of the Japanese, the sovereign lord and master of Paradise. He is represented as an invisible, incorporeal, and immutable substance, distinct from all the elements—who existed before nature; who is the source of every good, without beginning or end, infinite and unbounded, and the creator of the world. He is worshiped in a singular manner by some of his devotees, who drown themselves in honor of him. The self-devoted victim enters, in presence of the idol, into a little boat, gilt and adorned with silken streamers. He then dances to the sound of musical instruments; and fastening to his legs and neck some heavy weights, precipitates himself into the river. Others inclose themselves in a narrow space, walled round with stones, where they constantly employ themselves in calling upon his name, until they expire. He is represented mounted on a horse with seven heads, on an altar; this figure is emblematical of seven thousand years. The idol, itself, has the head of a dog, and holds in its hand a golden circle, which it is biting; he is clad in a rich robe, adorned with gold and precious stones. (Bell's Pantheon.)

Thunberg, who, in the year 1776, accompanied the Dutch embassy to the Japanese court at Jeddo, and who has described the temples of two of their gods—Darbud and Quanwan—which, on his return through Meaco, he was permitted to visit, says, that the Supreme Being is by the worshipers of Budd in Japan, called Amida; that the ancient and pure religion of that empire, however, is called the Sinto, which is that of the emperor, and that its temples contain no image of the deity, but only a mirror, placed in the centre with some pieces of white paper.

The following is the description given by that traveler of the temples and images of Darbud and Quanwan: "The temple of Darbud is the largest and most remarkable. It stands on ninety-six pillars, and has several entrances, which are very lofty, but extremely narrow. The body of the temple consists of two stories that run into each other, and have consequently a double roof; the uppermost of which is supported by several painted pillars of about two yards in diameter. The floor was formed of square pieces of marble. The only thing that was wanting, was light sufficient for so large and magnificent a building. The image of Darbud stood nearly in the centre, and was enough to strike the beholder with terror. It was in a sitting posture, elevated about two yards from the ground, with its legs crossed in the Indian manner, and gilt. The ears were long, the hair short and curled, the shoulders naked, the body covered with a wrapper, the right hand raised, and the left placed edgeway against the belly. To any one who had not seen

486

it, the size must appear incredible. I was assured that six men might sit on the palm of the hand in the Japanese manner, with their feet under them. It appeared to be well-proportioned, although it was so broad that its shoulders reached from one pillar to the other, which, to judge by the eye, appeared to be about thirty or thirty-two feet apart. I was next conducted to another temple nearly as majestic. Neither the heighth or breadth of it was extraordinary, but its length was great. This was sacred to Quanwan ; and his image, with those of his attendant deities in great numbers, was set up in this edifice. In the midst sat Quanwan, furnished with thirty-six hands ; near him were placed sixteen others, larger than the human size, but much inferior to that of Quanwan ; these occupied a separate room, partitioned to themselves ; on both sides were two rows of gilt idols, each with twenty hands. These were succeeded by several rows on each side of the others, of the size of a man, placed quite close to each other, the number of which I could not reckon. Those that were forward were the smallest, and those behind gradually larger, so that all the twelve rows might be seen very distinctly. The heads of the small idols were placed on their hands, and the whole number was said to amount to thirty-three hundred and thirty-three. These idols, as well as the sect that worship them, derive their origin from India. It is the sect of Buddah."

Xaca is probably the same with Budd or Budha, whose religion has extended itself from India over China and Japan, as many of the circumstances in the account of the life of the former, are conformable to what is related of the latter.

" Whence art mechanic wears her fairest forms." The Japanese, in some few branches of the manufacturing arts are, perhaps, unequaled by any people in the world. I have seen a Japanese sabre of admirable workmanship and inimitable temper ; such was its keenness as readily to sever a hair when suspended, and the person who showed it to me, said, that he had himself seen the proof of the excellence of its temper made by its cutting in two a tenpenny nail.

[27] " Imperial Jeddo's," &c. The capital of Japan. It is one of

the largest and most opulent cities in the East. The emperor's palace is square, and five miles in circumference; a part of the roof is said to be covered with golden plates.

[28] " And, vain of antique fame," &c. It has become of late almost as much the fashion to diminish, as it was during a part of the last century to elevate, the antiquity of the Chinese. But, without pretending to the least faith in their extravagant and absurd claims to antiquity, a reasonable share of it cannot well be refused to a people, who, it appears, from recent and undoubted information, have possessed a standard Dictionary of their language, from nearly two hundred years before our era. Such is the account given by the ingenious Mr. Marshman, who was at great trouble to collect information respecting those Dictionaries that were of established reputation in China. The earliest work of this kind, says he, and which is still appealed to as high authority, is mentioned in the Introduction to the Imperial Dictionary, as a compilation made by the learned men of the empire, under an Emperor of the Han dynasty, which occupied the throne about two hundred years before Christ.

[28] " In richest state, here cultivation reigns." Cultivation is carried to so great a height in China, that the inhabitants cultivate even the bottoms of their waters; and the beds of their ponds and streams produce crops that are unknown elsewhere. Their industry has discovered resources in a number of aquatic plants, several of which, as the Pi-tsi, or Water-chesnut, and the Linen-hoæ, are the greatest delicacies of a Chinese table. The government has caused this lost land to be cultivated in all the lakes, marshes, and waste grounds covered with water, which belong to the state. The canals that ornament the imperial gardens, and the ditches that surround the palace, are filled with it. The flowers and leaves of this plant cover those two immense sheets of water in the centre of Pekin, which are only separated by a bridge. The Pi-tsi grows only in the southern provinces; its leaves are as long as those of the bulrush, but hollow, and formed into a pipe, like the top of an onion. Its fruit is found in a cover formed by its root, in which

NOTES TO THE SECOND BOOK.

it is inclosed. When this husk is broken, the fruit may be extracted without injuring the plant. It is very wholesome, and has a delicate taste. (Natural History of China.)

[29] "She bids the Jaka and the Lichi bloom." The Jaka, or Tse-tse, is a fruit peculiar to China. Those of the southern provinces are very sweet; the seeds are black and flat, and the pulp extremely slimy and juicy. The tree which produces it is very beautiful; it is as large as the walnut-tree; the leaves in the spring and summer are of a bright green, but in autumn become of a beautiful red. The fruit is of the size of an apple; as they ripen, they assume an orange color, and when dried are as sweet as figs. The Li-tchi is of the size of a date; the stone is long and very hard, and covered with a soft juicy pulp of an exquisite flavor. This pulp is inclosed in a rough, thin rind, shaped at one end like an egg. This fruit is delicious, but is apt, when eaten to excess, to produce an eruption over the whole body. It is found only in the southern provinces.

[30] "Rears the rich Tea, unfolds her snowy flowers." Tea grows in the valleys, and at the foot of the mountains; rocky grounds produce that of the best quality. The root of this shrub is like that of the peach, and its flowers resemble the white wild-rose. It grows from five to six feet in height. The branches form a tufted top, much like that of the myrtle, and are covered with beautiful green leaves, that are narrow and about an inch and a half long.

[31] "Pay adoration to a human God." The city of Teshoo-Loomboo, the capital of Thibet, is the residence of the Grand, or Teshoo-Lama, who unites in himself, to a certain degree, both the spiritual and temporal power, and is revered as a god by the inhabitants of a vast extent of country, comprehending most of the tribes of Tartary, some of the people of farther India, and a great part of China, who annually send their ambassadors to render him homage, furnished with magnificent presents. He is thought to be immortal, and death as merely a

renovation of his youth. The priests who watch over and serve him, always taking care during his life to provide him a successor. For this purpose they select a beautiful child, resembling as much as possible the reigning Lama, whom they have educated under their immediate inspection with the utmost strictness, and who, within a certain period after the decease of his predecessor, is installed with great solemnity and magnificence. The number of priests immediately attached to the service of the Lama, for the performance of daily offices in the temple, amount to about seven hundred. A very singular and interesting account of an interview between the Teshoo-Lama and an officer in the service of the East India Company, may be seen in Sir W. Jones's Asiatic Dissertations, in which the effects of early instruction, exemplified in the propriety of conduct displayed by an infant of eighteen months old—the Lama being no more—almost exceeds credibility.

[32] "Its peopled wave where shining Canton pours." At Canton great numbers of the Chinese live constantly on the water in covered vessels or boats, and there are many of them who never quit these habitations. This is not the case at Canton, alone, but on all the large rivers of China. A circumstance not so surprising, when the immense population of that empire is considered, amounting to two hundred millions of inhabitants

[33] "What swarming cities crowd," &c. China is said to contain four thousand four hundred and two walled cities; and its towns and villages, the most of which are rich, commercial, and populous, are almost innumerable. The village of King-te-ching, in the province of Kiongsi, alone, is estimated to contain a million of inhabitants, who daily consume upwards of ten thousand loads of rice. This compact and populous village, which extends for a league and a half along the banks of a beautiful river, contains about five hundred furnaces for porcelain, which are in continual use. (General Description of China.)

NOTES TO THE SECOND BOOK. 105

³⁴ "Where the deep Kiang rolls his waters blue." The Kiang, from the depth and appearance of its water, called the blue river, by the Chinese.

"Nankin, thy piles," &c. The city of Nankin is of an almost incredible extent. Its inhabitants are estimated at three millions, and its walls are said to be fifteen leagues and a half in circumference.

³⁵ "Thy Porcelain Tower," &c. The Porcelain Tower of Nankin, one of the most splendid edifices in Asia, is upwards of two hundred feet in height, covered with the most beautiful porcelain tiles, and adorned with an infinite variety of gilt figures.

³⁶ "Great Confucius blest." Confu-tsee, or Confucius, the celebrated Chinese philosopher, was born about four hundred and fifty years before the Christian era. About the age of twenty he married and had a son, but soon after quitted his wife, in order to pursue his studies without interruption. Having acquired a high reputation for knowledge, he was solicited to accept the office of civil magistrate ; but preferring the less splendid, though not less important employment of instructing youth, he opened a school, which increased to such a degree that the number of his pupils amounted to no less than five thousand. He delivered the most excellent precepts of morality, and persuaded the women to lay aside their fantastic dresses and many ridiculous customs which prevailed among them, and to adopt others more suitable to the modesty and dignity of the female character. In close application to study, and in the constant practise of every public and private virtue, this great man lived to the age of seventy. The period of his existence was finally shortened by grief for the dissolute manners of his disciples, and he died, carrying with him to the grave the esteem and regret of the whole empire.

³⁷ "The purple Mutang," &c. Mou-tan, a shrub cultivated and held in high estimation by the Chinese. It is sometimes called Hoaouang, or the king of flowers. This plant shoots forth a number of

branches, which form a top nearly as large as those of the finest orange-
trees in boxes. They sometimes, but rarely, grow to the height of
eight or ten feet. The leaves of the Mou-tan are deeply indented, and
of a much darker green above than below. Its flowers, composed of
numberless petals, blow like a rose, and are supported by a calyx, com-
posed of four leaves. From the bottoms of the petals rise several
staminæ, which have small anthers of a rich gold color.

[38] "The Tallow grove," &c. The Tallow-tree is carefully culti-
vated by the Chinese, and planted in squares, or quincunxes. The
leaves are of a bright red, and the tree produces a very fine white wax
from which their candles are made.

[39] "Here art with life," &c. Among the various ingenious works
of art produced by the Chinese, one of the most extraordinary is a most
beautiful species of Porcelain, mentioned by du Halde, the secret of
making which is, at present, in a great measure lost. This, on being
filled with any pellucid liquor, exhibited upon the sides the figures of
insects, fish, plants, &c., which, on removing the liquor, immediately
became invisible.

[40] "Hence meanest arts," &c. "To such a height is the desire of
amassing wealth carried in China," (says M. de Guignes,) "that
there are no means, however base, but what are resorted to, to obtain it.
Whenever the Imperial Commissioners arrive in any of the provinces,
all the Mandarins hasten to anticipate their wishes and to offer them
presents. These, it can scarcely be expected they should refuse, since
the Emperor himself is accustomed to receive them to a very great
amount. This fondness for presents has from time immemorial pre-
vailed in China. A Viceroy, before taking possession of his office,
pays from sixty thousand to two hundred thousand francs; and there is
not a Commissioner or Viceroy who does not acquire, during his stay in
office, from two to three millions. I have known, myself, a Hopou of

Canton, on quitting his office, after a year's residence, carry off with him a million of dollars."

41 "The vast bulwark of yon massy pile." The celebrated wall of China, built to preserve that empire from the incursions of the Tartars, more than two thousand years ago, is five hundred leagues in length, thirty feet high, and of sufficient breadth to admit six horsemen with ease to ride abreast on its top.

THE
Charms of Fancy.

BOOK THE THIRD.

ARGUMENT OF THE THIRD BOOK.

INDIA beyond the Ganges.—Its Kingdoms. Cochin-China; Tonquin; Siam. Rivers Mecon and Menan. Superb annual procession of the Siamese Monarch. Empire of Ava. Description of the capital city of Pegu; Splendor of the Palace; Magnificent Temples, and Superstition of the Peguans. Islands of Sunda, Sumatra, Java. The Bohon Upas Tree. Borneo. The Ourang Outang. Celebes. The Opium Tree. Character of the Macassars. Molucca Islands. Indostan;—Its Rivers. Ancient Temple of Sum-nat. Islands of Salsette and Elephanta. Gigantic Sculptures of the Gods of India. Ruins of Kinnouge. Cities of the Mogul Empire. Imperial Palace at Delhi. Magnificence of the Court. Reflections on its empty pomp and ostentatious parade. Ancient Innocence and Simplicity of the Natives. Peace and Happiness of India before the Tartarian Invasion. Reflections on the Comparative Happiness of Wealthy and Indigent Countries. European Cruelties. Savagi, Chief of the Mahrattas, successfully opposes the subjection of his country by Aurungzebe. Hyder Ally. Persia. Its Poets.—Ferdousi, Janni, Hafir. Character of the Persians. Cyrus. Xerxes. The Magi. Zoroaster;—his Tenets. Persian Cities. Ruins of Persepolis. Gardens of Shiraz. Arabia. Description of the Desert. Attack and Destruction of a Caravan by the Arabs. Ruins of Palmyra. Longinus. Zenobia. Temple of the Sun. Egypt. The Nile. Alexandria. Pompey's Pillar. Cairo. The Pyramids, considered as the favorite seat of Superstition.

THE
CHARMS OF FANCY.

Book the Third.

From placid seats, by gay contentment own'd,
⁽¹⁾ Where Justice sits in majesty enthroned,
And sees a grateful realm with joy obey
The virtuous mandates of parental sway;
To lands where wealth his dazzling charms displays,
Where every jewel lights its gorgeous blaze,
Varies the view.—Lo! different climes appear,
Where torrid summer rules the blossom'd year—
Where India's Genius, on her eastern shores,
The despot rule of petty kings deplores.
    Here rice-clad Tonquin boasts her wide domains,
And fair Cambodia spreads her fertile plains:
Near, Cochin-China, highly favor'd soil,
Where lurks no pilfering thief in quest of spoil,

No hoary mendicant, with famine pale,
Implores compassion in a piteous tale.
  Here, rich in mines of gold, their genial store
O'er sparkling sands, Siam's fair rivers pour,   [tides;
Through blossom'd woods, thick-trembling o'er his
Through fragrance-breathing groves the Mecon glides;
Innumerous peacocks [2] midst the o'erhanging glooms,
Perch'd in proud state, display their gold-eyed plumes;
While, with reflected forms, the wave below
Gives back the colors of the April bow
Bright emblem of the clime! in sportive fold,
The beauteous Boiga [3] waves his length of gold;
O'er his bright form, with varying tinctures gay,
The richest colors dart a splendent ray:
In verdant lustre there the emerald gleams,
The sparkling topaz pours its golden beams;
And, with the sapphire's mild cerulean light,
The semblant ruby's crimson fires unite.
In floating myriads, lightning o'er the stream,
The twinkling [4] Fire-Fly wakes her nightly beam;
O'er the still wave the lambent splendor plays,
High leaps the fish, rejoicing in the blaze;

By flashing fits the living flames expire,
And the whole prospect glows one widely-waving fire.
　　Through bliss-inspiring scenes, through citied vales,
In mazy beauty, Menan gently steals;
Proud ⁽⁵⁾ Odian's walls the silver current laves,
The tall towers, sparkling, tremble in the waves:
With golden roofs far-bright'ning o'er the sky,
Itself a city, swells her palace high.
And lo! the massy gate, unclosing wide,
Rolls through the figured arch a dazzling tide.
The ⁽⁶⁾ circuit now begins, in annual state;
Around the monarch bands of nobles wait,
While, raised amidst the proudly-servile throng,
Borne on a towering elephant along,
O'er whose vast frame, in gem-starr'd trappings roll'd,
A crimson covering shines, with flowers of gold;—
In sovereign pomp the despot sits supreme,
Array'd in robes that mock the noontide beam.
A train of elephants, succeeding slow,
Swells the long order of the pageant show; [crowds,
The flower-strew'd streets are fill'd with gazing
The throng'd roofs tremble with unusual loads;

Where'er the proud procession passes, all
In base prostration to their idol fall,
As if some power divine, from opening skies,
Had burst in glory on their dazzled eyes.
   Bright in the splendors of imperial rule,
Here Ava's prince extends his high control—
Sees realms, the prize of war, his sceptre own,
And powerful princes bow before his throne:
Proud [7] Anacan reluctant homage yields,
And mourns Pegea her tributary fields;
Her ancient honors lost, her mighty name
Soil'd with disgraceful marks of vassal shame.
O'er the fair borders of yon azure flood,
Her city rises like a vernal wood,
Where domes in gilded pomp salute the skies,
And rows of trees in verdant bloom arise:
The golden lustre, mingling with the green,
Forms in assemblage bright a new, enchanting scene.
High o'er the rest, with glitt'ring turrets crown'd,
The castled palace lifts an ample round;
The [8] sculptured hall with every jewel beams,
Whence day perpetual pours in lucid streams;

500

Horrid in frowning gold, in silver dire,
Here giant forms in threat'ning ranks aspire;
Their sapphire zones an azure light disclose,
And crowns of rubies sparkle on their brows.
Innumerous spreading o'er her far-stretch'd plains,
Magnificent ascend the (n) idol fanes;
There, bright with gems, within their sacred shrine,
In gold horrific lie the forms divine.
No shapes so monstrous wildering fancy frames,
And none so hideous haunt the sick-man's dreams;
Yet these her priest-deluded sons adore,
As gods revere them, and as gods implore.

To Fancy's view now Sunda's islands rise,
Bright in all blooms that glow in tropic skies,—
Where the gay Orange hangs her fragrant fruit,
Their luscious clusters mild Bananas shoot;
Of taste embrosial, rich Ananas swell,
And the tall Cocoa rounds her milky shell.
Here, long Sumatra bends her deep'ning bays,
Where fields of Pepper blacken in the blaze:
From inland mountains, proud in savage gloom,
Whose central caverns ripening ores entomb,

Her numerous torrents whitening down the sides,
Through gold-strew'd channels lead their rushing tides;
Hence Indapoora [10] pours a sanguine train,
And blushes on, red-rolling to the main.

    Like some low mist, o'er settled ocean spread,
Fair Java rises from her wat'ry bed.
Here, rich Batavia lifts her shining towers,
And numerous cities grace the fertile shores:
But lurid wildness glooms the inlands wide,
Where the lone [11] Upas spires in deadly pride;
In sullen horror frowns the region round—
No lively verdure cheers the sick'ning ground:
For many a league no tree its honors rears,
No scatter'd shrub, nor lonely plant appears;
Each tainted gale, that sweeps the mournful heath,
With venom loaded, breathes immediate death;
No savage tenant of the shady grove,
With vent'rous footsteps, here attempts to rove;
No tuneful choirs here hail the opening day—
None vagrant round on careless pinions stray;
But all instinctive shun the dreary waste,
Where fate, exulting, rides the poison'd blast.

CHARMS OF FANCY. 117

    Bright o'er the rest the queen of islands smiles;
Vast [12] Borneo, rising midst her subject isles.
Gay wave her woods along the circling strand,
And groves of Camphor shade the scented land;
Of size gigantic, here the Ourang roves
Through the wild tangles of the searchless groves—
In human form the monster stalks along,
Grimly majestic, mid the savage throng.

    Near Celebes, in pride of nature drest,
Heaves her fair bosom o'er the wat'ry waste;
The woolly plant adorns her fertile vales,
And waves its yellow blossoms to the gales;
The [13] Opium spreads its dulling langours round,
And droops its nodding branches o'er the ground.
No sun e'er marks its glooms with cheerful ray,
No birds melodious hop from spray to spray,
No rustling breeze awakes the torpid boughs,
No noise ungrateful mars the deep repose:
Here Sleep, dull Power, his sway imperial spreads,
Hence o'er the world his drowsy influence sheds,—
Bids listless heaviness each sense invade,
And seals the leaden eye in slumber's shade,

Gives to the wretch a respite from his woes,
The toil-worn slave, the sweets of wish'd repose,
The seaman peace amidst the stormy main,
And soothes the anguish'd on the bed of pain.
    Skillful her sons, unrivall'd in the art
From hollow reeds to blow the poison'd dart:
Less sure of aim, where Lybia's woods expand
In glooms of horror o'er her hydra land,
The flitting [14] Serpent from the treach'rous bough,
Darts on the heedless passenger below:
Less instantaneous Fate's dark arrow flies
From the fell [15] Basilisk's envenom'd eyes:
A race of heroes, [16] whose unshaken souls
No abject fear of death, no pain controls;
Not Sparta's sons, for valor famed afar,
By old Lycurgus form'd to deeds of war,—
Not northern tribes, whom Odin's doctrines gave
With joy the terrors of the fight to brave,
A more intrepid spirit e'er display'd,   [vey'd;
Or with more calm contempt the frowns of death sur-
Not the wild Mohawk, nursed in human woe,
Amid the flames who taunts his cruel foe,

Whose savage pride of fortitude to quell,
Torture in vain exerts his utmost skill,
With more unshrinking stubbornness sustains
The varied round of vengeance' studied pains.
  Like distant clouds Molucca's islands rise,
Blue-skirting o'er the edge of southern skies:
There glows in yellow bloom the Nutmeg grove,
And dark-red honors crown the fragrant Clove;
Here birds of Paradise, in sportive rings,
Bright in the sunbeam, ply their silken wings,
Whose glossy plumes such vivid tints adorn
As gleam from dew-drops in the eye of morn.
Mark'd by his gorgeous hues and length of tail,
In waving curls loose floating on the gale,
Amid the rest the king distinguish'd shines,
And forms the order of their marshall'd lines;
Now in swift flight, on downy pinion, roves
Through walks of Cinnamon and Nutmeg groves;
Now on some tall tree's topmost bough, at ease,
Inhales the fragrance of the spicy breeze;
Or, when the shifting Monsoon's rage prevails,
And mad'ning tempests swell th' autumnal gales,

High o'er the clouds he wings his airy flight,
To azure realms and fields of purest light;
In conscious pride his subject-bands precedes,
Who joyful follow where their monarch leads:
Surveys, with eyes serene, the storm below,
Or marks the beauties of the prismy bow.

 O'er diamond realms, majestic, deep and strong,
In sacred pomp where Ganges moves along;
Where, by a thousand streams unknown supplied,
The Bunampooter [17] pours his mightier tide;
Or Indus rolls its wave, lo! prospects new,
Attired in splendor, open on my view.
Mid fair Cambaya's plains, in plenty drest,
Proud Ahmedabad lifts its regal crest;
Erst on yon shore, near Diu's present site,
Thy temple, [18] Sum-nat, rear'd its sacred height,
Before whose shrine adoring India bow'd,
And own'd, from earliest time, her greatest god;
While kings successive there their treasures pour'd,
And gifts of ages swell'd the countless hoard.

 See, farther south, where [19] Salsette's island lies,
And Elephanta's sculptured rocks arise;

As now amid their cavern'd walks I roam,
And vast Pagoda's subterranean gloom,
What sculptured wonders to my view unfold!
What forms terrific of gigantic mould!
With hideous frowns seem starting from the stone,
The work of nations, and of times unknown.
Here India's gods, a host in dread array,
The various symbols of their power display.
With look composed great Brama here appears;
His savage mien the dire Destroyer [20] rears:
Here Crishna [21] stands, the pride of India's plain,
And Vishnoo, glorious from the Tyrant [22] slain.

Near Ganges' wave, yon heaps of ruins claim,
And still preserve, Kinnouge, [23] thy mighty name!
How changed from that Kinnouge, the peerless seat
Of India's ancient kings, immensely great,
An empire in itself, afar renown'd,
The awe, the wonder of the realms around!
Wrapp'd in decay, have sunk thy towers and fanes,
Nor scarce a vestige of thy pomp remains;
Oft mid thy scenes, or where, in wealth array'd,
Bengal's fair capital her charms display'd.

Illustrious [24] Gour! the boast of ancient days,
Absorb'd in pensive thought, the native strays;
While, as he views, in ruins scatter'd wide,
The mouldering monuments of Hindoo pride.
His country's old renown his bosom swells;
On those proud times with raptured view he dwells,
Till, haply checked, at once the vision ends,
And terror's freezing tide each power suspends,
As, from the covert of some thicket near,
The Tiger's [25] hideous growl assails his ear,
Where, couch'd to earth, in act to spring, he lies,
And marks his destined prey with flaming eyes.

   Here ancient Lahor lifts her tower-crown'd brows,
In crimson beauty Agra's [26] palace glows;
And here, reflected in the Jumna's stream,
Thy domes superb, imperial Delhi, gleam.
High o'er the rest, with stately turrets crown'd,
Her royal palace looks sublime around;
And lo! the gates unclose, the court displays
Its dazzling wonders to my raptured gaze.
Retired in yon alcove of burnish'd gold,
Where wreathes the mimic vine in curling fold,

Green from whose stems the leaves of emerald shoot,
And glows the amethyst in purple fruit.
High on a gorgeous throne sublimely raised,
Thick starr'd with pearls, with every gem emblazed,
Sits the Mogul, [27] in show a sovereign god,
And monarchs tremble at his awful nod.
His diamond robes a wide effulgence stream,
Bright as a summer sun's unclouded beam;
The rainbow-splendor of whose glancing rays
Wide o'er the hall in trembling radiance plays:
Around his vassal kings and Omrah band,
With gold adorn'd and gay in jewels, stand.
So when the moon, in full-orb'd glory bright,
Resplendent beaming through the shades of night,
From heaven's blue zenith pours her light serene,
The host of stars surround their smiling queen,
But, gleaming faint, with feeble lustre shine,
Lost in the splendor of her rays divine.

 Vain mockery of power! Unreal show!
Joy's empty shade! The poor disguise of woe!
In vain the despot, mid encircling spears,
On terrors base his dome of greatness rears.

There still suspicion's pallid eye is seen,
And discontent exalts his gloomy mien,
And waits with watchful ken the fav'ring hour,
To rouse the pageant from his dream of power;
While at each blast he trembles on his throne,
Nor scarce can count one moment as his own.
Was it this poor pre-eminence to gain,
At best delusive, dangerous and vain,
To stand exposed amid the storms of state,
To the fierce Afghan, [28] and the barbarous **Tate**,
While foreign foes incursive arms prepare,
And near domestic treason plants its snare,
That, lost to justice and to honor dead,
Each tie of kin, each sense of friendship fled?
So oft in arms fraternal kings have stood,
And impious sons have blush'd with parents' blood:
Such tragic fates the race of Timur known,
While murder form'd the cement of the throne.
  But from the glare of courts, the pride of power,
Far different scenes the willing Muse allure;
Where, deck'd in simpler beauties, nature reigns,
And spring purpureal clothes the genial plains;

Where healthful temperance, of rosy dye,
Warms the flush'd cheek and sparkles in the eye;
Where, in cool ease, the harmless native, laid
Beneath the palm-tree, or the olive's shade,
As free from care the transient minutes move,
Recites the praises of his tawny love;
Or, fired to rapture, wakes his tuneful lays,
In hymns of gratitude, to Brama's praise.
Benignant Brama! Life-sustaining power!
From whose creative hand, in constant shower,
Its fated round of change still following, flows
Each good that man enjoys or nature knows;
Thrice happy land! his power indulgent fills
Thy plains with every fruit, with every gem thy hills.

Here, wild revenge, or ruthless lust of power
Ne'er gave the sword to reek with human gore;
But Innocence, unterrified by foes,
Securely smiled in undisturb'd repose.
Here, cheerful plenty, from her bounteous hand,
Spread the rich harvest o'er the fertile land,
And dove-eyed peace, in lucid robes serene,
With joy presided o'er the blissful scene;

Till from cold Scythia rush'd her savage brood,
Resistless, pouring wide a wint'ry flood.
O'er thy fair plains the impetuous torrent bends,
Dire desolation on its course attends;
The splendid structure to its fury yields,
And ripening treasures of thy waving fields;
Wild fly before it horror and dismay,
And death and havoc mark its dreadful way.
Then what avail'd the plenty of thy plains,
Thy golden treasures and thy jewell'd fanes?
Will nature's beauties, or the works of art,
To soft compassion melt the savage heart;
Or guardless wealth procure its feeble lord
A longer respite from the ruffian's sword?
Those boasted joys that wealthier climates know,
Too frequent prove the fatal source of wo.
Though nature there her gifts profusely pours,
And wealth exalting spreads his golden stores;
Though there the arts invite, the muses sing,
They ill repay the evils that they bring.
Their smiling plains, where vernal pleasures bloom,
And odorous trees exhale the rich perfume—

Their gold, their domes, magnificently gay,
But lure the robber to the tempting prey;
While colder climes, in penury secure,
Whose barren rocks no greedy foes allure,
Taught their own bliss by others' ills to prize,
No longer mourn their less indulgent skies;
But view, exulting in their happier state,
The woes severe that lovelier realms await.
So shines the fair, whose peerless graces move
The nymphs to envy and the youth to love;
Till, by some false seducer's arts betray'd,
Her beauty's victim, falls the hapless maid;
In ruin plunged, her charms no longer move
The nymphs to envy or the youth to love;
All join her fatal weakness to proclaim,
And scorn's cold sneer insults in pity's name.

But not alone from Scythia's savage train,
Has bleeding India mourn'd her children slain;
Thy polish'd sons, O Europe! lured by gold,
In these fair realms the blackest crimes unfold;
O'er her rich plains, like ravening wolves, they pour,
Let havoc loose, and bathe their steps in gore.

In vain the native, plunged in deepest woe,
For pity supplicates the ruthless foe;
In vain his glittering treasures trembling yields,
And the rich produce of his cultured fields.
No beam of pity sheds its kindly rays;
Through the cold breast unfeeling avarice sways;
Nor gifts, though pour'd in copious tides, control
That raging fever of the sordid soul;
The glittering present but incites desire,
And adds fresh fuel to the former fire.

Yet unrevenged has not Indostan view'd
Her ravaged regions drench'd with filial blood;
Fired by her wrongs, her braver children rose,
The stern avengers of their country's woes;
When Aurungzebe, defiled with brother's gore,
Through every crime attain'd the heights of power;
Each awe-struck Rajah, trembling at his nod,
In base submission crouch'd beneath the rod.
With generous pride and freedom's brave disdain,
Sevagi [29] simply scorn'd the servile chain—
Resolved no more to fill a shadowy throne,
Another's slave, in show a king alone;

But the proud Despot's utmost force defy,
And live a monarch, or a monarch die.
Each mode in vain the guileful tyrant tried,
That fraud could dictate or that power supplied.
The Prince, no stranger to the courtly wile,
And ambush'd treachery of its hollow smile,
His plots eluded, and his hosts compell'd,
With shame repulsed, to fly the routed field;
While to his country's wrongs his vengeful **sword**
Of Tartar blood a glad libation poured,
Till, often foil'd, the baffled foe gave o'er,
And bade the weary contest rage no more.
There too, illustrious boast of modern time!
India's support, the glory of her clime,
In whom thy nation, with admiring eyes,
Beheld anew her loved Sevagi rise—
Exalted Hyder! whose capacious mind,
Each vast resource of various war combined,
Thy prowess lower'd the plume of British **pride**,
And check'd the fury of their hostile tide;
Their cruelties avenged, and gave, in turn,
The insulting victor's haughty hearts to mourn.

515

But from these plains, embrued with native blood,
Where waves of crimson swell the blushing flood,
Lo! Persia's realm allures my eager sight,
Where polish'd ease and social joys delight.
Hail! Land, where genius fires the raptured soul,
Where love of fame conducts to honor's goal,
Where poetry her beams celestial sheds,
In brightest splendor, o'er her votaries' heads,
And views, with proud delight, her tuneful throng,
In rapture's strains, rehearse the magic song.

In epic state, thy great [30] Ferdousi reigns,
The mighty Homer of the Asian plains,
Whose strains sublime, with various beauties fraught,
With rich description and ennobling thought,
With equal force the raptured soul engage;
Mid scenes of peace, or mid the battle's rage,
Whether, serene in Feridoon [31] appears
The autumnal lustre of declining years,
Zal's [32] youthful form the bloom of spring displays,
Raduva [33] shines in beauty's peerless blaze,
Her death-doom'd Lord Afrasiab's [34] daughter mourns,
Or Rustem [35] dreadful in the battle burns

Pathetic Janu's [36] melting numbers move,
In strains accordant with the notes of love;
Replete with life his warm descriptions shine,
And waken'd passion breathes in every line.
As shines the rose still moist with evening's tears,
So bright Zulrica [37] mid her grief appears,
When from her sleepless couch she lifts her head,
The flattering vision of the morning fled.
Ill-fated fair one! thine the lot to prove
The bitter anguish of rejected love;
Though deck'd with charms the coldest heart to warm,
Each grace of mien, each elegance of form,
Absorb'd in grief, to black despair a prey,
Those charms neglected, pined in pale decay.

The force of beauty, and the power of wine,
In sprightly Hafir [38] mirthful odes combine;
Nature, to whom he sung, attuned his lyre,
And fill'd his bosom with her genial fire;
Around his brows her fragrant garland twined,
Where laurel-wreath'd the rose of Shiraz shined.
Enchanting Bard! thy artless verse shall please
While the rich Musk Rose scents the passing breeze;

While Shiraz' vines with purple clusters shine,
And flows the generous juice in sparkling wine!
    Though vile reproach thy sons, O Persia! stain,
As sunk in sloth, effeminate and vain,
Yet generous, hospitable, gay, refined,
To honor warm, to noble deeds inclined;
Though mild yet brave, though courteous yet sincere,
For winning manners famed, to genius dear;
With pride exulting, nature sees them stand,
Amidst the foremost of her favor'd band.
    Here Cyrus, crown'd with palms of conquest, shone,
Of kings the pride, the glory of a throne;
From hence, that fancied god, proud Xerxes, hurl'd
The bolts of terror o'er the Asian world;
When at his mandate pour'd her various host,
From distant regions, to Byzantium's coast,
O'er trembling Greece the floods of war to roll,
And freedom bend to tyranny's control.
Numerous as stars that gild the vault of night,
Ere rising Cynthia beams her placid light,

Whole realms are hid beneath the countless swarms,
And glows the prospect round one dazzling blaze of
arms.
Where'er, wide-sweeping, with resistless force,
The whelming myriads roll their wasteful course,
Exhausted fountains mourn their rivers dry,
And fertile plains in barren horror lie.
In vain the Hellespont's opposing tide
Rolls its deep flood and spreads a barrier wide;
The monarch wills, he gives the fatal word;
Submissive millions press to please their lord;
Sudden, as form'd by necromantic lore,
The bridge enormous spreads from shore to shore,
And o'er it, bright in pomp of martial state,
A world dispeopled pours its mighty freight.

  Here, learn'd in nature's works, the Magian
  choir,
With secret rites, adored the sacred fire,
While rose in Mithra's praise their early lay,
Mithra, the god who lights the lamp of day;
By Zoroaster [40] taught, whose faith convey'd
Sublimest truths, though veil'd in mystic shade.

Exalted Sage! whose heaven-illumined sight,
Mid prime effulgence, view'd the sire of light,
And pierced the central glooms of endless pain,
Where night's dark demon spreads his dire domain;
Thy tenets adverse powers contending show'd,
Author of evil one, and one of good—
Great Oromazes, [41] whence all blessings flow,
And Arimanius, source accurst of wo.

   As o'er the realm my airy course I bend,
What cities gay, in spiry pomp, ascend!
Here Ispahan exalts her regal head,
Here pearly Ormus' wealthy marts are spread;
Here Tauris smiles, beneath her blissful skies;
Here Kom's gay groves and Kashan's mosques arise;
In mouldering horror, o'er the lonely plains,
Persepolis extends her sad remains;
Far-famed Istakhar! [42] where, in rival pride,
With art's fair forms each charm of splendor vied;
While wonder still, with pleasure ever new,
On Jemsheid's palace, fix'd her raptured view,
Till Macedonia's king, by wine subdued,
By wanton Thais' false enticements woo'd;
520

To flames consign'd, in smould'ring ruin hurl'd,
That boast of art, and wonder of the world.
Now, grim, exulting o'er its desert space,
Lifts Desolation his destructive mace;
By ruin strew'd in mingled heaps around,
Fanes, arches, porticoes conceal the ground;
Columns on columns piled here meet the eye;
Here the rent architrave and broken cornice lie.
Triumphant still o'er time's all-conquering might,
Here winds the marble stairway's lengthening flight;
Here yet the imaged walls in glittering rows
The beauteous forms of sculptured art disclose,
Where mimic plants their flaunting foliage spread,
And sceptred monarchs lift the haughty head.
Through the cleft roof of yonder rifted pile
Spires the dark cypress, midst the nodding ile;
The lonely wall-flower opes her modest charms
Betwixt yon weeping Cupid's mangled arms;
Horrid with hoary moss, the aged thorn
Hangs its black berries o'er the broken urn;
The wild vine wreathes her antic folds around
Yon column, mark'd by time with many a wound;

The gate superb where watch'd the palace bands,
Its arch disjoin'd, in crumbling ruin stands;
The loose stone trembles from the nodding brow,
And waves its long moss o'er the pass below;
The sculptured hall where erst, in all the state
Of Eastern pomp, Darius proudly sate;
Where mighty Jemsheid, (43) from his throne on high,
With peerless beauty charm'd the dazzled eye,
A refuge for each reptile base behold!
There the green Serpent coils his venom'd fold,
There lurks the Aspic cold, the bloated Toad,
There the black Scorpion makes his dire abode.
No festal lamp now beams meridian light,
No sound disturbs the still repose of night,
Save when the Bittern wakes her dismal cries,
From the gray tomb the Screech-Owl's shrieks arise,
Or the wild Jackall, o'er the desert plain,
With howl lugubrious, calls his kindred train.

  But what perfumes delight my ravish'd sense?
What balmy odors mingled sweets dispense?
Borne on the pinions of the western gale,
 That breathes its fragrance o'er yon blossom'd vale,

Lo, there what fields in rich luxuriance glow,
What crystal streams in wide meanders flow!
There, in green beauty, long-drawn lawns retire;
There flowery groves in stately ranks aspire;
And one bright sky, eternally serene,
With purest azure decks the enchanting scene.
Not fairer bloom'd gay Eden's blissful shade,
In infant nature's earliest charms array'd;
Thy gardens, Shiraz, [14] spread their beauties here,
Where spring unfading blossoms through the year.
Less fair the scenes where bright Barradia [15] laves
Thy plains, Damascus! with his genial waves;
Less fair, Obolla, thy attractive shores,
Where lavish nature opes her richest stores;
Less fair the plain, amid whose landscapes gay,
Thy towers, Samarcand, sparkle to the day!
Here richest fruits, the growth of every land,
Ope in gay bloom, in ripening state expand;
From its dark green the golden Orange glows,
The downy Peach her cheek red-blushing shows;
In purple clusters, from the bending vine,
With tempting show, nectareous grapes decline;

Here fragrant flowers, of every vivid hue,
In soften'd lustre gleam, impearl'd with dew;
Their mottled leaves there gaudy Tulips spread;
Here the pale Lily hangs the pensive head—
Sad emblem of the Fair, in beauty's bloom,
With hopeless love slow-sinking to the tomb;
The friendly Jessamine, on yonder bower,
Wreathes, with the Woodbine sweet, her snowy
    flower;
In virgin diffidence, the blushing Rose
Here scarcely dares her opening buds disclose,
And there, full-blown, in matron pride unveils
Her crimson bosom to the wanton gales;
The Anemone, in scarlet lustre gay,
Expands her petals to the cheering ray;
Here boasts the Auricula her dress of gold,
The Polianthus' tinted leaves unfold,
And rich Ranunculus, of every dye,
That lights the morn, or paints the evening sky.
Beside yon flower-fringed stream, whose dimpling
    maze,
O'er yellow sands, in tuneful murmurs strays,

Long rows of Dates [46] in stately pomp ascend,
And o'er the wave their snow-bloom'd branches
 bend,
With shade inviting spread a cool retreat,
A grateful shelter from meridian heat.
The breeze, soft-rustling, scarcely curls the stream,
Bright in whose face the bordering Roses gleam.
Warm at his honey'd task, the Bee around
From flower to flower, low hums with busy sound,
Lulling, with murmurs soft, to transient rest,
Each rude emotion of the troubled breast.
Here painted songsters, of each beauteous dye,
Amidst the trees in wanton frolic fly,
Far trill around their melting notes of love,
And rapturous music vibrates through the grove.
Midst the green leaves, in scarlet plumage gay,
The little Red-bird wakes his tuneful lay;
Where yon broad plaintain spreads its shadowy
 leaves,
Her curious nest the little [47] Artist weaves;   [rude,
There, screen'd from storms, from each intruder
In their green dwelling, hides her callow brood;

Here the lone Charmer of the silent grove,
Tunes to the Rose [49] his nightly tale of love,
While, bathed in evening's tears, the beauteous flower,
More lovely shines, unconscious of her power.
Enamel'd Butterflies, of every hue,
The Topaz' yellow, and the Sapphire's blue,
The Emerald's green, the Ruby's crimson dyes,
With silver border'd and instarr'd with eyes,
Bedropp'd with gold and bright in gleaming pearl,
In gaudy pride their filmy wings unfurl.
O'er the whole scene the sounds of mirth prevail,
And Love and Pleasure fill the smiling dale.
  But, from these breezy groves, these fragrant bowers,
These favor'd walks of nature, deck'd in flowers,
To joy-deserted plains my course I bend,
Where wild Arabia's dreary wastes extend.
Here no clear stream in murmuring windings roves;
In blossom'd pride aspire no shady groves;
With flow'rets deck'd no verdant lawns appear;
No birds, their notes soft-warbling, charm the ear;

No Zephyrs round a grateful fragrance cast:
But breathes alone the suffocating blast.
  Now sultry mid-day glows—the source of light
Intensely flames from heaven's meridian height;
O'er the hot sands his rays reflected gleam,
Like waves bright-rolling in the morning beam;
Like fields of clover glistening with the rain,
When smiles the sun upon the moisten'd plain.
Fainting beneath the intolerable heat,
Its rage to shun, I seek some cool retreat.
In vain no tree, no verdurous beauties smile,
No limpid fountain glads the thirsty soil,
Nor human footstep marks the faithless waste,
For ever flitting with the driving blast.
One waste of sand far spreads, an ocean wide,
  Scarce with a few low tufts of withering furze supplied.
    Wild as the clime here oft, in murderous bands,
The Arabs, roaming o'er the burning sands,
Rush on the caravan, whose pious train
Direct their toilsome course to Mecca's fane.

In vain the feeble band attempt the fight—
Vain as resistance are their hopes of flight:
Now Murder waves on high the reeking blade,
And deep in gore those fiends of slaughter wade;
Their savage hearts no ray of pity feel,
Their hearts relentless as their murderous steel;
Nor sex, nor age their brutal fury spares:
In vain the matron's cries, the virgin's prayers,
In vain sweet childhood spreads its little hands,
Pity in vain enfeebled age demands—
The sportive infant yields his scarce-drawn breath,
And bends the snow-white sire his head in death;
The beauteous maid whom keener woes await.
In trembling horror views their envied fate;
One wide destruction wraps the hapless train,
And floods of crimson deluge o'er the plain.
Thus, when a hurricane, the scourge of heaven,
In darkening fury o'er these deserts driven,
Tears up whole plains in eddies whirl'd on high,
And blots with smothering clouds the lurid sky;
Here, haply journeying, sinks the pilgrim host,
In one wide sweep of dire destruction lost;

And, deep inhumed beneath o'erwhelming plains,
One fate involves them, and one grave contains.

   The sun, declining, darts a slanting smile:
My shadow lengthens o'er the burning soil.
Lo! swelling on the eye, blue mountains rise,
Their dim-seen summits mingling with the skies.
Thither my course I bend; in distant shew,
What wrecks of grandeur fill the imperfect view!
Now, from yon purple cloud, the setting ray
Smiles, the last farewell of departing day.
What golden gleams his sinking orb invest—
What reddening glories tinge the blushing West—
What painted clouds, swift-varying to the eye—
In fleecy volumes sail the evening sky!
Here, golden-edged, with flaming crimson glare,
And there the amber's milder tinctures wear;
In mimic rocks project the dark-blue brow,
Or swell convolved in whitening hills of snow.

   Now, thickening fast, gray twilight's shadows roll,
And night's black curtains wrap the darken'd pole;

While, slowly rising up the eastern sky,
Lifts the full moon her friendly lamp on high;
Shines the blue vault, with golden stars enchased,
A pleasing contrast to the dreary waste.
In mournful beauty, by the ray serene,
Bursts on my raptured view the gorgeous scene;
In stately rows here marble columns spread,
In single state there lonely rear the head,
Like groups of blasted oaks amid the wild,
Stripp'd of their verdure, of their limbs despoil'd;
Here from the base by time's rude tempests rent,
Like fallen pines, lie stretch'd in vast extent;
In mouldering fragments here o'erspread the sand,
Some broken there in shatter'd ruin stand:
In sullied pomp, half-sunk within the ground,
Lies the rich capital with foliage crown'd:
The spreading Eagle, [49] low in dust is laid,
Beneath yon rough palmetto's fan-like shade.
Thy ruins these, Palmyra! here once smiled
Thy splendid structures o'er the desert wild:
Here the faint traveler, with raptured eyes,
Mid barren sands beheld thy beauties rise.

Thus, when old Chaos heard creation's call,
And first, fair-gleaming, rose this beauteous ball,
Admiring angels view'd, with fond delight,
Revolving systems mid chaotic night;
Their golden lyres the tuneful seraphs strung,
The great Creator's praise enraptured sung;
The notes of transport wide o'er space were hurl'd,
And sweet Hosannas hail'd the new-born world.

Thy scenes oft heard the Sage divine rehearse
The laws of eloquence, and rules of verse—
Sublime Longinus! on whose tuneful tongue
The bending crowd in rapt attention hung.
Here reign'd Zenobia, o'er whose daring soul
No female weakness held its soft control;
With courage graced, with talents bright adorn'd,
The gay allurements of her sex she scorn'd;
O'er earth her pride aspired to stretch her sway,
And make imperial Rome her rule obey:
Beneath her reign, with wide-spread lustre, shone
Thy fame, Palmyra! till, by Rome o'erthrown,
Sunk in obscurity thy meteor rays,
Lost in the splendor of that solar blaze.

Yon marble pile, that, gleaming o'er the sands,
In proud pre-eminence of ruin stands,
Where the pale moon, between the column'd rows,
A line of lengthen'd light far-streaming throws;
The Sun's rich fane, with fair perfection graced
Of art Corinthian, charm'd the eye of taste.
Now, midst its gorgeous walks, his straw-built sheds
And clay-patch'd huts the swarthy Arab spreads;
And, in these once gay scenes of wealth and pride,
The savage tenants of the waste reside.

From burning sands, where vegetation dies,
Where no cool stream the crystal wave supplies,
To fairer scenes I turn, with keen delight,
Where far-famed Egypt's fertile plains invite—
Where meads unsown their crops spontaneous yield,
Spontaneous harvests gild the uncultured field
O'er these rich realms, in wealth-diffusing pride,
The Nile majestic pours his swelling tide.
Thou king of rivers! from thy source unknown,
In streams of plenty roll thy treasures down;
Thy floods wide-spreading various climates lave,
And future harvests smile beneath thy wave.

Here Alexandria's mingled scene displays
The wrecks of old and piles of modern days;
In Gothic state where Turkish mosques arise,
And low the Grecian fane in ruin lies.
High o'er the rest, proud spiring to the sky,
Thy pillar, Pompey, claims the admiring eye;
Ill fated Chief! whose various fortunes show
The height of grandeur and extreme of wo.
By the false Goddess' fickle favor raised,
Thy sun awhile with peerless lustre blazed;
O'er wond'ring worlds thy fame extended wide,
Thy rivals' envy and thy nation's pride—
Till, from the summit of thy splendor thrown,
Thy country's fate involving in thine own,
From servile hands thou found'st a shameful doom,
While barbarous shores scarce gave a furtive tomb.

Breathing blue plagues beneath her tainted sky,
Here swarming Cairo lifts her domes on high.
Lo, what vast wonders, swelling on the view,
In ken remote, like sloping mountains shew!
The enormous Pyramids there heave sublime
In all the hoary majesty of time;

O'er acres spread the solid masses tower,
Dark round their sides the low-hung vapors lour;
High in the heavens they rise, in boastful state,
And earth encumber'd shrinks beneath their weight;
Within their cells, her former loved resort,
Pale Superstition ⁽⁵⁰⁾ holds her gloomy court;
Her form distorted massy chains confine,
And round her limbs in tortuous bands entwine;
The gloom of awe, with mystery's strange grimace,
Sits on the sullen features of her face;
Her threat'ning eyes with deadly malice glare,
And on her darken'd brow frowns wild despair.
O'er her black robe each hideous shape is spread,
By fear e'er raised, or sickening fancy bred;
Around her breast enzoned in barbarous pride,
A cestus glows, with human crimson dyed;
Terror's black trump her better hand supplies—
Whene'er she bids its hideous clangors rise;
Uncommon horrors startle every breast,
Each form affrights in fearful colors drest;
All nature trembles at the infernal sound; [ground;
By earthquakes rent, deep groans the shuddering

534

Black clouds o'er heaven a sudden darkness pour,
In peals incessant doubling thunders roar;
Blue through the shades pale gleaming lightnings fly,
And meteors redden o'er the lurid sky;
With thrilling shrieks his dirge the Death-owl sings,
And birds ill-omen'd flap their dusky wings;
Wild, fire-eyed monsters ride the troubled air,
And damned demons howl in deep despair;
While spectres, rising from the yawning tomb,
Half show their airy forms and flit along the gloom.

NOTES TO THE THIRD BOOK.

¹ "Where Justice sits," &c. Kien Long, the present Emperor of China, who has considerably extended the limits of the empire by the conquest of several countries, amongst which is the rich and fertile kingdom of Bochara, is not less celebrated for his clemency and paternal affection for his subjects, than for the success of his arms; among the numerous instances of which, the following is not the least conspicuous. An earthquake having, in the year 1783, destroyed a great part of the island of Formosa, he ordered a general account of the loss of each individual to be taken, and the full amount to be paid from the royal treasury. This beneficent monarch, who is of a very advanced age, is also a poet of no inconsiderable merit.

² "Innumerous peacocks." The banks of the Mecon abound with wild peacocks, which make a most beautiful appearance on the trees that overhang that river.

³ "The beauteous Boiga." A most beautiful species of serpent in India, remarkable for the richness, variety, and brilliancy of its colors; is about three feet in length, but extremely slender in proportion, being only a few lines in diameter. When this serpent moves itself in the sun, it exhibits the various colors, together with the splendor of the most precious stones. The beauty of its appearance and gracefulness of its motion are still heightened in the eyes of the beholder, by its innocence; it even appears to receive pleasure from the fondlings of the young Indians. (Capeda.)

152   NOTES TO THE THIRD BOOK.

⁴ "The twinkling Fire-Fly." The Fire-flies on the rivers of Siam, are remarkable for their numbers, size, and brilliancy. These insects are common in America, and at times exhibit a phenomenon of a most beautiful and singular kind. I have seen them, in a warm evening in July or August, so numerous as to cover an extent of meadow of several acres, and throughout the whole, as if actuated by one soul, expand and close their wings at the same instant, at momentary intervals; now withdrawing their light, and now flashing on the view a wide-extended plain of animated fire.

⁵ "Proud Odian's walls." The capital of Siam.

⁶ "The circuit now begins." The King of Siam shows himself to his subjects but once or twice a year. He regularly makes an annual procession through the city, attended by his nayres and ministers of state, in which all the splendor of Eastern magnificence is displayed.

⁷ "Proud Arracan," &c. The kingdoms of Arracan and Pegu, formerly powerful and independent sovereignties, are now subject to the Emperor of Ava, and form a part of the Birman dominion. Between the years 1740 and 1750, a great revolution took place in the kingdom of Pegu, which rendered it subject to Ava, of which it is no more at present than a province. In 1783, the Peguans attempted to regain their independence, and acquired possession of Rangoon, the capital; but they were able to hold it only a few days, when they were reduced to subjection.

⁸ "The sculptured hall." The palace of Pegu is described by travelers as a very magnificent structure, containing a great number of gigantic figures, in gold and silver, ornamented with jewels. This was, no doubt, previous to the revolution which subjected it to Ava.

⁹ "Magnificent ascend the idol fanes." The temples or pagodas of the Peguans are very splendid; they differ, however, in shape from

those of the other parts of India. They are of a polygonic form, having a great many sides of about thirty feet in height, surmounted by a round spire, curving inwards like an inverted lily, and terminating in a point. At the top of the spire is fixed a ring or circle, to which are suspended a great number of small bells that are constantly agitated by the wind. Their priests are called Talapoys, and are distinguished by a loose dress of yellow cloth. They have their heads shaved and bare, are bound to celibacy, and in many respects resemble the priesthood of the Romish Church. There is also an order of priestesses, or nuns, who are bound by the same regulations, and wear the same habit. (*Hunter's Account of Pegu.*) The objects of worship of the Peguans are various; but with them, as in Siam, and in most of the countries of Eastern India, the principal object of adoration is Tommonacodom, whose worship is supposed, at some remote period, to have pervaded almost all the countries of the East, and is probably the same as Sumnat, whose temple was taken and pillaged by the celebrated Mahmud.

10 " Hence Indapoora pours a sanguine train." The waters of the Indapoora, a principal river in Sumatra, especially when swelled by rains, are of a dark-red color, which is supposed to be owing to the bark of a tree, of which there are great numbers on its banks.

11 " Where the lone Upas." The Bohon Upas, or Poison-Tree of Java, is about twenty-seven leagues from Batavia. It is surrounded on every side by high hills; the country for twelve miles around it is entirely barren. Its poison is of the most deadly and subtle kind, sudden in its operations, and infects the air to such a degree that neither man nor any other animal can exist within the distance of twelve or fifteen miles from it.

12 " Vast Borneo." The island of Borneo, the largest known in the world, excepting New Holland, produces vast quantities of Camphire. Here, too, is found the Ourang-Outang, or Wild Man of the woods; this animal has a greater resemblance to man than any of the

154   NOTES TO THE THIRD BOOK.

brute creation. He is of gigantic stature, being from seven to eight feet in height, and possessed of great strength; he has but little hair; his skin is black; his face wrinkled like that of an old man; his eyes are small—sunk deep in the head, and very near each other; his nose is flat, and his features, generally, have the appearance of those of a negro. He is said to be very ferocious and dangerous when attacked.

[13] " The Opium spreads," &c. There is said to be a certain tree or shrub in the island of Celebes, from which the natives collect great quantities of Opium, by making incisions in the bark.

[14] " The flitting Serpent." The Tree-snake, or Dart, a species of very venomous serpent, in Africa. It attaches itself to the branch of a tree, which it resembles in color, from whence it hurls itself with inconceivable velocity at the object of its aim.

[15] " From the fell Basilisk's envenom'd eyes." The Basilisk was supposed by the ancients to have the power of killing, by a glance of his eye, whatever animal he looked at.

[16] " A race of heroes." The natives of Celebes—the Macassars — are no less celebrated for their fortitude in supporting pain, than for their intrepidity in encountering danger, and in a very extraordinary degree unite the virtues of active and passive courage. They are endued with a very high sense of honor, and a keen sensibility to injury, resulting, probably, in a great degree, from their form of government, which nearly resembles the feudal system. Among the many instances of their unconquerable spirit which are furnished by the histories of the East, the following is selected, taken from the Memoirs of M. Forbin, a French officer of distinction, and related by Capt. Forrest in his Account of the Morgui Archipelago: That gentleman, who held an important command at Bancoc, in the service of the King of Siam, in the year 1686, ordered his Major, who was a Portuguese native of India, to disarm six Macassars. The officer, terrified at being ordered

on such a service, remonstrated with M. Forbin, and endeavored to dissuade him from executing his design. "What you propose, sir," said he, "is not practicable; I, who am a native of India, am well acquainted with this people. Believe me, when I assure you, that they cannot be taken alive; you must kill them before you can succeed. And I farther inform you, that if any attempt is made to seize their captain, who is in the tent, he and his few companions will put every man of us to death." M. Forbin, however, still persisted in his design, imagining that it might be effected with ease. Somewhat impressed, however, with the apprehensions manifested by the Portuguese, he took the precaution of placing twenty Siamese soldiers, armed with lances and muskets, at the entrance of the fort, and having approached within a short distance of the tent of the Macassars, he directed a Mandarin, who served him as an interpreter, to tell the captain from him, that he was sorry in being obliged to execute the orders he had received, to arrest him, but that he might feel assured that he should be treated with the greatest respect. The Mandarin did as he was ordered; but on his mentioning the word arrest, the six Macassars, to use M. Forbin's expressions, threw their turbans on the ground, seized their creeses, and rushed forward like so many demons, and instantly slew the interpreter and six Mandarins who were with him in the tent. M. Forbin with difficulty effected a precipitate retreat himself, by springing over the lances of the soldiers whom he had stationed at the entrance of the fort. The Macassars then set fire to their galley, to prevent it from falling into the hands of their enemies, and afterwards to a convent of Tellapoys, and killed the monks. In this desperate encounter three hundred and sixty-six Siamese, and a number of Frenchmen were killed, and but seventeen Macassars.

[17] "Here Birds of Paradise, in sportive rings." The Molucca, or Arrou Islands, are the favorite and almost the sole residence of the Birds of Paradise. "They are," says Mr. Pennant, in his account of the Spicy Islands, "natives of New Guinea, as well as those islands; are supposed to breed in the first and to reside there during the wet monsoon, but to retire to the Arrou Isles, about a hundred and forty

miles to the east, during the dry or western monsoon. In the east monsoon they moult their long feathers, but recover them in the west. They always migrate in flocks of thirty or forty, and have a leader, which the inhabitants of Arrou call the king, who is said to fly above the flock, which never desert him, but settle where he does. They constantly avoid flying with the wind, which ruffles and blows their loose plumage over their heads, and often forces them down to the ground, from whence they are unable to rise without some advantage; hard showers of rain are equally destructive to them. When they are surprised with a strong gale, they instantly soar to a higher region, beyond the reach of the tempest; there they float at ease in the serene sky, on their light flowing feathers, or pursue their way in security. During their flight they cry like starlings, but in the distress occasioned by a storm blowing in their rear, they express it by a note resembling the croaking of ravens." " When they alight, it is always on the highest trees, the king taking the lead."

" No birds have ever had so much fable mixed with their history. It was believed that they always remained floating on the spicy Indian air, and, of course, not to be in want of legs or feet, of which they were supposed to be destitute; that, when they wanted to sleep, they hung themselves by their two long tail-feathers to the boughs of a tree; that during their flight, even ovation and nutrition of their young were discharged in that element, the male receiving the egg in an orifice nature had formed for that purpose; that they subsisted on the dew, and had no evacuation like other birds. From their being so much in the higher regions, the Portuguese styled them Passaros dà Sol, or Sparrows of the Sun; the islanders, Manu-co-dewata, or the Birds of God; and most of the Europeans name them the *Birds of Paradise*. So happily did this opinion work on the petty kings of the isles, that, seeing them fall, as it frequently happened, dead from the heavenly regions, they became converts to the truth of the immortality of the soul." (Gen. Outlines.)

" The Burrampooter." This majestic river, which is superior in size to the Ganges, takes its rise in the mountains of Tibet, from whence the

Ganges also flows, but proceeding in an opposite direction, pursues its course to the south-east, through the kingdom of Tibet and near the confines of China, till suddenly turning to the south-west, it enters Bengal, and joins the Ganges about forty miles from the ocean. For more than sixty miles from its confluence with the Ganges, it is invariably from four to five miles broad." (Maurice's Indian Antiquities,)

[18] "Thy temple, Sum-nat." The temple of Sum-nat, situated on the coast of Guzurat, or Cambaya, was famous throughout the East for its immense riches and the worship paid to its idol, from the remotest antiquity, by the various nations of the Hindu religion. It was taken, after an obstinate and bloody siege, by the famous Mahmoud of Ghezny, who found in it an astonishing quantity of gold, silver, and precious stones, far exceeding the boasted treasury of the richest princes of antiquity. In this temple, to whose support two thousand villages with their territory had been appropriated by the several princes of Indostan, there were two thousand Priests, or Bramins, three hundred musicians, five hundred dancing girls, and three hundred barbers, who were employed to shave the devotees before their introduction to the god. (Idem.)

[19] "Salsette and Elephanta." The islands of Salsette and Elephanta, situated near Bombay, are famous for their remarkable caverns, or subterraneous temples, excavated in the solid rock, whose walls are ornamented with a vast number of gigantic figures of the deities and ancient heroes of India. These figures form a part of the rock to which they are attached, and are executed in a masterly style ; many of them are represented under the most monstrous forms, and with most hideous countenances ; others have a placid and serene look ; and some appear pensive and melancholy. The period of the execution of these stupendous monuments of labor and art is entirely unknown, but they are without doubt of the remotest antiquity, as neither history or tradition seems to have preserved the least account of them,

and as, both in point of design and execution, they are totally different from anything now remaining in India.

The chief pagoda of Salsette is eighty-four feet in length, forty-six in breadth, and forty in height to the middle of the roof, which is finely arched and supported by thirty-five beautiful pillars of an octagonal form, and of about five feet in diameter, their capitals and bases being richly ornamented with the figures of elephants, tigers, &c., wrought with great skill and proportion. That of Elephanta is about one hundred and twenty feet square, and eighteen in height; the roof is flat, and supported by four rows of columns of a very singular order; they are finely fluted, as are their capitals; their pedestals are square, and the shaft, which is round, gradually becomes larger towards the center, from either end. On the shore of the latter island are the statues of an elephant and a horse, as large as nature, cut on the rock with such skill, that at a small distance they have all the appearance of life. (Idem.)

[20] "The dire Destroyer." Seeva, or Shivah, the destroying principle; the third person of the Indian Godhead, which, according to their system, consists of Brama, the Supreme—the Creator; Veeshnoo, the Preserver; and Shivah, the Destroyer, or Punisher. In the cavern of Elephanta is a monstrous bust of this triple Divinity, with three faces, of which that in the midst measures five feet. (Idem.)

[21] "Here Crishna." Creeshna, or Krishen, the Apollo of the Indian Mythology, is represented as very beautiful, and as attended by the Nine Gopia, or Muses, and by the Raignies, or Godesses of Harmony.

[22] "And Vishnoo, glorious from the Tyrant slain." In one of his various incarnations, the god Veeshnoo is represented under the form of a lion-man, as bursting from a pillar, and seizing and tearing in pieces the giant Cansu, an inflexible and bloody tyrant, who, in order

NOTES TO THE THIRD BOOK.

to destroy him when a child, had ordered all the children in his dominions to be massacred.

23 "Kinnouge, thy mighty name!" The city of Kinnouge, or Canouga, was celebrated in ancient times for its amazing extent, the number and wealth of its inhabitants, and the splendid magnificence of its buildings. An extent of one hundred miles was occupied by its walls; within the city were thirty-thousand licensed shops, in which Betel and Areca were sold; it also contained three thousand jewelers, and sixty thousand bands of musicians, who paid a tax to the government.

24 "Illustrious Gour." The city of Gour, formerly the capital of Bengal, was one of the largest and most splendid cities of India. Its site, says Major Rennell, is at present occupied by a few straggling villages and thick forests, the resort of the Royal Tiger.

25 The Tiger's hideous growl." The Royal Tiger, the strongest and most terrible of that class of animals, is a native of India, but is principally found in the warm climate of Bengal. The following description of this animal is from M. D'Obsonville's Philosophical Essays: "The Royal Tiger, distinguished by a skin marked with blackish stripes upon a fawn-colored ground, sometimes grows to the height of four feet ten inches, and is about nine feet in length—measured from the high part of the head to the insertion of the tail. I have seen a skin that measured from the tip of the nose to the end of the tail, more than ten cubits. His roar begins by intonations and inflections—at first, deep, melancholy and slow; it presently becomes more acute, when, suddenly collecting himself, he utters a violent cry, interrupted by long, tremulous sounds, which altogether make a distracting impression upon the mind. It is principally in the night that he is heard to roar, when silence and darkness add to the horror, and his cries are repeated by the echoes of the mountains. At the gloomy and haggard aspect of this monster, who always appears to tremble with a ferocious joy at the

sight of the blood which he is about to drink, most other animals think only of flight, of which they are often incapable. If the Bear has not time to climb a tree, he is dead; the Dog, dismayed, has scarce a moment to utter a cry of despair, before he is seized and torn in pieces; in an instant, a large Bull is overthrown and dragged away with ease; the wild male Buffalo will dart at his enemy, but if he be alone, he is almost always overcome."

Within a short time since a striking and affecting instance of the ferocity of this animal was related, in the account published of the melancholy fate of Mr. Munroe, while on a hunting excursion with some of his friends, near the mouth of the Ganges. The following, communicated to a friend of the author by a gentleman, who, for several years had resided in India, and who received the account from an eye-witness of the horrid scene, exhibits a still stronger proof of their undaunted ferocity and determined pursuit of their prey, even in opposition to the generally received opinion, that fire affords a certain security from the attacks of all wild beasts: "A vessel with a number of passengers on board, was shipwrecked on one of the islands in the mouth of the Ganges. Having got on shore, as it was near night, their first care was to look out for some place where they might find shelter, and be secure from the attacks of the wild beasts, with which those islands abound. On searching around, they discovered on a rising ground, the ruins of an old pagoda, and collecting a quantity of wood, with which the island was covered, disposed it so as completely to surround the building. This, at night, they set on fire, and retiring under the walls of the pagoda, considered themselves as perfectly secure. Ere long the accustomed yell was up, and the woods resounded with the hideous roar of the tiger, intermingled with the cries of other wild beasts, who were roaming for their prey, and soon was discovered, by the light of the fire, the approach of a royal tiger of immense size. This animal traversed the circle with the most ferocious gestures, and having attentively eyed them for some time, at length sprang through the fire at a Gentoo merchant, who was standing, reclined, against a part of the ruins; but, deceived by the glimmering of the flames, so far overleaped his mark,

NOTES TO THE THIRD BOOK. 161

as to strike his head with violence against a projection of the wall Stunned by the blow, he fell to the ground, drawing with him the unfortunate merchant, whose robe he had caught in his paw, and still retaining his hold, in rolling over and over, passed through the surrounding fire, and soon recovering from the effect of the blow, tore his wretched victim in pieces in sight of his terrified companions. What rendered still more interesting and impressive the fate of the Gentoo, was the singular circumstance of his having had, as he informed them, a twelve-month before in the course of a journey that he had made, his only son, a youth of about fourteen, torn from his side by a monstrous tiger."

26 "In crimson beauty Agra's palace glows." This magnificent palace, which is of great extent, was built by Sultan Akber; the walls are of a species of the jasper, of a fine crimson color, highly polished, and make a most beautiful and splendid appearance in the sun.

27 "Sits the Mogul." The author is aware that this description cannot, with propriety, be applied to the present Emperor of Indostan. It is rather intended to represent the ostentatious magnificence of some of his immediate predecessors, than as descriptive of the state of an unfortunate monarch, who, after having been long retained on the throne, the mere phantom of power, by a few ambitious and designing chiefs, since the above lines were written, has, in the savage treatment he has met with, and the inhuman deprivation of his sight, furnished an additional lesson to princes of the emptiness of titles and the wretchedness of human grandeur.

28 "To the fierce Afghan and the barbarous Jate." Two nations in India, remarkable for their savage ferocity and spirit of independence, whom the monarchs of Indostan have never been able entirely to subdue. They have frequently proved very formidable to the inhabitants of that empire by their predatory incursions, particularly since the

NOTES TO THE THIRD BOOK.

decline of the house of Timur, and have lately conquered some of the richest provinces, and menaced the imperial throne itself.

[29] "Sevagi singly," &c. Sevagi, or Sewajee, Rajah, or Prince of the Mahrattas, whom Aurungzebe in vain endeavored to reduce to his subjection.

[30] "In epic state, thy great Ferdousi." Ferdusi, or Ferdousi, the great epic poet of Persia, lived at the end of the tenth and beginning of the eleventh century. He was born in the town of Lar, in the province of Tus, and kingdom of Khorasan. At that period, the court of Mahmoud, Sultan of Ghezny, was the general resort of men of learning and talents from all parts of the East. Mahmoud having been shown some of the productions of the young poet, sent for him to Ghezny. A history of Persia, in the Pehlevi dialect, from the earliest period of its monarchy, had been compiled from the ancient manuscripts and records of that country by order of the great Anushirwan. This book, at the victory of Cadesia, which sealed the fate of Persia and transferred the sceptre of Cyrus to the successors of Mahomet, fell into the hands of Said, the general of Omar, who, pleased with the romantic tales which it contained, preserved it from that fate, which involved in one general ruin the productions of genius, the monuments of art, and the invaluable records of ancient science. Champion, in his life of Ferdousi, adds, " that Said having presented it to Omar, that Caliph ordered it, as a book treating of such worldly affairs as are forbidden by the Prophet, to be thrown among the general plunder; that it fell to the lot of an Abyssinian soldier, who carried it as a present to his prince, and that by his direction it was translated into the Abyssinian language." This history, parts of which had already been translated by some of the principal poets at the court of Mahmoud, was put into the hands of Ferdousi. Animated with the enthusiasm of a poet and with zeal for the honor of his country, he resolved to make this history the subject of an epic poem, and the foundation of his future eminence. He, accordingly, began the work; and so pleased was the Sultan with

some passages of it that were shown to him, that he ordered a generous present to the author, and encouraged him to proceed in the completion of his work, by the most flattering marks of attention, and the promise of a piece of gold for every couplet that it should contain. After thirty years of unwearied application, devoted to this arduous undertaking, he completed the poem and sent it to the Sultan; a poem, containing sixty thousand couplets in rhyme, and " combining," says Sir William Jones, " all the energy of Dryden, with the sweetness of Pope." But the fruits of the royal bounty were intercepted by the Vizier of Mahmoud, a man equally vain and mean-spirited, who hated Ferdousi for his independent spirit and that noble pride which prevented his paying court to him, and led him to disdain his patronage on the terms of flattering his vanity by the incense of poetical adulation. Instead, therefore, of the expected reward, he only received as many small pieces of silver as the poem contained couplets. Irritated in the highest degree by this affront, and the mortifying disappointment of his expectations, he distributed the money among his servants, and in the bitterness of his soul, composed a satire against Mahmoud, filled with pathetic complaints and the most cutting reflections. This he gave to an officer of the court, requesting him to present it to the Sultan, whenever he should appear chagrined, as it was a poetical compliment calculated to soothe him at such a time. On this he immediately fled, and took refuge, for some time, in the court of Bagdad, from the indignation of the provoked monarch. He afterwards successively resided at the courts of several princes, who contended with each other for that honor, and from whom he received the highest favors. Ferdousi died at an advanced age, after having experienced various vicissitudes of fortune, and the disappointment of finding the reward of his talents and the labor of a life sacrificed to the treacherous schemes of malignity and the resentment of a deluded prince.

[31] " Whether, serene in Feridoon." Feridún, an ancient king of Persia, who freed that empire from the usurpation and tyranny of the line of Zohak; he is highly celebrated by the Persian poets and his-

NOTES TO THE THIRD BOOK.

torians for his heroism, benevolence, paternal love, power, and extent of his dominions. The following excellent maxim is attributed to him on resigning his sceptre to his grandson, Municheher: "The life of a king is a paper journal; happy is he, who, during his reign, inscribes only good actions therein." Ferdousi thus finely describes him, in Champion's translation:—

" White were his hairs, still ruddy was his face,
  The moon's mild rays around the monarch shone ;"
" War sparkled in his eye, though soft his language as the evening sky."

[32] " Zal's youthful form." Zalzer, or Zal, a famous Persian hero, the father of the celebrated Rustem, by the beautiful Raduva, princess of Cabul. In his infancy he was exposed by his father, Taum, generalissimo of the armies of Municheher, but was taken pity of, carried to a cavern, and there nursed and educated by the great Griffen, or Simergh; he was afterwards sought for, and received with great transport by his father, and appointed to the command of an army for the conquest of Zabulistan, where he fell in love with and married the fair Raduva.

Sadi, in his Gulistan, ascribes to Zalzer the following excellent advice to his son Rustem: "Never despise your enemy, however weak he may be ; for we frequently see a stream, small and insignificant at its source, become swollen in its progress, so as to carry away with it a loaded camel."

[33] " Raduva shines in beauty's peerless blaze." The following lines, descriptive of that princess, from the Seventh Book of Champion's translation of the Shah Nameh, appear to be much more felicitous than his version in general :—

" The sweets of paradise around her blow ;
  Her charms are radiant with celestial glow ;

NOTES TO THE THIRD BOOK.

Her jetty locks in graceful ringlets play,
Charm every sense, and steal the soul away;
Those jetty locks her blooming beauties shade,
And pierce the heart, to instant love betray'd.

" Even and white her well-form'd teeth appear,
Not the white-rose more delicately clear;
Nor the narcissus, which the florists prize,
Equals the beaming lustre of her eyes.
Her oval breast, no fancy e'er could paint,
Weak were all language, all expression faint."

[34] " Her death-doom'd lord, Afraziab's daughter mourns." The following passage of Ferdousi, from the French of M. Langles, is descriptive of the despair of Franhis, or Manizha, the beautiful daughter of Afraziab, on discovering her father's design of putting to death her husband, the young Siavesche :—
" Filled with inexpressible grief, the young princess tore from her hair the hyacinths, and in despair beat her tender bosom. She spread the musk of her tresses over the ivory of her beautiful forehead. The streams which flowed from her eyes inundated the roses of her cheeks, as this unfortunate fair thought of the cruel designs of Afraziab."

[5] " Or Rustem, dreadful in the battle burns." Rustem, the Persian Hercules, the principal hero of Ferdousi's poem, and with whose marvelous exploits Eastern romance is filled.

[36] " Pathetic Jami's melting numbers move." Noureddin Jami, the tenderest, most elegant, and harmonious of the Persian poets. He is the author of several poems of great merit; but the work to which he principally owes his fame, is his poem on the Loves of Joseph and Zulecia. This is said to abound with the finest poetical descriptions, the most beautiful and lively images, and the sweetest and most

NOTES TO THE THIRD BOOK.

harmonious versification. The following extract, translated by Sir William Jones, will convey some idea of the style of this elegant writer:

"In the morning, when the raven of night had flown away, the bird of dawn began to sing, the nightingales warbled their enchanting notes, and rent the thin veils of the rose-bud and the rose; the jasmine stood bathed in dew, and the violet also sprinkled his fragrant locks."

"Molla-Abd-errahman-ben-Ahmed-Jami flourished in the ninth century of the Mahometan era. He died about the year 1486 of the Christians. Among many other excellent productions, he is chiefly admired as the author of the beautiful poem of Joseph and Zulecia, the Baharistan or Residence of Spring, and his Divaun, or Collection of Odes and Sonnets. The Divaun of Jami, which, according to M. D'Herbelot, contains all the mystic theology of the Mahometans, is replete with passages of the most tender and amorous description, and, with an inconsistence, by no means unfrequent among the Persian writers. Religious poems, of a sublime and mysterious nature, are comprised in the same work with Erratic and Bacchanalian Odes and Sonnets; and the same person appears, as we read his different compositions, the enthusiastic and bigoted devotee, or the gay, voluptuous, and impassioned lover.

"But this poet, whether he pours forth the ejaculations of piety and devotion, or breathes the sentiments of passion, or the fondest love, uniformly maintains the greatest correctness and chastity of language." (Ouseley's Persian Miscellanies, Chap. 2.)

[37] "So bright Zulecia mid her grief appears." The celebrated wife of Potiphar.

Zulecia, or Zoolekha. According to Jami, this celebrated fair one was the only daughter of the King of Mauritania, a powerful monarch in Africa. At the age of thirteen years, a young man of wonderful beauty appeared to her in a dream, whose face, to use the words of the poet, "was as dazzling as the sun; he was tall, and strait as the cypress; his eye-brows were two bows, and his eyes quivers, filled with the all-conquering arrows of love; his smiling mouth was

NOTES TO THE THIRD BOOK.

like a bed of roses; his teeth rows of pearls, and his lips two strings of rubies." For a number of nights in succession was she haunted by the same image. So strong was the impression it made on her, that she became violently in love with the beautiful phantom. A deep melancholy took possession of her mind; her health was impaired, and at length, she fell dangerously sick. One of her attendants, who had been her nurse, and was tenderly attached to her, suspecting that her disorder proceeded from love, had the address to obtain from her the secret of her extraordinary passion. She immediately promised to leave no means untried to procure her the possession of the beloved object; and, as she was deeply skilled in magic, by the force of her spells she caused the beauteous phantom to re-appear, at the same time directing Zeleikha to question it, as to its state, the place of its residence, &c. It replied to her questions, that it was no angel, which, on its re-appearance, she had at first mistaken it for, but the actual representation of a youth, whose station in life was far inferior to hers; that he was a native of Canaan, in Asia; but that he was called by the decrees of fate to Egypt, where a brilliant fortune awaited him, which he was destined to share with her, after experiencing many perils and sufferings

At the same time, a similar vision had appeared to Joseph, the young son of Jacob. He dreamed that he saw a most beautiful woman, who informed him that she was called Zulecia, and that she was destined, one day, to be united to him; but that this happiness must be purchased by severe trials and a long course of suffering and affliction. The fame of Zuleikha's beauty, together with the great power and wealth of her father, induced many of the princes of Africa and of Asia, to send ambassadors to the Court of Mauritania to solicit her in marriage. The king, who loved his daughter with great tenderness, made known to her the arrival and the object of the envoys. Full of the idea of the lovely phantom and of her promised happiness in Egypt, she inquired of her father if either of these ambassadors were from that court. The king replying in the negative, she begged of him to dismiss these suitors, informing him, that she could never consent to quit her country for any other than that of Egypt, of which she had heard such wonders related. The fond and indulgent parent, desirous of gratifying the wishes of his daughter, immediately dismissed the ambassadors with a refusal, and dispatched a trusty messenger to Egypt, with directions to obtain information respecting the king of that country, and if he was unmarried, to concert measures so that he should be induced to demand the hand of Zulecia. The agent soon acquainted the king, that the King of Egypt was not only married, but that he was so immersed in the pleasures of his seraglio, that he had intrusted the cares of government wholly to his Vizier, who was the effective sovereign. That this man, whose name was Azir Katfer, had risen to this high rank from the lowest station, having been brought as a slave into Egypt from some part of Asia, and also that he was unmarried. The king communicated this intelligence to his daughter, who, imagining that she had discovered in this man the object of her love, by her earnest and repeated solicitations, at the same time assuring him that the oracle had predicted that she should find happiness only in Egypt, she finally overcame her father's objections, and he directed his messenger to offer his daughter in marriage to the Vizier. Katfer was greatly surprised and delighted at this proposal from so powerful a monarch, and immediately returned an answer expressive of the gratitude and honor he felt in the proffered alliance. Pharaoh with little difficulty was persuaded to consent to this union, which the crafty minister took care to represent to him as one that would add lustre to the crown. Accordingly, the most magnificent preparations were made for the reception of the princess and the approaching nuptials. On pretence of public business, the Vizier did not go to meet the princess till she came near Memphis. On entering that city, the curtains of her litter were for the first time drawn aside so as to allow them to see each other. Great was the surprise and disappointment of Zuleikha, on perceiving at first sight, that Katfer was widely different from the beautiful object of her constant meditations. She made known the bitterness of her disappointment to her confidante, the nurse, who had again recourse to her spells, and discovered that Katfer was not the person destined to render the princess happy. That, from a state of servitude he had been raised to the high station he held, in consequence of the most degrading artifices and the basest flattery to his sovereign; that, wholly incapable of exciting jealousy, even in the bosom of the most suspicious monarch, Pharaoh had first promoted him to the government of his seraglio, where he submitted to the meanest of employments, and afterwards to that of his dominions; that, his want of talents was supplied by cunning and boldness, which retained him in the important station he had obtained through artifice and meanness.

The marriage was, at length, celebrated with great pomp; and the Vizier, elated with the honor of having espoused the daughter of the King of Mauritania, treated her with the utmost deference and respect; built for her a most magnificent palace; provided for her service and amusement a numerous train of female slaves, and omitted no expense to please and gratify her. At this time it happened that the merchant who had bought Joseph of his brethren, (whose story is told by Jami, with circumstances nearly conformable to those related in Holy Writ,) arrived in Memphis. Having erected his tent on the great square of that city, he issued a proclamation by the crier, that he had for sale the most beautiful male slave that had ever been seen in Egypt. This being made known to Zulecia, her active imagination immediately conceived the idea that this must be the one prefigured in her dream; she, accordingly, sent her nurse in disguise to the tent of the merchant, to ascertain the truth of her conjectures. The nurse, on seeing Joseph, instantly recognized in him the phantom which she had raised by her charms, and communicated the pleasing information to Zuleikha. The latter readily persuaded Katfer to purchase him for her of the merchant.

Joseph, on his part, at their first interview, immediately recognized in his mistress the beautiful subject of his dream, of whom he had from that moment become enamored. But, governed by a rigid sense of honor and duty, he continued manfully to struggle with his passion, and successfully to resist her allurements and the various arts of seduction which she employed, until the madly-enamored Zulecia so far forgot her native modesty, as openly to court him. Disappointed in this last attempt, in the rage of unrequited love, she rejected, on the audacity of her slave, the suspicions of her fidelity, which some circumstances had excited in the breast of Katfer. At the same time, her love for Joseph induced her to employ all her influence with her husband to mitigate his punishment, and to change it from that of death to perpetual imprisonment. From this state of confinement he was released, in consequence of his interpretation of the dreams of two of Pharaoh's officers, and that of the monarch himself. From the gloom of a dungeon, he was now raised to the most splendid honors of the state. When Katfer heard of the preferment and honors bestowed on the slave whom he had imprisoned, such was his mortification and chagrin, that he sickened and soon after died. There remaining now no obstacle to the union of Joseph with his beloved Zuleikha, when the period of her mourning was completed, their nuptials were celebrated with great rejoicings throughout Egypt.

[38] "In sprightly Hafez, mirthful odes combine." Hafez, a celebrated lyric poet, the Anacreon of Persia, and the peculiar favorite of his countrymen, was born at Shiraz, where his tomb is still to be seen, which is held in the highest veneration by the inhabitants.

"Among the Persian poets, few, (says Sir William Ouseley,) are more worthy of being generally known than Hafez! None are more interesting to the scholar and searcher into Eastern manners. The terse morality of Sadi, and the lofty and sublime language of Ferdusi, claim and deserve the highest place in our esteem : but the Divan (or Collection) of Hafez, will always be the more popular work ; and his sweet simplicity and polished numbers must charm the most phlegmatic reader. In his works, we may discover the private life of a Persian ; become acquainted with his turn of mind, his thoughts, and occupation ; and learn many curious customs disregarded by graver authors. His fame throughout the East, (where a crowd of imitators has sprung up in every country,) is a strong evidence of his merits ; and his importance in Persia was rarely equaled and never exceeded in the darkest ages of superstition. Statesmen and warriors have not unfrequently stopped at his tomb, and rested their hopes on the decisions of the mysterious volume. Even the savage Nader confessed the inspiration of the poet; and yielding to the prejudices of his soldiers, perhaps his own, he treated the oracular answer as the surest presage of victory. In the correspondence of Asia, where poetry is intermixed with prose, the distichs of Hafez are often applied to the various vicissitudes of life; and both the scholar and the traveler will receive advantage from the study of this engaging poet." (Oriental Collections.)

There are but few of the Odes of Hafez that contain not some impressive moral reflection. The following stanza, from the Fifth Ode of Mr. Nott's translation, will probably recall to the reader's recollection one of the finest passages in Goldsmith's beautiful ballad of Edwin and Angelina :—

"O let not avarice tempt thy wild desires
 To toil for wealth in fortune's glitt'ring mine!
Small is the pittance mortal man requires,
 And trifling labor makes that pittance thine."

A sentiment of a similar cast occurs in the Eighth Ode :—

"O ask not alms at fortune's gate!
 But from her hated temple fly;
She gives her goblet's poison'd bait,
 She bids thee drink, then bids thee die.

"Two little handfuls of strew'd earth
 To build thy last abode suffice;
Then where the use, or what the worth
 Of mansions tow'ring to the skies?"

[40] "By Zoroaster taught." Zoroaster, or Zerdusht, an ancient Persian Philosopher; the founder of the sect of the Magi, or Worshipers of Fire. Much diversity of opinion appears to have prevailed respecting the time in which he lived; some supposing him cotempo-

rary with Abraham; while others affirm that he lived in the reign of Cambyses, the son of Cyrus. He is said to have been a king of the Bactrians, and to have given to the Persians their system of religion. He admitted one Supreme Being, the author of all good; and another, somewhat less powerful, who is the author of evil. His doctrine contains a pure morality; and a little moral and didactic work is attributed to him, the following passages from which, M. Anquetil has inserted in his Translation of the Zend-Avesta, or Sacred Book of the Magians, containing the laws and tenets of Zoroaster:—" God in his justice has decreed that men should be judged by the good and the evil which they have done; * * * * * that the good should inhabit the regions of light, and the wicked, hell. Let man abstain from all kinds of robbery and rapine; and, when he is in doubt whether an action be good or bad, let him not commit it." Zoroaster taught the Persians to adore the Divinity under the symbol of Fire. His doctrines have, even at this day, a great number of followers; they are denominated Guebres, or Gaures, and one of the suburbs of Ispahan is wholly inhabited by them.

[41] " Great Oromazes," &c. " And Arimanius," &c. The good and evil principles of the Magian religion. The first, the author of all good; the other, of all evil. The former was represented by light, and the latter, by darkness, as their truest symbols. The good power was called Gezad and Ormuzd; the evil demon, Aherinian, or Aherman. The Magi, generally, hold the first to be eternal; and the second, created. According to Theopempus, the Magians believe, that for the period of three thousand years these two gods, alternately, conquer and are conquered; that they will wage mutual war and destroy the works of each other, till at last Hadez, or the Evil Spirit, shall perish, and men become perfectly happy; their bodies requiring no food, nor casting any shadow, being perfectly transparent. (Bell's Pantheon.)

[42] " Far-famed Istakhar." The name by which Persepolis is known to the Orientals.

NOTES TO THE THIRD BOOK. 173

The ancient Persepolis, or Istakhar, was the capital of Persia, under the kings of the three first dynasties. The author of Leb-tarikh says, that Kishtasp established his residence therein, erected several temples to the element of fire, and excavated, for himself and his successors, sepulchres in the rocks of the mountains near the city. The ruins of columns and broken figures, which still remain, defaced as they were by Alexander, and mutilated by time, plainly evince that those ancient princes had made choice of it for the place of their interment. Their monuments must not, however, be confounded with the superb palace built by Queen Homai, in the midst of Persepolis, distinguished by the name of Tchilminar, or the Forty Watch-Towers; or, as some authors assert, by Giamschid.

One of the most magnificent monuments of the reign of Giamschid was the city of Istakhar, which had been begun by Tahmurath. This city, as completed by Giamschid, was of a wonderful extent, for it is said to have been twelve parasangs in circumference, which is equal to eighty French leagues, and to have inclosed within its walls not only a great number of palaces and pleasure-houses, but likewise many spacious parks and cultivated lands. This city, at present called *Gihil*, or *Tchil-minar*, from the forty columns erected in it, as some say, by Queen Homai, and according to others, by Soliman Ben David, was known to the Greeks by the name of Persepolis; and the Orientals have still a tradition, that, at the burning of that city by Alexander, seven stupendous structures built by Giamschid, were consumed, together with his palace. (D'Herbelot's Bibliothèque Orientale; Notes to Caliph Vathek, &c.)

Sir William Ouseley, in his Persian Miscellanies, has the following interesting remarks on the Ruins of Persepolis :—" But of those palaces the majestic ruins yet to be seen, while they remain a venerable record of the nation's former greatness, afford ample subjects for melancholy reflections on the decay of empires and the revolutions effected by time; for now, to use the words of a Persian poet—

'The spider holds the veil in the palace of Cæsar,
The owl stands sentinel on the watch-towers of Afrasiab.'

"To the mildness of a happy climate alone, are we probably indebted for the preservation of those sculptured figures and mysterious inscriptions, that still decorate the walls of the royal apartments of the magnificent palace of the Sons of Cyrus; one of the noblest productions of human labor and ingenuity.

"Yet, however considerable may be its majestic remains still to be seen above ground, it is most probable that, within the precints of the ruined palace, treasures much more precious, in the antiquary's estimation from long concealment, lie buried in the dust of more than twenty ages.

"And, that valuable and most curious subterranean fragments still exist at Persepolis, is an opinion which I have adopted, not merely from the probability that similar treasures lie hidden among all visible ruins of considerable antiquity, but from the positive testimony and strong conjectures of several ingenious travelers. Of the figures at the monument of Rustem, (in the vicinity of Persepolis, supposed to represent that *celebrated warrior and his favorite mistress,) the lower parts are concealed in heaps of stones and accumulated rubbish, which hide, perhaps, at the same time, some ancient inscriptions or interesting sculptures."

"In the beginning of this century, Mons. Le Bruyn published engravings of several hundred figures, cut in relief, which yet remained upon the walls. According to some travelers, Herbert, Mandelsloe, &c., the number of sculptures are so great, that it would require no common degree of industry in an able artist to make drawings of them all in the space of several months. When visited in 1627 by Sir

---

* "Near the ruined palace of Persepolis are shown the gigantic figure of a warrior and that of a female, who hold between them, each with one hand, something of an annular form, but proportionably large enough to go round the neck. To these figures, tradition has given the name of Rustum and his favorite mistress, probably the fair Princess of Sitaurgaun, the mother of Johraub." (Persian Miscellanies.)

Thomas Herbert, not only the images cut in the marble remained in perfect preservation, but even the gilding on the walls and on the drapery of some figures retained its original lustre. I have been assured by the Chevalier Clergeau de la Barré, that, among the ruins of Babylon and Persepolis, curious and valuable antiques are daily discovered. Among the most curious were several volumes of parchment, covered with characters hitherto undeciphered; and an emerald of two inches in length, containing the figure of Alexander, engraved with such exquisite art as to be discernible only when placed in a particular point of view, between the eye and the light."

A paper in the Oriental Collections, signed C. D. V., affirms, that the figures on the walls of the palace of Persepolis, or Tokchelminar, are supposed to represent the actions of Rustem.

¹³ " Where mighty Jemsheid from his throne," &c. Jemsheid, or Gemschid, the fourth King of Persia, of the first or Peishdadian dynasty. He is highly celebrated for his magnificence and the wisdom of his institutions, and is said to have built the splendid palace of Persepolis, which was called from him the Throne, or residence of Jemsheid. After a long and prosperous reign he was at length dethroned and put to death by the usurper Zohak. (Sir W. Jones, D'Herbelot, &c.)

" Jemsheid." This monarch is said to have received the addition of Schid to his name, which was Gem, or Giam, from the beauty and majesty of his countenance, which, like the sun, in Persian Schid, dazzled all beholders. After having subdued seven large provinces of Upper Asia, and enjoyed in peace a long reign—according to some writers, of seven hundred years—this prince became intoxicated with his greatness, and foolishly imagining that it would have no end, arrogated to himself divine honors, and caused his statues to be worshiped throughout his dominions. But the Almighty, to punish his pride, excited against him in his own family a terrible enemy. This was no other than his nephew, Schedad, son of Ad, King of Arabia, who sent against him a powerful army under the command of Zohak, the chief general of his forces. Giamschid, unsuspicious of an attack, and unpre-

NOTES TO THE THIRD BOOK.

pared, was easily defeated by Zohak, and compelled to save himself by flight, leaving his dominions to the usurper. Many valuable discoveries and useful inventions are ascribed to him; and the author of *Giame al Gavarikh* relates that, in digging the foundations of the city of Istakhar, a vase, formed of a single gem, was discovered, which contained two pints. This precious vase received the name of the Vase of the Sun, and is also known by that of the Cup or Concave Mirror of Giamschid. The Persian poets frequently allude in their writings to this vessel, attributing to it the property of exhibiting everything in nature, and even some things that are preternatural. The gem it was formed of, appears to have been the Carbuncle, or Oriental Ruby, which, from its resemblance to a burning coal, and the splendor it was supposed to emit in the dark, was called *Schebgerag*, or the Torch of Night. (D'Herbelot.)

44 " Thy gardens, Shiraz, spread their beauties here." The gardens of Shiraz are remarkable for their beauty and pleasantness, and highly praised by travelers.

45 " Where bright Barradia laves," &c. The vale of Damascus, the banks of the river Obolla, near Bagdad, the delightful plain of Sogd, on which stand the city of Samarcand, with the beautiful valley of Bavan, are among the fairest scenes in nature, and are distinguished by the appellation of the Four Paradises of Asia.

46 " Long rows of Dates." The flowers of this species of the Palm are elegantly disposed in long clusters, and are of a snowy white.

47 " Her curious nest the little Artist weaves." The Tailor-Bird. This curious little bird is a native of the East, more especially of India. It forms its nest in a singular manner, by joining together two or more leaves of some broad-leafed tree, as the Bananoe, or Plantain; this it effects by first perforating them with its little bill, shaped like an awl; it then draws them closely together, and firmly secures them by means

of a thread, formed of the fibres of the leaf, so as to render the nest impenetrable to the rain, and at the same time, from its position at the extremity of a limb, secure from the attacks of the serpent, or other enemies. Its color is a pale yellow, or straw color.

[48] " Tunes to the Rose," &c. This beautiful fiction, the passion of the Nightingale for the rose, is frequent in the poetical compositions of the East.

" The excessive delight which the (Bulbul,) Persian Nightingale, derives from the enjoyment of the rose's fragrance, affords a thousand beautiful allusions and allegories to the Eastern poets. In a line from one of Sadi's sonnets, he pays to his mistress the most delicate compliment that a Persian lover could express, by saying, ' Should the Nightingale once behold thy beauteous face he would no longer seek his beloved rose.'

" To account for this allegorical passion entertained by the Nightingale for the rose—the subject of so much beautiful imagery in Persian poetry—we must consider that the plaintive voice of that sweet bird is first heard at the same season of the year in which the rose begins to blow; by a natural association of ideas, they are therefore connected as the constant and inseparable attendants of the Spring. It is probable, too, that the Nightingale's favorite retreat may be the rose-garden, and the leaves of that flower occasionally his food; but it is certain that he is delighted with its smell, and sometimes indulges in the fragrant luxury to such excess, as to fall from the branch, intoxicated and helpless to the ground." (Ouseley's Persian Miscellanies, Chap. 5.)

As an appropriate appendage to this Note, I have selected the Seventh Ode of Hafez, in Mr. Nott's version:

> Pour the grape's empurpled tide;
> Lo! the youthful blooming flower,
> Now with cheerful brightness glows:
> Throw repentant cares aside,
> Seated in the festive bower,
> Richly perfumed with the rose

Led by jollity and song,
Wander where sweet beauty's train
In thy cultured garden blows;
So, the vernal groves among,
Chaunts the Nightingale his strain,
Where he finds his fav'rite rose.

Quaff thy bowl, 'twill glad thy heart;
Now the newly-drest alcove
Mantling foliage round thee throws:
All that pleasure can impart,
And the luxuries of love,
Wait the bidding of the rose.

See, the knotted clusters shine
In the gayly-spangled glade!
Heed not when their lustre goes:
But with friendship, and with wine,
In some pleasant, secret shade,
There enjoy the short-lived rose.

As the bird with mellow lay,
Fondly, Hafez, dost thou love
Those delights the Spring bestows;
Early buds shall strew thy way,
Let thy soul but grateful prove
To the Guardian of the Rose.

Thus likewise, Sadi, "The Spring is delightful! O Rose! where hast thou been? Dost thou not hear the lamentations of the Nightingale, on account of thy delay?"

[49] "The spreading Eagle," &c. The spread-eagle is an ornament which decorates some parts of the ruins of Palmyra. The leaves of the

Palmetto are hard, edged with a number of sharp points, and expand from the stem in form of a fan.

[50] "Dire superstition holds her gloomy court." The question, whether the pyramids of Egypt were erected in honor of their gods, or destined to receive the bodies of their kings, has long divided the literary world. In either view, however, they may well be supposed the seat of superstition, whether considered as temples or as tombs, as devoted to the dark mysteries of the Egyptian religion, or sacred to the repose of the dead; for superstitious prejudices, no less than the desire of perpetuating their names, must have operated on the minds of their founders to induce them, at such an enormous expense, and such a waste of labor, to raise these enormous edifices.

The Charms of Fancy.

BOOK THE FOURTH.

ARGUMENT OF THE FOURTH BOOK.

INVOCATION to the Genius of Melancholy.—Apostrophe to the Ruins of Thebes. Ruin, and his attendants. Grandeur of ancient Thebes. Sesostris: his exploits and character. Temple of the Sun: its former magnificence; sublimity of its ruin. Tomb of Osymandus: traditionary accounts of its splendor and opulence; haughty inscription of its Founder. Reflections on the pride and cruelty of the ancient Egyptian monarchs. Egypt celebrated for Arts, Laws, and Government, but debased by the most abject Superstition. Its present inhabitants: an ignorant, brutish, deceitful and barbarous race, scarcely preserving a trait of the ancient rational character, but that of superstition. Reflections suggested by the present state of Egypt and the East: whether a similar fate does not await the countries of Europe and America. Original subject resumed. Influence of Fancy: the sorrows and glooms of life cheered and alleviated by it; and its pleasures enlivened and enhanced. Comparative view of the advantages and disadvantages of a strong and ardent imagination: the pleasure derivable to its possessor, even amidst misfortunes in some degree proceeding from that source, from the very consciousness of its possession. Decline of Fancy in advancing years, with its total extinction in old age. Some exceptions to this general rule, exemplified in the instances of Homer, Sophocles, Sadi, Metastasio, &c. Conclusion.

THE
CHARMS OF FANCY.

Book the Fourth.

Thou Genius sad! whose melancholy sway
The awful, mournful, and sublime obey;
Who on some cliff enjoy'st the tempest's roar,
When maddening billows whiten all the shore;
Who oft explor'st, in midnight's silent gloom,
The hallow'd temple, or sequester'd tomb;
And oft, with pensive step, delight'st to stray
Where mouldering ruins woo thy lonely way;
Inspire my song—thy aid propitious lend,
As o'er yon dreary waste my course I bend,
Mid broken walls, cleft domes, and hoar remains
Of sumptuous palaces and gorgeous fanes.
   All Hail! ye solemn scenes, ye piles immense,
Ye mouldering relics of magnificence—

Ye sacred monuments of ancient time,
Which fill the bosom with an awe sublime!
Ere yet proud Rome in infant grandeur shone,
Or ere in Athens Science fix'd her throne—
Ere Corinth rose, of art the beauteous boast,
And tower'd in splendor o'er the Isthmian coast;
Ye taught a lesson sad: how short the date
Of earthly grandeur and of royal state!
How vain, how transitory is that power
Which monarchs covet and mankind adore!

Here Ruin reigns: his throne a mouldering mass,
O'ergrown with hoary weeds and matted grass;
A broken crown invests his hairless head,
O'er his lank form a tatter'd robe is spread,
Whose vileness, blended with the regal blaze,
The pomp of sordid majesty displays;
His tottering frame incessant palsies shake,
And Phthisis flushes on his wasted cheek;
Where'er around his baleful eyes he turns,
Falls some proud palace, or some city burns:
Near him a mutilated scroll is placed,
The imperfect characters of time defaced,

Of mighty empires and illustrious states.
Whose dust-polluted leaves contain the fates.
His grim attendants, ranged on either hand,
Obsequious wait their gloomy king's command:
In crimson robes, the Genius stern of War
Here stands, deform'd with many a ghastly scar;
His better hand a blood-stain'd falchion bears,
High in his left a flaming torch he rears;
In vengeful fires his bloody eye-balls roll,
And scenes of slaughter fill his ruthless soul;
The Earthquake dire here writhes his giant form,
And frowns the Spirit of the blackening storm;
Slow-creeping Time with scatter'd locks of gray,
And Rapine bending under loads of prey.
With thousands more, a wild terrific band,
Inspiring horror, near the tyrant stand.
 On this wild waste, where Desolation lowers,
The Queen of cities raised her lofty towers;
Majestic Thebes! thy ancient power how great,
How bright the glories of thy former state!
Far-distant nations trembling own'd thy sway,
Where Ethiops blacken in the vertic ray;

Where Nilus' fertile wave receives its birth,
And, pour'd with gushing fury, cleaves the earth;
Where o'er gold-sparkling sands the Ganges pours
His wave, wide-swelling to Indostan's shores.
Whene'er thy sons the rage of conquest led,
O'er neighboring lands the plagues of war to shed,
Pour'd from thy hundred gates, the rushing train
With horse and chariots darken'd all the plain;
Thick as when Summer beams his fervent rays,
The myriads floating in the noontide blaze;
Thick as the locusts, when the Prophet's wand
Waved desolation o'er thy guilty land.

 Here Art, fair plant, her earliest blossoms bore,
And Learning here first taught his simplest lore,
And here the subject east Sesostris sway'd,
Loved as a man, and like a god obey'd.
Though numerous realms beneath his conquests bled,
And wide the terror of his falchion spread;
Not his the views which meaner souls inspire,
Where low ambition wakes the hero's fire,
Whose great exploits all tend, with praiseless aim,
From slaughter'd hosts to gain a meteor fame;

572

By wisdom govern'd, and by virtue fired,
His soul sublime to higher praise aspired,
To join the world in ties of civil love,
The manners soften, and the mind improve,
Give the rude breast with generous warmth to glow,
Exult in social joy and melt in social woe,
With conquest's palm, of peace the olive bind,
"And shine the king and father of mankind." [arise,
    The scene, how changed! No more thy spires
No cloud-topp'd temples tower amid the skies—
No gorgeous domes their glittering sides unfold,
With sculptured marble graced and figured gold;
In crowded streets where throng'd the busy train,
Now solitude and dismal silence reign.
    Midst crumbling ruins, wide around it strew'd,
Where frowns yon massy pile, abrupt and rude,
With frequent rifts disjoin'd, with moss o'ergrown,
Waving its rank head o'er the tottering stone,
And o'er the plain a mountain-shadow throws,
The matchless temple of the Sun arose
Stupendous work! of art the wondrous pride,
Where regal gifts in ostentation vied;

Thy walls with conquest's sculptured trophies glow'd,
Where imaged kings in state triumphal rode
While captive princes, midst the gazing throng,
Drew the fierce victor's golden car along:
Before thy beauteous gates, a towering wood,
High raised in air, colossal statues stood,
And hideous sphinxes, ranged in long array,
Glared, from the marble, horror and dismay.
Here still the traveler views, with wondering dread,
In heaps on heaps, thy giant ruins spread;
Thy marble walls immense, that still withstand
The heavy stroke of wild destruction's hand;
Thy forms colossal tumbled to the ground,
In massy fragments rudely heap'd around;
Thy [1] pyramidal gates, which yet remain,
Thy broken sphinxes, scatter'd o'er the plain;
Thy numerous columns of enormous size,
That still in stately ranks high towering rise;
Thy inner dome, whose painted sculptures seem
Like works of magic, or a fairy dream,
 Whose beauties tempt even ruthless Time to stay,
 Nor yet to Ruin give his destined prey;

For still its golden [2] stars attract the eye,
Resplendent beaming from their azure sky;
Fresh, unimpaired, in pristine lustre gay,
Though ages since have roll'd their years away.

Reclined on yonder column's hoar remains,
That scarce the broken architrave sustains,
The sceptre dropping from his palsied hands,
The Genius sad of fallen Grandeur stands.
From his torn bosom bursts the frequent sigh,
The glistening tear starts trembling in his eye,
With anguish'd look, as he the waste surveys,
Where ancient splendor pour'd its dazzling blaze;
Where beauty beam'd her soul-dissolving smile,
Where plann'd the statesman his politic wile,
Where valor shone, in glittering armor drest,
And, awe-inspiring, moved the hoary priest;
In purple robes the haughty tyrant frown'd,
While servile millions prostrate trembled round.

Though dimm'd the rays that from his crescent [shine,
And soil'd the lustre of his robes divine,
Yet still superior, through the cloud of woe,
An awful majesty his features show;

His piercing eyes, replete with regal fire,
A solemn dignity of thought inspire.
So some tall oak, which many a year has stood
In towering pride, the monarch of the wood,
By the cold blasts of wintry age decay'd,
Resigns the leafy honors of its shade;
And though with verdure, unadorn'd and bare,
Nor genial spring its beauties can repair,
The sapless trunk, still awfully sublime,
Receives new honors from the hand of Time.

Where'er I turn my eyes, on every side
Wrecks of magnificence the champaign hide;
But, far the rest above, those ruins hoar,
That distant rise on Nilus' eastern shore,
Attract the view—my course I raptured bend,
Where, 'spiring high, yon Obelisks ascend.
A melancholy awe and sacred dread
Now thrill my soul, as o'er these scenes I tread:
Through the cleft wall the sun's declining beam
A broken radiance pours, in lengthening stream,
Gilding the blended heap, where, soil'd with dust,
The headless statue lies, and broken bust;

CHARMS OF FANCY.

The capital, hurl'd from its towering height,
Half-sunk beneath the prostrate column's weight;
And gilded frieze, whose mangled charms impart
A mournful pleasure to the feeling heart. [walls,
O'er the gray moss, which hides these mouldering
The spotted lizard unmolested crawls,
Through the long weeds, blown by the breeze aside,
In view romantic gleams their sculptured pride,
With stronger force which strikes the mind, as seen
Obscurely glimmering through the verdant screen.

 These vast remains magnificent proclaim
Some splendid structure of gigantic frame:
But not a trace remains, to inform the mind
By whom erected, or for what design'd;
Perhaps some ancient tyrant's proud abode,
Or temple sacred to some monster-god.
While, lost in dark conjecture's varying maze,
From thought to thought, perplex'd opinion strays;
Lo! old Tradition's reverend form appears,
Hoary his head, his figure bent with years;
Though Time's deep furrows mark his aged brow,
His eyes with fancy's youthful splendors glow;

On his plain robe Invention's hand has wrought
Each wild chimera of fantastic thought,
Which, o'er it strew'd profuse, conceal from view
The simple beauties of its native hue:
"No palace here," he cries; "no sacred fane
Extends its ruin'd honors o'er the plain;
Where these rude walls in shapeless fragments frown
In earth half-buried, and with weeds o'ergrown,
In Egypt's pride, by Osymandus rear'd,
Proudest of kings, a splendid tomb appear'd,
Who deem'd this work, his pledge of deathless fame,
To latest periods should extend his name;
For this, the sumptuous monument he raised,
Which, rich with sculptured gold and jewels blazed;
The vaulted dome like heaven's blue concave seem'd,
Where glittering stars with mimic lustre gleam'd;
On the high top a golden circle placed,
With mystic figures and inscriptions graced,
Shone brightly glowing in the noontide ray,
A rival sun, and pour'd an added day;
Here, living figures of the kings of old,
Whiten'd in stone, or beam'd with burnish'd gold;

Above the rest his statue, towering high,
A form colossal, fix'd the wandering eye,
Whose base, in gold, this proud inscription bore:"
"Let those who wish to know how vast my power,
My deeds how glorious, and my name how great,
Let them my meanest works but imitate."
How vain thy pride! thy empty boast how vain!
What traces now of all thy power remain?
The historian's pen refused thy pompous claim,
Nor gave thy actions to the roll of fame;
And Time's rude hand, which lays each beauty waste,
Has broke thy statues, and thy name erased;
Thy wealth, thy grandeur, thy extensive sway,
Alone Tradition's fabling tales display.

Unhappy Egypt! ever doom'd by fate
To bend beneath oppression's iron weight;
What empty vanity thy kings possess'd,
What wild delusion swell'd each tyrant's breast,
To dream that Fame's immortal laurels bloom
From the huge pyramid or sumptuous tomb!
These vain memorials of their pride to rear,
Source of the widow's moan, the orphan's tear;

Thy hapless sons to servile tasks were doom'd,
Thy millions sacrificed, thy wealth consumed,
Thy fertile plains, untill'd, neglected lay,
Thy towns dispeopled, or to want a prey.
The bright reward of honor to obtain
This waste of treasure and of blood how vain!
Not e'en the pyramids, whose wond'rous size
O'er ruin triumphs and decay defies,
Whose era [3] no recording annals boast,
In the thick gloom of earliest ages lost,
Their founder's memories have avail'd to save;
Whelm'd are their names in black Oblivion's wave.

O'er thy fair realms, elate in youthful pride,
Unfolding Science spread her empire wide,
And still, with mournful joy and fond regret,
She views thy scenes, her former loved retreat,
Whence first diffusive shone her quick'ning light,
While droop'd the world around in shades of night:
Such fond regret as feeling bosoms prove
From view of objects of a former love,
Though now no more their charms our peace molest,
And hush'd the passion that disturb'd the breast;

580

Yet Memory still awakes a thought severe:—
We once have loved, and once to them were dear.

For arts of rule, for moral wisdom famed,
Thy ancient people high distinction claim'd;
But o'er the brightening beams of mental light,
Dark Superstition drew the veil of night;
Or used, with aim perverse, the heavenly blaze,
Alone to lure through Error's devious ways.
Beneath her despot sway degraded, pined
The sense of freedom and the powers of mind;
The reptile vile, the monsters of the wood,
Or scaly terror of thy fertile flood,
The plant, the insect, challenged rites divine,
And vows absurd ascended at their shrine.

Here still the Demon holds despotic power,
Still o'er thy climes her baleful shadows lower;
While blank-faced Ignorance, in pride of heart,
Triumphant tramples on the wrecks of art;
Each worth, each science, banish'd from thy plains,
Of ancient time alone this vile reproach remains.
A wild, rapacious, cruel, treacherous race,
Nature's rude outcasts, and their clime's disgrace,

To feeling lost and dead to sense of shame,
Thy abject sons in strongest terms proclaim
What misery clouds, what vices taint mankind,
Unsway'd by order, nor by laws confined!
   Thus, o'er these climes as bends my airy way,
Where Power, grim despot, spreads his iron sway,
Where Desolation rears his baleful crest,
Mid scenes in vain by lavish Nature blest;
Mid luxury's riot waste, where Famine reigns,
And mouldering cities gloom the lonely plains;
While o'er their glories past pale Memory sighs,
What dreary prospects in idea rise!
Is this of realms the fate, the mournful end
To which must all inevitably tend?
Must each, in turn, lament the same sad doom,
By heaven prescribed for nations yet to come;
And, as their fame has shone, their empire spread,
Misfortune o'er them roll her deepening shade?
Ere long, perhaps, by barbarous rule opprest,
Shall Europe's realms this fatal truth attest;
Ere long shall, haply, o'er her beauteous land,
Stern Desolation wave his sterile wand;

CHARMS OF FANCY.

Her fairest plains to desert wastes be turn'd,
Her arts neglected, her refinements spurn'd,
While moss-grown walls and heaps of ruins rude,
Shall mark the place where once her cities stood:
Where gay Lætitia's splendid scenes are spread,
Shall the rank thistle wave its lonely head;
And London's domes, in wild destruction hurl'd,
Convey a future moral to the world.
Yon cities, too, in infant pride that rise,
And shine, Columbia! mid thy favor'd skies,
Some future day may see in dust o'erthrown,
With brambles shadow'd, and with brake o'ergrown;
Some future day, the traveler haply come
To view their ruins, from his distant home,
From western shores with brilliant cities graced,
The seats of science, elegance, and taste,
Where now Alaska lifts her forests rude,
Or Nootka rolls its solitary flood;
While o'er the spot, contemplative, he strays
Where Philadelphia caught the admiring gaze;
Mid ambient waves York's proud emporium shone,
Or fair Bostonia graced her eastern throne;

No peopled domes, no spires ascending high,
No scenes of culture please his pensive eye;
No human voice he hears—the desert plain
Knows but the Whippo'will's funereal strain,
The Hern's hoarse clang, or Sea-gull's lonely cry,
Join'd with the moan of winds, that sadly sigh
O'er many a shatter'd pile, and broken stone
Of sculptured form, in mournful unison :—
Save, haply startled at the human tread,
From some gray tomb, by withering fern o'erspread,
Slow rears the Rattle-snake his glistening crest,
And fills with deathful sounds the dreary waste.

 Yet may this prospect dark, this mournful **theme**,
Prove but a vision vain, a melancholy dream!
Lo! brighter scenes exulting Hope descries,
As o'er the future glance her radiant eyes;
With joy she sees the arts of peace expand,
And willing nations own the mild command;
Exulting, marks those blissful days unfold,
By poets sung, the favor'd age of gold,
When fierce contentions shall prevail no more,
No barbarous nations flood the **earth** with **gore,**

No ruffian bands the fairest climes annoy,
No savage victor conquer to destroy;
When realms, now sunk beneath barbarian sway,
Shall shine illumed with freedom's quick'ning ray:
E'en the fierce Turk shall feel the generous flame,
And fair Refinement grace his laurel'd name;
Those cities mouldering o'er the gloomy waste
Again shall rise with new-born lustre graced:
Again shall Thebes erect her head sublime,
Again Palmyra cheer the desert clime,
O'er their glad plains the smile of joy expand,
And jocund Plenty crown the fertile land;
Mid wildest tribes, to earth's remotest end,
The reign of Science and of Truth extend,
Humanity the bliss of worlds improve,
And all mankind unite in social love.

But quit, my Muse! description's lucid strain,
Nor further range o'er realms that yet remain;
Though Asia Minor's various cities smile,
In pomp alluring, o'er her blissful soil,
And Europe's sons and various customs yield
A pleasing subject and an ample field.

Some future poet, in his tuneful lay,
Shall sing each people, and each clime display;
Their manners show, their numerous sources trace,
And mark the difference of the human race,
When nations now unknown the Muse shall fire,
And give new music to her magic lyre.

 Such are the pleasures, such the prospects bright,
Thou pour'st, O Fancy! on the raptured sight;
Mid cheerless solitude's forsaken gloom,
Where sad-eyed Melancholy loves to roam,
In life's dark moments o'er the sinking soul
When chill Despondency's black shadows roll,
Or, rapture-wing'd, with cloudless sunshine gay,
Joy's halcyon season pours its vernal ray,
Thy fairy visions, with benignant power,
Cheer the lone sadness of the unsocial hour;
Gild the wild horrors of Dejection's gloom,
And Joy's bright Sun with brighter beams illume.

 Though cold declaimers, in severest strain,
Thy pleasures reprobate, thy sons arraign:
"For grant," they cry, "that Fancy's magic ray,
With fairer sunshine gilds of joy the day,

With deeper tinge she glooms the sable clouds,
When dire Despair, life's cheerful prospects shrouds,
With sharper stings impoints the venom'd dart,
When pale Affliction rends the tortured heart,
And far from Reason's road her lures beguile,
Where wild Projection plants its fatal toil:
So the pale Meteor, whose deceitful ray,
Shines to mislead, and lights but to betray,
When misty darkness wraps the cope of night,
Decoys the traveler with its wandering light,
Till, whelm'd in floods, or treacherous bogs beneath,
Too late he finds the illusion end in death.
Ixions vain, who chase thy phantoms fair,
Find their false Junos changed to empty air,
And, on the torturing racks of misery torn,
Too late their vain pursuits, and follies mourn."

  Though, thus adorn'd with candor's specious air,
The show of truth their warm invectives wear;
Yet lost in error's maze they wander wide,
Misled by prejudice and critic pride:
For that propensity, on all imprest,
The happy self-love of the human breast,

Impels the mind to turn the cheerless view,
From scenes Despondence paints in mournful hue,
To those thy flattering mirror gives to sight,
By hope's gay pencil drawn in colors bright.

 Even he who, sinking with distress and care,
Condemn'd misfortunes bitterest frowns to bear,
Compell'd the soul-corroding pangs to prove
Of treacherous friendship, or of hopeless love,
From wonted joys of ease and affluence torn,
To strive with pain, with indigence and scorn;
Or, in forsaken age, to shed the tear
Of grief paternal o'er his children's bier;
Whose woes, by thee with stronger force imprest,
With keener torment goad the afflicted breast,
Still finds a pleasure from the sense refined
Of nicer feelings and a nobler mind;
Nor would that pride sublime of grief forego,
For all the tasteless joys that Apathy can know.

 But ah! too soon thy pleasing visions fade;
Thy power declines as Age's frosts invade,
Or Sage experience, cruel, draws aside
Thy glittering veils, that Life's dark shadows hide.

588

CHARMS OF FANCY.

In that bright Season, when the flower of Spring
Unfolds its fragrance to the zephyr's wing,
When, with the charm of novelty imprest,
Youth's gay amusements fire the ductile breast,
And, eager as its pleasures we pursue,
All else unheeded 'scapes the careless view,
In that my favor'd age, with brightest dyes
Thou paint'st the future to our longing eyes;
Deck'd, by thy magic touch, with grace divine,
The charms of love, and joys of friendship shine;
One face of bliss Life's fair-drawn scenes display,
And smile alluring in perpetual May,
While schemes of happiness the mind employ,
Of unalloy'd prosperity and joy,
The fairy dreams of Hope's untutor'd train,
That mock the narrow bounds of Reason's reign:
And, e'en when envious Time's officious care
Divests thy pictures of their flattering glare,
Scarce can the soul, by thy bright prospects warm'd,
Resign the beauties that so long have charm'd.

In manhood's Summer, when, with scornful pride,
Youth's air-built whims and visions we deride,

While visions scarce less wild ourselves engage,
Interest's vain schemes, Ambition's madd'ning rage,
Though changed thy object with life's changing day,
Still thou presid'st with scarce diminish'd sway.
When Autumn's season of decay appears,
Thy powers declining with declining years;
By thee scarce bias'd, when the mind pursues
Its cool employments and its sober views,
With equal eye, contemptuous we survey
The little sports of Childhood's frolic day,
Spring's gay pursuits and wild romantic dreams,
And ardent Summer's visionary schemes;
And, as Experience' piercing beam despoils
Thy bright [4] Morganas of their magic smiles,
Surprised we view the blind mistakes of youth,
In following phantoms for the form of truth.

  Thus by degrees declines thy varying power,
As stooping years bring on the wint'ry hour;
When, lost to pleasure and to feeling dead,
Each bliss of hope, each fond endearment fled,
The icy heart no kind attachment knows,
No tender passion in the bosom glows,

While all the frosty eye alike surveys
With dull indifference, or with cold dispraise,
Till, in the wint'ry grave's all-shrouding night,
Sink the last gleams of thy expiring light.

Yet, e'en amidst this gloomy view, appears
Thy power superior, and thy influence cheers:—
Not all, though none escape the general doom,
Tread the same course, descending to the tomb,
Mid sinking years the like dull journey go,
Distinguish'd only by a change of woe;
For oft to life's last verge thy glow inspires
Those favor'd sons who boast thy genuine fires;
Through long-protracted years of want and pain
They feel thy influence, and thy warmth retain;
As erst in youth, in fairy dreams engage,
And with thy pleasures soothe the ills of age,
See Time obedient to thy mandates yield,
And nature's laws by Fancy's magic quell'd.

Thus great Mæonides, by want distress'd,
With age enfeebled and disease oppress'd,
Mid strangers thrown, a houseless wanderer, fain
A scanty pittance from his lyre to gain,

Still felt thy genial flame his bosom fire,
And Poesy's sublimest strains inspire;
And, while delighted crowds around him pour,
From each famed city of Ionia's shore,
As the high theme their wondering ears engage,
Of Troy's famed war and stern Pelides' rage,
The eyeless minstrel glow'd with youth again,
Forgot his woes, and triumph'd o'er his pain.

Thus, like the aged swan, whose latest breath
In tuneful notes preludes the approach of death,
The Athenian bard,* for matchless sweetness famed,
Still from the Tragic Muse distinction claim'd,
While Glory's hand, around his brows, was seen
To twine fresh laurels of unfading green,
Though Time, long since, his frosts had o'er him shed,
Plough'd his pale cheek, and shorn his hoary head.
O'er Persia's plains, where Shiraz' landscapes bloom,
And fields of roses waft a rich perfume,
Thus the famed Sage, mid years' increasing weight,
Still glow'd with Fancy's brightest fires elate;

* Sophocles.

In sweetest verse his moral precepts sung,
While Wit, delighted, o'er her Sadi hung.

    E'en *modern* times examples bright supply,
On which with pleasure dwells reflection's eye,
Like some clear lamp, whose gloom-dispelling **blaze**
E'en to the last a constant light displays,
To life's late close for powers of genius known,
Thus fair Italia's lyric poet shone;
Loved bard! whose life, in even course along,
Flow'd pure and blameless as thy classic song,
Taste's richest flowers shall mid thy ashes bloom,
While Virtue weeps o'er Metastasio's tomb.
Thus, with advancing years, in Darwin's lays
The sportive Muse more vivid tints displays,
Gives with thy brighter beams his verse to shine,
And pours new splendor o'er the polish'd line;
As, touch'd with frost, the hawthorn's berries glow
With deeper crimson mid surrounding snow.

    Like some tall oak that rears its vigorous form,
And bids defiance to the wint'ry storm,
While trees of brighter verdure, stretch'd around,
Mourn their reft honors scatter'd on the ground;

Thus gayly smiling mid the lapse of years,
Thy boast, Germania! unimpair'd appears:
Lo! at his bidding what strange shapes advance,
What forms fantastic weave the airy dance!
When to young Huon, in the desert wild,
On his bright car appears the lovely child,
Mid whose infantine smile, the eye's keen blaze
The fairy-monarch's dreaded mein bewrays,
His strains, accordant to the subject, thrill
The soul with transport, or with terror chill.

Thus has the Muse, unequal to the toil,
With daring footstep trod thy magic soil;
And thus presumed, with bold, advent'rous hand,
To sketch the beauties of thy fairy land:
Yet, ere her hands the varying lyre resign,
Fraternal love demands the grateful line.

To thee, allied by nature's tend'rest claim,
Whose least endearment is a sister's name;
To thee, while warm affection prompts the notes,
With joy the Muse the closing strain devotes.

If any merit grace these artless lays,
If any humble meed of modest praise,

Indulgence kind, with fav'ring smiles bestow,
To thee that merit and that praise I owe.
    Oft, when first starting on my young career,
Repress'd by diffidence and anxious fear,
While the chill'd verse in dull suspension hung,
The theme neglected and the lyre unstrung,
As to my view the various ills arose,
That envious spleen and prejudice oppose,
The storms that lower o'er each devoted head,
Whose luckless feet these paths presumptuous **tread,**
Oft hast thou urged my loit'ring course along,
And fired me to complete th' unfinish'd song.
    Form'd to improve the hour of social bliss,
To heighten pleasure and to soothe distress,
To grace the brilliant circles of the gay,
Do through life's noiseless vale contented **stray,**
With cool instruction sweet delight to blend,
The sage adviser and the cheerful friend;
A mind possessing, by improvement graced,
With genius brighten'd, and refined by **taste,**
A gen'rous heart, with tend'rest feelings **fraught,**
And all the ardor of ennobling thought;

595

With fortune's smiles enrich'd, to care unknown,
Thy morn of youth in cloudless splendor shone.
But ah! No human state exists secure;
No happiness is fated to endure;
Life, ever varying, knows no certain plan;
And frail's the tenure of the bliss of man.
False as the smiles that deck an April day,
And sooner with'ring than the flowers of May,
Our joys precarious no continuance boast,
Nipp'd in their bloom by pale affliction's frost;
On pleasure's steps the fiend of woe still treads,
And grief's deep gloom mirth's fairest smile succeeds,
E'en the gay hours with brightest transport warm,
Shine a sad prelude to th' impending storm,
While, more alluring as their prospects show,
Still heavier hangs the sable cloud of woe.
But, though the hopes of perfect bliss are vain,
Nor here the fairy holds her heav'nly reign,
Yet not unmix'd the stream of misery flows:
Some soothing sweets its bitt'rest waves disclose;
Some glitt'ring beams life's darkest shades adorn,
And pleasure's rose oft blooms in sorrow's thorn.

CHARMS OF FANCY.

To-day, though sadness wear her sable veil,
And gloomiest thoughts the troubled mind assail,
To-morrow hope unfolds her radiant face,
Joy's winning smiles her lovely features grace;
Before the splendors of her bright'ning eye,
The glooms disperse, the low'ring shadows fly.
Though sorrow's hand hath paled thy wonted **bloom**,
And thy fond hopes are shrouded in the tomb;
While each occasion gives thy tears to flow,
As memory opes afresh the source of woe,   [pears
And, view'd through grief's dark medium, **life ap-**
A weary journey through a vale of tears;
Yet mild-eyed comfort, on her healing wing,
To thee the heav'nly balm of peace shall bring,
Time's lenient hand shall lend its kindly aid,
And o'er thy sorrows draw its softest shade;
Hope in thy breast here would her seat **resume,**
And thence dispel dejection's mournful **gloom,**
While, to each wild excess alike **unknown,**
There calm serenity shall fix her throne.

NOTES TO THE FOURTH BOOK.

1 " THY pyramidal gates," &c. The gateways or entrances of the great temple at Luxor are very massy, and of a pyramidal form. The remains of the outer walls are forty feet in width at the base

2 " Still its golden stars." "Amongst the heaps of rubbish with which the village of Achmounain is surrounded, is a superb portico, that has suffered nothing from time. It is one hundred feet long, and twenty-five wide, and is supported by twelve columns, which have only a plain fascia, by way of capital. Each column is composed of three blocks of granite, forming in all sixty feet in height, by twenty-five in circumference. The block which rests upon the base is simply rounded, and loaded with hieroglyphics, which commence with a pyramid; the two others are fluted. The columns are ten feet distant from each other, except the two middle ones, which, serving for the entrance, leave an interval between them of fifteen feet. Ten enormous stones cover the whole extent of the portico; over them is a double row. The two middle ones, which rise in the form of a pediment, surpass the others in form and thickness. It is astonishing that the art of man has been able to elevate these prodigious masses of rock to the height of sixty feet. The frieze, which surrounds it, is covered with hieroglyphics very well carved. The figures are those of birds, of insects, of various kinds of animals, and of men seated, to whom others appear to be making offerings. This is probably the history of the time, the places, and the deity in whose honor this monument was raised. The portico was painted red and blue. These colors are effaced in many

places; but the lower part of the architrave, which surrounds the colon‑
nade, has preserved a gold color astonishingly lively. It is the same
with the ceiling, where the stars of gold shine upon an azure sky, with
a dazzling brilliancy. This monument, constructed before the Persian
conquest, has neither the elegance nor the purity of the Grecian archi‑
tecture ; but its solidity, which it seems impossible to destroy, its awful
simplicity, and its majesty, command admiration."—*Savary's Letters
on Egypt.*

³ " Whose era no recording annals boast." The same uncertainty
and difference of opinion is to be found in authors, both ancient and
modern, as to the period of the erection of these stupendous masses and
their founders, as prevails with regard to the object of their erection—
some ascribing them to Cheops, to Mœris, &c., some to Amasis, Busi‑
ris, or Sesostris, while others assert that they existed prior to the gene‑
ral deluge. Amidst this impenetrable cloud of uncertainty, the most
learned in Egyptian antiquities, until the language of the hieroyglyhics
can be deciphered, can form, at best, but ingenious conjectures, that
will bring us very little nearer to the truth.

The third volume of Oriental Collections contains on this subject a
letter from the Rev. Dr. Hales to Sir William Ouseley, an abstract of
which I shall here insert :—" The first pyramid was built by Apachnes,
the third of the Yksos, or Shepherd Kings, who, according to Manetho,
in the reign of Timaios emigrated from the East, subdued Egypt, and
grievously oppressed the inhabitants, for the period of two hundred and
fifty-nine years, when they were finally expelled, through the deserts
of Palestine, by Thammosis. This was begun about the year two thou‑
sand and ninety-six, before Christ, and completed about two thousand
and sixty-three. The two others were probably built during the long
reigns of the immediate successors of Apachnes—Anophis and Janias ;
and the expulsion of the Yksos occurred in or about the year nineteen
hundred and five, before Christ. The Egyptian priests, from a senti‑
ment of national vanity, or in order to conceal their subjection and
servitude, falsely attributed the building of the two great pyramids to

NOTES TO THE FOURTH BOOK.

two of their native sovereigns—Cheops and Cephrenes—who reigned long after; the first about the year one thousand and eighty-four, and the other one thousand and thirty-four, before Christ. In corroboration of this hypothesis, Dr. Hales observes, that Mr. Wilford notices the invasion of Egypt in ancient times, recorded in a Hindoo work, the *Maha-Calpa*, which gives the names of three of the Hindoo princes, who reigned there—Samo-Vatia, Bahya-Vatia, the Baion of Manetho, and the second in the list of his Shepherd Kings, and Ruema-Vatia, or Apachnes, the last of which, possessing great wealth, raised three mountains, called Rucanadri, Rajat-adri, and Retu-adri, or the Mount of Gold; the Mount of Silver, and that of precious stones, that is, the three great pyramids, coated with yellow, white, and spotted polished marbles. These pyramids were consecrated to Padma-Devi, (the Goddess of the Cotos, or white water-lily,) called also Paramasi, or the Chief Goddess."

4 "Thy bright Morganas." The Fata Morgana is a most beautiful aërial phenomenon, observable from the harbor of Messina, and some other places adjacent, in Sicily, at a certain height from the level of the ocean. In a clear, calm day of summer there rises, above the great current of air, a vapor, which acquires a certain density, so as to form in the atmosphere horizontal prisms, whose surfaces are so disposed as to reflect and represent in succession, like a moving mirror, for sometime, the objects on the coast, or in the country contiguous. They exhibit, by turns, the city and suburbs of Messina, trees, animals, men, and mountains.—Voyage Pittoresque, par M. Houel.

The time of the appearance of this phenomenon is when the sun has just risen above the horizon. After it has attained some height, the pictures become obscure and gradually disappear. The common people have given it the name of the Fata, or Fairy Morgana, from a belief entertained by them, that this appearance is produced by that celebrated Fairy.

* "O'er her Sadi hung." "The celebrated poet Sadi was born at

Shiraz, in the year 1175 of our era. He was the author of the Gulistan, or Bed of Roses; the Bostan, or Fruit Garden; the Molamaat, or Rays of Light, and a large Collection of Odes and Sonnets, alphabetically arranged in a *Diván*. The portrait of this celebrated poet was lately to be seen in a building near Shirawz, representing him as a venerable old man, with a long, silver beard, and flowing robes, holding in his right hand a crooked ivory staff, and in the left a charger of inincense. He lived to the advanced age of one hundred and sixteen years, and his tomb is still visited with the respect due to classic ground, at a little distance from Shirawz, his native city."—Ousley's Persian Miscellanies, Chapter 4.

The Gulistan of Sadi, of which there has been a recent translation, is a work abounding with many excellent precepts of morality and practical lessons of wisdom. In one of his Fables, or Stories, he relates that King Feridún, had written at the entrance of his palace, in letters of gold, the following sentence:—" Whoever thou art, recollect that the pleasures of this world are of no endurance: But place thy heart on Him who created it, for He will never disappoint thee! Put not thy trust in earthly power or riches; for time has produced and elevated many like thee, whom in the end it has destroyed. When the soul of the virtuous man is on the point of its departure, of what consequence is it to him if he dies on a throne, or in the street?"

THE
ENCHANTED LAKE

OF THE

FAIRY MORGANA.

FROM THE ORLANDO INAMORATO OF
FRANCESCO BERNI.

NEW-YORK:
PRINTED AND PUBLISHED BY ISAAC RILEY AND CO.
Logotypographic Office.

1806.

District of } ss. BE IT REMEMBERED, That, on the twentieth day of May, in the thirtieth year of the Independence of the United States of America, RICHARD ALSOP, of the said District, hath deposited in this Office, the Title of a Book, the right whereof he claims as Author, in the words following, to wit:

" The Enchanted Lake of the Fairy Morgana, from the Or-
" lando Inamorato of Francesco Berni."

IN CONFORMITY to the Act of the Congress of the United States, entitled " An Act for the Encouragement of Learning,
" by securing the Copies of Maps, Charts, and Books, to the Au-
" thors and Proprietors of such Copies, during the time therein
" mentioned."

EDWARD DUNSCOMB,
Clerk of the District of New-York,

PREFACE.

THE Orlando Inamorato, from which the following beautiful allegorical story is taken, is one of the most celebrated poems of Italy and rivals in popularity the Furioso of the immortal Ariosto.

This singular production was originally written by *Matteo Maria Boiardo*, count of Scandiano, a place dependent on the dutchy of Ferrara, and published in 1496, two years after the death of its author. Though Boiardo is admitted to have possessed an uncommon brilliancy of imagination, and a happy talent for invention, yet his work appears to have been little more than a compilation (principally from the fabulous chronicle of Turpin) of the various popular tales relative to the Paladins, or peers of Charlemagne, connected and enlivened by additions of his own *invention*, and rendered in some degree conducive to the general action, or actions of the poem. It is, however, principally indebted for its high reputation to the labours of FRANCESCO BERNI, a cotemporary of Ariosto, who improved and polished the style, harmonized the versification, added many stanzas and moral reflections, and as the title expresses, recast it, and has thus converted the rude structure of Boiardo into a magnificent Gothic edifice, which cannot fail of impressing the mind with wonder and delight, though the component parts are deficient in proportion, and frequently exhibit a strange and discordant mixture of materials.

This poem is of great length, consisting of three books, subdivided into numerous cantos. Its principal subject is the achievements of the celebrated Orlando, performed for the love of Angelica, daughter of Galaphron king of Cathay, and the adventures of the most renowned Paladins and distinguished Saracen knights, whose names are rendered familiar to the reader of English poetry by Mr. Hoole's well-known version of Ariosto. It contains three distinct epic actions; the siege of Albracca, by Agrican king of Tartary, a rejected suitor of Angelica—the invasion of France by Gradasso, king of Sericana, in order to obtain Rinaldo's horse and the sword of Orlando; and lastly, that of the same country by Agrimant, emperor of Africa, and Marsilius, king of Spain. This last adventure constitutes the principal subject of the Furioso of Ariosto, who has continued and brought it to a conclusion from the Inamorato, in which it is left imperfect. These different actions are interspersed with a great variety of separate adventures and stories in the manner of the Furioso, but less connected with the principal subject, and much more extravagant than those contained in that work.

Though, considered as a poem, the *Inamorato* is, in every respect, far inferior to the *Furioso*, yet it is certainly a very interesting, and it may be truly added a fascinating production. Its style, variety of adventures, allusions to common life, mixture of comic humour, occasional display of vulgar manners, and even its extravagance, are admirably adapted to render it a favourite with the people.

Were this poem possessed of no other recommendation, than that of giving rise to the *Furioso*, and having served as a model in many respects to the inimitable Cervantes, (who has frequently copied with the happiest success, the burlesque* style of Berni,) it would well deserve the attention of the classic reader. But the merit of the Inamorato, is not merely relative. The great variety of incident and wonderful

* It may not be impertinent here to observe, that the burlesque style derived its appellation from Berni, who first employed and perfected it, being originally called the Berniscan, and afterwards by corruption the burlescan, whence our English word burlesque.

adventures which it contains, cannot fail of pleasing all who delight in fiction. Many of the stories are interesting, and happily told, the descriptions are brilliant, sometimes sublime, and often display great beauty of imagery, and felicity of expression. The prognostics of the storm, previously to the sailing of Rodomonte from Africa, the tempest itself, and the demeanour of that daring chieftain, are delineated with a masterly hand, and would not suffer by a comparison with some of the best descriptions in poetry. It must be acknowledged, however, that the images are often low and disgusting, the stile frequently mean and vulgar, and that the retorts of the heroes, appear to partake more of the low buffoonery, and coarse invective of Lazzaroni, than the courtly stile of chivalry.

But it is not the intention of the translator of the following tale, to enter into a critical examination of the merits of the Inamorato; some account of the poem and its author, appeared to him requisite to be given, and he has only to observe that this version, not originally intended for publication, is chiefly designed to give some idea of that celebrated and singular poem, and is the first specimen of equal length, he presumes, that has hitherto been presented to the English reader. Though the entire work, is not, in

vii

his opinion, susceptible of an English dress; he proposes, should this be received with approbation, occasionally to furnish such other selections, as may appear best suited to the public taste.

With respect to the stile of the version, the translator readily acknowledges, that he has in some instances been induced to imitate that adopted by the late ingenious Mr. Way, in his version of the Fabliaux, which from the occasional introduction of antiquated words, he conceives admirably adapted to this species of composition, and best suited to the genius of the original.

R. A.

ERRATA.

Page 4 last line for " monster" read " monsters."
— 6 line 15 after " exclaimed" insert a semicolon.
— 9 line 13 after " shore" dele comma.
— 9 line 15 for " encircled round" read " fast lock'd around."
— 31 line 20 after fled, insert a comma.
— 38 line 9 after leaf, insert comma.
— — line 17 for " strange" read " strong."
Page 55 line 2 of the poetry, for " Profused" read " Profuse."
— 57 line 1 before " shouldst" read " but."
— 58 line 16 at the beginning, for " to" read " on."
— — line 19 after combat insert a comma.
— 68 line 11 for " elegant" read " excellent."

Her eyes she cast and now to heaven she threw

The Adventure of the Lake.

FROM THE SECOND BOOK OF THE ORLANDO INAMORATO OF
FRANCESCO BERNI.

YE who in stories of romance delight,
The spell-fram'd monster and intrepid knight,
List to the strange, the pleasing tale I tell
Of what the Count Orlando erst befel,
When he th'abode of fam'd Morgana sought,
And such high deeds and proud atchievements wrought.
  When now Orlando had, as late was seen,
Destroy'd the garden of Orgagna's queen,(1)
The monsters slain, the furious giants quell'd,
Each toil surmounted and each charm dispell'd,

He, by that sorceress fair attended, went
To free the captives in her dungeons pent,
On foot he far'd, his Brigliadoro lost,
And many a plain and weary mountain cross'd.
   As thus they pass'd, conversing on the way,
Along a devious road they chanc'd to stray,
Whose course conducted to a river's side
That deep and silent pour'd an ample tide:
A bridge, of structure strange, o'er-arch'd the flood,
On which, high-rais'd, a fence of iron stood,
Whose midmost part a narrow wicket show'd
That scarce admittance for a man allow'd.
Amidst a mead with gloomy cypress spread,
Beyond the bridge a turret rear'd its head;
Around the mead, slow-circling, roll'd the tide,
And in a deep dark lake expanded wide.
This was the spot, as erst you've heard me tell,(2)
Where such mishap the boldest knights befel,
The lake in which had Arridano thrown
The two brave friends and Amon's* valiant son.(3)

* Rinaldo.

Where Dudon since an equal fate had found,
In vain for prowess and for strength renown'd,
For 'gainst that robber's force no strength avail'd,
The bravest knights, the strongest champions fail'd.
The arms and vestments of each hapless knight,
By him or pris'ner made, or slain in fight,
As tokens of his fame and their disgrace,
Proud was he wont amid the grove to place:
High o'er the rest a cypress' trunk display'd
Rinaldo's mantle, arms, and beamy blade.
When now Orlando and the sorceress drew
To where the stream and bridge appear'd in view,
Pale grew her face, her limbs with terror shook.
And to the warrior thus, alarm'd, she spoke:
' O valiant knight, since cruel fate has led
' Our wand'ring steps this fatal path to tread,
' Since o'er us both destruction hovers near,
' Attend my words, and to my counsels hear!
' Within that tower a murd'rous robber dwells,
' Who all in deeds of villainy excels.
' Whome'er untoward fortune hither brings
' In yonder lake the ruthless villain flings,

'Strength more than human the charm'd ruffian shares
'And Arridano is the name he bears.
'Beneath the waters of the gloomy lake
'A far-fam'd fairy does her dwelling make,
'Morgana call'd, who erst, by magic's aid,
'A curious horn of wond'rous beauty made;
'Such power, 'tis said, the magic horn endued
'Whene'er 'twas sounded death the blast ensued.
'Long were the tale, and difficult to tell
'The num'rous victims of this potent spell:—
'Suffice to say, a knight who thither came,(4)
'Unknown to me his country or his name,
'The bulls subdued, the furious dragon slew,
'And armies springing from the earth o'erthrew.
'Enrag'd, the fairy saw her charm destroy'd,
'The boasted charm that long her skill employ'd,
'And this devis'd, the pride of magic lore,
'A spell surpassing all e'er known before;
'Against its force all human strength is vain,
'Who hither comes, comes only to be slain.
'Him hopeful to destroy, whose pow'rful arm
'Subdued the monster and dispell'd the charm,

'The vengeful fairy form'd this plot, should e'er
'Chance or adventure bold conduct him here.
'For this the mead, the lake, the bridge she wrought,
'For this, 'midst villains infamous, has sought
'This wretch most impious, whose unequall'd crimes
'Would shock the tenants of th'infernal climes:
'Beneath the fairy's gift, secur'd from harms,
'The caitiff combats in enchanted arms,
'And such the wond'rous spell, his force in fight
'Six times exceeds his adversary's might.
'Then since all human prowess here is vain,
'Nor strength however great the conflict can sustain,
'Tempt not the enterprize, thy death 'twill be,
'And mine is certain when depriv'd of thee:
'Our hope of safety sole remains in flight,
'If haply we have scap'd the ruffian's sight.'
Smiling, replied the knight.—' Nought here below
'Can make me turn; I dread no human foe.
'For thee my heart with pity glows sincere,
'Thou left alone a timid woman here;
'But comfort take and on my aid depend,
'For arms and courage succour sure will lend.'

'O fly sir knight! O turn from death away!
'Thy courage here in vain wouldst thou essay.
'Not fam'd Orlando aught could here avail;
'Here Charlemain and all his court would fail.
'I grieve my life to lose, but more I plain
'That thou a noble knight should'st here be slain;
'A woman I, of small account am found,
'Thou, courteous, wise, for deeds of arms renown'd.
These soothing words, accompanied with tears,
With feelings not unmov'd Orlando hears;
Wav'ring he stands, half-prompted to return,
While thoughts conflicting in his bosom burn;
Till o'er the bridge Rinaldo's arms on high,
Fix'd to the lofty cypress, caught his eye.
The arms he knew, and, weeping, thus exclaim'd
'O thou, the flower of knights, of champions fam'd
'The peerless pride! who hath thee thus disgrac'd?
'Who hath thee slain and here this trophy plac'd?
'By arts of treach'ry hast thou been assail'd,
'As else against thee worlds had ne'er prevail'd.
'Lov'd cousin mine! from Paradise O hear,
'To thy Orlando lend a pitying ear!

' Though late, by love bewildering led astray,(5)
' In passion lost, to jealousy a prey,
' I wrong'd thy worth; tho' 'twixt us twain arose
' From causes vain, the deadly strife of foes,
' I ever held thee dear; with tears, I own
' The fault was mine, and mine the blame alone:
' Forgive thy friend, and charge not his offence,
' To want of love, but alienated sense.'
 Orlando thus his kinsman's fate deplor'd,
And grasp'd his shield, and drew his shining sword,
The fated sword, 'gainst which no spells avail,
No strength of arms, no charmed helm or mail,
Whose virtue such, and such its keenness tried,
'Twould iron, steel or adamant divide,
By Falerina wrought, with magic skill,
As erst I've told, the Paladin to kill.
 By grief to fury wrought the knight impell'd,
On to the bridge his course impetuous held,
The iron barrier broke, in pieces hew'd,
And to the meadow swift his way pursued.
Beneath the cypress, Arridano lay,
And on Rinaldo's spoils, in pleas'd survey,

Exulting fix'd his eyes :—When, lo! the knight
In hostile guise advancing, met his sight;
Surpriz'd, his massy club the robber took,
Light sprung from earth, and thus fierce-threat'ning
    spoke :
' Wretch, whosoe'er thou art, prepare to die !
' Not all the powers in Paradise on high,
' Thee from my wrath and fury can defend,
' Nor Trivigante, or Macon here befriend.'
    Furious he spoke, and aiming from above,
With both his hands the dreadful mace he drove;
The mace descending with a thund'ring stroke
Dash'd the strong shield—the shield in shivers broke—
~~In wild contortions reel'd the knight around,~~
~~Stunn'd by the blow, and fell upon the ground.~~
To seize him quick the ruthless villain sped,
Intent to plunge him in the wat'ry bed,
The lake wherein full many a knight was thrown,
Of rank illustrious and of high renown.
The Count, tho' fallen, still was undismay'd;
As stoop'd his foe, he whirl'd the fated blade,
In vain th' enchanted shield oppos'd the stroke—
Th' enchanted shield it cleft, the corslet broke,

[margin: Stunn'd by the blow in giddy mazes round / The champion reels, & sinks upon the ground.]

And thence descending with resistless sway
Rent from his side the cov'ring mail away,
And slight a wound impress'd: with eyes on fire
Wild rag'd the giant with redoubled ire,
And heav'd the mace on high—his active foe
Light threw himself aside, and 'scap'd the menac'd
    blow,
While at his leg a stroke transverse he made—
The club descending met the keen-edg'd blade,
Sheer thro' the pond'rous mace the falchion went,
And to the ground the end divided sent.
Loud Arridano roar'd, like some wild beast
Reft of its young or close by hunters prest,
And furious seiz'd the knight, and to the shore,
With falcon speed the struggling champion bore,
And with him, in his arms encircled round,
Plung'd to the bottom of the lake profound:
Dash'd by the pond'rous fall the waters rave,
And boils in eddies white the closing wave.
  No longer there durst Falerina stay,
But wing'd by terror speeds her flight away,

Like some thin leaf that's shaken by the wind,
She trembles, starts, and often looks behind;
Whatever meets her sight, whate'er her ear,
In all she deems the dreaded robber near.
  Meantime, in cruel grasp together strain'd,
The hostile pair the lake's deep bottom gain'd;
Thence Arridano bore the struggling knight,
In vain contending 'gainst his magic might,
All might surpassing. Down a long descent,
Thus clasp'd, a dark and miry road they went;
At length, emerging from the dreary way,
A mead they reach'd with flowers and verdure gay.
Struck with the scene Orlando lifts his eyes,
And sees the light of day with wild surprise;
Soft breath'd the air around, and o'er his head
The magic lake's suspended waves were spread,
While from above, faint gleaming thro' the wave,
The sun's mild rays an added beauty gave.
Three miles in circuit stretch'd the lovely mead—
Around a wall of purest crystal spread,
Beyond, a little verdant mountain rose,
Rich with each varied flower that fragrant blows.

The ruthless villain, on this beauteous plain,
Was wont to spoil the captives he had ta'en.
When here the Count Orlando he had brought,
With ease to strip him of his arms he thought;
He, like the rest, discourag'd deem'd the knight,
Nor longer able to contend in fight.
Fallacious thought—far else had fate decreed!
Scarce from his iron grasp the Count was freed,
Scarce found himself releas'd, when, undismay'd,
Fierce on his foe he sprung with lifted blade,
The giant's helm the trenchant weapon found,
The enchanted helm it cleft, but fail'd to wound.
Nought reck'd the robber this—in proud disdain
He cried, ' Thy toil is here but labour vain,
' Such blows might serve to frighten flies away,
' But for this one a hundred I'll repay.'
 He said, and hurl'd on high the pond'rous mace,
Whose force had shook a mountain to its base;
Aside Orlando leap'd—with fruitless aim,
In thunder driven, the mace descending came,
Deep groan'd the solid earth beneath the stroke,
The mountain echo'd and the meadow shook.

Now 'twixt the twain a fiercer strife arose,
With deadlier ire inflam'd the battle glows,
This cloth'd in strength beyond all human might,
In valor that excell'd and skill in fight:
The giant wields his mace, with thundering sound,
Thick, heavy, fall the erring blows around;
In vain he strikes, for still his wary foe
With dext'rous speed eludes the coming blow,
Now foins, now feints, now shifts his ground and tries
Each varied stratagem that skill supplies.
Far else the robber fares—his streaming blood
From three deep wounds effused a crimson flood;
At length the knight the glad advantage spy'd
And drove his falchion thro' the caitiff's side,
Whose life-blood issuing with the fleeting breath,
Writhing he fell, extended pale in death.

   Freed from his foe alone the Count remain'd;
Nought else of life the silent mead contain'd;
Around in vain his anxious eyes are thrown,
He sees the mountain and the wall alone
Whose ramparts white, the mead encircling wide,
All access to the flow'ry mount denied.

Cut in the crystal rock, at length, he found
A lofty gate with sculptur'd figures crown'd,
Of rich device and workmanship most rare,
That in the world could nought with it compare.
Thither he came, and entering he survey'd
A story old, with wond'rous art portray'd.
Depicted there the lab'rinth's maze appear'd,
The Minotaur his form terrific rear'd,
There Ariadne bloom'd in beauty's pride,
While Theseus stood attentive at her side
As to his hands she gave the guiding clue,
And taught the means the monster to subdue.
With gold and pearls the rich mosaic shin'd,
And ev'ry gem its various hues combin'd;
There flam'd the topaz, glow'd the ruby's red,
Its prismy rays the lucid diamond shed,
The mimic sky with azure sapphires beam'd,
And in the verdure bright the emerald gleam'd.
  But little heed to this Orlando paid,
As small account of works of art he made;
The gate he left and downward held his way,
Where thro' the hollow'd rock a passage lay—

THE ADVENTURE

Along the dreary grotto's deep descent,
Four miles or more, a road obscure he went.
At length, the outlet reach'd, a flood of light
At once in splendor burst upon his sight,
Bright as the mid-day sun the radiance glow'd,
And fair each object round illumin'd show'd.
A river near him roll'd its lucid tide—
Beyond the stream a plain extended wide,
With pearls all cover'd and with jewels gay,
That o'er it heap'd in vast profusion lay.
Less num'rous shine the stars in winter bright,
When purest azure decks the vault of night;
With fainter hues, in number less, the flow'rs
That spring, with lavish hand, o'er nature pours.
This plain Morgana's secret treasure held,
Her countless wealth the fairy here conceal'd,
She who with partial hand her gifts bestows,
Riches to these and poverty to those.
Amidst th' innumerous gems a wond'rous stone
Far o'er the rest in dazzling lustre shone,
A flame of fire it seem'd—from this the light
Beam'd wide around in noon-day splendor bright.

A narrow bridge the stream extended o'er,
Which twenty paces stretch'd from shore to shore;
Fix'd at the farther end an image stood
Whose iron-frame a man in armour shew'd.
As near Orlando drew, the pass to try,
The image rais'd his pond'rous club on high—
Arm'd with his sword advanc'd th' intrepid knight,
But as the bridge he reach'd, with furious might
The figure dash'd his club—to atoms broke
The slender structure fell beneath the stroke.
Fix'd to the ground, the knight in wonder stood,
When, strange to tell, slow-rising from the flood,
In the same spot another bridge appear'd,
And o'er the wave its magic structure rear'd:
Again he fearless tries the pass to gain,
Again th' attempt the image renders vain.
Thus frequent foil'd, impatient of delay,
Since here no hope he sees to force his way,
He desp'rate ran, and, as with wings supply'd,
Arm'd as he was leap'd lightly o'er the tide.

When now the plain he reach'd, in bright display
Where the rich fairy's boundless treasures lay,

He saw what seem'd a king,—a figure crown'd,
Seated in state, with numbers standing round,
Form'd all of gold, and o'er them thickly strown
Pearls, rubies, diamonds intermingled shone.
All seem'd in high respect the king to hold;
Before him richly wrought in colour'd gold,
A table spread with costliest meats was plac'd,
Of rare procurance and of daintiest taste;
But from above, suspended by a thread,
A pointed sword hung threat'ning o'er his head,
And on his left stood one with bended bow,
As at the ford expectant of the doe.
Near on the right a second held his place,
Alike in form, in stature and in face;
Who in his hand an open scroll display'd,
Which bore these words, in letters fair portray'd:
' Small is the worth of riches and of state
On whose possession fear and peril wait;
And what of joy can silken pomp afford
When dire suspicion haunts its gloomy lord?'
Wretched appear'd the king, his jealous eye
E'er seem'd to dread some treason lurking nigh.

Of richest workmanship, before him placed,
A lily wrought in gold the table graced,
From whose proud top a bright translucent stone,
A carbuncle of wond'rous beauty shone.
Large was the place and square of form, the ground
With flint was paved, of flint the wall around.
Four roads adverse from this inclosure led,
O'er each of which a splendid gate was spread,
No opening else the massy wall contain'd,
Nor from without the light admittance gain'd,
The carbuncle alone with splendent ray
Pour'd wide around the noontide blaze of day.

 Not long admiring here Orlando stood,
But to a portal near his way pursued.
Dark was the entrance, not a ray of light
Pierc'd the thick vapours of surrounding night;
In vain to grope his way the warrior tried,
The dark obstructed road all pass denied—
Again he back return'd, and sought around
If other outlet might from thence be found,
In vain in eager search around he goes,
Dark and more dark each gloomy passage shows:

THE ADVENTURE

Awhile suspensive stood the knight, nor knew
What measures to adopt, what course pursue,
At length to thought recurr'd the precious stone
That like enkindled fire bright-blazing shone.
To take it he advanced—as near he drew
From the bent bow the ready arrow flew,
Struck from the lily's top the ruddy light,
And left the Count involv'd in hopeless night:
An earthquake shook the place, with fearful sound
Deep-groan'd on every side the rock around,
But he, whose courage danger never quell'd,
Unmov'd remain'd and firm his footing held.
At length the earthquake ceas'd, again the light
Diffus'd new lustre from the lily's height,
To seize the gem again Orlando tries,
Again the golden shaft unerring flies,
A direr earthquake heaves the trembling ground,
And deeper darkness spreads its glooms around.
Once more the darkness fled, the stone once more
Resum'd its place—still brighter than before.
The knight who now perceiv'd th' attempt was vain
If still as erst pursued, the gem to gain,

OF THE LAKE.

His buckler took and wide before it spread—
From the bent bow his shaft the archer sped,
But vain the shaft its course unerring held
The covering shield its feeble stroke repell'd.
Without obstruction then the stone he took,
And by its guiding light the place forsook.

But as the Count by chance directed went,
Not to the right hand gate his course he bent,
Which upwards by a smooth and easy way
Had soon conducted to the light of day,
But where the left a downward passage shew'd,
'Mid more than stygian gloom, the road pursu'd
On to th' impervious prison, where confined,
Full many a knight and damsel hopeless pined:
Where Dudon, where Rinaldo pensive stray'd,
With Brandimarte since them a prisoner made,
Whom there Morgana lured by artful wiles,
With love pretended and fallacious smiles.
Down a long marble stairway's deep descent
A mile of strange and crooked road he went,
So twisted, so obscure, that ne'er the knight
Had thence his way explored without the light,

THE ADVENTURE

But 'midst its windings lost and midnight gloom,
In endless wanderings there had found his tomb.
The bottom reach'd, at distance he descried
What seem'd a fissure in the cavern's side,
Thither, still guided by the friendly ray,
With slow and cautious step he bent his way.
At length a portal he perceiv'd that gave
A joyful outlet from the gloomy cave,
Whose cornice rough, engraved this sentence held.
 ' O thou, whose steps hath fortune here impell'd,
' Know that with ease an entrance thou can'st gain,
' But think not to return—the thought is vain
' Unless you first th' elusive fairy seize,
' More light than air, more changeful than the breeze,
' Who round the mountain, round the meadow green
' Incessant whirls, nor ever fix'd is seen,
' Who bald behind like withered age appears,
' And o'er her forehead fair her tresses wears.'
 The Count, whose mind on other thoughts was bent
But slight attention to th' inscription lent.
The gate he passed and onward held his way
Where fair below a lovely meadow lay,

OF THE LAKE.

Rapt in delight the scene around explores,
And treads the herbage gay with vivid flowers,
For not within the world's encircling bound
A place so passing beauteous could be found.
Serene the air, the sky of purest blue
Exceeded far the sapphire's radiant hue,
Wide stretch'd beneath the flower-enamell'd mead
Of tenderest green a beauteous carpet spread,
Adorn'd with balmy shrubs and blossom'd trees
That threw their perfumes on th' enamour'd breeze,
Whose boughs at once the bursting bud unfold,
Gleam gay with flowers and glow with vegetable gold.
At distance from the gate a wall appear'd,
That cross the mead its glittering rampart rear'd,
And form'd a mirror of transparent stone
From whence the garden bright reflected shone.
  Thither his course th' admiring Count pursued,
When 'midst the mead a fountain fair he view'd;
Enchas'd with precious stones of every kind
Immix'd with costliest pearls the fountain shin'd,
There on the herbage green extended lay
Wrapp'd in soft slumber's folds, th' enchanting
    Fay—

In her bright features and attractive mien
Such winning grace, such loveliness was seen,
As would with pleasure fill the heart of woe,
And give despair with new-born hope to glow;
O'er her fair face a lovely smile was spread,
Slender her well-turn'd limbs and form'd for speed,
No locks behind their graceful length unfold,
But o'er her forehead wave in curling gold,
Thin were her glossy robes of white and red
That still when caught the grasp elusive fled.

In wonder and delight his senses chain'd,
Fix'd to the spot the Paladin remain'd;
As gazing on her with enraptur'd sight
He stands, these words arrest the wond'ring knight,
'Why stand'st thou loitering thus? Ah! seize the
    'prize,
'Seize the bright trait'ress who before thee lies;
'Unless those roving limbs thou dost confine,
'Fatigue and pain and sorrow will be thine.'
Surpris'd he turn'd, and guided by the sound,
Soon reach'd with silent step the crystal mound,
Which near the fountain rose, so clear and bright
No spot it shew'd, nor aught obstructed sight.

When thither come, beyond the rampart clear,
He Dudon sees, a hapless captive there—
Each sees and knows, and at the other's sight
In bitter tears laments each noble knight,
They stretch their arms in vain—th' opposing space
Forbids to meet, forbids the fond embrace.
Meantime, Rinaldo, Brandimarte drew near,
Lock'd arm in arm the valiant chiefs appear:
When them Orlando saw no bounds he kept,
But wildly raved with rage, with sorrow wept.
Their story heard he felt still keener grief,
Since nought of hope he found to yield relief,
The crystal wall three feet in thickness spread,
And high in air arose its glittering head,
Nor human strength or art could aught avail
To force th' inclosure, or its height to scale.
He sees his friends nor yet can aid impart,
He sees them near while torture wrings his heart—
Stung with the thought, by mad'ning rage impell'd,
Prepar'd to strike the wall his sword he held.
When, with one voice—' O stay !' the prisoners
    ' cried,
' O stay ! or ruin sure will us betide—

'For such the spell that should the wall you see
'Defaced or broken in the smallest be,
'With it we sink within the cavern's gloom,
'And find at once our prison and our tomb.'
   A damsel then, who sunk in sorrow seem'd,
Whose pallid features still with beauty beam'd,
Approach'd and said, 'Here all attempts are vain,
'But by one way cans't thou admittance gain,
'Yon splendid gate that only passage shows,
'That bright with diamonds, and with emeralds
      glows.
'But there nor courage, strength, or skill avail,
'There threats are empty, flattery's arts will fail,
'Nought can the gate unclose, the passage free,
'Unless Morgana yield the fatal key—
'But that to gain, with shame, fatigue, and toil,
'Must thou her flight pursue for many a mile,
'That slight compared to this wilt thou esteem
'Thy former toils, and light each suffering deem,
'Thus her to follow o'er the desert wild,
'With certain pain, by treach'rous hope beguil'd.
'But virtue e'er prevails, with that to friend
'Who perseveres will conquer in the end.

' Thou see'st these noble knights, these damsels fair,
' Who captive pine in bonds of pale despair,
' On thy exertions sole depends their fate,
' From thee alone their rescue they await.
' But turn, Sir Knight, no longer here abide,
' As chance the fairy may not thee have spied,
' And to the fount with speed again repair,
' For haply still you'll find Morgana there.'
 To this the impatient warrior nought replied,
But back returning sought the fountain's side.
New risen from sleep he there Morgana found
Who lightly skimm'd the verdant marge around
In graceful dance, the while she sweetly sung,
And on the notes enraptur'd echo hung.
Turns not the leaf so lightly to the wind
As turn'd the fairy, now to earth declin'd
Her eyes she cast, and now to heaven she threw,
While thus her song the charm'd attention drew.
 ' Whoever seeks for wealth, or joy desires,
' Whom pleasure prompts, or proud ambition fires,
' Let him but seize this golden lock of hair
' Which o'er my forehead waves in ringlets fair,

' And I will make him blest, his wishes grant,
' Fulfil each hope, anticipate each want ;
' But when occasion smiles with aspect gay,
' To seize the favor let him not delay,
' For slighted once I never more return,
' But turn my back, and leave the wretch to mourn.'
Thus sung the fairy constant whirling round,
So light that scarce her footsteps press'd the ground;
But when she saw the Count she turn'd and fled,
The fountain quitting and the flowery mead,
And up a rugged mountain took her way,
In which inclos'd a little valley lay ;
Thither, full closely, he her flight pursued,
And reach'd at length a place more wildly rude
Than knows Arabia, or the desert sand
Where hot Zaara's shifting plains expand ;
Rugged with stones, with brambles mantled o'er,
A place so dreary ne'er was seen before.

And now dark grew the sky—in murky clouds,
Still thick'ning fast, the sun his radiance shrouds,
The wind wild rises, loud the tempest roars,
Rain mix'd with hail-stones o'er the desert pours,

Dread bursts the thunder, blue the lightning gleams,
Wide flashes round, or darts in arrowy streams,
Thick spreads the mist o'er mountain and o'er plain,
And heaven appears dissolv'd in floods of rain.
Still grows the tempest—fled the light of day,
Alone the lightning lends its lurid ray,
Rent by the wind the trees uprooted lie,
The beasts affrighted from their coverts fly,
And foxes, doves, the serpent's venom'd brood,
Slain by the storm lie scatter'd o'er the wood;
For no protection, no defence avails,
When dread misfortune's bitter storm assails!

O'er the rough mountain, 'mid the gloomy dells,
Through dangerous ways the Count his course impels,
Where the big torrents foaming down the steep
The banks and rocks in one wide ruin sweep,
While far is heard the crash and echoing groan
Of falling forests by the wind o'erthrown.
Yet little recks he this—but still proceeds,
Nor danger nor fatigue his course impedes,
Still holds the chace resolv'd to take the fay
Or that his life the vain attempt should pay,

But each new step fresh obstacles supplies,
Toil grows on toil, on perils perils rise;
When lo! wild wailing from a cavern came,
Meagre and pale, a lothly-looking dame,
Soil'd were her vestments coarse, of earthy dye,
And in her hand she waved a whip on high,
With which she ceaseless scourg'd herself, and tore
The quiv'ring flesh, and bath'd her sides in gore.
Pitying the knight this meagre form beheld,
And ask'd what cause such conduct strange impell'd.
To whom the hag: ' In me Repentance know,
' Stranger to peace, of every joy the foe—
' Whom fortune shuns I seek, with him I stay,
' Nor quit his couch by night, his side by day;
' And since she thee forsook on yonder mead,
' I thy companion come, by fate decreed
' To haunt thy steps, and while she flies from thee
' Shalt thou be follow'd and be scourg'd by me:
' Nor strength or bravery will avail thee aught,
' Unless with all-enduring patience fraught.'
' Patience,' replied the Count, ' may suit the slave,
' But ill that coward virtue fits the brave:

' Think not to beat me like some losel base,
' And that I'll tamely yield to such disgrace,
' But o'er this dreary desert guide my way,
' And as a friend my wearied footsteps stay.'
   He said, and turn'd abrupt, with quicken'd speed
To chace the fairy who at distance fled,
When the wild form her frantic cry began,
And, with strange gestures, circling round him ran,
And oft with shameful stripes his shoulders beat,
As one condemn'd the penal scourge to meet.
With rage, chagrin and shame Orlando burn'd,
And tow'rds the hag with furious look he turn'd
And threaten'd death—yet answer none she made,
Nor to his threats the least attention paid,
But as he 'gan the fairy to pursue
She wav'd her whip and follow'd him anew;
Still, constant as his shade, where'er he goes
She follows close, and oft repeats her blows.
Enrag'd at length, with iron-clenched fist
He at her face a furious blow addrest,
That stroke he deem'd the hag would sure have sped,
And from her malice him for ever freed,

But wound nor harm receiv'd his wayward foe,
Whose airy form, impassive to the blow,
No more resistance offer'd to the stroke
Than a thin vapour, or a wreath of smoke:
And as he turn'd the weary chace to urge,
Again she beat him with the cutting scourge.
To madness stung, the Count each method tries,
And now his fist and now his heels he plies,
But vain his strength, his skill, his efforts all,
On empty air his idle blows still fall.
Convinc'd, at length, no force of mortal arm
Could work that female fury aught of harm,
Again he hastes the fairy to pursue
Who now had almost vanish'd from his view;
But at his back again, with hideous cries,
Her scorpion lash that fell Megæra plies:
Howe'er so fast he speeds, where'er he wheels,
Still, close, Repentance follows at his heels,
Beats him with bitter stripes, with taunts derides,
With insult mocks and fierce upbraidings chides.

    The Count, tho' madd'ning passions fir'd his breast,
Yet curb'd his ire, his struggling rage represt,

Resolv'd, since fruitless all his efforts were,
Perforce with patience arm'd each ill to bear.
Nor more he turns, nor more the strife renews,
But, with increasing zeal, the fairy swift pursues.
As the fleet greyhound holds the hare in chace,
So seem'd the contest, and so swift the race;
Brambles and shrubs in vain his course oppose,
He rends the brambles, and the shrubs o'erthrows,
Wide scatter'd round the thorns and bushes lay,
And broad behind him op'd a beaten way.

Now keener grows pursuit, more tardy flight,
Still near and nearer draws the ardent knight,
Who deems the prize his own, and thinks with ease
The elusive fairy's lovely form to seize.
Fallacious hope! for e'en when seiz'd the fay
Slips from the disappointed grasp away.
To take her oft with eager hand he prest,
And now her person caught, and now her vest,
But her thin robes, of shining white and red,
As oft as caught his grasp elusive fled
Their subtle texture still his hold deceives,
And in the moment of expectance leaves.

But, as his fortune will'd, amid the chace
As tow'rds the knight she turn'd, with smiling face,
With ready hand, at length, the lock he caught,
The golden lock, so long, so vainly sought.

Hush'd was the storm at once, and chang'd the scene,
Blue shone the sky, the air became serene,
Where the wild mountain rear'd its rugged head
A plain delightful cloth'd in verdure spread,
And late where brambles fill'd the obstructed road,
Now fragrant flowers in vivid beauty glow'd,
The bloodless form her persecutions ceas'd,
And thus, with soften'd mien, the knight address'd.
' Watch well, Sir Knight, that precious lock of gold
' Which fav'ring chance permits thee now to hold,
' And guard the important charge with strictest care,
' Lest Fortune 'scape and leave thee to despair;
' For when this fairy wears her loveliest mien,
' When most subdued she seems and most serene,
' Then dread her flight, nor her false smiles believe,
' Who trusts in her she surely will deceive,
' For on her faith can none dependance have,
' As light as air, unstable as the wave.'

OF THE LAKE.

Thus spoke the form and to the grotto fled,
'Mid whose lone glooms a life recluse she led.
  With threats severe and mild entreaties join'd,
The Count who held the Fairy still confin'd
Of her the key requir'd: When thus she spoke,
With pleasure's semblance false, and smiling look.
' Submiss, Sir Knight, I thy behests attend,
' And to thy wishes yield, thy pleasure bend:
' Those pris'ners all at thy disposal are;
' For one alone, I my request prefer,
' A youth, of royal Monodante the son,
' Whose grace and blooming charms my heart have
     won;
' In him is all my bliss, for him I sue,
' O take him not, or take me with him too ;
' Leave me that youth, Sir Knight, I thee request
' By that high valour that inspires thy breast,
' And by thy god, nor give me e'er to mourn,
' Reft of my love, from every pleasure torn.'
The Count replied, ' My word I pledge to thee
' That youth to leave if thou wilt give the key,

'But thee I will not loose, as much I fear
'That o'er that rough and desert road, I ne'er
'My way shall find; then let us be agreed—
'With me shalt thou return ere thou art freed.'
   He said, the Fairy from her glittering vest
Drew forth the fatal key, and thus the Count address'd.
'Undaunted knight! this key of silver take,
'But use with caution lest the lock you break,
'For should that hap thou'lt meet a wretched doom,
'Plung'd in the horrors of the cavern's gloom,
'And with thee all the knights imprison'd there
'Sunk in th' abyss the same sad fate will share;
'Not worlds can save thee, nor my art can show
'The means of rescue from that gulph of woe!'
From this the knight the ready inference drew,
That rarely found are those, in number few,
Who know the gifts of fortune to enjoy,
And can with skill her silver key employ.
   Now tow'rds the garden, through the meadow gay,
The Count proceeded with the beauteous Fay,
Still closely held, and o'er a flow'ry road
The portal reach'd that bright with diamonds glow'd.

There, by discretion taught, with ready skill
He turn'd the key obedient to his will
Through each intricate ward, the bolts unclose,
And open flies the gate and free the passage shows.

The knights and damsels from confinement freed
Rush joyful forth and throng the verdant mead;
Each to the Count his grateful tribute paid,
And thank'd his God for such unlook'd for aid.
All issued thence with joy and mirthful cheer,
Him saving whom the fairy held so dear,
That youth Ziliantes call'd, so passing fair
That shone his beauty far beyond compare.
Weeping, alone within the gate he staid,
And curs'd his cruel fate, and loud lamentings made.
The Count with sorrow saw a youth so fair
Thus plung'd in grief, a prey to wild despair;
But tho' he pitied much his hopeless woe,
Yet would he not his plighted word forego.

And now the captive band, from durance freed,
Led by Orlando to the gate proceed
That form'd the entrance to the gloomy way,
Amid whose winding vaults their passage lay.

Thither they enter'd all, and up its flight
Of marble steps soon reach'd the cavern's height,
And issuing thence the paved area gain'd,
Whose bounds the Fairy's wealth immense contain'd,
The figur'd king and those who 'round him stood,
All form'd of gold, with pearls and rubies strew'd.

   The prisoners much these forms, admiring, ey'd,
And heaps of jewels spread on every side,
But fearful of some trick, or magic snare,
Not one adventur'd aught to handle there.
Rinaldo sole, whom no such fears alarm'd
Whose eager eye those heaps of wealth had charm'd,
Seiz'd a large seat of gold, of pond'rous weight,
And with it loaded, hasten'd towards the gate.
The Count, who saw him thus, advis'd in vain
To quit his hold, and let the seat remain,
Nor like some burden'd mule himself to lade.
To whom, keen taunting, thus Rinaldo said:
' I knew a monk who preach'd the sacred word
' And each indulgence censur'd as abhorr'd,
' Who urg'd the crowd through fasting to repent,
' And made his theme the saving grace of lent;

' And on his doctrine had he so improv'd,
' That scarce with toil his load of flesh he mov'd.
' Like that fat friar art thou, who quite content,
' With well-fill'd belly, preach'd in praise of lent,
' His constant subject self-denial made,
' And to roast capon great devotion paid.
' On you the Emperor wealth and rank bestows,
' And each new day some added favour shews.
' Rich cities you possess and castles fair,
' And Count of Brava and of Anglante are;
' While I a wretched fortress scarcely own,
' And Lord of Mount Albano am alone,
' Where oft to bed I supperless should go,
' Did I not seek it in the plain below;
' And when good fortune throws it in my way
' To help myself to aught I'll not delay;
' For this I hold—no scandal e'er proceeds
' From taking booty to supply our needs.
   Conversing thus, at length they reach'd the gate
Which led from thence, when, wond'rous to relate,
A furious wind, forth issuing from the rock,
Amon's brave son with force resistless struck

Full in his breast, and back in his despite
For twenty paces drove the struggling knight;
The rest th' impetuous wind nor harm'd nor mov'd,
Nor save Rinaldo one its fury prov'd:
But he, undaunted at the strange event,
Leap'd light from earth, and to the portal went,
His prize still bearing, but when reach'd, once more
The wind impell'd him from the fatal door,
And, like a wither'd leaf at distance cast,
Or thistle's down the sport of every blast.
Much were the rest alarm'd, Orlando most,
Who deem'd the knight would rue it to his cost,
And greatly fear'd he there would meet his fate,
And death instead of gold his rash adventure wait.

Rinaldo wondering saw, with anger wild,
His wishes frustrate and himself thus foil'd,
Yet still with strange desire the seat he ey'd,
And firm resolv'd, whatever might betide,
From thence the golden prize away to bear,
Nor will remonstrance heed, intreaty hear.

But since he well perceiv'd th' attempt was vain,
When loaded with the seat the pass to gain,
He rais'd it high in air, and round him whirl'd,
With matchless force against the opening hurl'd.
The stone not swifter issues from the sling,
Or feathery arrow from the sounding string,
Than by the vigour of that arm impell'd,
The pond'rous seat its course impetuous held;
But, by the blast repell'd the massy weight
Recoil'd in thunder from th' impervious gate.

Around Rinaldo press'd the anxious train,
And with intreaties urg'd him to abstain
From farther proof, since vain his efforts were,
But with them quit and leave th' enchantment there.
Urg'd by his friends, convinc'd, at length, that ne'er
He thence the spell-protected gold could bear,
With much reluctance left the knight behind
The prize regretted and his comrades join'd.
Thence went they all, and forth their way pursued,
For miles ascending o'er a rugged road,

And faint and weary reach'd the mead at length,
Where late that robber of unequall'd strength
Held his dread won, and glorying in his might,
On high had plac'd the armour of each knight,
From thence all took their own without delay,
And straight departed each one on his way.

THE END.

NOTES.

NOTES.

(1) '*DESTROYED the garden of Orgagna's queen.*'—Orlando, after having slain Agrican, king of Tartary, left Albracca, at the request of his mistress Angelica, in order to destroy the enchanted garden of Falerina, queen of Orgagna. On his way thither he released a damsel, who was suspended by her hair to a pine tree, by fighting with and overcoming a knight, who guarded her. This damsel, whose name was Origilla, soon after took an opportunity of requiting this service, by stealing his horse, Brigliadoro. He then continued his journey on foot; and having arrived in the kingdom of Orgagna, saw a large croud of people armed, some on horseback and others on foot, who had with them, as prisoners, two knights and a lady, whom they were conducting to the garden for the prey of the dragon who guarded the gate. Orlando, having attacked the guards, slain most of them, and dispersed the rest, released the prisoners, who proved to be his nephews, Gryphon and Aquilante, and the lady the one who had so treacherously deprived him of his horse, which she then rode. By her artifice and pretended sorrow, however, she soon

obtained the forgiveness of the easy Count, who having mounted his horse, took her up behind him and pursued his way towards the gate of the garden, in company with the brothers; but conceiving a jealousy of Gryphon, from his attention to the damsel, of whom he had himself become foolishly enamoured, he rudely ordered them to depart. After this he alighted, and seating himself on the grass with Origilla, near the wall of the garden, began to declare his passion to her. He had not been long in this place, when a lady seated on a white palfrey came up, and thus addressed him. Wretched man! What misfortune has brought thee hither! Dost thou not know that this is the garden of Orgagna, and that thou art within two miles of the gate? And while thus exposed to certain destruction, thou dost idly trifle and loiter here. The Count politely thanked her for the interest she appeared to take in his welfare, but informed her that it was his intention to go into the garden, and that if she could give him any aid or counsel in the undertaking, he should ever consider himself indebted to her. The lady then informed him that the garden was the work of a celebrated enchantress, who had a palace in it to which she occasionally retired, where she employed herself in framing a magic sword for the purpose of killing a celebrated knight in the west, called Orlando, who was said to be invulnerable, and whom the enchantress had discovered by her art was destined to destroy her garden; that she was at that time there, having repaired thither the preceding day; but that in order to obtain admission, it was requisite to continue chaste for three days, and that only at sunrise could he enter the garden. She then gave him a little book, which she informed him contained a complete description of the place, which it would be necessary for him to consult whenever any difficulty should occur.

The lady then departed; and Orlando being obliged to wait until morning before he could undertake the adventure, laid himself down on the grass and fell asleep. Origilla profited of this opportunity to effect her escape, in order to rejoin Gryphon, for whom she had conceived a violent passion, and taking Durindana, the celebrated sword of the knight, she mounted Brigliadoro and rode off with the utmost speed.

Orlando, when he awoke in the morning, finding himself a second time deceived, was extremely mortified; but what more particularly embarrassed him at this time was the loss of his sword. As he was resolved, however, not to relinquish the adventure, he broke a large bough from an elm, and stripping it of its leaves and branches, formed it into a club, and with this weapon proceeded towards the gate. The sun was just rising as he reached the gate, which fronted the east; at that moment it flew open, and the dreadful dragon who guarded it, shook his wings, lashed his tail and hissed aloud. The knight, however, undauntedly approached, and, as the monster extended his jaws to swallow him, gave him a violent stroke upon the head. This only served to increase his fury, but the champion still continued to ply him with blows and, leaping upon his back finally broke his skull with the massy club.

The dragon being slain, the gate shut of itself, the wall of the garden closed so that no aperture could be perceived, and the knight found himself completely a prisoner. In looking around he discovered a fountain to which he repaired to refresh himself, and cleanse his hands and face from the blood and dust. On approaching it he perceived a figure of a man in marble, from whose breast the stream issued and formed a rivulet of cool and transparent water, bordered with flowers and herbage; a beautiful little tree stood on each side of the fountain, in the midst of the fresh verdure which surrounded it, and the image bore this inscription on its forehead, ' *By this river is the road to the beautiful palace of the garden.*' Thus directed, the knight resolved to follow the course of the river; as he proceeded he was filled with surprize and delight at the singular beauty of the place.

> May's genial hand had o'er the lovely scene
> Her richest mantle thrown of emerald green.
> Flowers of a thousand tints the ground o'erspread,
> And thro' the air refreshing fragrance shed.
> Here plains delicious meet his ravish'd eyes,
> There verdant knolls, in gentle swell arise,
> Where groves of pine and balmy fir displayed
> A beauteous prospect and delightful shade,

Mid whose green boughs the birds, in wanton play,
Delighted sport, or trill the am'rous lay:
Beneath their umbrage herds of deer are seen,
Some stretch'd at ease, some feeding on the green;
While midst them kids in sportive gambols bound,
And timid hares range fearlessly around.

He at length came to the palace which was situated on the side of a little green eminence, and of most wonderful architecture, the walls being entirely covered with plates of gold, enamelled with various colours, and the door, which was very large, thickly studded with rubies and diamonds. The knight on entering perceived a lady dressed in white who held a highly polished sword in her hand, in which, as in a mirror, she was viewing herself. When she perceived Orlando, she fled with precipitation; but the knight pursued and overtook her in the meadow, and having taken the sword from her, threatened to put her to death unless she would instruct him how to quit the garden. But his threats were of no avail, she would not even deign to reply. He tried the effect of soothing words and of flattery, to as little purpose; she obstinately persisted in her silence, and appeared to take pleasure in his embarrassment. Finding, that neither persuasion nor menace would succeed, he led her to a beach tree that was near, and there bound her fast with long and flexible branches of elm: at length recollecting the book which the lady had given him, he drew it from his bosom, and examining it, discovered that the first step requisite for him to take was to proceed to a gate which opened towards the south, and which was guarded by a furious bull who was armed with one horn of iron and another of fire, whose strokes no armour could resist; but that it was necessary for him before arriving there, to pass by a very dangerous lake.

He then left the lady bound to the tree, and, pursuing the directions of the book, filled his ears and helmet with roses, so as to exclude the least sound, and went forward to the lake.

> Small was the lake but deep, beneath whose wave,
> By pleasure lur'd, had numbers found their grave:
> Through the pure crystal of its lucid flood
> Distinct each object at the bottom show'd.
> Soon as the knight approach'd its flow'ry side
> A gentle motion heav'd the placid tide,
> The boiling waters rose with gurgling sound,
> And sparkling bubbles lightly danced around;
> When slow emerging from the wave was seen
> A beauteous Syren of attractive mien,
> She look'd a damsel fair, but cautious held
> Her monster form beneath the wave conceal'd.
> But when she sang the notes so sweet and clear,
> In rapture struck on each enchanted ear—
> From their green haunts the savage beasts repair,
> And quit their boughs the winged tribes of air—

What numbers flock from grove, from hill and plain,
Charm'd with the music of her melting strain,
But as the shore they reach'd, the spelful sound
In deepest slumber all their senses bound.

Orlando, then pretending to listen, lay down as if asleep, which the Mermaid perceiving, came on shore with an intent to draw him into the lake, but as she came within his reach the knight caught her by her long hair, and dragging her into the meadow, to which she could oppose no resistance but her singing, cut off her head; then unclosing his ears, he stained his helmet, his vest and armour completely with her blood. Having done this, he repaired, as directed, to the Southern Gate; as he approached it, the wall of flint stone which formed the barrier of the garden disparted, and a brazen gate flew open from which rushed the bull roaring fearfully, and wildly tossing his head, armed with horns of fire and of iron, and such was the strength and keenness of the latter, that it would pierce the best tempered armour. Orlando leaped aside, and aiming a blow at his head fortunately struck the iron horn and severed it at the root. But notwithstanding this loss, the bull attacked him with so much fury with his horn of fire, that he could scarcely keep his feet, and so dreadful was the flame that the Count would inevitably have been consumed by it, had he not have been preserved by the blood of the Mermaid, which was the only charm capable of resisting its violence. After an obstinate conflict he at length succeeded

H

in killing the bull, when the earth opened and swallowed up the body, and the gate which till then was open, suddenly closed, and the wall resumed its former appearance.

Again the knight found himself inclosed, but consulting the book, he discovered another gate which opened towards the West, and was under the guard of an ass, a most singular animal. On his way towards this gate he perceived at a distance a very large and lofty tree; having examined the book, he unbound his shield from his arm, and fastening it upon his helmet, directed his course towards the tree, keeping his eyes constantly fixed upon the ground. As he came near, a large bird flew from among the branches with a rustling noise, and assailed the Count; this bird whose plumage was of a golden colour, had the face of a woman, with long flaxen hair, and wore a crown upon her head; she was armed with long and sharp talons, which had the hardness of iron, and from her body exuded a liquid, which on touching the eyes instantly produced blindness, and rendered the wretched victim her easy prey; this formidable bird as he approached kept constantly circling around the knight, shrieking dreadfully, and let fall in great quantities that liquid substance, which was like boiling oil; it fell upon his shield and upon his breast, but did no injury to his eyes, which were effectually secured by the projection of his buckler. At last, pretending to be blind, he fell upon the ground and began to grope among the herbage, the bird then descended and seized him with her talons by the corslet, when with a back-stroke, he divided her in twain.

Orlando having slain this monster, replaced his shield upon his arm, and continued his way to the gate, which as he came near it opened of itself.—This gate, as has been said, was guarded by an ass, who was entirely covered with an impenetrable armour of golden scales; his tail, which was long, was sharper than the keenest sword, and could cut in pieces the strongest armour, and his ears were two ells in length, and as flexible as the tail of a serpent. When he perceived the knight, he ran furiously towards him, braying dreadfully, but Orlando, with his sword, against which no enchantment could avail, cut entirely through the scales, and laid bare one of his sides; with his long ears he however caught hold of the champion's shield and wrested it from his arm, when the knight with a stroke of his sword separated them from his head. Upon this the ass turning around, struck the knight, with his sharp tail and hewed his armour to pieces, yet he who was invulnerable, remained unharmed. The next attack of the Count was more successful; he struck the ass upon the hip and cut it entirely through; the monster fell, and began to bray and roar most hideously, while Orlando continuing his blows, at length severed the head from the body. Immediately the head began to whirl swiftly around, the earth shook with violence, and opened, and closed again after having received the body of the ass.

NOTES.

In the mean time, the gate had disappeared, and no vestige of it was to be seen. Orlando, then directed his course towards the North, as the book described an outlet in that quarter by which he might escape ; but it was necessary in the first place, to overcome a monstrous giant, who guarded it, and who was enchanted in such a manner, that if he was slain, two more ferocious and powerful would arise from his blood, and these possessing and communicating the same property, would in like manner proceed to multiply themselves to infinity.

> As to the north the Count pursued his way
> He saw a vale that fair before him lay,
> Thick spread with flowers and level was the ground;
> Th' enchanting spot a lovely fountain crown'd ;
> Near which, in order rang'd, on ev'ry side
> Were tables spread with costliest cates supplied,
> Which wide around delicious odours cast,
> And lur'd the trav'ller to the rich repast,
> In cups of gold the sparkling nectar glow'd,
> And the parch'd lip with strong temptation woo'd.
> Lur'd by the smell, attracted by the sight,
> Though much these dainties charm'd the wond'ring knight
> Yet fearful of some trick, some hidden snare,
> Again the faithful book he cons with care—
> There full display'd, and stripp'd of its disguise,
> Clear shows the fraud to his enlighten'd eyes—
> Beyond the fountain cloth'd with roses red,
> Its verdant boughs a thorny thicket spread,

662

Beneath whose close embow'ring shade conceal'd
A cruel Faun her watchful station held;
Her form uncouth, above a woman show'd,
And fair with beauty's charms resplendent glow'd,
But foul beneath, in many a monstrous fold
Its venom'd train a hideous serpent roll'd—
A chain she held which round the fountain led,
And midst the flowers conceal'd its toils entangling spread.
Ah, wretched he! destruction's fated prey,
Of sense the slave, who thither bends his way!
Beneath those treach'rous viands opes the grave,
And death smiles grimly o'er the gelid wave—
Caught in the mazes of the circling chain,
When once approach'd, t' escape he tries in vain,
And to her bower compell'd, the monster's prize,
Press'd in her stifling grasp in horror dies.

The Count cautiously avoided the fountain, and hastily advanced towards the thicket. The Faun on seeing him approach, attempted to escape, but was soon overtaken and slain by him as she made no resistance. Then continuing his course towards the north, he saw the giant standing on a bridge, which was at a small distance from the gate, armed with a sword. As the knight came up the giant aimed a furious blow at him, but he eluded the stroke and smote him with the enchanted sword, on his right side with such force, that he cut him in twain. The giant fell dead, and his blood flowed in large quantities; the knight now supposed that he should meet with no further obstacles to his departure, but when the blood reached the farther part of the bridge, a large flame instantly kindled around it, and ascending on high soon formed itself into a giant, still larger and more terrible than the first, and soon after another like him appeared, both of whom had the faces of serpents.

Orlando was now much perplexed what course to pursue, but he fearlessly went to the gate, which the giants had barred, and notwithstanding their opposition seized the bar and broke it into pieces. Upon this they both attacked him with their scimetars, but to this he paid little regard. Convinced that he could never succeed in his enterprise by killing them, he resolved to adopt a different plan; he sheathed his sword and ran and seized one of the giants, and lifting him with unequalled strength from the ground, whirled him around and threw him on his back. But while thus employed he was exposed to the blows of the other, leaving him therefore, he ran upon his companion, and laid him in his turn on the ground. But finding this measure ineffectual, and that he could not quit the garden, as the giants constantly opposed themselves to his attempts, he at length pretended to be afraid, and ran into the plain expecting that they would pursue him, but they whom the charm had constituted the keepers of the gate, would not quit the bridge. Finding it fruitless after several attempts to lure them from their station, he, at length, recollected the chain which the Faun had spread around the fountain; thither he went,

NOTES.

and taking it returned with it to the bridge. He then seized one of the giants and threw him to the ground, and bound him with the chain, after which, in like manner, he confined the other.

The giants being bound, nothing further obstructed the departure of Orlando; but at leisure now to reflect, he bethought himself that he should have done but little towards the accomplishment of his engagement, should he depart without destroying the garden. He again consulted the book, and discovered that in the centre of the garden grew a tree, from which if the topmost bough was plucked, the garden would immediately disappear.

Determined to complete the adventure, he returned to the place where he had left Falerina bound to the beech, where she still remained, and proceeding onwards, came to the middle of the garden.

> Just in the midst, the beauteous tree arose,
> Profused with foliage from unnumber'd boughs,
> Distinguish'd o'er the rest, afar ascends
> The bough on which the garden's fate depends,
> Nought could with this in beauteous shew compare,
> High rose the glittering shoot, erect in air,
> Nor from a Scythian bow, with force impell'd,
> E'er to that height, its course an arrow held.
> Small was the trunk, the branches wide were spread,
> Each day the tree its fleeting foliage shed,

While still renew'd the thorny leaves were seen
Each day reviv'd to shine in vernal green,
And 'midst the foliage, beauteous to behold,
Gleam'd the rich boughs with fruit of burnish'd gold.

This fruit was very large and ponderous, and held only by a slender twig, so that if any one approached the tree, the branches were shaken, and he was beat to the ground and crushed beneath the weight of the heavy fruit, which fell on every side. Orlando, who was apprised of the danger, formed for himself a kind of lattice work covering, from the interwoven branches of elm and osier, and covering it with earth and moss, placed it upon his head.— Guarded in this manner, he approached the tree, the fruit of which showered down upon him in such quantities, that he was scarcely able to support himself beneath the weight. When he came up to it with one stroke of his sword he separated the trunk, and the tree fell.

A violent earthquake ensued, the sky was obscured with clouds, thick darkness shut the surrounding scenery from his sight, and amidst the gloom arose a large and resplendent fire. At length the earthquake ceased, the darkness was dissipated, and the sky again became serene: but the wall and the garden had entirely disappeared, nor was there a vestige of the fountain or the palace left. The lady alone was to be seen, still bound to the tree, bitterly lamenting the destruction of her garden.

She no longer persevered in her former obstinate silence, but in a mild voice, thus addressed herself to Orlando.—' Valiant

'knight, I am conscious that I deserve death, shouldst thou now
'inflict that punishment on me, thou wouldst in my fate involve that
'of many valiant knights and damsels who are my prisoners.
'Know then that I contrived this garden, which required the ut-
'most exertion of my skill for seven months, in order to revenge
'myself for the injuries I had received from a knight called Arri-
'antes, and a damsel who is named Origilla : I shall not detain you
'with a relation of their villainy, but shall only observe that nei-
'ther of them have fallen into my hands. Many captives have been
'taken at this garden, but much the greatest number have been
'sent to me from a bridge which I caused to be built over a large
'river, and gave it in keeping to a crafty old man, who allured
'many thither, and such was the device, that whosoever came was
'sure to be taken. He has a number at present in his possession,
'and such is the nature of the spell, that were you to kill me, the
'bridge and tower would disappear, and they would all perish.
'But if you will consent to release me, I solemnly promise
'you that I will set at liberty those prisoners ; and if you cannot
'confide in my word, take me with you, released, or bound as I
'am, and I will free the prisoners and destroy the tower
'and bridge in your presence.——Take then your choice,
'either of destroying them with me, or of permitting them to
'escape.' The Count, who was far from wishing to put her to
death, released her, and desirous to free the prisoners, depart-
ed with her for the bridge.

NOTES.

(2) *The two brave friends and Amon's valiant son.*—Rinaldo having left Albracca, accompanied by Astolpho, and the two friends Iroldo and Prasildo, Saracen knights, whom he had released from the guards of Falerina, on his journey met with a damsel who was weeping bitterly; she implored their aid to preserve her sister from a cruel robber who had seized her, stripped her of her garments, and bound her to a tree, where he whipped her in the most barbarous manner. The knights fired with indignation at this story, followed the damsel, who conducted them to the bridge of the Lake, beyond which, in the meadow, bound to a cypress, she shewed them her unfortunate sister, whom the ruffian still continued to scourge.

Iroldo dismounted the first, and passed the bridge, the wicket being too narrow to admit a horse. When the robber saw him, he quitted the damsel, and taking his iron mace, soon extended him to the ground; after which he took him up, and carrying him to the lake threw him in. Prasildo, who thus saw himself deprived of a friend whom he loved with the sincerest affection, solicited Rinaldo, who had prepared himself for the combat with so much earnestness, to permit him to revenge his friend, that he yielded to his request; but he had no better success than his companion, he was beat to the earth by the robber, and thrown into the lake.

Rinaldo, filled with the sincerest regret for the loss of these affectionate friends, then passed the bridge, and began a furious combat with the robber, the contest was long and arduous; the knight sought in vain to slay his enemy as he was secured from harm by enchanted armour which was impenetrable to his blows; the robber on his side, in vain sought to strike the knight with his ponderous mace, for such was his vigilance and activity, that he constantly eluded his strokes. At last tired of this fruitless contention, he threw his mace at the champion with such just aim that he struck him transversely with the massy weapon, and dashed his shield in pieces. Such was the violence of the blow, that Rinaldo fell, though he soon recovered his feet; but scarcely had he arisen, when the robber rushed upon him, and seizing him round the body, ran with him to the lake, intending to throw him in as he had done the others. Rinaldo however, struggled so forcibly, and held him so fast, that finding that he could not disengage himself from his grasp, he sprung with him into the water. Astolpho, the mournful witness of the fate of his companions then came into the meadow, and after waiting in vain for some time for the reappearance of the robber, and bitterly lamenting the loss of his friend Rinaldo, released the damsel who was bound to the tree, and departed, taking with him Bayardo, the horse of Rinaldo.

(3) Rinaldo, the son of Amon, and cousin of Orlando, was one of the most renowned Paladins of the Court of Charlemagne, and in prowess and wonderful achievements, scarcely inferior to Orlando.

(4) *Suffice to say, a knight who thither came.*—An adventure of Orlando, evidently copied from the stories of Jason and Cadmus In one of Orlando's excursions, a lady, came up to him seated on a palfrey, whose trappings were of silk, she had in her hand a book, and suspended to her neck a horn of most beautiful workmanship, it was white ornamented with gold and coloured enamel and set with precious stones. She informed Orlando that if he was disposed to undertake the achievement of the most brilliant adventure that had ever employed the valour of a knight, he must sound the horn which she had with her three times. The adventure consisted in killing a monstrous dragon, in subduing and yoking two furious bulls, and in ploughing with them a certain quantity of land and sowing it with the dragon's teeth, from which a crop of armed men would arise, and lastly in destroying these enemies.

After much fatigue and hazard, the knight achieved this adventure, when the lady offered to furnish him with the means of taking a white stag, belonging to Morgana, the fairy of riches, which was so fleet as to defy pursuit, and had horns of gold, which he shed and renewed six times each day. But the knight, declined the offer, as he had but little regard for wealth, glory being the idol of his pursuit.

(5) *Though late by love bewildering, led astray.*—This passage alludes to a furious combat between Orlando and Rinaldo, at the siege of Albracca, whither the former had gone as the champion of

NOTES.

Angelica, against Agrican and the other knights who had besieged her. Rinaldo, who after he had drank at the enchanted fountain of Merlin, had conceived the most violent hatred for Angelica, joined himself to her enemies, and fought against her with the bitterest animosity.

After the battle between the two knights, Angelica, apprehensive for the safety of Rinaldo, whom she loved with an ardour equal to his hatred of her, and desirous to free herself of an importunate suitor, persuaded Orlando to undertake the adventure of the garden of Falerina, as above related.

ADDITIONAL NOTES.

" *Where Dudon since an equal fate had found.*"—See page 3, line 1.

One of the Paladins or twelve Peers of Charlemagne. The weapon employed by this redoubtable champion was a heavy mace, which he wielded with so much dexterity and effect, that he from thence obtained the appellation of *Dudon of the mace*.

" *Nor Trivigante, nor Macon here avail.*"—See page 8, line 8.

In the romances of chivalry these names frequently occur. In those writings the Saracens are uniformly confounded with the Pagans, and represented as adoring Macon or Mahound (a corruption of Mahomet) Apollo and Trivigante; the latter rendered by the old English writers Termagaunt, whence the derivation of that word as applied to a shrew. What were the particular character and attributes of this god, it is, I presume, at present difficult to define; but from an extract from an old legend of Guy of Warwick, in Bishop Percy's Reliques of ancient Poetry, it would seem as if the romanceer supposed him the same as Apollo.

" So help me Mahoune of might,
And Termigaunt my god so bright."

As the writers of those times, however, were more distinguished for their abhorrence of Mahometanism, than a knowledge of its tenets, or their classical learning, it was not unusual for them

ADDITIONAL NOTES.

to apply similar attributes to distinct mythological characters, and those which were opposite and discordant to the same deities.

" *With Brandimarte since them a pris'ner made.*"—See p. 19, l. 16.

Brandimarte was the companion and bosom-friend of Orlando, by whom he had been converted to Christianity. The loves of this amiable hero and his wife, the tender and beautiful Flordelisa, form a very interesting part both of the Inamorato and Furioso; and his adventure at the sepulchre of the Fairy is one of the most pleasing stories contained in the former—an abbreviation of which in prose has been given to the public by the author of that elegant poem, the Lay of the last Minstrel, in one of the notes to his learned and interesting work, the Minstrelsy of the Scottish Border. As a happy exemplification of the manner of Berni, of his mixture of the grave and ludicrous, and occasional felicity of expression, the translator offers the following short passage from that story....Having overcome a giant of a very singular form, and a knight, after a long and bloody conflict, he is accosted by a lady, and directed, as the only means of extricating himself from the castle in which he finds himself inclosed, to remove the covering from a marble sepulchre, and to kiss the first object which should present itself. The knight removes the massy stone—a serpent of hideous appearance immediately raises itself in the tomb, and opening its mouth, hisses aloud and shews its formidable fangs. Brandimarte draws back, and claps his hand to his sword, but the lady with a fearful countenance and trembling voice calls to him to desist, assuring him that an attempt to injure the serpent would prove their mutual destruction, and exhorting him to kiss it as the only means of safety. "What! (said the warrior) do you not see how she grins and shews her teeth, which look as if they were formed on purpose to bite off noses, and makes such a hideous step-mother's face at me, that it is enough to frighten one? On the contrary (replied the lady) she invites you with a benignant countenance, approach her, be not afraid nor do as many others have here done, sacrifice your life to your fears. The knight again slowly approached, as this kind of kissing had, in his opinion, very little to recommend it, but as he inclined himself towards the serpent, she appeared so fierce and horrible that his blood was chilled, his face became as cold as a stone, and he thus said to himself. If I am destined to perish here, it may be as well another time as now, but at any rate I am resolved that I will not contribute to it myself. Would I were as sure of going to, heaven, as I am that, should I incline myself a little more, this monster would spring at my face, and catch me by my nose or some other part. I see how it is others have been caught by this same trick; and the lady has given me this counsel in revenge for the death of the knight whom I have slain. Thus saying he began to retire, resolved no more to approach the tomb. The lady perceiving this, was filled with despair, and thus reproached him, " Ah! coward, what wouldst thou do? Why art thou so base of heart? a baseness which will most surely

ADDITIONAL NOTES.

end in thy destruction. O thou of exceeding fear and of little faith, the path of safety is open to thee, but thou believest me not! Animated by this cutting reproach, the knight again returned to the sepulchre, and his fear changing into shame, the hue of the violet became tinged with the colour of the rose. He yet hesitated for a moment, alternately prompted by fear and hope. At length impelled by a desperate courage, he drew near and kissed the serpent; cold to the touch as ice was her mouth, which had before appeared like fire. The serpent immediately began to change, and by degrees assumed the figure of a damsel."

" *From taking booty to supply our needs.*"—See p. 37, l. 18.

This trait is in exact conformity with the character of Rinaldo, as described in the old romances. In the combat between him and Orlando at the siege of Albracca, before noticed, the latter reproaches him with his robberies. And at the burning of Don Quixote's Library, Cervantes makes the curate say, that " Signor Rinaldo de Montalban and his companions were greater thieves than Cacus."

GLOSSARY.

Betide, to befal, to happen to.
Durance, confinement, imprisonment.
Erst, formerly, long since, before.
Fare, to go, to travel, to be in any state good or bad.
Fated, secured by enchantment, or gifted with the property of being invulnerable or impenetrable; or when applied to a weapon, as in the present instance, endued by magic with the power of piercing or cleaving the hardest substances. This word is probably derived from the Italian *Fata*, a Fairy, as in the popular traditions of almost every European nation, the fairies are supposed to have possessed the skill of fabricating armour and weapons of this description, which they were accustomed to bestow upon those champions, who were so fortunate as to obtain their favour. The Scandinavian mythology had also its elves or duergars, a species of being in most respects resembling the fairy, and endued with the same wonderful art of framing charmed swords and impenetrable armour. See the very ingenious dissertation of Walter Scott, Esq. on the fairies of popular superstition, prefixed to the tale of Tamlin, in the second volume of Border Minstrelsy.

GLOSSARY.

Faun, in its common acceptation, a sylvan deity, one of the attendants of Pan. For what reason the author has given this appellation to this monster, who seems to have been the prototype of Milton's Sin, it is somewhat difficult to determine.

Fay (from the French, *Fee*) a Fairy.

Guise, manner, external appearance.

Lore, learning, doctrine, instruction.

Lothly, loathsome.

Losel, a worthless fellow, a vagabond.

Passing, exceeding, surpassing in point of excellence.

Perforce, of necessity.

Reck to regard, to care for.

Submiss, humbly, with submission.

Spoil, to despoil, to strip, to plunder.

Trenchant, sharp, cutting.

Won, habitation, place of accustomed resort.

A POEM;

SACRED TO THE MEMORY

GEORGE WASHINGTON,

LATE PRESIDENT OF THE UNITED STATES, AND COM-
MANDER IN CHIEF OF THE ARMIES OF THE
UNITED STATES.

Adapted to the 22d of Feb. 1800.

By RICHARD ALSOP.

" ——— borne to distant lands thy deeds sublime
Shall brighten as they mark the page of time,
And ages yet unborn, with glad acclaim,
Pronounce a WASHINGTON's illustrious name."

CHARMS OF FANCY.

HARTFORD:

PRINTED BY HUDSON AND GOODWIN.

1800.

679

TO

Mrs. MARTHA WASHINGTON;

AS A SMALL TRIBUTE OF ESTEEM TO HER VIRTUES,

AND

A TESTIMONY OF INDIVIDUAL SYMPATHY IN HER AFFLICTION AND THE PUBLIC MISFORTUNE,

THE FOLLOWING

POEM

IS RESPECTFULLY INSCRIBED,

BY

HER DEVOTED

AND

OBEDIENT SERVANT,

RICHARD ALSOP.

A POEM.

Why on this day when erst, in smiles array'd,
Each cheerful mien the signs of joy display'd;
When the gay pomp of military show
With sprightly ardour gave each breast to glow;
When the scarr'd veteran, fill'd with honest pride,
Resum'd his war-worn garb, and martial stride;
When feeble age rekindling vigour knew,
And sportive childhood still more frolic grew;
With added charms when beauty smil'd serene,
Prepar'd to grace the festive birth-night scene?
Why o'er the city spreads this death-like gloom?
Why round display'd the insignia of the tomb?
Why sounds yon passing knell in accents slow,
And strings each heart in unison of woe?
Why o'er those martial bands gay standards wave
In mournful pomp the colours of the grave?
Why droops yon veteran soldier's hoary head,
His honest pride, his wonted ardour fled?

Why heaves the breast of Age that tort'ring sigh?
Why mark'd with gloom is Childhood's frolic eye?
Why does the fair absorb'd in grief appear,
As down her cheek slow steals the unbidden tear?

Has that dire fiend, who holds unseen his way
In midnight's shades, or midst the glare of day,
Again resum'd his wasteful fell career,
Arm'd with new wrath with terrors more severe?
Does each amid the gen'ral suff'ring mourn
A friend or father from his bosom torn?
Does age lament his sole surviving stay,
Or childhood weep a parent snatch'd away?
Do floods of grief the cheek of beauty lave
To mark a father's or a lover's grave?
Ah, no! the Pestilence' malignant breath
Wastes not our cities with the blast of death,
In icy chains the noxious fiend is bound,
And purest gales salubrious breathe around.
These marks of woe no private loss the cause,
No private grief the tear from millions draws,
But all a guardian, friend and sire deplore;
The great, the immortal WASHINGTON's no more.
One sign of mourning o'er the land is spread,
Columbia weeps her guardian genius fled,
While from her children bursts one general moan—
' Our friend, our father, our protector's gone.'
Hence this revolving day which gave him birth,
Erst mark'd with joy and consecrate to mirth,

At this sad period gives our tears to flow,
And wakes anew the bitterness of woe.

   Illustrious shade! the muse would fain essay
Her humble tribute to thy worth to pay,
With trembling hand amid thy laurels twine
A wreath of roses round thy hallow'd shrine;
Fain would her lyre to notes sublimer raise,
To sing thy virtues and record thy praise;
Yet midst thy various worth, thy talents rare,
The brilliant deeds that mark thy great career,
Where shall she fix? amidst that field of light
The splendid how select when all is bright?

   Now, fancy-borne, mid vales enshrin'd in woods,
Where Mononghela roll'd its winding floods,
She sees thy morning sun's auspicious ray
Unfold the promise of the brightest day;
When calm midst scenes of death, from slaughter's hand
Thou sav'dst the relics of the British band,
While veteran bosoms shook with panic dread,
Their general slain, all hope of safety fled,
Sure of their prey grim-smil'd the painted brood,
And yells of triumph echoed through the wood.

   When stern Oppression o'er Columbia's plains
In pride exulting shook her ready chains,
Secure of conquest, and from realms afar
Sent forth the fiends of ravage and of war;

On thee thy country turn'd an eye of hope,
In thee she saw her shield, her firmest prop,
Gave thee her raw untutor'd bands to guide,
Yet new to scenes of blood, in arms untried,
To oppose a host inur'd to war's alarms,
In slaughter nurtur'd, and unmatch'd in arms;
And soon thy genius gave that host to mourn
Its pride neglectful and its haughty scorn.

Foil'd on Bostonia's heights, the foe again
With crouded navies shade the western main;
With British legions join'd, a numerous throng,
Of uncouth semblance and of barb'rous tongue,
Germania sends;—the wide-extended host
Fills with the gleam of arms Manhattan's coast.
In vain Columbia's sons attempt the field,
By numbers press'd her gallant squadrons yield,
O'er heaps of slain insatiate carnage strides,
And cold dismay o'er every heart presides.
The foe exulting, of his victory vain,
Already sees in bonds the captiv'd train,
And waits but morn to seal Columbia's doom,
And shroud her freedom in eternal gloom.

What pangs, great Chief, thy bosom must have wrung!
What cares on that portentous hour have hung;
Yet still unruffled thy capacious mind
Its arduous plans delib'rately combin'd.

Led by thy care, amid the shades of night,
The troops in solemn silence speed their flight;
No sounds tumultuous their retreat betray,
Or crowds confus'dly press'd obstruct the way,
But Order reigns : while, sav'd from ruin's hand,
Beyond all hope they reach the adverse strand.

When morning came the baffled foe beheld
With deep surprize the wide-deserted field,
His cares eluded, and the prostrate prey
Torn, as by magic, from his grasp away.
But still of conquest sure, with greedy eye
He marks the period of subjection nigh;
He sees 'gainst myriads fir'd with martial pride,
With every means t' insure success supplied,
Of ill-appointed troops, a scanty band,
And terror wild pervade the hopeless land.
Yet with that scanty band, too weak to oppose
In open field the numbers of its foes,
In partial conflict oft thou dar'dst their force,
And check'd the conqueror in his wasteful course :
Till thy keen eye the eventful moment view'd
On which thy country's fate suspended stood;
As o'er Cesarea's plains, by riot led,
The foe in scornful negligence were spread.
Tho' deepest glooms the face of night deform,
And howls the spirit of the wintry storm,
Tho' mounds of floating ice their passage stay,
And snow and hail obstruct the slipp'ry way,

B

Cheer'd by thy voice the ardent bands proceed,
Nor know fatigue, nor cold nor danger heed.
While morn beheld on Trenton's blood-ftain'd field,
The war-tried veterans of Germania yield.

Scarce could the wondrous tale belief obtain,
E'en fanguine fancy fear'd to find it vain.
Soon fpreads the welcome news from fhore to fhore,
Hope's funken eye is mark'd with fmiles once more,
Again, of new-born confidence poffeft,
Each feels frefh ardour kindling in his breaft.

Yet midft the brilliant deeds which rais'd thy name,
And fpread o'er diftant climes thy martial fame,
On every fide thou faw'ft new perils prefs,
New fcenes of trouble rife and dire diftrefs.
Scarce in the field a few brave troops remain'd,
Fir'd by thy zeal, by gen'rous pride retain'd;
Thofe few unpaid, with want fevere diftrefs'd,
By cold affail'd, by hunger keen opprefs'd;
While, proud in added ftrength, the foe again
Infpir'd with hopes more fanguine fought the plain.
Yet with thofe few thou held'ft his force at bay,
His meafures thwarted, or perplex'd his way,
And kept his cohorts, with defult'rious arms,
Fatigued by watchings, harrafs'd with alarms:
Till Monmouth gave the wond'ring world to admire
Thy Fabian coolnefs join'd with Cæfar's fire.

On that fam'd day, in equal conteſt tried,
Thou met'ſt the flower of Britain's martial pride.
There, when the ſultry ſky, with ſcorching breath,
Join'd with the ſword to ſpeed the work of death,
While faint with toil the ſquadrons droop'd around,
And the ſpent ſoldier ſunk without a wound,
By vet'ran legions urg'd the ranks gave way,
Thy prowefs chang'd the fortune of the day;
Mid walls of ſteel and ſhowers of waſting fire,
Thou led'ſt the charge, and mad'ſt the foe retire:
Who gladly ſeiz'd the welcome veil of night
To ſhroud his terrors, and conceal his flight.

Tho' check'd on northern plains, the foe ſurvey'd
Like painted clouds his dreams of conqueſt fade;
Yet ſtill o'er ſouthern climes his waſteful courſe
He roll'd impetuous, in reſiſtleſs force;
There proudly glorying in his might, he ſtood,
Mid trophied piles, with laurels ſteep'd in blood,
Nor deem'd that ſoon his proſtrate pride muſt mourn
Thoſe blood-ſtain'd laurels from his temples torn;
Till, from his flattering viſions rous'd too late,
He ſees around him ſpread the ſnares of fate,
His ſchemes all fruſtrate;—by thy ſkilful wiles
Himſelf entangled mid deſtruction's toils.
Depriv'd of aid, no ſhew of ſuccour nigh,
Deſperate the fortune of the field to try,
His numbers leſſen'd and of hope bereft,
Nor e'en in flight the means of ſafety left,

He yields his arms, submissive to thy doom,
To captive chains transferr'd the victor's plume.
Thus by thy genius forc'd their arms to yield
The admiring world two mighty hosts beheld,
Elate in confidence and martial pride;
While York-Town's palms with Saratoga's vied.

Their force diminish'd and their ardour fled,
Their bravest chieftain foil'd and captive led,
The astonish'd foe, with consternation fill'd,
Saw their last hope in death-like torpor chill'd,
Their glitt'ring visions sunk, to rise no more;
And wearied gave the fruitless contest o'er.
Returning peace diffus'd her cheering ray,
And raptur'd freedom hail'd the auspicious day.

Lo, the rich prize that urg'd thy efforts gain'd,
Thy hopes fulfill'd, the glorious goal attain'd,
On freedom's base thy country's weal secur'd,
Her claims acknowledg'd and her rights ensur'd,
From war's alarms in quiet calm repos'd,
Thou saw'st the period of thy labours clos'd!
Beheld, with joyful eye, the fav'ring hour
To quit the staff of delegated power;
And while a nation's raptur'd tears display'd
The grateful tribute to thy virtues paid,
Gladly retir'd'st, from scenes of active strife,
To calm enjoyments of domestic life:
Nor would'st accept Columbia's proffer'd meed,
The grateful guerdon to thy toils decreed;

Thy patriot spirit all reward declin'd,
Save that which rises from the approving mind,
That high reward which conscious virtue knows,
The bliss supreme that rectitude bestows.

 Thence by thy country call'd to toils of state,
Of public cares to assume the important weight,
She saw thy fame with added splendors glow,
New beams of glory radiate round thy brow.
—But from the arduous toil, the task severe,
The Muse despairing shrinks in conscious fear;
To trace that brilliant course the hope were vain
Though eagle's pinions should her flight sustain:
For were the eye, with fix'd undazzled sight,
To mark the progress of yon orb of light?
While morning vapours dim its golden rays,
Or fleecy clouds obstruct the noontide blaze,
Tho' each with ease beholds its blunted ray,
And notes its passage mid the realms of day,
Yet when in cloudless splendor pours its beam
No eye can bear the fierce effulgent stream.

 Deeply engrav'd on every breast remain
The great events that mark'd thy civic reign—
Thou found'st Columbia sunk in pale decay,
Lost in disunion, to despair a prey,
Rais'd from that verge of death she soon became,
While added vigour nerv'd her glowing frame,
Reliev'd from penury smil'd her cheerful swains,
And prosperous plenty gladden'd o'er her plains;

While foreign powers that saw, with scornful eye,
Her fancied term of diffolution nigh,
Beneath thy sway, adorn'd with fresher bloom,
Wond'ring beheld her rescued from the tomb.

When o'er pale Europe, fix'd in dread aghast,
War breath'd his dire exterminating blast,
Fell slaughter stalk'd with garments steep'd in gore,
And frown'd the fiend with rage unknown before;
Thy watchful genius, with prudential care,
Preserv'd thy people from the woes of war.
Though guileful France her treacherous lures dis-
 play'd,
Now threats employ'd, now artifice essay'd,
To plunge Columbia in the dire affray,
And o'er her counsels gain pestiferous sway,
And left no dark insidious means untried
From thee, their sire, thy children to divide;
While in the accurs'd attempt base faction join'd
To spread her poisons o'er the public mind,
And fought with gratitude's pretended claim,
And prostitution foul of freedom's name,
To gain the crowd, by semblance false betray'd,
By sounds deceiv'd, its dark designs to aid:
Mid slander's shafts, mid faction's clamours rude,
In calm unruffled dignity thou stood,
Still thy firm course with step unwavering held,
Nor check'd by murmurs, nor by threats repell'd,
But, with fix'd eye, undeviously pursued
The guiding star that mark'd thy country's good;

And gave the baffled Gaul, at length, to know
That freedom's sons are anarchy's worst foe.

 The louring cloud deep-fraught with ruin past,
In calm Columbia settling from the blast,
Her laws, her rights on firmer basis plac'd,
Her arm invigour'd, and her sinews brac'd;
With eager joy to Vernon's much-lov'd seat,
Its shades alluring, and its calm retreat,
Glad thou retird'st, imperial rule declin'd,
Power's splendid robes for vestments plain resign'd:
There, pleas'd o'er scenes of culture to preside,
To illume its science and its labours guide,
Thou saw'st thy presence every bosom cheer,
One glad'ning smile of bliss around appear.
Yet when, anew, thy country claim'd thy aid,
Thou left'st the patriarch joys of Vernon's shade,
From haughty foes her threaten'd rights to shield,
And lead her squadrons in the embattled field.

 Exalted Chief—in thy superior mind
What vast resource, what various talents join'd!
Temper'd with social virtue's milder rays,
There patriot worth diffus'd a purer blaze
Form'd to command respect, esteem inspire,
Midst statesmen grave, or midst the social choir,
With equal skill the sword or pen to wield,
In council great, unequall'd in the field,
Mid glittering courts or rural walks to please,
Polite with grandeur, dignified with ease;

Before the splendors of thy high renown
How fade the glow-worm lustres of a crown,
How sink diminish'd in that radiance lost
The glare of conquest, and of power the boast.
Let Greece her Alexander's deeds proclaim,
Or Cæsar's triumphs gild the Roman name,
Stripp'd of the dazzling glare around them cast,
Shrinks at their crimes humanity aghast;
With equal claim to honour's glorious meed
See Attila his course of havoc lead!
O'er Asia's realms, in one vast ruin hurl'd,
See furious Zingis' bloody flag unfurl'd.
On base far-different from the conqueror's claim
Rests the unsullied column of thy fame;
His on the woes of millions proudly bas'd,
With blood cemented and with tears defac'd;
Thine on a nation's welfare fix'd sublime,
By freedom strengthen'd and rever'd by time.
He, as the Comet, whose portentous light
Spreads baleful splendor o'er the glooms of night,
With chill amazement fills the startled breast,
While storms and earthquakes dire its course attest,
And nature trembles, lest, in chaos hurl'd,
Should sink the tott'ring fabric of the world.
Thou, like the Sun, whose kind propitious ray
Opes the glad morn and lights the fields of day,
Dispels the wintry storm, the chilling rain,
With rich abundance clothes the smiling plain,
Gives all creation to rejoice around,
And life and light extends o'er nature's utmost bound.

Though shone thy life a model bright of praise,
Not less the example bright thy death pourtrays.
When, plung'd in deepest woe, around thy bed,
Each eye was fix'd, despairing sunk each head,
While nature struggled with severest pain,
And scarce could life's last lingering powers retain:
In that dread moment, awfully serene,
No trace of suffering mark'd thy placid mien,
No groan, no murmuring plaint escap'd thy tongue,
No louring shadows on thy brow were hung;
But calm in Christian hope, undamp'd with fear,
Thou saw'st the high reward of virtue near,
On that bright meed in surest trust repos'd,
As thy firm hand thine eyes expiring clos'd,
Pleas'd, to the will of heaven resign'd thy breath,
And smil'd as nature's struggles clos'd in death.

Ill-fated Country—lo, of aid bereft,
Thy spear is broken and thy buckler cleft!
What arm shall now a firm support bestow,
And shield thee harmless from the threat'ning foe;
Who, mid the storm, with fearless hand shall guide
Thy course in safety o'er the troubled tide?
See Faction lift on high his hateful head,
O'er his dark brow unwonted smiles are spread,
His lurid eye malignant triumph glares,
And joy infernal every feature wears!
For now no more that piercing eye he fears,
No more that voice, with terror thrill'd, he hears;

That eye, from whose bright beam he shrunk dismay'd,
And veil'd his treasons in the midnight shade;
That fateful voice which levell'd in the dust
His plots nefarious, and his high-rais'd trust;
For, lo, in slumbers of the grave repos'd,
Hush'd is that voice, that eye in darkness clos'd!

Is't not enough that o'er these fated shores,
In sullen gloom, the fiend of discord lours;
With foreign foes domestic traitors join,
Our weal to barter and our rights resign?
That Pestilence, with wide-destroying hand,
Sweeps in fell triumph o'er the mourning land,
Marks with new victims each returning year,
And gains fresh fury in his dread career;
While dooms his rage unsparing each to mourn
The ties of kindred or affection torn,
And, o'er a friend's or brother's early grave,
The tear to stream, the sigh of anguish heave?
Are all these ills, are all these suff'rings vain;
Could not a nation's doom a respite gain?
But while the cloud, portending ruin, spreads,
And deeper rolls the thunder o'er our heads,
At this dread period must his country's stay,
Torn by the cruel hand of fate away,
Must WASHINGTON to realms of splendor borne,
Thus leave his people guardless and forlorn?—

Unpitying heaven!—But, lo, from opening skies,
What white-rob'd form descending meets my eyes!

Bright beams of glory o'er his temples twine,
And in his eyes celestial lightnings shine.
He speaks ;—in silence all is hush'd around,
And sinks the listning breeze in calm profound.
' Short-sighted mortal ! by what fury driven
' Dar'st thou arraign the high behests of heaven,
' What rashness wild, what madness of despair,
' Prompts thee to doubt the Almighty's guardian
   ' care ?
' Say, dost thou murmur that the harvest's Lord
' The ripen'd ear has in his garner stor'd ?
' Would'st thou complain that, freed from ills of
   ' life,
' From this low vale of sorrow and of strife,
' With honours laden, and in full of time,
' To realms of joy and feats of bliss sublime,
' Great WASHINGTON has wing'd his raptur'd way;
' And walks with angels mid the blaze of day ?
' Learn that the ills you plain are light to those,
' Deep-stamp'd in blood, offending Europe knows.
' Behold, sublime that mighty Angel stand !
' The Book of Fate unfolded in his hand,
' His sun-bright mien dispensing terrors dire,
' A cloud his footstool, and his robes of fire.
' Around, obedient to his high decree,
' Employ'd his ministers of vengeance see,
' O'er guilty realms the wrath of heaven to pour,
' And scourge mankind with ills unknown before !
' Tho' o'er these shores the purple fiend presides,
' And mid the tainted air in triumph rides ;

' O'er eastern regions see yon demon lour,
' Yon hideous fury bath'd in human gore!
' Lo! in her train what lesser fiends appear,
' War, famine, havoc, desolation drear!
' She, the worst monster hell's dark limits know,
' The bane of law, religion's deadliest foe,
' With craft insatiate cruelty combines,
' And fair in freedom's stolen vestments shines;
' While, lur'd by phantom fires and flattering wiles,
' The prey suspectless rushes to her toils,
' Where'er around her with'ring step is seen
' The harvest dies and fades the blasted green,
' Order proscrib'd retires, and, smote with dread,
' Pale Industry conceals his hunted head,
' Religion views his servants stretch'd in blood,
' And hurl'd to earth the altars of his GOD,
' Right sinks before her trampled in the dust,
' And yields the reins to licence and to lust:
' Nor sex nor state can stay her brutal rage,
' The tears of childhood, nor the locks of age;
' Vain beauty pleads;—no shelter from the sword
' To her lov'd spouse the consort's arms afford,
' Stabb'd on the mother's breast the infant dies,
' And spurn'd contemptuous age expiring lies:
' With gloating eyes she feasts on human woes,
' And drinks the blood warm-trickling as it flows.
' Then cease to murmur at the afflicting rod,
' But bow submissive to the will of GOD,
' And taught by others woes, convicted, own
' That mercy e'en in chastening still is shown.

' Freed from the world, refign'd its load of cares,
' Though WASHINGTON the blifs of angels fhares,
' Yet, not unmindful of Columbia's weal,
' Still glows his breaft with love and patriot zeal,
' Her guardian Spirit, ftill with fhielding hand,
' He turns the ftorm that thickens o'er her land,
' With generous pride her ardent youth infpires,
' Directs her ftatefmen and her warriors fires :
' His name, his bright example long fhall prove
' Her bond fecure of union and of love,
' Shall urge her fons to emulate his worth,
' And wake each flumb'ring virtue into birth :
' Adhering firmly to his precepts pure
' To lateft time her freedom fhall endure,
' If not feduc'd, to foreign wiles a prey,
' She madly caft the precious boon away.'—
—Fleets the fair form ; but ftill the voice I hear,
Still its laft accents ftrike upon my ear.
Reprov'd and humbled I my error fee,
And bend in reverence to the high decree.

Ye Youth, Columbia's pride, to whom has heaven
In facred truft her future welfare given;
On whom devolves the high the important charge,
Her rights to guard, her happinefs enlarge;
Fix'd to whofe courfe immutably remains
Her blifs or woe, her liberty or chains !
O let your PATRIOT FATHER's precepts reft
Deep in your hearts indelibly impreft !

Let his example bright your souls inspire,
To virtue kindle and to glory fire;
Teach you the yells of Faction to despise,
Unmasque his arts and strip his thin disguise;
To spurn, with generous pride and mark'd disgrace,
The attempts insidious of a foreign race
To spread their baleful influence o'er your land,
Direct its councils and its strength command,
What means soe'er their end to gain they try,
Or force employ, or artifice apply,
If with the tiger's glare they mark the prey,
Or crafty serpent's subtleties display.
Nor e'er seduc'd let discord's fiends abhorr'd
Tempt you to draw the parricidal sword,
Your country's breast to wound with mortal blow,
And lay the bulwark of her safety low :
But, friends to order, firm, in union'd band,
Around your government collected stand,
That edifice on equal freedom rear'd,
By reason sanction'd, and by truth rever'd.
Let dire disunion, party rage expire,
And one great object all your bosoms fire,
Bid local hate and jealousy subside,
The offspring mean of ignorance and pride ;
And teach the world Columbia's sons alone
One glorious object of contention own,
By virtuous acts, disinterested zeal,
And fond devotion to their country's weal,
With unremitting ardor to pursue
The path that WASHINGTON has op'd to view.

Ere yet the Muse in silence close the strain,
While still her hands the sinking lyre retain,
To thee, RESPECTED MOURNER, would she pay
A solemn tribute in the heart-felt lay,
Awake the strings to sympathetic woe,
And bid the notes of consolation flow.
But who shall venture with presumption rude,
On sorrow's sacred silence to intrude;
May no rash voice disturb that deep repose,
AFFLICTED MOURNER hallow'd be thy woes!

[PUBLISHED ACCORDING TO ACT OF CONGRESS.]

ARISTOCRACY.

An Epic Poem.

———— DE BELLARE SUPERBOS.

PHILADELPHIA:
PRINTED FOR THE EDITOR.
1795.

PREFACE.

AT a time like the prefent, when the Liberties of the People are in danger; when the executive and legiſlative powers have united to denounce the POPULAR SOCIETIES; and when there is great reaſon to fear that the ſupineſs of the friends of Liberty will enable its enemies to accompliſh its deſtruction; it behoves every lover of his country, every advocate for the equal rights of man, to awake from the dream of deluſive ſecurity, and exert every energy of his nature, to enlighten and preſerve his fellow-citizens.

The DEMOCRATIC SOCIETIES have been ſtigmatized with the opprobrious epithets of Anarchiſts and Diſorganizers; they have been loudly rated as wanting in political knowledge, and deſtitute of integrity; and the public has been earneſtly called upon, not to conſider them with the eye of friendlineſs and approbation, but with the determined frown of indignation and contempt.

An enquiry naturally ariſes here—What have theſe people done? Wherefore are we required to ſuſpect or deteſt them? It would be out of place, were I here to enter into a formal juſtification of their principles and conduct; neither do I deſign it. It muſt be left to time, and to the unbiaſſed judgment of future generations, to determine candidly on this great queſtion.

But whether the Democratic Societies have, or have not, been ſucceſsful in the demonſtration; there can be no doubt, in the mind of every intelligent obſerver of the condition of our country, that a dangerous Coalition exiſts (*actively*, if not *formally*) to deſtroy the general influence of the people; or, at leaſt, ſo to modify it, as may be moſt advantageous to the perſonal aggrandiſement of the Coalition.

Thoſe who are beſt acquainted with the hiſtory of theſe States, as well while under the authority and controul of Great Britain, as ſince the acknowledgement of their independence, have not failed to obſerve that this ſpirit of Ariſtocracy has manifeſted itſelf in various ways, and under very various forms, at different times.

PREFACE.

The design of the British Ministry, beyond dispute, was to establish the political and religious supremacy of their country over ours. A plan was undoubtedly in agitation to saddle us with an hereditary nobility; and a sufficient number of *right reverend* bigots was to be distributed among us, who might wield the weapons of opinion in support of that power which gave them being, and maintained them in the enjoyment of its advantages. The revolution disconcerted these measures. But though, for awhile, it prevented any attempts to carry them into execution, it did not destroy that secret longing which had been excited by the artifices of the vile instruments of the mother country.

It might be *dangerous*, and it certainly would be *imprudent*, to develope the secrets of all succeeding attempts. These, fortunately for America, have hitherto failed of success. GOD grant that all future similar designs may be equally ineffectual! The surest means of causing them to be so, is, early to alarm the public mind concerning all men and all motions which appear to aim at the establishment of an undue influence in the hands of any particular description of citizens; and (the Honourable Legislator will pardon me if I misapply his words) " *gibbet them to public* " *detestation.*" This is the more necessary, as it is impossible to determine to what excesses even that assumption of power, which is apparently most innocent, may lead those who exercise it: and, as there is reason to fear, there are those in exalted stations who would gladly sing " the ditty of Republicanism," in derision, at the funeral of LIBERTY.

My enquiries have led me to examine, with more than common attention, the subject of *Policy*, especially the policy of the United States: and this, because it appears evident to me, that, hitherto, our government is only a government of expedients; and that the *great principle*, by which the complicated affairs of this vast continent are to be directed, is not yet discovered. To this end, the most exact scrutiny has been made into the history, manners, circumstances, &c. of this country; and, above all, into the characters and situations of those persons who have at different periods taken the lead in civil, social, military, and political life, throughout the several States. It was in the course of this scrutiny that the following POEM (the first Book of which is now given to the public) fell into my hands.

The Author of this work was, as acknowledged therein, concerned in one of those plots against the liberties of the people, of which I have taken notice; and, I have good reason to believe, more deeply implicated in it than he assumes to be in the Poem. At any rate, he was the confidential friend of the man most active in its promotion. To the furtherance of this scheme, not Americans only, but Foreigners also, were associated; and all their projects were near being carried into effect, by the assistance of a number of Foreign Envoys—*three, in particular*—though but one (probably for poetical reasons) is taken notice of in the Poem. The causes of their failure are exhibited at large in the work itself.

The Author submitted in silence to the demolition of his hopes; and solaced himself by composing this Poem at his country-seat, whither he had retired, and where he died a few years since,— with the reputation of a great Patriot! The manuscript, which probably was never intended for publication, at length passed into my hands. Hitherto I have kept it (even from the knowledge of my most intimate friends), together with copies in his own handwriting of a few of the Author's original letters, as a precious evidence of the factious designs of certain aspiring characters in our country; and nothing but our present alarming situation could have induced me to make it public, while so many of the personages commemorated in it are yet alive. But the lust of power, when once excited, however it may be repressed for a time, can never be extinguished but with life. And when I see the same spirit, which has been so often subdued, again starting into action —and my countrymen again likely to become its victims—I should be wanting in that patriotism by which I profess ever to be guided, were I to be deterred by fear of *any man*, however exalted in station, from making every possible exertion in their behalf.

The publication of this Poem, at this time, appeared to me to promise some advantage to the general cause of Liberty. It may awaken some attention to our present condition; and, by shewing (even under the guise of interested praise) the means which *have been* used to acquire undue consideration and power, teach my fellow-citizens to look warily about them, and see whether like designs are not now forming, and whether they ought not to be on their guard. It may serve to " counteract certain *political here-* " *sies*,"—I repeat it again, " *certain political heresies*—which " have sprung up among us " And it may excite them to a recollection, that ARISTOCRACY has ever imposed itself upon the necks of all former Republics, till, by its increasing weight, it has sunk them in slavery; and rouse into action that energy of Freemen, always superior to the force of Oppression.

PREFACE.

In respect to the literary merit of the Poem, it is probable the opinions of men will differ, as their own prejudices and wishes are exposed or flattered. I shall attempt no vindication of it in a critical point of view. But I ought to exculpate the Author from one charge, to which he may, in the opinions of those who do not read attentively, have exposed himself: I mean that of *self-vilification*.

It is observable that the writer every where represents himself and his friends as influenced solely by *self-interest:* and it may seem improbable that such a confession should proceed from any one who was really so influenced. The following extract of a letter, by the same hand, will determine the Author's own opinion on this question. The letter is written to the friend here celebrated under the name of ARISTUS, and bears date November, 1786.

"Let others think as they please: we, who have such ample experience, have long since discredited the dream of disinterested benevolence. Surely no dispute can be more ridiculous than those which have arisen on this subject, unless it should be those respecting the propriety of employing (what are called) iniquitous means to obtain a good end. Opinions of this sort are well enough to amuse the vulgar; and to be played off on those weak, but well-designing men, who must have Scripture for every thing they do." And, in another letter to the same person, he says—" In the prosecution of this design, I have no doubt of your inflexible adherence to that maxim which has so long been the governing rule of our actions, *That if the* END *is desirable, we are not to hold question respecting the* MEANS. Our motto should be RESPICE FINEM, but not in the sense of the Philosopher."

A more serious objection seems to lie against the machinery of the Poet. Nor do I know of any justification of it, other than by supposing it a mere play of the fancy: for it could not be meant by him to insinuate that the designs of his friend were infernal; and it is certain that the Author regarded Heaven and Hell, Providence and Futurity, equally fabulous as the theology of the Greeks or Hindoos, and alike the property of every dealer in rhyme—to be the elegant decorations of the Epopea, or the ponderous ornaments of the Sonnet.

Here, then, the Editor takes his leave, for the present, of the reader; assuring him, that, if this First Book of 'ARISTOCRACY'

PREFACE.

shall be esteemed of value, the remaining ones shall be presented to him with all convenient expedition. The Editor, indeed, designed at first to have published the entire work: but was deterred from so doing, by a fear lest its size would prevent that general circulation which might be secured by a less immediately expensive mode of publication.

Philadelphia, January 5th, 1795.

N. B. The Notes are by the Editor.

ARISTOCRACY.

BOOK FIRST.

INTRIGUES, and Heroes, whose unequall'd toil
Dar'd Freedom's progress many a year to foil;
For many a year Columbia's realm who bow'd,
Leading, metereous, the deluded crowd:
Illustrious Chiefs! who hop'd aloft to rise,
And shine distinguish'd in the people's eyes;
Themselves alone the helm of state to guide,
Floating triumphant o'er the subject tide:
Illustrious Chiefs! who sought the bliss divine,
In lordly pomp and titled pride to shine;
While, bent beneath their oligarchic sway,
Their native land should tremble and obey;
With those from European shores who came,
Brethren in toil, and partners of their fame:
What counsels led, what various means employ'd;
What foes they conquer'd, what success enjoy'd;
What Fates malign against their aims arose,
And bade, in sad despair, their labours close;
While grief and rev'rence all my soul inspire,
I sing, responsive to the mournful lyre.

Hail, hallow'd Sages! venerated Names!
Of war and peace, ye bright conducting flames!
Columbia's glory, Nature's pride and boast!
Though now deserted, desolate, and lost,
O may your fame o'er Time's dark rage prevail,
And your immortal compeers bid ye hail!
And may this verse, which bears to future days
That fame, receive a portion of your praise!
From one it flows, like you, who scorn'd to feel
Fraternal interest in the common weal;

Like you, who strove distinction proud to gain,
Shar'd in your triumph, and divides your pain.

 Hail, native stream! O ROWA, hail to thee!
Whose sweet wave winding seeks the neighb'ring sea;
Whose flow'ry banks the pastoral city claim,
Which proudly bears the Albion Virgin's name.
How chang'd the times, since, fill'd with youthful fires,
Ambitious thoughts, gay hopes, and warm desires,
With great ARISTUS I was wont to rove
(His earliest friend) through ev'ry skirting grove;
And on thy margin join in frolic play;
Or with the hook delude the finny prey;
Or, plunging in thy waters, joy'd to lave,
And breast with eager strife thy downward wave!
Alas! how little did each youngling mind
(To ev'ry brighter view alike inclin'd)
Foresee the sorrows which, in slumbers mild,
Portentous hung o'er each advancing child!
In all the sky of life, our searching eye
No danger saw, no mis'ry could descry.
Our sun of fame ran on his glorious way,
And blest the nations with his setting ray.
We saw him scatter each contending fire,
To match his radiance that should dare aspire;
Nor sink, till, following his resplendent course,
His phœnix offspring rose with equal force.
Ah! dread deception!—fatal view obscure!
Illusive vision!—medium most impure!—
What clouds burst threat'ning from the frowning north!
What fearful flames, what thunders issue forth!
Wide o'er th' horizon see their volumes roll,
And Night tempestuous hangs o'er either pole.

 Now, bent with grief, with disappointment worn,
I seek thy shore, O ROWA! most forlorn.
While great ARISTUS' lordlier soul obtains
On —— bank some solace of his pains,
By thee, O melancholy Stream! my days
Shall slowly pass; while, catching notes of praise,
Drawn from my mournful, yet resounding lyre,
Thy echoing woods shall loftiest deeds inspire.
Yes, native Stream! by thee the song shall rise,
Which bears thy heroes to the distant skies:
Along thy margin shall ARISTUS' name
Re-echo'd reach its well-deserved fame;

B

And ev'ry Chieftain's, who, with him allied,
Fell in his cause, or struggled at his side.
What though Contempt and foul Derision join
To dim the lustre of their great design;
And Hate and Infamy, united, shed
Their sickly dews on each illustrious head !
What though, like them, by ev'ry ill deprest,
Shame, grief, and anger fill the Poet's breast ?
Yet shall his ardent and immortal lays
To future ages give their wond'rous praise :
And future ages shall exalt the song,
Which dares, in hallow'd strains, their praise prolong;
And ev'ry sage, and ev'ry youth, shall say—
" Such were the men who scorn'd the people's sway."*

   Sinking, the Sun withdraws the lightsome day,
His slant beams trembling on the water play ;
With dazzling lustre all the windows glow
Of yon high dome, which fronts the wave below;
Mild through the ambient wood the splendour streams,
And hills and thickets feel the level beams.
There great ARISTUS, fill'd with anxious cares,
Wanders absorpt, nor aught of pleasure shares.
His nobler mind aspires to nobler state,
And execrates the slow designs of Fate.
Down the slope way his path the hero takes,
And now the darkness of the vale he seeks :
Uneasy thoughts within his bosom rise,
And tears of indignation fill his eyes.
At length, with sorrowing, but resentful tones,
Burst forth, in sad soliloquy, his moans.

   ' What Fates disastrous all our labours thwart,
' The toils of Genius, and th' attempts of Art !
' In vain we strive, in vain our might essay,
' And see each promis'd aid our will obey;
' What strength soe'er, and blest events conjoin,
' Some Power adverse still foils the bold design.
' Fair plans are form'd, immense resources league ;
' Prudence and passion, frankness and intrigue ;

* Our Poet follows the example of Horace, Ovid, and other great men, in prophesying great reputation to himself hereafter. How far this prediction of his may be true, we will not pretend to determine. That which relates to his heroes will be accomplished exactly at the period when the art of printing is forgotten, and the whole world subjected to a new feudal system.

‘ All parts in happiest unison progress;
‘ In ev'ry State we seem to meet success;
‘ The long-sought end within our reach appears;
‘ Secure, we give the idle wind our fears;
‘ Glowing with joy, extend th' expectant hand,
‘ And half secure the boon, the prize command;—
‘ When, unforeseen, some hidden strength prevails,
‘ Our prospects perish, and our project fails.

‘ Is there (which yet I question if there be)
‘ Some Power, exalted over Time and me?
‘ One who, with ev'ry wickedness at war,
‘ Still makes the virtuous his unceasing care;
‘ Supports their souls 'mid danger's fierce alarms,
‘ And guards them safe from sorrows and from harms?
‘ Who gives to Truth the blest reward of joy,
‘ And bids the arts of Vice its peace destroy?
‘ —No!—still be this of vulgar tongues the theme;
‘ Let Priests, and men priest-ridden, hug the dream:
‘ Nature alike her various bounty grants;
‘ With equal care supplies her children's wants,
‘ Whether, of Christian or of Pagan race,
‘ To Christ or Brahma they their tenets trace;
‘ Or whether, following their forefather's path,
‘ They bow to Moses' or Mohammed's faith.
‘ From action, not belief, their good they gain,
‘ And Industry and Art the prize obtain:
‘ Superior power from art superior flows;
‘ He best can govern men, the most who knows.
‘ Such are my thoughts——yet some mysterious power
‘ On all my noblest efforts seems to lour:
‘ Untoward Fate, or all-deciding Chance,
‘ Bids with slow steps my mighty schemes advance;
‘ And though, with Cunning, Industry conspires,
‘ Still damps, with long delay, my glorious fires.

‘ Of late, how vast the prospect rose to view,
‘ When last each chieftain to his post withdrew!
‘ When union'd councils promis'd bright success,
‘ And fav'ring Fortune seem'd to woo and bless!
‘ And now in order meet, and due array,
‘ Art after art commenc'd our bold display;
‘ Month following month new promises arose,
‘ Portentous omens to suspectless foes;
‘ Events unhop'd for came to aid our cause,
‘ And foil, in our behalf, opposing laws.
‘ Yet, ah! when flatt'ring thus our fortunes shone,

' Their splendour lessen'd, from some cause unknown ;
' And faint, and fainter now, alas! they fade,
' While frowning storms our fairest skies invade.
' Yet not entirely were the cause o'erthrown,
' But every chief seems stupified to stone;
' Action, suspended, rests; one listless soul
' Throughout infests the wide and torpid whole:
' Else why, neglected, should events arise,
' Which, ably us'd, might near secure the prize?
' Events, which, moulded by our plastic care,
' Would all our worst disasters well repair.

' But does not *Self* each hero's bosom fire?
' And shall that vital spark, subdu'd, expire?
' Expire, while countless honours live to crown
' Its bold exertions with deserv'd renown?

' Yes, let the rich abjure, the poor despise;
' 'Tis *Self* alone which charms each mortal's eyes.
' By this prest on, we ev'ry danger dare,
' In peace that's hidden, or reveal'd in war.
' Still then shall men, with pride enormous, boast
' Of souls, to all but public welfare lost?
' And though in one dull course they onward move,
' Unsway'd by threaten'd wrath, or proffer'd love,
' The idle farce of Patriotism sustain,
' And bask in all the sunny light of gain?
' Fierce indignation rises in my breast
' When I behold their toils by Fortune blest:
' While we, who vary as each coming day
' In different forms shall public will display—
' And strive, beneath this mask of patriot zeal,
' Our proud aspiring wishes to conceal—
' Or yet, with shew of independent mind,
' Press on, to ev'ry vulgar interest blind,
' Still find the bright reward before us fly,
' And rigid Fate each fond request deny.

' And such must be the curst estate of those
' Whose exaltation from the people flows;
' Who on their fickle voice for power depend;
' Servants to all, yet calling each a friend.

' But O when titled place, and gainful might,
' O'er a whole realm maintain usurped right,
' How blest the man who revels in the joy,
' With strength to make, and vigour to destroy!

' And thanks be thine, O CUNNING! Goddess dear!
' If, though remote, for me such good appear.
' Yes, fond Presumption bids me hope, ere long,
' Aided by thee, to bend the vulgar throng;
' With titled friends, in pomp sublime, to move,
' And hold by Fear what now I gain by Love.
' For though self-interest all my actions sway,
' Nor other motive these my friends obey,
' Yet mutual interest here with pers'nal blends,
' And mutual aid subserves our private ends.
' Each seeks for power, yet each perceives how vain
' Would be the struggle, place or power to gain,
' Without the aid of others to procure,
' Without the aid of others to insure.
' Most fortunate in this my hopes appear;
' Blest be thy name, O CUNNING! Goddess dear!
' Where'er I look, dependents greet my view,
' Pow'rful to serve, to all my wishes true.
' Their friend I seem; I aid their petty suits;
' Yet draw, from all their toils, the noblest fruits:
' Nor most distinguish'd 'mid the mighty whole,
' Yet guide their force, and act the moving soul.

' But why, O why so languid and so slow?
' Why rage they not with action's fiercest glow?
' Now, when events so full of promise rise,
' And clothe in brighter hues our changeful skies?
' Alas! I fear some new-found motives sway
' To other schemes their selfish minds astray;
' Some fairer project leagues with adverse powers
' Those very souls the most engag'd in ours.'

He paus'd, as lost in thought; then, lifting high
His hand, while lightnings flash'd from either eye—

' By ev'ry Power of Hell (if such there are)
' And by my mightier, dearer Self, I swear!
' If once they swerve—from me no after aid
' Shall any gain; but, all their wiles display'd,
' Th' astonish'd people shall their purpose know,
' Though, lost, I sink beneath the whelming woe.'*

* Every literary reader will admire the accuracy and taste with which our author has, in this speech of his hero, imitated the pure models of antiquity, and the most celebrated epic poets of modern ages. The striking turns of thought, and variations of passion, which appear throughout—even the very inconsistencies

Thus, preft with various cares, Aristus ftray'd;
And now his footfteps fought the thicker fhade,
Where deeper darknefs reign'd, with ftillnefs join'd,
Luring to graveft thought the anxious mind.

And now, where central fire and Night profound
In ten-fold horror loweft Hell furround,
'Mid Pandemonium's walls, in awful ftate,
High on a throne exalted, Satan fate.
Around, in order meet, on either hand.
Powers and Dominions, Thrones and Princes ftand :
Afphaltic lamps, with intermitting light,
(A fickly ray !) fhot through encircling Night :
All were attentive :—when, in accents dread,
Shaking the fable horrors of his head,
The fearful filence thus the Monarch broke,
And Hell's unfathom'd caverns fhudder'd as he fpoke :—

' Tartarean Potentates, fubmiffive hear !
' And you, ye tenants of the nether fphere !
' While, not unwilling, now your King unfolds
' The fecret purpofe which his bofom holds.

' Since, fprung from Chaos, felf-fupported ftood
' The earth, and round it roll'd the fubject flood,
' Ye know, O Powers ! with what embitter'd rage,
' 'Gainft man, and his proud Maker, war we wage.
' How vaft our triumphs, ev'ry fiend can tell,
' Who views the fiercely-flaming lakes of hell.
' Difeafe and Death we introduc'd, and made
' Unfeemly forrow Heaven's high courts invade ;
' And, while his angels wept, man's overthrow
' Hung round th' Eternal's throne the gloom of woe;
' And (height of victory ! our glory's crown !)
' Bade on the crofs expire his lov'd, his only Son.

' Nor hence, in faith's and prophecy's defpite,
' Around the globe has e'er declin'd my might.
' Beneath my yoke fee Europe finking low,
' And Afia ftoop, and feeble Afric bow :
' O'er half the weftern world my fway extends,
' And, flowly yielding, now the other bends.
' This to promote, new projects now I frame :
' For this, attention to my voice I claim.

themfelves of Aristus—indicate the moft profound knowledge
of the human heart, as well as a judgment formed according to
the unadulterated rules of the antients.

ARISTOCRACY.

' Wide spread o'er fair Columbia, cloth'd with power,
' And strength obtaining each swift-passing hour,
' What names rever'd, subservient to my sway,
' Rise, and increase with each successive day!

' Long have I seen, with heart-distracting grief,
' That land to all distress'd extend relief;
' Seen sacred order ev'ry boon bestow,
' And drive far distant ev'ry threat'ning foe.
' I fear'd that there, indeed, at length would rise,
' Belov'd of men, and cherish'd by the SKIES,
' A mighty Empire, whose resistless force,
' The world involving in its spreading course,
' Beneath one *plan* would ev'ry State combine,
' The good of man their great, their sole design;
' And hence would flow wealth, liberty, and ease,
' And all earth hail the reign of moral peace.

' But, lo! to Hell more pleasant prospects shine,
' And fair Columbia hastens to be mine.
' Even now, immers'd in dark surrounding shade,
' ARISTUS roams, the spirit and the head.
' His mighty soul now labours to extend
' My spreading sway, himself my dearest friend:
' Rous'd by his arts, through each divided State,
' Obedient to his will, of influence great,
' At whose command the stubborn people move,
' Their power his union'd friends with zeal improve.
' And now, from Europe's shores, th' obedient wind
' Wafts to their aid, of no discordant mind,
' A chosen Chief:——
' Even now his anchors bite the joyful strand,
' And, hark! the people welcome him to land:
' The thund'ring cannon from their ramparts roar,
' And shouts redoubled shake the trembling shore.

' And you, ye Powers! be 't yours with every art
' To gain fresh converts, and fresh aid impart;
' Assistant rumours and deceptions frame,
' And every soul with new-born rage inflame.
' And be ye faithful——for, by Hell I swear,
' What Power soe'er to thwart my will shall dare,

* For an attempt to explain this circumstance, see Preface. The additional lines, descriptive of the joy of the people, firing of cannon, &c. must have existed only in the imagination of the Poet, since nothing of the kind did happen at the time referred to.

' In fiercest league with Heaven's eternal ire
' The quenchless flames of Hades shall conspire
' To whelm the wretch; who, deep in ruin hurl'd,
' Shall prove th' immeasurable wrath of either world.'

He ended threat'ning—and terrific struck
His trined spear against the flaming rock
Whereon his throne uprose. The Powers around
In wild dismay swift vanish'd at the sound:
All Hell with horror shudder'd—while a stream,
To Earth far shot, of pale sulphureous flame,
With momentary ray illum'd the shade
Where, lost in thought, the sad ARISTUS stray'd.
A secret hope quick fill'd his throbbing breast,
And homeward now with eager haste he prest:
For black and stormy Night around him roars,
And ————'s billows thunder on his shores.*

* Before the reader passes on to a future Book, it may be proper to remark,—That the commendations on the execution of this Poem are by no means meant as extended to the sentiments therein expressed. This, the Editor trusts, is sufficiently apparent from his Preface. Such exclamations of admiration as the author forces from us by the charms of his verse, may be passed over, without their being looked upon as any way implicating us in the villainy of the friends of ARISTUS And here it becomes us to give the author all due credit for the sublime use he has made of machinery so common as that of the infernal regions. But while the editor beholds it with wonder, he confesses his inability to explain the difficulty, which is apparent, in endeavouring to account for its particular application in this Poem, and by a professed friend of the heroes celebrated. Perhaps the reader will think some light is thrown upon this dark subject in the succeeding Books.

END OF BOOK FIRST.

ARISTOCRACY.

An EPIC POEM.

—Debellare SUPERBOS.

ADVERTISEMENT.

THE favorable reception which the First Book of ARISTOCRACY has met with from an indulgent Public, encourages the Editor to proceed in the Publication; and, agreeable to his engagement, to present the Second Book to the notice of his Fellow-Citizens. As he expected, various judgments have appeared respecting the Work; but he is happy to observe that all have not misapprehended him. While he acknowledges, with gratitude, his obligations to some, who have been pleased to express themselves favorably of his principles and design, he thinks it his duty to declare that he has been grossly misconceived by others: and he further esteems it incumbent upon him to make known his determination not to be deterred from the exercise of, what he considers, an inalienable right, by the threatened, or actual, interference of any man; how highly soever he may rank in the good opinion of a certain description of Americans.

PHILADELPHIA, *March* 26th, 1795.

ARISTOCRACY.

BOOK SECOND.

WASH'D by the tempest of the gloomy night,
Mild rose the morn, in blushing beauty bright.
Cheerful the hinds awake, from short repose,
Cheerful the city's busy swarms arose.
But, on his couch, to troublous dreams a prey,
In interrupted sleep, Aristus lay.
Vainly he languish'd for refreshing rest—
Unkind deserter of the anxious breast—
And vainly strove in Lethean dews to steep
Th'increasing woes of his perturbed sleep;
When now, from Satan sent, a bolder dream,
On quivering wings, with ampler message came;
And, lightly hovering o'er th'unconscious Sage,
Bade visionary scenes his mind engage.
Aristus saw—when lo! before his eyes,
A stately dome majestic seem'd to rise:
Wide opes the portal, wide the hall expands,
And, full in view, a sumptuous banquet stands.
Around, of various ages, different tongues,
From many doors, rush in the num'rous throngs;
And, with obeisance low, and studied phrase,
Of endless gratitude, and pompous praise,
To one, unknown, aloft, to view display'd,
The gathering crowd their uncouth homage paid.

Astonish'd at a scene so strange, the Chief
Dar'd not withhold, yet scarce could grant belief;
And round him look'd, with anxious doubts opprest—
When thus the Man unknown the Chief addrest.
" Why stands Aristus wrapt in mute suspence?
" Why bears he still his lethargy of sense?
" Rouse thee Aristus! burst thy slothful bands!
" Thy genius asks it, and the time demands.
" Behold, from distant —— ——'s favouring realm,
" I come, in might thy rivals to o'erwhelm.
" By me shall Order's tyrant spells be broke—"
The Vision vanisht, and the Hero 'woke.

As when an army, far from friendly aid,
Retiring, flee the land they dar'd invade;
And, night succeeding night, a short repose,
Prone on his arms, is all the warrior knows;
What time the morning casts a doubtful gleam,
Hear sudden burst the foe's revengeful scream;
The loud drums beat, sonorous trumpets sound;
Rude clash of arms, and horses shake the ground;
Start from deluding sleep, and rush to war—
So, from his couch, Aristus sprang—with fear.
What could the portent mean? In deep amaze,
He turns it in his mind a thousand ways;
Doubt after doubt disturbs his labouring brain;
And all his long conjectures prove in vain.
At length, joy-stricken, and with glad surprize,
" Can it be so?" the enraptur'd Hero cries—
" O if it be, in nature's ample round,
" Blest as Aristus, can there one be found?"

Scarce had he ended, when the door expands,
And in his presence faithful Janus stands.
" O Chief belov'd!" began the duteous slave—
" Your kind attention let your servant crave.

  " A gallant vessel, from the —— —— shore,
" The gale of eve within our harbour bore.
" Strait to the strand our eager townsmen fly,
" And raise to Heaven the loud, rejoicing cry:
" The crew re-echo, and, with agile bound,
" Spring from the lofty sides, and tread the ground.
" Upon the distant deck, of noblest height,
" A man majestic met our wondering sight;
" Who, slow descending, with a splendid train,
" Seem'd proudly pleas'd, our peaceful shore to gain.
" Envoy to us, we learnt, the stranger came:
" Each breast with rapture kindled at his name:
" Loud thundering cannon hail'd him to our shore,
" And shouting thousands to his mansion bore;

" And, on this day, this morn, with coftly care,
" A feaft fraternal for his fake prepare*."
As one, who meets a serpent in his way,
Stands riveted to earth, in pale difmay;
But, flow recovering from his icy dread,
Exclaims in rapture when he finds it dead;
So far'd the Chief: his foul within him died,
So near the vifion with the truth allied†;"
But, when he found his warmeft hopes furpaft,
Afide the apprehenfive gloom he caft;
Bade faithful Janus from the room depart,
And feafted on the rapture of his heart:
Then, iffuing forth, exulting in his thought,
High on his chariot thron'd, the neighbouring city fought.

Meantime, with busy care, and zealous hafte,
The people ftrove to build the rich repaft.
Three days of feafting all the city knew,
Nor on the fourth to homely fare withdrew.
But thou, O Mufe, the tedious tafk forego
To deck, in lofty verfe, the loathfome fhow;
Wafte not thy powers o'er Bacchanalian boards;
Kings be thy theme—Chiefs, Minifters, and Lords.
Yet fay, O fay, when now from crowds retir'd,
Crowds who his perfon gaz'd, his fpeech admir'd,
What thoughts within the Envoy's bofom dwelt,
What hopes he harbour'd, and what wifhes felt.
Silent a while the lonely room he courf'd,
Then, from his lips, thefe accents, joyful, burft.

" O glorious prefage of moft fure fuccefs!
" What aid unlook'd for comes, my caufe to blefs!
" O fortune happier, more refplendent, far,
" Than all the trophies of victorious war!
" The recompence of art, how high, how great!
" Thy art, ——— ———, wife Minifter of State.
" Great was the project, and profound the plan,
" The faireft empire fince the world began,

* Notwithftanding the remarkable coincidence of this relation with the paffage, in the fpeech of SATAN, noticed in the Firft Book, the Editor, (from the difficulty he meets with in attempting to connect thefe circumftances with the arrival of any Foreigner to this country) ftill adheres to his opinion—That they are mere poetical additions to the fact.

† Behold here a new proof of the Poet's profound knowledge of the human heart. ARISTUS, who believes neither in the exiftence of God, or Futurity, this very ARISTUS is terrified by a dream. An accidental refemblance between what paft in fleep, and what took place in reality, fhakes his foul with dread, who fears not to deny an intelligent Creator.—O mad philofophy!

" With rude divifion, in the midft to tear,
" And to ourfelves fecure the nobleft fhare.
" Wonderful thought! but Fate's fevere decree
" Withheld the bleft accomplifhment from thee.
" By thee the deep foundation firm was laid,
" And by thy hands the mighty arches made;
" But I, more glorious in my nation's eyes,
" Shall bid the fuperftructure reach the fkies.
" Thou, luckless Sage! waft fated to contend,
" And find a foe in him fuppos'd thy friend;
" But I, more happy, fee no power oppofe,
" Even thofe I fear'd feem chang'd, to friends, from foes.
" Two men, at moft, thy mighty plans defpoil'd;
" While, for my fake, a nation has run wild.
" Statefman rever'd! from thine eternal home,
" Behold the hour of bright fuccefs has come;
" Nor turn aftonifh'd, tho' thou chance to fee
" Thy difappointed fchemes fucceed with me*.
" Thy pupil I, with all thy wifdom fraught;
" Taught by thy leffons, by thine errors taught.
" Thou know'ft the Statefman owns no binding rules,
" Learnt in the precincts of pedantic fchools;
" Nor heeds opinions which would bind his faith
" To one fole mafter, one unvarying path;
" But, as his intereft and his judgement guide,
" Forfakes the weaker for the ftronger fide;
" Abjures this hour what he maintain'd the laft,
" And mourns, in outward guife, his follies paft.
" Kings, Lords, or People, as their powers prevail,
" Still ever find him in the heavier fcale;
" And now, with duteous loyalty he bends;
" Now, feems devoted to his patrons' ends;
" And bellows now, among the people's friends.
" Nor lefs does he conform, as beft befalls,
" To thofe, mid whom his fate as *Envoy* calls;
" A Courtier there, all frippery and grimace;
" Here a bald Patriot, ftript of gaudy lace,
" Cropt hair, unpowder'd, and unfhaven face;

* There is no paffage, in the whole of this Poem, which has appeared more obfcure to the Editor than the foregoing. The blank might readily be filled by inferting the name *Dundas*—as that is the name of a well-known Minifter of State; and moreover the difpofition of the fyllables is agreable to the melody of the verfe. But the apoftrophe to the Spirit of this Minifter (whoever he is) forms an objection to the idea of its being Mr. *Dundas*, as he is ftill living. On confulting a literary friend, to whom I fhewed this Book, as I was preparing the notes, &c.—and ftating my difficulties in attempting to folve the queftion—he fuggefted, that, poffibly, a recurrence to the Hiftory of the Treaty of Peace of 1782, might afford a folution.—The reader muft determine.

" His form and language fitting each extreme,
" His good, his object—theirs, his constant theme.
" Nor to externals is his trust confin'd ;
" Interest more strong than flattering words can bind.
" This well consider'd, faithfully applied,
" Instant, what legions range upon my side.
" Where men are free, how powerful is the press !
" If fitly gain'd, how certain is success !
" Some proper presents to their chiefs, shall raise
" The noisy vulgar to be loud in praise.
" And lo ! where-e'er I move, around they throng,
" My name and fame, the burthen of their song;
" Feast follows feast, and, as my voice declares,
" Patriot or traitor, every man appears.

" O Goddess ! object of my early vows,
" Transcendent CUNNING! deign my cause espouse !
" If former failures have my spirit prov'd,
" And shewn, successless, how sincere I lov'd ;
" If ever on thy shrine my gifts were rear'd ;
" If ever to thy throne my prayers preferr'd ;
" Grant me, O Goddess, in this doomful hour,
" The blest assistance of thy favouring power !
" O bid delusion, ignorance, and rage,
" And rankling envy, in my cause engage !
" So shall thy servant to thy next decree,
" Bow the low head, and bend th'obedient knee."
Thus spake the ENVOY—while his bosom hides
The guile which o'er his secret thoughts presides.

With the fifth morn, his home ARISTUS sought;
His heart with joy, with schemes his head was fraught;
For, on that day, his house and social board
Were doom'd to greet the ENVOY, by their Lord.
He came ; the feast was spread ; the gen'rous wine
In the cup sparkles ; all their faces shine.
And now the Sun, declining, sought the main,
And eve commenc'd her mild and sober reign ;
Fled were the dishes, and the mingling fume,
Of coffee and tobacco, fill'd the room ;
When, from his lofty seat, the mighty MAN,
To great ARISTUS, earnest, thus began.

" Say, noble Chief, nor deem th'inquiry bold,
" To me, thy country's annals deign t'unfold.
" Her wars and sufferings thro' the east resound,
" And bear her glory to earth's farthest bound:
" Pale Europe trembles at her growing fame,
" And shuddering views fair freedom's spreading flame :
" Warm'd by thy genius, France, (her fetters broke)
" Shakes from her galled neck, the tyrant yoke ;

B

" And, to th'aftonifh'd univerfe declares,
" Like you fhe feels, like you, for freedom, dares*.

" But of events fo glorious, to inquire,
" Would fhew a carelefs mind, a mean defire;
" Confpicuous and fublime, they feize the heart,
" Nor afk affiftance from th'hiftorian's art.
" No! rather let me learn the fecret caufe
" Of what exifts—of parties, fyftems, laws.
" What fchemes ambition, rivalry, and fear,
" And pride, and honefty, fucceffive rear.
" In fhort, from independence, to this hour,
" The varied hiftory of wavering power."

" O Sage renoun'd!" Aristus fwift replies—
" On actions paft I turn unwilling eyes.
" The melancholy tale my grief renews,
" Which briefly now my mournful voice purfues:
" For, had you thrice his patience at command,
" The fabled dweller of the Uzzian land†;
" And were my lungs endued with triple ftrength;
" They both muft fail, if all were told at length.

" When now the foe had flown our fatal fhore,
" And hoftile laws and arms were fear'd no more,
" The bond of union, eommon danger wrought,
" Each independent State contemn'd as nought.
" Provincial jealoufies, and perfonal hate,
" Of ancient origin, and later date,
" Hid, in the ftruggle for the general weal,
" No longer could their hateful forms conceal.
" Paffions, opinions, interefts, mingling, warr'd,
" 'Till frighten'd Peace for diftant flight prepar'd.
" A paffing mention, given to each, will fhow
" All that is ufeful, at this hour, to know;

* Nothing could be more confiftent with the principles on which the Envoy acted, than this addrefs to Aristus. Aristus, the native of a republic, and fuftaining an office of high truft and dignity in the councils of that republic, would not be fuppofed hoftile to liberty. We fhall fee, hereafter, with what addrefs he difclofes his real feelings; and how readily the Envoy, once acquainted with them, adapts his language and conduct to them.

† Aristus, it is obfervable, lofes no opportunity of cafting contempt on all which is *commonly* deemed facred. Such ever is the fpirit of Ariftocrats. Having fucceeded in gaining a belief of their fuperiority over their fellow-mortals, they glory in defpifing what others venerate; and having deprived men of their rights, they audacioufly would rob the Deity of his fupremacy.

" And well will point, with what succeeds combin'd,
" To present knowledge thy discerning mind.
" For this, great ENVOY, with attentive ear,
" The brief, but just, enumeration hear.

" The *friends of Britain*, ere the war began ;
" With *those*, who, fearful, from the contest ran :
" *Men*, sore chagrin'd, their mounting wishes crost ;
" And *Men*, who venturing all, that all had lost :
" Honest of heart, but obstinate of head,
" And by the craft of subtiler men misled,
" *Those*, who each State a separate State desir'd ;
" Who thought—(their brains by wild ideas fir'd)
" That virtue dwelt in rustic guise alone,
" To science, arts, and polisht life, unknown ;
" With *those*, who hop'd, by aid of these to rise,
" The nine-days' wonder of admiring eyes ;
" The petty lordlings of a petty town :
" With these, be join'd, the pedant and the clown—
" *That*, who would go the way his fathers went ;
" And *this*, on endless innovation bent :
" To these more powerful partizans succeed,
" A people's formidable foes decreed,
" *Spirits*, once banisht the restraints of law,
" Who but in anarchy their interests saw ;
" And *souls*, disdaining ever to obey,
" Who hop'd to rear an oligarchie sway :
" All these, with subdivisions, endless, vex'd,
" The agitated Nation long perplex'd.
" Loud howl'd the storm ;—in each divided State,
" Foul demons urg'd the furious work of fate.
" TENDER, who laughs at violated right :
" UNFUNDED PAPER, imp of stygian night ;
" Fierce COMMUTATION, with a hundred tongues,
" Sounding the peal of visionary wrongs ;
" EXCISE and IMPOST, brother friends accurst ;
" TESTS, by wild-ey'd Fanaticism nurst ;
" And DEBT, the Monster, whose terrific mouth
" Threaten'd engulphment to to the tardy South ;
" With thousand others, whose mishapen frame
" Still balks description, and still wants a name*.

* We observe the *Aristocrat* throughout this passage. ARISTUS gradually discovers himself to the ENVOY. *Unfunded Paper* is ranked among the plagues of a country. *Excise* and *Impost*, too, are put in the list ; but the real meaning must be shewn. ARISTUS is speaking of the times preceding the present Constitution, when an unequal Impost and Excise were levied in several of the States. This it is that excites his hate ; not that universal burthen, under which, good democrats now groan.

" While thus, from day to day, from hour to hour,
" Diffention gather'd an increafing power;
" The Nation's Council flighted or condemn'd,
" Its calls unheeded, its requefts contemn'd;
" While State with State, by clafhing views enrag'd,
" And felfifh aims—in contefts fierce engag'd;
" And each, at home, to difcord dire a prey,
" Saw threat'ning clouds deform the beauteous day;
" As the laft project to protract their fate,
" The *felf-call'd** fages of the nation met.
" (The pledge his honour)—whatfoe'er he hears—
" Or who the fpeaker, ev'ry ftatefman fwears,
" Whate'er the import, from his friends or foes,
" No power on earth fhall tempt him to difclofe.
" O farce ridiculous! a ftatefman's oath!
" A ftatefman's honour! fhallow, fhallow both!
" This ******* proves, who held the bond fo light,
" He fcarce preferv'd it for a fingle night.
" Nor longer much, tho' bound by ev'ry tie,
" Sacred in honour's and in friendfhip's eye,
" The far-fam'd Sage, **'s chofen one,
" That prince of turn-coats, peerlefs ***.
" Of thefe enough; a different fcene, erewhile,
" Shall greet thine eye, and wake th'approving fmile:
" Nor need we fear, if e'er our purpofe afk
" Their plaufive aid, to load them with the tafk.

" Meantime, conven'd, th'affembled nation fate,
" And op'd, in folemn form, the grave debate.
" Long were their toils"—" But where," the Envoy cries,
" Where was Aristus?" Swift the Chief replies—

" Exalted Man! forgive my wounded pride,
" Which ftill its fore chagrins would feek to hide.
" O couldft thou think it?—yet, by Hell†, 'tis true—
" Curft be th'occafion, and the rival too!
" Yes—tho' as yet upon my chin appear'd
But youthful down, my ardent fword I rear'd,

---

* This feems to be a very awkward and obfcure fneer upon the Federal Convention of 1787; the epithet "felf-call'd" being equivocal; tho' defigned, as I fuppofe, to convey the fame meaning with the French expreffion *foi-difant*. Aristus, the enemy of Republicanifm, would involve, in one general cenfure, all who favour it, in any fhape.

† Profanity—another characteriftic of Ariftocracy: this is the fecond time that Aristus has fworn by Hell. Profanity, I have been told, was deemed by him a defirable accomplifhment: nay, I have fomewhere heard that he even thought it an effential part of *female* education.

" And rush'd to combat in my country's cause;
" (For thus was call'd, my passion for applause—)
" Yet was I left, neglected, and alone,
" While HE, capricious Fortune's favour'd son,
" Lost be the memory of his hated name!
" Who still precedes me in the walks of fame;
" Who, as I mount, still towr's above my flight,
" With Jacob-craft*, despoil'd me of my right."

Here tears of anguish, such as, erst, in Heaven,
When from their seats his haughty pow'rs were driv'n,
From SATAN fell—ARISTUS shed: his rage,
The bitter drops, flow falling, half assuage;
And now, in some faint sort, his calm renew'd,
The interrupted tale he thus pursued.

" Long were their toils, their very walls within,
" Discordant interests kept perpetual din;
" Systems, opinions, facts, in ferment strange,
" Now here, now there, their several powers arrange;
" Those ask too much, and these too little give,
" Some credit all, and some will none believe.
" At length the offspring of their union'd might,
" Bursting its prison doors, arose to light;
" Republican proclaim'd—tho' (half reveal'd)
" Its robe, one badge of slavery ill conceal'd;
" Yet so robust of form, that all might say,
" Such strength, with ease, could tear the badge away.—
" And now, thro' jealousy, or fear, or hate,
" Fierce opposition rose in many a State:
" Furious were all, and 'mid the foremost those
" Who at the birth had labour'd to oppose.
" GERRY, whose alter'd mind, in one short year,
" Led him its firm supporter to appear:
" Poor YATES, and LANSING obstinate and warm,
" Once prejudic'd, whose spleen no art can charm:
" Thee, LUTHER MARTIN, whose loquacious tongue,
" Thy State throughout, the loud alarum rung:
" But chiefly thee, implacable of zeal,
" Redoubted MASON! challenger of steel!
" With *Cutting-box*, in letters large, thy *Hand*
" Long time spread terror thro' th'astonish'd land.——
" Nor with less fury fresh opponents rose,
" Foes to itself, or to its framers foes;
" Some, long since, steep'd in dull oblivion's stream,
" And some, still known to memory by name.
" A few, by changing, or by constant hate,
" Yet held aloft, and rank'd among the great.—

† An early religious education supplies ARISTUS with numerous Scripture allusions; yet observe how careful he is to shew his contempt for the principles in which he was instructed, by his parents.

" But thefe to name would ampler time demand ;
" The event, well known to every diftant land,
" Afks not the detail, nor requires the care"—
" But where," the Envoy cries, " ah tell me where !
" Where was Aristus ? Which contending fide
" Chofe thee its guardian, genius, glory, guide ?"

" O Man rever'd !"—the Hero fwift return'd—
Red were his eyes, his cheeks with anger burn'd ;
" Silent, at home, neglected, I remain'd ;
" Nor added fortunes, nor diftinctions gain'd."
" And what the caufe?" the Envoy quick demands.
Solemn, Aristns lifts on high his hands—
" Were not my profpects dreft in livelier hue,"
He cries, " I well might bid a long adieu,
" A lafting farewell, to all craftful aid ;
" Craft then fo ill, my numerous cares repaid.——
" Silence, I hop'd, whate'er th'event fhould prove,
" Would ftill fecure me either party's love.——
" Alas ! by each diftrufted or abjur'd,
" I long their hate or their neglect endur'd.
" Thanks be to Cunning, whofe returning aid,
" Again has rais'd me, from misfortune's fhade ;
" Firm in my caufe a numerous hoft allied,
" Their guardian I—their genius, glory, guide.

" But turn we now—behold, with wond'ring eyes,
" From Chaos' realms, a realm well order'd rife ;
" An Empire organiz'd now ftarts to birth ;
" A Phœnix 'mid the empires of the earth.——
——" Curft be the hour ! forever curft the day !
" Annual, thou Sun, withhold thy gladfome ray !
" Vanifh ye ftars ! thou moon, thy beams deny !
" And let fubftantial night begloom the fky !—
—" Thofe moft abhorr'd, detefted by my foul,
" Arm'd with frefh power, the weftern world controul:
" He, to whofe love a rival was preferr'd ;
" And He, the rival who my progrefs barr'd ;
" Out-ftep'd me firft, and all my after days,
" In camp and forum, bore away the praife.

" From hence, great Envoy of a people kind,
" Thou fee'ft confirm'd my doubtful, wavering mind.
" Hopelefs the fummit of that power to gain,
" Which, with fuch care, I labour'd to obtain ;
" Behold me now the foremoft to oppofe,
" Leagued with the deadlieft of its conftant foes.
" Deep rankling in my breaft, to grief a prey,
" My hated rival's high advancement lay :
" Should chance remove him from his lofty place,
" And, (what I wifh'd) my name the title grace,
" Still would the memory of his earlier fame,
" Blaft all my joys, and tarnifh all my name.

" What then remain'd ? What purpose, project, plan,
" Might bow the statesman, and disgrace the man ?
" Could I, superior, o'er my rival rise,
" Next to his Patron in the people's eyes—
" Then might I hope the Empire's highest seat ;
" Then see my rival humbled at my feet ;
" The utmost object of my vows be found :
" And pride, ambition, and revenge, be crown'd.
" But, if successless, with redoubled might,
" Each marshall'd band should urge th'unceasing fight,
" 'Till, tottering, from its base, the Fabric fall ;
" Destruction's giant mace demolish all ;
" While from the ruins, our invigor'd sway,
" Should rear an oligarchic dome to mock the day.

" Such resolutions working in my breast,
" Disturb'd my days, my nights depriv'd of rest ;
" For now my soul no glittering prospect cheer'd,
" Nor blissful presage of success appear'd ;
" Fancy's gay pictures far and farther fled ;
" Dampt were my transports, almost hope was dead.
" But then, when sinking 'neath increasing woes,
" Nor chance seem'd left of triumph o'er my foes,
" Effulgent, from his cloud, the sun of joy
" Burst—and, with dazzling glory, thro' the sky,
" Urging his beauteous and resplendent way,
" Dispell'd the mists of grief that long obscur'd my day.
" Nor think, *Gay Dweller* of our sober shore,
" Fancy's fond dreams I spread thine eyes before ;
" But mark, from hence, events how wond'rous spring,
" And to thy aid unnumber'd forces bring :
" Yes, to thy aid, if silent thou, and bold,
" Firm in our cause thy riper purpose hold.

" Well order'd, now, intelligent, discreet,
" The new-form'd Councils amicably meet ;
" Mutual indulgence, mutual candour, shine ;
" And gentlest temper, more than half divine.
" Wide spread the tidings, ecstacy and love
" Grow strong, and little jealousies remove.
" Dumb were opposers, stopt the slanderous mouth ;
" The North was silent, silent was the South ;
" Deep in her cavern, PARTY, with her train,
" Sunk, in despair her empire to regain.

" Hark ! what dread sounds the startled ear arrest ?
" Lo ! what fell forms the Councils fierce invest !
" Loud roars the fearful din ; around,
" The walls with clamor and with rage resound ;
" Full in the midst, aloft see PARTY rear
" Her hateful form,—and lo ! her train appear !

" O * * * ! thou loft, thou wretched man !
" Thou who waft form'd on Nature's ampleft plan !
" Thy mind with learning's richeft treafures fraught ;
" And made more rich by thy energic thought :
" Thou on whofe voice a liftening nation hung,
" Bleft but to hear the accents of thy tongue ;
" Whofe grateful hearts with earneft wifhes beat,
" To fee thee deck their empire's higheft feat ;
" Who thought no gift too mighty for thy worth,
" And deem'd thy country bleft to give thee birth ;
" Who, at each eve, at each returning morn,
" Afk'd Heav'n thy life with glory to adorn ;—
" O moft unhappy ! what difaftrous force,
" Far from the right impell'd thy devious courfe ?
" What envious dæmon urg'd thee to deftroy
" Thy growing hopes, a people's growing joy ?
" Say, what infernal what malicious fiend,
" With hellifh arts divorc'd thee from thy friend ;
" And, from thy heart, in one detefted day,
" Rent honour, truth, and happinefs, away ?
——" Aw'd by his genius, by his fame outfhone,
" A blow fo dire, with glory, I might own ;
" Have triumph'd in his pain, and rofe more bright,
" At his declining and enfeebled light :
——" But thou, who every faint, (if faints there are),
" Had heard unending, changelefs, friendfhip fwear ;
" Who each returning eve, each daily fun,
" With him beheld, in council, action, one ;——
" Sure on thy face fhould fit enduring fhame,
" Remorfeful anguifh fhake thy guilty frame,
" And infamy eternal blaft thy name.

" Now hope reviv'd, and hence increafing power
" Marks our fwift progrefs to the prefent hour.
" Once, to their force, fo great a leader found,
" At home rever'd, and through the realm renown'd,
" Afide th'oppofers their concealment threw,
" And fir'd with tenfold rage the war renew.
" But HE, from whom their hope and courage flow'd
" Not yet in open oppofition glow'd ;
" The veil of candour ftill conceal'd his aim ;—
" Candour his once—and well eftablifh'd fame :
" Timid of heart, implacable of foul,
" Long, o'er his fpeech, his fears maintain controul.
" But lo, from Europe, now a Chief returns,
" Within whofe breaft undaunted courage burns;
" Who, with the force with which his mind conceives,
" To his bold thoughts the aid of action gives ;
" And, well inftructed in the courtier's art,
" Purfues, remorfelefs, a determin'd part.——
" Now friends increafe, and fee, in every ftate,
" Where nought but fulfome praife was heard of late,

" The groaning preſs diſcharge its factious load,
" And ſpread its venom'd ſlanders all abroad.——
" Drawn from his hole, unwilling SINBAT ſee,
" Lur'd by the golden treachery of a fee ;
" His *Maſter's* ſpirit guides his venal preſs ;
" His proſe ſtalks forth in ſtarch and pompous dreſs ;
" Soft tinkling rhimes with leaden luſtre glow ;
" And froth and calumny the land o'erflow.

" Swift from my proſpect now the clouds withdrew,
" And future glories open'd on my view ;
" Nor did I fail to bleſs the bounteous day ;
" But well reſolv'd to brook no more delay,
" I tried each art, each known expedient us'd,
" Here favours offer'd, terrors there infus'd ;
" 'Till from his ſeat, an abſent rival thrown,
" I found the hard-earn'd dignity my own.
" Hence a kind preſage of ſucceſs I drew ;
" More firmly fixt my purpoſe to purſue.
" Still to be gain'd ſuperior power appear'd ;
" When he ſhould fear me, whom I long had fear'd.
" But yet no ſyſtem gave our ſcatter'd bands
" The ſtrength which every arduous taſk demands ;
" Scarce to each other were the leaders known,
" Or yet their intereſts deem'd alike, and one.
" Mark then, while I the ſecret ſource diſcloſe
" Whence the firſt compact of our forces roſe.

" Thrice had the Sun his annual circuit trac'd
" And half of his remaining diſtance paſs'd,
" Whoſe hop'd completion brings the joyful day,
" The ſure renewer of expiring ſway.
" Think, thou exalted, thou attentive, SAGE,
" What fears, what wiſhes, in my boſom rage :
" Each artifice I us'd, employ'd each plan,
" That e'er was practis'd, or devis'd by man ;
" Yet was I forc'd my warmeſt wiſh to hide,
" Delay's ſoul-piercing injury abide ;
" And all my power, and all my art, to bend,
" A wretch I loath'd and hated to befriend."

Here pauſ'd the Chief : with grief and rage oppreſt,
Deep ſighs convulſe his ſwelling, labouring breaſt ;
Tears fill his eyes : but ſhame, and native pride,
Aid him in ſilence his diſtreſs to hide ;
A feeble ſmile his countenance illum'd,
While thus th'unfiniſh'd ſtory he reſum'd.

END *of* BOOK SECOND.

ORIGINAL POETRY.

AN ELEGY,
Written in February 1791.

By Mr. Richard Alsop.

Dark is the hour and lone, o'er icy plains
    The wandering meteors gleam a deadly light;
Wild howls the blast amid descending rains,
    And forms funereal flit along the night.

Retir'd from scenes where Pleasure's airy wand
    Gilds the light moments with delusive joy,
Where Mirth exulting leads her festive band,
    Far other scenes my pensive soul employ.

The clouds of death that gloom the baleful year,
    The days of joy, alas, so lately fled!
While Friendship bids its sympathetic tear
    Stream in remembrance of the much-lov'd dead.

My friend, but now, of every bliss possest
    That love connubial can on man bestow,
When mutual wishes warm the mutual breast;
    Behold the prey of life-consuming woe.

Of late, how fair the beauteous prospect show'd,
    How lovely glittering in the morning's eye;
But long ere noon, like April's painted cloud,
    Or hues that tinge the summer's evening sky,

The fairy hopes that raptur'd Fancy drew,
   The dream of future bliss that shone so bright,
On Fate's swift pinions vanish'd from the view,
   And sunk in shadows of eternal night.—

What notes of woe in mournful cadence swell
   Along the Western breeze from climes afar,
Mix'd with the dying groan, the savage yell,
   And all the horrid dissonance of war!

And lo! mid gliding spectres dimly seen,
   Pale as the mists that Autumn's car surround,
A form superior lifts his pensive mien,
   While on his bosom glares the shadowy wound.

" Behold," he cries, " the band who lately bled,
   " Mid western wilds in glorious conflict slain;
" While recreant troops in pale confusion fled,
   " Ignobly left unburied on the plain."—

Far opes the view, sublime in savage pride
   A wild unbounded frowns on Fancy's eye;
Tall rise the trees, and o'er savannahs wide
   The rank grass trembles to the breeze on high.

With torrent sweep, amid a night of woods
   Where scarce the sun a livid glimmering lends,
A blood-stain'd river rolls his foaming floods,
   And o'er the plains in wild meanders bends.

Lo! this the scene where War, with bloody hand,
   Wav'd his red standard o'er the carnag'd ground;
Where wild-eyed Horror led the tawny band,
   And fell the brave with dear-bought laurels crown'd.

Here, grim with gore, beneath the inclement sky,
  Smote by the parching ray and driving rain,
The mangled forms of breathless warriors lie,
  All pale extended on the lonely plain.

In slaughter'd heaps, around promiscuous cast,
  Mid savage chiefs Columbia's sons are spread,
While, breath'd from polar snows, the northern blast
  Shakes its cold pinions o'er the unburied dead.

For them no more shall morning gild the sky,
  No more shall May unveil her radiant charms,
No more shall Joy illume the sparkling eye,
  Or Glory's voice excite the soul to arms.

Near yon grey rock by withering leaves conceal'd,
  Amyntor lies, benevolent and brave;
Whose duteous hand a father's age upheld,
  And smooth'd his dreary passage to the grave.

Not far, a corse distinguish'd o'er the rest,
  Of noble stature and heroic mien;
Deep opes the wound that gor'd his manly breast,
  And his pale features wear a smile serene.

Too well alas! that much-lov'd form I know,
  Those features pale with gory dust o'erspread,
O'er whom has Friendship mourn'd in bitterest woe,
  For whom Affection's tenderest tears are shed.

Still, still in Fancy's view recurs the day
  When war's black demons pour'd their hideous yell,
When left expos'd to savage rage a prey,
  Thy gallant band beside their leader fell.

Opprest with toil, while countless foes surround,
   Thy arm, thy voice, the fainting troop inspir'd;
And e'en when sinking with the deadly wound,
   Thy latest breath their martial ardor fir'd.

Lamented Hero, far from weeping friends!
   No funeral honours to thy corse were paid,
And no memorial o'er thy grave extends
   To mark the lonely spot where low thou'rt laid.

Yet what avails to please the senseless clay,
   " The trophied tomb," the monumental bust,
Or recks the spirit mid the realms of day,
   The empty rites attendant on its dust.

A fairer wreath shall friendship's hand bestow,
   A fairer tribute shall thy shade receive,
Than all the idle pageantry of woe,
   Than all its pompous monuments can give.

Long, long shall Memory's ardent eye recall
   Thy worth, thy milder virtues to her view;
Thy Country long lament her hero's fall,
   And o'er thee Fame her brightest laurels strew.

O'er the lone spot where rests thy mouldering form,
   Shall opening spring her mildest breezes wave;
And Flora's hand with every fragrant charm
   Deck the soft turf that forms thy verdant grove.

There the Wild-Rose in earliest pride shall bloom,
   There the Magnolia's gorgeous flowers unfold,
The purple Violet shed its sweet perfume,
   And beauteous Meadia wave her plumes of gold.

Rest much-lov'd Chief with thy Jer——a bleft,
  Amid yon realms of light, yon feats of joy,
Where hush'd is forrow in perpetual reft,
  And pleafure fmiles unconfcious of alloy.

From that calm fhore with pitying eye furvey
  The varying fchemes of man, the bufy ftrife,
The vain purfuits that fill his " little day,"
  And tofs with ceafelefs ftorms the fea of life.

While feraphs, bending from their thrones of gold,
  With fongs of triumph hymn thy foul to peace;
And to thy raptur'd eye, with fmiles, unfold
  The happy manfions of eternal blifs.

VERSIFICATION

Of a Passage from the Fifth Book of Ossian's Temora.

BY THE SAME.

THE hofts like two black ridges ftood,
  On either fide wild Lubar's ftream;
Here Foldath frown'd a darken'd cloud,
  There Fillan fhone a brightening beam.

Their long fpears glittering in the wave,
  Each hero pour'd his voice afar;
Gaul ftruck the fhield, the fignal gave,
  At once both armies plung'd in war.

Steel pour'd its flashing gleam on steel;
  The fields two rushing torrents glow,
That whitening foam, in mingled swell,
  O'er the dark rock's projecting brow.

He comes, with fame immortal crown'd,
  His faulchion lays the heroes low;
Death rides the shadowy blasts around;
  Thy paths O Fillan warriors strew!

Between two rocks in fissures rent,
  Brave Rothmar stood, the warrior's pride;
Two aged oaks, that winds had bent,
  Their branches spread on either side.

Silent he shades his friends in flight,
  While his dark eyes on Fillan roll;
Fingal beheld the approaching fight,
  And all the father fill'd his soul.

As falls the stone of Loda, hurl'd
  From trembling Drumanard's high cliff,
When angry spirits rock the world;
  So Rothmar fell, blue-shielded chief.

Young Culmin's friendly steps are near;
  His eye the bursting tear o'erflows;
Wrathful he cuts the empty air,
  Ere yet with Fillan's mix his blows.

He first with Rothmar bent the bow,
  Along his own blue-winding streams;
And mark'd the dwelling of the roe,
  As shone the fern with morning beams.

ORIGINAL POETRY.

"Why Youth would'ſt thou provoke the might
   Of that bright beam, that waſting fire?
Unequal were your ſires in fight;
   Retire, Culalluins's ſon retire!"

Lone in her hall, his mother caſts
   Her eyes o'er Strutha's winding ſtreams;
Wrapp'd in a whirlwind's eddying blaſts,
   Her ſon's thin ſpectre faintly gleams.

His dogs ſtand howling on the plain,
   Red his ſuſpended ſhield with gore;
"And is my fair-hair'd hero ſlain?
   Pale does he lie on Ullin's ſhore?"

As pierc'd in ſecret lies a hind,
   Panting her wonted ſtreams beſide;
The hunter views her feet of wind;
   Culalluin's ſon thus Fillan eyed.

In a ſmall ſtream his hair is roll'd,
   His blood flow wanders o'er his ſhield;
Still graſps his hand, with dying hold,
   The ſword that fail'd in danger's field.

"Thou'rt fallen ere thy fame was known,"
   Said Fillan, muſing o'er the ſlain;
"Elate, in hopes of thy renown,
   Thy father ſent thee to the plain.

Perhaps, his ſtreams grey bending o'er,
   His dim eyes ſeek thee on the heath;
In vain,—for ah! returns no more,
   His ſon extended pale in death."

Wide o'er the heath, in terror loſt,
  The flight of Erin Fillan pour'd;
But, man on man, falls Morven's hoſt,
  Before the rage of Foldath's ſword.

Undaunted, Dermid meets his courſe;
  The ſons of Cona wake the fight;
But cleft his ſhield, by Foldath's force,
  And far is ſpread his people's flight.

The exulting foe with haughty boaſt,—
  " Go Malthos, go to Erin's lord;
And bid him guard blue ocean's coaſt,
  Leſt Morven's king eſcape my ſword.

For cold muſt Fingal lie in gore,
  Near ſome low fen his tomb ſhall riſe
Without a ſong, while hovering o'er,
  Half hid in miſt, his ſpirit flies."

In darkening doubt ſtood Malthos bold,
  He knew the boaſter's heart of pride;
Around his gloomy eyes he roll'd,
  And plung'd in war with ſullen ſtride.

In Clono's narrow vale, two trees
  Dark-bending o'er the rolling flood,
Shook their broad branches to the breeze;
  There Duthno's ſon in ſilence ſtood.

The blood is ſtreaming from his thigh;
  A rock ſuſtains his aſhen ſpear;
His boſſy ſhield lies broken nigh;
  " Why Dermid, why that burſting tear?"

"I hear the battle roar afar,
  Alone my people on the plain;
No shield is mine to stem the war,
  And weak and slow my steps of pain.

Shall Foldath then prevail in fight?
  Ere that in death shall Dermid lie;
Again stern chief I'll prove thy might,
  Again thy fiercest rage defy."

He seiz'd his spear the strife to join,
  When Morni's son before him stood;
"Stay Dermid stay, no shield is thine,
  Thy trembling steps are mark'd with blood."

"Chief of Strumon give thy shield,
  Oft has it stemm'd the battle's force;
This arm may yet sustain the field,
  May yet repel yon boaster's course.

Behold that stone, with moss o'erspread,
  Where spires the waving grass so high;
There low a kindred chief is laid—
  And there in night let Dermid lie."

Slowly he rose the hill's tall brow,
  And view'd the troubled field of death;
The gleaming ranks of fight below,
  Disjoin'd, and broken o'er the heath.

As fires at distance, seem by night
  Now lost in smoke, in darkness drown'd,
Now rear on high their streams of light,
  As cease or blow the winds around;

So met the battle from afar
  Broad-shielded Dermid's eager eye.
Amidst the varying scene of war
  The chief of Morna towers on high;

Like some black ship, in lofty pride,
  Dark rider of the billowy plain;
Wide sporting o'er the echoing tide,
  When winter rules the stormy main.

Dermid with rage beheld his course,
  He rush'd to meet the gloomy foe;
But fails the wounded hero's force,
  And tears of pride his eyes o'erflow.

He sounded thrice his bossy shield,
  And thrice on Foldath call'd aloud;
Foldath with joy the chief beheld,
  And lifted high his spear of blood.

As some vast rock whose rugged side
  Is mark'd with streams of many a storm;
So look'd, with wandering blood bedyed
  The gloomy chief of Morna's form.

Each host, appall'd, in terror flies,
  From the contending fierce of Kings.
At once their gleaming points arise,
  With speed of lightning Fillan springs.

The haughty foe, with trembling, view'd,
  That dazzling beam of early fame;
That swift, as issuing from a cloud,
  To save the wounded hero came.

In founding strife as on the gale
   Two broad-wing'd eagles fierce contend;
So, on Moilena's far-spread vale,
   The chiefs in gloomy battle bend.

Low on his shield is Foldath laid,
   Pierc'd by the youthful hero's spear;
Nor o'er the fallen Fillan staid,
   But onward roll'd the storm of war.

Malthos beheld the warrior low,
   Low laid on Lubar's winding shore;
His bosom melts in generous woe,
   And hatred fills his soul no more.

He seem'd a rock, down whose grey sides
   The desart waters trickling stray;
When slow the sailing mist divides,
   And gives its blasted trees to day.

Thus to the dying chief he said,—
   " Say shall thy mossy stone ascend,
Where Ullin's dark green hills are spread,
   Or Morna's woody vales extend?

There, where the sun looks forth serene,
   On blue Dalrutho's bordering glades;
Fair Dardulena's steps are seen,
   Thy daughter, pride of Erin's maids."

" Rememberest thou," the chief reply'd,
   " The maid, because no son is mine,
To roll the battle's deathful tide,
   And in revenge in arms to shine?

I am reveng'd, for not in vain
   Has shone the lightning of my spear.
Amidst the tombs of those I've slain
   My narrow house, O Malthos! rear.

Oft shall I leave my airy fold,
   To hail the spot where low they lie;
When, spread around me, I behold,
   The rank grass of their graves on high."

His spirit rush'd on eddying winds,
   And came to Dardulena's dream;
As, wearied with the chace of hinds,
   She slept by blue Dulrutho's stream.

Her bow unstrung is near her placed,
   The breezes fold her raven hair;
Each charm of youthful beauty graced
   The love of chiefs, the blue-eyed fair.

From the dark skirts of Morna's wood,
   Her father's ghost, pale bending, gleam'd;
At times his bloody form he shew'd,
   Then hid in shrouding vapors seem'd.

She rose in tears, her soul divin'd
   The chief in death was lowly laid;
To her a beam of light he shin'd.
   When folded in his darkest shade.

ORIGINAL POETRY.

HABAKKUK, Chap. III.

BY THE SAME.

THE Lord of Hosts from Teman came,
  From Paran's mount the Almighty God,—
The heavens his glory wide proclaim,
  And bent the earth beneath his nod.

As light his awful brightness show'd,—
  There was the hiding of his power;
On burning coals Jehovah trode,
  Dire mov'd the pestilence before.

He stood, and measur'd earth and air,
  He look'd, apart the nations fled,
The eternal mountains scatter'd were,
  And hills perpetual bow'd the head.

I saw when Midian's curtains shook,
  I saw pale Cushan's tents in woe;
Say, did the streams thy wrath provoke?
  Against them did thine anger glow?

Did e'er the deep his God displease,
  That on thy horses thou did'st ride?
Thy path was thro' the troubled seas,
  In heaps roll'd back the astonish'd tide.

The mountains saw, they trembling shook,
  The o'erflowing waters passed by,
The mighty deep in horror spoke,
  And lifted up his hands on high.

The rolling stars their courses stay'd,
    The sun and moon stood still in fear;
Before thine arrows blaze they fled,
    Before the lightning of thy spear.

With rivers did'st thou cleave the earth,
    And naked made thy dreadful bow;
Thou marched in indignation forth,
    And laid in dust the heathen low:

Thou wentest forth on Israel's side,
    To save from death thy chosen race;
Thy sword has smote the heathen's pride,
    And everlasting are thy ways.

Altho' the fig-tree shall not shoot,
    Nor grape the withering vine shall yield,
The olive shall withhold her fruit,
    And blasted be the herbag'd field;

Tho' in the fold the flock shall die,
    And in the stall no herd shall be,
Yet on the Lord will I rely,
    Yet, O my God! will joy in thee.

ORIGINAL POETRY.

Runic Poetry.

TWILIGHT of the GODS;
OR
DESTRUCTION of the WORLD.

FROM THE EDDA, A SYSTEM OF ANCIENT SCANDINAVIAN MYTHOLOGY.

BY THE SAME.

A TIME shall come, a barbarous time,
Dark shadowed o'er with every crime,
When ties of kin shall cease to bind,
In love's soft bands, the human mind:
When sons their fathers' blood shall pour,
And brother blush with brother's gore:
When, lost to every tender care,
Not one his dearest friend shall spare;
And man, oppress'd with bitterest woes,
Wish the sad scene of life to close.

   Winter, clad in wild array,
Then shall hold his direst sway;
The sun withdraw his golden light,
And veil the world in darkest night;
The winds with wildest rage contend;
The snow in ceaseless storms descend;
The earth in icy fetters bound;
And desolation glare around.

Uncherish'd by one genial ray,
Three such winters pass away.
Portents dire shall then succeed;
The Monsters from their chains be freed:
Dreadful, in his fiery car,
Giant Rymer * rush to war;
The Serpent † roll his hideous train
Deep beneath the billowy main,
Whose lifted waters, wildly swell'd,
Wide o'er the earth shall be impell'd;
In thousands men resign their breath,
And throng the gloomy courts of death;
His prey the screaming eagle seek,
And tear the dead with gory beak;
The Earth in dread convulsions heave;
Its wonted course the river leave;
The tottering mountain headlong borne,
From its deep base resistless torn;
Rent from their roots, whole forests fall;
And one vast ruin spread o'er all.
Floating on the whelming tides,
Fate's black Ship ‡ in triumph rides;

---

* Rymer—One of those Giants who, according to the Edda, are in continual enmity with the Gods, and shall, in co-operation with the Evil Genii, eventually overpower them.

† The Great Serpent—or Serpent of Midgard, is said to have been cast by the Gods into the ocean; where he soon became of such an enormous size as to encircle the earth.—Midgard—the Residence, or Fortress of the Deities.—

‡ The Ship of the Gods, or of Fate, in which the Host of the Evil Genii, &c. arrives.

Perfidious Loke § directs her courfe,
Leader of the giant force.
Fenris ‖ burfts his iron chain;
Nought his fury can reftrain;
His noftrils fparkling flames expire;
His eye-balls flafh terrific fire;
Urged by rage, by vengeance driven,
He rends the beauteous fun from heaven:
The Serpent floods of venom pours
O'er the wide fea and circling fhores;
Rocks rufh on rocks, together hurl'd;
Deftruction triumphs o'er the world;
From the torn concave of the fky,
The affrighted ftars confus'dly fly;
The vaults of heaven in funder rend;
The Evil Genii fwift afcend;
Pour'd from the fouth, in terrors dire,
Before them moves the Prince of Fire,
Surtur * the Black, in flames array'd—
Shines like the fun his waving blade,
The fign of death; with him their might
The Serpent, Fenris, Loke, unite;

---

§ Loke,—the Evil Being: in the higheft degree malicious and deceitful.

‖ Fenris,—or the Wolf,—of all the others a monfter moft dreaded by the Gods; who by ftratagem confined him with a magic chain; which he breaks at the diffolution of nature.

* Surtur,—the deftroying Principle; fuppofed to refide in the South, in the flaming Gulf of Mufpelfheim; leader of the Evil Genii, who are to deftroy the Univerfe by Fire.

Succeeds a death-determined hoſt,
The hideous Giants of the Froſt.
His crooked trumpet Heimdall†† takes,
With potent breath the blaſt awakes;
Far heard thro heaven's remoteſt bound,
Pours the ſhrill clangor of the ſound;
Loud crows the Cock, the bird divine,
Whoſe creſts in golden glory ſhine;
Hoarſe from beneath, with diſmal cries,
The Herald black of death replies;
Trembles the ſacred Aſh ‡‡ with dread,
And groaning ſhakes its lofty head;
All nature's fill'd with wild affright;
The Gods, convened, prepare for fight.
A mid-day ſun is Odin §§ bold,
Far beaming in his arms of gold;
Againſt the Wolf ‖‖ he bends his courſe,
And Frey * encounters Surturſ's force.
The enormous ſerpent Thor† aſſails;
The God's reſiſtleſs might prevails;

---

†† Heimdall,—the Centinel of Heaven.

‡‡ The Sacred Aſh of Ydraſil, under which the Council of the Deities is held.

§§ Odin, the firſt and moſt powerful of all the Gods.

‖‖ Fenris.

* Frey,—a Deity repreſented as clothed in white; and ſuppoſed to preſide over the productions of the earth.

† Thor,—the firſt of the ſons of Odin, and ſtrongeſt of the Gods; who preſides over the thunder; and whoſe office it is to protect the injured and oppreſſed.

But short his joy, he sinks in death,
From the Monster's venom'd breath.
By each others falchions slain,
Loke and Heimdall press the plain.
The snow-white God §§ resigns his life,
By Surtur slain in furious strife.
Rushing from the dark abodes,
Death denouncing to the Gods,
Hideous howls the Dog of night;
He meets with Tyr ‖‖ in mortal fight;
Long the contest fierce they wage,
And victims fall of mutual rage.
Goddess, * weep! thy cares are vain—
Odin falls, by Fenris slain.
Swift to vengeance Vidar †† flies;
By his hand the monster dies:
Wild Destruction, hovering o'er,
Waves her banner dipt in gore;
O'erpower'd the heavenly legions fall,
And Death's dark billows close on all.
The gloomy Prince, ‡ with conquest crown'd,
Dreadful scatters flames around;
In one wide conflagration driven,
The raging fires ascend to heaven;

---

§§ " The snow-white God,"—Frey.
‖‖ Tyr,—a Deity answering to the Roman Mars.
* The Goddess Friga, or Freya,—the Mother of Odin.
†† Vidar, a Son of Odin.
‡ " The gloomy Prince:"—Surtur.—

Sinks the world to ruin's power,
And time itself exists no more.

 Bursting from existence' grave,
O'er the bosom of the wave,
Lo! a new-born World unroll'd,
Far more beauteous than the old,
Smiles adorn'd with loveliest green;
Spring unfading decks the scene;
The eagles, soaring mid the breeze,
Their fishy prey on mountains seize;
The earth her fruits spontaneous yields;
Rich harvests glad the uncultured fields;
Unknown to grief, to torturing pain,
There eternal pleasures reign.
Then, from seats of orient light,
In divinest glories bright,
Comes forth the great, the all-powerful One,*
Incommunicate, alone,—
Who was ere Time began his race,
Or being fill'd the vast of space;
And, unchangable, supreme,
Thro endless ages is the same.
There a Palace glows, more bright
Than the sun's meridian light,

---

 * This Being is entirely distinct from Odin, and the other Gods of the Scandinavian Mythology; who had their birth soon after the creation of the World, and who perish with it.

Where the virtuous shall reside;
And, as pleasure rolls its tide
Undebased by pain's alloy,
Know an eternity of joy.

EXTRACT FROM THE
CONQUEST OF SCANDINAVIA;
BEING THE INTRODUCTION OF THE FOURTH BOOK.

BY THE SAME.

O DIN *having defeated the Scandinavians in several great battles,* WOLDOMIR, *the druidical sovereign of Scandinavia, reduced to the utmost distress, obtains the assistance of* GRYMER, *Prince of the Saraceni,—a Scythian Tribe,— the hereditary foe of* ODIN; *and having assembled his forces on an extensive plain, near the banks of a river, prepares to attack the Enemy, who are encamped on the opposite shore.—The present Book commences with the Night preceding the engagement.*

NOW Night, in clouds involv'd, her mantle drew,
   And deepest darkness veil'd the etherial blue;
Dire heard afar, with wild and hollow roar,
Hoarse groan'd the woods along the rocky shore;
Loaded with vapours dank and drizzling rains,
The chill North-east shrill whistled o'er the plains;
Pale shone the phantom fires, whose boding light
In tenfold horror vests the storms of night;

And, wildly yelling thro the dreary shade,
Shriek'd the sad spectres of the unburied dead;
Involv'd in anxious cares, and gloomy thought,
When Mondak's* Son the tent of Ulfo sought.
Ulfo the old, renown'd for magic lore,
From Volga's flood to cold Kamschatka's shore;
Amid the gloom of Scythian forests bred,
Where Altai lifts on high his wintry head;
Among a savage race, rapacious, rude,
Wild as the storms that toss the Caspian flood,
As thunder dreadful, bursting from the cloud,
When Night o'er Altai hangs her sable shroud.
Olaf his sire, in fields of death renown'd,
As chief in war, the stern barbarians own'd,
Sprung from that race accurst, whose demon sway
The hoary Giants of the Frost obey,
The same stern soul which mark'd his sires of yore,
The same fell hate to Woden's laws he bore,
The same inspir'd the son, whose rebel pride
The God derided, and his power defied.
In nature vers'd, to him each plant was known
That blooms mid Scythia's snows, or Afric's torrid zone;
Each secret power that earth's dark bosom hides,
That rules in ocean, or in air presides.
To him had Grymer sent, o'er realms afar,
With costly gifts, to win him to the war,
When first imperial Woldomir implor'd,
In Scandinavia's aid, the hero's sword;

---

* Grymer.

ORIGINAL POETRY.

Nor lefs impell'd by envious hate, he came,
Of Odin's glory and of Woden's name.

 Intent to folve the dark decrees of fate,
In deep enquiry fix'd, the Wizard fate;
When, Grymer entering, from his feat he preft,
With eager hafte, and thus the Chief addreft.
" Say, at this hour, when o'er the dreary plains,
In all her horrors, Night funereal reigns;
While fhrieks of terror on the blaft arife,
And the black tempeft howls along the fkies;
At this untimely hour, what potent caufe
Forth from his tent the Prince of Scythia draws?"

 " O Sire of magic!" thus the Prince replied,—
" My Shield in battle, and my counfels' guide,
Full well to thee is known what weight of care
Hangs on the vaft uncertainty of war;
What anxious fears a leader's peace annoy,
Poffefs his foul, and every thought employ.
The chief who hopes in glory's walks to fhine,
And round his brows the palms of conqueft twine,
When war's dark tempeft fpreads its horrors round,
Not in the bowers of thoughtlefs Eafe is found;
Not on the lap of Sloth reclines his head,
By proud Prefumption's flattering glare mifled;—
Which oft the vainly confident betrays,
And lights to ruin with its phantom blaze;—
But, when the hour of battle hovers near,
Neglects no caution, tho' he knows no fear.
By cares like thefe impell'd, I hither come,
Of reft neglectful, mid the dreary gloom;

While, wide around, the camp in silence lies,
And slumber seals the wearied soldier's eyes:
For lo! to morrow wakes the rage of fight,
When morning opes the golden gates of light;
To morrow gives my eager arm to dare
This scourge of Scandia's realms, this pest of war;
Gives me, perchance, that first of joys to know,
The joy of vengeance on a hated foe.
For that fell hate, which steel'd our sires of yore,
Which dyed so oft in blood Jaxartes' shore,
That hate my breast with all its rage inspires,
Sublim'd, by rival love, to fiercer fires.
Yes! still revenge has set that day aside,
When, scorn'd my passion, and my suit denied,
Hermanric's daughter gave her heaven of charms,
Detested thought! to Odin's happy arms.
But tho' my soul delights where Danger rears
His awful crest, amid the strife of spears,
And glows with transport in the fierce alarms,
The shock of battles, and the din of arms;
Tho', in comparison, the foe are lost
Mid the vast numbers of our warlike host;
Yet not, in vain security, reclin'd,
The events of battle fill my anxious mind.
Perchance the Gods, too partial to the foe,
Our strength may wither, and our hopes o'erthrow;
For Odin long has prov'd their guardian care,
By Woden shielded in the storms of war;
And still the favoring God his aid affords,
And bears him harmless mid descending swords.
How oft has Scandia mourn'd her heroes' doom,
Swept, by that arm, in thousands, to the tomb!

Before his might her hosts have shrunk away,
Like mountain snows before the vernal ray.
Then let the all-conquering force of spells be tried,
And range the Powers of magic on our side;
Bid panic terror hover o'er their fight,
Chill the pale foe, and turn their steps to flight;
So may thy friend a double triumph prove,
And, with a nation's wrongs, avenge his slighted love."

The monarch ceas'd,—the words the wizard took,
While sarcasm smil'd contemptuous in his look.
" Dread'st thou that feeble race ? Can Grymer's soul
Thus bend to phantom terror's vile controul?
Do thoughts like those which little minds debase,
Become the leader of a warlike race?
Thy mighty Woden, and his Gods, at most,
A narrow sway, and power precarious boast.
In time's first day-spring, when as yet the earth
Knew not its place, nor ocean roll'd to birth;
Alone one torpid, vast abyss, was seen,
Uncloth'd with form, undeck'd with cheerful green;
Ere man the breath of first existence drew ;
Those sons of Bore the mighty Ymir slew,
By fraud his race confin'd, usurp'd the sway
O'er the blue mansions of unclouded day.
Yet still in fear their ill-got rule they hold,
Still dread the day, when vengeance uncontroll'd
Shall burst its chains, and, in destruction hurl'd,
A fiery deluge wrap the sinking world.
Then go, and Valhall's feeble Gods despise,
For Powers more mighty in thy aid shall rise ;—

Those Powers who o'er the gloom of night preside,
Live in the storm, and on " the whirlwind ride;"—
Shall whelm in dust the foes presumptuous boast,
And roll dark ruin o'er their prostrate host."

 The Wizard ceas'd—with brightening hopes inspir'd,
The Scythian monarch to his tent retir'd.

 Forth from his camp the dire Enchanter stray'd,
Mid the weird horrors of the midnight shade,
Till a lone dell his wandering footsteps found,
Fenc'd with rough cliffs, with mournful cypress crown'd,
There stay'd his course: with stern, terrific look,
Thrice wav'd on high, his magic wand he shook;
And thrice he rais'd the wild funereal yell
That calls the spirits from the abyss of hell.
When, shrilly answering to the yell afar,
Borne on the winds, three female forms appear;
Dire as the hag who, mid the dreams of night,
Pursues the fever'd hectic's trembling flight.
With gestures strange, approach the haggard band,
And nigh the wizard take their silent stand.
Near, in a rock, adown whose rugged side
The lonely waters of the desart glide,
O'ergrown with brambles, op'd an ample cave,
Drear as the gloomy mansions of the grave.
Within, the screech-owl made her mournful home,
And birds obscene that hover round the tomb;
Dark, from the moss-grown top, together clung,
Ill-omen'd bats, in torpid clusters, hung;
And o'er the bottom, with dank leaves bestrow'd,
Crept the black adder, and the bloated toad.

Thither the magic throng repair'd, to form
Their spells obscure, and weave the unhallow'd charm.
Muttering dire words, thrice strode the wizard round;
Thrice, with his potent wand, he smote the ground;
Deep groans ensued; on wings of circling flame,
Slow-rising from beneath, a Cauldron came;
Blue gleam'd the fires amid the shades of night,
And o'er the cavern shot a livid light.

  Now op'd a horrid scene : all black with blood,
The infernal band, prepar'd for slaughter, stood.
Two beauteous babes, by griffons borne away,
While lock'd in sleep the hapless mothers lay,
Whose smiles the frozen breast to love might warm,
And e'en the unsparing wolf to pity charm,
The hags unveil'd; and sportive as they play'd,
Deep in their hearts embrued the murderous blade;
Their dying pangs with smile malignant view'd,
And life's last ebbings in the sanguine flood.
Now, mix'd with various herbs of magic power,
In the dark cauldron glows the purple gore:
The Night-shade dire, whose baleful branches wave,
In glooms of horror, o'er the murderer's grave;
The Manchineel, alluring to the eye,
Where, veil'd in beauty, deadliest poisons lie;
The far-fam'd Indian Herb, of power to move
The foes of nature to unite in love,
The serpent race to infant mildness charm,
And the fierce tiger of his rage disarm,—
Known to the tribes that range the trackless wood
Where mad Antonio heaves the headlong flood;—

ORIGINAL POETRY.

The * Monster plant that blasts Tartaria's heath;
And Upas fatal as the stroke of death:
Boil'd the black mass, the associate fiends advance,
And round the Cauldron form the magic dance.
Three times around, in mystic maze they trod,
With hideous gesture, and terrific nod;
While Runic rhymes, and words that freeze the soul,
From their blue lips, in tones of horror, roll.
The wizard rais'd his voice, the cavern round,
Wild-shuddering, trembled at the fearful sound;
In mute attention stood the haggard throng,
As thus he woke the incantatory song.

 From the dreary realms below,
  From the dark domains of fear,
 From the ghastly seats of woe,
  Hear! tremendous Hela, hear!

I.

Dreadful Power! whose awful form
Blackens in the midnight storm;
Glares athwart the lurid skies,
While the sheeted lightening flies;
When the thunder awful roars;
When the earthquake rocks the shores;

---

* BAROMETZ, Tartarian Lamb:——A plant found in Tartary and the northern parts of China: It is covered with a very beautiful kind of furze or wool, of a bright yellow, and in its form has some resemblance to a LAMB, appearing to stand upon four legs, from so many roots to which it is attached. It is said to be of a nature so destructive to every other species of vegetables, that none will live within its vicinity.

Mounted on the wings of air,
Thou rul'st the elemental war.
When Famine brings her sickly train;
When Battle strews the carnag'd plain;
When Pestilence her venom'd wand
Waves o'er the desolated land;
Rush the ocean's whelming tides
O'er the foundering vessel's sides;
Then ascends thy voice on high;
Then is heard thy funeral cry;
Then, in horror, dost thou rise
On the expiring wretch's eyes.

From the dreary realms below,
  From the dark domains of fear,
From the ghastly seats of woe,
  Hear! tremendous Hela, hear!

II.

Goddess! whose terrific sway
Nastrande's realms of guilt obey;
Where, amid impervious gloom,
Sullen frowns the serpent Dome;
Roll'd beneath the envenom'd tide,
Where the sons of sorrow 'bide;
Thee, the mighty Demon host;
Thee, the Giants of the Frost;
Thee, the Genii tribes adore;
Fenris owns thy sovereign power:
And the imperial Prince of Fire,
Surtur, trembles at thine ire.

Thine, the victor's pride to mar;
Thine, to turn the scale of war;
Chiefs and princes at thy call,
From their spheres of glory fall;
Empires are in ruin hurl'd;
Desolation blasts the world.

From the dreary realms below
  From the dark domains of fear,
From the ghastly seats of woe,
  Hear! tremendous Hela, hear!

III.

Queen of terror, queen of death!
Thee, we summon from beneath.
From the deep infernal shade;
From the mansion of the dead;
Nieflehm's black, funereal dome;
Hither rise, and hither come!
By the potent Runic rhyme,
Awful, mystic, and sublime;
By the streams that roar below;
By the sable fount of woe;
By the burning gulph of pain,
Muspell's home, and Surtur's reign;
By the Day when, o'er the world,
Wild confusion shall be hurl'd,
Rymer mount his fiery car,
Giants, Genii, rush to war,
To vengeance move the Prince of Fire,
And heaven, and earth, in flames expire!

> From the dreary realms below,
>   From the dark domains of fear,
> From the ghastly seats of woe,
>   Hear! tremendous Hela! hear.

He ceas'd—the flames withdrew their magic light,
And, cloth'd in deeper horrors, frown'd the night.
At once, an awful stillness paus'd around,
Hush'd were the winds, and mute the tempest's sound,
One deep, portentous, calm o'er nature spread,
Nor e'en the aspin's restless foliage play'd;—
Such the dire calm that glooms Carribean shores
Ere, rous'd to rage, the fell Tornado roars:—
Not long, for lo! from central earth releas'd,
Shrill through the cavern sigh'd an hollow blast;
Wild wails of woe, with shrieks of terror join'd,
In deathful murmurs groan along the wind;
Peal following peal, hoarse bursts the thunder round;
Redoubling echoes swell the dreadful sound;
Flash the blue lightnings in continual blaze;
One sheet of fire the kindling gloom displays;
And o'er the vault, with pale, sulphureous ray,
Pour all the horrors of infernal day.
Now heav'd the vale around, the cavern'd rock,
The earth, deep trembling, to its center shook,
Wide yawn'd the rending floor, and gave to sight
A chasm tremendous as the gates of night.
Slow from the gulph, mid lightnings faintly seen,
Rose the dread form of Death's terrific Queen;
Of wolfish aspect, and with eyes of flame,
Black Jarnvid's Witch, her fell attendant, came;

Than whom, no monster roams the dark abodes,
More fear'd by friends, more hated by the Gods.

More frightful, more deform'd, than Fancy's power
Pourtrays the demon of the midnight hour,
In hideous majesty, of various hue,
Part fallow pale, and part a livid blue,
A form gigantic, awful Hela frown'd;
Her towering head with fable serpents crown'd;
Around her waist, in many a volume roll'd,
A crimson adder wreath'd his poisonous fold;
And o'er her face, beyond description dread,
A sulphury mist its shrouding mantle spread.
Her voice, the groan of war, the shriek of woe
When sinks the city whelm'd in gulphs below,
In tones of thunder, o'er the cavern broke,
And nature shudder'd as the Demon spoke.

"Presumptuous mortal! that, with mystic strain,
Dost summon Hela from the realms of pain,
What cause thus prompts thee rashly to invade
The deep repose of death's eternal shade?
What, from the abodes of never-ending night,
Calls me, reluctant, to the climes of light?"

"Empress supreme! whose wide-extended sway
All nature owns, and earth and hell obey;
The solemn call no trivial wish inspires;
No common cause thy potent aid requires;
The dooms of empires on the issue wait,
And doubtful tremble in the scale of fate.
The glow of morn, on yon extended heath,
Will light the nations to the strife of death.

There Saracinia's sons their force unite
With Scandia's monarch, Woldomir, in fight;
By strength combin'd, proud Odin to o'erwhelm,
The fierce invader of the Scandian realm;
By Woden favor'd with peculiar grace;
Friend of the gods, and odious to thy race.
Then, in the impending fight, thy succour lend,
And o'er our host thy arm of strength extend;
The hostile bands, protected by thy foes,
With dangers circle, and with ruin close;
With wild dismay their shrinking ranks pervade;
Whelm their pale numbers in the eternal shade;
And wing, with certain aim, the missive dart,
Or point the faulchion, to the leader's heart."

Thus Ulfo spoke—and Hela thus return'd.
" Know, while in primal night creation mourn'd,
The eternal cause, the great, all-ruling mind,
The various term of human life assign'd;
Irrevocably firm, the fix'd intent
No power can vary, and no chance prevert.
Mark'd, by the fates, for years of bloody strife,
Rolls the long flood of Odin's varied life;
Nor is it ours the stern decree to thwart
By open violence, or by covert art.
Yet still the power is left us to annoy,
Whom rigid heaven denies us to destroy;
And, tho of life secure, the hostile chief,
The wretched victim of severest grief,
Shall mourn his arms disgrac'd, on yonder plain,
His laurels blasted, and his heroes slain."

She ceased ;—in thunder vanishing from view,
The fiends, the cauldron, and the hags withdrew.
Back to the camp the Inchanter sped his way,
Ere, o'er the east, arose the first faint glimpse of day.

FOR THE PORT FOLIO.

*Ode to the Sheer Water. By the late Richard
Alsop, Esq.*

Whence with morn's first blush of light
  Com'st thou thus to greet mine eye,
Whilst the furious storm of night
  Hovers yet around the sky.

On the fiery, tossing wave
  Dost thou, calmly cradled, sleep,
When the midnight tempest raves
  Lonely wanderer of the deep!

Or from some rude Isle afar
  Castled midst the roaring waste,
With the beams of morning star
  On swiftest pinions dost thou haste?

In thy mottl'd plumage dress'd
  Light thou skim'st the ocean o'er,
Sporting round the breakers' crest,
  Exulting in the tempest's roar.

O'er the vast rolling wat'ry way
  While our trembling vessel's borne,
And my eyes with glad survey
  Watch the effulgent lamps of morn—

As through yon clouds its struggling beam
  Around a parted lustre shed,
And bright beneath the effusive gleams
  Each mountain billow lifts its head—

Far seen, while glittering in the ray,
  At distance, o'er th' expanse so blue,
White sided domes, and villa's gay
  Aspiring rise to Fancy's view.

From wave to wave, swift skimming light,
  Now near and now at distance found,
Thy airy form with ceaseless flight
  Cheers the lone dreariness around.

Through the vessels' storm rent sides
  When the rushing billows rave,
And with fierce gigantic strides
  Death terrific walks the waves—

Still on hovering pinions near
  Thou pursuest thy sportive way;
Still uncheck'd by aught of fear,
  Calmly seek'st thy finny prey.

Far from earth's remotest trace,
  What impels thee thus to roam?
What hast thou to mark the place
  When thou seek'st thy distant home?

Without star or magnet's aid
  Thou thy faithful course dost keep,
Careless still— still undismay'd,
  Lonely wanderer of the deep!

VERSES TO THE SHEARWATER—ON THE MORNING AFTER A STORM AT SEA.*

Whence with morn's first blush of light
   Com'st thou thus to greet mine eye,
Whilst the furious storm of night
   Hovers yet around the sky?

On the fiery tossing wave,
   Calmly cradled dost thou sleep,
When the midnight tempests rave,
   Lonely wanderer of the deep?

Or from some rude isle afar,
   Castled 'mid the roaring waste,
With the beams of morning's star,
   On lightning pinion dost thou haste?

In thy mottled plumage drest,
   Light thou skimm'st the ocean o'er,
Sporting round the breaker's crest
   Exulting in the tempest's roar.

O'er the vast-rolling watry way
   While our trembling bark is borne,
And joyful peers the lamp of day,
   Lighting up the brow of morn;

* This piece, we believe, has never before been printed.

As through yon cloud its struggling beams
  Around a partial lustre shed,
And mark at fits with golden gleams
  The mountain billow's surging head;

Whilst the long lines of foamy white,
  At distance o'er the expanse so blue,
As domes and castles spiring bright,
  Commingling, rise on fancy's view—

From wave to wave swift skimming light,
  Now near, and now at distance found,
Thy airy form, in ceaseless flight,
  Cheers the lone dreariness around.

Through the vessel's storm-rent sides,
  When the rushing billows rave;
And with fierce gigantic strides,
  Death terrific walks the wave,

Still on hovering pinion near,
  Thou pursuest thy sportive way;
Still unchcck'd by aught of fear,
  Calmly seek'st thy finny prey.

Far from earth's remotest trace,
  What impels thee thus to roam?
What hast thou to mark the place
  When thou seek'st thy distant home?

Without star or magnet's aid,
  Thou thy faithful course dost keep;
Sportive still, still undismay'd,
  Lonely wanderer of the deep!

HYMN TO PEACE.

Written at the conclusion of the last War with England.

While as yet with guilt unstained,
  Man through Eden happy strayed,
PEACE, the seraph, sole remained,
  Guardian of its blissful shade;
When from duty's path declined,
  Him the tempter lured astray,
The angel-guard his charge resigned,
  Weeping sped to heaven his way—
    Hail, thou bright celestial form,
      Soft descending from above,
    Calming Discord's furious storm,
      Child of Mercy, child of Love!

But when earth's wide regions o'er,
  Far the deluge flood was hurled,
While the ark the patriarch bore
  Midst the ruins of the world,
Thou, commissioned from on high,
  Didst repress the raging wave,
Arched the rainbow o'er the sky,
  To the dove the olive gave—
    Hail, thou bright celestial form,
      Soft descending from above,
    Calming Discord's furious storm,
      Child of Mercy, child of Love!

And when midst exulting heaven,
  Loud hosannas hailed the birth
Of a God and Saviour given
  To redeem the sons of earth,
Thou receiv'dst th' Almighty word—
  Go! o'er Bethlehem fix the star,
And bid the nations sheathe the sword
  Through remotest realms afar—
    Hail, thou bright celestial form,
      Soft descending from above,
    Calming Discord's furious storm,
      Child of Mercy, child of Love!

Long has War's unsparing hand
  Heaped the bloody fields with dead,
And through every Christian land,
  Want, dismay and sorrow spread,
Now the clouds of sorrow flee,
  Wars and fierce contentions cease;
We, in choral hymn, to thee,
  Hail thy coming, heavenly Peace—
    Hail, thou bright celestial form,
      Soft descending from above,
    Calming Discord's furious storm,
      Child of Mercy, child of Love!

HYMN TO PEACE

HAIL thou bright celestial form!
Soft descending from above,
Calming discord's furious storm,
Child of mercy! child of love!

While as yet to guilt unknown,
Man through Eden, happy stray'd,
PEACE, the seraph, stood alone
Guardian of its blissful shade;
When from duty's path declin'd
Him the tempter lur'd astray,
The angel-guard the charge resign'd
Weeping sped to *heaven* his way.

But when earth's wide regions o'er,
Far the deluge flood was hurl'd,
While the Ark the Patriarch bore,
Midst the ruins of the world,

Thou, commision'd from on high,
Did'st repress the raging wave;
Arch'd the rainbow o'er the sky
To the dove the olive gave.

And when midst exulting Heaven
Loud hosannahs hail'd the birth
Of a God, and Saviour given
To redeem the sons of earth,

Thou received'st th'Almighty word,
"Go, o'er Bethlem fix the star
"Bid the nations sheathe the sword
"Through remotest realms afar."

Long has war's unsparing hand,
Heap'd the bloody field with dead,
And through every Christian land
Want, dismay and terror spread.

Now the clouds of sorrow flee;
Wars and fierce contentions cease:
We in choral hymns to thee,
Hail thy coming, heavenly PEACE!

Hail thou bright, &c.
                    22nd February 1815

THE OATH OF HANNIBAL

From Silius Italicus—Book 1st.

Translated by R. ALSOP

By birth distinguished, by his prowess more,
The first command renown'd Hamilcar bore:
The chief indignant view'd his country's doom,
Disgrac'd and humbled by the arms of Rome,
And sought each means assiduous to inflame
His son with hatred of the Roman name,
When Reason first her glimmering dawn display'd,
And first his lisping tongue imperfect words essay'd.

   Just in the centre of the city flood
(In the dark bosom of a sacred wood,)
A fane in honor of Eliza rear'd,
By Carthage with religious awe rever'd.
Here baleful yew and larch obscur'd the ground,
And cypress cast a mournful gloom around:

No cheerful sun, in noontide splendour bright,
Through the close branches pour'd enlivening light,
But gloomiest night eternally display'd
Her sable pinions o'er the dreary shade.
Here, as 'tis said, the love-distracted queen
Clos'd, of a hapless life, the weary scene:
The mournful statues of her royal race
(Great Belus' progeny) adorn'd the place.
With Belus, Agenor, the nation's fame,
And ancient Phenix, whence Phenicia's name!
Sad Dido stood before her much-lov'd lord;
Beneath her feet was placed the Dardan sword.
To Gods celestial and infernal rais'd,
An hundred altars in long order blaz'd:
Here, in dishevell'd hair, the hoary priest,
In black attire and Stygian garments drest,
Invok'd aloud, with wild terrific yell,
The powers Ætnean, and the Gods of Hell.
Then the torn earth, opprest with terror, shook;
Through the dun shade dire screams of horror broke,
Sulphureous lightnings gleam'd a pallid ray,
The kindling altars flash'd with sudden day,
Then spectres, shrieking, shot athwart the gloom,
Compell'd by songs of magic from the tomb;
Eliza's statue trembled from its base,
And briny drops bedew'd the marble face.

These dark recesses stern Hamilcar sought;
Hither, with him, young Hannibal he brought:
With anxious care the sire his son survey'd,
No change of hue the signs of fear betray'd,
Nor wild Massylian priests, with fearful howl,
Nor barb'rous rites dismay'd his steadfast soul;
Nor the dire threshold, wet with human gore,
Nor Stygian flames, evok'd by magic lore.
With fond paternal kisses then he prest
The godlike boy, and clasp'd him to his breast,
And thus bespoke,—"The sons of Troy disgrace,
With stipulations vile, our Tyrian race;

But should opposing fate deny to me
My country's honour from this stain to free,
Thine, O my son! shall be the future praise,
Against proud Rome destructive wars to raise;
E'en now her youth with dread thy rising wait,
And Latian mothers mourn their offspring's fate."
By such incitements fir'd, he fierce reply'd,—
"When age maturer shall my councils guide,
By land, by sea, with sword and wasting flame,
Will I pursue that loath'd, detested name.
By thee, O Mars, terrific God of war!
By thy dread manes, mighty queen, I swear!
Tarpeian rocks and Alpine cliffs in vain
Shall lift their heights my vengeance to restrain;
No faith of treaties shall my arms confine,
No holy reverence for the powers divine,
No terms my settled enmity controul,
Or to soft peace dispose my vengeful soul."

 Then fell a sable victim to the power,
The tri-form'd Goddess of the midnight hour;
The priest explores, with *auruspicial* art,
The limbs yet quivering and the beating heart;
With skilful eye the various signs surveys,
Then thus, aloud, the will of fate displays.
"What routed bands o'er pale Ætolia pour?
What lakes are smoking with Idean gore?
Far off, what rocks immense to heaven ascend,
On whose aërial heights thy camps depend?
And lo, the pass is gain'd!—Dire havoc reigns,
And fires Sidonian light Hesperian plains;
O'er men and arms, in crimson billows roll'd,
I see the Po a bloody shroud unfold!
Here shall thy victor arms, 'mid fields of blood,
Raise thy third trophy to the thundering God.
Alas! what sudden clouds in tempest roll,
While flames terrific kindle o'er the pole?
Events of import vast the Gods prepare,
And Jove in thunder rushes to the war.
More to disclose the Queen of Heaven denies,
And veil'd in deepest shades the future lies."

DESCRIPTION OF HANNIBAL

From the same—By the same.

SWIFTLY his furious course he thither prest;
Far gleam the fatal lightnings of his crest.
So, scattering bloody fires, the comet's blaze,
With flaming train, barbarian realms dismays;
Its torch portentous, in continual stream,
Wide o'er the heavens emits a ruddy beam;
From the red star terrific sparklings hurl'd,
Menace destruction to the astonish'd world.
Before him standards, arms, the embattled host,
Swiftly recede in wild confusion lost;
Both armies tremble—from his massy shield
A glancing splendour lightens o'er the field;
His javelin's fiery point sends forth afar
A dreadful radiance through the ranks of war.
So the Ægean sea, rough, swelling high,
Heaves its tumultous billows to the sky,
When wintry Caurus howls, with hideous roar,
The uplifted waters tumbling to the shore,
With dread the shivering sailors stand aghast;
Hoarse sounds the surge, and, maddening with the blast,
Wide o'er the trembling Cyclades is cast.
Not flaming brands, nor all the missile showers,
Incessant pouring from the hostile towers:
Nor rocks, from engines thrown, avail to stay
Or check the ardent chief's resistless way.

A SONG.

From the Italian.

BY R. ALSOP.

COME fair Iola let us love!
   For swift the winged minutes move,
With speed more rapid than the dart
That strikes the bounding leopard's heart.

That tender flower will soon decay,
Transient and fleeting is its day;
That flower of youth, thy beauties bloom,
Cold withering Age shall soon consume.

At eve, beneath the ocean's bed,
The beauteous planet hides his head;
But with the dawn's returning light
In new-born splendour rises bright.

Stern Winter rends, with tempests rude,
Its verdant foliage from the wood;
But Spring restores, with brighter hue,
And bids its beauties bloom anew.

But of our age the youthful flower,
No genial spring can e'er restore;
And once when set in shades of night
No morn relumes our vital light.

In the drear regions of the tomb,
Amid Oblivion's endless gloom,
Amid eternal Horror's frown,
No voice of love is ever known.

Ah! then, while yet the power we have,
Ere Time resumes the boon he gave;
While still with freshest tints it glows,
Ah let us pluck the blooming rose!

Inspir'd by love, our hearts disdain
The censures of that hoary train;
To lovers stern, of love the foe,
Whose frigid breasts no passion know.

Then fair Iola let us love!
For swift the winged minutes move,
With speed more rapid than the dart
That strikes the bounding leopard's heart.

DESCRIPTION OF AN AFRICAN SERPENT

From the 6th Book of Silius Italicus

Translated (1782) by RICHARD ALSOP

Its turbid wave, where wide Brigada pours,
Through wilds and deserts to the Lybian shores,
And o'er the far-stretch'd plains diffuses wide
A stagnant water and polluted tide,
In search of plants we came—which o'er that land
Penurious Nature spreads with scanty hand.

Near the steep bank an aged forest stood,
Whose horrid gloom imbrown'd the bordering flood;
Through the thick boughs no quivering sun-beam play'd,
But dusky darkness wrap'd the dreary shade,
And hoary mists, which putrid fens exhale,
With pois'nous vapours clogg'd the tainted gale.
Within the wood a winding cavern lay,
Whose dire recesses ne'er admitted day;
E'en at the thought wild terrors still arise,
And chilling fears my panting heart surprise,
A monstrous serpent, venomous and dread,
Whose length immense and hundred cubits spread;
Whom in her anger earth vindictive bore,
The grove infested, and polluted shore.
No era e'er disclos'd to mortal eyes
A pest more fell, or of superior size.
Seiz'd by surprise, along the shady stream,
The furious lion oft his prey became;
And flocks and herds that hither sought retreat
From the fierce fervors of meridian heat;
Or birds, attracted to the noisome wood
By putrid carcases and fœtid blood:

Limbs half devour'd, and bones dispers'd around,
The air infected, and defiled the ground.
When swoln with blood, and surfeited with prey,
In the black cave the hideous monster lay;
Or oft, when heated with his fervent food,
Sought the cool shelter of the rapid flood,
Nor wholly sunk beneath the wave remain'd,
But on the adverse shore his head sustain'd.
Of this unconscious, nor of aught afraid,
I went to explore the secrets of this shade,
With Umbrian Havens and Aquinus bred,
Where snow-clad Apennine exalts its head.
Approaching near, our minds dire horror fill'd,
With panic fears our shivering limbs were chill'd;
Yet still we enter, and the nymphs adore,
And God unknown, whose waters lave the shore;
And, tho' with terror thrill'd, our way pursu'd
To the dark centre of the fatal wood,
When from the entrance of the cave profound
A stygian whirlwind rush'd with fearful sound.
No fiercer blast rude Eurus ever pour'd
From his cold chambers with bleak tempests stor'd;
Infernal hissings from the gulph accurst,
With sprinkling rain, and storms loud howling, burst.
Pale with dismay, we heard the earth resound,
And felt quick tremblings shake the solid ground,
When from the cave, by spectres usher'd, roll'd,
The monster fell in many a hideous fold.
Arm'd with such snakes, the earth-born Giants strove
To arrest the thunder from imperial Jove;
Such as Amphytrion's mighty son subdu'd,
Where snaky Lerna rolls its poisonous flood,
And such secur'd the Hesperian garden fam'd,
With golden fruit whose trees far-glittering flam'd.
His monstrous head from earth to heaven he rais'd;
In his dread front terrific splendours blaz'd;
From his black mouth, a flood of venom cast,
The air infected with a pois'nous blast.
With palpitating hearts, in vain, we fly,
And for assistance raise a piteous cry;

Wide o'er the wood his hiss shrill-startling rolls,
And dark'ning fears distract our boding souls.
Condemning the rash enterprise too late,
Unhappy Havens found a dreadful fate;
In a large oak conceal'd, he sought to elude
The watchful serpent, who his flight pursued;
And, scarce could I myself believe it true,
His monst'rous folds around the tree he threw,
And close encircling, tore it from the ground;
Rent from its deepest roots it fell with rushing sound;
Then seizing in his fangs the youth dismay'd,
With outstretch'd arms in vain imploring aid,
In his black jaws absorb'd the struggling prey,
Who, living, buried in his entrails lay.
Hapless Aquinus on the stream rely'd,
And swiftly swam across the rapid tide;
In vain his efforts, 'midst the river caught,
Him to the shore the frightful monster brought,
And there a horrid scene my eyes survey'd,
As on his quiv'ring limbs, while yet alive, he prey'd.

From the dire place, in headlong flight I sped,
Impell'd by wild dismay, and wing'd with dread,
And to the camp escap'd, inform'd the chief,
In broken accents and a flood of grief;
At the sad tale his eyes with tears were fill'd,
And pity for their fate his bosom thrill'd;
But love of fame, with dauntless valour join'd,
To scorn of danger fir'd his generous mind,
Which equal shone, both in surprise by night,
In hosts embattled, and in single fight.
Fir'd with impatience to avenge the slain,
He bade the equestrian squadron seek the plain;
And ardent first advanc'd with matchless speed,
Exciting with the spur his foaming steed.
The troops obey—and instantly prepare
The vast *balistae* and machines of war,
And to the field the spear immense convey'd,
Which oft proud turrets in destruction laid.

Soon as the coursers reach'd the adjacent plain,
And hollow tramplings echoed through the den;
Rouz'd at the tumult, forth the dragon came,
Emitting from his jaws sulphureous flame;
From his broad front terrific lightnings fly,
And sparkling fury glows in either eye;
High rais'd in air, he lifts his head above
The topmost branches of the towering grove;
His forky tongues in quick vibrations fly,
And, darting upwards, lick the azure sky.
When first the trumpet's martial notes he hear'd,
In deep surprise his form immense he rear'd;
And with his back reclin'd, his length comprest
In sinuous folds beneath his scaly breast;
Then swift unloosing his contorted train,
His glittering bulk extended o'er the plain;
And on the shore advanc'd the sight to try,
While wild amazement look'd from every eye.
When near approach'd, the troops beheld their foe,
Congeal'd awhile, the blood forgot to flow:
Scarce could the rider rule his trembling steed,
From whose black nostrils pitchy flames proceed.
With scornful pride, as he the host survey'd,
In threat'ning motion wav'd his lofty head;
Now fir'd to rage the gory corse he tears,
And high in air the mangled carcase rears;
Now his strong orbs convolves, in wanton play,
With strict embrace around his shapeless prey;
Now the black flesh absorbs and crimson tide,
Then his voracious jaws, expanding wide,
Disgorges broken bones and clotted gore,
And leaves the limbs half-eaten on the shore.
With rising terrors every bosom chill'd,
To panic fears the bravest soldiers yield;
At length the squadrons in confusion fly,
With pallid cheek and wildly-glaring eye,
In vain the eagles should their flight restrain,
With them ignobly hurried o'er the plain;
When thus the leader stopp'd their shameful flight,
The recreant bands inciting to the fight.

"Shall the Italian youth, in arms renown'd,
Inferior to a Lybian snake be found?
Does his vast yawn your timorous souls affright,
Or empty blasts pale cowardice excite?
Unaided I to meet his rage will go—
This hand alone shall quell your dreaded foe."
He said—and fearless straight approaching near,
From his strong arm discharg'd the massy spear;
With force Herculean hurl'd, the weapon flies,
And in a whirlwind cleaves the liquid skies.
The flying lance the advancing monster found,
And in his forehead deep impress'd a wound;
Fix'd in his head the point firm-rooted stood,
And in vibrations play'd the quiv'ring wood:
In loud acclaim straight plausive voices rise,
While mingled shouts of triumph rend the skies.
Stung with the smart with tenfold rage he burns,
And all on Regulus his fury turns;
For, new to pain, no vent'rous steel before
E'er his bright form distain'd with streaming gore.
Nor had his vengeance sought his foe in vain,
To madness fir'd by agonizing pain;
Had not the Chief, well skill'd to rule the steed,
By art eluded his impetuous speed;
Turn'd to the left he fled, with loosen'd rein,
The serpent swift pursuing o'er the plain,
With flexile back, in undulating course,
The various mazes of the flying horse.
Nor Marus' hand slept idle by his side,
Next in his venom'd blood my spear was dyed;
For now the fainting steed, opprest with pain,
The unequal strife no longer could maintain,
While close behind the foe, fierce threat'ning hung,
And brandish'd o'er his back his triple tongue;
That fateful moment I my javelin threw,
And on myself his vengeful fury drew.
The cohort next their brandish'd weapons plied,
And each in turn the monster's rage defied;
From a balista hurl'd, at length, a rock
His course arrested with a thundering stroke;

Stunn'd and disabled by the forceful blow,
No more with ardour he pursues the foe;
No more his head he raises to the skies;
No more its wonted aid the wounded spine supplies.
And now deep crimson'd in his vital blood,
Fix'd in his side the *mural javelin* stood;
And showers of arrows clos'd his eyes in night,
Whose glaring orbs diffus'd a baleful light.
He now lay faintly gasping on the shore,
His shining form with wounds all cover'd o'er,
And from his deadly mouth pour'd forth a flood
Of verdant poison, mix'd with clotted blood;
Transfix'd with spears, to move, in vain, he try'd,
Yet menac'd still with jaws distended wide,
When in hoarse thunder from an engine fled
A pond'rous beam, and lopp'd his hideous head;
Then on the bank outstretch'd, expiring, broke
From his black mouth pale wreaths of pois'nous smoke.
From the sad river burst the notes of woe,
And broken murmurs from the gulphs below,
The gloomy cave, the banks and grove around,
In mournful concert, echoed back the sound.

ADDRESSED TO AN INFANT BOY WITH A SMALL TOY-WATCH.

By the late Mr. Alsop.

SWEETLY smiling cherub child,
   Blooming in this infant spring;
In whose breast no care resides,
   Nor grief has fixed its bitter sting.

From one by tender ties affin'd,
   One, who holds thy welfare dear,
This small pledge of love receive,
   Present of the opening year.

Emblem of thy little day,
   Scarce past *one*, it points the hour;
Yet a little, and will pass
   Childhood's sweetly blooming flower.

To thy artless, fond caress,
   Infant play, and painted toys;
Of youths the herald, will succeed
   Boyhood's sports, and ruder joys.

Swift the sportive years have flown,
   'Neath the feathered foot of time;
Lo! the youth, a boy no more,
   Glows elate in manhood's prime.

Other objects now engage,
   Loftier views the mind employ;
Ill exchanged, the happy sports
   Of the once contented boy.

May this little mark of love,
    Thy dark eyes with pleasure light:
And when older grown, no more
    Infant plays and toys invite.

Not unsuccessful may it prove,
    But impress the important truth;
The golden moments not to lose,
    That deck the brilliant morn of youth.

May improvement stamp each hour,
    Well employed each day be found;
Each month new store of knowledge yield,
    With added worth each year be crowned.

For oh! too soon, with course unmarked,
    The fleeting hours away will glide,
'Till days, and months, and years have past
    In time's forever ebbing tide.

INSCRIPTION FOR A FAMILY TOMB.

O thou, by fortune or reflection led,
To view this gloomy mansion of the dead,
O'er the sad spot, as casual roams thine eye,
Where cold in dust our mouldering relics lie,
Permit not sacrilege, with insult base,
To spurn our ashes, or our bones displace.
Nor let the voice of impious mirth presume
To break the hallowed silence of the tomb.
Reflect that youth, that beauty, now no more,
Here sleep, unconscious of the form they wore:
Here genius low on earth extends his head,
His high-souled schemes of glittering fancy fled;
Here moulder hearts that once were prompt to feel
Love's melting glow, and Friendship's fervid zeal;
Hearts that with thine might boast as bright a flame,
As gay a spirit, animate their frame;
Who once like thee, in pleasure's sportive ray,
Passed the short sunshine of life's summer's day.

And thou, when, wearied with this mortal strife,
Exhausted nature brings the eve of life,
From wintry storms a refuge safe shall crave,
And find with us that refuge in the grave.

THE POETRY

OF THE

MINOR CONNECTICUT WITS

ELIHU HUBBARD SMITH

EDWIN AND ANGELINA;

OR

THE BANDITTI.

AN OPERA, IN THREE ACTS.

NEW-YORK:
Printed by T. & J. SWORDS, No. 99 Pearl-street.
—1797.—

Copy-right secured according to Law.

To Reuben *and* Abigail Smith, *Lichfield, Connecticut.*

My dear Parents,

I CAN *not resist the feelings which impel me to seize this first, and perhaps only, opportunity, of publicly testifying to you my respect and affection.—To you I am indebted, not merely for life, but for instruction and example happily calculated to explain, and impress me with a sense of, its value, and the inestimable purposes to which it may be applied. If, in my past or future conduct, any conformity to your desires and precepts appear; if, by any past or future exertions of mine, the welfare of mankind be in any degree promoted; to your cares, to your vigilance, to your virtues, will it be owing. It is, therefore, a simple act of justice, to make my first acknowledgments to you.—The panegyric of a poet, on his patron, may justly be suspected; but who will venture to question the sincerity of a son, who dedicates to his parents?—Nor need your modesty be wounded, by this public mark of my esteem. Should my conduct prove me worthy to claim relation to you, it will best pronounce your eulogy: my follies and my vices can only affect myself.—Accept then, my dear parents, this new proof of my sincere and filial love.*

E. H. SMITH.

PREFACE.

AN Author, of some reputation, has declared it as his opinion, that every Preface should be historical; and explain, not only the design of the work it precedes, but the circumstances and motives which led to its composition. It would ill become me to controvert a doctrine so convenient for my present purpose. Authors, it is true, are apt to measure the respect of others for their productions, by the estimation in which they are held by themselves. In this they may be, and often are, deceived. Yet, perhaps, they do not greatly err, when they suppose the history of their performances would not be unpleasing to those who have thought the performances themselves worthy of their attention. Such an error, at least, is venial; and will, I hope, be pardoned by those who may deem the succeeding statement unnecessary.

The principal scenes of the following Drama were composed in March, 1791; as an exercise, to beguile the weariness of a short period of involuntary leisure; and without any view to theatrical representation. From that time, till the month of October, 1793, they lay neglected, and almost forgotten. An accident then bringing them to recollection, several short scenes were added, agreeable to my original design; and the whole adapted to the Stage. The piece was presented to the *then* Managers of The Old American Company, for their acceptance, the December following; but the peculiar situation of the Theatre prevented any attention to this application, till June, 1794; when, on a change in the management, it was

was accepted. An interval of six months, and a further acquaintance with the Stage, had convinced me that the Piece might undergo alterations, with advantage. These were undertaken, immediately: the loss of a comic character, which was now rejected, was supplied by two new scenes; additional songs were composed; and a Drama of two acts, in prose, was converted into the Opera, in its present form, in the course of the succeeding month. The inherent defects of the plan were such as could not be remedied, without bestowing on the subject a degree of attention incompatible with professional engagements; and which I, therefore, thought myself justified in withholding. But should this performance meet the same generous indulgence, in private, with which it was received, in public, I shall neither attempt to disarm Criticism of her severity, nor be ashamed of this feeble effort to contribute to the rational amusement of my fellow-citizens.

New-York, Feb. 15, 1797.

P. S. It may not be improper to observe, (though the reader can scarcely be supposed uninformed, in this particular,) that the first, second, third, fifth and sixth songs, in the third Act of the following Drama, are from Goldsmith; and all, except the first, from the Ballad of "Edwin and Angelina." I have taken the liberty to make a slight alteration in the second, to accommodate it more perfectly to my purpose; and it will be obvious that, in the principal scene between Edwin and Angelina, I have availed myself of the sentiments, and, as far as possible, of the very expressions of the Author.

PERSONS OF THE DRAMA.

SIFRID,	Mr. HODGKINSON.
EDWIN,	Mr. TYLER.
ETHELBERT,	Mr. MARTIN.
WALTER,	Mr. CROSBY.
EDRED,	Mr. MUNTO.
HUGO,	Mr. MILLER.
BANDITTI.	
ANGELINA,	Mrs. HODGKINSON.

The Scene lies in a Forest, on the northern extremity of England; and in a Cavern, and the entrance of a Hermitage, in the Forest.

Time, that of the Representation.

The Reader is desired to correct the following Errors of the Press, which occur in the subsequent Pages.

Page 14, line 4th from the bottom, for "joys" read *joy*.
Page 39, line 6th from the top, for "pluming" read *plumy*.
Page 67, line 9th from the top, for "the" read *he*.

EDWIN AND ANGELINA.

ACT FIRST. SCENE I.

SIFRID *enters, as from an Engagement.*

SIFRID.

AWAY! detested thought! .... I will not think!
Visionary forms, phantoms of horror,
Hover not around me!——A murderer!
A Youth so beautifully form'd withal;
Of such magnanimous and warlike soul;
'Twas damnable!——A robber!——Observant,—
Watching the unsuspicious step of Wealth,
And with infuriate, with relentless rage,
Marring the works of nature and of man!——
——Damnation! And what to me is Nature?
What, but a treacherous and detested guide,
Leading my footsteps up the height of heaven,
To hurl me thence precipitate to hell?
What Man? but a dark savage, furious for his prey,
And arm'd with subtiler skill, by reason's aid,
To seize, and to secure, it? Full of wiles,
When powerless; empower'd, a gaunt hyæna,
Snatching at life, and gluttonous of death.
'Twas man that bow'd, opprest, destroy'd me,
Girded with power, that ravisht every blessing;
Ease, liberty, and love:—that cast me forth,

B   Drove

Drove out, a monster, from the haunts of men,
To foam and chafe, to prowl for prey, and shake,
With fierce alarms, these wild resounding woods.
——O woods, ye woods, who lift your towering trunks,
And wave your dark tops in the northern breeze,
Safe from the barbarous and despoiling axe;——
Thou cavern'd rock, grotesque and rude, whose top
The mountain-laurel, and whose shelving side
The gadding frost-vine, cover and adorn;——
And ye, ye fountains, whose translucent streams,
Irriguous, beautify the forest wild,
Bursting, white-foaming, from this rocky cave,
Fit haunt of souls like mine!—O bear me witness!
To you alone my sorrows I unfold;
Covering my face with smiles, or, on my brow,
Bearing the stern look of revengeful war,
Before my fellows:——O be witness ye!
Once I was happy: competence and ease,
And glorious freedom, blest me; and, supreme,
Extent, and height, and crown, of every joy,
Love, ardent and sincere, I felt, I knew,
And saw return'd, successful. No remorse
Steept its foul bitter in my cup of bliss.
—Remorse!—stern God of Vengeance! why remorse?
Was it not man, proud man, insulting man,
Tyrannous, and boastful of his noble blood,
That tore, with ruffian hand, my joys away?
Do I not right to make him smart for this?
To spoil him of his wealth, strip him of power,
And o'er his rich domains spread wasting war?
—Thou know'st, inscrutable God! thou knowest well,
That never on the weak my vengeance came;

That I have never ſtript the poor, but ſav'd
His humble cot, and ſpar'd his little flock.

 The mountain ſtreams, full, deep, and wide,
  By bounds uncheckt, majeſtic, flow,
 Roll peaceful down the ſloping ſide,
  And bleſs the ways thro' which they flow.

 But, if proud man ſhall dare reſtrain,
  Foreſts nor rocks withſtand their force;
 They thunder headlong to the plain;
  And deſolation marks their courſe.

 Yet, o'er the low and humble vale,
  Gently, their waters they diffuſe;
 Green ſprings the blade, and, thro' the dale,
  Each faded flower its bloom renews.

SCENE II.

Enter, to SIFRID, EDRED *and* WALTER; *as from purſuit.*

SIFRID. EDRED. WALTER.

SIFRID *(As they enter.)*
Welcome, brave chiefs! What? have you juſt return'd?
Say, did we not the conflict well ſuſtain?
With valorous and gallant uſe of arms?
   EDRED.
O noble chief! moſt terrible this night!

Moſt fierce and deadly this our laſt encounter!
If we, in each attempt, ſo much muſt dare,
Hazard ſo much; nought but increaſe of ſtrength,
Or the moſt deſperate prowefs, can uphold us.
Alarm already ſpeaks of us.
          WALTER.
                    Be it ſo.
Strong in our nature, and inur'd to toil,
Of ſuffering patient, and reſolv'd of mind,
We fight with double 'vantage: while the cauſe,—
Thrice damn'd oppreſſion,—which the ſtrength impairs
Of tyrant lordlings, gives us growing force.
Think you that men, men like themſelves endow'd,
Or to themſelves ſuperior, long will bend,
To the low duſt, the knee,—and ſtoop the head,
To ſlaviſh vaſſalage, and feudal pride?
And tremble in a miſ-nam'd Noble's preſence?
It cannot be: ſoon will they ſpurn the yoke,
Fly to our aid, and emulate our zeal.
If not,—we are ourſelves,—we have a chief,—
And, Sifrid at our head, we dare oppoſe
The utmoſt front of tyrannous invaſion.
          SIFRID.
Thanks my friend!
Nor of your love, nor courage do I doubt:
But all muſt not be valorous as him
With whom we laſt contended. To my ſoul,
Us'd as I am to carnage and to blood,
The blow, which caus'd his death, gave many pangs.
When he beheld his dear companions ſlain,
With ſuch a generous diſregard of life
He fought; ſuch brave indignancy, that he,
                              Of

Of all the band of love, alone was left;
The single wearer of detested life;
I could have snatcht him to my soul, kist him,
And call'd him brother. But why lament him?
The world has cast me out, and let it perish!
    EDRED *and* WALTER.
'Tis nobly spoken, Captain!
     WALTER.
       Now, by my soul!
Did I not hope to spread devouring flame,
And shake, o'er peers, the desolating scourge;
Were not my earnest expectation, soon,
Death in the van, and ruin in the rear,
To raze the castle, mine the haughty towers,
And bow their sky-assailing heads to earth;
Existence were my scorn, my very hate,
The heavy vengeance of the angry heavens.
     SIFRID.
O we have suffer'd foul, foul wrongs, my brother!
And, by the arm of God! we will have right,
Have sweet revenge!
    EDRED *and* WALTER.
     We will!
     SIFRID.
       But where are they,
Our bold compeers, and brothers, in this cause?
They were not wont, with such a leaden pace,
Behind their chief to loiter.
     EDRED.
      Nor do they.
Fiercely they urge pursuit, if chance their steps
May yet o'ertake two recreant knaves, who fled,
Diverse, their braver friends most base forsaking.
      SIFRID.

SIFRID. *(Agitated, and to himself.)*
And muſt there be more blood? and more of murder?
EDRED.
Of blood?
WALTER.
Of murder?—What means our Captain?
SIFRID. *(To himſelf.)*
Almighty God! thou know'ſt 'twas not my fault—
That I was clean of hands, humane of heart——
Had rather died myſelf, than wrong'd a brother——
WALTER.
Sifrid! Thou prat'ſt! By heaven! I am aſham'd;
I bluſh for thee:——Think on thy duty chief!
SIFRID. *(Still inattentive.)*
And him I thought my friend—whoſe ſoul I deem'd
The very fount whence truth and honor flow'd——
Demons of hell ſhall torture him for this!
WALTER.
Why now I know thee: throw aſide this gloom:
Obſerve how fair the day, and what its promiſe.
EDRED.
See how the glowing ſun ſhoots his fierce beams,
Urging the traveller, o'ercome with heat,
To ſeek the ſhady covert of theſe woods.
Obſerve! and baniſh ſorrow from thy ſoul.

 The ſafe and calm retreat of peace,
 May court and cheriſh thoughts like theſe,
  And draw, from ſadneſs, ſweeteſt joys;
 But, 'mid the loud alarms of war,
 A ſterner tone the ſoul ſhould ſhare,
  And ruder ſcenes its hopes employ.

SCENE

SCENE III.

The Banditti shout, behind the Scenes, and show themselves, coming down the Avenues, bringing HUGO *bound.* EDRED *speaks as they enter.*

SIFRID, EDRED, WALTER, BANDITTI, *and* HUGO.

EDRED.
Hark! 'tis our friends! that shout bespeaks success.

(By the Band.)
Here let mirth, let pleasure dwell;
  Hence all grief and sadness fly;
Glory brightens up our cell;
  Riches all our wants supply.

(Single Voice.)
When wars surround, and dangers rise,
The wise and brave should shun surprize;
With steady valour meet their rage,
With sober courage battle wage.

But, when the doubtful conflict's past,
And triumph crowns their arms at last;
When all its treasures wealth imparts,
Care swift should vanish from their hearts.

(By the Band.)
Here let mirth, let pleasure dwell;
Hence all grief and sadness fly;
Glory brightens up our cell;
Riches all our wants supply.

ALL BANDITTI.
Long life to Sifrid!
SIFRID.
Welcome, thrice welcome,
Noble brothers! Now, by my head I swear,
It joys me much to see you thus return;
So full of life, of spirit, and of joy;
With numbers so entire; after such rude
And dangerous conflict. Triumph like to this
Our Band knew never,—victory so complete.
FIRST BAND.
Never, our Captain: some half-score except,
Who fell, sore prest by numbers, all return.
SIFRID.
'Tis well. But say, who is this captive slave?
FIRST BAND.
A trembling, coward knave; a very fool;
Whom we, deceiv'd, pursu'd; mistaking him
For one of nobler sort, and bolder heart,
Who somehow hath escap'd us.—*(To Hugo.)* Sirrah,
 knave!
Hold up thy head.—*(To Sifrid.)* So full is he of fear,
As yet, our Chief, we nought have learnt of him.
SIFRID. *(To Hugo.)*
Captive! resume thy courage man! Look up!
There shall no harm be done thee—Fear'st thou yet?
Fellow,

Fellow, I swear to thee upon my sword,
Nay, by my head I swear, no mischievous,
Or deadly evil, shall be practis'd on thee.
Who? What thou art? Why here? Briefly unfold.
    HUGO.
Dread Sir, have mercy on me! Nought am I,
But a poor slave, the follower of a lord,
Who, thro' this country, seeks a wandering maid;
For whose dear love all comfort he foregoes.
But yester-morn, he join'd him to a band,
Of noble knights, who sought the North of Wales;
For better safety, travelling together.
Alas! most sad mischance! none of that band,
My master's self except, now tastes of life.
    SIFRID.
And he?
    HUGO.
  He, he alone, escap'd; urging
With wondrous speed, down the steep rock, his flight.
    SIFRID.
Haste thee! disclose his name and quality.
    HUGO.
'Mid England's Peers, the first;——Earl Ethelbert.
    SIFRID.
Earl Ethelbert!—Thunder of Heaven!—What he?—
And roam these woods?—He here? within my power?
Why yes!—'tis well!—Now, by the arm of God!—
Vengeance!—revenge!—O! it is well!—'tis well!—
  EDRED. *(To Walter.)*
What may this mean?
    WALTER. *(To Edred.)*
    Speak to him, Edred.
  C   EDRED.

EDRED. *(To Walter)*
                                      I will.
Captain! brother! friend! Sifrid!—What ails thee?
What dreadful paſſion agitates thy ſoul?
                SIFRID.
Can he love?—Curſes blaſt his love!—No—no——
I will have ample, will have ſweet revenge!
                EDRED.
Sifrid!—He hears me not.—Sifrid, my friend!
Are we not ſworn to thee?—Tell us thy wrong.
                SIFRID.
Forgive me! O my good friends, forgive me!
I have done much injuſtice to your love,
Thus long to hide it from you; but will now——
                    (To the Band.)
Bear hence that ſlave, and ſee him cloſe confin'd!
Then, my kind brothers, haſten to return;
For I would bare my heart, and nought conceal.

    The generous heart, diſtreſt with ſhame,
        Still, ſtill would hide its grief;
    Nor e'er the inglorious reaſon name,
        While far is yet relief.

    But when redreſs at length appears,
        Its wrongs conceal'd no more,
    Each friend the ſhameful ſecret hears,
        And aids revenge's power.

SCENE

SCENE IV.

The Banditti return.

SIFRID. EDRED. WALTER. BANDITTI.

  SIFRID. *(To those who enter.)*
My brothers, it is well.—'Mid all my griefs,
Much does it joy my soul to find such friends.
    FIRST BANDIT.
Captain, we love you.
    SIFRID.
      Nay, I know it well,
And now confide my story to your love.
——'Twas my most hapless lot my birth to gain
In the same city with Earl Ethelbert.
His sire, of the first rank, (as sure you know,)
Was wealthy; and reported generous.
I was of noble birth—but—poor.—While young,
Distinction proud was neither known nor felt:
Like passions, and resembling taste, were ours;
And in sweet friendship's bands united us.
    EDRED.
And what could interrupt?—He did not dare——
    SIFRID.
Observe!—To manhood now arriv'd, his sire
To France dismist him, hoping his improvement.
——O fatal error! thus alone to trust,
Remote from friends, in life's most dangerous prime,
         Gay.

Gay, inconsiderate, and warm-glowing youth!——
——'Twas there his passions gain'd the mastery;
And he, profuse of wealth, unaw'd by rule,
And ignorant of restraint; flatter'd, caress,
His every humour studied; all his wants,
His passions all, supplied; grew vain, debauch'd,
Selfish and mercenary, false and cruel,

EDRED.
Ha!—I see——The Earl——

SIFRID.
                    Give heed!—It so befel,
Himself far off, and rioting in joys,
His father died.   Then, and not till then, he,
To receive, at once, estate and title,
From abroad, return'd.

EDRED.
                Splendidly, no doubt;
With dissolute and arrogant demeanor.

SIFRID.
Most true.—In place exalted, he no more
His former friend recogniz'd; now, indeed,
A simple husbandman, of manners plain.
Nor did neglect alone content his soul;
Which, first estrang'd, soon hurried on to hate,
And urg'd his hand to deeds of foul oppression.

WALTER.
Most execrable villain!

SIFRID.
            I was weak———

WALTER.
Damn'd, damn'd villain!

SIFRID.

SIFRID.
               Nor yet was quite subdu'd,
Tho' deeply wounded, the true love I bore him.——
To struggle was but vain. His rank and power,
Banisht all hope, and might defy all strength.
Convinc'd, I left my farm; becoming tenant
To a neighbouring Lord. There I saw, and lov'd,
The daughter of a man like me.
               WALTER.
               And Ethelbert——
The Earl——
               SIFRID.
    Wealth, alone, she had not.—I scorn'd it.—
               WALTER.
And she?——
               SIFRID.
    Had not heard of affectation:
I was belov'd.
               EDRED.
    And you were happy?
               SIFRID.
                         No!
               EDRED.
No?
               SIFRID.
O, no! This lord, this Ethelbert, this Earl,
Must have—O foul appendage! shame to rank!
A Mistress.
               WALTER.
        And he did strive——
               SIFRID.
                    Strove to gain,
                         Betray,

Betray, corrupt, my Emma.
WALTER.
Thief! villain!
SIFRID.
Submissive, tender, complaisant, and mild,
The importuning lover long he play'd:
But she was constant; and with armed force,
At night, he bore her captive to his tower.
WALTER.
Ruffian accurst!
SIFRID.
Nor knew we where she was.
He tried all arts; but she, inflexible,
To faithlessness or shame, did death prefer.
ALL BAND.
Noble woman!
EDRED.
The Earl———
SIFRID.
With disappointment rais'd to frantic rage,
And furious that to him I caus'd denial;
He nor restrain'd, nor limited his hate.
Me, he procur'd imprison'd;———basely fed;———
WALTER.
Tyrant!
SIFRID.
I had forgiven him,———but he held,
In vile captivity, my love; and hop'd,
By long attention, to o'ercome her hate.
A year past on; he caus'd report be spread,
Nay, told her, I was dead. And then—*(wildly.)*
EDRED.

Edred. *(Alarmed.)*

Sifrid!

Sifrid.

Didſt ever know what 'twas to love, good Edred?—
Alas! I've known.—Haſt ever known the bliſs
Of love return'd? And heard the gentle " Yes"
Fall from the trembling lip of bluſhful maid?—

Edred.

Captain!

Sifrid.

This have I known.—And when thou look'dſt
To bear thy treaſure home, did ſome one come,
One whom thou ne'er hadſt wrong'd, good Edred? one
On whom thou'dſt laviſht all thy friendly ſtore?
Came ſuch an one between thy love and thee?
Say, did his baleful arm ſunder ye, then?
Doom her to death, and tell thee ſhe was dead?
Knew'ſt thou ſuch grief?—And yet—*This* I have
  known.——*(A pauſe—Sifrid covers his eyes.)*

Edred.

Captain, 'twere well,
Weak, and o'ercome with ſorrow, as thou art,
To ſpare recital of what yet remains.

Sifrid.

No, my good Edred, no! I feel renew'd:——
I thank thee that thou'ſt rouz'd my memory:——
What follows is moſt brief.
When now ſome years had ſeen me thus impriſon'd,
I forc'd eſcape; nor of my friends, nor kin,
I ſtay'd to learn; but fled. Our former Chief,
As well you know, receiv'd me. And hence my deeds,
My fortune, and my various life, you know.
                                            But

But let them pass:—Ethelbert roams these woods,—
You are brave;—I am your leader;——and you——
                EDRED.
Have sworn to obey——
                SIFRID.
                    And will support me?
                ALL.
To death.
            SIFRID.
        Dear friends—I cannot speak—my tears,
They best can tell how truly I do thank you.——
—But we must scour the woods, and keep the watch.—
You Rino, guard the entrance: we will swift
Enclose the forest: Vengeance the watch-word,
And revenge the aim.—He can not escape.

  Whene'er Oppression dares to urge,
   With lash, or steel, on man her claim,
  The dastard basely bears the scourge,
   And meanly meets the poignard's aim.

  Not so the brave, with lion heart,
   He e'en her deadliest rage defies;
  Victorious triumphs o'er her art;
   Or, not triumphing, nobly dies.

  Or yet, awhile her chains he bears,
   'Till Heaven the favoring signal gives;
  Then, of revenge the sword he rears;
   And, while the Tyrant dies, he lives.

END OF ACT I.

ACT SECOND. SCENE I.

A different part of the forest. ANGELINA *enters, disguised in the habit of a Pilgrim.*

ANGELINA.
With melancholy steps, hopeless I wander;
And no repose, no sheltering shed, discern.
───O Edwin! how has vanity repaid me!──
With wreck of happiness, and loss of peace.
Hated by thee, myself I hate, and find,
From solitude, whence ease I hop'd, new pains.──
──'Mid these wild woods, hostile, or full of fear,
Where'er I come, the beasts menacing howl,
Or fly, as from some desolating fiend.
The warblers cease their songs, or flit away,
And on the distant trees' soft-waving tops,
Insult my sorrows with their merriest notes.
The forest green, and every budding plant,
Flowers, and the springing blade, and mantling vine,
All the full blessing of the spring enjoy;
And to my soul new melancholy add.───
───My tears incessant flow!──Alas! how sad,
How desolate is life; when but to think
On those whom most we love, afflicts us most.

The foft, and gently-pleafing woe,
Which two fond hearts, divided, know,
　　The foul with fweeteft fuffering moves;
But O! when guilt with abfence joins,
Grief it to agony refines,
　　And fires to rage the breaft that loves.
　　　　　　　　　　　　[*She goes out.*

SCENE II.

ETHELBERT *enters from the oppofite fide.*

ETHELBERT.
What have I not encounter'd? Famine; flood;
The tyger's haunts; and fierce and dangerous battle.
———True, I efcap'd; I live; but vainly live:
Alas! Heaven fmiles not on my enterprize.
———And can it be? am I the fame? unchang'd?
And is it Ethelbert that danger braves?
Why toil has been my hate; my very jeft
Was conftancy; and love, my fixt contempt.
—O Angelina! peerlefs maid! a world
Of unknown beauty, haft thou op'd unto me.
Tranfporting fight! were not the glorious fcene,
By recollection of foul crimes, obfcur'd.
———O Sifrid! Emma! not of pangs like mine,
Tho' ye are wretched both, by me made wretched,
Not of fuch pangs, fuch anguifh, are ye flaves.
Yours is the grief which from oppreffion fprings,
And even 'mid all your woes doth innocence,
With its fweet peace, your forrowing fouls fupport.
　　　　　　　　　　　　　　　　　But

But I—a very wretch—(whofe tongue hath dar'd
At all of facred ufe to fcoff; whofe hand,
Still hath atchiev'd whate'er wild paffion prompted;)
The fport of agony,—know no relief.
——Thou Angelina! it is thou, whofe voice
Hath lur'd me back, to virtue, from perdition.
Thou flieft:—in vain I feek thee;—and in vain
The woods I penetrate. Day and the night
Slow pafs, and on my faint and weary way,
Sorrowing I fee returning morning break.

  The lover, journeying to his fair,
  Beholds, with joy, the day appear,
   To light him on his fhort'ning way;
  But ah! if far from her he roam,
  Unwifht, he fees the morning come;
   For diftance grows with every day.
         [*He goes out.*

SCENE III.

   A<small>NGELINA</small>. *returns.*

    A<small>NGELINA</small>,
Fainting, enfeebled, in a ceafelefs round,
I wander ftill. Each opening lures my fteps
To fome contiguous path; and that, alas!
With wily bend, conducts to whence I mov'd.
Fatigue and grief o'erpower and weigh me down.
  (*A paufe, fhe leans againft the fide fcene.*)
——Sweet are the days of youth, when innocence.
           Lives

Lives in the breaſt, and heightens every charm.
But ah! with years' increaſe, joy flies afar;
Like the young bird, who leaves his native clime,
When ſummer fails; but not like him returns.

   The bird, when ſummer charms no more,
      Forſakes his native clime,
   And wantons o'er the ſouthern vales,
      Which feel perpetual prime.
   Yet when the ſeaſon ſmiles again,
      Raptur'd he ſeeks his favorite plain.
   But joy, as riper days advance,
      To younger boſoms goes;
   Nor e'er returns, for hapleſs man
      No ſecond ſummer knows.

SCENE IV.

ETHELBERT *enters, from the oppoſite ſide, without obſerving, and unobſerved by*, ANGELINA.

ANGELINA. ETHELBERT.

ETHELBERT. *(To himſelf.)*
Whence is that voice ſo ſweetly melancholy?
Do the celeſtial denizens of air
Viſit this foreſt? Or is all around,
As ſure to me beſeems, enchantment ſtrange?
     ANGELINA. *(Seeing him.)*
Heavens! it is Ethelbert!
                     ETHELBERT.

ETHELBERT.
                    Which way foe'er
My footsteps stray, still the same spot appears,
Unbidden, and restrains my further course.
And when reflection tells me I am here,
And wherefore here; and when it all reviews,
Which here hath past; I startle at myself;
And question hold if it be truth.
                    (Observing Angelina.)
                    Pilgrim!
I pr'ythee stay.—Nay,—whither dost thou fly?
I am no robber that would do thee harm;
But a most hapless man, here lost, and here
Enforc'd to wander.—Nay, do not leave me!
                    (Catching hold of her garment.)
Leave me not here alone, unhelpt to perish!
Silent!—still silent!——*(Discovering who it is.)*
                    Angelina! Heaven!
        ANGELINA.   *(Aside.)*
Lost! lost, forever!
        ETHELBERT.
And is it thee? Indeed? And have I found thee?
O fate! I thank thee! She is found! is safe!
Speak to me, Angelina! art thou well?
Uninjur'd? Safe? Ah! how hast thou escap'd
The numerous perils which beset thee round?
How have thy delicate and tender limbs
Sustain'd the fierce extremes of temperature?
The sickly mists of day, and dews of night?
—Speak, O speak to me, my Angelina!
——And is it possible, that while the tears,
Of transport, for thy safety, bathe my cheeks;
                                    O, is

O, is it possible! that thou with such
Cold, cold demeanor, can'st receive me?
ANGELINA.
Ethelbert! beware!
Withhold me not; nor follow thou my steps.
Now thou dost know what most I wisht conceal'd,
Let it content thee; and do thou release me.
ETHELBERT.
Release thee?—Astonishment! Impossible!
Hast thou not lost thy way? deceiv'd, perchance,
By the wild beauty of some favorite walk,
Skirting thy lov'd paternal towers, 'till Eve
O'er thee, unconscious, cast her starless shade;
And conjur'd up some demon, whose false lamp,
With devious glare, betray'd thee 'mid these horrors
Have I not sought, and found thee? And shall not
My hand conduct thee to thy native dome?
ANGELINA.
Never.
ETHELBERT.
Never!—What frenzy hath possest thee?—
Never?—Never return?—It cannot be.
ANGELINA.
See'st thou not where we are?—Release thy hold.
ETHELBERT.
Think'st thou I would enforce thy stay?—O, no!
(Loosing his hold.)
ANGELINA.
'Tis well: I know thee now.—When to the world
I voluntary farewell bade——
ETHELBERT.
O, no! *(With great vehemence.)*
Thou

Thou doſt not mean it. No, it cannot be,
That hither thou haſt ſtray'd of choice. What charm
Have theſe drear foreſts, and huge craggy rocks,
For one, like thee, the idol of the world?
—O do not let thy hate of Ethelbert
Urge thee, thus madly, to renounce that care
With which he will, inviolate, reſtore thee.
     ANGELINA.
Earl Ethelbert!
     ETHELBERT.
      Doſt thou diſtruſt me then?—
I ſwear, upon the honor of a Peer:
And ſurely thou may'ſt truſt his oath, whoſe heart,
With holieſt love, adores thee.—If thou didſt know
How many days of grief, how many nights
Of ſleepleſs anguiſh, thy departure caus'd;
Sure they would plead within that gentle breaſt,
For ſome ſmall gracious token of compaſſion.
—O think how hard the lot of Ethelbert;
Leaving the accuſtom'd pleaſures of his ſtate;
Anxious, diſtracted, for thy loſs; theſe woods,
Horrid with every dreadful death, exploring;
Fir'd with the hope to ſhield thy precious life,
And ſafe reſtore thee:—Think what pangs are his
To find his zeal repulſt; and, in the ſtead
Of kind regard, to meet thy fiercer ſcorn.
     ANGELINA.
Hear Ethelbert. To thee, thou knoweſt well,
I ne'er have us'd deceit; but have been frank.
Why ſhould my words want credit with thee, then?
I do aſſure thee, on a maiden's faith,
That not unwillingly I roam theſe woods.
          Nor

Nor do thou follow me.—Think not I scorn thee.—
No, Ethelbert: e'er since I saw thy change,
Thou hast possest esteem: and nothing more
This heart can give thee.—Farewell:—and leave me.
            ETHELBERT.
Too beauteous maid! do not! O do not ask it!
If thou *wilt* wander here, vouchsafe me leave,
(I will not speak of love,) to be thy guard.
Nay, do not frown!—O thou shalt ever find me
Most submissive. All day I will provide,
And bring thee food; and all the live-long night,
Thou sleeping, guard thee from approaching harm.
            ANGELINA.
It may not be. My purpose needs no aid.
Farewell.   *(Turning, and proceeding.)*
            ETHELBERT.
      Stop, I conjure——Angelina!
            (She looks back, and stops.)
Thou must not go!—Heavens! think what perilous,
What dreadful fates surround thee. These dark woods,
" Tangled with horrid thorn;" these ruinous rocks,
Frowning with death; shouldst thou escape these ills,
On thy dank couch the hissing snake may dart,
And rabid wolves hem in thy daily walk.
Should Heaven protect thee from such foes as these,
Who, who shall save thee from more savage men?
Men, who do live on violence and lust?
Think, Angelina! think before thou mov'st!
O! it were more dreadful than any death.
            ANGELINA.
Sure, Ethelbert, thy passion doth obscure
Thy sight. Consider well this garb. Who knows,
                                        Thus

Thus far from winding Tyne, Earl Orgar's daughter?
What man but, seeing me, shall deem *me* man?
And of such holy sort, that he shall feel
His duty bind him, to defend, not harm, me?
ETHELBERT.
What garb can hide thy loveliness? What garb
The ruffian hand of violence disarm?—
But if thou'st no compassion on thyself,
Still let humanity restrain thy steps.
Whate'er of good I have, to thee I owe it.
By thee half-torn from vice, yet not confirm'd
In virtue. And wilt thou, after such toil,
And in this feverous state of soul, forsake me?
Say, wilt thou not pursue, perfect, thy work?
Has Ethelbert been led to virtue's path,
And will his guide, his angel guide, even there,
Desert him?—O! for pity's sake relent!—
Who, when thou'rt gone, shall aid my tremulous steps,
And warm my doubting heart to virtuous deeds?
ANGELINA.
Thou know'st but little of the power of virtue,
If thou dost doubt its efficacy here.
Be virtuous,—thou must, perforce, be happy.
Be virtuous,———
ETHELBERT.
Ah! what is virtue, without
(What constitutes its worth) the bright reward?
Be then compassionate.—I do not ask,
I *will* not ask, for love.
(Kneeling and seizing her hand.)
Hear me!—I swear,
By every sainted soul, in yonder heaven,

Thou shalt be safe, be free. I conjure thee
Hear me! 'Tis for thyself, for thy own life,
For thy own peace, for thy eternal peace,
I plead. Speak, Angelina!
    ANGELINA.
        Urge me not:
Seek not reproach: Releafe my hand.
    (A rufhing noife is heard.)
    ETHELBERT.
        Hear'ft that?
It is our foes, the ruffians of the wood!
Hafte, ere they rufh upon us; for they come:
The dry leaves ruftle, and the foreft fhakes.
Yield to my care! By all in earth and heaven
Thou valueft, I adjure thee! Let us fly!
   (A loud fhout, and the Banditti appear.)
I will defend thee with my life.

SCENE V.

(As Ethelbert turns to defend, Angelina efcapes. The Banditti, with Sifrid at their head, rufh in, furround and feize Ethelbert; who is able to make but fhort refiftance.)

  ETHELBERT. SIFRID. BANDITTI.

    SIFRID.
Bind, and bear him to the Cavern.
   (The Banditti bind Ethelbert, and bear him out.)

        SCENE

SCENE VI.

Sifrid, *alone.*

Sifrid.

How shall I act? What do? What purpose choose?
My soul, at thought of cruelty, recoils;
Deeply as he has wrong'd me.—Shall I bear,
In bondage rigorous, his spirit down?
Or shall I throw concealment off; reject
All temporizing means; and, front to front,
Load him with accusation and reproach?

 The mother, anxious for her child,
 Whose country calls him to the field,
  Danger and glory long comparing;
  And each, herself, in fancy, sharing;
 Still, with fond arms, the youth constrains;
 Nor thinks, embracing, she detains.

 So, in my changing, wavering, mind;
 To different acts, by turns, inclin'd;
  On direful vengeance now resolving;
  And now some milder fate revolving;
 No settled purpose bears the sway,
 And long, and longer, grows delay.
      [*He goes out.*

SCENE VII.

The inside of the Cavern: Ethelbert *discovered, bound, walking in front of the Stage: the* Banditti *silent, in the back part of the Scene, keeping guard.*

Ethelbert. Banditti.

    Ethelbert. *(To himself.)*
Heavens! to what dreadful fate am I reserv'd?
These are no common thieves. Untoucht remains
Whate'er of worth, whate'er of use, I had.
Nor hold they ought of converse with each other;
Nor yet, to my enquiries, make reply.
Their Chief,—what majesty!—I shrunk, dismay'd,
Before the piercing terrors of his eye.
Knowledge of him most surely I have none.
Why should I start!—but that the sense of guilt,
For crimes against so many men committed,
Makes me to fear in every man a foe:
Perchance in him.

SCENE VIII.

Ethelbert. Banditti. Sifrid.

    Sifrid. *(To the Banditti.)*
        Remove the prisoner's bonds,
And leave us to ourselves, my gentle friends.
    (The Banditti unbind Ethelbert, and go out.)
                      SCENE

SCENE IX.

Ethelbert. Sifrid.

(Sifrid walks about—agitated—occasionally stopping, and measuring Ethelbert with his eye—at length he exclaims.)

SIFRID.
Monster! thou'rt now within my power.
  ETHELBERT. *(With surprize.)*
           Monster!
    SIFRID.
Thou know'st me not?
    ETHELBERT.
     No.
    SIFRID.
       My form, familiar erst,
Hath then the hand of time so far defac'd?
Or have foul injuries, from thee receiv'd,
Destroy'd the well-known features of my youth?
Or rests the cause with *thee?* 'Tis dignity,
Perchance, above remembrance elevates.
Or do thy cruelties a hell so great,
So fierce, become, thou fear'st new punishments,
Should recollection shew thee who I am?—
Think of the man thou most hast wrong'd—and then,
Know me for Sifrid.
    ETHELBERT.
  Sifrid!
         SIFRID.

SIFRID.
Yes, Sifrid.
And doth my name, alone, banish the colour
From thy changing cheek?—Tremble at my wrath.
Base man! doth not that name, within thy breast,
Awake more tortures than thou fear'st hereafter?—
O wretch! wretch!
ETHELBERT.
I do confess——
SIFRID.
No—no—no—
Do not:—Confession ill becomes thee now.
ETHELBERT.
Nay, hear me! I——
SIFRID.
Would talk of palliation:—
O thou hast sinn'd beyond its utmost reach,
And hardly can the hand of Heaven itself
Erase so deep a blot.
ETHELBERT.
But yet——
SIFRID.
O, no!—
Didst thou not force me from my home?
ETHELBERT.
I did.
SIFRID.
With hell-born cruelty pursue me?
ETHELBERT.
'Tis true.
SIFRID.
Captive, in chains, shut from the sun, the air,

All

All intercourse of friends, by thy command,
For months, for years, I languisht.
Thy villain hand each *little* good rent from me;
Or ever, with interposition rude,
Prevented its advance.—No pleasing sounds——
Not even the pluming warblers' of the spring,
To all her offspring, Nature's common gift,
Ever approach'd me:—but, instead, deep groans;
The felon's rattling chains, the murderer's oaths;
And,—worse than all,—thy proud insulting taunts.
And more—Monster of inhumanity!—
And more—Didst thou not tear my Emma from me?
Within a noisome cell confine? Weary,
With offers of vile lust, her virgin soul?
Say, didst thou not?

    ETHELBERT.
      All, all is true.
    SIFRID.
Yes, yes! And do I live to see thee here?
The dark assassin of my love? my life?—
Wretch! what dost thou deserve?

    ETHELBERT.
        To be heard.
    SIFRID.
           Heard?
And is there aught, that's villainous, undone,
Which, in this little space of life, allow'd,
Thou hop'st to do?—Or, can thy speech recall
Past times; retrace the years of frantic grief;
And once more place me where I erst was happy?
Oh, no!—Thou'st fill'd the measure of thy guilt;
Triumph'd o'er every sacred tie, that binds,
            In

In fellowship, the man to man.—-And what,
Plung'd as thou art in crimes, is left to do?
Is there, of justice, one unbroken law?
           ETHELBERT.
Tyrant! beyond all patience hast thou urg'd me,
And I will speak.—Justice!—Talk'st thou of justice?
Shew me in all the ample page of right,
In all truth's code, a rule, or even a plea,
To confecrate, or to excuse, thy trade.
Robber! thou can'st not.—Him does it become,
The armed leader of a ruffian band,
To hold difcourfe of justice? And shall he,
Who strips the unwary traveller of life;
The midnight door of sleeping wealth who breaks;
Who tears, from age, its honor, and from youth,
From *helpless* youth, its innocence;
Shall he of justice question?
           SIFRID.
              Villain!
           ETHELBERT.
Villain to thee! Shew me the plunder'd stores,
Rent from the industrious tenants of my fields.
Difclofe the vast incalculable sum,
Swept from the puissant nobles of the realm.—
Ha! dost thou shake with rage? grow pale with shame?
Conceal it, Sir; it ill becomes a thief.
           SIFRID.
Monster! if any guilt is mine,—tremble!
Yes, tremble for thyself, the accurfed cause!
Who, tearing from me all that life endears;
Exalting each dark passion of my soul;
Hast made me breathe with nought but fell revenge —
                        —O hadst

—O hadst thou torn all wealth, all honor, from me;
Made me still poorer than the wandering wretch,—
Sordid petitioner of daily food;—
Heapt to the heavens, imprisonment, and pain;
Sicken'd all ears with tales of infamy;
And still hadst left my Emma to be mine;
I had been blest; had loaded thee with blessing;
And Heaven had seen me spotless and devout.
                ETHELBERT.
Emma *is* yours.
            SIFRID. *(Fiercely.)*
        Hast thou not murder'd her?
        ETHELBERT. *(With horror.)*
No!—no!
            SIFRID. *(With terrible fury.)*
        Villain! hast thou not murder'd her?
                ETHELBERT.
She lives.
            SIFRID. *(Wildly.)*
    Not dead?
                ETHELBERT.
            She lives, to love and bless thee.
                SIFRID.
    (Faintly; and laboring for breath and utterance.)
Oh! it can not be!—It can not!—can not!
Merciful Heaven!—this tumult of my soul!
*(He leans against the Cavern. After awhile, as though
he supposed it some new imposition in Ethelbert, he
starts; and drawing a dagger, seizes Ethelbert by the
arm.)*
Most damn'd impostor!—
*(Ethelbert remains unappalled. Sifrid, looking on his
face, observes it—drops the dagger, and exclaiming)*
            F   He

He could not do it!—*(Sinks into a reverie.)*
ETHELBERT. *(After a short silence.)*
Sifrid!—He hears me not.—Thy Emma lives.
She lives, indeed; and thee alone requires;
Whose hop'd return will all her joys renew.
    SIFRID. *(Starting from his reverie.)*
And whence is this?—From thee?
    ETHELBERT.
                O, heap not shame,
Too vast already, on my humbled head!
For I will all disclose; nor dare conceal
Aught of near import, so thou be compos'd.
    SIFRID.
Speak on. Thou hast my promise.
    ETHELBERT.
The tears of Emma, silent as they fell,
Soften'd my flinty heart. Compassion, then,
A guest unknown before, enter'd my breast.—
Who does not know what sweet affinity
Love bears to gentle sorrow?—Now, indeed,
A purer flame shot thro' my alter'd soul.
The grief, the modestly-reproachful woe,
Unwavering, matchless, constancy, of Emma,
Chill'd every glow of passion, bent my heart,
Reprov'd my guilt, and humbled me to silence.
Affection builds not on remorse. I shunn'd,
I fled, her presence;—but, to feel the force,
And sink the slave, of Angelina's beauty.
I saw, and lov'd:—lov'd; and of love became
The thrall successless.—Was *I* unhappy?—
Had not my murderous hand rent the fond ties,
Dissolv'd the fairy bliss, canker'd the buds of love?—

Frenzy

Frenzy poffeft me;—and remorfeful grief,
With agonies fo dreadful, fhook my frame,
That reafon totter'd on her throne; and hope,
That I fhould e'er revive, my friends forfook.
Thy Emma then———
    SIFRID. *(Furioufly.)*
      What didft thou fay of Emma?
    ETHELBERT.
O, be calm, my friend! Let thefe tears declare
I am repentant. Thy forrowing Emma
Confol'd and ferv'd me, with unceafing care;
And once again to life reftor'd me.
    SIFRID. *(With ecftacy.)*
        She did!
    ETHELBERT.
Hence, every vice caft off, with earneft zeal,
I ftrove my many mifchiefs to repair.
What could I do for Emma? Half my wealth
Was proffer'd, but refus'd.
    SIFRID. *(Proudly.)*
      No doubt it was.
    ETHELBERT.
With care folicitous, o'er all the realm,
My trufty flaves difpatcht, ftill fought thee out.
Meantime, with her I lov'd, my fuit advanc'd not.
With pleas'd regard fhe faw me turn from vice;
And witneft kind refpect, but never love.
At length fhe fled. With unremitting zeal,
I fought her long; each town and village fearching.
In vain.—This day, as full of grief I ftray'd,
Whether by chance, or Heaven's conducting hand,
The long loft fair I found; when, captive made,
           Hither

Hither have I been led, in some poor sort,
The wrongs on thee enforc'd, to expiate.
    SIFRID.
To expiate?—O Emma! dost thou live?—
Would I could grant thee more than my forgiveness.
    ETHELBERT. *(Kneeling.)*
And canst thou then the injuries forget——?
    SIFRID. *(Raising him.)*
Come to my soul, thou man of blest repentance.
    ETHELBERT.
O, nobleness divine!   *(They embrace.)*
    SIFRID. *(After a pause.)*
    Our band, with speed,
Shall circle, and shall scour the forest thro'.
To them each part well known, the wandering Fair
Shall soon be found, and peace again be thine.
    ETHELBERT.
Excellent man! how greatly have I wrong'd thee!

    Duet.

  Sweet are the fleet and flying hours,
   Serene, when friendship lives:
  But sweeter far their joyful course,
   When love, once lost, revives.

  For who can heave the sorrowing sigh,
   Regretful of the wrong,
  When fond forgiveness fills the eye,
   And trembles on the tongue?

   END OF ACT II.

ACT THIRD. SCENE I.

A Hermitage: EDWIN, *disguised as a Hermit, sitting in the entrance; in profound contemplation. He rises, and comes, slowly, forward.*

EDWIN.
O Memory! thou fond deceiver;
  Still importunate and vain;
To former joys recurring ever;
  And turning all the past to pain.

Thou, like the world, the opprest oppressing;
  Thy smiles increase the wretch's woe;
And he who wants each other blessing,
  In thee must ever find a foe.
            (Walks in great agitation.)

How sad! and, yet, how true! How many suns
Have cours'd their daily round; how many moons
Have silver'd o'er this dell, and sunk in night;
Since first I enter'd!—Yet, nor the jocund
Sun, nor moon soft-smiling, cheer my soul.
In vain, the hermit's sacred robe invests me;
In vain, at earliest morn and deepest night,
I kneel before my rustic altar; press,

                                   With

With trembling lips, the crucifix; and ftrive
To frame fome apt, and well-according prayer;
Love and defpair ftill triumph in my breaft.
Angelina!—Angelina!—This cell,
Thefe dark and dreary woods, alone reply;
Alone make anfwer to my mournful cries.
Time! thine are the fpendthrift's promifes!
And life! thou'rt full of agony! Ah where!
Where fhall the wretched find fome fure repofe?

SCENE II.

As EDWIN *is flowly croffing the Stage,* ANGELINA *enters—at firft, not feeing him.*

EDWIN. ANGELINA.

ANGELINA.
Now am I fafe, and baffled is purfuit;
But, faint and loft, I know not where to fly.
(Seeing Edwin.)

Turn gentle hermit of the dale,
  And guide my lonely way,
To where fome rock o'erfhades the vale,
  From fiercely-blazing day.

For here, forlorn and loft, I tread;
  With fainting fteps and flow;
Where wilds, immeafurably fpread,
  Seem length'ning as I go.
EDWIN.

EDWIN. (*Turns, and advances.*)
Pilgrim! fatigue sits heavy on thy frame;
Let me support thee: thou hast gone too far.
          (*Assists her.*)
    ANGELINA.
Indeed, my father, I have greatly stray'd;
And, much I fear, shall find no place of rest.
            (*Sighs.*)
    EDWIN.
Let not affliction prey upon thy mind:
Each path, that hither leads, or hence, I know.
With me, the night, repose; and ruddy morn
Shall light thee thro' the wood; myself thy guide.

  Then turn, my son, and freely share
    Whate'er my cell bestows;
  My rushy couch, my frugal fare,
    My blessing, and repose.
        (*He leads her into the cell.*)

SCENE III.

The inside of the Cavern. ETHELBERT *alone.*

    ETHELBERT.
With what a generous and unceasing care
Does Sifrid seek to serve me! Could I once,
What my full soul is anxious to disclose,
Unfold; and draw him from this fatal snare;
All would be well.

SCENE IV.

Enter, to ETHELBERT, SIFRID—*with a wild and distracted air; as having just dismiss the* BANDITTI; *and without observing* ETHELBERT.

ETHELBERT. SIFRID.

SIFRID. *(To himself)*
They're gone; all gone; at last I am *alone!*
Would I had been *so* ever! Never known man!
Had perisht ere my eyes were op'd to light!
Or wither'd, an untimely fruit!—O where!
Where are the golden visions that, but now,
Ravisht my soul, with ecstacies of joy?
Where now the treacherous hope which made thee mine,
Too faithful Emma? Never more shall I,
With arms of love, encircle thee. No more!—
Would God that *I* had died,—that *thou* hadst died,
Ere this accursed hour of dark despair.
That we were slumbering in the peaceful grave.
Now, when shall I know peace? Never! never!—
O that I knew not that thou still didst live!
That yet I thought thee dead! Then, as before,
I now should rise, fierce-panting for revenge.
Thy fancied death—my own foul wrongs—despair—
United, would urge on my furious hand;
And make the work of death seem just and joyful.
But now,—horrible state!—tho' heaven itself
Entices me to turn;—tho' I do know

Where

Where it will plunge me;—ſtand upon the brink;—
Tottering;—I muſt—*(ſtarting back)* horror! horror!
ETHELBERT.
                    Sifrid!
          SIFRID.
Who calls upon that wretch? *(Seeing Ethelbert.)* **And**
    is it thee?   *(Tenderly.)*
          ETHELBERT.
'Tis me, 'tis Ethelbert, it is thy friend!
Why doſt thou look thus wildly on me, Sifrid?
What is it that ſo ſhakes thy frame? What **cauſe—?**
          SIFRID.
Have I not cauſe enough,—Eternal Powers!
Have I not cauſe enough, for my diſtreſs?
          ETHELBERT.
Whence is this dreadful paſſion which deſtroys thee?
Art thou not maſter of thy native fields?
Is not thy Emma free, and faithful to thee?
Does ſhe not languiſh for thy quick return?
          SIFRID.
Ay, but my oath! For I am bound; have ſworn.
          ETHELBERT.
And think'ſt thou any oath hath force to bind
Againſt the eternal ordinance of Heaven?
Believe it not.—What haſt thou ſworn to do?
To murder and deſpoil, is 't not?—Beware!
The poſitive injunction ſure is plain;
Caſting ſtern condemnation in thy face.
          SIFRID.
Ay, but my truth is pledg'd; my honor giv'n;
And were eternal death the ſure event,
I've ſworn upon my ſoul,—and muſt go on.
          G   ETHELBERT.

ETHELBERT.
Horrid, but powerlefs, oath.
SIFRID.
Immutable!
O agony fupreme! I fee my fate.—
Emma!—yes, thee I muſt leave:—Forever!
I muſt fulfil my deſtiny of death.
The wrath of Heaven falls heavy, and I fink.
(*A ſhort pauſe.*)
ETHELBERT.
O be calm, my deareſt friend! Let fweet peace
Soft fettle on thy foul, and footh its woes.
SIFRID.
Never more fhall peace vifit this bofom.
ETHELBERT.
Nay, think not fo!—it fhall, my friend, it fhall.
Obferve the pleafing profpects that invite thee.
Untoucht, thy hamlet, and paternal fields:
Thefe, by thy care, fhall thrive; there fhalt thou live;
And, with thy Emma, fee thy joys renew'd.
SIFRID.
Never again, will joy be mine!
ETHELBERT.
It will.—
Leave but thefe fcenes, and, 'mid thy native fhades,
Gain independence from the cultur'd foil;
Thou fhalt be truly happy.—Here, around,
On every fide, danger approaches fwift.
The alarmed nation haftens to deftroy thee.
Toils, dangers, and diftrefs, and many deaths,
Perchance of thy beſt chiefs, moſt fure await thee.
If fortunate at firſt; it can not laſt;
Unfortunate,

Unfortunate, thy people's, and thy, lot,
How dreadful! The reverse, how sweet! Where thou,
Where they, a ready pardon, from the throne,
Procur'd, secure, the joys of peace may taste;
And life steal on, serene, to honor'd age.

SIFRID.
O I do see how many, many joys,
I might, full sure, obtain! But, I have sworn.

ETHELBERT.
And will not they, to whom thy oath is given,
Like thee, discern the danger, and avoid it?
Dost thou not think thy brothers of the war
Would share thy toil?

SIFRID. *(With frantic ecstacy.)*
   They will!
(Suddenly relapsing into despair.)
      No! they can not.
I must still live a very wretch.

ETHELBERT. *(A pause.)*
   Sifrid!
What mean'st thou? Wherefore can they not?

SIFRID.
       Ask not.
Leave me, my friend, to perish. Thy kindness
Can not, now, avail me.

ETHELBERT.
   Sifrid, I can not,
Must not, leave thee.—Explain what thou dost mean.

SIFRID.
Are we not bound by mutual oaths, to death?
Is it not death to him who first shall dare
Request a change? And how shall I, who fram'd,
     Propos'd,

Propos'd, the oath; exacted their acceptance;
Dare, firſt, to ſeek exemption from its bonds?
O, would they but relent; unite, with me,
In more endeared toils; *(to Ethelbert)* thou wilt have rais'd
A weight that preſſes me to deep perdition.

ETHELBERT.

Thy paſſion, Sifrid, doth unman thy ſoul;
And makes thee eſtimate the danger more
Than reaſon will allow.—Cheer up my friend!
And when, from this their ſearch, thy Band return,
Do thou addreſs them with a manly zeal:
Point but their way, and I will fields beſtow,
Untill'd, thro' fear of their deſpoiling hands,
Which ſoon would bud and bloſſom, by their aid.

SIFRID.

'Tis well!—I am reſolv'd! It can not be
But only death.—Emma! I can not bring
Thee hither;—and, without thee, this little,
Little day of life, were agony; were death.—
I will addreſs them.

ETHELBERT.

Fear not; they will comply.
Pardon, and rural wealth, ſhall crown the act;
And fairer ſuns ſhall riſe to gild thy day.

SIFRID.

Moſt generous man! I can not ſpeak my thanks.

When, in our youth, a friend we find,
Of like deſires, congenial mind,
What joy the generous paſſion gives!
Within the ſoul what tranſport lives!

But

But when, where fixt had envious fate,
Suspicion dire, and causeless hate,
Reviving love awakes its fires,—
What bliss the unlook'd for good inspires!
       [They go out.

SCENE V.

The Hermitage: Edwin *and* Angelina *discovered, sitting in the entrance of the cell: a small table spread; and covered with a variety of fruits.*

   Edwin. Angelina.

    Edwin.
Scarce dost thou taste my fruits:—O be not sad!
I will conduct thee, with the early dawn,
Where terminates the forest.
    Angelina.
      Ah! Father!
I fear I then shall be more distant far,
Than ever, from my journey's wisht-for end.
       (Sighs.)
    Edwin.
Unhappy Youth! what dost thou wish? what seek?
    Angelina.
I seek in vain.—I seek—for—happiness. *(Sighs.)*
    Edwin.
Is happiness thy wish; here rest; here dwell.
Remote from courts, and palaces, and kings;
From domes of grandeur, and from halls of wealth;
         Far

Far from the poisonous city's busy hum;
From Passion's reign, and fierce Ambition's war,
Borne on the winnowing gale, flies Happiness.
She loves, with Peace her sister, to reside
In cottages and vales; by running streams;
In woods; and on the cliff's rude, hanging brow:
For there, if yet, perchance, on earth they dwell,
Meets she Integrity, and sober Toil;
And Innocence, and sweet Simplicity:
And oft the Hermit's cell she deigns to visit;
With Piety her guide, and mild Repose
Her fair attendant.—This, then, be this thy——
    ANGELINA.
And do meek Piety and Peace, in truth,
Visit so often then thy cell, my Father?
    EDWIN. *(Apart.)*
That question!—Be still my heart!—*(To her.)* Dost
  thou doubt!—
But whence, poor Youth, the sorrows of thy breast?
The rose still blooms upon thy cheek; nor there
Trace I the characters of villain guilt.
Yet, oft ambitious is the youthful mind.
Say, dost thou thirst for Power?   *(She sighs.)*
      Ah! remember!
'Tis but of momentary worth alone;
Lifting the proud heart of forgetful man
Above the worship pure of Heaven. It draws
From Virtue's paths; and all her smiling train,—
Even Fortitude, depart: and when appear
Misfortune and her frightful troop, the soul,
Debas'd, no longer can itself support.

      ANGELINA.

ANGELINA.

Father, I wish it not.

EDWIN.

And what is Wealth?
What, but, like Power, corrupter of the heart?
To every ill exposing more the man,
And hard'ning more to sense of others' grief.
Avarice and pride increasing; and the soul
Binding to earth, not lifting up to heaven.
Does it, on man, one virtuous wish bestow?
Or brings it happiness?

ANGELINA.

Alas! it does not.
Power might be mine; and Wealth I can command;
But where, ah! where, is happiness?

EDWIN.

Poor Youth!
And hast thou *dreamt* of Friendship? Fixt thy soul
Upon a fancied friend, and found him false?
—O Phantom, subject of eternal praise!
Man's foul betrayer, murderer of his peace;
Of wealth and fame thou still-attendant shade;
The base deserter of the cheated wretch;
What art thou, visionary fiend, that man
Should ever be condemn'd to think thou art,
(Tho' thou wert never seen,) and still to seek thee?—
(To her.) Grieve not for this;—our earthly lot is woe;
And we but bare our bosoms to the stroke,
The assassin's stroke, when we embrace a friend.
Say, dost thou mourn for one as such suppos'd?

ANGELINA.

O, no! I never yet so blessed was
As, even in fancy, to possess a friend.

EDWIN.

EDWIN.

And Love,—Love hath, perhaps, tormented thee?
Haſt to a fair-one ever op'd thy ſoul?
Haſt lov'd? to be the jeſt, the ſcoff, the ſcorn,
The play-thing, of a heart inſenſible?
(She ſighs deeply.)
Thy only anſwer is of ſighs and tears.—
O Heaven! and hath ſincerity again,
Again hath truth been wounded?
(To her.) Haſt thou lov'd?
(She ſighs more deeply, and appears greatly agitated.)
Let her be thy ſcorn!—Ha! know'ſt thou not yet,
That air, not truth, is meaſure of affection?
—Almighty Father! wherefore did thy wrath
Create me man? Was it to ſee all worth,
And every bright perfection of the mind,
Humbled before the arrogance of wealth?
Falſe pride of birth? and tyranny of power?—
Know'ſt thou not this?—The heart of man, himſelf,
Theſe have beguil'd; and, of his daughter's peace,
Have made her ſire the aſſaſſin.

ANGELINA. *(In tears, and lifting up her hands.)*
O, my God!

EDWIN. *(Not noticing her emotion.)*
For theſe hath woman, vain, and trifling wretch!—
(All fond deſires, and ſweet affections ſhunn'd;
Each nobler paſſion of the ſoul caſt off;)
Rejected love: deceiv'd,—deſtroy'd,—ſpurn'd it,
With acrimonious, with inſulting ſcorn.

ANGELINA.

ANGELINA.
(Starting up with wildness, clasping her hands, and pressing them to her head; her hat, at the same time, falling off, and her long hair floating down her back.)
Gracious, gracious God!—Spare me!—O spare me!
EDWIN.
What do I see?—a woman?
(She sinks faintly into his arms.)
It is herself!
She dies!—Angelina!—What shall I do?—
(Distractedly.)
Soft!—she revives!—I'll throw me at her feet,——

ANGELINA. *(Reviving.)*
Where am I?—where?
EDWIN. *(Apart.)*
Discovery might destroy my only hope.
ANGELINA. *(More revived.)*
Where have I been?
EDWIN. *(Supporting her.)*
Compose thyself, my Child!
Be calm; and tell me whence these transports wild;
And let me sooth the sorrows of thy soul.
ANGELINA. *(With great emotion.)*
I can not speak!
EDWIN. *(Tenderly.)*
Sit down.—Be not disturb'd.
I am, myself, the very child of woe,
And can disclose whence consolation springs.
ANGELINA.
My tears prevent all utterance.
EDWIN.
'Tis well.—
Yes,

Yes, let them flow. Compofure flies afar
From where fit mute Defpair and tearlefs Anguifh;
But gently lights, where Grief her facred dew
Sheds 'round the mourner. *(A paufe.)*

ANGELINA.

Thou art too kind, my Father.—Ah! forgive
A wretch, whofe feet, unhallow'd, have difturb'd
Thy cell ferene of piety and peace.

EDWIN. *(Apart.)*

Of peace?—alas! *(To her.)* Do not condemn thyfelf:
The Power who rules is good; and our weak feet,
Tho' often he permit to ftray, yet ftill
'Tis but a devious path, to good conducting.

ANGELINA.

I gain fweet hope and courage from the thought.
And fure compaffion dwells within thy breaft;
And thou wilt pity one who hath been led
Aftray by love; who feeks for peace, but finds
(The fole companion of her way) defpair.

EDWIN. *(Paffionately.)*

Defpair!—Proceed, my child.—*(Apart.)* What fhall
I hear?

ANGELINA.

How fhall I fpeak of happy times, which, erft,
Saw me, the daughter of an ancient Earl,
With wealth's proud fplendors, blandifhments of eafe,
And art's and nature's, copious ftores, furrounded?
Ador'd, and fung, by every neighbouring Chief;
While flattery, with mufic join'd its voice;
Echoing along the winding banks of Tyne?
—O blifsful days of innocence and peace!
Early, how early loft!

EDWIN.

EDWIN.
   Ceaſe not, thou fair——
  ANGELINA.
Frequent and numerous were the ſuing crowds,
To the warm proffers of whoſe love, real,
Or yet pretended, ready ear I lent;
While my young mind, intoxicate, drank in
Delicious draughts of flattery.
   EDWIN.
    Deteſt——
  ANGELINA.
Deteſtable indeed.—Among the reſt,
Moſt ſimply clad, but grac'd with virtue's guiſe;
Not arm'd with wealth or power, but full of worth;
Whoſe mind was wiſdom's throne; a Youth was ſeen.
Ah! how my boſom panted at his ſight!
Of love he never ſpake; and with diſdain,
Moſt noble of the flatterer's art——
  EDWIN. *(Paſſionately extending his arms.)*
    My An——
   (Partly recollecting himſelf.)
Speak! what of him!
  ANGELINA.
   Amazement! What mean'ſt thou?
Know'ſt thou aught——?
  EDWIN. *(Recollecting himſelf, yet heſitating.)*
   Pardon—forgive me, daughter!—
Be not alarm'd!—Go on—I nothing meant!
The thoughtleſſneſs of youth did cauſe my warmth.
  ANGELINA.
The muſk-roſe, which unfolds its tender flowers
Unto the early ſun; the dew, which loves to hang
         Its

Its trembling lustres on the silver bell,
The lily of the vale; his purer mind
But faintly emulate. The rose, the dew,
With charms inconstant shine: their charms were his;
But, woe to me! mine was their constancy.—
Wretch that I am! I trifled with his love,
Scofft at his pain, who only liv'd for me!

    EDWIN. *(Agitated.)*
Haste thee———!
   ANGELINA.
   Wretched woman!—on what far shore,
What land unknown, murder'd by thy disdain,
Hath he, who lov'd thee, died?—And died for thee?
(She walks about—in extreme agitation—Edwin re-
 garding her fixedly, and with an attitude evidencing
 the most entire and distressful concern.)

 But mine the sorrow, mine the fault,
  And well my life shall pay;
 I'll seek the solitude he sought;
  And stretch me where he lay.

 And there, forlorn, despairing, hid,
  I'll lay me down, and die;
 'Twas so, for me, that Edwin did,
  And so, for him, will I.

    EDWIN.
(Forcibly, and passionately, clasping her to his breast.)
" Forbid it Heaven!"
  ANGELINA. *(Endeavoring to disengage herself.)*
   Man———
       EDWIN.

EDWIN.

Turn, Angelina, ever dear,
  My charmer, turn, to see
Thy own, thy long-lost, Edwin, here;
  Restor'd to love and thee.

Thus let me hold thee to my heart,
  And every care resign:
And shall we never, never part?
  My life! my all that's mine?

No, never, from this hour to part;
  We'll live and love so true,
The sigh that rends thy constant heart,
  Shall break thy Edwin's too.

(They embrace.)

SCENE VI.

ETHELBERT, SIFRID, *and* BANDITTI, *burst through the Wood, and advance hastily.*

(Angelina shrieks faintly, and clings to Edwin—who raises his staff, in defence,—while, with his left arm, he supports her.)

EDWIN. ANGELINA. ETHELBERT. SIFRID.
BANDITTI.

ETHELBERT.
Tis she! and in another's arms!—

Hermit!

Hermit!
Release——
ED WIN.
Robber! thou dieſt if thou advance.
ETHELBERT.
See'ſt not our numbers?—Wherefore ſhould I hurt thee?
EDWIN.
Single, unarm'd, I will defend my charge,
" Againſt a world in arms." *(To Angelina.)* Fear not, my love!
Heaven combats on the ſide of right.
ETHELBERT. *(Angrily.)*
Old man, Provoke me not!
EDWIN.
Proud boy, away! *(To her.)* Be calm.
(To him.) Dare not!—*(To her.)* My Angelina——
ANGELINA. *(Faintly, and looking up to him.)*
O, forbear! Riſk not thy life!
ETHELBERT. *(Fiercely.)*
Hermit, be brief. By heaven, Nought ſhall detain her.
EDWIN.
As thou valueſt life, Advance not.
SIFRID.
Peace! let me be heard, my friends.—
Holy man, we come not here to injure thee:
Far be from us impiety ſo baſe.
Earl Ethelbert moſt dearly loves the maid

Whom thou withhold'st: and surely thou dost know
Of what fierce quality and fiery power
Is love; and wilt forgive impetuous speech.
He seeks but to restore her to her friends,
And gain her hand: for, he doth so adore,
Above all earthly good he prizeth it.
And why should'st *thou* detain? why not release,
And give, her to his wish?—His noble soul
Disdains a force superior to employ.—
Be obstinate no more—but yield——

   EDWIN. *(With great firmness.)*
         Never.

   ETHELBERT.
I would not harm that reverend form, or dash,
Against the earth, thy sacred head;
But, wert thou young, thy life should answer me,
For thy high insolence, old man!

   EDWIN. *(Throwing off his disguise.)*
         Off! off!
Ye trappings of dishonorable peace!
Array of bondage, vestments of disgrace!
Hence, the monk's cowl, and hermit's staff! and now,
Come forth thou sword of ancestry heroic!
(To Ethelbert.) Villain! I dare thee!

   ETHELBERT. *(In great surprize.)*
         Edwin!

   EDWIN. *(Fiercely advancing.)*
         Edwin, Lord!

   ETHELBERT. *(With great emotion.)*
The saviour of my *life!*
The murderer of my *love!*
         EDWIN.

EDWIN.
                    Nay, hang not back!
We stand upon the perilous brink of death,
And one must surely leap.
          ETHELBERT. *(Greatly agitated.)*
                    Almighty God!
Whence?—wherefore?—why is this?—My life!—my
     love!
Gratitude!—Passion!—It can not—can not be!—
                              (Walks distractedly.)
Come to my breast each noble sentiment?
Arm, arm my soul, and make it all your own,—
That I—*(irresolutely)* I can not do it—*(firmly)* I will—
That I may spare his love, who sav'd my life.
          (All stand in a posture of surprize.)
               EDWIN.
Why do we wait?
               ETHELBERT.
               After ingratitude
So base, if with repentant heart I come,
Say, noble Edwin, canst thou yet forgive me?
Angelina, daughter of heaven, canst thou?
               EDWIN.
Whene'er Earl Ethelbert becomes himself,
He shall not want a friend.
     *(Edwin drops his sword; they meet, and embrace.
          Angelina advances.)*
               ETHELBERT.
                    Angelina,
I owe thee all:—compassionate my woes;
Forget my errors; if thou canst, forgive.
(Angelina places one hand in his—the other in Edwin's.)
                              ANGELINA.

ANGELINA.
When Edwin pardons, I can ne'er refuse.
　　EDWIN. *(Drawing her towards him.)*
My Angelina!
　　ETHELBERT.
　　　Excellent woman!
(To the Band.) My friends, one myftery remains to you.
It is to Edwin that I owe my life;
Refcu'd, at rifk of his, from men whofe fouls
No mercy knew. Already had they ftript
And bound me; and their reared fwords
Menac'd my death; when, (a delivering fpirit,)
He came, with lightning fpeed—withering their powers.
Three fell beneath his hand; and, to the fourth,
Humbled, and full of promifes, he gave
Life, freedom, and fecurity.—Bleeding,
Nor confcious of my ftate, me he convey'd
To where attention dwelt; and only left,
When, in returned ftrength, vigorous he faw me.
But—O how!—how fhall I relate the reft?
Vain-glorious, cruel, execrably bafe,—
In the remembrance, Sifrid, of thy woes,
Learn thou the fhameful hiftory of his.

SCENE

SCENE VII.

Enter WALTER *and* EDRED, *with other* BANDITTI.

EDWIN. ANGELINA. SIFRID. ETHELBERT.
WALTER. EDRED. BANDITTI.

SIFRID. *(To Walter, &c. as they enter.)*
Happily arriv'd, my friends!
   ETHELBERT. *(To Sifrid.)*
        Remember!
   SIFRID. *(To Ethelbert.)*
I do.—*(To the Banditti.)* My friends! Hear all.
To my fond arms, Earl Ethelbert restores
The woman of my love; unto my care,
My fields paternal, and my earliest home.
     WALTER.
Sifrid!
     SIFRID.
  Nay, more——
     WALTER.
       Chief! think upon thy oath!
And how thou'rt bound to us, and we to thee!
Think of the forfeit too!
(The Banditti draw their swords, and encircle Sifrid.)
   SIFRID. *(To the Band.)*
        Deem not that I,
So used to blood and death, shall shrink with fear.
I know my life is forfeit; and that you,
As most shall please, may spare, or may exact it.
           I have

I have well weigh'd the terms, and place that life,
Now more than ever dear, upon the iſſue.—
If it ſhall pleaſe you to allow me chance,
I will unfold my purpoſe.
WALTER.
(Looking round upon the Banditti, who nod their aſſent.)
'Tis granted.
SIFRID.
For myſelf, I plead not. I will not ſtrive
To move your pity for a wretch, who, long,
From all the valued, baniſht; finds, at length,
The happineſs he loſt, within his reach.
No!—for yourſelves, it is, I plead; for you,
By many union'd toils, to me endear'd.—
'Tis not to me alone, this noble Earl
(Pointing to Ethelbert.)
Doth offer good; he, generouſly, to you,
Extends his manors, and invites acceptance.
WALTER
And is this thy mighty purpoſe? For this
Haſt thou forſworn thyſelf, and purchas'd death?
What charm, think'ſt thou, to tempt us from our woods,
Is there in vaſſalage?—Are we not free?
And ſhall we ſtoop to bondage? *(To the Band.)* What
    ſay You—
Shall we be bond or free?
ALL BANDITTI.
Free!
SIFRID.
Curſt be he
Who ſhall attempt to make ye ſlaves.—My friends!
Ye do miſtake:—Not vaſſalage, but wealth,

Is

Is offer'd;—not bonds, but independence.—
Think of the value of the proffer'd boon!
To your own hearts I speak; what hath revenge
Of pleasure so unmixt, as rural ease,
And independent toil?—Weigh, and compare,
This mighty mass of good, with that estate
In which you stand.—Behold, by you arouz'd,
The assembled vengeance of the nation haste,
Wide desolation o'er your shades to pour.
What can you do to stem this torrent?
    WALTER.
              Die.
  SIFRID.
And will thy death, the death of these brave men,
Confer such lasting glory on your names,
As to have cast revenge aside, when penitence,
With outstretcht arms, implor'd you to forgive?
What glory can arise, from spurning life,
When ready pardon waits, when wealth invites,
And nature and humanity beseech?
Let me not plead in vain! O! as in scenes,
Where danger and where death hideous appear'd,
Where rapine and destruction arm'd the hand,
I have been oft your guide; let me still lead
Where peace doth spread her shades, and where
Dwells sweet humanity!—If not,—'tis well!—
Here strike!—I bare my breast! the heart within
Beats only for your good.—Here plunge your swords!
For, without Emma, never more shall joy
Visit the soul of Sifrid; never more
Will he seek for revenge in fields of death.—
Why do ye linger?
    WALTER.

WALTER. *(Sheathing his sword.)*
'Twas man's oppreffion made me what I am;
Let it be due to man that I become
Such as I ought to be.—
    EDRED. *(Replacing his sword.)*
           Walter hath fpoken.
    SIFRID.
Shall I then lead? and will you follow me?
    ALL BAND. *(Putting up their fwords.)*
We will.
    ETHELBERT. *(To the Band.)*
    My friends! this your refolve is fure
The very work of Heaven. *(To all.)* O! we will form
A little world of love; all wrongs forgot,
And all our errors: for all have errors;
Nor is the Libertine's, nor Robber's, life,
More falfe to nature than the Anchorite's.
    EDWIN.
All muft, indeed, amend: all will amend.
Our energies, long time, fo ill-directed,
Henceforth, with wondrous joy, fhall blefs the land:
While men fhall fay——
    SIFRID.
        Not deeply, in their fouls,
Could Vice her dark, polluted feat have fixt,
Who could, fo eafily, her chains caft off,
And bow their wills to Virtue's rightful fway.

    Chorus.
  Now burft the fhout of joy around,
  And let the foreft wide refound.
                Peace,

Peace, henceforth, forever reigns;
And laughing Plenty loads our plains;
Then burſt the ſhout of joy around,
And let the foreſt wide reſound.

SIFRID.
Fierce Deſpair,
   EDWIN.
    And frantic Grief,
  BOTH.
Find, at length, unhop'd relief:
  ANGELINA.
Wayward Beauty,
   ETHELBERT.
     Brutal Luſt,
  BOTH.
Learn to feel, and dare be juſt.

Chorus.
Burſt, then, the ſhout of joy around,
And let the foreſt wide reſound.

ETHELBERT.
The waters of the living fount,
 Daſht in caſcades, in columns toſt,
Nor nurſe the root, nor ſwell the blade,
 Waſted in foam, diſperſt, and loſt;

But, iſſuing in a gentle ſtream,
 Thro' ſmiling meads, rejoicing ſtray;
Perennial flow; and fruits, and flowers,
 And living verdure, mark their way:
       Chorus.

Chorus.
Loud burſt the ſhouts of joy around,
And plains, and foreſts, wide reſound.

EDWIN.
The mineral, ſleeping in the mine,
Decks not the board, nor glows in coin,
　While droop the languid arts;
Refin'd, its power, where'er it flies,
Bids new-born wonders round ariſe,
　New energy imparts;

Chorus.
While burſt the ſhouts of joy around,
And plains, and buſy ſhores, reſound.

ANGELINA.
The meteor gilds the face of night,
The pilgrim truſts the faithleſs light,
　And ſinks in lonely death;
But, by the moon's ſerener ray,
Unharm'd, the wanderer ſpeeds his way,
　O'er many an unknown heath;

Chorus.
And ſwells the notes of joy around,
And bids the peaceful ſhades reſound.

SIFRID.
When, arm'd with terror, thro' the ſky
　The light'nings flaſh, the thunders roar;
When ruſh the tempeſts, from on high,
　Howl o'er the ſea, and ſweep the ſhore;

The whelm'd ship sinks, the cottage falls,
And ruin every heart appals:

But, when the lively breezes blow,
   And fan, with gentle gales, the land;
Or bid their airy currents flow,
   And swell the sail that quits the strand;
Smooth glides the ship, the cottage smiles,
And gay content each heart beguiles;

Chorus.
While bursts the shout of joy around,
And earth and heaven the strain resound.

E N D.

DEMOCRACY;

AN

EPIC POEM,

By AQUILINE NIMBLE-CHOPS, Democrat.

CANTO FIRST.

NEW-YORK:

PRINTED FOR THE AUTHOR.

863

CONTENTS.

SUBJECT *proposed*—*Invocation*—AQUILINE *invoketh the Genius of Confusion*—*telleth what she is not*—*commenceth with the grand Meeting at the* TONTINE—*counteth their numbers*—*enquireth the cause*—*maketh a shrewd conjecture*—*fine simile of locusts and frogs, with a singular allusion to bread-trays*—*sage remarks on patriotism*—*Crowd becometh impatient*—*Mr. M———k harangueth*—*nominateth* GRIPUS—GRIPUS *chosen Chairman*—*adjournment to* CITY-HALL—*dextrous manner of opening a lock*—*'Squire Pomposo remonstrateth, and enquireth the cause*—*second adjournment*—*Chieftans described*—*violent contest between* TAR *and* CITIZEN PIG-TAIL—*Citizen presseth forward*—*TAR presseth backward*—*Crowd clamoureth, and Citizen retreateth*—*eloquent speech of M———k*—*beautiful simile of Frogs, with an allusion to Town-Meetings*—*a new speaker appeareth*—*Poet recounteth his pedigree*—*pathetic lamentation of the speaker for the absence of his brother*—*a ray of hope*—*elegant game at* "*Slap-Chops*"—*excellent logic and metaphysical observations*—*reasons for fighting* ALGERINES—*better reasons for continuing peace with* BRITAIN—*excellency of Bankruptcy, a fine family piece*—*deficiency in the Federal Treasury accounted for*—*timidity of Congress reprehended, and reasons assign'd*—*new praise of Bankruptcy, and noble illustration*—*Indian expedition*—*new manufactures established*—*scurvy observations on* BROOM-MAKERS—*speech concluded*—*strange figure, and a* GOLDEN PIG—FIGURE *waxeth mad*—*severely reprehendeth abuse of honest occupations, and departeth*—*Committee chosen with additions*—*great exultation of M———k*—*M———k's third speech*—*strange spectre appeareth*—*speaketh*—*interrupted*—*how a* CRANE *may be mistaken for an* OWL—*spectre proceedeth*—*Citizens depart with Huzzas*—*which are finely described.*

CANTO I.

WHAT deeds of glory grace thefe latter days,
Of earth the wonder, and of men the praife;
How, while, around, all fingle defpots die,
Tumultuous throngs the vacant thrones fupply;
From democratic fway what bleffings fpring;
Say, heavenly *Mufe*, and aid me while I fing.
    Not *thee* I call, by whofe diviner aid,
Mæonia's Bard the fate of Troy pourtray'd;
Nor *thee* upborne by whofe adventurous flight,
Milton effay'd the empyrean light;
But *thee*, who fpringing from the central realm,
Where Chaos rules, rejoiceft to o'erwhelm,
By force fupported, and by fraud maintain'd,
Whate'er of good and fair mankind hath gain'd.
Thee I invoke, for unto thee belong
The factious bankrupt, and the noify throng;
Thee I invoke, for unto thee pertains
The fubject matter, and recording ftrains.
    Now had the Sun, who, with peculiar grace,
This day had burnifh'd up his aged face,
O'er half the welkin lafh'd his courfers on,
And glow'd incumbent o'er the melting noon;
When, mid the dome where Mocha's berried pride
With vaporous fragrance every room fupplied,
From every part conven'd, in trim array,
The *guardians of the land* their powers difplay.
Not lefs in number, o'er the Egyptian land,
Came *flies* and locufts, call'd by Mofes' wand;
Nor with much milder notes, from every *tray*,*
The frogs hoarfe-croaking, hymn'd their new-gain'd fway

---

* Vide Exodus, chap. 8th, verfe 3d.—" And into thy bread-trays."

But fay, O mufe! what powerful motive draws?
For this event, unfold the mighty caufe?
What could induce four hundred men to come,
Their fhops forfaken, and forgot their home,
Perhaps not e'en a marketing prepar'd,
And doubtlefs fome good time and money fpared;
What could impel the fhow-man to forego
The certain profits fpringing from his fhow?
What could engage the cobler to permit
'Prentice and journeyman the *laft* to quit?
While angry cuftomers with half-dreft pate,
And beards impatient for the razor, wait,
What madnefs urg'd the barber to difmifs,
Puffer and fhaver to a fcene like this?
How could the Printer, while news-mongers fwear,
With hands unfili'd direct his devil there?

While with found hub, and with uninjur'd fpoke,
The ring unflaw'd nor yet the tiring broke,
The Wheel of Government moves on, by day,
No man fhould ever from his bufinefs ftray:
But private intereft never fhould controul
The vaft, and nobler intereft of the whole.
Hence, when diforder mars the wheel of ftate,
Its courfe impedes, or turns, by force, or weight,
If the ring burft, or if the tiring break,
The fpoke is fhatter'd or the hub fhall crack,
Ballads and pictures, lafts and awls, fhould fly,
Razors fhould fall, and puffs neglected lie,
No news fhould fpread, but every arm contend
Who firft, and beft, the failing wheel fhould mend.
This was the caufe, the wond'rous caufe, which led
Four hundred human creatures by the head;
For mighty M———k had inform'd the town
That fome had fwore the wheel fhould be o'erthrown;
That Algerines had given it many a hack,
And Briton's Sons had made the hub to crack;

Wherefore he begg'd them to convene with speed,
(This day the unspotted patriot had decreed.)
That its sad state might undergo inspection,
And, after wise debate, and sage reflection,
They should resolve what measures to pursue,
To mend the old one up, or make a new.
But left the minds of people uninform'd
By this fine figure should be too much warm'd,
And such full well the honest chieftain knew
Compos'd the ranks of his upholding crew—
He plainly said by wheel he wish'd to paint
That sorry thing the Federal Government.

   Now, mid the room where Commerce' Sons appear'd,
Disorder foul its brassy forehead rear'd;
Without, more loud, the noisy croud demand
Why idly thus their comely leaders stand.
Deep thoughts revolving in his anxious breast,
Which groan'd beneath a nation's cares oppress,
With sable front, the mighty M——k rose,
Bawl'd "Order," and the tumult feebler grows.
" Sure, at this time, the public good requires
" Some Chairman fill'd with patriotic fires;
" One who, with tried *integrity*, unites
" A *settled liking* to the people's rights.
" And such an one, methinks hard by I see;
" And GRIPUS, once an Alderman, is he."
   He said—around they swing their greasy caps,
And cheer'd his soul with oft-repeated claps.
" Order!" the new-appointed chairman cries—
And every note of praise in silence dies.
Again his form the mighty M——k rear'd—
And as so many friends this day appear'd,
And as the present place was found so small,
Propos'd adjournment to the City Hall.
" Proper!" a voice exclaim'd; and all around—
" Proper!" the echoing walls amazed resound.

(8)

Forth moved the cavalcade, and now repair
Where the huge City Hall affails the air;
Nor of the adjoining court requeft the key,
But *modeft*, break the lock to gain them way:
They enter in---and wond'rous to relate,
Enclos'd within thofe walls the *worthies* fate,
Thofe very walls, from whence, obferv'd with awe,
A frantic CONGRESS gave the country law.
Ah! little did IT think how foon decrees
Which *friends to liberty* could never pleafe,
Such as now met their hated rule to bow,
Muft, where they rofe, receive the fatal blow.
Ah! little did IT think how high-foul'd men
Would, in this place, their native rights regain;
And, warm'd with freedom's democratic fire,
Make law and reafon *equally* expire.

Now much debate, and various founds, arife,
Several fage fpeeches, and as fage replies,
And nought was done---'till 'fquire POMPOSO rofe,
With mouth wide-open'd, eager to oppofe.
That 'Squire fo fam'd for copper coinage erft,
Of noble coiners fure the very firft;
That worthy 'Squire for honefty fo known,
Flefh of their flefh, and of their bone a bone,
That all fuppos'd him:---"Who"---aloud he bawls---
" Hath now conven'd the people in thefe walls?
The price of Weftern land is rifing, fure---
Who dares to think that we are growing poor?
I've lately fpeculated there myfelf,
And hope to gain no little fhare of pelf;
If not, another bankruptcy will do---
And if for me, why will it not for you?
This to a fortune is the readieft way---
Who call'd this meeting here---again I fay?"

With rage inflam'd, and eager to reply,
Full many a form now rear'd itfelf on high;

When, once again some unknown voice informs,
That round the Hall the gather'd people swarms;
And hints, while hidden from the public fight
The leaders fate, they marr'd the people's right.
The rest applaud, they rush the house without,
And with their fellows join the general shout.
    Meantime the Chairman, with important airs,
Leading his suite, ascends the lofty stairs;
Forth marching then, hat off, with solemn gait,
Fix'd in the balcony invites debate.
In order rang'd, and by his side, appear,
Full many a youth, and veteran chief severe,
Of various aspect, and of various fame,
But few deserving of exalted name:
These few the Muse, as suits her purpose best,
Shall dignify, and raise above the rest.
    Plac'd on the right, with ruddy face, and round,
With portly belly, and with look profound,
Of doubtful views, but much with learning blest,
A son of Esculapuis stood confest.
By him a being star'd, of monkey mien,
A famous actor on the factious scene,
And who, distinguish'd for his splendid share,
The Muse shall to a future mention spare.
Perch'd on the left, the mighty M———k shone,
O'er all conspicuous for his visage known.
Reader, hast ever seen, at show or fair,
That comely, sable thing, yclept a *Bear?*
Doubtless thou hast—thy notion then is good—
Such, and so looking, mighty M———k stood;
And now had spoken—but a sad affray
O'er all the balcony spread wild dismay.
A little onward stood the noted Tar,
The dup'd ringleader of the wordy war;
He who, presiding o'er the men who swear,
No private citizen should titles wear,

Himself an appellation proud retains,
Nor titled salutation e'er restrains;
Who, for equality a bawler loud
Struggles for eminence amid the crowd.
Puff'd with the importance of his present fate,
The room of three he fill'd in haughty state;
Behind, and straining for a forward place,
And watchful of the too much wasted space,
Citizen PIG-TAIL prest a spot to gain,
But met the fury of the SAILOR'S cane.
Once more tenacious of his equal right,
He labor'd forward, with redoubled might;
Once more the democratic TAR, enraged,
With his sharp stick the citizen engaged.
Vociferous the crowd cry out below,
" The rash intruder o'er the railing throw"—
Aghast affrighted PIG-TAIL backward shrinks,
Nor longer of his rights invaded thinks.
The tumult hush'd, and " Order" cried once more,
M——k essay'd his voice's utmost power.

"Friends! friends!" he cried—"for purposes most great,
You've been call'd hither, freely to debate;
About who call'd you hither make no clatter,
You're here--who gave the notice---'tis no matter—
Whether the *Card* TOM, DICK, or HARRY, wrote,
Or he who now solicits you to vote:
You need not plague yourselves about such stuff,
You're here---as I have said---and that's enough.

" The Algerines take all our ships, I swear,
And captive all your men to slavery bear;
CONGRESS 'tis true, have talk'd about a fleet;
But damn the English, they perform'd the feat;
They turn'd the pirates on us, let's requite,
And take good care that they get nothing by't.
The English take your vessels, steal your goods,—
Let's fight them, every man, curse take their bloods!

Wait not for negotiation---that won't do---
But fight 'em, burn 'em---beat 'em, black and blue.
I'll tell you what to do:---we owe them cash:
We'll plague 'em---yes, we'll make a noble crash.
They ca'n't recover debts 'mong us, they say---
Why that's the very thing---let's never pay.
Do as I've done; break, break's, the happiest plan,
And keep your cash yourselves unto a man.
They can't get money of us, now they groan---
We'll have it always so---and give 'em none.
" And now I beg to know, if any dare,
Against the people's right to meet declare?
Let's wait a bit, to see if one dare come,
And say you all had better stay'd at home."
  Here clos'd the wond'rous speech, hoarse---braying, loud,
In tones of thunder echoing from the croud,
The murmurs of applause, resounding far,
In one deep column rush'd upon the ear,
While separate sounds, their light detachments spread
Lurk'd in the rear, or skirmish'd at the head:
Thus when the vernal sun's prolific ray,
Paints with rich flowers the Verdant robe of May,
When the green citizens of ponds prepare
To hold their first town-meeting of the year;
Some leading frog, with croaking talents blest
For strength of lungs, distinguish'd o'er the rest,
Perch'd on his chair of log, in solemn state
With notes sententious, opes the grave debate,
'Tis silence round,---at length begins the strain,
The notes applausive echo o'er the plain,
Deed, deeper swells the undulating sound,
And one vast croaking vibrates o'er the pond.
---Fir'd with the sounds, ambitious to obtain
An equal share of honorary gain,
Proud of descent from sires before the flood,
Near, on the right, a younger leader stood,

O'er the drawn features, of whose solemn mien,
A sort of stupid dignity was seen,
While quite expressive of its owner's mind,
Up from his mouth, his hauty nose inclin'd,
Seem'd as if, mounting to the realms of air,
It scorn'd the usual intercourse to share;
Transmitted pure his heritage by birth,
Through a long line of sires of equal worth;
That firm integrity, that godlike pride,
Inflexible in truth, in virtue tried,
That candid spirit which, nor lust of power,
Nor interest's potent sway could e'er allure,
From honor's paths to steer a devious way,
In him combin'd diffus'd a brighter ray.
With much complacence, in himself he view'd,
The mighty atlas of the haughty brood;
To wit, 'twas true, he made no great pretence,
For want of wit, with him, was proof of sense;
And nature kindly had that want supplied,
By no small portion of conceit and pride.
—All ardent now he stood to view confest,
Put forth his hand, and, thus, the crowd addrest,
In solemn tones, which, many a day before,
Were cut and dried, all ready for this hour.
" Hear what I speak, and list to what I say,
Ye Cits, conven'd on this important day,
This day, which Faction shall with pride behold,
When future ages have their courses roll'd,
And celebrate with glee the auspicious hour,
Which gave new strength to her declining power;
This day to *Anarchy* forever dear
By sorrowing Freedom, mark'd with many a tear,
When wild misrule, with renovated fire,
Shall bid all law and decency expire,
And blest Confusion with her flag unfurl'd,
Spread consternation o'er the trembling world.

" Much I lament that on this glorious day,
My far fam'd brother BILLY is away,
Ah haplefs brother, what a lot is thine!
Doom'd, at a diftance from this place to pine,
By fate's tyrannic laws forbade to fhare
In Scences like this, to thee for ever dear;
Yes, nobleft brother! in thy favor'd breaft,
The hawk, *Democracy*, had built her reft,
Impregn'd by Faction there had hatched her brood,
And train'd them up to rapine and to blood;
Each principle oppos'd to order, fhone,
And bleft Confufion there had fix'd her throne.
Full well you know, nor need I now repeat
The vaft fum total of his merits great;
Full oft his peerlefs deeds to you have fhown,
How dear he holds your interefts, and *his own*.
Had he been here at leaft one hundred men,
To thefe four hundred would have added been,
Then had the Prefs, which, with impatience, waits,
To give our doings to our Sifter States;
Whofe types now fix'd for fifteen hundred ftand,
Been but deficient of two thirds the band.
But fince 'tis fo, what boots it to regret?
Lo! brighter pictures grace the page of fate.
To my rapt view, prophetic vifions rife,
And Scenes of glory burft upon my eyes;
A younger brother, in fome future day,
Shall all our W———m's various worth difplay:
In the mean time, I'll do what'er I can,
To fill the place of that exalted man:
But now the bufinefs which us hither brought,
Seems to demand fome little fhare of thought.
That, we've a right to meet's a thing moft plain,
'Tis one of the prerogatives of man;
Some Animals, of folitary kind,
Are much, to keeping by themfelves inclin'd;

" Others gregarious are, of thefe is man,
The great *chef d'œuvre* of wife nature's plan;
And if gregarious, he, of courfe, muft then,
Be born to affociate with his fellow-men;
And having thus by force of logic, quite,
Prov'd that our meeting is a native right,
I now proceed moft ably to unfold,
Thofe things of which you need not here be told.
How the bafe Briton, with infulting pride,
Firft "*flaps our chaps*" on this, then t'other fide;
How Algiers' infidels intent on gain,
Your goods have plunder'd and you fhips have ta'en;
Forbear ye Infidels, ye little deem!
Whom moft you injure, by this plundering fcheme;
Know, that long fince, by right prefcritive held,
Our race their coffers have by plunder fwell'd.
And fhall thefe thieves thus boldly dare invade,
Our facred rights, and fpoil the fwindling trade?
Forbid it, Heaven! for fhould they thus go on,
We foon fhall find our wonted harveft gone.
For this good caufe, with them I'd have you fight,
Nor let the knaves deprive us of our right;
But let me, here, a caution interpofe,
For tho' 'gainft Britain fierce my anger glows,
Yet not with mighty M————k would I join,
At once, to crufh a wonderful defign.
Not yet with Albion let us venture war,
A future time will anfwer better far;
Now while with willing heart fhe credit grants,
Still let her Sons fupply our utmoft wants.
Deeply indebted, at the prefent hour,
Increafing debt fhall place her in our power.
One confifcating act all dues fhall pay,
While by her lofs, for many a glorious day,
Th'mportant warfare fhall we ftrong maintain,
From breach of faith, deriving ample gain.

"Nor let the fear of infamy affright.
Our race have tried, and know the thing is right,
Scarce of the name, one single soul survives,
But, by this conduct, now in splendor lives;
And tho' to all the world the truth's confest,
Is still of public confidence possest.
—The Sons of Britain and of Algiers join'd,
And with the Western Indians both combin'd,
By depredations, cause the doleful want
Which makes of cash our treasury so scant.
And does not Congress know these things are true,
Who dares to say they don't? they do, they do;
And what's the cause of all this timid care,
To keep the country from the glorious war?
The reason's this, a foolish one enough,
They dread a bankruptcy, and such like stuff.
Now, for my part a bankruptcy I deem,
A noble, kind of heaven-invented, scheme;
To make a fortune, 'tis the readiest way,
He is a fool who calculates to pay.
If precedents they want, I have them plenty,
Our name alone, affords not less than twenty
This is the mode by which a man can live,
Set up his *Coach*, and brilliant *concerts* give;
And this to CONGRESS, I should recommend,
As means best fitted to attain that end.
—Should we pretend much longer in this way,
And such poor councils all our measures sway;
'Ere long the Savage Tribes in hostile pride.
In light Canoes may down the Mohawk glide,
The *Caughnawaga*, *Onondagoe* band,
And *Powtowatimies*, shall rule our land;
Then will those dogs compel us to become
Artificers of basket and of broom,
And, death to honor! e'en our noble race,
A vile Broom-maker's calling, may disgrace.

" Then since the CONGRESS are so stupid grown,
  So lost to sense, 'tis time to claim your own;
  And in this period of distress and pain,
  To take yourselves of government the rein."
—He ceas'd; the applausive tumult swell'd around,
And neighbouring domes re-echoed back the sound.
When fir'd to rage, a form most strange appear'd,
And high in air, his angry visage rear'd;
In feudal pride, like some old baron big,
He swell'd high mounted on his GOLDEN PIG.
Firm in his right, for lance, a brush he held,
A trunk's rough lid supplied the place of shield,
On which, with brazen nails, inscrib'd was seen,
" I'll brush them out, egad, I'll make them clean;"
And ever, and anon aloud he'd cry,
" I'll keep him straight, depend on't that will I,"
" What's this I hear," the angry figure cried,
" Why these reflections base, thou son of pride!
  And have I wish'd so long this day to see,
  To hear Broom-makers, made a jest by thee?
  Dost thou pretend, with appellations vile,
  The unspotted honour of our craft to soil?
  Broom-maker's, hear it Sir, and shrink dismay'd,
  Are own first cousins to the *Brusher* trade,
  Broom-making, Sir's an occupation good;
  Nor could it much disgrace your noble blood:
  Better from honest means, a living draw,
  Than eastern affluence, from a bankrupt law.
  But ne'er attempt to touch this string again,
  I scarce can now my boiling wrath restrain,
  For if thou dost, by this good shield I swear,
  Whose skin it's owner's back no more shall wear,
  My brood of pigs, your carcase shall assail,
  Whet the sharp Tusk, and whisk the curly tail."

* This redoubted personage is employed, by the D. S. to watch over the conduct of the President of the United States—(to whom this verse refers) and to keep him strictly within the line of his duty.

—He ended, threatning, and with anger fir'd,
Straight from the meeting with his pi g retir'd.
  Now different voices, from amidst the crowd,
For a Committee bellow'd out aloud.
"Fifteen!" cried some---some "ten"---and "twenty" some
And hideous tumult shook the frighted dome.
"Order!" cries Gripus---"friends! to try your mind---
Unto the highest number I'm inclin'd:
Shall your Committee be of twenty made?"
The union'd *ay* the people's mind displayed.
Such was the found as, mid some spacious stye,
Where hogs are kept, some frighted hog should fly,
He first, with long-drawn squeal his gladness tells,
And one deep grunt their answering joy reveals.
Again the might, M———k ardent rose:
"My friends!" he cried---"I hasten to disclose,
What, for your sakes, to save you trouble here,
Those, who most love you, form'd with toil severe.
Last night, in sage convention, eighty men,
'We ne'er shall look upon their like again.'
Compos'd a *List* of sixteen, who would serve,
And never from your interest dare to swerve.
First, if you please, I'll read the *Roll* all o'er,
And then read one by one, 'till we've a score."
  "Proper!" a voice exclaim'd---and all around---
"Proper!" the echoing walls amazed resound.
  Read was the *Roll*---and one by one the *Sage*
Who fill'd the Chair, their fury to assuage,
Had now proceeded to re-name the men,
When tumult shook the astonish'd streets again.
  Scarce had *himself* the people's plaudits known,
"P——— R. L———! let him be one!"
The crowd exclaim'd:---tho' not upon the *List*---
P——— was put---and call'd on to assist.
"C———c N———!" now some exclaim'd
And some the son of Æsculapius nam'd.

The crowd perfift, with energy of foul,
And add thefe names to the illuftrious *Roll.*
" Let the remaining place be fill'd, 'tis meet,
By *Colonel* SCANTLING, now of Water-ftreet."
Thus cried the throng—when mighty M——k rofe—
" My friends!" faid he—" I fpeak not to oppofe;
To PENN's fair city SCANTLING ftout is fent,
To aid our views upon the Government.
Our democratic bretheren, there, requir'd
One of like foul, with like diftraction fir'd;
With us united, and in concert ftrong,
They hope refiftance to difmay ere long.
SCANTLING is there, nor will he foon be back:
So choofe *your humble fervant---White* ———"
Loud rung the applaufes---and full foon complete
Their lov'd committee all the people greet.
Of whom, for wife *Report* of *Office* known,
The pious GOOD Os, early choofe was one.
Now mighty M——k, by fuccefs infpir'd
With bold, refiftlefs, elocution fir'd,
Perch'd as he was, on balcony fo high,
The crowd who watch'd his moft expreffive eye.

" With joy, O friends—with rapture vaft I view,
What union'd hearts this day's proceedings fhew.
Sure from this day democracy fhall rife,
Spread thro' the earth, and triumph o'er the fkies;
Before its power all Government fhall fly,
And at its prefence each Republic die;
An age of Gold once more delight the earth,
With years not number'd from a faviour's birth;
Decades, not weeks, our days fhall hence divide,
And o'er the globe democracy prefide.
Such, fuch effects, from your *Refolves* fhall flow,
Which beft, I think, fome future day will fhow.
Not at this time can your committee frame,
Such *Refolutions* as your zeal would claim;

Some day next meek we better can procced."
" Thurfday !" the crowd exclaim'd—and Thurfday was
  decreed.
  Again he fpeaks—" By that time we fhall have,
The prudent doings of *Boftonians* brave ;
Thofe men fo fam'd for true, confiftent merit,
And not behind us much in proper fpirit.
Them will we join, with them go hand in hand,
Fall if they fall, and if they ftand we'll ftand.
No *act of milk and water* fhall be ours—
Fragrand and ftrong as urinary fhowers,
To our foes fores no comfort fhall *it* give,
But make them fmart, while yet *it* lets them live."
  As when vaft billows break upon the fhore,
Applaufe now burft, in one tremendous roar ;
Hats, caps, and wigs, and leathern aprons, flew,
And puffs of wondrous fize, and jerkins blue.
  Not lefs the noife when, mid the watery way,
The wounded whales in anger lafh the fea ;
Not lefs the noife when, 'neath beleagur'd walls,
The deep mine burfts, the whelmed city falls ;
Nor lefs the rout when, out of *Meeting* read,
The mighty M——k bent his fable head.
  Soon was the tumult hufh'd, and foon was heard
A voice, but neither face or form appear'd.
At length, beneath the Chairman's arm, was feen,
Of wondrous afpect, and of fearful mein,
A human head, if head it might be nam'd,
Which fcarce to man the leaft refemblance claim'd.
Like the full moon, but of a darker dye,
The vifage was ; difaftrous beam'd an eye
On either fide of what was meant for nofe,
Which from each cheek quadrangularly rofe.
Below a chafm tremendous op'd to view,
Whence, with hoarfe groans, thefe words the fpectre drew:
  " As yet of fhips delay'd, and men mifus'd,

Of veſſels captur'd, and of wealth abus'd,
Whether by Algerines the miſchief came,
Or yet by Britons of notorious ſhame—
No proper liſt—no facts by them believ'd
From any place, has CONGRESS yet receiv'd."
"You lie!" the croud exclaim—"I have not ly'd!"
Sternly the hedious mouth, direct, replied.
Tumult and rout now drown'd the ſpeaker's voice,
His own all vanquiſh'd by the people's noiſe.
"Order!" ſage GRIPUS ſcreams—and P— R.
Begs that the throng the ſpeaking *Crane* would hear.
"He! he a *Crane*!" cried one, with horrid howl—
"I ſwear, he's couſin-german to an OWL."
"Hear him!" again the Chairman bellows loud;
And huſh'd in peace, attentive ſtood the crowd.

"I hope that our Committee will take care
A long account, for CONGRESS, to prepare,
Of all the michiefs by the Britiſh done,
And brand the devils every mother's ſon."

"Huzza! huzza!" thro' all the ſtreets reſounds;
"Huzza! huzza!" from every wall rebounds;
The diſtant lanes reverberate the roar,
And echoes break on either River's ſhore.

END OF CANTO FIRST.

EPISTLE

TO THE AUTHOR OF THE BOTANIC GARDEN.

For unknown ages, 'mid his wild abode,
Speechless and rude, the human savage trode;
By slow degrees expressive sounds acquired,
And simple thoughts in words uncouth attired.
As growing wants and varying climes arise,
Excite desire and animate surprize,
Gradual his mind a wider circuit ranged,
His manners soften'd, and his language changed;
And grey experience, wiser than of yore,
Bequeath'd its strange traditionary lore.

Again long ages mark the flight of time,
And lingering toil evolves the *Art* divine.
Coarse drawings, first, the imperfect thought reveal'd;
Next, barbarous forms the mystic sense conceal'd;
Capricious signs the meaning, then, disclose;
And, last, the infant alphabet arose:
From Nilus' banks adventurous CADMUS errs,
And on his Thebes the peerless boon confers.

Slow spread the sacred art, its use was slow:
Whate'er the improvements later times bestow,
Still how restrain'd, how circumscrib'd, its power!
Years raise the fruit an instant may devour.
Fond SCIENCE wept; the uncertain toil she view'd,
And, in the evil, half forgot the good.
What tho' the sage, and tho' the bard inspired,
By truth illumined, and by genius fired,
In high discourse the theme divine prolong,
And pour the glowing tide of lofty song;
To princes limited, to Plutus' sons,
Tyrants of mines and heritors of thrones,

EPISTLE

The theme, the song, scarce toucht the general mind;
Lost, or secluded from opprest mankind.
Fond SCIENCE wept; how vain her cares she saw,
Subject to Fortune's ever-varying law.
Month after month a single transcript claim'd,
The style perchance, perchance the story, maim'd;—
* The guides to truth corrupted, or destroy'd,
A passage foisted, or a painful void,
The work of ignorance, or of fraud more bold,
To blast a rival, or a scheme uphold;—
Or, in the progress of the long review,
The original perisht as the copy grew;
Or, perfect both, while pilgrim bands admire,
The instant prey of accidental fire.
Fond SCIENCE wept; whate'er of costliest use,
The gift and glory of each favouring Muse;
From every land what genius might select;
What wealth might purchase, and what power protect;
The guides of youth, the comforters of age;
Swept by the besom of barbaric rage,—
Scarce a few fragments scatter'd o'er the field,—
Frantic, in one sad moment, she beheld.
" Nor shall such toil my generous sons subdue;
" Nor waste like this again distress the view!"
She cries:—where Harlem's classic groves
Embowering rise, with silent flight she moves;
She marks LAURENTIUS carve the beechen rind,
And darts a new creation on his mind:
A sudden rapture thrills the conscious shades;
The gift remains, the bounteous vision fades.
Homeward, entranced, the Belgic Sire returns;
New hope inspires him, and new ardor burns;
Secret, he meditates his art by day;
By night fair phantoms o'er his fancy stray;
With opening morn they rush upon his soul,
Nor cares, nor duties, banish nor control;
Haunt his sequestered path, his social scene,
And, in his prayers, seductive, intervene;

* The four following lines were supplied by a friend.

TO Dr. DARWIN.

Till, shaped to method, simple, and complete,
The filial ear the joyful tidings greet.*
—First, their nice hands the temper'd *letter* frame,
Alike in height, in width, in depth, the same;
Deep in the *matrices* secure infold,
And fix within, and *justify*, the *mould;*
The red *amalgam* from the cauldron take,
And flaming pour, and, as they pour it, shake;
On the *hard table* spread the *type* congeal'd,
And smooth and polish on its marble field;
While, as his busy fingers either plies,
The embrion parts of future volumes rise.
—Next, with wise care, the slender *plate* they choose,
Of shining steel, and fit, with harden'd screws,
The shifting *sliders,* which the varying line
Break into parts, or yet as one confine;
Whence, firmly bound, and fitted for the *chase,*
Imposed, it rests upon the stony base;
Till, hardly driven, the many-figured *quoins*
Convert to *forms* the accumulated lines.
—Then, with new toil, the upright frame they shape,
And strict connect it by the solid *cap;*
The moving *head* still more the frame combines;
The guiding *shelf* its humbler tribute joins;
While the stout *winter* erring change restrains,
And bears the carriage, and the press sustains:
The *platten* these, and *spindle* well connect,
Four slender bars support it, and direct,
As the high handle, urging from above,
Downwards and forceful bids its pressure move:
Beneath, with *plank* the patient *carriage* spread,
Lifts the smooth marble on its novel bed,
Rides on its wheeled *spit* in rapid state,
Nor fears to meet the quick-descending weight.
—Last, the wise Sire the ready *form* supplies,
With cautious hands and scrutinizing eyes;

---

* Laurentius first confided the secret of his discovery to his son-in-law.— The reasons for the subsequent deviations from historical accuracy, will be obvious to the poetic reader.

EPISTLE

Fits the moist *tympan*,—(while the Youth, intent,
With *patting balls*, applies the sable paint,)
Then lowers the *frisket*, turns the flying *rounce*,
And pulls amain the forceful *bar* at once;
A second turn, a second pressure, gives,
And on the sheet the fair impression lives.
Raptured, the Youth and reverend Sire behold,
Press to their lips and to their bosoms fold;
Mingle their sighs, ecstatic tears descend,
And, face to face, in silent union blend:
Fond SCIENCE triumphs, and rejoicing Fame,
From pole to pole, resounds LAURENTIUS' name.

Hence, doom'd no more to barbarous zeal a prey,
Genius and Taste their treasured stores display;
Nor lords, nor monks, alone, the sweets procure,
But old and young, the humble and the poor.

Hence, wide diffused, increasing knowlege flies,
And error's shades forsake the jaundiced eyes;
Man knows himself for man, and sees, elate,
The kinder promise of his future fate;
Nations, ashamed, their ancient hate forego,
And find a brother, where they found a foe.

Hence, o'er the world,—(what else perchance conceal'd,
Supprest for ages, or fore'er withheld,
To one small town, or shire, or state, confined,
In merit's spite to long neglect consign'd,
The sport or victim of some envious flame,
Whence care nor art might rescue nor reclaim,)—
Flies the BOTANIC SONG; around
Successive nations catch the enchanting sound,
Glow as they listen, wonder as they gaze,
And pay the instructive page with boundless praise:
For not to Britain's parent isle alone,
Or what the East encircles with her zone,
The bounty flows; but spreads to neighbouring realms,
And a *new hemisphere* with joy o'erwhelms.

TO Dr. DARWIN.

Here, read with rapture, studied with delight,
Long shall it charm the taste, the thought excite;
And youths and maids, the parent and the child,
Their minds illumined, and their griefs beguiled,
By all of fancy, all of reason, moved,
Rise from the WORK invigor'd and improved.

Nor only *here*, nor only *now*, enjoy'd :—
Where opes the interior desolate and void;
Where Mississippi's turbid waters glide,
And white Missouri pours its rapid tide;
Where vast Superior spreads its inland sea,
And the pale tribes near icy confines stray;
" Where now Alaska lifts its forests rude,
" And Nootka rolls her solitary flood;"*
Where the fierce sun with ray severer rains
His floods of light o'er Amazonian plains;
Where, land of horrors! roam the giant brood,
On the bleak margin of the antarctic flood;
In future years, in ages long to come,—
When redient Justice finds again her home;—
Known, honour'd, studied, graced with nobler fame,
Its charms unfaded, and its worth the same,
To vaster schemes shall light the kindling view,
And lift to heights no earlier era knew.
Some ardent youth, some Fair whose beauties shine,
In mind, as person, only not divine,—
In halls where Montezuma erst sat throned,
Whom thirty princes as their sovereign own'd;—
In bowers where Manco labour'd for Peru,
While the white thread his blest Oëlla drew,—
Where Ataliba met a tyrant's rage,—
Entranced, shall ponder o'er the various page;
Or, where Oregon foams along the West,
And seeks the fond Pacific's tranquil breast,

---

* This couplet is from an unpublished Poem of my friend Mr. Richard Alsop; a poet who, were his ambition equal to his talents, would appear among the poets of his time " *velut inter ignes luna minores.*"

EPISTLE TO Dr. DARWIN.

With kindred spirit strike the sacred lyre,
And bid the nations listen and admire.

 Hence keen incitement prompt the prying mind,
By treacherous fears nor palsied nor confined,
Its curious search embrace the sea, and shore,
And mine and ocean, earth and air, explore.

 Thus shall the years proceed,—till growing time
Unfold the treasures of each differing clime;
Till one vast brotherhood mankind unite
In equal bands of knowlege and of right:
Then, the proud column, to the smiling skies,
In simple majesty sublime shall rise,
O'er Ignorance foil'd, their triumph loud proclaim,
And bear inscribed, immortal, DARWIN's name.

E. H. SMITH.

New-York, March, 1798.

Ella-Birtha-Henry Poems

THE VOLUNTEER LAUREAT,
AN ODE ;
For the BIRTH-DAY of the PRESIDENT of the UNITED STATES.

OFT has the Poet's venal song,
  Correctly mean, and elegantly low,
Told the false plaudits of the courtly throng,
And wak'd a smile on guilty Grandeur's brow.
  But here hath Virtue's guardian hand
Torn from the Syren, Adulation's power
The Man, whose praise—*the voice of every land*—
Hangs on the lips of every parting hour.

  Here, can no Poet's venal song
Echo the praises of a courtly throng ;
Nor the poor wealth of many a powerful State,
Buy a new honor for the truly great :
  For here, the Muse's noblest lays
  But speak a Nation's answering praise ;
  And here, can heaven-descended verse
Nought but the glories of his name rehearse.

Daughter of Heaven ! awake the enobling lyre !
Breathe thy full influence ; every cord inspire ;
Exalt the soul to dignity of song ;
Swell every note, and every strain prolong.

The answering Spirit trembles o'er the strings ;
Things, more than earthly, dance before my sight ;
Hark ! with her voice the empyrean rings ;
The Past, lies all reveal'd ; the Future lives in light.

  " The voice of Horror echoes far ;
  " Responds, the direful whoop of war ;
  " Thunders, the mighty tube of death ;
  " The knife red gleams upon the heath ;
  " Groans load the air, shrieks rend the skies ;
  " The crimson standard wildly flies ;
  " Impatient slaughter loudly calls ;
  " The Chief of Tho'tless Valor falls.
  " 'Gainst all the terrors of the field,
  " The Chief of Virtue rears his shield ;
  " Secure, the train diminish'd move ;
  " And weeping Britain smiles in love.

" See, demon Danger's horrid form,
" With dire Oppression strong allied,
" Hangs o'er the land—and wakes the storm ;
" And swells, of deep calamity, the tide.
" See, in their train Destruction stalk ;
" And Giant Vengeance threatening walk ;
" And red-clad Envy ride the empoison'd gale ;
" And jealous Grandeur spread the impatient sail.

" Greatly inspir'd, his country lifts her voice—
" See Danger trembles at his awful name ;
" Tyrant Oppression views her fainting flame ;
" And gasping Freedom breathes but to rejoice.

" Dark o'er the field of Liberty and Right,
" Of sad Dismay, hangs low the deepen'd gloom :
" Wide spreads the flash of *Trenton's* bloody light ;
" And Freedom, glorying, rises from the tomb.

" Strong in himself—he scatters wide the storm ;
" Calms the wild raging of the troubled tide ;
" O'erthrows Destruction ; Vengeance joins his side ;
" And Envy kneels in Adoration's form.

" Lin'd with red Hosts the ramparts shine ;
" Oppos'd, the brother armies join ;
" The brazen Thunders ope their throats ;
" On all the air the Tempest floats :
" Their Captives guarded, see the bands retire,
" And jealous Grandeur at the view expire.

" His Country sav'd, o'er Cincinnatus great,
" He tills the soil, and guides the arts of Peace.
" But see ! new Glory bursts the womb of Fate !
" New toils demand him from the promis'd ease !

" The voice of millions lift him o'er the realm
" Which once his valor from oppression freed ;
" Powerful in virtue, now he rules the helm—
" In War—in Peace—the blest of Heaven succeed.

" O born to grace and dignify mankind !
" Years long await thee—Time himself shall stay
" Till thou hast op'd, resplendent on the mind,
" Th' immortal brightness of the *moral day*.

" Tis thine to spread new virtue o'er the Earth ;
" To breathe the soul of liberty in man ;
" To brace Creation to a glorious birth ;
" And charm Perfection to complete the Plan."

Favor'd of Heaven ! the Muse in rapture faints,
Thy grateful country strives, in vain, to sing ;
The Earth uplifts her hands in joy—the Saints
Respond in Peans to each speaking string.
" Long may'st thou live"—the Soul of Nature cries—
" Greatest of Mortals—Favorite of the Skies."   ELLA.

SONNET I.
Sent to Miss ——— ———, with a Braid of Hair.

FAIR shews the rose, but soon its beauty fades,
   And soon its balmy-breathing fragrance fails;
     The downy peach, sweet pear, DECAY assails,
And clustered purples of the vine invades.

Nor does alone the vegetative realm
   Feel the destroyer's over-bearing power;
He joys in ruin, cities to o'erwhelm,
     To shake the column, and to sink the tower.

Nor yet can Beauty, radiant as the morn,
   Escape his wrath. The rosy cheek he pales;
   O'er all the lily of the skin prevails;
And *flowing honors that the head adorn.*
    The soul, refined in sentiment and truth,
    Derides his power, and smiles eternal youth.

ELLA.

SONNET II.
Sent to Mrs.——— ———, with a Song.

BLEST is the *Poet* if his songs can raise
   Some kindred genius that will catch the fire,
     With answering notes awake the trembling lyre,
And give to far posterity his praise.

Yet double pleasure fills his aged days,
   If chance, responsive to his fond desire,
     While from the lips of youth the notes aspire,
In the warm breast the flame of virtue blaze.

And still a greater pleasure, should he spy
That while from Virtue's breast the music flows,
Caught by the song, the voice, the speaking eye,
In every heart the illustrious purpose glows.
Even he, the Poet, nobler worth should warm
By virtue, greatly rous'd, in ———'s form.   ELLA.

TO ELLA.

STRIKE, ſtrike again thy ſilver-ſounding lyre
ELLA, thou darling of the God of verſe;
Again in thy clear, claſſic ſtrain, rehearſe
DECAY's fierce ravage, with a poet's fire.

So when the fainting Sun's laſt golden rays,
   Have glimmer'd o'er the foam-white billowy ſea,
I've heard a Seraph's voice in heav'nly lays,
   Oft bid me think on dread ETERNITY!

"Thy feeble ſtar now ſhoots its paley beam,
   "Dim'd by diſeaſe, o'er life's tempeſtuous ſurge,
   "And ſoon the murmuring waves ſhall ſound thy dirge,
"While deep thy ſtar is ſunk beneath the ſtream.
   "Then ſhall it riſe in the bright *realms of Truth*,
   "Deride DECAY, and ſmile eternal *Youth*."

                                   BIRTHA.

SONNET III.

Sent to Miſs. ——— ———,

NOW o'er the world hath ſober Evening ſpread
   Her ebon-tinctured veil—the ſtars appear—
   The ſmiling Moon in mildeſt beauty clear,
As on my hand I preſs my penſive head.

While not on earth is heard one echoing tread,
   Look thro' the Southern upraiſ'd window near.
   Down on my cheek tear courſes after tear—
I think on abſent *friends*, on pleaſures fled.

Now all *their* actions living in my ſight
Awake new, mournful, pleaſures in my ſoul,
And each memento gives a freſh delight.
Do not ſuch joys my fair one's mind controul?
They do—I ſee th' aſſenting tear deſcend—
And ſhe will love this trifle for the friend.

                                     ELLA.

SONNET.

THE incense-breathing Lily rears her head,
  On the fair bosom of the dark green vale;
    While youthful zephyr borne along the gale,
Steals her perfume and wantons on her bed.

  The new-born Rose, all dripping with the dew,
    With magic spell attracts the Poet's eye;
    Amidst the lucid tears, its blooming hue
  Looks lovlier, and assumes a deeper dye.

'Twas thus of late I saw a lovely Maid,
  Pure as the silver lily of the vale;
  But *Syren pleasure* blew her sullying gale,
And o'er her *bosom* cast a sombre shade.
  Now like this blushing Rose, the Fair appears,
  Her vernal cheeks suffus'd in silv'ry tears.

BIRTHA.

ODE.
TO BIRTHA.

POOR, and unknown, a stranger to the great,
  While now, with holy veneration deep inspir'd,
To *Him*, whose virtue glads the extending *state*,
  Wak'd by the voice of *Truth*, my soul to song is fir'd.

And now, while Friendship, trembling o'er the strings,
Breathes on the lyre unutterable things,
  And steals its ancient, and neglected store:
Hark! o'er the wild-resounding air,
What music floats, in varied numbers near,
  And winds, in wildering echoes, down the dashing shore!

Again, in full, deep sounds, it loads the swelling gale;
  And now, it softly undulates the breeze;
And now, *a small, still voice*, the notes my soul assail,
With calm delight responsive; now they seize,
In bolder swellings, on the impassion'd *mind*,
  That feels *its* different *powers* refin'd,
As now, with many a slowly-solemn pause, they fail.

O Thou, whose fingers from the answering lyre
  Draw sounds so flattering to the Youth of Song,
Deep from my soul the grateful sighs aspire,
  That hail the enjoyment which they would prolong.

Life hath trifling joys to give;
Not in *Life* doth pleasure live;
Tomb of pleasure, *tomb* of joy,
Ever anxious to destroy:

Shrouding in thy narrow space
Every virtue, every grace.
Tyrant! soon thy reign is o'er,
Radiant glory bursts thy door.

Love, who all thy power defies,
Rising, mingles with the skies.
Now, even now, I scorn thy wrath—
Glory brightens round my path.

Now thy yawning gates unfold,
While the powerful charm is told.
See, my soul, in fancy rise—
BIRTHA, seraph, opes the skies.
        E L L A.

SONNET IV.

ADOWN the melancholy stream of life
 Who joys the vessel of his Years to guide?
 Nor fears the roarings of th' incertain tide,
The inclement Winter, or the Ocean's strife?

And who, regardful of his certain end,
 Can bear the incessant struggles of his Youth;
 Force thro enticement to an age of truth;
And welcome Death as freely as his friend?

Who, that when Poverty's torpedo hand
Has chill'd even Charity's soft-answering soul;
When green-eyed Malice hunts him thro the land,
Can smile serene, superior to the whole?
He, who the paths of Rectitude has trod—
His friends—*his life, his conscience, and his God.*
        E L L A.

SONNET.

BEHOLD that woe-wild Maiden in yon Cell!
    Poor haplefs Maiden! once the Village boaſt!
    O'er ev'ry Glaſs her name was ſung the toaſt,
The praiſe of KATE on every tongue would dwell.

Her boſom tender as the callow Dove,
    She liſt'ned to the tale of WILLIAM's tongue;
Her Eye would dart the penſive-looks of love,
    And only WILLIAM charm'd her with his ſong.
But when the faithleſs Lover, caught her heart;
    Loſt to the *laws* of honor, *voice* of truth,
    Loſt to the *generous* ſentiment of youth,
Her name he ſullied by a *villain's* art;
Remorſe now forces the nerve-ſhaking ſigh,
While fierceſt madneſs fires her ſparkling Eye.

                      BIRTHA.

TO ELLA.

NO ſkill I boaſt, no forceful art,
    To ſhake the nerves of ELLA's heart;
Save ſuch as from the Thruſh's throat,
Is uſher'd in her feeble note,
When ſitting on the hawthorn buſh,
She whiſtles to her fellow Thruſh.

But ELLA, doſt thou think to find,
Hid in my lines, the artful, *flattering* mind?
    Far from the tow'ring city was I rear'd,
Where pois'nous *flattery* ever vig'rous grows;
    In earlieſt youth my Parents I rever'd,
To what their *virtue* taught, my ſpirit bows:

Here have I liv'd and heard ſweet Nature's voice,
Where Brandywine rolls on with ruſhy-noiſe;
The ſtream from many murm'ring rills ſupplied,
Along a curving channel pours his tide;
'Ere long the flood its mazy windings leaves,
And ſwift from clift to clift down daſh the waves;
Now ſweeping round beneath a lofty hill,
With rapid force it whirls full many a mill.
Below, the ſmoother current, ſpreading wide,
Full freighted Barks along its boſom glide;
Above, the trees their verdant branches ſpread,
And o'er the tinkling ſtream throw their deep ſhade;

Here oft entranc'd—I've flowly ftepp'd along,
And heard the Robin's folitary fong;
Touch'd by his thought-exciting note,
    I caft my tear-wet eyes around,
    Beheld the richly flower'd ground,
    Whilft borne on zephyrs airy wing,
The fpirits of the blufhing Beauties float;
And over fwelling hill, and delving dale,
    Their fweeteft odours fling,
Upon the bofom of the flowing gale;
Then fading, fink in earth,
And when the Spring returns again come into birth.
But Man, when fome few hafty hours have flown,
    Drops in the yawning grave,
Nor lives again on *Life*'s e'er changing wave;
Where throbs of anguifh tear the feeling breaft,
And from the heavy *lid* fteal nature's healing reft;
But, " pleafing, dreadful thought!" mounts into worlds
    When the rofy-color'd morn!   [unknown.
Came lightly tripping o'er the hills,
Dancing on the dimpling rills,
    And lucid pearls pour'd from her dewey horn:
Here have I heard the warbling Lark awake
The voice of Echo, fleeping in the brake,
And as the heaven-taught bird pour'd out his foul,
The lift'ning Fairy half his mufic ftole,
And blew the thrilling founds from grove to grove,
Till nature feem'd to breathe but harmony and love.

The foft-eyed Turtle breath'd her plaintive note,
Soul-tend'ring notes! which on clear æther float,
And oft prophetic, tell the tardy fwain,
To fhield his harveft from the coming rain.

When the creative God of Day,
His flaming Car drove down the Weftern fea,
And fober Evening's twilight grey,
Borne on the wings of Time had pafs'd away.
Along the curling wave in radiance bright,
The fair Moon fhot her filver fhafts of light,
And all was filent as the cave of Death,
    Where fhadowy beings walk,
    Who ne'er prefume to talk,
Nor ruffle filence with a founding breath:
There have I ftood, and wrapt in Thought fublime!
Mark'd the quick flight of light'ning-footed Time!
Or gaz'd with rapture on the worlds on high,
Till my full foul would breathe th' extatic figh,
And the big pearl ftart from my glift'ning eye.

While late I press'd my downy bed,
And sleep her poppies bound around my head,
A heav'nly Phrenzy seized on my soul,
And swift as lightnings dart from pole to pole,
A host of Beauties rush'd upon my sight,
By Fancy, clad in changeful robes of light!
   I saw again the verdant grove
   Its wild, luxuriant foliage move,
   And heard the plumy Songsters shout their love.
   I heard again the dashing wave,
   Its wild and rocky borders lave.

I saw thy Spirit, like the Bird of Jove!
On never-failing wings, mount to the sky;
With eyes of light'ning pierce the realms above,
And hail the GOD OF MUSIC, thron'd on high.
Charm'd with thy air, he gave a heav'nly Harp,
And bade *thee* pour the music sweetly sharp;
   Then sweep the golden strings,
And rouse the deeper tones—and form the awful Pause,
   That opes the sacred springs
Of joy sublime, and wafts the spirit up to Nature's **Cause**!
Then wake the swelling sounds to roll
In bursting floods of harmony upon the panting soul.
He, o'er thy form a sky-dipt mantle threw,
Where silver stars glow'd on th' etherial blue;
And bade thee to old Earth descend, and take
Thy Lyre, and from the strings the sleeping Music wake.

I saw thee in the shady Grove alight,
Whose woven branches caught the blaze of light;
Thy rosy fingers careless swept the Lyre,
And drew the music-breathing Spirit from each wire.
Lur'd by the sounds of thy sweet Strings,
The feather'd Warblers dropp'd their wings,
   And listen'd to thy melting tone,
   Still more enchanting than their own!

Borne on the undulating breeze,
Thy heaven-taught Notes my Spirit seize,
And waft it to the sky:
Now sweetly soft they ling'ring die;
Now in awful solemn sound,
Float on the Air around;
The deep majestic base most sweetly clear,
Now bursts upon my ear;
And where the rushing Waters roar,
" It winds in wild'ring echoes down the dashing shore."

The thrill of rapture darting through my breaſt,
My nerves with heav'nly anguiſh ſhook,
And I awoke!
But found no *fiction* broke upon my reſt;
For now the truths unfold,
In thy nervous Song is told,
What e're I heard, or ſaw, and as I read, " my ſoul, my
ELLA, " Seraph, opes the Skies."   [fancy riſe,"
Delaware, April 10, 1791.

SONNET, V.

"SAY, what is Life?" the ſons of ſorrow cry—
  " Is it to breathe a lingering age of woe
    " In vegetative being here below?
  " To eat, to drink, to ſleep, and then—to die?"
" Is it in Pleaſure's airy rounds to fly?
    " To laugh, to dance?"—the ſouls of Joy would know—
      " To plunge in lewdneſs, and no care beſtow
  " On what may greatly fit us for the ſky?"
No.—Tis the Twilight of a heavenly Day,
  Whoſe radiant glories opening on the Soul,
Shall raiſe, and bear it, from itſelf away,
    Far o'er the bounds of this terreſtrial pole,
Wak'd to new rapture by the living lay,
  Where GOD informs the immeaſurable whole.
                                        ELLA.

SONNET VI.
TO EGWINA.

GO verſe, ſoft-whiſpering, to EGWINA ſay—
  'Tis not that rich complexion's lucent white,
    Tinged with the Roſe's fragrance-bluſhing light,
O'er all her lovely features loves to ſtray;
Nor yet, that Nature, with a fond diſplay,
    Hath ſpread her auburn treſſes on the ſight,
      And fram'd her lips the ſeal of ſweet delight,
And op'd her eyes reſplendent on the day;
Tell her 'tis not, that o'er each motion, Grace
Sheds a ſoft luſtre, as ſhe deigns to move,
Giving new beauties to the ambient place;
That every tho't, and all my ſoul, is love.
But, that her mind, its radiant worth to prove,
Imprints the ſoul of Beauty on her Face.   ELLA.

ODE TO *BIRTHA*.

SOFT o'er my soul the voice of music breathes,
  Waking the sympathies which thrill delight.
    The Mental Spirit hails seraphic light,
    Heavenly Visions fill the sight.
  Glory hangs immortal wreaths;
  Joy the Harp divine unsheaths;
    Echo answering as it rings,
    Female Virtue strikes the strings.

Nearly allied the trembling *Passions* live:
And all the *Emotions* of the human mind,
In mystic bands united, fondly give
Mingling responses, tremulously join'd.
Now tranquil *Pleasure* softly moves along.
Touching the cord to which mild *Melancholy*'s voice,
In answers low, awakes the sigh-exciting song,
Making sweet *Pity*'s tear-suffused eyes rejoice,
As now, in awful tho't sublime,
She sees the immortal *Spirit* triumph over *Time*.

O Thou whose soul, responsive, wakes the lyre!
Throw off, of gorgeous praise, the rich attire,
  And, with united labours, let us toil,
To raise the mind to energy of tho't;
  To bid Morality attractive smile;
And deep impress what Heaven itself hath taught.

O let us strive, with union'd hearts sincere;
To form the patriot soul to deed severe;
  To draw the sympathetic tear;
To bid of love the generous transports glow;
  The ennobling warmth of friendship flow;
    And kind compassion's hand
      In extacy expand,
    To soothe Misfortune's woe.

O let us wake the *Imaginative Powers*
Whose smiles give pleasure to the passing hours;
  Whose kind progression weans the heart
    From earth, and all its low concerns,
  And bids it, anxious, wish that better part,
That home, for which the immortal Spirit yearns;
Which draws it, sweetly, from this sad abode,
To Heaven, to Happiness, to GOD.

This be our praise---That Virtue, Truth, inspire;
And Human Bliss, breathes o'er the echoing lyre.
                                    E L L A.

SONNET,

Written after hearing a SONG sung by several SISTERS.

Hark!—hear'st thou not the sweetly swelling strain
Of warbled music float along the air?
Soft are the sounds,—the Sister band how fair!
How high flies rapture when it springs from *P*yn**.
So round the lyre the heavenly Mutes stand,
   And charm the changing soul with varied joy;
So Ella's lays the feeling heart command,
   And faintly hide Apollo in the boy.
Hail charming group! for you shall Fancy rise,
   To you young Love his earliest homage pay;
   And while our souls on softened flav'ry stray,
Your *Minds* preserve the conquests of your *Eyes*;
   Till ripe you fall, as Heaven and Fame approve,
   From Beauty's branch, into the lap of Love.

                              HENRY.

SONNET, VII.
TO THE SUN.

Hail Son of Morning! thou, whose orient Smile,
   While now the dew-drop twinkles on the rose.
   And richest fragrance o'er the champaign flows,
Awakes the slumbering laborer's daily toil.
Do e'er thy ruddy splendors gild the pile,
   As o'er the earth their circling glory glows,
   Where modest Virtue's unseen hand bestows
Joys that the cares of Misery oft beguile?
O! if thou dost,—to that sweet cherub say—
   'Tho Time, dim-sighted, overlook thy worth;
' Tho Fame shall fail thy merit to display;
   ' Nor glory deck thee, hallow'd of the earth;
' Yet thou shalt shine in GOD's eternal day—
   ' The heir immortal of a heavenly birth.

                              ELLA.

ODE TO HENRY.

WHAT blifs the voice of Mufic gives,
   While tranfport in the bofom lives,
While virtue, borne on every found,
Spreads love and happinefs around!
   The Soul in purer vifion fees
The ills of human life retire;
   And Adoration loads the breeze,
With praifes that to Heaven afpire.

How few the happy power poffefs
The fympathizing heart to blefs
With pictures of ideal joy,
Which ftrengthen virtue, not deftroy!
   They are the Mufe's favorite care;
Perfection thro' their fouls fhe breathes;
   And crowns them, faireft of the fair,
With Glory's never-fading wreaths.

And *He* whofe fong *their* voice infpires
With holy Pleafure's warm defires;
With power the trembling lyre to move
To accents of immortal love;
   Shall, robed in modeft merit, fhine
His country's wonder, and its praife;
   While, bending at her moral fhrine,
To Truth he confecrates his lays.

Him fhall the love of nations hail,
Born o'er Oppreffion to prevail;
Virtue's own hand fhall round his tomb
Twine circlets of immortal bloom;
   The Loves eternal incenfe burn;
The Mufes there the Lyre fhall place;
   And Glory fhall the fimple urn
With HENRY's name, in tranfport, grace.

                              E L L A.

SONNET VIII.

TO THE *MOON*.

BEND from thy throne fair Empress of the Night,
    And as thou look'ſt o'er earth with eye ſerene,
    Marking thy ſhadowy paintings on the green,
And brightening Heaven with ſilver-ſtreaming light—
O! if in all thy courſe, divinely bright,
    Thou ſee'ſt one wretch, in felon malice mean,
    Debaſe the varied beauty of the ſcene;
Or one fell murtherer burſt the bands of right;
Dart thro' his ſoul, ſeverely bright, a ray
    Whoſe living ſplendor ſhall his hand arreſt;
And to his guilty-conſcious ſpirit ſay—
    ' Tho thou may'ſt live unknown to Law's beheſt,
' And hide thy deeds from mortals, and the day—
    ' Yet Conſcience' worm ſhall rankle in thy breaſt.'

ELLA.

TO ELLA.

AH! vainly Ella, do I hear
Thy lute complain, in notes ſo clear,
As would ſeduce an angel's ear;
That bids me check the ſong of praiſe,
And give to *other themes*, my lays.

To fierce diſeaſe and grief a prey,
In pain I paſs the lingering day.
No more I raiſe the ſprightly ſtrain,
    Or warble the melodious ſong,
That fill'd the breaſt with envied pain,
    And could the joys of life prolong.

Now, when the *glowing orb* of day,
    Hath ſunk, beneath the weſtern wave;
With melancholy heart I ſtray
    To hear the ſtream his border lave.

Or like some pilgrim press the yielding grass,
   And wet my sandals with the nightly dew,
A sprig of laurel breaking as I pass.
   To *thee* I say the *honoring branch* is due.

My dangerous course along the vale I take,
   Beneath the hanging rock, that seems to shake
With ev'ry blast, and threatens on my head
     Its crushing weight to roll;
     But my undaunted soul,
Enjoys the scene, nor feels the chill of terror spread.

Now, near a cavern dark, and wild,
   With folded arms I stand,
Like melancholy's gloomy child;
     I heave the swelling sigh;
     Upon the passing gale;
     While from my ever-streaming eye;
       Adown my cheeks, so wan and pale,
The tears incessant drop upon my hand.
There I hear the moping owl,
His dismal whoopings roll,
Upon the heavy ear of night,
In sounds that would thy soul affright.

But Oh! my bursting heart!
So tortur'd by the fang of grief,
In other scenes would seek relief:
On fancy's rapid wing I'd dart
Where horror with his staring eye,
And upright hair,
Sits gazing on the fiery sky,
When sulphurous lightnings fly,
And swell the soul to wild despair.

Where the vex'd wave with mad'ning roar,
Rolls thundering on the craggy shore,
And aims with ev'ry dreadful shock,
To burst apart the flinty rock;
When still like wretched man! in vain
He strives his purpose to obtain;
Mad to despair, he flies again
And clamours to his parent main.

                    BIRTHA.

TO ELLA.

ALIGHTED from the azure sky,
　A Seraph stood before my sight,
And checked awhile the anxious sigh,
　　And pointed to the Realms of Light.
Celestial Youth his Features fired,
His Eye the Breast with Hope inspired,
Virtue's own Hand his Temples crown'd,
And Glory shed her Day around.
'Twas ELLA!—wrapt in awe I stood,
And thrill'd with joy the Vision viewed.
　Soft as the gentlest shower descends,
　　His soothing accents flowed,
And, winding thro' the maze of Song,
In playful eddies poured along,
　Till Nature sighing—sinking bends,
　　And Life a pause bestowed.

Cease, ELLA, cease thy 'witching Song,
Nor lure me from the earthly throng;
Too frail to shine in Virtue's Train,
Too weak to wake the heavenly Strain,
In vain with borrowed Art I soar,
For fickle Fancy smiles no more.
　The feeble *Meteor's* transient blaze
Unnoted sinks in Night;
　But Nature lives in *Sol's* bright Rays,
And Nations bless his Light.

　　　　　　　　　　HENRY.

ODE
TO BIRTHA.

AND does disease thy bosom grieve?
O had I known it at an earlier hour,
　I would have strove thy sorrows to relieve,
Have torn thee from the tyrant Sickness' power,
　And bade thy aching breast delight receive.
　I would have sat the lingering, painful, eve,
With various talk the lonely moments cheer'd;
　Have, with unwearied hand, thy head sustain'd
Whole nights; and soothed thee as thou had'st complain'd;
And heal'd thee with affection long endear'd.

For I have known the hand of hard difeafe;
  Have felt oppreffive ficknefs at my foul;
    Seen death-like palenefs o'er my features fpread;
And mark'd the life-fupporting current freeze,
    From hollow eyes, of blue defpair, the big tears roll;
      And join'd, in anguifh'd fancy, with the dead.

Yet then, even then, I caft a lingering look
  On all the bufinefs of beloved mankind;
While each adieu, each fond farewel, I took,
  Still left a wifh, for one more view, behind.
'Twas then new pleafures burft upon my mind,
New wifhes agitated all my breaft;
  And hope, and paffion, and affection, join'd,
With life-reviving health again my bofom blefs'd.

Such are the joys I offer to thy view.
  For what a greater tranfport can afford
Than to behold affection, virtue new,
  And lovely goodnefs, o'er creation pourd?
To fee refinement new-born raptures fhew?
  And happinefs, by you, to earth reftored?

    To fee the enchanting fmile
    Of fweet benevolence expand,
And o'er the human face diffufe new light;
What hath fuch power affliction to beguile,
And foothe the woe-worn heart with comfort bland?
What greater pleafure can the foul delight?

      To let Imagination ftray,
      And wanton in celeftial day;
      To fee Creation's fecond birth.
    And Heaven, defcending, blefs the Earth;
    To view new beauty clothe the plain,
    And rapture hail Meffiah's reign;
    To mark death, anguifh, and difeafe,
    And vice, no more pollute the breeze;
    To fee perfection's glorious heirs,
    Triumphant o'er life's little cares,
    To new attainments daily grow;
    With nobler virtue hourly glow;
    And, bofom'd in immortal peace,
    In God's felicity increafe;
    To love with frefher truth inclined;
    And gaining on the eternal Mind:
What nobler tranfports can the foul poffefs?
What richer joy the fympathetic bofom blefs?

                E L L A.

ODE TO *HENRY*.

WITH what an anxious, trembling, joy,
  Doth Modesty his powers employ!
While earnest pantings fill his breast,
He shrinks with shadowy fears distrest.
    Warm'd with Fancy's glowing fire,
    HENRY can tny soul desire
    Far from Virtue's aid to fly?
    Virtue daughter of the sky.

C I had hoped, with fond delight,
With thee, ambitious, to unite;
With thee to wake the answering lyre;
With thee the strength of truth inspire.
    Now thou fli'st the doubtful field
    Yet untried, I see thee yield;
    Shun the stormy face of day,
    Which to glory points the way.

We might have join'd, with studious care,
To chase from earth the fiend Despair,
To wake new tenderness and truth,
New virtue, in the soul of Youth.
    Might have bade true friendship rise;
    Love regardless of disguise,
    Merit garb anew the mind;
    Worth the glory of mankind.

To us the Muse have oped her store
With luxury unknown before;
Our fainting souls with strength have fired;
Our song with energy inspired.
    Now a tear her cheek bedews—
    " Henry hath forgot the Muse.
    " Slights the power whose constant care
    " Makes him lovely to his fair.

" Tell him, altho the fires of even,
" Before the Sun, are lost in heaven;
" Like, are the Muse's splendid rays,
" The *glory of the latter days.*
    " Radiance gilds the Poet's sky;
    " Heavenly visions fill his eye;
    " Time's dominions unconceal'd,
    " All Creation lies reveal'd."

                                    E L L A.

SONNET TO *REFLECTION*.

THE *Lord of light* has journey'd down the sky,
    And bath'd his coursers in the foaming wave;
The twinkling star of Ev'en too, hastes to lave,
Her silver form, and vanish from my eye.

Now dusky twilight flings her sombre shade,
    O'er the bright beauties of the silent vale,
The aspin trembles not, the verdant blade,
    No longer nodding answers to the gale.

Come sweet Reflection! hither pensive Maid!
    Direct thy wandering steps, and on this stone,
Worn by no travellers feet, with moss o'ergrown,
Repose with me in solitude's deep shade.
    Then shall I know the height of human bliss,
    And taste the joy of *other worlds* in this.

                  BIRTHA.

LAURA and MARY.

"WHY drops the pearly tear from LAURA's eye?
    That eye which used the love-lorn mind to cheer;
Why heaves that bosom thus the far-fetch'd sigh?
What grief afflicts the maid to friendship dear?

Form'd with the power the coldest heart to warm,
With innate beauty glowing in thy breast;
What from thy bosom can contentment charm,
Or break with momentary woe thy rest?

Can she whose presence never fails to give
New life, new joy, on whom she deigns to smile;
Thus like a turtle solitary live,
And all admirers of their hopes beguile?"

" Alas my Mary! nought can e'er avail,
To sooth the gathered tumults of my soul;
Or, wakening comfort for a girl so frail,
To calm my sorrows, or my griefs control.

Not all the pleasures that this world affords,
Can give one moment to my soul of peace;
Nor all the flattering emptiness of words,
Make glad this conscience with its wonted ease.

Short are the joys triumphant beauty gives,
With hurried steps full quick they flit away;
E'en while the triumph in the bosom lives,
We droop with night, and sicken with the day.

But O my MARY! nought can e'er reprieve
My soul from sorrow, or my bosom cheer;
Or bless the heart, that fluttering to deceive,
Has stretch'd my EDWARD on a watery bier.

Pleased with the tho'ts of conquest, and of fame,
I spurn'd the youth, forgetful of his love,
Whose crimson blushes spoke the burning flame—
Hard was my heart—nor sighs, nor tears, could move.

At length, dejected with my base disdain,
And worn with sorrow, and corroding care,
He plunged, at midnight, in the billowy main,
And left these fields, and left this vernal air.

'Twas then I found, nor pride, nor wealth, nor praise,
Could pour one beam of comfort on my mind;
Twas then I wish'd, that with an answering grace,
I'd heard his vows, and never been unkind.

Full many an eve I've dew'd the green-clad earth
With stern Repentance' bitter-dropping tear;
Full many a day I've fled the house of mirth,
And brooded o'er the memory of my dear.

Thus, thus, my Mary! torn from every joy,
And pierced with Conscience' terrifying dart,
In tears, and sighs, my moments I employ,
Nor tears, nor sighs, can ease my broken heart."

Here as she paused, a sudden thunder shook
The groves around; the darken'd forests roar;
The trees that mantled o'er the winding brook,
Scared at the sound, forsook the waved-wash'd shore.

Terrific lightning blazing round their heads
In one large sheet the wide-stretch'd forest veil'd;
And new-form'd thunder shook again the meads,
And chafed the lightnings that their forms assail'd.

At once a voice, stern as the winter's roar,
That chill'd their vitals, and that froze their blood;
Bade the loud grumbling thunder vex no more
The trembling forest, and the frighten'd flood.

At once a deeper flash o'erspread the sky;
A louder peal convulsed the trembling ground;
The lightnings vanish'd from the pain-fed eye;
And thunders wavered with a distant sound.

Sudden a form, with which the angelic host,
Nor Raphael's self in majesty could vie,
Chased the dark thunders from the quaking coast,
And oped the purpling regions on their eye.

Then, with a look that pierced thro' LAURA's heart,
And crop'd the withering roses of her cheek—
" Thou wretch" he cried, " no comfort I impart;
No joys for thee the swift-wing'd minutes seek.

He who, with tears, thy favors once implored
Another holds by Hymen's sacred band;
No more to wander from the nymph adored,
No more to quit, for vile disdain, the land.

Content shall bless him in the works of peace,
Fame shall his footsteps in the war attend;
Rend from a Cesar's brow the withering wreaths
To deck the worthier temples of my friend.

His wife, sweet partner of his every joy,
Adorn'd with all the virtues of the fair,
Shall bless his life in love without alloy,
Love free from sorrow and perplexing care.

In all her looks is sentiment express'd;
In every action dignity and grace;
O! form'd from every age new praise to wrest—
And scatter blushes o'er a Portia's face.

She, tinged with health's inimitable dye,
Shall pass the spring and summer of her life;
Rise, with a nation's blessings, to the sky,
Her only Epitaph—" This was a Wife."

But thou, shall sicken with the coming eve;
Drop, unlamented, to the narrow grave;
No grateful memory to thy kindred leave;
No hand assist thee, none shall wish to save."

Again fresh lightnings sheeted o'er the skies;
Again fresh thunders rock'd the trembling ground;
The vision vanish'd from her eager eyes,
And lightnings quivered at the parting sound.

ELLA.

ODE,

WRITTEN ON LEAVING THE PLACE OF MY NATIVITY.

HIGH up the heavens the Sun in radiance moves,
 Gilding thy varied beauties, happy *Place*,
Whose charms, by birth and time endear'd, my spirit loves,
And mourning leaves, a diftant way to trace.

 Now let me check the rifing figh
  To mark, with melancholy eye,
   Thy fcenes which, lingering, from my view retire:
  Thy domes, flow-moving from the fight;
  Thy Lake, which gleams a fainting light;
   Thy dim-difcovered fpire.

 Dear fcenes of youthful joy—farewel!
Farewel the *Street* which evening hail'd her own,
Charm'd with the fcattered moonlight o'er it thrown,
Liftening, with fweet attention, while the knell
Rung o'er the echoing fields, of Summer's early bell.
Farewel the *Street*, where winter, robed in fnow,
Roar'd with wild tempeft in the ear of night;
Where Friendfhpip, powerful, could his might o'erthrow,
And win Affection's houfe of calm delight.

 Farewel thou venerable *Dome*,
Where the mild Sabbath call'd my conftant feet.
Still let me think how frequent on thy feat,
Deep-mufing tho't hath found a heavenly home.

 For there the foul, when bigot rage was raifed,
And fiery zeal threw crimfon o'er the face,
 Or when the vengeance of the Lord was praifed,
And torture fhook the tenements of grace;
  Or prieftly warmth upraifed the rod;
 Or Dullnefs nodded o'er the word of God;
Could look with mild complacency around;
  And aye where inborn worth was found,
Or goodnefs glow'd upon the face of youth,
  Or native innocency fhone,
Or beauty foften'd on the lip of truth,
  Or dove-like Purenefs fix'd her throne;
   Could gaze with fond delight,
   Grow better at the fight,
  Grateful would fwell for what was given,
And rife, in glowing rapture, up to heaven.

To the still-winding *River's* moonlight banks;
The slowly-rising *Hill*, which leads along
To where the *Grove*, rich scene of Quips and Cranks
And side-supporting laughter, becks the jocund throng;
One pensive, last farewell, now loads my sorrowing song.

    Farewel dear *Inmates* of my soul!
    Now let no grief your minds controul;
    Now heave no silent, secret, sigh;
    Or hang in tears the mournful eye;
    Or lift the hands, in anguish wrung;
    Or wake to speech the flattering tongue.
    Is't not enough in pain to part?
    Spare, spare, the agonizing heart.

    Science hails me to her seat;
      Bright *Ambition* urges on;
    Fame to *Glory* tempts my feet.
      ' Seize on knowledge ere 'tis gone.
    ' *Learning* opes her varied stores;
    ' *Age* his stream of treasure pours;
    ' Meek-eyed *Piety* requires;
    ' Mild *Humanity* desires;
    ' *Pity* points, thy gain, the skies;
    ' Come!' the *Voice* of *Nature* cries.

Father of Heaven! I bow with soul resign'd,
  My former joys shall aid my better part;
All meaner cares be banish'd from my mind
  My toils my Country claims, and God my heart.

                E L L A.

TO ELLA.

HARK! while I found my trembling shell,
And bid the nymph, sweet echo tell;
Where on her velvet couch she lies,
Hid from the gairish burning skies;
How the soul-enlivening sound
Of thy enchanting lyre,
Was borne on Ether's waves around,
From each soft-speaking wire.

'Twas when beside the wizard stream,
I saw the sun's last golden beam,
With yellow tip the aspiring heads,
Of time-contending oaks, the king of shades!
I saw the night flies buzzing round,
I heard the beetle's humming sound :
My soul to sober thought inclin'd,
Thus ran the current of my mind.

No longer now my cheeks disclose,
The beauty of the budding rose ;
No longer, as in former days,
I joy, the sprightly laugh to raise.
O! then each lovely, summer's night,
'Twas my enraptured soul's delight,
To tread the lonely silent vale,
And " drink the spirit of the gale :"

Or when the cloudless moon on high,
Beam'd forth her radiance from the sky ;
To wander o'er the airy hill,
Where pattering falls the lucid rill ;
And see the wild flow'rs shining bright,
Crown'd with the *tears of weeping night*.

But O! the wondrous change!
Now, it delights me not to range,
The fields and vallies, bright and gay,
With beauties of the *laughing May*.

When the shrill spirits of the coming storm,
　　Their shrieks of terror pour along the wind;
And fiercer raging all the grove deform,
　　The branches tear, and shatter down the rind:
When heav'ns bright fires descending from on high,
An awful day flash thro' the gloomy sky;
And from their dwellings the hoarse thunders roar,
And dusky torrents down the vallies pour:
'Tis then my soul enjoys the dreadful hour,
And bows my God! in rev'rence to thy power.
'Twas thus I mus'd, when borne along the air,
Thy heavenly notes came trembling on my ear;
Sweet as the gentlest showers
Of spring, descending on the flowers,
When murmuring Zephyr sinks to rest,
Soft-sighing on the lily's breast.

Ah! would'st thou with thy arm sustain
My wearied form, and soothe my pain?
And wouldst thou all the lingering Eve,
With thy soft sounds my soul relieve?
And hast thou learn'd the healing charm,
　　The power to bid the tyrant sickness fly?
O! hither come, extend thy potent arm,
　　And bid the *beam of Hope* stand sparkling in my eye!

Ah! now, ev'n now, this very hour,
I confess thy magic power!
Charm'd with thy notes divine,
No more my troubled soul,
O'er scenes of horror loves to brood,
No more my freezing blood,
In lazy tides doth roll;
Bright in my eye the tears of rapture shine,
Thro' all my nerves I feel a tremor run,
Now cold as Zembla's snow, now fervid as the sun.

O! may thy generous sympathising heart,
Ne'er feel the anguish of affliction's dart;
May streams of earthly treasure on thee flow,
That thou, the pure celestial joy may'st know,
To bid the beggar smile, and cheer his *house of woe.*

　　　　　　　　　　　BIRTHA.

SONNET to JOY.

HAIL! heaven-descended Queen! to thee I breathe
    This fervent song, the incense of my soul!
Too long has sorrow's dripping cypress wreathe
    O'er-reach'd the source, whence liquid pearls would roll.

Thy soul-reviving Form! I now behold
    In radiant beauty burst upon my sight,
    Thy clear blue eye, beams with a pure delight,
* Adown thy shoulders wave thy locks of gold.

O'er all thy figure glows a nameless grace,
    A beauty that no mortal can behold,
When the soft smile illumes thy blooming face;
    And not declare thee of celestial mould.

O! dwell with me thou angel from the sky,
And bid the Maid tear-loving sorrow fly.
BIRTHA.

* "*And wave thy shadowy locks of gold.*"
Dr. DARVIN's address to May.

SONNET IX.
To Mr. JOHN TRUMBULL.

TRUMBULL! to thee, with hesitating hand,
    I wake the tremulously-breathing lyre;
    Fearful that Age, altho the Muse inspire,
Should weep that Modesty had lost command.

Tis not, alone, that energy divine
    Lives o'er the canvass, as thy pencil moves;
That tint perfects the exquisite design,
    And *life* is present; that my soul approves:

But, that thy Spirit brooding o'er the immense
    Of unknown Beauty, to existence gave
The *plan*, where Wisdom, Liberty, and Sense,
    The high-soul'd Patriot, and the Warrior brave,
Live, with the appropriate character of face,
In all the *pencil's* manners-painting grace.
ELLA.

ODE,
TO BIRTHA.

WITH every changement of the varying mind
  New feelings animate the mortal frame;
  And new sensations of the body, claim
A soul to equal sympathy inclined.

  See Malice on the face imprint
A dimpled smile, the down-drawn lip that strains,
  Half bend the brow, and place the eye asquint,
And shrink, with expectation, all the veins.
  See pale Consumption o'er the sage's soul
Spread idiot weakness, infantine distress,
  Raise with false hope, with faithless joy controul,
With fancied, groundless agony depress.

While with invigorating health we tread,
  And Youth, with dewy fingers, binds
    Her crown of roses round the head,
  Borne on the winged winds,
    Imagination strays.
Wherever *Nature's* hand *her* charms displays—
  Be it to see "the rich-hair'd Youth of Morn"
Impearl the fragrance-breathing thorn;
  To see the mist wind slowly o'er the hill;
Or hear, from unseen bank, loud burst the gurgling rill;
  Or Zephyr rustle sweet the woods among
Whose thickets swell with melody and song;
  To hear the voice of Industry resound;
The ploughman whistling o'er the loamy ridge;
The shepherd's tinkling bell that talks around;
And hoofs loud rattling o'er the village bridge;
Or torrents foaming down the mountain's breast;—
  There doth imagination love to rest.

But when the fallow hand of Sickness spreads
  Wan desolation o'er the human face,
  No more imagination loves to trace
The sportive beauties of the laughing meads.

But the drear cavern, and the darkfome dell,
  The wild faint-gleaming with the meteor's light,
The diftant watch-tower's hollow-founding bell,
  And tempefts brooding o'er the inclement night;
Blue, fulphur-breathing, flames, from church-yard paths that rife,
  Dim, fhadowy forms, that dance before the fight,
The quick-departing flafh, that wraps the fkies,
  And horror's fcream, the melancholy foul delight.

When deep difeafe hangs heavy on the mind,
  Such fympathetic grief the body feels,
  That he but half reftores, who only heals
The woe with which the anguifh'd fpirit pined:
For health muft give new vigor to the frame
Ere foft Contentment can the bofom claim.

So, if the hand of agony diftrefs
  The fuffering body with diftracting pain,
  No earthly medicine can fo well fuftain,
No coftly cordial can fo truly blefs,
As the calm foul, to providence refign'd—
The fteady funfhine of the immortal mind.

O then, my BIRTHA! from the fcenes
Where gloomy Contemplation loves to dwell,
From mufing Melancholy's cell,
  Your wounded fpirit call,
  To where eternal love the foul ferenes,
And Heaven's own finger's " drefs the dreary ball."

Read and reflect, reflect and read;
  Make it your conftant ftudy and employ,
The grand, affecting, folemn, truths to heed,
  Which wake, of pious hearts, the moral joy.
Thefe as you ftudy, torn from dreary views,
  New blifs fhall animate your foul,
    New ftrength your body brace;
    With fweet delight the fancy trace
The lighter paths of moral dues,
  And fee contentment light the mental pole.

By foft degrees, the fcenes which *former days*
  On your imagination pictured fair,
Shall rife, bedeck'd with joy-reviving rays,
  And from your bofom chafe the monfter Care.
Then Happinefs, with powerful arm,
  Shall wreft his poignard from Difeafe,
  And from the features that were born to pleafe,
Scatter, of felon Sicknefs, far the fallow charm:
Again fhall bid health fparkle from your eye;
  In every ftep bid laughing pleafure dance;
  Young Love the dimpling cheek with fmiles enhance;
And Youth, in glory burfting from the fky,
  With Beauty's rich, inimitable grace,
  Throw her celeftial rofes o'er your face.   E L L A.

The following little Poem was written as a testimony of the Author's respect for the talents of Mr. RALPH EARL, a Painter of the school of WEST, and one whom nothing but misfortune has hindered from making a conspicuous figure among the great artists in the profession of Painting.

A FRAGMENT.

* * * * * * * * * * * With steady hand,
There EARL marks out the deep-expressive line.
Fix'd o'er the work intent, the colours spread—
Thro the thin white deep blushes now the red;
And here the violet, mingling with the blue,
Spreads loose in flowing folds of azure-shining hue.

* With form embodied, Force, and Vigour stand;
   And Eloquence extends the hand;
   And sober Tho't contracts his brow;
   And Sadness wipes the tears that flow
   In softly-sympathetic woe.
   Still at his touch new forms arise;
   The soul sits sparkling in the eyes;
   Speech opes the lips; the throbbing heart
   Seems thro the swelling breast to start:
The turgid muscles aid the vivid strife,
And all the form bursts trembling into life.

  † Simplicity, with ardent gaze,
   Stands fix'd in deep amaze;
And agitated Rapture lifts his trembling hands;
   Bent o'er the piece young Genius stands;
   While Tenderness, with tearful eye,
   Strives to suppress the rising sigh;
And Superstition lifts the affrighted cry.

                                 ELLA.

* *Refering to several Paintings by Mr. EARL.*
† *The effect which the sight of them produces on different characters.*

THE SMILE.
SONNET to CAROLINE.

Hast thou not seen upon some night serene,
  The silver moon with smiling radiance beam—
  Illume the grove—enliven every stream—
And add new charms to every lovely scene?

So charming CAROLINE thy angel-smile
  On day or night unequall'd joy bestows,
Does the sad breast of grief and pain beguile,
  And stays the tear which else forever flows.

In thy soft smile the soul of sweetness lives,
  That grace, which shines exalted over art—
  Which speaks the friendly and the feeling heart,
And ev'ry virtuous wish and transport gives.
  Then lovely CAROLINE thy smile repeat;
  I fear not there the *poison of deceit.*

HENRY.

TO *ELLA.*

Again thy sweetly warbled strain,
  Thou leader of the choral train;
Again thy sweeping harp I hear,
That long has charmed my ravished ear.

New vigour to my soul thy words impart,
With softer pleasures touch my wounded heart:
The moral lore that flows along thy line,
Might well befit a PLINY to rehearse;
The bold descriptive beauties of thy Verse,
Would bright on TITIAN's glowing canvas shine.

When closed the blazing eye of day,
And on my downy couch I lay,
Deep musing on thy moral lore;
The God of Sleep around me threw
His mantle dipped in slumbrous dew;
And thus arose my fervent pray'r—

O! thou from whom creation sprung!
O! send from thy bright realms above,
Some faint to cheer me with thy love,
And bid me raise the rapturous song—
For I have heard thy spirits, who on high
Possess the plains of yon cerulean sky;
Have oft, in pity to the mortal race,
Descending closed them in their pure embrace;
And whispering soothing music to their breast,
Charmed all the tempests of the soul to rest—
Scarce had the words escaped my moving tongue,
Yet on my lips the trembling accents hung;
When lo! a form descending from on high,
On silver plumes thro' yonder orient sky:
Wide flows in circling locks her golden hair,
And plays with every eddying of the air.
Her filmy robes white as the falling snow,
Around her form in graceful foldings flow.
Her bright blue eyes beam forth a gentle light,
And fix and charm at once the gazer's sight.
When near she moved I saw bewitching grace,
And heavenly beauty lighten up her face.
Now by my side upon the earth she stood,
Her quickened glance warmed all my chilly blood.
High waving in the air a sky-blue wand,
She bade me follow to yon lofty land;
The path she led, with joyous heart I flew.
'Till near the high and verdant hill I drew;
Then turning round she took my trembling hand,
And waved again her bright cerulean wand:
Soft as the sound of some angelic lute,
Sweet as the breath of Orpheus' mellow flute,
Her words in rapt'rous warblings poured along,
And thrilled my trembling soul with heavenly song.
Behold! she said, that lovely country round,
With nature's richest gifts and beauty crowned,
There purest joy flows thro the circling year,
The happy people know no pain, nor fear;
Their queen am I, from realms of light I came,
Fair virtue's offspring, *blue-eyed Hope* my name."
She ceased; then rose before my ravished sight,
Enchanting scenes in nature's beauty bright;
Here spreads a wide and ever verdant plain,
And waves the yellow life-supporting grain:
There grandly rise the proud aspiring hills,
Between whose rocky chinks slide down the rills.
Here in majestic beauty towering high,
The branching groves shoot to the cloudless sky;
The feathered warblers hop from spray to spray,
And hold their tuneful strife till closing day;

Then pours the plaintive Nightingale her notes,
And all night long her melting mufic floats—
Along the walks of thofe e'er b'ooming bowers,
Forever fpring new crops of fragant flowers.
The priftine colors of the fun are feen
With countlefs changes waving o'er the green—
Rich fculptured figures formed of blazing gold,
Attract the eye, and firm the fenfes hold—
Here *Dove-like Innocence*, engaged in play,
With frolic lambs prolongs the happy day;
There *Charity* throws from her copious ftore,
Till the glad fuppliants ceafe to afk for more:
Here, with celeftial fire in her eye,
Mild Faith with firmnefs gazes on the fky,
And *Adoration* pours her fong of praife,
While tears of rapture wander down her face.
There o'er white curling lakes the nodding trees,
Wave flowly to the gentle paffing breeze;
And wildly-grand around deep rocky caves
Return the echo of the dafhing waves.
Here chryftal mountains fhoot into the fky,
And with the fun in fplendor feem to vie;
Where rife the rugged rock an awful height!
The fheeting torrent holds my wandering fight:
From fteep to fteep down dafh with thundering roar
The mad'ning waves, and foam along the fhore.
" Lo faid the maid there burfting from the ground,
A bubbling fountain cafts its waters round;
And fee behind, where opens yonder bower,
The virtuous fouls enjoy the rapturous hour:
There many a harp, and many a breathing flute
Is heard; refponding founds the filver lute;
Whilft ravifhed with the melody of found
The vocal chorus pour their fongs around.
Thus all the bleft their happy days employ,
And each contributes to the other's joy;
Their grateful incenfe rifes up to heaven,
And for their praife a double joy is given:
Know thou, fhe faid, whoe'er purfues the path
That leads to *Virtue* and unwavering *Faith*,
Shall hail me Queen! and where they dwell fhall rife
A fcene like this, enchanting to their eyes;
The fpheres fhall warble mufic in their ear,
And all creation harmony appear."
Now ceafed her voice, fhe clap'd her filver wings,
And rifing to the fky thro Ether fings.

BIRTHA.

ODE TO TIME.

THOU waſt ere Worlds began to be,
And ſhalt continue to eternity.
Tho' oft the Painter's pencil, oft the Bard,
On canvas, or on Fancy's airy ſcene,
Hath ſhewn thee laughable, with griſly beard,
Stiff-ſtarting from a peaked chin;
A few white hairs thin-ſcattered round thy head,
Thine eyes turn'd grey with age;
Thy noſe quite ſhrivel'd, like a pointed hook,
Thy viſage bearing all a wrinkled wizard look:
Bent down and crooked was thy form,
And tottering on thy weak, lank legs,
Like ſome ſlim reed amid the ſhaking ſtorm:
Thy blood poor, miſerable dregs
Of life, crept thro' each wind-puff'd vein,
Which ſeem'd as tho' 'twould burſt with ev'ry ſtrain:
Thy long and dangling arms a ſcythe ſuſtain,
To lop off men as they cut down their grain!
Moſt laughable indeed! thus to deform
A God in power firſt, as firſt in form!

But look ye Painters! hear ye Bards this truth!
His face ſhall ever bloom unfading Youth.
Bright golden locks adorn his head,
   Majeſtic beauty ſeems his form;
Where'er he ſteps, his awful tread
   Sounds like the thunder of the ſtorm.

Imperial *Rome!* once Miſtreſs of the World!
Who rear'd her palaces, her towers on high,
Bade her tall obeliſks ſhoot to the ſky!
In ruin lies, by *his* ſtrong arm of power hurl'd:
Tall fanes, proud palaces and arches thrown
By *his* ſlight touch come headlong down;
The dreadful weight the mountains ſhakes around,
And hills and vales the horrid roars rebound.
Some broken arch, or nodding tower,
Falls prone to earth each paſſing hour;
And oft the wary traveller hears the ſound
Of ſome lofty column broke,
By *Time's* rudely ſhattering ſtroke,
When down it comes loud-craſhing on the ground.

Behold yon figure ſtarting on the ſight!
His awful brow around,
With palm and laurel bound;
His forceful eye, with genius bright,
Seems now in Fancy's view to roll,
And ſpeak the *bloody Cæſar's* warlike ſoul!
But *Cæſar!* thou art gone!
And *Time* ſhall bid thy ſtatue follow ſoon.

The spacious Forum where great TULLY's voice,
A clear and swelling torrent pour'd along,
'Till the tumultuous faction check'd their murmuring noise,
And mute—with dumb attention hark—as to the song
Of ORPHEUS, did fierce CERBERUS of old,
When *he* with *music's tongue* his tender story told;
Touched by *Time's* destructive, potent wand,
Lies in ruins mouldering on the land.

From *Rome* the Muse now turns her eagle-eye,
To where the sun burns in the western sky—
Where *Niagara* loud and strong,
Her deep, majestic current rolls along:
From many a noble stream and lake supplied
The rushing tide,
With rapid force, most dreadful roars;
While echo swells the solemn sound upon its solitary shores;
But lo! the boiling flood check'd by a rocky mound,
It madly foams, and whirling round,
In one stupendous sheet,
From the dizzy awful height,
Fierce rushing, flashing, falls headlong thundering to the ground.
The trembling groves and caves around
For many a league the dreadful shout resound—
And while the bellowing flood, 'midst craggy rocks below
Boils into foam; above the heaven-depicted bow
In rapture holds the wondering traveller's eye;
And all his senses whirl with heavenly extacy.
But hold, my Muse! repress thy airy flight;
Nor give thy rapid soul to sweet delight;
For e'en those haughty rocks, that rear on high
Their shaggy heads, and rend the vaulted sky
With their loud-roaring sounds sublime,
Shall bow beneath the shattering hand of *Time:*
And ere thrice ten times the God of Day,
Hath drove his flaming, annual car,
Adown the rosy West;
My slender frame of clay,
With Time and fierce Disease at war,
May moulder into dust:
These grief-strung nerves of mine may cease to move
In sad vibrations to the voice of Love;
With many a hapless Bard whose tender breast,
Now knows no more the goading thrust
Of penury, or pride his nerves of feeling tear.
But hold! ah hold thy lifted hand!
Nor lowly bow,
Beneath thy awful blow
The Father of Columbia's favor'd land:
Oh spare! the glorious Patriot spare!
Nor give the stroke of fate
Until his equal shall appear,
To fill with equal dignity the lofty Chair of State.

BIRTHA.

A FRAGMENT,
IN IMITATION OF SPENSER.

AH me! how black misfortune clouds the day!
How joy is banish'd from the human mind!
How pleasure flies at like the evening ray,
Ne can we e'er its lovely footsteps find.
And still unheedful, to the present blind,
We let the joyous moments slip along;
Still to ourselves eke careless and unkind,
We pass e'er straying from the happy throng,
Ne join the easy dance, ne sootly raise the song.

Yet now, regardful of life's little space,
And wisely yielding with obeisance still,
Let me no more the pleasant scene deface
With griefs responsive to the murm'ring rill,
And moans loud echoing o'er the neigh'bring hill.
O let me hide my sorrows in the night,
And bow submissive to the Eternal will;
Then Time shall load each moment with delight,
And o'er my soul shall shine the Muse's living light.—

'Twas when the Sun had climb'd the azure steep,
And shed his yellow influence on the earth;
Had driven the roaring tempests 'neath the deep,
And call'd the green creation into birth;
When lively Youth, gay Health and buxom Mirth,
Scatter'd the Summer's joys the world around;
When the neat housewife from her kitchen hearth
Had thrown the ashes on the garden ground,
And with green boughs and flowrets it had crown'd;

Then, where Libanus which is hight the new*
Spreads all around its ever varied scene,
And pours a rich creation on the view,
Stray'd from mine home, in spritely youth I been,
Then, with fresh joy I ken the smiling green,
The distant mountains frowning on the vale,
The lofty woods which shew their heights atween,
The speckled flocks thick nibbling in the dale,
And leaves, and flutt'ring birds, ay flying in the gale.

---

* *New Lebanon springs, in the state of New-York—commonly called the* Pool.

Aid me, O Mufe! the varied joys to tell
Which in this region of delight appear;
To mark the forrows which muft here ay dwell;
The joys, and woes, which call the differing tear.
What curious Nature hath ypighted here
Ay torturing pain fore'er to drive away,
And eafe the grief of many tirefome yeare;
Or to add comfort to the prefent day;
Eke her unkindnefs joying kindly to o'erpay.†

From the fmooth plain we rife the craggy hill
That tortuous windes its lengthened way along;
Leave on the left the hoarfe ay clacking mill,
And reach the dome, meet burthen of a fong.
The dome e'er fwarming with the bufy throng,
That with a different purpofe feek the place,
In pleafure's paths to wander all among;
Or dry the *tear* from forrow's faded face,
Which the foft hand of Love delights away to chafe.‡

Straught from the morning to the falling ray,
Full many a foot the building fpred, I ween,
And its front proudly to the fouthern day
Uprearing pleafant, from afar was feen.
Flank'd with a broad *Piazza* round it been—
Meet *place* to walk, and fpend the fummer's morn;
And from its edge to view the diftant fcene,
When the fun, rifing, all things doth adorn,
And gild the flowers, and dew-drops gliftening on the thorn.

† *Thefe waters have proved a radical cure in many cafes of rheumatifm, and in fcrophulous affections; and have relieved many other complaints. One fingular cafe of their efficacy in Spafmodic difeafes is daily exhibited there, and is worth relating. A Mr. Hitchcock, who keeps the Bath Houfe, has lived there many years unable to remove. He appears perfectly well. Generally once a day—fometimes lefs often, and fometimes oftener, he is feized with ftrong convulfions; his mufcles appear to be drawn into knots—which I have feen of the fize of a large egg. In this fituation, unable to fupport or affift himfelf, he is carried to the bath, ftripped and rolled in. The effect is inftantaneous. He immediately jumps up perfectly recovered; and is commonly free till nearly the fame time next day.*

‡ *Much company refort here in the months of July, Auguft, September and October, for the purpofes of pleafure, and recovering health.*

Here, when the orient blushes o'er the earth,
I walk, regardful of the enchanting view.
What charms the voice of Summer wakes to birth!
What beauty trembleth through the lucent dew!
Far round the horizon rise the mountains blue!
In distant prospect mingling with the sky;
And here the woods in varied foliage shew;
Yielding soft pleasure to the roving eye,
That longs the innumerous sweets of nature to descry.

At distance still, and o'er a beauteous plain
A village breaketh through the tufted trees:
Where industry renews her daily pain,
And labor sigheth on the careless breeze.
Here, tho' rich plenty laugheth o'er the mees,
In antic vesture robed Religion walks,
Her face in sorrows drest, all hearts doth freeze,
And with a frigid hand creation balks;
While in her train wan Care, with Pain united, stalks.§

Here, while the eye doth glisten with delight
To see what pleasaunce liveth o'er the scene,
Yet doth compassion's tear bedim the sight.
O Heaven! shall *Virtue* of celestial mien
The soul of nature, and creation's queen,
Reign but to spread destruction on mankind?
Shall *Piety*, bedeck'd in God's own sheen,
Live but to seal damnation on the mind—
Whose very soul is love with adoration join'd?

        E L L A.

§ *This refers to the sect called* Shaking Quakers. *About two miles from the Pool they have a handsome church; and a large house in which near an hundred persons live.—Their devotion consists principally in dancing and singing. These exercises are carried on to their own extreme emaciation.—They are very laborious, and have generally the character of scrupulous honesty.—The women and men live in different parts of the same house; the married persons have no connection with each other, and all marriages are prohibited. Their dress is extremely simple. The men wear short coats and short hair. The women are, generally, dressed in a white short gown and skirt, and in small close long-eared caps.—The sect seems to be rather diminishing, as the natural means of increase are cut off; few proselytes are gained; and the severity and constancy of their fatiguing exercises carries them off in a few years —This denomination of religionists made its appearance about ten years since. The head of them was the former mistress of a British officer. She called herself the Elect Lady; and lived to see her principles adopted by a considerable number of people in the north part of the States of New-York and Massachusetts, and some parts of Vermont —They call themselves Christians—but their exact principles I am unacquainted with.*

SONG.

AWAY each soft and tender bliss—
  The laugh of joy—the glance of love—
The gay discourse—the heart of peace—
  The hours, which winged with rapture, move.

A friend, once wont to give and share
  Each transport of the fleeting year,
A semblant angel, good and fair,
  To every thought and feeling dear;

Explored my unsuspecting heart
  In smiling Friendship's faithless guise,
Exulting found a tender part
  Where lives soft peace and where it dies.

And there—ah there! her causeless hate
  Impressed an undeserved blow,
That sealed with endless grief my fate,
  And plunged me deep in hopeless woe.

Then trust not, Youth, the melting air,
  The thrilling touch, refined embrace;
Since Treachery has a form so fair,
  And Malice wears so sweet a face.

HENRY.

ODE.

THE FAREWELL.

HOPE, holy sister of the cherub Peace!
  Thy path celestial thro' the heavens I trace,
As now, reclining on the amber breast
  Of yon far-sailing cloud,
Thou deign'st thy hallowed form to rest,
  Thy beauties half enshroud.

Yet, tho' thy glories faintly fill the sight,
Fair Queen I know thee, and adore thy might.
  Thy robes of snowy white I know;
The golden lock that o'er thy shoulder strays,
And on the skirting of the cloud doth throw
The splendor of the solar blaze;
  Thy skyey mantle now I spy,
That, backward floating, on the breezes plays;
  The dim mists now thy visage fly,
  I meet the comfort of thine eye.

Offspring of Virtue, Consolation's child!
  Thy power, thy kindness, and thy love, I bless;
  And with adoring heart thy care confess,
Whose condescension mild,
  Hath spread new calmness o'er my BIRTHA's soul,
Bid new-born transport' thro' her bosom stray,
  Their tides fresh spirits thro' her vessels roll,
And sweet Contentment o'er her features play.

Henceforth my idle song shall cease,
  No higher comforts can I give
  Than those which in her bosom live,
Thy voice serene hath spoke, and all her soul is peace.

****

———Go little Lyre, unbend thy useless chords,
  Untune each speaking string;
No more my voice of youth shall give thee words,
  My feeble touch responsive bid thee ring.
For now severer Study lifts her voice,
  And chides the lingering accents of my lay;
Points to the waiting object of my choice,
  That shuddering trembles at each fond delay.

Now cares await me, and the frugal toil
  That builds, of Competence the peaceful dome,
  And gives, at length, the happy haven home.
Perchance, in days to come, may Leisure smile,
  And fond Remembrance give thee to my sight,
    Not all unused thy warblings to awake,
    Not unacquainted to arouse delight,
To soothe the sad, the warm to love excite,
And bid, with deepest dread, the soul severely shake.

And then, perchance, in happiest union join'd,
  Thy chords, kind answering to my song,
  May pour some happy strain along,
And please, of Wisdom's Sons, the taste refined.
                              ELLA.

OCCASIONAL ADDRESS

Spoken by Mr. HODGKINSON, *on the opening of the* NEW THEATRE, *in New York, Monday, the 29th of January, 1798. Written by the late Dr.* E. H. SMITH.

WHEN the first prows attain'd the Atlantic shore,
One rude, uncultur'd face, the region wore;
Nor useful art, nor genial science smil'd,
Nor social order charm'd the mighty wild;
But, 'mid his woods, the native savage ran,
And beast, but scarce distinguish'd from the man.
Wide where Virginia spreads her golden plains,
Debark, successive, the adventurous trains:
With different zeal, 'mid bleaker skies, a band
Of pious exiles seize the desert land;
With patient step the doubtful gloom they dare,
And brave the rage of inexperienc'd war;
Destin'd thro' scenes of fearful strife to pass,
And bid, sublime, on virtue's solid base,
In ample strength, thy tower, O Freedom! rise,
Pride of the young and idol of the wise.

From like beginnings *our* adventurous race,
The recent history of *their* fortunes trace;
Like your bold sires, the fathers of the *stage,*
Of fate uncertain, brav'd the ocean's rage;
Of future æras caught prophetic views,
And sought a land scarce conscious of the muse.
Long years of labour mark'd their dubious way,
And fickle Favour oft withheld her ray;
But, as the shades of prejudice withdrew,
Fair, and more fair, the cheering prospect grew,

Till light and life the brightning scene endear'd,
And the gay bow of promis'd peace appear'd.
—O! if in future, as in former days,
Their true descendants meet your generous praise,
Propp'd by your smiles, this *stage*, a stately tower,
Lifts its proud front, and scorns misfortune's power.
    Great is the task, and nice the art required,
To raise such scenes as Dryden erst desir'd;
But greater still, and far more nice the art,
To fix the impressive moral in the heart;
To voice, form, feature, motion, accent, give
Appropriate force, and bid the picture live.
This asks the poet's fire, the player's skill,
Minds that discern, and souls that know to feel;
Applause, that cherishes as well as cheers,
And time, that mends, and softens, and endears.

    When first the spell of Gothic art was broke,
And, from its tedious trance, the Drama woke,
Mysteries and masks the new-born stage disgrac'd—
The monkish structures of perverted taste,
And many a year, and many a lustrum fled
'Ere Giant Shakespeare rear'd his hallowed head;
'Ere Britain's earlier Roscius grac'd the scene,
And the first Barry mov'd, and look'd a queen.
With patient ear our wise forefathers heard;
With kind applause the actor, poet, cheer'd;
Till, by successive trials, well sustain'd,
Nature and skill the improving pair attain'd;
From infant weakness rose the scenic art,
And truth and genius charm'd the hearer's heart.

    Let not your fiercer, more impatient doom,
Blast our young flowrets in their timid bloom;
But shield them from the inclement skies, and hope,
In future years, a rich and various crop.

If nobler toils, if triumphs more sublime,
Your boast and glory to remotest time,
To different scenes the glowing mind impell'd,
The watchful senate and the embattled field,
And chiefs and sages, theme of every tongue,
Awak'd alone the consecrating song;
While the neglected stage, from foreign shores;
A motley mass! deriv'd her various stores;
Yet now, by you encourag'd and allow'd,
Dramatic bands your native scenes shall crowd,
And native bards awake the slumbering lyre,
While gain and glory goad them and inspire;
Proud competition struggle for the bays,
And find a new existence in your praise.
So shall new Bettertons and Booths arise,
New Quins and Garricks ravish and surprize;
Another Pritchard charm with various powers,
And Woffington and Clive again be ours.

So shall some modest Congreve's juster wit,
With keener sallies more your taste delight;
Some happier Jonson's classic humor charm,
Some gayer Cibber spread no chaste alarm;
Some livelier Farquhar virtuous wishes move,
Some Steel inflame with pure and lawful love;
A graceful Cowley elegantly sway;
Another Inchbald point her sex the way;
Another Sheridan, with nobler zeal,
Convulse with mirth, or teach the heart to feel;
An active Holcroft, sovereign of the stage,
To perfect morals form a future age.

So shall a loftier Dryden rouse your fears,
A tenderer Rowe beguile you of your tears;
With wonderous verse a virtuous Otway scourge
Unheard of crimes and half to madness urge;
With thrilling horror shake the secret soul,
And give the tears of agony to roll;

A perfect Shakespeare, nurst by every muse,
Shake from his manly locks the pearly dews
Which the fond graces, all delighted, shed,
When their fair fingers, round his infant head,
Twin'd flowers and laurels from Parnassus' height,
And rule the scene with uncontested right;
Grief, rage, despair, and joy, and hope, and love,
Destin'd, by turns, their monarch's art to prove,
Vanish, appear, or perish, or revive,
As the soul's master bids them die or live.

    Then shall this STAGE of fame, of praise, secure,
Like this fair empire flourish and endure;
Alike in ample strength and beauty rise,
Pride of the young, and idol of the wise.

NEW YEAR's WISH.*

By Dr. ———.

TO you, my young friends, while I write,
    Kind wishes spontaneous arise;
And does ought my rude passions excite,
    They are hush'd by benevolent sighs.
A muse, in the form of a Dove,
    Hovers round, and dispels every fear;
She bids me each talent improve
    To hail you a HAPPY NEW YEAR!

Her mandates I cheerful obey,
    As her smiles I would strive to procure;
For the lines that my wishes convey,
    May her favors in future secure.

---

* First published in No. 85, of the Gazette of the United States; and originally addressed, by the author, to a circle of his female friends.

On you, my young friends, may she smile,
    That your verse may with melody flow;
And may joy all your sorrows beguile,
    Nor an hour be reserved for woe.

When WINTER shall sternly appear,
    And Nature in gloom be array'd;
When the Mariner shudders thro' fear,
    Lest his bark should by winds be betray'd;
Then, in safety, well shelter'd from snow,
    May you all, putting sorrow aside,
In domestic tranquility know
    All the joys of a social fire-side.

When SPRING in young beauty shall smile,
    And charm following charm shall unfold;
In rapture beholding the while,
    May your portion be pleasures untold.
May each songster that chirps on the spray,
    May each floweret that blows in the field,
For you be more cheerful and gay,
    For you its choice fragrances yield.

When SUMMER shall sultry advance,
    And flocks from their sports shall retire;
May each youth, who declines the light dance,
    Your charms, and your virtues admire.
May the grape-vine form Arbors of ease,
    While the eglantine skirts them around;
And then may the fresh balmy breeze
    Waft perfumes from each neighboring ground.

When AUTUMN his treasures shall bring,
    When each fruit tree shall bend with its load;
May your hearts ever gratefully sing,
    The hand that such blessings bestow'd.
Thus sweetly shall time roll away,
    Nor shall you once wish it in haste;
And the YEAR that commences to-day,
    Far happier shall be than the past.

Then, when WINTERS and SPRINGS shall decay,
    When SUMMERS and AUTUMNS are o'er,
And PHOEBUS, the Prince of the day,
    Shall wake the glad Seasons no more:
To you, each forgeting her mirth,
    May beauty immortal be given;
May you change the faint joys of this earth,
    For transports uncloying in heaven.

From a Gentleman, to a Lady, who had presented him with a CAKE HEART.

BY THE SAME.

WITH eager haste I homeward flew
    My precious gift to unfold;
I saw, and at the flattering view,
    My transports thus I told.

Thou beauteous semblance of the heart
    That warms Lucinda's breast,
Come, and each gentle joy impart
    As to my soul thou'rt press'd.

But still, tho chaste delight full oft
   To my fond heart you give,
Yet thou, say what I will, no soft
   Impression canst receive.

O had Lucinda, lovely fair,
   Deign'd but her own to have given,
The gift I'd cherish with that care
   As if 'twere sent from heaven.

In my own bosom it should lie,
   By no rude passion toss'd;
And, hush'd to love, it should supply
   The place of mine that's lost.

THE POETRY

OF THE

MINOR CONNECTICUT WITS

LEMUEL HOPKINS

EPITAPH

On a Patient killed by a Cancer Quack.

By Dr. Lemuel Hopkins.

Here lies a fool flat on his back,
The victim of a Cancer Quack;
Who lost his money and his life,
By plaister, caustic, and by knife.
The case was this—a pimple rose
South-east a little of his nose;
Which daily reden'd and grew bigger,
As too much drinking gave it vigour:
A score of gossips soon ensure
Full three score diff'rent modes of cure;
But yet the full-fed pimple still
Defied all petticoated skill;
When fortune led him to peruse
A hand-bill in the weekly news;
Sign'd by six fools of diff'rent sorts,
All cur'd of cancers made of warts;
Who recommend, with due submission,
This cancer-monger as magician;
Fear wing'd his flight to find the quack,
And prove his cancer-curing knack;
But on his way he found another,—
A second advertising brother:

But as much like him as an owl
Is unlike every handsome fowl;
Whose fame had rais'd as broad a fog,
And of the two the greater hog:
Who us'd a still more magic plaister,
That sweat forsooth, and cur'd the faster.
This doctor view'd, with moony eyes
And scowl'd up face, the pimple's size;
Then christen'd it in solemn answer,
And cried, "This pimple's name is CANCER."
" But courage, friend, I see you're pale,
" My sweating plaisters never fail;
" I've sweated hundreds out with ease,
" With roots as long as maple trees;
" And never fail'd in all my trials—
" Behold these samples here in vials!
" Preserv'd to shew my wond'rous merits,
" Just as my liver is—in spirits.
" For twenty joes the cure is done—"
The bargain struck, the plaister on,
Which gnaw'd the cancer at its leisure,
And pain'd his face above all measure.
But still the pimple spread the faster,
And swell'd, like toad that meets disaster.
Thus foil'd, the doctor gravely swore,
It was a right rose-cancer sore;
Then stuck his probe beneath the beard,
And shew'd them where the leaves appear'd;
And rais'd the patient's drooping spirits,
By praising up the plaister's merits.—

Quoth he, "The roots now scarcely stick—
"I'll fetch her out like crab or tick;
"And make it rendezvous, next trial,
"With six more plagues, in my old vial."
Then purg'd him pale with jalap drastic,
And next applies th' infernal caustic.
But yet, this semblance bright of hell
Serv'd but to make the patient yell;
And, gnawing on with fiery pace,
Devour'd one broadside of his face—
' Courage, 'tis done,' the doctor cried,
And quick th' incision knife applied:
That with three cuts made such a hole,
Out flew the patient's tortur'd soul!

Go, readers, gentle, eke and simple,
If you have wart, or corn, or pimple;
To quack infallible apply;
Here's room enough for you to lie.
His skill triumphant still-prevails,
For DEATH's a cure that never fails.

THE HYPOCRITE's HOPE.

BY THE SAME.

BLEST is the man, who from the womb,
    To saintship him betakes,
And when too soon his child shall come,
    A long confession makes.

When next in Broad Church-alley, he
    Shall take his former place,
Relates his paſt iniquity,
    And conſequential grace.

Declares how long by Satan vex'd,
    From truth he did depart,
And tells the time, and tells the text,
    That ſmote his flinty heart.

He ſtands in half-way-cov'nant ſure;
    Full five long years or more,
One foot in church's pale ſecure,
    The other out of door.

Then riper grown in gifts and grace,
    With ev'ry rite complies,
And deeper lengthens down his face,
    And higher rolls his eyes.

He tones like Phariſee ſublime,
    Two lengthy prayers a day,
The ſame that he from early prime,
    Had heard his father ſay.

Each Sunday perch'd on bench of pew,
    To paſſing prieſt he bows,
Then loudly 'mid the quav'ring crew,
    Attunes his vocal noſe.

With awful look then riſes ſlow,
    And pray'rful viſage four,
More fit to fright the apoſtate foe,
    Then ſeek a pard'ning power.

Then nodding hears the sermon next,
　From priest haranguing loud;
And doubles down each quoted text,
　From Genesis to Jude.

And when the priest holds forth address,
　To old ones born anew,
With holy pride and wrinkled face,
　He rises in his pew.

Good works he careth nought about,
　But *faith* alone will seek,
While Sunday's pieties blot out
　The knaveries of the week.

He makes the poor his daily pray'r,
　Yet drives them from his board:
And though to his own good he swear,
　Thro' habit breaks his word.

This man advancing fresh and fair,
　Shall all his race complete;
And wave at last his hoary hair,
　Arrived in Deacon's seat.

There shall he all church honours have,
　By joyous brethren given—
Till priest in fun'ral sermon grave,
　Shall send him straight to heaven.

ON GENERAL ETHAN ALLEN.

BY THE SAME.

LO Allen 'scaped from British jails,
   His tushes broke by biting nails.
Appears in hyperborean skies,
To tell the world the bible lies.
See him on green hills north afar
Glow like a self-enkindled star,
Prepar'd (with mob-collecting club
Black from the forge of Belzebub,
And grim with metaphysic scowl,
With quill just pluck'd from wing of owl)
As rage or reason rise or sink
To shed his blood, or shed his ink.
Behold inspired from Vermont dens,
The seer of Antichrist descends,
To feed new mobs with Hell-born manna
In Gentile lands of Susquehanna;
And teach the Pennsylvania quaker
High blasphemies against his maker.
Behold him move ye staunch divines!
His tall head bustling through the pines;
All front he seems like wall of brass,
And brays tremendous as an ass;
One hand is clench'd to batter noses,
While t'other scrawls 'gainst Paul and Moses.

Psalm LXXXVII.

The Church the Birth Place of the Saints; or Jews and Gentiles united in the Christian Church.

1 GOD in his earthly temple lays
 Foundation for his heavenly praise;
 He liked the tents of *Jacob* well,
 But still in *Sion* loves to dwell.

2 His mercy visits every house
 That pay their night and morning vows;
 But makes a more delightful stay,
 Where churches meet to praise and pray.

3 What glories were describ'd of old
 What wonders are in *Sion* told!
 Thou city of our GOD below,
 Thy fame shall *Tyre* and *Egypt* know.

4 *Egypt* and *Tyre*, and *Greek* and *Jew*,
 Shall there begin their lives anew:
 Angels and men shall join to sing
 The hill where living waters spring.

5 When GOD makes up his last account
 Of natives in his holy mount,
 'Twill be an honour to appear
 As one new-born and nourish'd there.

THE POETRY

OF THE

MINOR CONNECTICUT WITS

THEODORE DWIGHT

MOLL CAREY. Note A.

[Appeared in the Connecticut Courant, published at Hartford, Ct., March 3d, 1803.]

"SONG TO BE SUNG AT THE CLOSE OF THE REPUBLICAN EXERCISES, WITHIN THE HOUSE AT NEW HAVEN, MARCH 9, 1803."

1. Ye tribes of Faction join,
    Your daughters and your wives,
   Moll Carey's come to dine,
    And dance with Deacon Ives. Note B.
        Ye ragged throng
        Of Democrats,
        As thick as rats,
        Come join the song.

2. Old Deacon Bishop stands, Note C.
    With well befrizzled wig,
   File-leader of the band,
    To open with a jig.
        With *parrot*-toe,
        The poor old man
        Tries all he can
        To make it goe.

3. Director Powel leans, Note D.
    And takes a pinch of snuff,
   His words like little beans
    His neighbors' pockets stuff.
        Let all who please
        Their footsteps ply,
        And from him fly,
        Or stay and sneeze.

4. But oh! what human pen
    Can Abraham's self describe, Note E.
   The first of mortal men,
    The last of Treason's tribe.
        With mighty voice
        The patriot cries,
        Let earth and skies
        And Hell rejoice.

5. Rejoice, that man is free
    From Law, and Moral Strife,
   From Truth, and Decency;
    From shame,—and eke *his* wife.

Here let me stop;
My box of Glass
Will never pass
With "This side up."

6. Behold a motley crew. Note F.
Comes crowding o'er the Green,
Of every shape and hue,
Complexion, form and mien.
With deafening noise,
Drunkards and Whores
And Rogues in scores,
They all *rejoice*.

7. In meek and humble state,
"Old Porpoise" holds his way; Note G.
The Virtues on him wait,
And Graces round him stray,
While at his side,
Black, white and gray,
In wanton play
"Seven young ones" ride.

8. The Candidate was there, Note H.
Our David at his back; Note I.
Potter and Heylager, Note J.
The friend of White and Black;
Lo, as he goes,
A negro fume
Thro' every room
Regales each nose.

9. All energies at play,
The amusements now begin;
A few without doors stay,
But fun-alive's within.
With fainting voice
And closing eye,
The songsters cry,
"We—will—rejoice." Note K.

10. Moll Carey leads the van,
And boldly scours the field,
She takes them, *Man* by *Man*,
And makes the stoutest yield.
Great Potter pants,
And Kirby crawls,
And Wolcott falls, Note M.
And Bishop faints.

11. All pale the Deacons stand,
  And see their troops expire;
 Each begs, with wig in hand,
  Permission to retire.
   Moll opes the door
    And bids them fly,
   And never try
    Their courage more.

12. Thus every year we'll meet,
  And keep Thanksgiving Day.
 We'll drink, rejoice and eat,
  And then forget to pay. _{Note N.}
   Thus shall our Wives
    And Daughters find
   How very kind
    Is Deacon Ives.

NOTES.

NOTE A.—*Moll Carey* was the keeper of a noted house of ill-fame at that day in New York.

NOTE B.—*Deacon Ives.* Levi Ives was or had been a Deacon of a Presbyterian Church in New Haven. He was a popular and successful practitioner of medicine, a man of unblemished character and was universally esteemed as a member of society. His offense consisted in preferring Mr. Jefferson to Mr. Adams for President of the United States. He was father of the late Prof. Eli Ives of that city.

NOTE C.—*Deacon Bishop.* Another old and venerable citizen of New Haven, whose character was equally unblemished with that of Deacon Ives, and whose offense was the same.

NOTE D.—*Director Powell.* Capt. Powell was a fussy old Englishman, excessively addicted to snuff-taking. In 1786 he kept a grocery store at the head of Long Wharf, subsequently was auctioneer who occasionally imported and sold large collections of second hand books. He was an active and violent Jeffersonian, and acted the part of Sancho Panza for certain other aspiring politicians, and was an early applicant for and expectant of office under Mr. Jefferson. The day on which

Abraham Bishop was installed collector of customs at New Haven, Capt. Powell and others of his kin dragged a loaded cannon to the front of the office and was about to discharge it. Mr. B. ran out to the gun and urged Capt. P. not to fire it off. The latter persisted in his determination. "Hush! hush! Captain," says Mr. B. "We have got our appointment and secured all we want. It is better to be quiet and lie low than to disturb the public by firing a salute. "Yes!" responded the Captain. "You have obtained the Collectorship, but what in h—l have I got for my pains and labors?" The gun was removed undischarged, and the Captain soon after was appointed Tide-Waiter.

NOTE E.—*Abraham's self*. Abraham Bishop, an able, energetic and ardent leader of the Jeffersonian party in Connecticut. He was son of the aforesaid Deacon Bishop, graduated at Yale in 1778, and a member of that distinguished class which embraced such talented men as Joel Barlow, Josiah Meigs, Asher Miller, Zephanias Swift, Uriah Tracy, Noah Webster, Oliver Wolcott and Alexander Wolcott.

Near the close of the last century he strongly opposed the measures of Mr. Adams' administration of the General Government, and especially the relations that subsisted between Church and State in Connecticut. His voice and pen were active in assailing his opponents. He was author of several publications of great efficiency and well adapted to their occasions, but at this day forgotten. All of them are preserved in my library. The earliest was "THE GEORGIA SPECULATION UNVEILED," a transaction he charges with covering an unparalleled amount of fraud and swindling.

"CONNECTICUT REPUBLICANISM," an oration on the extent and power of political delusion, delivered in New Haven on the evening preceding Commencement, Sept., 1800. This was, perhaps, his second publication.

"ORATION DELIVERED AT WALLINGFORD, CT., March 11th, 1801, before the Republicans of Connecticut." A large edition was published and extensively circulated. It was on this occasion, as before stated, that the song of Jefferson and Liberty was first sung in public, and that oration of Mr. Bishop's had much to do in drawing out the song of Moll Carey.

"PROOFS OF A CONSPIRACY against Christianity and the Government of the United States, exhibited in several views of the union of Church and State in New England," was his fourth publication, which appeared in 1802, and was the last of his party publications. About that period he received the appointment of Collector of Customs at New Haven, a lucrative office. His political enemies, who were numerous and virulent, said that after that appointment he followed out his policy of *lying low*, as he suggested to Capt. Powell. The only apparent deviation from that course subsequently was a review of and answer to Timothy Pickering's Letter on the subject of the Embargo, which was of a very different character from his earlier political publications.

Domestic troubles caused him to obtain a divorce from his first wife, to which the author of Moll Carey alludes; a matter of no concern either of that author or of the public.

Mr. Bishop was a gentleman in his manners, of extensive knowledge, an artful and shrewd politician, an implacable enemy, a firm and enduring friend, and an active and useful citizen.

NOTE F.—*Behold a motley crew.* A fancied but incorrect view of the character of Jeffersonians assembling on the occasion of those festivals. The average of character was about the same in the two parties. Both contained good, bad and indifferent elements. A majority of wealth and education was on the side of the Federalists, who selfishly claimed to be the friends of decency and order, exclusively. At the present day, with "Moll Carey" before us, we can see little to sustain their claim to exclusive decency. Nor from the intolerant *Ten Letters* of Noah Webster to Dr. Priestly, do we discover any special claim to "good order."

The other party contained numerous poor but worthy people, who were debarred the elective franchise under the unequal and partially administered Laws of the State. Without a written constitution and under no control except the Charter of King Charles II., the Legislature passed laws best suited for party purposes and to curtail the rights of that poorer class of people who very generally were Jeffersonians.

The platform of the ruling party was an incongruous mixture of politicks and religion. It was satirically written of it,—

"Politicks and true Religion,
As much alike as Dove and Pige.

Any one who failed to square his views fully with that party creed, was condemned as an *Infidel and Anarchist*, the catch words of that party.

NOTE G.—"*Old Porpoise.*" Pierpont Edwards, a man of great talents, but his moral character would not bear too close examination. That seventh verse undoubtedly abounds in about an equal amount of truth and poetic license.

NOTE H.—"*The Candidate.*" Ephraim Kirby was for many years the Democratic candidate for Governor of Connecticut. He was a native of Middlebury, Vt.; served as a private in a cavalry company under General Washington; was severely wounded while watching the advance of General Howe, near the head of the Elk; lost a portion of his brain by a sabre-cut, and for several years, also, entirely his mind. Instantaneously his consciousness and mind returned, when he exclaimed, "Where is Eagle?" the name of the horse he was riding when he was cut down more than three years before. He studied Law after the close of the Revolution, settled in Litchfield, where he had few peers as a worthy citizen and jurist. The jaundiced and inflamed eye of party could hardly detect a flaw in his character. The Honorary Degree of A.M. was conferred on him in 1787 by Yale College. Mr. Jefferson appointed him Territorial Judge after the purchase of Louisiana, when he removed to Mobile, where he died in 1804. He was succeeded by one far less popular as Democratic candidate for Governor of Connecticut. The late hostess, Mrs. Barnum, of the far-famed Barnum's Hotel of Baltimore, was Col. Kirby's sister; and our eminent Ohio physician, surgeon, anatomist, naturalist and artist, Theodatus Garlick, M.D., now a resident of Bedford, Cuyahoga Co., Ohio, is a nephew of theirs. It is said that the Confederate General, Kirby Smith, who early in the Rebellion threatened to attack Cincinnati and caused Gov. Todd to call out the "Ohio Squirrel Hunters," was a son of the late Col. Joseph Smith of Litchfield, who was distinguished on the Canada frontier during the late war with Great Britain, and grandson of Ephraim Kirby. Joseph Smith married Kirby's daughter.

NOTE I.—"*Our David.*" The Rev. David Austin, an able clergyman settled over a Presbyterian congregation in Elizabethtown, N. J., afterwards in Bozrah, Connecticut. Late in the last century he became imbued with certain views in regard to the Millenium, akin to Millenarism, and subsequently with Jeffersonianism. He thought he clearly saw in the rise and progress of the French Revolution, of the first Napoleon, and the political revolution in the United States, a fulfillment in part of REVELATIONS. He was suspended or dismissed by his society and declared by his former friends to be insane, when he ardently attached himself to the Jeffersonian party.

As an orator and public speaker I have never heard him excelled. In those positions Thomas Corwin occupied a much lower level.

He graduated at Yale College in 1779, in the next class after Abraham Bishop, and died in 1831.

NOTE J.—"*Potter and Heylager.*" Jared Potter, M.D. (my grandfather), was a lineal descendant of the 5th generation from John Potter, one of the signers of the Plantation Covenant, in Deac. Newman's Barn, at New Haven, June 4th, 1639; born at East Haven, Sept. 25th, 1742; graduated at Yale in 1760; studied medicine, first under Dr. Herpine, in Milford, and then under the Rev. and Med. Doctor Elliott of Killingworth, Conn., and commenced practice in 1763.

Though brought up in a strict Presbyterian family, and amidst the practical workings of slavery and the slave trade, he during his collegiate course became strongly imbued with Universalism and anti-slavery sentiments, which he undeviatingly sustained through life.

In many of his beliefs and habits he was a Quaker, though he never conformed to the use of language which marks that sect. At the time of his marriage, in 1764, Samuel Forbes, a merchant and shipper of slaves, presented the bride, his daughter Sarah Forbes, with a wedding gift,—a black slave boy some 16 years old. With this gift the bride was highly gratified and the groom equally disgusted, and to the latest hours of their lives it was a cause of bickering between them.

The Doctor would never acknowledge the boy a slave, though he kindly allowed him to become a member of the family. The latter soon became a sailor, accumulated property and ultimately settled in Wallingford as a successful farmer, under the name of Jack John. He was admitted as a Freeman and he regularly voted at every election in Wallingford for twenty-five years, though he was as black as the ace of spades. When he died, a plain brown sandstone slab was erected over his grave, and which to-day occupies the exact geographical center of the cemetery of that town by a *special act of Divine Providence*. (Vid. Meriden Republican.)

His reputed master, thinking that to even nominally hold a slave was an imputation upon his Quaker reputation, caused emancipation papers to be drawn up in legal and highly technical form, setting the slave free, and to be entered on the township records in 1772, where they may now be seen.

He was distinguished for kindness, benevolence and universal philanthropy, extended equally to high and low, rich and poor, *white* and *black*. This trait of character, "The friend of white and black," was virtually true, which called for the vile insinuations of the author of Moll Carey.

Heylager was a well-bred Englishman, with rather aristocratic manners, an ardent Jeffersonian, a professed admirer of republican institutions, a disciple of Wilberforce and a resident of New Haven. Of course his offenses were unpardonable.

NOTE K.—" *We will rejoice.*" An allusion to the emphasis thrown on that line of Jefferson and Liberty by the choir at the Wallingford Festival in 1801.

NOTE L.—"*And Wolcott falls.*" A lawyer by profession, Collector of the Port of Middletown, a member of the class of eminent men of Yale who graduated in 1778, and of the Wolcott family, of which Connecticut may well be proud. He was a man of worth, talents and unimpeachable character, guilty only of thinking for himself, a crime of the kind committed by his kinsman Oliver Wolcott in 1818, when he ran as candidate for Governor on the Toleration ticket, which resulted in the separation of Church and State, and a written Constitution for that State.

These Festivals or Rejoicings were held annually for a number of years; the last, I believe, at Litchfield, and for the special purpose of encouraging and relieving Selleck Osborn, the talented poet and editor of the Witness, who had long been incarcerated in a dark and loathsome criminal's cell, by a *Starr Chamber* Court. for some trivial editorial in his journal, such as every party paper at this day contains without attracting attention.

The convention of his friends, some thousands in number, formed in line, marched by his grated window and each one, with difficulty, reached the editor's bleached hand, extended through the iron grating, and bestowed verbal good wishes and others more substantial tokens in form of coin and bank bills.

These transactions have all occurred in the enlightened State of Connecticut within my recollection.

JARED P. KIRTLAND.

East Rockport, Cuyahoga Co., O.,
August 27, 1874.

PROFESSOR WILLIAM C. FOWLER:

My Dear Sir—In accordance with your request I have forwarded to you the songs of "Jefferson and Liberty" and "Moll Carey." I have taken the liberty to add certain statements and Notes which may not square with your views and sentiments. From different stand points the same objects will present different aspects and perspectives to different beholders. You have above *my views*. My views, according to Dean Swift, are "orthodoxy." Other folks' views are "heterodoxy." The *facts* you have. They are historical. The *views* you can adopt or reject, as you please.

Eighty-one years press heavily on me. I have no amanuensis and I have neither strength nor leisure to re-write and make corrections.

I am your obliged friend and humble servant,

JARED POTTER KIRTLAND.

Sept. 3, 1874.

SELECTED POETRY.

*From the New-Haven Gazette, and Connecticut Magazine, for 1788.**

TO THE PRINTER.

THE distress which the inhabitants of Guinea experience at the loss of their children, which are stolen from them by the persons employed in the barbarous traffic of human flesh, is, perhaps, more thoroughly felt than described. But, as it is a subject to which every person has not attended, the Author of the following lines hopes that, possibly, he may excite some attention, (while he obtains indulgence) to an attempt to represent the anguish of a mother, whose son and daughter were taken from her by a Ship's Crew, belonging to a Country where the GOD of Justice and Mercy is owned and worshipped.

"HELP! oh, help! thou GOD of Christians!
  "Save a mother from despair!
"Cruel white-men steal my children!
  "GOD of Christians, hear my prayer!

"From my arms by force they're rended,
  "Sailors drag them to the sea;
"Yonder ship, at anchor riding,
  "Swift will carry them away.

---

* This Poem was originally printed in the above-mentioned Paper, February 21st, 1788, in rather an incorrect manner. It is now offered to the public, with the amendment of the errors reprehensible at its first appearance.

" There my son lies, stripp'd, and bleeding;
  " Fast, with thongs, his hands are bound.
" See, the tyrants, how they scourge him!
  " See his sides a reeking wound!

" See his little sister by him;
  " Quaking, trembling, how she lies!
" Drops of blood her face besprinkle;
  " Tears of anguish fill her eyes.

" Now they tear her brother from her;
  " Down, below the deck, he's thrown;
" Stiff with beating, thro' fear silent,
  " Save a single, death-like, groan.

" Hear the little creature begging!"—
  ' Take me, white-men, for your own!
' Spare! oh, spare my darling brother!
  ' He's my mother's only son.

' See, upon the shore she's raving:
  ' Down she falls upon the sands:
' Now, she tears her flesh with madness;
  ' Now, she prays with lifted hands.

' I am young, and strong, and hardy;
  ' He's a sick, and feeble boy;
' Take me, whip me, chain me, starve me,
  ' All my life I'll toil with joy.

' Christians! who's the GOD you worship?
  " Is he cruel, fierce, or good?
' Does he take delight in mercy?
  ' Or in spilling human blood?

'Ah! my poor distracted mother!
 'Hear her scream upon the shore.'—
Down the savage Captain struck her,
 Lifeless on the vessel's floor.

Up his sails he quickly hoisted,
 To the ocean bent his way;
Headlong plunged the raving mother,
 From a high rock, in the sea.

ODE TO CONSCIENCE.

BY THEODORE DWIGHT, ESQUIRE.

HAIL Conscience, faithful inmate of the breast!
   Thy smiles can charm to sweetest rest,
Thy frowns can wake the keenest woe,
Without thy aid even heaven would grow
A cheerless void of deep distress,
And angels want the power to bless.

When great Jehovah's voice creation form'd,
   When worlds unnumber'd sprang to instant birth;
When morning stars to ecstacy were warm'd,
   And man stood ruler of the boundless earth,
Thou in the realms of light and love,
Did'st dwell embosom'd with the Etherial Dove.
" Where Guilt shall dare extend her reign,
" And Satan stretch his dark domain,
" There let the tides of horror roll,
" And torture rend the sinking soul."
The GODHEAD spoke,—Creation round,
Deep trembled to its utmost bound.

ORIGINAL POETRY.

Hail mighty Conscience! hail!
   When the black deed of guilt is done,
Thou mak'st the quivering wretch turn pale,
   And startle at the sun.
When Murder fearless of thy power,
   Lifts up the fateful knife,
And in the dark and midnight hour,
   Destroys the guiltless life;
High swells thy awful voice:
Awaking at the fearful sound,
The fiends of vengeance gather round;
   The villain starts at every noise,
His soul, to judgment summon'd, shakes,
His frame convuls'd with horror, quakes;
'Till urg'd to fate by all-resistless fear,
He owns his crime, and dies the victim of despair.

   When the quick tide of life swells high,
   And Pleasure hourly wantons nigh,
   The Sceptic braves thy stern command,
   Nor dreads thy executing hand.
   But when the powers of life decay,
   And sickening nature wastes away,
   When Age brings on a lengthening train
   Of weakness, dire disease, and pain,
   When Death uplifts its horrid form,
   And Justice wakes the avenging storm;
   Torn with distracting doubts and fears,
   Thy terrors thunder in his ears;
   Pale spectres haunt the shades of night,
   Deep blushes meet the morning light,—

> Above he sees the tempest lower,
> And floods of wrath around him pour,—
> Wide yawns beneath the world of woe,
> Where waves of burning vengeance flow.

Impell'd by conscious guilt he strives to fly,
Far from the light of God's all-searching eye,
And plunging headlong in the midnight shade,
Calls rocks and hills to shield his guilty head;
'Till robb'd of Hope,—life's latest stay,—Despair
Breathes the faint wishes of unutter'd prayer:
In dread suspence, his last sad refuge fled,
His schemes all frustrate, his delusions dead,
Heaven shut from view, annihilation vain,
He shrinks from life, and flies to endless pain.

> Not such thy lot, O man* divine!
> Peace on the bed of death was thine.
> Calm with a retrospective view,
> Thy mind look'd past existence thro;
> In bright, and regular array,
> And blazing on the face of day,
>   The deeds of virtue stood;
> Conscience beheld them as they shone,
> Approv'd and hail'd her darling son,
>   And God pronounc'd them good.
> And when the messenger of death,
> Receiv'd thy faint expiring breath,
> Soft slumbering on the bed of peace,
> Thy voice bade every sorrow cease,

---

* Mr. Addison.

While to the world's astonish'd eye,
Thou shew'd'st with what repose a virtuous man can die.

   Hail Conscience! hail the good man's friend!
     Thy smiles thro' life his steps attend;
     And on his dread departing day,
      Impart a sweet, and gladsome ray,
To cheer his soul, to sooth his dying breath,
To light his path-way thro' the vale of death,
And ope his prospect to awaiting Skies,
Where Faith looks forward with prophetic eyes,
And sees unmov'd the moon in blood expire,
The sun in darkness, and the earth on fire,
Stars, planets, systems, into ruin hurl'd,
And the last trumpet rend a guilty world.

LINES ON THE DEATH OF WASHINGTON.

Far, far from hence be satire's aspect rude,
No more let laughter's frolic-face intrude,
But every heart be fill'd with deepest gloom,
Each form be clad with vestments of the tomb.
From Vernon's sacred hill dark sorrows flow,
Spread o'er the land, and shroud the world in wo.
From Mississippi's proud, majestic flood,
To where St. Croix meanders through the wood,
Let business cease, let vain amusements fly,
Let parties mingle, and let faction die,
The realm perform, by warm affection led,
Funereal honors to the mighty dead.

Where shall the heart for consolation turn,
Where end its grief, or how forget to mourn?
Beyond these clouds appears no cheering ray,
No morning star proclaims th' approach of day.
Ask hoary Age from whence his sorrows come,
His voice is silent, and his sorrow dumb;
Enquire of Infancy why droops his head,
The prattler lisps—"great Washington is dead."
Why bend yon statesmen o'er their task severe?
Why drops yon chief the unavailing tear?
What sullen grief hangs o'er yon martial band?
What deep distress pervades the extended land?
In sad responses sounds from shore to shore—
"Our Friend, our Guide, our Father is no more."
  Let fond remembrance turn his aching sight,
Survey the past, dispel oblivion's night,
By Glory led, pursue the mazy road,
Which leads the traveller to her high abode,
Then view that great, that venerated name,
Inscribed in sunbeams on the roll of Fame.
No lapse of years shall soil the sacred spot,
No future age its memory shall blot;
Millions unborn shall mark its sacred fire,
And latest Time behold it and admire.
  A widow'd country! what protecting form
Shall ope thy pathway through the gathering storm!
What mighty hand thy trembling bark shall guide,
Through Faction's rough and overwhelming tide!
The hour is past—thy Washington no more
Descries, with angel-ken, the peaceful shore.
Freed from the terrors of his awful eye,
No more fell Treason seeks a midnight sky,
But crawling forth, on deadliest mischief bent,
Rears her black front, and toils with cursed intent.
Behold! arranged in long, and black array,
Prepared for conflict, thirsting for their prey,
Our foes advance,—nor force nor danger dread,
Their fears all vanish'd when his spirit fled.
Oft, when our bosoms, fill'd with dire dismay,
Saw mischief gather round our country's way;
When furious Discord seized her flaming brand,
And threatened ruin to our infant land;
When faction's imps sow'd thick the seeds of strife,
And aim'd destruction at the bliss of life;
When war with bloody hand her flag unfurl'd,

And her loud trump alarm'd the western world;
His awful voice bade all contention cease,
At his commands the storms were hush'd to peace.
  But who can speak, what accents can relate,
The solemn scenes which marked the great man's fate!
Ye ancient sages, who so loudly claim
The brightest station on the list of Fame,
At his approach with diffidence retire,
His higher worth acknowledge, and admire.
When keenest anguish rack'd his mighty mind,
And the fond heart the joys of life resign'd,
No guilt, nor terror stretch'd its hard control,
No doubt obscured the sunshine of the soul.
Prepared for death, his calm and steady eye,
Look'd fearless upward to a peaceful sky;
While wondering angels point the airy road,
Which leads the Christian to the house of God.

LINES ADDRESSED TO A MOTHER, WHO HAD BEEN ABSENT FROM HOME SEVERAL WEEKS, ON HER SEEING HER INFANT CHILD ASLEEP.

Wrapp'd in innocent repose,
Lost to all its little woes,
See that lovely infant rest,
On the pillow's downy breast.
Wearied with the toils of day,
Little frolics, childish play,
Frequent joy, and frequent grief,
Nature yields a short relief.
Say, my sleeping cherub, say,
Whither doth thy spirit stray?
Art thou flown to realms above,
On some angel's wings of love,
Where, array'd in purest white,
Dwell the sainted sons of light,
Hymning round the eternal throne,
Praise to God's Almighty Son?
Or dost thou now at random roam;
Through creation's nightly tomb,
Borne by Death's insidious power,
To his temporary bower?

Hush the thought!—I see thee smile!
Dreams thy little heart beguile;
O'er thy sweet, enchanting face,
Steals inimitable grace.
Say, my little cherub, say,
Whither doth thy spirit stray?
Hark!—his answering smile replies—
"Far from hence my spirit flies;
Borne on Fancy's wing, I move
To a mother's arms of love,
And clasp'd in sweet embraces, rest
On her balmy angel-breast.
Here the tides of pleasure roll,
Rapture charms the licensed soul,
Here divinest transports play,
Here affection loves to stray,
Here I share the envied kiss,
Sink in pleasure, drown in bliss.
Spotless as the beams of light,
Crowding on the ravish'd sight,
Ever new its beauties rise,
Charming unforbidden eyes.
Hark!—My mother's voice benign,
Speaks in harmony divine"—
Peaceful here, my infant rest,
On your raptured parent's breast.
Here no hand shall enter rude,
No unhallow'd eye intrude;
In this paradise of joy,
Dwells no spirit to destroy;
But, on Virtue's spotless throne,
Thy happy Father reigns alone,
Licensed here alone to move,
Bathing in voluptuous love,
Pleasure here without alloy,
Pours an endless stream of joy,
While its blissful currents roll,
Through the mazes of his soul.

THEODORE DWIGHT.

WOMAN.

Nor less shall thy fair ones to glory ascend,
And genius and beauty in harmony blend;
The graces of form shall awake pure desire,
And the charms of the soul still enliven the fire;
Their sweetness unmingled, their manners refined,
And virtue's bright image impress'd on the mind.
With peace and soft rapture shall teach life to glow,
And light up a smile on the aspect of wo. Dwight.